THE GREENWOOD GUIDE TO AMERICAN POPULAR CULTURE

THE GREENWOOD GUIDE TO AMERICAN POPULAR CULTURE

Volume II

Edited by M. Thomas Inge and Dennis Hall

GREENWOOD PRESS
Westport, Connecticut • London

Library of Congress Cataloging-in-Publication Data

The Greenwood Guide to American popular culture / edited by M. Thomas Inge and Dennis Hall.
p. cm.
Includes bibliographical references and index.
ISBN 0–313–30878–0 (set : alk. paper)—ISBN 0–313–32367–4 (v. 1 : alk. paper)—
ISBN 0–313–32368–2 (v. 2 : alk. paper)—ISBN 0–313–32369–0 (v. 3 : alk. paper)—
ISBN 0–313–32370–4 (v. 4 : alk. paper)
1. Popular culture—United States. 2. Popular culture—United States—History—Sources.
3. Popular culture—United States—Bibliography. I. Inge, M. Thomas. II. Hall, Dennis.
E169.1.H2643 2002
306.4'0973—dc21 2002071291

British Library Cataloguing in Publication Data is available.

Library of Congress Catalog Card Number: 2002071291
ISBN: 0–313–30878–0 (set)
0–313–32367–4 (v. 1)
0–313–32368–2 (v. 2)
0–313–32369–0 (v. 3)
0–313–32370–4 (v. 4)

First published in 2002

Greenwood Press, 88 Post Road West, Westport, CT 06881
An imprint of Greenwood Publishing Group, Inc.
www.greenwood.com

Printed in the United States of America

The paper used in this book complies with the
Permanent Paper Standard issued by the National
Information Standards Organization (Z39.48–1984).

10 9 8 7 6 5 4 3 2 1

For
Donária Carvalho Inge
and
Susan Hall

They stood by their men.

CONTENTS

EDITORIAL CARTOONS

Paul Somers

The editorial cartoon has been a facet of American culture much longer than the comic strip, and it was taken seriously at an earlier date. No matter how poorly drawn or how tasteless, a widely distributed cartoon attacking a public figure could not be ignored. It is one thing to read historians' accounts of what a devious leader President [the name of your choice here] was and another to see—and sometimes to feel right in your belly—page after page of cartoons dramatizing that opinion with dozens of different metaphors and allusions.

Although editorial cartooning has a long history in the United States, it originated in Europe. The key words—"cartoon" and "caricature"—derive from the Italian *cartone*, "a large sheet of paper," and *caricare*, "to exaggerate, change, or overload." The eighteenth-century Englishman William Hogarth, whose moral indignation led him from fine art to satirical engravings denouncing the evils of his society, may be considered the first cartoonist. His successors, Thomas Rowlandson, George Cruikshank, and, especially, James Gillray, inspired emulation. In the nineteenth century other Englishmen such as John Tenniel, David Low, and Ronald Searle, along with the Frenchmen Honore Daumier and Jean Louis Forain, influenced American artists. American editorial cartoonists have reflected the political and social moods of the nation, refining and simplifying their work to ensure the maximum impact on a public with little time to ponder the complex drawings and lengthy captions of earlier times. Despite the competition from newer media and the libel suits, protests, and boycotts mounted against newspapers, the power of a single drawing endures.

Herbert Block (Herblock) has defined the editorial cartoonist as "the kid who points out that the Emperor is without his clothes." From Ben Franklin to Mike Ramirez, America has produced a long line of artists—left, right, and center—idealists and cynics whose work has tried to keep politics honest. Unfortunately, the political or editorial cartoonists who have not also been accepted by "high culture" enthusiasts as painters, printmakers, or major illustrators have been relegated to secondary positions, as have so many artists in a variety of popular culture categories.

Thus, although early editorial cartoons or drawings by the most famous have been collected and celebrated, research into late nineteenth- and twentieth-century editorial cartooning has become a legitimate concern for scholars and collectors only in the last few decades. Indexes are incomplete; independent bibliographical and biographical guides appear in limited numbers; collections are erratically cataloged, and serious critical analysis of editorial cartooning and cartoonists—artistic, political, historical—is just beginning to realize its potential. In addition to these opportunities for research, there is much work to be done in the social sciences to examine and identify the underlying mechanisms to see how—or if—they work.[1]

HISTORICAL OUTLINE

American editorial cartooning probably began in 1747 with "Non Votis" or "The Waggoner and Hercules." Benjamin Franklin is credited with the designing and/or drawing of this, which he used in his pamphlet. Franklin is also associated with the second oldest extant political cartoon, actually the first political cartoon to appear in an American newspaper, the famous "Join or Die," variously "Unite or Die," published in his *Pennsylvania Gazette* for May 9, 1754. The engraver was Paul Revere, whose 1770 engraving "The Boston Massacre" was widely circulated for its propaganda value. Revere had copied a drawing by Henry Pelham, stepbrother of John Singleton Copley.

Shortly before the Revolution, Franklin reputedly designed the cartoon "Magna Britannia: Her Colonies Reduced" for distribution in England, hoping that the symbolic representation of Britannia fallen from its place of eminence at the top of the globe, its limbs (each bearing the name of a North American colony) severed, would help sway England toward a more lenient colonial policy.

The year 1788 saw "The Federal Edifice," the country's first cartoon series, published in Major Benjamin Russell's Boston *Massachusetts Centinel*. Thanks in part to the shortage of newsprint and the great expense of engravings, few cartoons appeared during this period; librarian-scholar Frank Weitenkampf lists a mere seventy-eight produced before 1828. An exception to the busy cartoons of the day was drawn by Elkanah Tisdale in 1812, who added a few pencil strokes to the map of Governor Elbridge Gerry's ingeniously contrived Essex County senatorial district, thus creating the dragonlike "Gerrymander" and giving a word to our language.

Considering the bitterness of partisan politics that characterized the early years of the republic, it is surprising that there are so few cartoons of George Washington, who was scurrilously derided by his foes. William Murrell surmises that "too ardent" patriots have destroyed unflattering cartoons of the father of our country. Thomas Jefferson was not so fortunate, as several cartoons survive that mock his Gallic and democratic proclivities. In fact, the first American cartoon designed for newspaper reproduction in the *New York Evening Post* in 1814 dealt with Jefferson's highly unpopular Embargo Act.

Although Franklin, Tisdale, and others were well known, Edinburgh-born William Charles was the first to become famous here primarily as a political cartoonist.

He drew heavily upon the works of English cartoonists James Gillray and Charles Rowlandson and left no disciples after his death in 1820, but he deserves to be remembered, nevertheless, for popularizing the political cartoon.

The next phase in the history of American editorial cartoons was initiated by the development of lithography, which was much faster than woodcuts and engravings. The first lithographed cartoon appeared in 1829; thereafter, lithographed cartoons flourished. Most of them were marketed by the firms of Henry R. Robinson and Currier & Ives. The Currier & Ives firm sold some 10 million copies between 1840 and 1890, only some eighty of which titles were political cartoons. As the Civil War approached, the firm often marketed cartoons, sometimes drawn to order, on both sides of a controversial issue.

Although Currier & Ives documented the midcentury discord with its lithographs, especially those dealing with the presidential campaigns of 1856 and 1860, the Civil War, and Abraham Lincoln, other emerging media would soon make lithography obsolete and would begin another phase in American editorial cartooning. Englishman Henry Carter arrived here in 1848, changed his name to Frank Leslie, and by the mid-1850s was embarked on a series of magazine ventures, the most successful of which was *Frank Leslie's Illustrated Newspaper* (later, *Frank Leslie's Illustrated Weekly*). Other Leslie publications included *The Jolly Joker*, *Cartoon*, *Chatterbox*, and *Phunny Phellow*. An impressive list of artists was employed by Leslie, as well as by *Vanity Fair*, *Harper's Weekly*, and the scores of other publications that appeared and disappeared abruptly. The Anglo-Irishman Frank Bellew was popular before the war, and his elongated caricature of Lincoln is still remembered. Other featured artists of the time include William Newman, Edward Jump, Frank Beard, William Henry Shelton, and many others. The most notable of these "others," of course, were the German Thomas Nast and the Viennese Joseph Keppler.

Born in Landau, Germany, in 1840, Thomas Nast came to New York City at the age of six. He became deeply interested in art, especially in the work of the great English cartoonists John Leech and John Tenniel and painter and book illustrator John Gilbert. Nast said that he was indebted to Tenniel for his striking use of animals as symbols. He studied drawing at the Academy of Design and at age fifteen won a job with *Frank Leslie's Illustrated Weekly*.

During the Civil War, his illustrations for *Harper's Weekly* were extremely popular. He soon turned to a more emblematic, less reportorial style, which was sometimes allegorical and nearly always emotionally powerful. So effective a voice for the Union did he become that Lincoln called him "our best recruiting sergeant."

The South had its own German-born artist, Adalbert J. Volck, a Baltimore dentist who is known for a few excellent caricatures, most notably, twenty-nine "Confederate War Etchings." He portrayed Lincoln as a clown, an African American, a woman, and a harem dancer. Apparently, he gave up cartooning after the war.

Nast, however, continued to draw, and his style evolved into caricature. Ultimately, it was through his battle against the Tweed Ring that he made his mark as one of America's most powerful editorial cartoonists. Incensed by the corruption of the Irish Catholic Boss Tweed, Nast began to fire his volleys from the pages of *Harper's Weekly*; he took Tammany Hall's own tiger and made it into a fearful symbol of marauding lawlessness, to be used against Tweed in the election of 1871. Tweed lost and went to jail in 1873. He escaped from jail in 1875 and fled to Spain, where he was arrested by customs officials who recognized him from one of Nast's cartoons.

The Reconstruction period also saw the brief career of perhaps the first African American editorial cartoonist, Henry Jackson Lewis, who, according to Draper Hill, was an indirect disciple of Thomas Nast. A topographical and architectural artist from Pine Bluff, Arkansas, Lewis had sold drawings to *Harper's Weekly*, some of which were engraved by Sol Eytinge. In 1888, after Democrats passed segregation legislation, he went with his family to Indianapolis, where he drew for the *Freeman*, self-described "Harper's Weekly of the Colored Race."[2]

Unfortunately for Thomas Nast, right and wrong would never again be so plainly distinguishable as they had been during these exhilarating times. His attacks remained formidable, but he was sometimes at a loss for a target, as his own Republican Party proved susceptible to corruption. Indeed, in 1874 he first began to represent his lumbering, uninspired party as an elephant. Nast quit *Harper's* in 1887 and lost much of his effectiveness. His investments failed, and by 1902 he had no choice but to accept the post of U.S. consul to Guayaquil, Equador, where he died in December of the same year. But he left behind such long-lasting symbols as the Tammany tiger and the Republican elephant, the less memorable rag baby of inflation, and the Democratic donkey, which he did not create but did popularize.

While Stephen Hess and Milton Kaplan give Nast his due for advancing the profession, they see him as "a rare, isolated phenomenon" [who] "left no disciples or school of cartooning, as Keppler would do" (102). Richard Samuel West, however, asserts in the introduction to *Best Political Cartoons of 1978* that Nast is the father of the indignation school, symbolic and powerful. His disciples, especially Robert Minor and D. R. Fitzpatrick, would dominate the early twentieth century. On the other hand, West asserts, Keppler's brand of lighter satire and florid style have more frequently prevailed in the century-plus since the two giants drew. But more of this later. Whichever view is correct, and subsequent trends support West's, Nast demonstrated by his influence on public opinion that a popular, forceful editorial cartoonist is someone to be reckoned with.

The passing of Nast did not leave a vacuum, however, for there arose the comic weeklies. Joseph Keppler, who came to St. Louis in late 1867 or early 1868, when he was twenty-nine, started two German-language comic weeklies, both of which failed. In 1872, Keppler went to New York and drew for Frank Leslie's magazines. He and printer Adolph Schwarzmann founded a German-language weekly, *Puck*, in 1876 and an English version in March 1877. The magazine thrived and in less than ten years had a circulation of 80,000. An excellent cartoonist himself, Keppler employed many of the best artists of the time.

Puck's heyday partly overlapped Nast's decline. By 1884, Nast was disgruntled by the Republicans' nomination of the corrupt James G. Blaine and expressed himself in a cartoon. Keppler being a Democrat, he and *Puck* joined in and revived an idea that he had used against Grant: the tattooed man. Bernard Gillam drew the scandalous series, depicting the husky Blaine in his undershorts, covered with tattoos representing his opponents' allegations of "Corruption, Bluster, anti-Chinese Demagoguery, etc." The Republicans responded with Frank Beard's cartoon in *Judge*, dramatizing a rumor that Grover Cleveland was the father of an illegitimate child. Perhaps the most telling shot in this cartoon war was "The Royal Feast of Belshazzar Blaine and the Money Kings," drawn by Walt McDougall for the *New York World*. Displayed on thousands of billboards around the state, the cartoon contributed to Blaine's defeat in New York. According to Charles Press, this marked the real beginning of daily editorial cartooning as a profession.

One of *Puck*'s two great rivals, *Judge* was founded in 1881 by dissatisfied *Puck* cartoonist James A. Wales. Perhaps the pro-Republican *Judge*'s most famous symbol was the "Full Dinner Pail," cartoonist Grant Hamilton's embodiment of the prosperity of Republican William McKinley's first administration.[3] As Stephen Becker points out, these "Full Dinner Pail" cartoons drawn by Hamilton and by Victor Gillam represented an advance in cartooning technique because of their greater simplicity and, therefore, immediacy, as compared to the crowded panel cartoons of the late nineteenth century. Writing in 1959, Becker denied Keppler any legacy, a judgment that would stand until Richard S. West's revision, beginning in the late 1970s. Intervening decades and shifts in popular taste unforeseen by Becker have restored Keppler's school to preeminence (see later).

The third great comic weekly of the period was *Life*, founded in 1883 by *Harvard Lampoon* graduates led by J. A. Mitchell and Edward S. Martin. Much, although not all, of its satire was social rather than political.

A contemporary of these periodicals, the San Francisco *Wasp*, has received considerably less attention. Said to be the first magazine in the United States to use color cartoons over an extensive period of time, *The Wasp* provided, in addition to its graphic wit, a forum for Ambrose Bierce, who edited the publication from 1881 to 1886 and, in his columns "Prattle" and "Devil's Dictionary," more than held up his end of the magazine's commitment to satire. Although it appeared in various forms from August 5, 1876, to April 25, 1941, *The Wasp*'s heyday came between 1876 and 1894.

There was no dramatic ringing down of the curtain on the great comic weeklies, with their elaborate lithographed cartoons, as *Judge* lasted until 1939 and *Life* until 1936, when it transformed into the modern pictorial publication. *Puck* survived for seventeen more years after its founder's death in 1901. Slowly, inexorably, they became obsolete as the dailies arose with their short lead times and immediate cartoons.

The lasting legacy of the weeklies (including the earlier *Harper's Weekly*, which merged into the *Independent* in 1916) is the forum that they provided for the two giants of editorial cartooning, Nast and Keppler, whose considerable influence is noted earlier. Keppler's "students" included Bernard Gillam and James A. Wales. Add Frederick Burr Opper and his "protégé" Eugene (Zim) Zimmerman, who would be major figures in the new era of editorial cartooning.

Newspaper cartooning developed gradually; James Gordon Bennett had started the *New York Telegram* in 1867 and had used sensationalism to boost sales. In the first regular use of cartoons in a newspaper, Bennett printed a front-page cartoon in the *Telegram* every Friday. Joseph Pulitzer, who bought the *New York World* in 1883, made an even bigger impression with editorial cartoons such as the devastating "Feast of Belshazzar," mentioned earlier. In 1885 he introduced the first comic strip, Richard F. Outcault's *The Yellow Kid*, thus further exploiting the graphic possibilities of the newspaper. William Randolph Hearst took over the *New York Journal* in 1895 and began the great circulation war, bringing with him from San Francisco Homer Davenport. Hearst snatched Frederick Burr Opper from *Puck* in 1899. Although critics have been condescending toward his technique, Opper was a cartoonist of great versatility and popularity, with a successful comic strip, *Happy Hooligan*, and several telling series of political cartoons, such as "Alice in Plunderland" and "Willie and His Papa." His career was unusual because of its variety and length and also because he was one of the few cartoonists able to make the changeover from the comic magazines, with their complicated, multifigured cartoons, to the daily newspapers, whose deadlines necessitated a more direct style and simpler designs.

By the turn of the century, editorial cartoons were featured regularly in newspapers all over the country. This proliferation so alarmed the politicians who were the target of these drawings that between 1897 and 1915 the legislatures of California, Pennsylvania, Alabama, and New York formulated anticartoon legislation. Only two states passed anticartoon bills: California's 1899 law was widely ridiculed and never enforced, but Pennsylvania's 1903 law was more formidable. Cartoonist Charles Nelan drew gubernatorial candidate Samuel Pennypacker as a parrot in *Philadelphia North American* cartoons. Upon winning, Pennypacker pushed through the Pennsylvania legislature a law prohibiting the drawing or publishing of any caricature or cartoon for the purpose of exposing a person to ridicule. Nelan and the *North American* defied the governor, and he eventually backed down. Although there were a few subsequent cases filed under the anticartoon law after that, its force had dissipated, and it was repealed in 1907. Not until the late twentieth century would there be another such concerted legal assault on political cartooning.

The war with Spain provided cartoonists with inspiration for a while, but Theodore Roosevelt literally sustained them for years. His teeth, mustache, and glasses made him easy to draw. He was a favorite subject for two of the early twentieth century's best-known cartoonists: John T. McCutcheon and Jay N. (Ding) Darling. Charles Press has put them at the head of a group of cartoonists that he labels "bucolic."

John Tinney McCutcheon was one of the most notable of a large group of outstanding midwestern cartoonists active around the turn of the century. He drew editorial cartoons and nostalgic panels and illustrated books, such as his famous *Boys in Springtime*. Of his political cartoons for the *Chicago Tribune*, perhaps the best known are his 1932 Pulitzer Prize winner, "A Wise Economist Asks a Question," and "The Mysterious Stranger" (Hess and Kaplan 133).

Another durable midwesterner was Jay N. (Ding) Darling of Iowa. His "The Long, Long Trail," a 1919 tribute to Teddy Roosevelt, has often been reproduced. The duration of his career is shown by the dates of his Pulitzer Prizes, 1924 and 1943; he received his last award when he was sixty-six. Darling's cartoons are generally populist, gently antipolitician, and antistrike. Other midwestern cartoonists include Darling and McCutcheon's contemporary, Charles Bartholomew (Bart) of the *Minneapolis Journal*, R. C. Bowman of the *Minneapolis Tribune*, also known for *Freckles and Tan*, a series of books of humorous verse illustrated by Fanny Y. Crory; and J. H. Donahey of the *Cleveland Plain Dealer*. Also count Gaar Williams, author of the nostalgic *Among the Folks in History* and onetime editorial cartoonist for the *Indianapolis News*; and Billy Ireland of the *Columbus* (Ohio) *Dispatch*.

In approximately the middle of these men's careers came the next major event in American history: World War I. During the three years of war before the American entry, major U.S. newspaper cartoonists, all but one of whom favored intervention on behalf of the French and English, kept busy drawing German atrocities. The interventionist artists included W. A. Rogers and Nelson Harding of the *Brooklyn Eagle*. Dutch artist Louis Raemaekers, whose work appeared in the Hearst papers, is generally considered to be better than the Americans who drew for the Allied cause. The lone pen wielded in defense of neutrality belonged to Luther D. Bradley of the *Chicago Daily News*, who died early in 1917.

With the United States in the war, a Bureau of Cartoons, set up under the direction of George J. Hecht, successfully channeled cartoonists' work into the war effort by suggesting topics and otherwise maximizing the propaganda value of cartoons. Luther Bradley was the only cartoonist for an important newspaper to oppose the war, but the radical cartoonists also opposed it and gained prominence in the development of modern political cartooning. Much of their work appeared in *The Masses* (1911–1917) and *Liberator* (1918–1924), because their uncompromising political views were unacceptable to the mainstream. They did not put their shoulders to the wheel of the cause but instead produced cartoons such as Robert Minor's in 1915, which presented the army medical examiner's idea of the "perfect soldier," a muscular giant with no head.

Three of the radical cartoonists who were most important and most content to be called cartoonists were Boardman Robinson, Art Young, and Robert Minor. Robinson was the most influential in terms of his effect on subsequent generations of political cartoonists, partly by virtue of his pioneering technique of using crayon on grained paper, as Daumier and Forain had done before him, and partly because of his position as an instructor at the Art Students League in New York from 1919 to 1930. Among those whom he influenced may be listed his fellow cartoonists Robert Minor and Clive Weed, as well as Oscar Cesare, Rollin Kirby, and Edmund Duffy.

Robert Minor was a successful and highly paid cartoonist by the time he was twenty-seven. He gave up this eminence, however, to draw cartoons that reflected his socialist and antiwar beliefs. He simplified his style to increase the impact of the intensely political cartoons that he drew for *The Masses*.

Art Young achieved probably the widest distribution of any of the radical cartoonists, partly because he was originally a Republican and came to socialism relatively late in life, after he had been on the staffs of several major newspapers, with his work appearing in *Judge*, *Life*, and *Puck*. He was one of *The Masses*' first cartoonists. With *The Masses* editor Max Eastman, Young was also sued for libel unsuccessfully by the Associated Press and was prosecuted in vain by the government under the Espionage Act for obstructing recruitment into the armed forces.

In spite of government suppression, *The Masses* in its various forms had provided a forum for some of the best cartoonists of the period; indeed, art editor John Sloan, along with George Bellows and George Luks, was an acclaimed artist of the Ashcan school. This exceptional degree of talent, coupled with a technique perfectly suited to the expression of moral outrage, has made the names and influence of the radical cartoonists last longer than those of their more moderate contemporaries.

Woman suffrage was the subject of much ridicule and had long been an issue that lent itself perfectly to cartooning. Not all magazines and cartoonists opposed suffrage, though. *Judge* championed the cause. Lou Rogers, among its top artists, is one of several neglected woman cartoonists. Painter Nina Allender drew for the *Suffragist*. Rose O'Neill, whose work appeared in *Puck* in the 1890s, is remembered as a personality and as the creator of the Kewpie Dolls, while her cartoons for suffrage are overlooked. The work of these and other women cartoonists, including Blanche Ames Ames, Cornelia Barns, Edwina Dumm, Fredrikke Schjöth Palmer, May Wilson Preston, Ida Sedgwick Prope, and Alice Beach Winter, some praising women voters and others vilifying its opponents as rumpots, helped sway public opinion and gain ratification of the Nineteenth Amendment shortly after the end of the war.

In 1922 the first Pulitzer Prize for editorial cartooning was awarded, to Rollin Kirby of the *New York World*. If winning prizes is any indication, he dominated editorial cartooning in the 1920s, triumphing again in 1925 and in 1929. (Nelson Harding won in 1927 and 1928.) Kirby studied art in Paris under James McNeill Whistler. His most famous creation was Mr. Dry, the spirit of Prohibition. As mentioned earlier, Joseph Keppler Sr. had drawn a Prohibitionist, and other 1920s cartoonists used the figure, but it was Kirby's that caught the public's imagination. Scholars consider him a transitional figure between the early, multifigure cartooning and the single-figure panels that dominated American political cartooning through the prime of Herblock, Mauldin, Conrad and others, well into the transitional period of the 1960s and 1970s.

Many of the best comic artists of the 1930s drew social, rather than political, cartoons for magazines such as *The New Yorker*, *Vanity Fair*, and *Life*. The depression, however, along with Federal Disaster Relief (FDR) and the National Recovery Administration (NRA) Eagle, gave editorial cartoonists plenty of inspiration. As it happened, most publishers and therefore most cartoonists opposed Roosevelt.

Edmund Duffy, who has been called Kirby's heir, won three Pulitzer Prizes in the next decade: 1931, 1934, and 1940. Just as Rollin Kirby's famous "Mr. Dry" was not represented in any of his prizewinning cartoons, so Duffy's chinless little Ku Klux Klansman was also overlooked by the judges. Like Kirby, Duffy was influenced by Boardman Robinson, and he is credited by Stephen Becker with continuing Kirby's move away from the crowded panels of the nineteenth century and toward the single-figure cartoon of those dominant figures of the mid-twentieth century, Herblock and Bill Mauldin.

The 1930s also gave cartoonists the slant-eyed figure of Japanese militarism and the easily caricatured Mussolini and Hitler. Daniel R. Fitzpatrick, in a style reminiscent of Boardman Robinson, made effective use of the swastika as a symbol of oppression. Fitzpatrick, who had won a Pulitzer Prize in 1926, would add another in 1955.

Also during the 1930s, Oliver Harrington began to establish his reputation. The first important African American cartoonist, Harrington held a B.F.A. degree from Yale University. He began drawing in Harlem, where he was friend to such Harlem Renaissance figures as Langston Hughes and Wally Fisher. Harrington cre-

"The Public Sneak," cartoon from the *Birth Control Review*, 1918. Courtesy of the Library of Congress

ated "Bootsie," an African American "Little Man" who was syndicated in several African American newspapers between 1933 and 1963.

During the war, Bill Mauldin's work in *Stars and Stripes* provided a welcome contrast to the patriotic propaganda. His drawing style reflected the influence of the radical cartoonists rather than the busy, hopeful *Chicago Tribune* artists. He was a combat veteran himself, and his characters, Willie and Joe, were survivors, not heroes. The public—and his fellow infantrymen—took to them immediately. In 1945, when he was twenty-three, Mauldin became the youngest artist ever to win the Pulitzer Prize in editorial cartooning. His popularity continued after the war, with some diminution; his style and the savagery behind it were too grating for a public that wanted amusement, not a crusade. Dissatisfied, he retired from cartooning in 1948. When he returned in 1958, with the *St. Louis Post-Dispatch*, he had switched to a lighter grease pencil and opened up his cartoons. As his Pulitzer Prize in 1959 for an anti-Russian cartoon showed, the targets were fatter. The civil rights struggles of the 1960s provided him with the southern redneck to ridicule. As Hess and Kaplan write, "[I]n the 1960's, when the issue was Civil Rights, *the* cartoonist was Bill Mauldin" (160). Overall, Mauldin may be said to have moved in the same general direction as his liberal counterpart, Herbert Block.

By his own testimony uncomfortable with the "liberal" label, Herbert L. Block ("Herblock") worked as a cartoonist throughout the 1930s. He received the Pulitzer Prize in 1942, but his preeminence generally began after the war. He was one of the first cartoonists to resist the anticommunist hysteria, going so far as to challenge Senator Joseph McCarthy himself. "Mr. Atom," Herblock's sinister personification of the bomb, ranks among the most effective cartoon symbols of the mid-twentieth century. Winning a Pulitzer again in 1979, he continued to be a force through the 1990s.

A more recent addition to the top echelon of the mid- to late twentieth century is Paul Conrad. An Iowa devotee of "Ding" Darling, he left the *Denver Post* in 1964 for the *Los Angeles Times*. Lawsuits filed by Mayor Sam Yorty and the Union Oil Company attest to Conrad's impact there. Stephen Hess and Milton Kaplan's 1975 inclusion of Conrad in the "big four" with Herblock, Mauldin, and Oliphant was not universally accepted, but he is unarguably one of the very top cartoonists of recent decades, winning Pulitzer Prizes in 1964, 1971, and 1984. He retired from the *Los Angeles Times* in 1993 but continued to draw five cartoons a week for the Los Angeles Times Syndicate.

Among the younger men who challenged the dominance of Herblock and Mauldin is Patrick Oliphant, who came from Australia in 1964 to work for the *Denver Post* and won a Pulitzer in 1966. Inspired by British cartoonist Ronald Searle, Oliphant has, in turn, influenced other artists with his fine, exuberant line and emphasis on sheer humor. He is considered by some to be the preeminent editorial cartoonist drawing in America today. A true satirist, he gets his laughs at the expense of the foolish, no matter what party or profession they represent. Formerly with the *Washington Star*, he, like an increasing number of artists, has no local newspaper affiliation, instead drawing directly for syndication.

The early 1960s saw the rise of the so-called New Wave, a term used to include Hugh Haynie of the *Louisville Courier-Journal*; Bill Sanders of the *Milwaukee Journal*; the resurgent Bill Mauldin, whose *Let's Declare Ourselves Winners—and Get the Hell Out* (1985) represented his first collection in twenty years; and other, generally liberal cartoonists such as Tony Auth of the *Philadelphia Inquirer*. Especially hard-hitting and somewhat younger, at least in terms of national prominence, were Tom Darcy of *Newsday*, Bill Shore of the *Los Angeles Herald Examiner*, and Paul Szep of the *Boston Globe*. A "second beachhead" was established by Don Wright of the *Miami News* (Pulitzer, 1980), who has influenced Mike Peters of the *Dayton Daily News* (Pulitzer, 1981), Doug Marlette of the *Atlanta Constitution* (Pulitzer, 1988), Bob Englehart of the *Hartford Courant*, and Dwane Powell of the *Raleigh News Observer*. Three Pulitzers went to antiwar cartoonists: 1968—Eugene Payne, 1970—Tom Darcy, and 1971—Paul Conrad.

Jim Borgman of the *Cincinnati Enquirer* defies classification, in that he is more interested in keeping the debate over issues alive than in crusading for a certain ideology. He won a Pulitzer in 1991. A humane cartoonist who often attains high impact is Draper Hill of the *Detroit News*, who is also a leading American authority on the history of the editorial cartoon.

Conservative cartoonists include Don Hesse of the *St. Louis Globe Democrat*, Charles Werner of the *Indianapolis Star*, Tom Curtis of the *National Review*, Wayne Stayskal of the *Tampa Tribune*, Dick Wright of the *Providence Journal*, Dick Locher of the Tribune Media Services (Pulitzer, 1983), Chuck Asay of the *Colorado Springs Gazette Telegraph*, Steve Benson of the *Arizona Republic* (Pulitzer, 1993), and Mike Ramirez of the *Memphis Commercial Appeal* (Pulitzer, 1994). Gary Brookins of the *Richmond Times-Dispatch* and Bob Gorrell are considered mostly conservative in philosophy. Jeff MacNelly of the *Richmond News Leader* and, later, the *Chicago Tribune*, winner of three Pulitzer Prizes, came closer than any of the other conservatives to the free-swinging hilarity of Oliphant. Indeed, so popular was MacNelly (who died in 2000), vying with Oliphant for the lead in the number of syndicated subscribers, that his numerous imitators earned the title of "the new school" or the sobriquet "MacNelly clones," depending on who is calling the names. William A. Henry III lists several "clones": Jack Ohman of the *Portland Oregonian*, Steve Benson of the *Arizona Republic*, Tim Menees of the *Pittsburgh Post-Gazette*, Bob Gorrell of the *Charlotte Observer*, and Kate Sally Palmer of the *Greensboro News*.[4] In May 1994, freelance editorial cartoonist Bruce Tinsley began syndicating "The Fillmore File" with King Features. This conservative strip features Mallard Fillmore, a reporter who is, as his name indicates, a duck.

The period saw a blurring of the boundaries between comic strips and editorial cartoons, although the idea of a comic strip touching on political issues was hardly new; Al Capp, born Alfred Gerald Caplin, had broken that ground decades ago, with his parables of Dogpatch and its leading citizens, Li'l Abner, Daisy Mae, and Mammy and Pappy Yokum. Walt Kelly's Pogo the Opossum and his friends in the Okefenokee Swamp frequently dealt with political issues and personalities, such as the Jack Acid (John Birch) Society and Simple J. Malarkey (Senator Joseph McCarthy). Kelly's approach to satire was more subtle and whimsical than Capp's.

According to Kalman Goldstein, "Abner and Pogo had a tremendous impact on the next generation of cartoonists; Jules Feiffer, Garry Trudeau and Robert Crumb are among those who have openly acknowledged this influence." He goes on: "Neither Doonesbury nor Bloom County would likely have achieved a mass syndication without the prior successes of Capp and Kelly, and *Mad Magazine* is almost unthinkable" (82).

Disagreement arose as to whether or not Garry Trudeau and Jules Feiffer's use of the strip medium instead of the single panel disqualified them as editorial cartoonists, although the winning of the Pulitzer Prize by Trudeau in 1975 and by Feiffer in 1986 is strong evidence on their behalf. At any rate, it was impossible to deny Trudeau's popularity among young people and liberals. Feiffer has been effective since the late 1950s, not only in his merciless forays against the liberals' nemeses but also in his equally merciless exposure of the self-deception and hypocrisy to which so many liberals fall prey.

Antistrip cartoonists to the contrary, the 1987 Pulitzer Prize was awarded to relative newcomer Berke Breathed, creator of the strip *Bloom County*, setting off a veritable tempest in an inkpot. Breathed at least partly supplanted Trudeau on campus. He dropped *Bloom County* in August 1989 in favor of *Outland*, which ended on March 26, 1995.

Absurd is the word for *Washingtoon*, the world of yet another strip cartoonist, Mark Alan Stamaty, of the *Village Voice* and the *Washington Post*, and his style exemplifies his attitude: crude, caption-crowded drawings with rules of perspective and proportion deliberately ignored. Although he is uncompromisingly liberal and attacked the Reagan administration's policies and the gutless gullibility of the voters without devoting space to liberal foibles, his barbs are not without empathy. After working for years with the *Washington Post*, he switched in 1994 to *Time* magazine. Jim Borgman's "Wonk City" replaced "Washingtoons" in the *Post* and also appeared in the artist's home paper, the *Cincinnati Enquirer*. Its busy panels recall McCutcheon's "Bird Center" and others. King Features began to syndicate "Wonk City" early in 1995.

A small, but growing, number of women are active in the profession. Etta Hulme of the *Fort Worth Star-Telegram* has served as president of the Association of American Editorial Cartoonists. Kate Salley Palmer is syndicated and has worked for newspapers in South Carolina. Linda Boileau draws for the *Frankfort* (Kentucky) *State Journal*, and Linda Godfrey is a freelancer whose cartoons appear in Wisconsin newspapers. Of the younger women editorial cartoonists, Signe Wilkinson, self-styled "attack Quaker," moved from the *San Jose Mercury* to the *Philadelphia Daily News* in 1985 and won the Pulitzer Prize in 1992. M. G. Lord studied under Garry Trudeau at Yale. Also at Yale at that time was Bill Mauldin, who encouraged her and helped her to get a job on the *Chicago Tribune*. She subsequently went with *Newsday* in 1981 at the age of twenty-four and published *Mean Sheets* in 1982. More recent additions to the profession are Washington, D.C.-based Ann Telnaes of North American Syndicate and Californian Marie Woolf of the Almeda Newspaper Group, Chicago Sun-Times Features, and *Mad Magazine*.

There are few African American cartoonists and even fewer African American editorial cartoonists. The undisputed dean of these is the late Oliver Harrington, whose early days are recounted earlier. During World War II he was a war correspondent for the *Pittsburgh Courier*. Working for the National Association for the Advancement of Colored People (NAACP) after the war, he was so outspoken that he moved to Paris to avoid prosecution as a communist. In Berlin on a business trip when the Wall was erected, he was trapped behind the Iron Curtain. During these Cold War years he drew for European publications. Although he had moved on from Harlem to a world stage, lampooning racism and injustice in South Africa and elsewhere, he still commented on American society and politics. Harrington returned to his native country briefly in 1972 and at length in 1992. He died in 1995 in Berlin.

Brumsic Brandon, creator of "Luther," which was syndicated by the Los Angeles Times Syndicate, is a syndicated editorial cartoonist for several African American papers. His daughter said that her father was influenced "a lot" by Ollie Harrington.[5]

Rupert Kinnard uses his talents as an editorial cartoonist to write his black, gay-perspective comic strips. He created the comic strip "Cathartic Comics," published in the *San Francisco Sentinel* and *San Francisco Weekly*, featuring the characters B. B. ("Brown Bomber") and the Diva. A more traditional cartoonist is Louisianan John Eaves Slade. As the title of his first collection, *But I Am Too a Black Cartoonist!—Really!* suggests, he prides himself on work that cannot be "automatically pigeonholed."[6] Overall, however, editorial cartooning remains an overwhelmingly white, male profession.

In the early 1980s, syndication, both by individual artists and by groups of artists "packaged" together, became widespread. Cartoonists just out of—or still in—college were suddenly exposed to mass audiences. While no one denies the importance of this phenomenon, critics disagree as to its effect. On one hand, it does enable cartoonists to reach a larger audience. Also, it helps some to increase their income while letting the syndicates take care of business details. Among the drawbacks is the fact that young artists may be thrust into national prominence before they are ready. Apprentice mistakes may be made, if not before a national readership, at least under the unforgiving eye of editors who subscribe to the syndicate. Insofar as the profession of editorial cartooning is concerned, the availability of inexpensive syndicated packages makes it less likely that midsize newspapers will be willing to hire a beginning artist, even at a low salary. Also, a syndicated cartoonist is likely to look increasingly to a national audience, at the expense of local issues. According to William A. Henry, "syndication tends to soften the most ascerbic cartoonists."[7]

Regardless of this trend away from the local cartoon, several artists continue to deal heavily with local issues alongside national and international concerns and in spite of the greater money and fame available outside their own backyards. Although affiliated with the *Christian Science Monitor* from 1986 to 1996, Jeff Danziger produced *Danziger's Vermont Cartoons: Political and Otherwise*. Jerry Fearing published *Minnesota Flavored Editorial Cartoons* himself. Another Minnesota artist, Ed Fischer, is represented by several volumes of cartoons (he leaves the lutefisk out of the national ones). George Fisher, frequently cited as the most effective of the local cartoonists, has compiled several anthologies of Arkansas cartoons, including *Old Guard Rest Home* and *God Would Have Done It If He'd Had the Money*. Paul Szep of the *Boston Globe* left United Features Syndicate because his commitment to the syndicate prevented him from drawing as many local cartoons as he would have liked. The "Troubletown" cartoons of Lloyd Dangle are set in San Francisco. Some other prominent cartoonists with local emphasis include Bob Engelhart of the *Hartford Courant*, Draper Hill of the *Detroit News*, Paul Rigby of the *New York Daily News*, and Ben Sargent of the *Austin American Statesman* (Pulitzer, 1982).

In the litigious 1980s, the shadow of libel suits fell again across the editorial cartoonist's drawing board. Although no editorial cartoonist to date has lost such a libel suit, the mere frequency of their filing is becoming a factor for both editors and cartoonists to consider. Referring to the inclusion of "malicious intent" in the legal definition of libel, *Philadelphia Inquirer* editor Eugene Roberts was quoted on a *Donahue* show as responding to a politician's suing because a cartoonist had held him up to ridicule: "My goodness, a political cartoonist holding up a politician to ridicule. That's not libel, that's a job description."[8]

A list of unsuccessful suers and their suees in recent years would include Los Angeles mayor Sam Yorty and Paul Conrad, Massachusetts governor Edward King and Paul Szep, and former Ohio Supreme Court justice James Celebreze and Milt Priggee. Political evangelist Jerry Falwell sued *Hustler* publisher Larry Flynt over an ad parody depicting the evangelist committing incest with his mother in an outhouse. A jury awarded Falwell $200,000 for "emotional distress," but the decision was reversed by the Supreme Court in a unanimous decision. Although this was not an editorial cartoon, *Hustler* was attacking Falwell on political grounds, and the "emotional distress" precedent could have had far-reaching effects on cartoonists' First Amendment protection.

In spite of the outcome of such cases, corporations and public figures continue to sue newspapers over editorial cartoons, with local ones giving the most offense. These legal developments continue to be worrisome to editors and cartoonists, as the time and expense of defending against even the most far-fetched of libel suits may intimidate all but the most fearless—or deep-pocketed—publishers.

Litigation is not the only obstacle to cartoonists' expression, as increasingly intransigent readers tend to boycott or at least picket at the drop of a pen. In the winter of 1992, Don Wright and Jack Ohman drew syndicated cartoons that offended autoworkers. In response to Wright's and Ohman's cartoons criticizing American workmanship, readers canceled subscriptions, auto dealers withdrew ads, and readers telephoned their anger in several cities in the Midwest and New York.

Garry Trudeau continued to stir up controversy. In 1989 a few newspapers dropped a series on AIDS, fearful that readers might interpret the gallows humor of Trudeau's character as making fun of AIDS victims. Twenty-five clients refused to print his 1991 strips spotlighting the Federal Drug Enforcement Agency's suppressed—and subsequently leaked—file on Vice President Quayle's alleged cocaine use.

While affronts to the dignity of public figures may draw lawsuits, cartoons criticizing religious groups will draw lightning. Cartoonists drawing such lightning include Doug Marlette (*New York Newsday*), who offended Catholics; and Joel Pett of the Lexington, Kentucky, *Herald Leader*, who ran afoul of conservative Christian readers over the abortion issue.

In the early 1990s, issues of censorship often came under the catchphrase "political correctness." To members of a profession whose job it is to offend everyone, any increase in public sensitivity is cause for concern.

In an economically significant development, several editorial cartoonists have branched out and begun drawing comic strips. One of the earliest and most successful of these side ventures was Jeff MacNelly's apolitical *Shoe* in 1977. Others include Mike Peters' *Mother Goose and Grimm*, and Wayne Stayskal's *Balderdash*. Pat Oliphant's *Sunday Punk*, which ran briefly in 1984, often dealt with social or political issues. Doug Marlette's *Kudzu*, begun in 1981, features the hypocritical evangelist Rev. Will B. Dunn, star of "There's No Business Like Soul Business." Many other editorial cartoonists, too numerous to list here, have tried their hands at comic strips, with varying degrees of success.

If some editorial cartoonists have sought artistic outlet (and increased earnings) in less political forms, others have expanded the comic art form more in the direction of the novel, while retaining elements of social and/or political criticism. Jules Feiffer wrote the cartoon novel *Tantrum* about a forty-two-year-old man who wills himself back to the age of two yet retains all the desires and knowledge of an adult. Art Spiegelman, who with Francoise Mouly edited *Raw*, "The Comics Magazine for Damned Intellectuals," has taken "Maus" from the pages of *Raw* to the book-length *Maus: A Survivor's Tale*. In this black-and-white story of the Holocaust as Spiegelman's parents lived it, Jews are depicted as mice and the Nazis as cats. The resulting incongruous hybrid is as close to literature as it is to comics.

In the 1980s came a resurgence of the political cartoon, due in part to the increasingly visual nature of our society. In general, the period saw a trend toward originality of style, with an increasing emphasis on humor for its own sake, perhaps a by-product of the political "honeymoon" of the early Reagan years. In a series of sharp attacks that lasted more than a decade, critics were quick to assail the new trend. As early as 1981, journalist William A. Henry III wrote, in his damning "The Sit-Down Comics," that the new generation seems to be trying to anesthetize the social conscience (54). In 1982 Oliphant repeated an earlier assessment that he had made for the *Los Angeles Times* in which he criticized

MacNelly and Peters as being "predictably bland" and for having "diluted the business." With the intensity that has made him an outspoken guardian of the art, he stated: "Political cartooning's too valuable to just be a vehicle for gags."[9]

Randall Harrison observes in *The Cartoon, Communication to the Quick* that many cartoonists "have moved away from the crayon-solid figure and the somber comment" and that, influenced by such modern illustrators as Ronald Searles, they favored sketchy, fine-line caricatures and approached their targets "with rapier wit rather than broadaxe attacks" (78). He sees the tendency toward more humor and less ideology as a result of the change in newspapers resulting from the passing of strong, politically opinionated publishers like William Randolph Hearst, Captain Joseph Patterson, and Colonel Robert McCormick. "The modern editorial cartoon may inform, and may persuade, but, above all, it must attract" (79).

By the mid-1980s, a backlash set in, with some cartoonists launching cartoon barbs at the president and his oft-indicted associates. Among the critics of the new geniality was Bill Sanders, then of the *Milwaukee Journal.* While praising the talented new artists entering the profession and seeing a "quantum leap in the quality of humor and the use of the gag motif," he warned that integrity of political cartooning was threatened by the "lack of substance and ideology" and denounced the "gag groupies" who serve up "sugar-coated placebos."[10]

Perhaps the trend toward more humor stemmed from the popularity of President Reagan himself; whatever might go awry in foreign or domestic afairs, the vast majority of the public found itself unable to blame the friendly, cheerful man who resided at 1600 Pennsylvania Avenue for eight years. If cartoonists had built careers and won Pulitzers at the expense of Richard Nixon and Jimmy Carter, they grew fat and sassy during the administrations of Ronald Reagan. His earlier career as a "B" movie actor, playing roles as cowboys, war heroes, "the Gipper," and friend of Bonzo the chimp, invited numerous metaphors. A survey of the hundreds of cartoons of Ronald Reagan would probably find the western motif the most common one, often positive at first but frequently showing the cowboy president as overwhelmed or trigger-happy in later years. Reagan's face, redolent in wrinkles and wattles, and his big ears, along with a his dyed-black pompadour, inspired competition among cartoonists. Most artists portrayed him as amiable, if increasingly bemused, during his second term. Only Paul Conrad drew the mean Reagan, the one with the pursed lips and hard eyes, whom he sometimes depicted as Reagan Hood, who robs from the poor and gives to the rich.

The question of President Reagan's intellectual capability had been an issue all along. In 1981, Garry Trudeau sent television reporter Roland Hedly on a tour of the cobwebbed catacombs of Ronald Reagan's brain. During the presidential primary season in 1984, Lee Judge of the *Kansas City Times* drew the proverbial ring filled with political hats, including a space helmet for former astronaut John Glenn, a beanie for Gary Hart, and a dunce cap for Ronald Reagan. As Ronald Reagan's mental decline accelerated in the last two or three years of his second term, the pack closed in. Generally, the president's neck and head (except for the pompadour) grew smaller, and his suits grew bigger.

Appropriately, cartoonists dramatized Ronald Reagan's exit in show business terms. In late July 1991, Bob Gorrell of the *Richmond News Leader* drew him taking one last bow, holding onto the curtain, an American flag, as flowers shower onto the stage: "Exit, stage right." Oliphant presented a back view of the Reagans sitting in an empty theater. The retiring president waves good-bye to his own image as a cowboy, in turn waving good-bye, while riding off into the sunset.

The subsequent revelation of the president's Alzheimer's disease took the zest out of the jokes, as Steve Benson learned at the end of August 1996. Known for his savage attacks on liberals and Democrats, Benson drew Nancy Reagan reminding the Republican convention that "Ronnie's legacy must never be forgotten." On the large television screen in the background an ancient, disheveled Ronald Reagan says: "What poor? What Blacks? What women?" Newspapers all over the country received angry letters, and their editorials listing Benson's impeccable conservative credentials and explaining the history of editorial cartooning and the concept of metaphor were dismissed. Whether the operant factor was President Reagan's still-considerable popularity or heightened awareness of Alzheimer's, the episode showed that a cartoonist must avoid the increasing number of red flags that enrage the public bull.

While the mid- to late 1980s and early 1990s lacked the national crises of Vietnam and Watergate for inspiration, they were not without interest. Tension and terrorism in the Middle East provided figures such as Yasser Arafat, Muammar Qaddafi, the Ayatollah Ruhollah Khomeini, Saddam Hussein, and others, who offered irresistible targets for ethnic stereotyping.

The 1984 presidential campaign found cartoonists drawing "many more cartoons of Geraldine Ferraro than of George Bush" and portraying her favorably for the most part. For the balance of the 1980s and the early 1990s, cartoonists had fun with President George Bush and Vice President Dan Quayle. Trudeau drew President Bush as an invisible man with an evil twin and Vice President Quayle as a tiny, floating feather. Oliphant pictured Bush as a very thin, schoolmarmish figure carrying a purse.

After Bill Clinton's victory over George Bush in the 1992 election, cartoonists had to deal with a new and at first baffling face. Clinton's square jaw and prebulbous nose, along with his fondness for Elvis Presley, provided some early guidance, as did his playing of the saxaphone on a late-night television show during the campaign. When asked if the liberal Clinton would be treated gently by members of the predominantly liberal cartooning profession, Kevin Siers of the *Charlotte* (North Carolina) *Observer* pointed out that so-called liberal cartoonists who savaged the Bush and Reagan administrations are the "same cartoonists who shrank Jimmy Carter into a dried-up, ineffective dwarf, easy pickings for mad ayatolahs, killer rabbits and has-been actors."[11] By 1997 cartoonists were drawing Clinton with the deer-in-the-headlights eyes reserved for failing presidents. Oliphant remarked early in 1997 that Clinton is "boring, but his scandals are getting better. . . . Scandals, China, the Millennium, Paula Jones. I can't wait!"[12] In the vein of his shorthand representation of Dan Quayle as a feather and comparable to Nast's reducing of Gratz Brown to a mere tag on Horace Greeley's coattail, in the mid-1990s Trudeau represented Clinton as a waffle and Speaker of the House Newt Gingrich as a bomb with a burning fuse.

The scandals predicted by Siers, Oliphant, and others soon materialized in the form of Whitewater and Monicagate (aka Zippergate). The president's skill at evading his Republican pursuers invited additional metaphors in October 1998, as Jim Borgman drew Clinton as Houdini, Jim Larrick of the *Columbus* (Ohio) *Dis-*

patch drew the president as the Roadrunner, and Mike Luckovich drew Special Prosecutor Kenneth Starr as Elmer Fudd to Clinton's Wascally Wabbit.

Somewhat apart from all this, ignoring such superficial phenomena as politicians and political parties, are underground and alternative artists who have rejected or simply ignored the entire social and political system. With modest financial expectations, they and their small presses need not be concerned with the restrictions of corporate publishers and editors or deterred by the prospect of alienating readers. In the 1990s, some alternative cartoonists such as Ted Rall, Dan Perkins ("Tom Tomorrow"), and Nina Paley found a degree of acceptance, but not much remuneration.

While it remains to be seen whether any of the recent technological advances are comparable to the earlier developments in lithography and newspaper printing, improvements in technology were nevertheless a factor in the latter part of the twentieth century. On March 16, 1965, John Chase pioneered the first regularly scheduled editorial cartoon to appear in color on television. Other trailblazers include, from the mid-1970s, Bill Daniels, WSB TV, Atlanta; and Hugh Haynie, WSOC TV in Charlotte, North Carolina. In 1981, Mike Peters, with his animated cartoons on the *NBC Nightly News*, became the first network political cartoonist. Ranan Lurie animated political cartoons for the *MacNeil-Lehrer Newshour* in 1986. John Slade on New Orleans television in 1996 tried projecting his editorial cartoons the way weathercasters do. Annual meetings of the Association of American Editorial Cartoonists take up such problems as the difficulty of drawing with a computer "mouse" and the advantages and disadvantages of transmitting cartoons by fax.

The revolution in electronic communication has put some cartoon services on the information highway. On April 1, 1995, United Media introduced a World Wide Web site, "The Inkwell" (http://www.unitedmedia.com/inkwell), which makes available on-line the work of nine comic artists and ten editorial cartoonists. Commercial on-line services such as Prodigy, CompuServe, and America Online also offer cartoons. Developments continue at a dizzying pace. The opening of a new medium raises a host of issues regarding rights and royalties. An increasing number of artists post cartoons on their own Web sites. The American Association of Editorial Cartoonists (http://detnews.com/AAEC/AAEC.html) provides an on-line version of its *Newsletter*, posting stories from its own and other publications, as well as providing sample cartoons. *Wittyworld*'s Web site is discussed later.

The debate about how important humor is to editorial cartooning, begun in the early 1980s, continued through the 1990s. Three other factors influenced the future of editorial cartooning at the end of the twentieth century: a diminishing number of jobs, with fewer newspapers, fewer of which have full-time editorial cartoonists; editorial timidity of corporation-owned newspapers, as nervous advertisers and touchy readers have editors and publishers looking over their shoulders; and a "shrinking pool of shared imagery resulting from poor education."[13] James R. Beniger looks on the brighter side, finding less labeling and more commonality among recent cartoons.[14] Widespread familiarity with public figures through television has removed at least one impediment to immediacy. So the cartoonists may have lost Salt River, as well as most of Shakespeare and the rest of the western classics (some enterprising scholar should check to see if this is true), but they have gained (?) an ever-changing gallery of television personalities and commercials that flickers across the television screen of our national consciousness.

HISTORY AND CRITICISM

The first real historian of the subject was Philadelphia-born James P. Malcolm, a fierce loyalist whose 1813 book, *An Historical Sketch of the Art of Caricaturing*, describes a very few caricatures dealing with the American war, while touching on Asian and European caricatures but emphasizing the British. In 1862, Richard Grant White provided for *Harper's New Monthly Magazine* a survey of caricature from the time of the Egyptians up to the present in France and England, concluding with a plea for caricaturists to exercise restraint. In "The Limits of Caricature" in 1866, *The Nation* pointed out technical weaknesses in American caricature and concluded that "upon the whole, we can hardly esteem caricature as an agreeable or particularly useful art; for fairness and good nature are almost impossible in the practice" (55).

American scholarly consideration of editorial cartooning may be said to have begun in 1878, with James Parton's *Caricature and Other Comic Art*. Parton traced the history of caricature from Roman times to his own, devoting the final thirty-odd pages to early and later American caricature from Franklin to Nast. The study is still worthwhile and includes 203 illustrations.

A few years later, Arthur Penn noted "The Growth of Caricature" in *The Critic*, citing Parton as a source. He commented on the failure of American imitations of *Punch* and on the success of *Puck*, while criticizing it for weakness in pictorial social commentary. Joseph Bucklin Bishop wrote in *The Century* in 1892 that political caricature in the United States dates from Andrew Jackson's first administration. His 1904 book, *Our Political Drama, Conventions, Campaigns, Candidates*, uses this material with few a changes, while reprinting numerous political cartoons. Bishop reworked basically the same graphic and historical material for *Presidential Nominations and Elections*.

Several scholarly milestones from the early part of the twentieth century are worth seeing, beginning with Arthur Bartlett Maurice and Frederick Taber Cooper's *The History of the Nineteenth Century in Caricature*. While emphasizing French and British caricature, the authors devote considerable attention to the American forms, including Currier & Ives, Nast, *Puck*, and *Judge*, and to the rise of the daily newspaper cartoon at the close of the century. Frank Weitenkampf's *American Graphic Art*, which appeared in 1912, was revised and enlarged in 1924. It was reprinted in 1970 and was a source for many subsequent researchers. Weitenkampf examines caricature from Franklin up to the newspaper cartoonists of his own time. The twenty-two-page chapter "Comic Paper and Daily Press" deals with early comic periodicals and continues with a survey of artists active at the time of writing. He continued his consideration of editorial cartooning as a serious art form in 1913 with his illustrated article "American Cartoonists of Today," which appeared in *Century*.

Twenty years later came the first volume of William Murrell's indispensable *A History of American Graphic Humor*, which ranges from the earliest wood engravings through the Civil War. In addition to an extensive background, the book provides 237 illustrations, listing the source or location of each. Murrell's comments, necessarily brief, are nevertheless historically and aesthetically worthwhile. Published in 1938, Volume 2 uses 242 illustrations in taking us through the presidential campaign of 1936. Both volumes have an index, bibliography, and list of illustrations. Between these two publication dates, Murrell's concise and useful "The Rise and Fall of Cartoon Symbols" appeared in *The American Scholar*.

Thomas Craven's copiously illustrated *Cartoon Cavalcade* presents strip and humorous cartoons as well as some editorial ones, spanning from 1883 to 1943. Essays by Craven relate the graphic humor of various periods to events and attitudes of the time.

The next year, 1944, saw the publication of historian Allan Nevins and Frank Weitenkampf's *A Century of Political Cartoons*. In addition to an excellent, nine-page introductory essay on caricature and cartoon, it explicates some 100 significant cartoons and chronicles the history of American political cartooning from 1800 to 1900.

Journalism professors have commented on editorial cartoons. Frank Luther Mott mentioned some historical highlights of the subject in *American Journalism*. Professor Henry Ladd Smith documented "The Rise and Fall of the Political Cartoon" in the *Saturday Review* in 1954, labeling the first quarter of this century the "golden age of the political cartoonists" (9).

Dealing primarily with journalism is Peter Marzio's *The Men and Machines of American Journalism*, which merits mention here because it emphasizes the impact of technology on the print medium and on the graphic arts, with some attention to editorial cartooning.

Stephen Becker's *Comic Art in America* is an important work, even though it devotes only one chapter (fifty-five pages) to editorial cartooning. Its strengths include the numerous illustrations and detailed coverage of the Pulitzer Prize years, 1922–1958. Popular rather than scholarly, *New York Times* correspondent and editor (as of 1982) Samuel A. Tower's *Cartoons and Lampoons: The Art of Political Satire* presents historical background and topical issues, with numerous full- and half-page reprints of widely available cartoons.

Stephen Hess and Milton Kaplan's *The Ungentlemanly Art* remains the definitive book on American editorial cartooning because of its comprehensiveness and its documentation of both print and graphic sources. Perhaps the authors lose some of the advantage of currency by devoting only 54 of the book's 173 pages to the chapter on "Newspapers, 1884–1975," even in the revised edition. After the introduction, subsequent chapters are arranged according to media: "Copper Engraving and Woodcut," "Lithography and Early Magazines," "Magazines," and "Newspapers." The revised edition of 1975 is only slightly revised, adding a dozen or so new bibliographical references and some then-current cartoons. The long-awaited update of *The Ungentlemanly Art* is *Drawn & Quartered: The History of American Political Cartoons* by Stephen Hess and Sandy Northrop. Thoroughly updated but scaled down, at 164 7" × 9" pages versus 252 7 ½" × 10" pages, it necessarily condenses some of the early history. There are numerous illustrations, many new to this volume. Although it supplements, rather than replaces, the 1975 book, *Drawn & Quartered*, with its conscientious updating of recent history as well as trends in the profession of editorial cartooning, is altogether worthwhile.

Charles Press' *The Political Cartoon* was published in 1981. Written from a political scientist's point of view, this extensively illustrated book emphasizes the role of editorial cartoonists in a democracy. Press devotes several chapters to an anecdotal history of American editorial cartooning. The chapter "Since World War II" is particularly welcome for its coverage of then-contemporary cartoonists, especially members of the "New Wave."

A collection of essays rather than a survey, Roger A. Fischer's *Them Damned Pictures: Explorations in American Political Cartoon Art* is less adulatory than previous studies as the author faults earlier scholars, himself included, for taking too seriously the profession's paid practitioners. Fischer analyzes the evolution of visual symbolism with the intent "to raise questions in need of further scrutiny rather than to provide definitive answers" (xviii–xiv). Well written and insightful, this book adds much to the study of editorial cartooning. It includes bibliographical references and over 100 full- and half-page illustrations.

A welcome update is *Graphic Opinions: Editorial Cartoonists and Their Art*, edited by Jack Colldeweih and Kalman Goldstein. The 1998 volume reprints interviews, biographical data, and sample cartoons for two dozen cartoonists, four of them Pulitzer winners, between their mid-thirties and late forties.

Other works, more restricted in subject matter, include Joan D. Dolmetsch's *Rebellion and Reconciliation: Satirical Prints on the Revolution at Williamsburg*, a catalog of caricatures collected in colonial Williamsburg. The book is worth seeing both for the topical background and for the prints themselves.

Among the anthologies dealing with early years in American history are Donald H. Cresswell's invaluable *The American Revolution in Drawings and Prints. A Check-list of 1765–1790 Graphics in the Library of Congress* and Michael Wynn Jones' 1975 book, *The Cartoon History of the American Revolution*. Also specialized is Clarence Saunders Brigham's *Journals and Journeymen*, a contribution to the history of early American newspapers. *Early American Prints* by Carl W. Dreppard has a twenty-page chapter on "Early American Caricatures."

Kenneth M. Johnson's *The Sting of the Wasp* has as its subject the San Francisco humor magazine *The Wasp*, which has received far less attention than its contemporaries *Puck* and *Judge*. Johnson's folio work reprints twenty cartoons, along with twenty pages of hard-to-find historical background.

Ralph E. Shikes' *The Indignant Eye* concerns the artist as social critic in prints and drawings from the fifteenth century to Picasso. In addition to providing an illustrated history of European protest art, Shikes devotes a seventy-page chapter to "The United States since 1870" and deals with the major cartoonists from Keppler and Davenport up through the radical cartoonists.

A book even more specialized than Shikes' is Richard Fitzgerald's *Art and Politics* (based on his 1970 dissertation), which tells the story of *The Masses* and *Liberator* in the first chapter and devotes a thoroughly documented chapter each to Art Young, Robert Minor, John Sloan, K. R. Chamberlain, and Maurice Becker. There are several helpful reference lists.

The Masses has inspired another fine work, Rebecca Zurier's *Art for the Masses (1911–1917): A Radical Magazine and Its Graphics*. This catalog is a retrospective of the artwork from *The Masses*. Zurier's animated essays chronicle the magazine's brief, but tumultuous, life and place the graphics in their social and historical context. The 450-page folio volume *Images of American Radicalism* by Paul Buhle mixes cartoons with posters and photographs.

Thomas Nast's "Emancipation" poster, 1865. Courtesy of the Library of Congress

Our national symbol inspired Alton Ketchum's thorough study *Uncle Sam: The Man and the Legend*, which reprints numerous cartoons and traces the evolution of America's symbols. More inclusive works that include folk art and other artifacts as well as cartoons are *The Bird, the Banner, and Uncle Sam: Images of America in Folk and Popular Art* by Elinor Lander Horwitz and *Tippecanoe and Trinkets Too* by Roger A. Fischer.

Narrowly restricted chronologically is Anne Marie Serio's twenty-one-page monograph *Political Cartoons in the 1848 Election Campaign*. It reproduces nine seldom-reprinted political lithographs by various engravers.

Mary and Gordon Campbell's *The Pen, Not the Sword*, an extensively illustrated anthology of the period of Nast, Keppler, Gillam, Opper, and other artists of the end of the nineteenth century, is accompanied by some confusing background essays.

Commemorative volumes include *The Image of America in Caricature & Cartoon*, which reproduces the exhibition presented at the Amon Carter Museum in Fort Worth, Texas. Explanatory material includes a two-page overview of American cartoons and caricatures and thirty-seven pages of American history related to cartoons. Each of the 263 cartoons is accompanied by a brief paragraph that analyzes its background and point of view. *The American Presidency in Political Cartoons: 1776–1976*, by Thomas C. Blaisdell Jr. and Peter Selz, reprints 113 cartoons, mostly black and white, from the Berkeley University Art Museum's bicentennial exhibition, along with introductory essays by the editors.

Two other books, Lynne Deur's *Political Cartoonists* and Jim Ivey's brief handbook, *U.S. History in Cartoons: The Civil War through WWII*, have some value, even though they seem to be aimed at secondary school readers.

Several books approach history and criticism from an insider's point of view; Syd Hoff's *Editorial and Political Cartooning* is discussed later, along with John Chase's *Today's Cartoon*. In *Great Cartoonists and Their Art*, cartoonist-collector Art Wood reproduces 120 cartoons from his collection, which features comic strip artists but includes a number of editorial cartoonists, with anecdotal reminiscences. Roy Paul Nelson's *Comic Art and Caricature*, mentioned later, discusses the art and its practitioners. *The Cartoon, Communication to the Quick* was written by Randall P. Harrison, identified as a "cartoonist as well as a communications researcher" (of the University of California, San Francisco). The thoroughly indexed book is helpful for its presentation of overall communications and graphics theory, as well as for its coverage of world and U.S. editorial cartooning.

Another group of books deals primarily with world cartooning, but several merit our attention because they devote some space to Americans: John Gilbert Bohun Lynch's *A History of Caricature*, C. R. (Charles Robert) Ashbee's *Caricature*, and Michael Wynn Jones' *The Cartoon History of Great Britain*. Draper Hill's three books, *Mr. Gillray, the Caricaturist*; *Fashionable Contrasts: 100 Caricatures by James Gillray*; and *The Satirical Etchings of James Gillray*, shed light on an English artist who had great influence on Americans.

Wider in scope but shorter in length, Clifford K. Berryman's booklet, *Development of the Cartoon*, is interesting primarily because its author was a well-known cartoonist. H. R. Westwood's *Modern Caricaturists*, with an introduction by David Low, has a chapter on Rollin Kirby and one on D. R. Fitzpatrick. More recently, *Mightier than the Sword* by W. G. Rogers surveys important European cartoonists and caricaturists, but it seems aimed at a high school audience. While it provides more illustrations, Bevis Hillier's *Cartoons and Caricatures* touches only briefly on American cartoonists. *The Cartoon* by John Geipel, however, has fifteen pages on Americans, eclectically mixing editorial with social cartoonists.

Although Ralph Shikes and Steven Heller's *The Art of Satire* deals primarily with the satirical drawings of thirty-four painters of the nineteenth to mid-twentieth centuries, especially the French, it does include works of Americans George Grosz, John Sloan, and Ad Reinhardt. *Political Graphics: Art as a Weapon* by French historian and medievalist Robert Philippe is heavily continental in its approach and lavishly illustrated with poster and cartoon art from the past 500 years. Similar to Philippe's book in its emphasis is *The Art of Caricature* by British art historian Edward Lucie-Smith. Most of the meager American samples are nonpolitical. A study of Victorian taste valuable to students of caricature is Roy T. Matthews and Peter Mellini's *In "Vanity Fair"*, which includes caricatures of American politicians by Thomas Nast and others probably by James Montgomery Flagg. Colin Seymour-Ure and Jim Schoff's *David Low* makes it clear why the English cartoonist was so important and so influential for those to follow.

Philosopher-psychologist Sam Keen compiled the international images of *Faces of the Enemy* to support his thesis that "we create the enemy . . . by projecting our own fears, inadequacies and self-hatred onto others." The book's 318 small reproductions, 116 of them in color, aim to illustrate this and the "universal" tendency to dehumanize.

Difficult to categorize is *A History of Komiks of the Philippines and Other Countries* by Cynthia Roxas and Joaquin Arevalo Jr. Although it deals primarily with comic strips and comic magazines, it is still worth mentioning. Of special interest to students of American political cartoons is the changing way in which Filipino artists have depicted Uncle Sam.

Roy Douglas has compiled four books of cartoons with commentary on the historical background. In general, they are unindexed and reprint few American cartoons but nevertheless have marginal value for scholars desiring to compare our cartoonists with their European contemporaries: *Great Nations Still Enchained, 1848–1914*; *The Great War, 1914–1918*; *Between the Wars, 1919–1939*; and *The World War, 1939–1945*.

Steven Heller and Gail Anderson's *The Savage Mirror: The Art of Contemporary Caricature* celebrates the renaissance of caricature in the United States and Great Britain from the 1950s to the 1990s. "The New Wave" takes up over half of the book with running commentary on the 1960s generation of caricaturists and their works.

A recent (1994) and most ambitious work, *Cartoonometer: Taking the Pulse of the World's Cartoonists*, edited by George Szabo and John A. Lent, has numerous illustrations, some in color, and eighteen profiles. "Cartoonometer" refers to a survey of "over five thousand cartoonists" worldwide.

Free of the fetters of censorship, profitability, and respectability, underground comics constitute a scandalous cousin of mainstream editorial cartooning, one that rejects all the premises of our society and government, not just a particular candidate or party. Three works on the subject are Les Daniels' *Comix: A History of Comic Books in America*, Dave Schreiner's *Kitchen Sink Press: The First 25 Years*, and Mark James Estren's *A History of Underground Comics*.

Underground comic artist Trina Robbins wrote *A Century of Women Cartoonists*, which is wide in scope and only incidentally concerned with editorial cartooning. Nevertheless, the volume is significant for its examination of women cartoonists in the larger political sense. More valuable to students of editorial cartooning are Alice Sheppard's *Cartooning for Suffrage* and William Cole's *Women Are Wonderful! A History in Cartoons of a Hundred Years with America's Most Controversial Figure*. Sheppard's volume gives the reader biography, illustrations, and feminist interpretation, reprinting over 200 illustrations, the overwhelming majority by women, with an index and a bibliography. Cole's book is worth seeing for a general impression of the representation of women in cartoons from mid-nineteenth to mid-twentieth centuries with only three women cartoonists represented.

Book-length treatments of ethnic topics include Gary L. Bunker and Davis Bitton's *The Mormon Graphic Image, 1834–1914*, *The Coming Man: 19th Century American Perceptions of the Chinese*, Rudolf Glanz's *The Jew in Early American Wit and Graphic Humor*, and L. Perry Curtis' *Apes and Angels; The Irishman in Victorian Caricature*.

Several books study individual cartoonists from the early period. Paul Revere's heavy representation is in proportion to his historical importance. One of the more recent is of the most use to students of political cartooning: *Paul Revere's Engravings* by Clarence Saunders Brigham. Less helpful to students of editorial cartooning than Brigham's biography is Elbridge Henry Goss' *The Life of Colonel Paul Revere, with Portraits, Many Illustrations, Fac-similes, etc.*, although it reprints more of Revere's engravings than do most of the biographies. W. L. Andrews' limited edition *Paul Revere and His Engraving* is helpful, but scarce (170 copies printed). Esther Forbes' *Paul Revere and the World He Lived In* reprints Henry Pelham's letter accusing Revere of plagiarism, as well as a few washed-out reproductions.

Some short studies deal with lesser-known engravers Amos Doolittle and William Charles: William A. Beardsley's *An Old New Haven Engraver and His Work: Amos Doolittle* catalogs some sixty of Doolittle's engravings and appends a brief biography. The little pamphlet *William Charles, Early Caricaturist, Engraver and Publisher of Children's Books* by Harry B. Weiss includes a six-page biographical sketch and reproduces some of Charles' illustrations and one political cartoon.

David Claypool Johnston, American Graphic Humorist, 1798–1865; Catalog, by Malcolm Johnson, catalogs "an exhibition held jointly by the American Antiquarian Society . . . and others in March, 1970," listing the drawings and cartoons shown, as well as their owners at the time. Its biographical essay merits mention here.

About Currier & Ives are the books *Currier and Ives* by F. A. Conningham and *Currier and Ives, Printmakers to the American People* by Harry T. Peters. Peters has also written *America on Stone*, which is conceived as a tribute to the vast number of lesser-known lithographers of the period.

Appropriately, Thomas Nast is also well represented. The definitive biography is Albert Bigelow Paine's *Th. Nast: His Period and His Pictures*, warmly written with a wealth of personal details. Paine includes rare early drawings and sketches among the 450 illustrations that he reproduces and treats Nast, whom he had met, with contagious admiration and affection. An antidote to this subjectivity is Morton Keller's *The Art and Politics of Thomas Nast*, which sees bigotry as much as altruism behind Nast's campaign against the Irish-Catholic Tweed. The large-format book reproduces 241 cartoons and illustrations, mostly full-page. A third book on Nast—and the scholar would be wise to consult all three—is *Thomas Nast: Political Cartoonist* by J. Chal Vinson, which emphasizes in its forty-one-page text the events of Nast's life more than his personality and reproduces 154 drawings.

Cartoonist-scholar Draper Hill is working on a massive biography of Thomas Nast. At the time of writing, publisher John Adler was preparing a CD-ROM, *The World of Thomas Nast*, with contributions by Draper Hill, Roger Fischer, Richard West, Alice Caulkins of the Mcculloch Hall Historical Museum, and others. Also projected is a CD-ROM version of *Harper's Weekly*, 1857–1865.

For the other cartooning giant of the nineteenth century, Joseph Keppler, there is Richard Samuel West's *Satire on Stone: The Political Cartoons of Joseph Keppler*. This painstakingly researched and diligently footnoted commentary explicates the cartoons and explains the political background of Keppler's times. Useful features include 147 full-page, black-and-white reproductions and *Puck* covers, nearly all by Keppler himself, as well as sixteen color plates; an index; a cartoon index; an appendix with brief biographies of "Keppler's Colleagues and Students"; a "selected," but useful, bibliography; and a list of "Primary Sources" giving locations of Keppler materials.

Quite unscholarly, yet fascinating and engaging, is the rare *Homer Davenport of Silverton* by Leland Huot and Alfred Powers. The large, amateurish volume includes much information about this little-studied figure as well as poorly reproduced sketches, cartoons, and portraits.

An outstanding work about this period that focuses upon a historical figure rather than a single cartoonist is Albert Shaw's *Abraham Lincoln*. This intriguing, two-volume work chronicles Lincoln's political career against the background of the times. It is profusely illustrated by cartoons, lithographs, portraits, and daguerreotypes on a wide variety of historical figures and events, not just Lincoln himself. The book has value for the student of Lincoln as well as for the student of editorial cartooning.

For a study of the British cartoonists' view of the Civil War, see William S. Walsh's *Abraham Lincoln and the London Punch*. This small-format volume reproduces fifty-five cartoons full-page, along with a running commentary on the cartoons themselves and the magazine's editorial policy.

Three books on Rosie O'Neill are Shelley Armitage's *Kewpies and Beyond: The World of Rose O'Neill*, which attempts to reclaim O'Neill's work as more feminist and generally subversive than other critics have allowed; *Titans and Kewpies: The Life and Art of Rose O'Neill* by Ralph Alan McCanse, which mentions O'Neill's affiliation with *Puck*, primarily in regard to her relationship with literary editor Harry Leon Wilson; and *The Art of Rose O'Neill*, an exhibition catalog edited by Helen Goodman, who also wrote an accompanying essay.

For a selected list of theses and dissertations in the humanities and social sciences dealing with editorial cartoons, see *Editorial Cartooning and Caricature: A Reference Guide* by Paul P. Somers Jr.

Of the books about individual figures, several deal with the radical cartoonists; three of these are titled *John Sloan*: one by Albert E. Gallatin, one by Bruce St. John, and another by Lloyd Goodrich; add to these Van Wyck Brooks' *John Sloan; A Painter's Life*. Other biographies of the radical cartoonists include Joseph North's *Robert Minor*, Albert Christ-Janer's *Boardman Robinson*, and Louis Lozowick's *William Gropper*.

John Canemaker's *Winsor McCay: His Life and Art*, is an excellent study of an artist whose considerable popularity in the early part of this century has been all but forgotten. Although his greatest achievements came in the fields of the comic strip and cartoon animation, his work for the Hearst papers has earned him a place in the history of editorial cartooning.

Billy Ireland by Lucy Shelton Caswell and George A. Loomis Jr. provides biographical background for the longtime cartoonist for the *Columbus* (Ohio) *Dispatch*. This folio volume also reprints 100 pages of his editorial cartoons and a like number of pages of his feature, "The Passing Show."

Illustrated with cartoons and photographs, Peter Marzio's *Rube Goldberg* is at once biographical and critical. Although necessarily emphasizing the humorous cartoons and wacky inventions that constitute Goldberg's contribution to our culture and even to our language, it does devote two chapters to the editorial cartoons.

David L. Lendt's *Ding: The Life of Jay Norwood Darling* details Ding's life as conservationist, New Deal activist, and cartoonist, in that order. The book does, however, reproduce some fifty cartoons, with explanations of how they represent specific political positions.

John W. Ripley and Robert W. Richmond compiled *Albert T. Reid's Sketchbook; Fads, Foibles & Politics: 1896–1908*. This little volume celebrates the life and career of Kansas artist Albert Turner Reid and reprints many editorial cartoons.

Works dealing with those pioneers of strip political commentary Al Capp and Walt Kelly deserve mention here, beginning with Kalman Goldstein's perceptive article in *Journal of Popular Culture* and Rick Marschall's interview "The Truth about Al Capp." In *Li'l Abner: A Study in American Satire*, Arthur Asa Berger considers "Li'l Abner" primarily as social criticism and concludes: "It is, perhaps, debatable as to how much specifically *political* satire there is in 'Li'l Abner' " (157).

Walt Kelly: A Retrospective Exhibition to Celebrate the Seventy-fifth Anniversary of His Birth, at Ohio State University in 1988, includes some biographical essays, such as Steve Thompson's "Highlights of Pogo," which recaps key episodes and issues. Mark Burstein's *Much Ado: The Pogofenokee Trivia Book* gives details about characters, episodes, and bibliography in question form, while reprinting a few strips and panels.

Kelly's widow Selby wrote *Pogo Files for Pogophiles*. This volume would be valuable for its copious illustrations alone, but it also provides detailed explanations of characters and events, as well as political and social issues of the times. Norman F. Hale's *All-Natural Pogo* examines the philosophy behind Pogo but eschews the politics.

New Orleans cartoonist John Chase is the subject of Edison Allen's *Of Time and Chase*, which features twenty pages of biography by Allen and an introductory page for each section. Allen reprints nearly 500 cartoons, chronologically arranged, three to six to a 10" × 10" page, concluding with several pages of Chase's color cartoons that appeared on WDSU TV in New Orleans from 1965 to 1968.

Several editorial cartoonists have written autobiographies: *Art Young: His Life and Times*; *Drawn from Memory* (John T. McCutcheon); *This Is the Life!* (Walt McDougall); *As I Saw It* (D. R. Fitzpatrick); *Zim: The Autobiography of Eugene Zimmerman*, edited and annotated with introductory commentary by Walter M. Brasch; *Rube Goldberg vs. the Machine Age*, edited by Clark Kinnaird; Bill Mauldin's *A Sort of Saga* (the artist's boyhood years); *Osborn on Osborn* (Robert Chesley Osborn); *The Best of H. T. Webster* (provides a five-page biographical sketch); *My Well-Balanced Life on a Wooden Leg* and *The Hardhat's Bedtime Story Book* (Al Capp); Martin Levin's *Five Boyhoods: Howard Lindsay, Harry Golden, Walt Kelly, William K. Zinsser and John Updike* (Walt Kelly's early life); *Dark Laughter: The Satiric Art of Oliver W. Harrington* and *Why I Left America and Other Essays* (editor M. Thomas Inge); and *Herblock: A Cartoonist's Life* (Herbert Block).

ANTHOLOGIES AND REPRINTS

Anthologies, published collections of editorial cartoons, and exhibition catalogs fall roughly into three categories: those that are arranged around a specific historical period; those that are concerned with a particular historical event, issue, or significant political figure; and those that collect a single political cartoonist's work. The latter category is too large for consideration in this chapter. See Richard Samuel West's bibliographies, mentioned later; and Appendix 5, "Selected Bibliography of Single-Artist Anthologies, excluding Illustrated Volumes," in Paul P. Somers Jr.'s *Editorial Cartooning and Caricature*. Exhibition catalogs are valuable sources of editorial cartoon reproductions, but they are frequently difficult to find, since they are usually printed in small numbers and indifferently distributed. Rare ones like the Toledo Museum of Art's *Catalogue [of] American Political Cartoons of Other Days, 1747–1872* and the Library Company of Philadelphia's *Made in America: Printmaking, 1760–1860* are quite scarce.

The first category, historical period, features several exhibition catalogs: Elizabeth Buckley's *Political Cartoons in Art & History: England, France & America, 1750–1890* catalogs an exhibition held at the Sierra Nevada Museum of Art in Reno, October 16–November 16, 1980, reprinting sixteen of the forty-three cartoons and caricatures originally exhibited and an essay by Dr. Buckley.

In addition to the the three anthologies dealing with early years in American history discussed earlier there is R. T. Haines Halsey's " 'Impolitical Prints': The American Revolution as Pictured by Contemporary English Caricaturists. An Exhibition," a catalog of an exhibition at the New York Public Library in November 1939. *American Printmaking, the First 150 Years* is a catalog by the Museum of Graphic Art of an exhibition of "the former Middendorf Collection of Americana" with text by Wendy J. Shadwell, a list of engravers, and a list of collections most frequently recurring. Bernard F. Reilly Jr.'s *American Political Prints, 1766–1876: A Catalog of the Collections in the Library of Congress* encompasses 758 separately published, single-sheet items in its 640 pages. *Two Centuries of Prints in America; A Selective Catalogue of the Winterthur Museum Collection* by E. McSherry Fowble is a large-format reproduction of nearly 400 prints from the collections of the Henry Francis du Pont Winterthur Museum in Charlottesville. Another collection of early prints is *Made in America; Printmaking 1760–1860; An Exhibition of Original Prints from the Collections of the Library Company of Philadelphia and the Historical Society of Pennsylvania, April-June, 1973.* Three books showcase the work of Paul Revere: *Paul Revere's Boston, 1735–1815*, a catalog of an exhibition at the Boston Museum of Fine Arts; *Paul Revere, a Picture Book* by the New York Metropolitan Museum of Art; and *Paul Revere: Artisan, Businessman, and Patriot—the Man behind the Myth*.

Another volume by Bernard Reilly, *Drawings of Nature and Circumstance*, is based on the Library's Caroline and Erwin Swann Collection. The catalog for Syracuse University's Martin H. Bush Exhibition of June 1966, *American Political Cartoons (1865–1965)*, gathers work by Thomas Nast and a dozen others. Rollin Kirby's *Highlights* is a chronologically arranged anthology of sixty full-page cartoons that Kirby drew for the *New York World*.

Drawing the Iron Curtain: Cold War Cartoons 1946–1960 is an illustrated catalog of a Caroline and Erwin Swann Memorial Exhibition, May 23–August 16, 1996, in the Oval Gallery of the Madison Building, Library of Congress, Washington, D.C. An international anthology of note is Steven Heller's *Man Bites Man*, which collects satiric art from 1960 to 1980.

Art Wood's *Great Cartoonists and Their Art*, cartoonist Jerry Robinson's *The 1970s: Best Political Cartoons of the Decade*, and Richard Samuel West and Richard B. Freeman's rare *The Best Political Cartoons of 1978* deserve prominent mention. Robinson's anthology is arranged chronologically by year. In addition to numerous American cartoons, this collection has a strong international representation, presenting the international perspective on such issues as Vietnam, Kent State, and Watergate. Freeman and West's well-selected anthology features the work of major editorial cartoonists. Also among the better anthologies in this group is *The Gang of Eight*, for which eight of America's most important cartoonists have selected twenty of their favorite cartoons. The book emphasizes the 1980s and includes an essay by each cartoonist. *Stars & Swipes* anthologizes cartoons by Doug Marlette, Mike Peters, Ben Sargent, and Don Wright.

Charles Brooks' *Best Editorial Cartoons of the Year* series, published annually since 1973, reprints cartoons by a number of editorial cartoonists. The collection depends on submissions from the artists, and in some recent editions a number of important cartoonists have not been represented.

The Foreign Policy Association has put out an excellent series of anthologies using editorial cartoons to illustrate commentary on historical events: *A Cartoon History of U.S. Foreign Policy since World War I*, *A Cartoon History of U.S. Foreign Policy 1776–1976*, and *A Cartoon History of United States Foreign Policy from 1945 to the Present*.

Joe Szabo edited *The Finest International Political Cartoons of Our Time*, three volumes with work by sixteen Pulitzer Prize-winning cartoonists and others from over fifty countries.

In the second category, events and issues, several anthologies and exhibition catalogs focus on events, special topics, or regions of the country: Michael Ricci and *Witty World* editor Joseph George Szabo compiled *Was It Worth It? A Collection of International Cartoons about Columbus and His Trip to America* (introduction by John A. Lent) for the 500th anniversary of said trip. The Statue of Liberty's centennial celebration was the occasion for another controversial anthology, Dani Aguila's *Taking Liberty with the Lady*.

Alice Sheppard's fine scholarly work, *Cartooning for Suffrage*, which has over 200 illustrations, is discussed earlier. A hostile, contemporary treatment of the topic may be found in Pulitzer Prize winner Nelson Harding's *Ruthless Rhymes of Martial Militants*. See also "Ding" Darling's *Dedicated to Home Brew, Suffragettes and Discords: Successors to Wine, Women and Song*. Arthur Bartlett Maurice edited *How They Draw Prohibition*, which reprints nearly 100 anti-Prohibition cartoons.

Graphics '75: Watergate: The Unmaking of a President: Lexington, January 12–February 9, 1975 was organized and edited for the University of Kentucky Art Gallery by Richard B. Freeman. Maury Forman and David Horsey edited *Cartooning AIDS around the World*, and Terry B. Morton edited *"I Feel I Should Warn You . . .": Historic Preservation Cartoons*, with an introductory essay by Draper Hill.

A number of anthologies specialize in war cartoons. *American Caricatures Pertaining to the Civil War* is one of several important Civil War collections. It was first published in 1892 and variously titled *Caricatures Pertaining to the Civil War* and *American Caricatures*. Other significant anthologies include the contemporary *The American War: Cartoons by Matt Morgan and Other English Artists* and Mark E. Neely's *The Confederate Image: Prints of the Lost Cause*. George McCullough Anderson edited and published *The Work of Adalbert Johann Volck; Who Chose for His Name the Anagram V. Blada, 1861–1865* with over 100 reproductions of work by the Confederate Volck, "V. Blada."

A generous sampling of Spanish-American War cartoons can be found in *Cartoons of the War of 1898 with Spain; from Leading Foreign and American Papers*. One-artist anthologies dealing with this war include Charles L. Bartholomew's *Cartoons of the Spanish-American War by Bart* and Charles Nelan's *Cartoons of Our War with Spain*.

World War I is the subject of several collections, including George Hecht's *The War in Cartoons*, which anthologizes 100 cartoons by twenty-seven cartoonists. Artists with individual collections of cartoons on World War I include Louis Raemaekers, *America in the War* and *Raemakers' Cartoon History of the War*; Luther

Bradley, *War Cartoons from the Chicago Daily News*; and Boardman Robinson, *Cartoons on the War*.

A fascinating volume published before the United States entered World War II is *What America Thinks*. Its 1,495 pages are filled with newspaper reports faced by full-page cartoons, representing U.S. public opinion as expressed in newspapers on events ranging from Munich to the fall of France (November 11, 1938–February 8, 1941).

The *Chicago Tribune* published two books, one early and one later in the war. *War Cartoons by McCutcheon, Orr, Parrish [and] Somdal* appeared in 1942. In 1944 the *Tribune* brought out *Thunderer of the Prairies; A Selection of Wartime Editorials and Cartoons, 1941–1944*. While the first volume had concentrated on the threat from Japan and the Axis powers, in this book the enemies are mostly Franklin D. Roosevelt, the New Deal, and Democratic "crackpots," whom editorals characterized as "Fascists" (June 17, 1942) (45). American cartoons on the war appear in several international anthologies, such as the contemporary *The Pen Is Mightier: The Story of the War in Cartoons*, edited by J. J. Lynx, and the more recent *World War II in Cartoons* by Mark Bryant and *The World War, 1939–1945* by Roy Douglas. Zbynek Zemen's *Heckling Hitler* is another international anthology that reprints a few Americans. *Original Political Cartoons of World War II*, compiled and published by Joseph F. Carpentier and Alfred S. Scarcelli, reprints 245 cartoons, mostly by Burt Thomas, which were printed in the *Detroit News* between 1939 and 1941.

Several individual artists offered their own collections of World War II cartoons. Reg Manning created *Little Itchy Itchy, and Other Cartoons*. Polish immigrant Arthur Szyk, already famous as an illustrator of the Bible, *Canterbury Tales*, *Arabian Nights*, *Andersen's Fairy Tales*, and *Grimm's Fairy Tales*, mocked Hitler and his allies in *The New Order* and *Ink & Blood*. Other cartoonists who put out wartime collections are John Churchill Chase, *40 Cartoons in Wartime*; Jerry Doyle, *According to Doyle: A Cartoon History of World War II*; and Elmer R. Messner, *The War in Cartoons*.

The Gulf War inspired collections: *Mother of All Windbags*, a small booklet with some sixty cartoons by major cartoonists, and *The Mother of All—Defeats, Retreats & Miscalculations*, which also reprints works by several well-known cartoonists. Victor Harville (*Now That's the Way to Run a War*) and J. D. Crowe (*Daze of Glory: Images of Fact and Fantasy Inspired by the Gulf War)* also marketed anthologies.

Three regional collections focus on the state of Texas: H. Bucholaer's extremely rare *Texas Question*, Robert F. Darden's *Drawing Power; Knott, Ficklen, and McClanahan: Editorial Cartoonists of the Dallas Morning News*, and *Cartooning Texas*, edited by Maury Forman and Robert A. Calvert. Forman and Rick Marschall edited *Cartooning Washington*.

Two deal with Florida: *Florida's Editorial Cartoonists: A Collection of Editorial Art with Commentary*, edited by S. L. (Stanley L.) Harrison, and the exhibition catalog *Political Cartooning in Florida 1901–1987*. Other states are represented by *Provocative Pens: Four Cleveland Cartoonists, 1900–1975*, an exhibition catalog compiled by Carolyn S. Jirousek; and *Marylanders in Cartoon*, which anthologizes caricatures by Siegel, J. C. Fireman, and others. Turn-of-the-centuury caricatures are collected by the Newspaper Cartoonists' Association of Michigan in *A Gallery of Pen Sketches in Black and White of Our Michgian Friends "As We See 'Em."*

Political campaigns have inspired a number of published cartoon collections as well, with anthologies of campaign cartoons, including *The Political Campaign of 1912 in Cartoons* by Nelson Harding, and Gib Crockett and Jim Berryman's cartoons in the *Washington Evening Star* anthologies for the campaigns of 1948 (with Clifford K. Berryman), 1952, 1956, and 1968 (Crockett alone). The *Chicago Tribune* put out Carey Orr's *1952 Cartoons from the Chicago Tribune*. In the mid-1950s Pierce G. Fredericks edited *The People's Choice: The Issues of the Campaign as Seen by the Nation's Best Political Cartoonists*. Jeff MacNelly's *The Election That Was—MacNelly at His Best* presents fifty-six pages of MacNelly cartoons from the 1976 campaign. *Political Satire '84* was published in conjunction with the exhibition October 5–28, 1984, at the Florida State University, Fine Arts Gallery.

Several volumes anthologize cartoons from recent elections. *Campaign: A Cartoon History of Bill Clinton's Race for the White House* was compiled and edited by Mary Ann Barton and Paul C. Barton. *A Window on the 1992 Campaign* collects political drawings by Oliphant, Levine, Sorel, and Conrad. A treasure for the Rare Book rooms is *Congress Drawn . . . , and Quartered!*, A Portfolio of Editorial Cartoons from a 1985 exhibition, with a regular edition limited to 500 numbered copies.

Of the anthologies dealing with public figures, perhaps the most numerous are those pertaining to presidents. Similarly, exhibitions have produced printed anthologies or exhibition catalogs. One of the most ambitious is Blaisdell and Selz's *The American Presidency in Political Cartoons: 1776–1976*, discussed earlier. *Oliphant's Presidents: Twenty-Five Years of Caricature* catalogs an exhibition organized by the Art Services International of Alexandria, Virginia, in conjunction with the National Portrait Gallery of the Smithsonian Institution, Washington, D.C.

Moving on to collections specializing in a particular president, an early one, which contains John Tenniel drawings, is William S. Walsh's *Abraham Lincoln and the London Punch*. Lincoln cartoons also appear in two rare volumes by Rufus Rockwell Wilson: *Lincoln in Caricature*, which reproduces thirty-two cartoons; and *Lincoln in Caricature; 165 Poster Cartoons and Drawings for the Press*. Two books by Albert Shaw deal with Lincoln: *Abraham Lincoln in Contemporary Caricature*, and the two-volume *Abraham Lincoln; His Path to the Presidency* and *Abraham Lincoln; The Year of His Election*, treated in greater detail earlier.

Luther D. Bradley celebrated William McKinley's exploits in a collection: *Wonderful Willie! What He and Tommy Did to Spain*. Another of Albert Shaw's anthologies built around a single political figure is *A Cartoon History of Roosevelt's Career*. Yet another Roosevelt anthology, Raymond Gros' *T. R. in Cartoon*, is international in scope. John T. McCutcheon's impressions of the head Rough Rider are collected in *T. R. in Cartoons*. In the 1920s "Ding" Darling weighed in with *Calvin Coolidge: Cartoons of His Presidential Years* and *As Ding Saw Hoover*.

James N. Giglio and Greg G. Thielen edited *Truman in Cartoon and Caricature*. C. D. Batchelor's *Truman Scrapbook* is a single-artist anthology of Truman cartoons. The National Cartoonists Society issued *President Eisenhower's Cartoon Book*, a volume of friendly cartoons. "Captain Raymond B. Rajski, USAF, Ret.," as he calls himself, compiled a special commemorative volume, *A Nation Grieved; The Kennedy Assassination in Editorial Cartoons*. A single-artist collection is Jim Dobbins' *Dobbins' Diary of the New Frontier*.

Oliver W. Harrington's editorial cartoon about race relations in the South. Courtesy of the Library of Congress

LBJ Lampooned, edited by Sig Rosenblum and Charles Antin, contains graphic criticism of Lyndon B. Johnson by forty international and American cartoonists. Rosenblum and Antin also collaborated on *LBJ Political Cartoons*, an exhibition catalog that reproduces 135 cartoons, many full-page. For an individual artist's impressions of the Texas president, see Scott Long's "*Hey! Hey! LBJ! Or He Went Away and Left the Faucet Running*."

Given Richard Nixon's controversial personality and actions, it is no surprise that so many books of individual cartoonists' work have been devoted to him and to Watergate: Jules Feiffer's *Feiffer on Nixon*, Garry Trudeau's *Guilty, Guilty, Guilty!*, Paul Conrad's *The King and Us*, Paul Szep's *At This Point in Time*, Mike Peters' *The Nixon Chronicles*, Ranan Lurie's *Nixon-Rated Cartoons*, Bill Sanders' *Run for the Oval Room . . . They Can't Corner Us There!*, John Branch's *Would You Buy a Used Cartoon from This Man?*, Robert Warren's *Nixon Made Perfectly Clear*, and Herbert Block's *Herblock Special Report*.

President Nixon's immediate successors did not inspire the same intensity on the part of editorial cartoonists. Gerald R. Ford himself is listed as the author of *Humor and the Presidency*. Chapter 4 reprints twenty half-page or full-page cartoons. *Car(ter)toons; or, The Un-making of the President 1976* is an eighty-page sampler of cartoons on the Carter–Ford contest, which lacks most of the "big names." *Augusta Chronicle* cartoonist Clyde Wells paid considerable attention to his fellow Georgian Jimmy Carter in *The Net Effect*.

Ronald Reagan provided ample inspiration for editorial cartoonists. Fred Barnes edited *A Cartoon History of the Reagan Years*, arranged chronologically from "1980: The Rise of Reagan," to "1987: The Legend Hits Bottom," with over 300 cartoons. Another telling anthology of Ronald Reagan cartoons is Carew Papritz and Russ Tremayne's *Reagancomics*, with 128 cartoons by nearly fifty artists, nearly all of the best known and many others.

Many cartoonists authored their own anthologies: Tony Auth's *Lost in Space: The Reagan Years*, Herbert Block's *Herblock at Large* and *Herblock through the Looking Glass*, Jules Feiffer's *Ronald Reagan in Movie America*, George Fisher's "*There You Go Again!*," Garry Trudeau's *In Search of Reagan's Brain* and *Doonesbury Dossier*, Dwane Powell's *The Reagan Chronicles*, Jim Borgman's *The Great Communicator*, Jeff Danziger's *The Complete Reagan Diet*, Tom Toles' *Mr. Gazoo*, and Mike Peters' *Win One for the Geezer*.

Eyes on the President: George Bush, edited by Leo E. Heagerty, reprints numerous editorial cartoons by thirty different cartoonists, nearly full-page, with commentary. Matt Tolbert's *Read My Lips: The Unofficial Cartoon Biography of George Bush* is a black-and-white comic book in a paperback book binding, illustrated by Neil Grahm and Mark Braun. President Bill Clinton from Arkansas proved ripe for hillbilly jokes, as perpetrated by the likes of Doug Marlette: *Faux Bubba*.

Some anthologies deal with more than one president: Steven Heller's anthology *Jules Feiffer's America: From Eisenhower to Reagan* contains 400 strong cartoons from twenty-five years of Feiffer's work arranged by chapters that are devoted to seven presidents.

Margaret F. Viens' *Never Underestimate: The Life and Career of Margaret Chase Smith through the Eyes of the Political Cartoonist* collects 200 chronologically organized cartoons by some 130 cartoonists, upon which was based a more selective exhibition at the Margaret Chase Smith Library in Smith's hometown of Skowhegan, Maine, April–June 1993. Speaker of the House Sam Rayburn is the subject of *Impressions of Mr. Sam: A Cartoon Profile*, edited by H. G. Dulaney and Edward Hake Phillips.

100 Watts: The James Watt Memorial Cartoon Collection, edited by Carew Papritz and Russ Tremayne, is a strong anthology that includes 100 cartoons by thirty-six American editorial cartoonists. All "100 Watts" are critical of George Bush's controversial secretary of the interior.

Evan Mecham, colorful governor of Arizona, inspired anthologies. Dr. Mark Siegel's edited collection *The World according to Evan Mecham* features mostly local cartoons critical of Mecham. Steve Benson, Pulitzer Prize-winning cartoonist for the *Arizona Republic*, gathered his Mecham cartoons in *Evanly Days!* Dwane Powell and Jesse Helms put cartoons together with quotations from the North Carolina senator in *100 Proof Pure Old Jess*. Former football star O. J. Simpson was not a political figure, but his trial became a political issue. Jerry and Jens Robinson edited *OD'd on O. J.*

The radicalism of the early twentieth century stimulated artistic expression, much of it centered around *The Masses* and *Daily Worker*. *Red Cartoons from the Daily Worker* was published 1926 through 1929. The list of artists reads like a who's who among radical cartoonists. *The Worker* brought out an anthology years later. Striking in its red-and-white paper cover, *A Selection of Drawings from the Worker, 1924–1960* has a foreword by Joseph North and features several *Worker* artists. Art Young's *The Campaign Primer* was published in a revised edition as *The Socialist Primer*.

12 Cartoons Defending WPA is a publication of the American Artists Congress, while *Living in the U.S.A.* is a product of the radical movement of the 1970s, with the Rising Up Angry newspaper of Chicago listed as the author. A contemporary work, published by "Philadelphia Resistance," is Edward S. Herman's *The Great Society Dictionary*, with five cartoons by well-known underground cartoonist Rob Cobb. More in the mainstream is *Them: More Labor Cartoons* by Gary Huck and Mike Konapacki.

A forerunner of numerous antiwar and specifically antinuclear weapons anthologies appeared in 1946 at the onset of the nuclear age: Robert Osbsorn's *War Is No Damn Good!* concludes with his famous drawing of a nuclear mushroom cloud in the shape of a skull facing one of an endless field of crosses. *Thin Black Lines: Political Cartoons & Development Education*, written and compiled by Colm Regan, Scott Sinclair, and Martyn Turner, anthologizes work from all over the world with the purpose of teaching peace.

Several others appeared in the 1980s. Steven Heller's *Warheads: Cartoonists Draw the Line* samples editorial art and political cartoons that deal with the nuclear threat. John Trever has two anti-nuclear anthologies: *Freeze* and *Trever's First Strike*, with text by Gene Copeland. In *Art against War*, D.J.R Bruckner, Seymour Chwast, and Steven Heller gather antiwar art from the last 400 years. The National Campaign to Stop the MX [Missle] compiled *MX Cartoon Book* to further its cause.

Cartoonists and Writers Syndicate held an international exhibition in Washington, D.C., at the end of 1993. The catalog *Human Rights as Seen by the Leading Cartoonists* has 127 pages, one cartoon per page, with some Americans represented. *Getting Angry Six Times a Week*, "a portfolio of political cartoons" by fourteen major cartoonists, edited by Alan F. Westin, is an anthology of civil liberties cartoon "galleries" originally planned or published by the now defunct *The Civil Liberties Review*, a bimonthly magazine of the American Civil Liberties Union.

Collections of feminist humor sometimes incorporate cartoons. Examples include *Pulling Our Own Strings*, edited by Gloria Kaufman and Mary Kay Blakely, and *Pork Roast: 250 Feminist Cartoons*. The Ohio State University Libraries publish catalogs in conjunction with their fine series of exhibitions, *The Festival of Cartoon Art*. *1989 Festival of Cartoon Art* is a handsome, 8½" x 11" volume celebrating two exhibitions: the appearance of the Smithsonian's traveling exhibit, *Great American Comics: 100 Years of Cartoon Art*, which appeared in Columbus from October 15 to November 26, 1989; and *Women Practitioners of "The Ungentlemanly Art,"* which appeared on the Ohio State campus from October 16 to November 30, 1989. A thirty-page essay, "The Comics," by M. Thomas Inge traces the development of the satirical comic strip from Al Capp and Walt Kelly to G. B. Trudeau. Lucy Shelton Caswell, curator of the Cartoon Research Library at Ohio State University, has written a twenty-page essay, "Seven Cartoonists," to accompany the *Women Practitioners of "The Ungentlemanly Art"* exhibit.

Two exhibition catalogs emphasize ethnic cartoons. The theme of Ohio State's 1992 Festival of Cartoon Art was *Cartoons and Ethnicity*, and the exhibition was held in the Philip Sills Exhibition Hall at Ohio State University, October 26–December 11, 1992. Aesthetically pleasing like its predecessor, the catalog contains an illustrated, thirty-five-page essay by John J. Appel, "Ethnicity in Cartoon Art." Lucy Shelton Caswell has provided a biographical sketch of Oliver Harrington, some of whose cartoons are reproduced. Lists of the exhibits accompany.

The Coming Man: 19th Century American Perceptions of the Chinese, has 137 illustrations. *Jews in American Graphic Satire and Humor* catalogs a number of ethnic political cartoons selected from an exhibit of the John and Selma Appel Collection. Gary L. Bunker and Davis Bitton's *The Mormon Graphic Image, 1834–1914* reproduces 129 cartoons and examines the historical, political, and sexual aspects of anti-Mormon sentiment. *The Jewish Political Cartoon Collection* features the work of Lou Golden, "long-time cartoonist for *Boston Jewish Times.*"

The best sources of cartoons, newspapers and magazines are popular subjects of anthologies. *The Sting of the Bee* centers around cartoonists' work for a single newspaper, the *Sacramento Bee*. The loosely arranged collection compiled by Kenneth M. Johnston features the work of Arthur Buel, Newton Pratt, and Dennis Renault. *The Art of the Dart: Nine Masters of Visual Satire* is a catalog for the exhibition held at the Gryphon Gallery in Michigan with a historical essay by Draper Hill.

Attwood's Pictures commemorates Francis G. Attwood's busy, full-page drawings for *Life* at the turn of the century. Two collections represent *New York Times* graphics: Jean-Claude Suares' *Art of the Times*, featuring thirty-one different artists; and Harrison Salisbury's *The Indignant Years*. Although the latter collection emphasizes articles, the artwork is worth seeing.

Pulitzer Prize-winning cartoons/cartoonists have their collections. An early anthology, Dick Spencer III's *Pulitzer Prize Cartoons*, reproduces on full pages the Pulitzer winners from 1922 through 1950. John Hohenberg's *The Pulitzer Prize Story*, which appeared in 1959, was revised and updated in 1980. Hohenberg reproduces cartoons along with prizewinning features and editorials. Gerald W. Johnson's *The Lines Are Drawn*, like Hohenberg's book, is more current than Spencer's. It includes Pulitzer Prize-winning cartoons for the years 1922–1958, accompanied by essays based on the cartoons' historical contexts.

Several miscellaneous anthologies and exhibition catalogs are worth seeing. The Salon International de la Caricature (International Salon of Cartoons) issues an anthology in conjunction with an international exhibition and judging held annually since 1964. The 1968 volume, no. 5, for example, reprints some 150 cartoons, and several of the international cartoons deal with U.S. politics and foreign policy. The College Art Association of America's *Catalogue of the Salon of American Humorists* commemorates a benefit exhibition to aid needy artists and for the College Art Association in December 1933.

Worth seeing are two catalogs commerating exhibitions associated with the Ohio State Cartoon Research Library, especially the 1983 *Festival of Cartoon Art*; and the 1986 *Festival of Cartoon Art* was also commemorated by a catalog, which reproduces ten editorial cartoons. The catalog lists some 400 cartoons from the 1980s, with political ones heavily represented.

Two works discussed earlier are *Great Cartoonists and Their Art*, which reproduces 120 cartoons from Art Wood's collection; and *The Image of America in Caricature & Cartoon*, published by the Amon Carter Museum of Western Art, Fort Worth, Texas.

With advances in technology, including the World Wide Web, mentioned earlier, some graphic works are available on CD-ROM. Art Spiegelman's *The Complete Maus* and Garry Trudeau's *Doonesbury Flashbacks: 25 Years of Serious Fun* are two early ones.

RESEARCH COLLECTIONS

Traditionally, research collections of editorial cartoons have been difficult to locate because such collections were not fully reported or cataloged. The dreaded word "ephemera" sometimes appears in the very name of the collection. The papers of any person, famous or otherwise, may include cartoon scrapbooks or even originals. Although progress has been made in recent years, specific holdings of editorial and political cartoons continue to be irregularly cataloged within general cartoon collections.

The 1993 edition of Lee Ash's *Subject Collections* lists three pages of cartoon collections in the United States, Canada, and Great Britain. Some collections are described more fully than others, but approximately three-quarters of the listings are of interest to students of American editorial cartooning. There is no discernible change from the 1985 edition.

The Image of America in Caricature & Cartoons, published by the Amon Carter Museum of Western Art in 1976, is still helpful, though dated. It concentrates on U.S. collections; the Canadian and British references are included primarily where there are holdings directly related to U.S. history and culture. The list of private collectors is necessarily incomplete. *Directory of Special Libraries and Information Centers—1996* is also helpful. See the index under the search heading "Caricatures and Cartoons."

The National Union Catalog of Manuscript Collections may be searched for the name of an individual cartoonist. Such an exercise is superseded by an electronic search of the Research Libraries Information Network, or RLIN. Long an institutional service, RLIN is now available on the World Wide Web. Searching the World Wide Web may be fruitful, as university libraries now have home pages on the Internet. Few have progressed to the point of itemizing cartoon collections at this time. If a researcher thinks that a particular library has collections of editorial cartoons, it is often possible to gain some information over the Internet.

Other electronic searches, such as First Search and SIRIS, may yield information about collections. Another technique for locating unrecorded or unreported collections, especially for cartoonists who did not acquire major or national reputations, is to consult the newspaper libraries where they worked and the libraries in the locales where they were best known.

The most diverse collection of caricatures and cartoons is probably to be found in the Library of Congress, in the Division of Prints and Photographs, which is continually enlarging its editorial cartoon holdings. The Library of Congress has four major collections of political cartoons. See Annette Melville's *Special Collections in the Library of Congress*.

The most extensive of the four is the Caroline and Erwin Swann Collection of nineteenth- and twentieth-century drawings, which includes approximately 2,200 editorial cartoons, comic strips, and single caricatures. It has been cataloged, and access is, for the most part, available to the public on-site. There is an unpublished finding list available in the reading room. Access to the item-level records, but not to the images, is also available through LOCIS (Library of Congress Information System).

The Cartoon Drawings Collection comprises some 6,535 drawings and ten prints by over 500 artists, with another 2,000 drawings added recently. Information regarding cartoons can be found on the Digital One-Box system within the Prints and Photographs Reading Room or through LOCIS.

About 600 American cartoons from 1798 to 1900 are also collected in the Library of Congress's Political Cartoon Print Collection, which is international in scope. The American portion of the collection has been cataloged, and a published catalog of items up to 1876 has been published as *American Political Prints, 1766–1876: A Catalog of the Collections in the Library of Congress* by Bernard F. Reilly Jr. (discussed earlier).

In addition, the Cabinet of American Illustration, which is primarily a set of drawings for American magazine and book illustrations, contains approximately 200 editorial and political cartoons, including work by Thomas Nast and Joseph Keppler. A major preservation program is in progress to restore these drawings. These catalog records are also available to researchers through LOCIS, and a database catalog is available at the Library of Congress. The Photoduplication Office (telephone: [202] 707–5640, fax: [202] 707–1771) can provide contact prints from a photographic negative for a fee. Those wishing to duplicate cartoons and caricatures should either know the call number or be able to send a clear photocopy identifying the image as belonging to the collections of the Library of Congress. Prices vary and are lower if the library has already made a negative of the drawing. Copyright restrictions apply. The Copyright Office conducts searches for a fee.

Correspondence to the Prints and Photographs Division should be addressed to Prints and Photographs Division, Library of Congress, Washington, D.C. 20540–4730. Inquiries regarding cartoons should be addressed specifically to the Curator of Popular and Applied Graphic Art, Prints and Photographs Division, Room LM-339, Madison Building, 1st and Independence Streets, S.E., Washington, D.C. 20540–4730, (202) 707–6394, fax: (202) 707–6647 (the entire division), and (202) 707–1486 (curatorial area).

Another major repository for printed cartoon art is the Ohio State University Cartoon, Graphic, and Photographic Arts Research Library, which has as its primary, long-term goal the development of comprehensive collections (published works, manuscript materials, and original cartoons) in the history of American cartoon art. Founded in 1973, by 1994 the library held over 14,000 books, more than 1,400 serial titles, over 202,500 original cartoons, and more than 1,900 linear feet of manuscript materials. According to Professor Lucy Shelton Caswell, curator, the library has cartoons by hundreds of people. The library has 25 cartoons or more (for some more than 1,000) from the following cartoonists, with gifts arriving regularly: Charles L. Bartholomew (Bart), Brian Basset, Ned Beard, Jim Borgman, Eugene Craig, Bill Crawford, Edwina Dumm, Bob Engiehart, John Fischetti, Karl Hubenthal, Billy Ireland, Walt Kelly, Jack Knox, Ed Kuekes, John Lane, Jim Larrick, Dick Locher, John T. McCutcheon, G. T. Maxwell, Frederick Burr Opper, Ray Osrin, Eugene Payne, Mike Peters, Art Poinier, Milt Priggee, Jeff Stahler, Burt Thomas, Edmund Valtman, L. D. Warren, Charles Werner, Harry Westerman, Gaar Williams, Scott Willis, and Larry Wright, among others.

Several individual collections are noteworthy; the Woody Gelman Collection has most of Winsor McCay's editorial cartoons, either as original drawings, proofs, or tear sheets. The Charles Press Collection of 2,000 books, gift of the Michigan State University editorial cartooning scholar, is available. The business aspects of cartooning are documented in the Ohio State Library's Toni Mendez Collection, the records of her many years representing cartoonists as a licensing agent. United Feature Syndicate has donated a very large collection of United and NEA syndicate proofs. The library became the permanent archive for the Association of American Editorial Cartoonists in 1984; the National Cartoonists Society named the library as its archival depository in 1985.

Complete runs of two important periodicals on editorial cartooning, *The Puck Papers* and *Target*, may be found in the Richard Samuel West Collection, which includes correspondence and manuscripts, totalling eighteen linear feet. (The library has long runs of *Punch*, *Puck*, *Cartoons*, *Cartoonist PROfiles*, *Harper's Weekly* [the Nast years], *New York Illustrated News*, and *The Masses*.) Recent additions to the West Collection give Ohio State more than 90 percent of all published collections of political cartoons. In 1993, United Media donated to the library over 83,000 original cartoons by 113 artists, designated as the Robert Roy Metz Collection. It should be noted that these numbers are constantly growing, as new contributions are made to existing collections and new collections are donated.

Triennially since 1983, the Ohio State Cartoon Research Library has sponsored *A Festival of Cartoon Art*, featuring presentations by working cartoonists and scholars as well as historical exhibits and original artwork by current cartoonists. In 1991, the library established a biographical registry, comprising clippings and other difficult-to-obtain biographical information. The library has itemized finding aids. It has built a database of editorial cartoons searchable by artist, caption, topic, and what is shown (i.e., frog, cowboys, etc.) and intends ultimately to link up actual pictures to the database. According to Professor Caswell, materials in the library are available to qualified researchers upon request following their registration as users. Inventory lists and other finding aids are available for each collection. Researchers are encouraged to make advance arrangements prior to coming to the library. Materials in the Cartoon Research Library, including collections, are now entered on OSCAR, the university's on-line catalog, accessible through Gopher/telnet—or the World Wide Web. (See *Directory of Special Libraries and Information Centers 1988* and "The Ohio State University Cartoon, Graphic, and Photographic Arts Research Library," *Inks* I [February 1994], 34–37, which were used in the preparation of this entry.)

Correspondence should be addressed to curator, Ohio State University, Cartoon, Graphic, and Photographic Arts Research Library, Wexner Center, Rm. 023L, 27 W. 17th Ave. Mall, Columbus, Ohio 43210–1393; phone: (614) 292–0538; fax: (614) 292–6184; E-mail: cartoons@osu.edu.

Established in 1954, the Archives of American Art exists to encourage research in American art history and to preserve valuable collections. Its 12 million items ("seventy-five thousand works of art on paper") may be searched electronically, through Smithsonian Institution Research Information System (SIRIS), Research Libraries Information System (RLIN), or the Internet. The Archives has a World Wide Web page, tied in with that of the Smithsonian Institution, with which it has been associated since 1970. Documents located through one of these searches may be accessed at one of the branches listed above or borrowed through Interlibrary Loan, Balcony 331, 8th and F Streets, NW, Washington, D.C. 20560, (202) 357–2781; 5200 Woodward Ave. Detroit 48202; (313) 226–7544; 1285 Avenue of the Americas, New York 10019; (212) 399–5015; 87 Mount Vernon St., Boston 02108; (617) 565–8444; 1151 Oxford Rd., San Marino, Calif. 91108; (818) 405–7847 (in the Huntington Library).

For holdings of over 100 other libraries, see Paul P. Somers Jr.'s *Editorial Cartooning and Caricature*.

REFERENCE WORKS AND PERIODICALS

Encyclopedias and General Works

Amon Carter Museum of Art. *The Image of America in Caricature & Cartoons*. Fort Worth, Tex.: Amon Carter Museum of Western Art, 1975, 1976.

Chase, John. *Today's Cartoon*. New Orleans: Hauser Press, 1962. Yearbook of 140 then-practicing cartoonists, including Chase himself. Two-page entries include photos, biographical data, representative cartoons, and informal commentary for each.

Deur, Lynne. *Political Cartoonists*. Minneapolis: Lerner, 1972. Brief biographical sketches of some major cartoonists, together with photos of the artists and sample cartoons.

Dictionary of American Biography. New York: C. Scribner's Sons, 1958–1964. Biographical descriptions of well-known, deceased cartoonists.

Feaver, William. *Masters of Caricature: From Hogarth and Gillray to Scarfe and Levine*. Ed. Ann Gould. New York: Knopf, 1981. Brief biographies and artwork examples of 243 caricaturists of historical and current importance provide basic introductions to many important figures in the field. Marginally useful bibliography.

Groce, George C. *The New York Historical Society's Dictionary of Artists in America, 1564–1860*. New Haven, Conn.: Yale University Press, 1957. Brief entries for Nast but not Keppler, Robert Minor but not Art Young.

Hoff, Syd. *Editorial and Political Cartooning*. New York: Stravon Educational Press, 1976. Unscholarly book includes 700 cartoons by 165 cartoonists. Hoff provides informal background and sometimes makes instructive aesthetic judgments. One section, "The Old Masters," covers from the ancient Chinese and Egyptians to British and American cartoons of World War I; another, "The Moderns/U.S. and Canada," proceeds alphabetically from Cal Alley to Doug Wright.

Horn, Maurice, ed. *Contemporary Graphic Artists*. Detroit: Gale Research, 1986– . Three volumes feature bibliographies and critical articles on more than 100 graphic artists, including fifteen editorial cartoonists. Cross-indexed by artists' names, occupations, and subjects.

———, ed. *The World Encyclopedia of Cartoons*. New York: Chelsea House, 1980. Two-volume reference staple includes a significant amount of material on U.S. editorial cartoonists, plus an overview of caricature and cartooning, 1,200 cross-referenced entries, indexed by proper names, subject, illustration titles, and country.

Mott, Frank Luther. *The New-York Historical Society's Dictionary of Artists in America, 1564–1860*. New Haven, Conn.: Yale University Press, 1957. Five volumes, indexes magazines, "Cartoons," and individual cartoonists.

Schwarzlose, Richard Allen. *Newspapers, a Reference Guide*. New York: Greenwood Press, 1987. Includes some biography and bibliography for cartoonists strongly associated with newspapers.

Sloane, David E. E., ed. *Magazines and Comic Periodicals*. New York: Greenwood Press, 1987. More up-to-date, collects detailed essays on 100 most important magazines (excluding *Harper's Weekly*), giving history, publication dates, bibliographies, and locations of copies. Treats 400 lesser-known magazines at shorter length. Index entries include "cartoons, political," listing several but not all of the periodicals that employed editorial cartoons and several individual artists noted for their magazine affiliations.

Taft, William H. The *Encyclopedia of Twentieth-Century Journalists*. New York: Garland, 1986. Presents more than 1,000 biographical sketches of journalists but is of limited value to students of editorial cartooning. Emphasizes editors, reporters, photographers, and publishers but does cover a few major editorial cartoonists.

Thorndike, Chuck. *The Business of Cartooning*. New York: House of Little Books, 1939. How-to book provides thumbnail sketches of a few political cartoonists, including C. D. Batchelor, "Ding" Darling, and John McCutcheon.

Who Was Who in American Art: Compiled from the Original Who's Who in America. Chicago: A. N. Marquis, 1899– .

Who's Who in American Art. New York [etc.]: R. R. Bowker, 1936/1937– .

Bibliographies

Although general encyclopedias, art reference works, and journalism indexes and bibliographies lend some help with the best-known figures in the field—especially those who also have "high culture" reputations—few indexes, bibliographies, or biographical dictionaries deal exclusively or comprehensively with editorial cartooning or political cartoonists. The most comprehensive bibliographies that deal primarily with editorial cartooning appear in the major history and criticism books, such as Hess and Kaplan, Hess and Northrop, and others listed later. For recent bibliography, students will want to consult not only the standard library references and on-line databases but the "Reviews" sections of cartooning journals such as *Inks*, *Witty World*, and *AAEC Notebook*.

Hess, Stephen, and Sandy Northrop. *Drawn & Quartered: The History of American Political Cartoons* (updates *The Ungentlemanly Art*). Montgomery, Ala.: Elliot & Clark, 1996. Index and five pages of bibliographical references.

Hess, Stephen, and Milton Kaplan. *The Ungentlemanly Art*. New York: Macmillan, 1975. Revised edition, with a longer bibliography. No page numbers in periodical entries, and the items are not annotated.

Kempkes, Wolfgang. *The International Bibliography of Comics Literature*. Detroit: Gale Research; New York: R. R. Bowker, 1971. Deals almost entirely with strips and contains only a few items on editorial cartooning.

Lent, John A. *Animation, Caricature, and Gag and Political Cartoons in the United*

States and Canada: An International Bibliography. Westport, Conn.: Greenwood Press, 1994. Seventy-four-page chapter, "U.S.: Political Cartoons," with 1,138 entries. Other sections list artists from Auth to Zimmerman, providing a mixed list of works by and about each figure and "Anthologies," thematic collections, and individual anthologies.

———. *Comic Art: An International Bibliography*. Drexel Hill, Pa.: [Author], 1986. This well-indexed, 156-page compilation does not deal exclusively with American editorial cartooning but includes 1,197 bibliographical entries broken down alphabetically and by continent and country. Books, journal articles, monographs, and conference reports, as well as seminar papers and fugitive materials, are included. Almost half of the entries deal with American materials, and editorial cartoonists are strongly represented in the selection.

Matthews, J. Brander. "The Comic Periodical Literature of the United States." *The American Biblioplast* 7 (August 1875), 199–201. A bibliographical essay that is still of value today.

Nelson, Roy. *Cartooning*. Chicago: Contemporary Books, 1975. Deals with social and strip as well as editorial cartooning, with some annotation. A number of items are American history references that have only indirect bearing on editorial cartooning.

Price, Warren C. *The Literature of Journalism, an Annotated Bibliography*. Minneapolis: University of Minnesota Press, 1959. Among the standard references in journalism; should be consulted. Indexes "Cartoonists & Cartoons," plus several cartoonists by name, indexing a very few anthologies by individual cartoonists.

Price, Warren C., and Calder M. Pickett. *An Annotated Journalism Bibliography, 1958–1968*. Minneapolis: University of Minnesota Press, 1970. The updated supplement to the previous entry.

Shikes, Ralph E. *The Indignant Eye*. Useful bibliography and valuable annotated list on recent and American cartooning. Boston: Beacon Press, 1969.

West, Richard Samuel. "A Contribution toward a Bibliography of Works by American Political Cartoonists." Washington, D.C.: R. S. West, 1990. Excellent work with a revised edition with V. Cullum Rogers in 1992 (Washington, D.C.: R. S. West, 1992).

———. "Selected Bibliography of Political Cartoon Collections," *Inks* 1 (November 1994), 47–49 and *Inks* 2 (February 1995), 43–49. A more readily available version of the preceding source.

Lists of Prints

Conningham, Frederic A. *An Alphabetical List of 5735 Titles of N. Currier and Currier & Ives Prints*. New York: F. A. and M. B. Conningham, 1930. For the collector, "lists every known print published by N. Currier and Currier & Ives" (as of the book's publication date, 1930).

Cresswell, Donald H. *The American Revolution in Drawings and Prints. A Checklist of 1765–1790 Graphics in the Library of Congress*. Washington, D.C.: U.S. Government Printing Office, 1975. Invaluable, the most complete single source of American and British prints from this period.

Currier & Ives: A Catalogue Raisonne/Compiled by Gale Research Company; with an Introduction by Bernard F. Reilly. Detroit: Gale Research, 1984. Massive, two-volume work with 7,450 entries and 1,000 two-by-five-inch illustrations, listed alphabetically by title and accompanied by detailed information. Concordance, subject index with some 150 entries under "Political Cartoons," indexes for artists and lithographers, chronology index, views, and illustrations.

Keller, Morton. *The Art and Politics of Thomas Nast*. New York: Oxford University Press, 1968. Brief annotations for a number of significant Nast studies.

Reilly, Bernard F., Jr. *American Political Prints, 1766–1876: A Catalog of the Collections in the Library of Congress*. Boston: G. K. Hall, 1991. Incorporated into the Library of Congress (LOC) database on the World Wide Web, it encompasses 758 separately published, single-sheet items in its 640 pages, plus 800 cross-indexed prints. Photo negative numbers allow readers to order copies of the public domain prints from the Library's Photoduplication Service.

Weitenkampf, Frank. *Political Caricature in the United States, in Separately Published Cartoons . . . an Annotated List*. 1953. New York: Arno Press, 1971. Indexes chronologically some of the most important editorial cartoons. Provides locations as well as descriptions for 1,158 cartoon entries.

West, Richard Samuel. *Satire on Stone: The Political Cartoons of Joseph Keppler*. Urbana: University of Illinois Press, 1988.

Periodicals

About Editorial Cartooning (Secondary Sources)

There are a number of mainstream periodicals of historical importance for students of editorial cartooning, but only a few current periodicals deal exclusively with the subject, and one of the most useful has ceased publication. In some of the remaining periodicals, editorial cartooning shares space with strip and social cartooning.

Cartoonist Profiles. Published quarterly since winter 1969, covers all kinds of comic art but is worth seeing for its attention to editorial cartoonists. Comprehensive index in the 100th issue, December 1993, 10–20.

Inklings. The Museum of Cartoon Art and Hall of Fame of Rye Brook, N.Y., published a dozen issues between fall 1975 and summer 1978. The new International Museum of Cartoon Art in Boca Raton, Florida, resumed the publication of *Inklings* in spring 1993 as an eight-page newsletter.

Inks: Cartoon and Comic Art Studies. Columbus: Ohio State University Press, February 1994–1997. Published three times a year, *Inks* began in February 1994. Lucy Shelton Caswell was editor, and Richard Samuel West was associate editor for political cartoons. The indispensable illustrated journal was discontinued after the November 1997 issue (vol. 4, no. 4).

Puck Papers. Narberth, Pa.: R. S. West, Autumn 1978–Summer 1981. Richard Samuel West edited this first reliable periodical devoted exclusively to American political cartooning.

Target. Warminster, Pa.: R. S. West, K. B. Mattern, Jr., 1981–1987. West's quarterly successor to *Puck Papers*, even more impressive than its predecessor. Excellent articles and interviews make this publication (now in the Cartoon Research Library at Ohio State University along with *Puck Papers*) a valuable research tool.

Witty World. North Wales, Pa.: WittyWorld, Summer 1987–December 1998. Enterprising international cartoon quarterly published by Joseph George Szabo; first appeared in summer 1987. Downsized to *WittyWorld International Cartoon Bulletin* with issue no. 1 in 1996 with a promise to continue the development of *WittyWorld*'s site on the World Wide Web. It offers a News Wire, Calendar, Who's Who (biographical information on international cartoonists, including some American editorial ones), Gallery, Marketplace, Directories, Honors & Awards, Censorship, Links (including several editorial cartoonists), Our History, and a link to the editors for "Questions/Comments." The print *WittyWorld* ceased publication with no. 34 (December 1998).

Trade Publications

AAEC News. Encino, Calif.: Association of American Editorial Cartoonists, August 1959–April 1965.

AAEC Newsletter. Wilmington, Del.: Association of American Editorial Cartoonists, September 1972?–May 1973.

AAEC Notebook. Washington, D.C.: Association of American Editorial Cartoonists, 1973– . Reviews of new books, interesting behind-the-scenes information, and Draper Hill's featured "History Corner." The association's publications are generally distributed only to members, but special requests are usually honored. The Ohio State University Cartoon, Graphic, and Photographic Arts Research Library holds a complete run of this publication, as well as the association's other publications. The society's Web site is discussed earlier. The AAEC's address is 4101 Lake Boone Trail, Suite 201, Raleigh, N.C., 27607.

Editor and Publisher. New York: Editor and Publisher, December 1927– . Weekly feature, "Syndicates/News Service." Features stories and articles about developments and controversies relevant to the trade, births—and deaths—of cartoon features, hirings and firings, and such trade minutiae as an artist's changing syndicates. Annual directory of syndicated services lists syndicates and their clients, both writers and artists.

National Cartoonists' Society Album. New York: The Society, 1965– . Edited by Mort Walker, about every seven years since 1965. The National Cartoonists' Society, which is less concerned with editorial cartooning, publishes this and others. Enough editorial cartoonists are intermixed with magazine artists and strip cartoonists who are members of the society to make one wish the publication were more readily available to nonmembers (Ohio State, Michigan State, and some other university libraries have them).

National Cartoonists Society Newsletter. (Originally *The Bulletin*). Since July 8, 1948. Reuben Award issues, usually appearing in April or May, are variously titled *The Cartoonist* and *The American Cartoonist*. The 1990s issues are parodies of magazines, tabloids, or newspapers, such as *[This Is Not Really] People Weakly*, May 17–20, 1991; *NCS Guide*, May 12–15, 1994; and *National Cartoonist Society Geographic*, May 26–29, 1995. Available to members only. Mail relating to the

American Cartoonist should be sent to the editors, P.O. Box 20267, New York, N.Y. 10023–1484; (212) 627–1550.

Academic Publications

The annual meetings of the Popular Culture Association and the American Culture Association frequently include an interesting selection of papers on American editorial cartooning. For additional new articles appearing in journals, readers are advised to consult on-line journal article indexes such as ACAD (Expanded Academic Index) and PSYC (PsycINFO). Of additional help are the following journalism and media periodicals:

Journal of American Culture. Bowling Green, Ohio: Bowling Green State University, Spring 1978– .

Journal of Popular Culture. Bowling Green, Ohio: Bowling Green State University, Summer 1967– .

Journal of the Thomas Nast Society. Morristown, N.J: The Society, 1987– . Scholarly articles, reprints of cartoons, facsimile reprints of auction catalogs, and so on. Vol. 10, no. 1 (1996) reprints an index of the first ten volumes from Vol. 1, no. 1 (1987).

Journalism and Mass Communication Quarterly (formerly *Journalism Quarterly*). Columbia, S.C.: Association for Education in Journalism and Mass Communication, March, 1924– .

Masthead. Washington, D.C.: National Conference of Editorial Writers, Spring 1949– . Occasionally publishes significant articles.

Media History Digest. Philadelphia: Media History Digest Corp., Fall 1980–Fall 1985. Devoted an entire nine-article issue to cartoons and comics, including articles on caricature history, Thomas Nast, and political cartooning.

Newspaper Research Journal. Memphis, Tenn., November 1979– . Publishes an occasionally relevant article.

Washington Journalism Review. Washington, D.C.: Washington Communications Corp., October 1977–1993. Publishes an occasionally relevant article.

Cartoons Only (Primary Sources)

At the time of writing, several publications were reprinting editorial cartoons. *Newsweek* reprints three editorial cartoons per week on the "Perspectives" page. The *Washington Post* reprints about twenty in its national weekly edition from some 300 submissions by cartoonists of all varieties of affiliation. The *New York Times* "Week in Review" section reprinted the work of forty cartoonists, twenty-three of them appearing just once, in a six-month period. Many other newspapers, such as the *Charlotte Observer* and the *Detroit News and Free Press*, also publish year-end "Best of" anthology pages.

Bull's Eye; The Magazine of Editorial Cartooning. Lynnbrook, N.Y.: Bull's Eye Publications, June 1988– . Reprints conservative cartoons, as well as liberal ones, along with interviews, book reviews, and features on Pulitzer Prize winners along with copious numbers of cartoons—five to six per page—arranged thematically according to current issues. A wide sampling of syndicated cartoonists, with an index of artists in later numbers.

The Civil Liberties Review. New York: J. Wiley, Fall 1973–January/February

1979. First a quarterly, then a bimonthly magazine of the American Civil Liberties Union in the mid-1970s. Publishing ten sets of "Galleries" of individual cartoonists beginning with vol. 3, no. 6 (February/March 1977) and continuing through the final issue.[15]

Comic Relief. Eureka, Calif.: Page One Publishers & Bookworks, 1989– . A monthly in comic book format, with newsprint pages and a glossy cover featuring a color editorial cartoon. The table of contents lists contributing editorial cartoonists, about thirty per issue, well known and not so well known, mainstream and alternative.

Liberal Opinion Week. Vinton, Iowa: Living History: Cedar Valley Times, 1990– . Each issue reprints some forty cartoons. Contributing cartoonists listed on the back.

The National Gallery of Cartoons. Has also been titled *The National Forum* and *National Forum Gallery of Cartoons Featuring America's Leading Editorial Cartoonists*. Fairfax Station, Va.: Associated Features, 1991–1992. Continued by *Gallery of Cartoons*, Supplement to *National Forum*. Burke, Va. Reprints well over 100 cartoons per issue, as many as six decent-sized cartoons to a page, with a wide representation of well-known and lesser-known artists.

Political Pix. Norwich, Vt.: Ambience, 1987–1990. Reprinted six pages of cartoons weekly, as many as six to a page, in various sizes, with the artist's signature plus the printed name of the newspaper. Ninety-one issues in the Richard Samuel West collection in the Cartoon Research Library at Ohio State University. Try interlibrary loan for this scarce publication.

We're Living in Funny Times. [Cleveland Heights, Ohio]: Susan Wolpert and Raymond Lesser, 1985– . A tabloid of syndicated humor, including cartoons, both social and political; has enough editorial cartoons to make it worthwhile. Tends to favor alternative cartoonists—Nina Paley, Dan Perkins (Tom Tomorrow), Alison Bechdel ("Dykes to Watch out for") and Ted Rall—but Jules Feiffer and other established names also appear. Some of the artists are indexed on the back page.

NOTES

1. See LeRoy Carl, "Editorial Cartoons Fail to Reach Many Readers," *Journalism Quarterly* 45 (Autumn 1968), 533–35, citing studies that found that a high percentage of readers came to interpretations that were "in complete disagreement" with the cartoonists' intended meaning (534).

2. See Draper Hill, "The United States' First Black Editorial Cartoonist?" *AAEC Notebook* (Spring 1991), 16–18.

3. Arthur Bartlett Maurice and Frederick Taber Cooper attribute the creation of this symbol to Nast, in 1874. *The History of the Nineteenth Century in Caricature* (New York: Dodd, Mead, 1904), 279.

4. "The Sit-Down Comics," *Washington Journalism Review* (October 1981), 22, 27.

5. David Astor, "An Unexpected Hit at Cartoon Festival," *Editor & Publisher* 28 (November 1992), 29.

6. Dubuque, Iowa: Kendall/Hunt, 1995.

7. "The Sit-Down Comics," 23.

8. Paul Duke, "If a Cartoonist's Pen Draws Blood, Victims Can Return the Favor," *Wall Street Journal*, August 2, 1985: 1, 14.

9. "Quintessential Cartooning: The Art of Pat Oliphant, Part II," *Target* (Autumn 1982), 5, 6.

10. "Using the Knife," *Target* (Spring 1982), 13.

11. "Kevin Siers: Making the Political Personal," reprint from the *Charlotte Observer*, in *AAEC Notebook* (Winter 1993), 13.

12. "Patrick Oliphant: A Talk and Presentation," James Madison College Founders Circle Dinner, Michigan State University, East Lansing, April 13, 1997.

13. Signe Wilkinson, in Nancy M. Davis, "Signe Wilkinson," reprint from *Presstime*, in *AAEC Notebook* (Spring 1995), 19–20.

14. James R. Beniger, "Does Television Enhance the Shared Symbolic Environment? Trends in Labeling of Editorial Cartoons, 1948–1980," *American Sociological Review* 48 (February 1983), 106.

15. Published with interviews in *Getting Angry Six Times a Week*, discussed earlier and listed in its bibliography.

BIBLIOGRAPHY

Aguila, Dani. *Taking Liberty with the Lady*. Nashville, Tenn.: EagleNest, 1986.

Allen, Edison. *Of Time and Chase*. New Orleans, La.: Habersham, [1969].

American Antiquarian Society. (C. S. Brigham). *Paul Revere's Engravings*. Worcester, Mass.: American Antiquarian Society. 1954. Rev. ed. New York: Atheneum, 1969.

American Artists Congress. *12 Cartoons Defending WPA*. New York: The Congress, [193-?].

American Caricatures Pertaining to the Civil War. 1892. Variously titled *Caricatures Pertaining to the Civil War* and *American Caricatures*. New York: Brentano's, 1970, 1971.

American Political Cartoons (1865–1965). Martin H. Bush Exhibition. Syracuse, N.Y.: Syracuse University Press, 1966.

Amon Carter Museum of Western Art. *The Image of America in Caricature & Cartoon*. Fort Worth, Tex.: Amon Carter Museum of Western Art, 1975, 1976.

Anderson, George McCullough, ed. *The Work of Adalbert Johann Volck*. [Baltimore: George McCullough Anderson], 1970.

Andrews, W. L. *Paul Revere and His Engraving*. New York: C. Scribner's Sons, 1901.

Antin, Charles, and Sig Rosenblum, eds. *LBJ Lampooned*. New York: Cobble Hill Press, 1968.

Appel, John, and Selma Appel. *Jews in American Graphic Satire and Humor*. Cincinnati: American Jewish Archives, 1984.

Armitage, Shelley. *Kewpies and Beyond: The World of Rose O'Neill*. Jackson: University Press of Mississippi, 1994.

The Art of the Dart: Nine Masters of Visual Satire. Grosse Pointe, Mich.: Gryphon Gallery, [1987].

Ash, Lee. *Subject Collections: A Guide to Special Book Collections and Subject Emphases as Reported by University, College, Public and Special Libraries and Museums in the United States and Canada*. 7th ed. Rev. and enl. New Providence, N.J.: R. R. Bowker, 1993.

Ashbee, C. R. *Caricature*. London: Chapman and Hall, 1928.

Attwood, Francis Gilbert. *Attwood's Pictures*. New York: Life, 1900.

Auth, Tony. *Lost in Space: The Reagan Years*. Kansas City, Mo.: Andrews and McMeel, 1988.

Bartholomew, Charles L. *Cartoons of the Spanish-American War by Bart*. Minneapolis: Journal Printing, 1899.

Batchelor, Clarence Daniel. *Truman Scrapbook*. Deep River, Conn.: Kelsey Hill, 1951.

Beardsley, William A. *An Old New Haven Engraver and His Work: Amos Doolittle*. [New Haven], Conn., 1914.

Becker, Stephen. *Comic Art in America*. New York: Simon and Schuster, 1959.

Benson, Steve. *Evanly Days!* [Phoenix, Ariz.]: Phoenix Newspapers, 1988.

Berger, Arthur Asa. *Li'l Abner: A Study in American Satire*. 1970. Jackson: University Press of Mississippi, 1994.

Berryman, Clifford K. *Berryman Cartoons*. Washington, D.C.: Saks, 1900.

———. *Berryman's Cartoons of the 58th House*. Washington, D.C.: C. K. Berryman, 1903.

———. *Development of the Cartoon*. Columbia: University of Missouri Bulletin, 1926.

Berryman, Clifford K., James T. Berryman, and Gibson M. Crockett. *The Campaign of '48 in Star Cartoons*. Washington, D.C.: Evening Star, 1948.

Berryman, James T., and Gibson M. Crockett. *The Campaign of '52 in Star Cartoons*. Washington, D.C.: Evening Star, 1952.

———. *The Campaign of '56 in Star Cartoons*. Washington, D.C.: Evening Star, 1956.

Best Editorial Cartoons of the Year. Ed. Charles Brooks. Gretna, La.: Pelican, 1973– . Annual.

Bishop, Joseph Bucklin. "Early Political Caricature in America." *The Century* 44 (June 1892), 219–31.

———. *Our Political Drama, Conventions, Campaigns, Candidates*. New York: Scott Thaw, 1904.

———. *Presidential Nominations and Elections*. 1916. New York: C. Scribner's Sons, 1971.

Blaisdell, Thomas C., Jr., and Peter Selz. *The American Presidency in Political Cartoons: 1776–1976*. Berkeley, Calif.: University Art Museum, 1976. Rev. ed. Salt Lake, Utah: Peregrine Smith, 1976.

Block, Herbert. *Herblock: A Cartoonist's Life*. New York: Macmillan; Toronto: Maxwell Macmillan Canada; New York: Maxwell Macmillan International, 1993.

———. *Herblock at Large: "Let's Go Back a Little . . ." and Other Cartoons with Commentary*. New York: Pantheon Books, 1987.

———. *Herblock through the Looking Glass*. New York: Norton, 1984.

———. *Herblock Special Report*. New York: Norton, 1974.

Borgman, Jim. *The Great Communicator*. Cincinnati, Ohio: Colloquial Books, 1985.

Boston Museum of Fine Arts. *Paul Revere's Boston, 1735–1815: Exhibition, April 18–October 12, 1975*. Boston: Department of American Decorative Arts and

Sculpture, Museum of Fine Arts: distr. by New York Graphic Society, 1975.
Bradley, Luther D. *War Cartoons from the Chicago Daily News*. Chicago: Chicago Daily News, 1914.
———. *Wonderful Willie! What He and Tommy Did to Spain*. [New York]: E. P. Dutton, 1899.
Branch, John. *Would You Buy a Used Cartoon from This Man?* Chapel Hill, N.C.: Chapel Hill Newspaper, 1979.
Bredhoff, Stacey. *Draw!: Political Cartoons from Left to Right*. Washington, D.C.: National Archives and Records Administration, 1991.
Brigham, Clarence Saunders. *Journals and Journeymen*. Philadadelphia: University of Pennsylvania Press, 1950.
———. *Paul Revere's Engravings*. 1954. Rev. ed. New York: Atheneum, 1969.
British Museum. Dept. of Prints and Drawings. *Catalogue of Prints and Drawings in the British Museum* [London]: By order of the Trustees, 1870–1954. Vols. 1–4 prepared by F. G. Stephens; Vols. 5–11 by M. D. George; Vols. 5–11 have title: *Catalogue of Political and Personal Satires Preserved in the Dept. of Prints and Drawings in the British Museum*.
Brooks, Van Wyck. *John Sloan; A Painter's Life*. New York: Dutton, 1955.
Bruckner, D.J.R., Seymour Chwast, and Steven Heller. *Art against War*. New York: Abbeville Press, 1984.
Bryant, Mark, ed. *World War II in Cartoons*. New York: Gallery Books, 1989.
Bucholaer, H. *Texas Question*. [New York]: J. Baille, 1844.
Buckley, Elizabeth. *Political Cartoons in Art & History: England, France & America, 1750–1890; Catalogue of an Exhibition Held at Sierra Nevada Museum of Art, Reno, Oct. 16–Nov. 16, 1980*. Reno, Nev.: The Museum, 1980.
Buhle, Paul. *Images of American Radicalism*. Hanover, Mass.: Christopher, 1998.
Bunker, Gary L., and Davis Bitton. *The Mormon Graphic Image, 1834–1914*. Salt Lake City: University of Utah Press, 1983.
Burstein, Mark. *Much Ado: The Pogofenokee Trivia Book*. Richfield, Minn.: Spring Hollow Books, 1988; updated and expanded, Forestville, Calif.: Eclipse Books, [1988?].
Campaign: A Cartoon History of Bill Clinton's Race for the White House. Comp. and ed. Mary Ann Barton and Paul C. Barton. Fayetteville: University of Arkansas Press, 1993.
Campbell, Mary, and Gordon Campbell. *The Pen, Not the Sword*. Nashville, Tenn.: Aurora, 1970.
Canemaker, John. *Winsor McCay: His Life and Art*. New York: Abbeville Press, 1987.
Capp, Al. *The Hardhat's Bedtime Story Book*. New York: Harper and Row, 1971.
———. *My Well-Balanced Life on a Wooden Leg*. Santa Barbara, Calif.: John Daniel, 1991.
Carpentier, Joseph F., and Alfred S. Scarcelli. *Original Political Cartoons of World War II*. Garden City, Mich.: J. Carpentier, 1994.
Car(ter)toons; or, The Un-making of the President 1976. Ed. Sandra K. Brown. Houston, Tex.: Praxis Financial, 1976.

A Cartoon History of the Reagan Years. Ed. Fred Barnes. Washington, D.C.: Regnery Gateway, 1988.

Cartooning AIDS around the World. Ed. Maury Forman and Dave Horsey. Dubuque, Iowa: Kendall/Hunt, 1992.

Cartooning Texas: One Hundred Years of Cartoon Art in the Lone Star State. Ed. Maury Forman and Robert A. Calvert. College Station: Texas A&M University Press, 1993.

Cartooning Washington: One Hundred Years of Cartoon Art in the Evergreen State. Ed. Maury Forman and Rick Marschall. Spokane, Wash.: Melior, 1989.

Cartoonometer: Taking the Pulse of the World's Cartoonists. Ed. George Szabo and John A. Lent. North Wales, Pa.: WittyWorld Books, 1994.

Cartoons and Ethnicity. Columbus: Ohio State University Libraries, 1992.

Cartoons of the War of 1898 with Spain; from Leading Foreign and American Papers. Chicago: Belford, Middlebrook, 1898.

Caswell, Lucy Shelton, and George A. Loomis Jr. *Billy Ireland*. Columbus: Ohio State University Libraries, Publications Committee, 1980.

Chase, John Churchill. *40 Cartoons in Wartime*. New Orleans: Higgins Press, 1945.

———. *Today's Cartoon*. New Orleans: The Hauser Press, 1962.

Christ-Janer, Albert. *Boardman Robinson*. Chicago: University of Chicago Press, 1946.

Cole, William. *Women Are Wonderful! A History in Cartoons of a Hundred Years with America's Most Controversial Figure*. Boston: Houghton Mifflin, 1956.

Colldeweih, Jack, and Kalman Goldstein, eds. *Graphic Opinions: Editorial Cartoonists and Their Art*. Bowling Green, Ohio: Popular Press, 1998.

College Art Association of America. *Catalogue of the Salon of American Humorists; A Political and Social Pageant from the Revolution to the Present Day*. [New York?: College Art Association of America?], 1933.

The Coming Man: 19th Century American Perceptions of the Chinese. Ed. Philip P. Choy, Lorraine Dong, and Marlon K. Hom. Seattle: University of Washington Press, 1995.

Congress Drawn . . . , and Quartered! Lakeville, Conn.: Kenneth Weir, 1985.

Conningham, F. A. *Currier and Ives*. Cleveland: World, 1950.

Conrad, Paul. *The King and Us*. Los Angeles: Clymer, 1974.

Craven, Thomas. *Cartoon Cavalcade*. New York: Simon and Schuster, 1943.

Cresswell, Donald H. *The American Revolution in Drawings and Prints. A Checklist of 1765–1790 Graphics in the Library of Congress*. Washington, D.C.: U.S. Government Printing Office, 1975.

Crockett, Gibson M. *The Campaign of '68 in Star Cartoons*. Washington, D.C.: Evening Star, 1968.

Crouse, Russell. *Mr. Currier and Mr. Ives*. Garden City, N.Y.: Doubleday, Doran, 1931.

Crowe, J. D. *Daze of Glory: Images of Fact and Fantasy Inspired by the Gulf War*. San Diego: Crowe's Dirty Bird Press, 1991.

Curtis, L. Perry. *Apes and Angels; The Irishman in Victorian Caricature*. Washington, D.C.: Smithsonian Institution Press, 1971.

Daily Worker. Red Cartoons: From the Daily Worker. Chicago: The Daily Worker, 1926–1929.

———. *Red Cartoons of 1927 from the Daily Worker and the Worker's Monthly.* Chicago: The Daily Worker, 1927.
———. *Red Cartoons from the Daily Worker 1928.* Ed. Walt Carmon. New York: The Daily Worker, 1928.
Daniels, Les. *Comix: A History of Comic Books in America.* New York: Outerbridge and Dienstfrey; distr. by E. P. Dutton, 1971.
Danziger, Jeff. *The Complete Reagan Diet.* New York: Quill, 1983.
———. *Danziger's Vermont Cartoons.* Barre, Vt.: Times Argus, 1978.
Darden, Robert F. *Drawing Power; Knott, Ficklen, and McClanahan: Editorial Cartoonists of the Dallas Morning News.* Waco, Tex.: Markham Press Fund of Baylor University, 1983.
Darling, Jay N. *As Ding Saw Hoover.* 1954. Ed. John M. Henry. Ames: Iowa State University Press, 1996.
———. *Calvin Coolidge: Cartoons of His Presidential Years Featuring the Work of Syndicated Cartoonist Jay N. "Ding" Darling, August 1923–March 1929.* Ed. Edward Connery Lathem. Plymouth, Vt.: Calvin Coolidge Memorial Foundation, 1973.
———. *Dedicated to Home Brew, Suffragettes and Discords: Successors to Wine, Women and Song.* Des Moines, Iowa: Des Moines Register and Tribune, 1920.
Deur, Lynne. *Political Cartoonists.* Minneapolis, Minn.: Lerner Publications, 1972.
Directory of Special Libraries and Information Centers 1988, 1996. Detroit: Gale, 1988, 1996.
Dobbins, James J. *Dobbins' Diary of the New Frontier.* Boston: B. Humphries, 1964.
Dolmetsch, Joan D. *Rebellion and Reconciliation: Satirical Prints on the Revolution at Williamsburg.* [Williamsburg, Va.: Colonial Williamsburg Foundation]. Charlottesville: University Press of Virginia, 1976.
Douglas, Roy. *Between the Wars, 1919–1939.* London: Routledge, 1992.
———. *Great Nations Still Enchained, 1848–1914.* London: Routledge, 1993, 1995.
———. *The Great War, 1914–1918.* London: Routledge, 1995.
———. *The World War, 1939–1945.* 1990. London: Routledge, 1991.
Doyle, Jerry. *According to Doyle: A Cartoon History of World War II.* New York: G. P. Putnam's Sons, 1943.
Drawing the Iron Curtain: Cold War Cartoons 1946–1960. Washington, DC: Library of Congress, 1996.
Dreppard, Carl W. *Early American Prints.* New York and London: Century, 1939.
Echoes of Revolt: The Masses, 1911–1917. Ed. William L. O'Neill. 1966. Chicago: Elephant Paperbacks, 1989.
Ellis, Fred. *1929 Red Cartoons Reprinted from the Daily Worker.* New York: Comprodaily, 1929.
Estren, Mark James. *A History of Underground Comics.* 3rd ed. Berkeley, Calif.: Ronin, 1993.
Fearing, Jerry. *Minnesota Flavored Editorial Cartoons.* Scandia, Minn.: Fearing, 1988.
Feiffer, Jules. *Feiffer on Nixon.* New York: Random House, 1974.
———. *Jules Feiffer's America: From Eisenhower to Reagan.* Ed. Steven Heller. New York: Alfred A. Knopf, 1982.
———. *Ronald Reagan in Movie America.* Kansas City, Mo.: Andrews and McMeel, 1981.

———. *Tantrum*. New York: Alfred A. Knopf, 1980.
The Festival of Cartoon Art. Columbus: Ohio State University Libraries, 1986.
The Festival of Cartoon Art/ Introductory Essay by Alan Gowans; Exhibits Organized and Catalog Compiled by Lucy Shelton Caswell. Columbus: Ohio State University Libraries, 1983.
The Finest International Political Cartoons of Our Time. 3 vols. Ed. Joe Szabo. North Wales, Pa.: WittyWorld, 1992–1994.
Fisher, George. *"There You Go Again!"* Fayetteville: University of Arkansas Press, 1987.
———. *God Would Have Done It If He'd Had the Money*. Little Rock, Ark.: Rose Publishing, 1983.
———. *Old Guard Rest Home*. Little Rock, Ark.: Rose Publishing, 1983.
Fischer, Roger A. *Them Damned Pictures: Explorations in American Political Cartoon Art*. North Haven, Conn.: Archon Books, 1995.
———. *Tippecanoe and Trinkets Too*. Urbana: University of Illinois Press, 1988.
Fitzgerald, Richard. *Art and Politics*. Westport, Conn.: Greenwood Press, 1973.
Fitzpatrick, D. R. *As I Saw It*. New York: Simon and Schuster, 1953.
Flautz, John. *Life: The Gentle Satirist*. Bowling Green, Ohio: Bowling Green State University Popular Press, 1972.
Forbes, Esther. *Paul Revere and the World He Lived In*. Boston: Houghton Mifflin, 1988.
Ford, Gerald R. *Humor and the Presidency*. New York: Arbor House, 1987.
Foreign Policy Association. *A Cartoon History of United States Foreign Policy since World War I*. New York: Random House, 1967.
———. *A Cartoon History of United States Foreign Policy: 1776–1976*. New York: Morrow, 1975.
———. *A Cartoon History of United States Foreign Policy from 1945 to the Present*. New York: Pharos Books, 1991.
Fowble, E. McSherry. *Two Centuries of Prints in America; A Selective Catalogue of the Winterthur Museum Collection*. Charlottesville: University of Virginia Press, 1987.
Fredericks, Pierce G., ed. *The People's Choice: The Issues of the Campaign as Seen by the Nation's Best Political Cartoonists*. New York: Dodd, Mead, 1956.
Gallatin, A. E. *John Sloan*. New York: E. P. Dutton, 1925.
The Gang of Eight. Boston: Faber and Faber, 1985.
Geipel, John. *The Cartoon*. London: Newton Abbott, David, and Charles, 1972.
Getting Angry Six Times a Week. Ed. Alan F. Westin. Boston: Beacon Press, 1979.
Giglio, James N., and Greg G. Thielen, eds. *Truman in Cartoon and Caricature*. Ames: Iowa State University Press, 1984.
Glanz, Rudolf. *The Jew in Early American Wit and Graphic Humor*. New York: Ktav Publishing House, 1973.
Golden, Lou. *The Jewish Political Cartoon Collection*. New York: Shapolsky, 1988.
Goldstein, Kalman. "Al Capp and Walt Kelly: Pioneers of Political and Social Satire in the Comics." *Journal of Popular Culture* 25 (Spring 1992), 81–95.
Goodman, Helen. *The Art of Rose O'Neill*. Chadds Ford, Pa.: Brandywine River Museum, 1989.
Goodrich, Lloyd. *John Sloan*. New York: Macmillan, 1952.
Goss, Elbridge Henry. *The Life of Colonel Paul Revere, with Portraits, Many Illus-*

trations, Fac-similes, etc. 1891. Boston: H. W. Spurr, 1902. Freeport, N.Y.: Books for Libraries Press, 1971.

Graphic Opinions: Editorial Cartoonists and Their Art. Ed. Jack Colldeweih and Kalman Goldstein. Bowling Green, Ohio: Bowling Green State University Popular Press, 1998.

Graphics '75: Watergate: The Unmaking of a President: Lexington, January 12–February 9, 1975. Ed. Richard B. Freeman. Lexington: University of Kentucky Art Gallery, 1975.

Gros, Raymond. *T. R. in Cartoon*. New York: Saalfield, 1910.

Hale, Norman F. *All-Natural Pogo*. New York: Thinker's Books, 1991.

Halsey, R. T. Haines. " 'Impolitical Prints': The American Revolution as Pictured by Contemporary English Caricaturists. An Exhibition." *Bulletin of the New York Public Library* 43 (November 1939), 795–828.

Harding, Nelson. *The Political Campaign of 1912 in Cartoons*. Brooklyn, N.Y.: Brooklyn Daily Eagle, 1912.

———. *Ruthless Rhymes of Martial Militants*. Brooklyn, N.Y.: Brooklyn Daily Eagle, 1914.

Harrington, Oliver. *Dark Laughter: The Satiric Art of Oliver W. Harrington*. Ed. M. Thomas Inge. Jackson: University of Mississippi Press, 1993.

———. *Why I Left America and Other Essays*. Ed. M. Thomas Inge. Jackson: University Press of Mississippi, 1993.

Harrison, Randall P. *The Cartoon, Communication to the Quick*. Beverly Hills, Calif.: Sage, 1981.

Harrison, S. L. (Stanley L.), ed. *Florida's Editorial Cartoonists: A Collection of Editorial Art with Commentary*. Sarasota, Fla: Pineapple Press, 1996.

Harville, Victor. *Now That's the Way to Run a War*. Little Rock, Ark.: Merritt, 1991.

Heagerty, Leo E., ed. *Eyes on the President*. Occidental, Calif.: Chronos, 1993.

Hecht, George. *The War in Cartoons*. 1919. New York: Garland, 1971.

Heller, Steven. *Man Bites Man*. New York: A and W, 1981.

———, ed. *Warheads: Cartoonists Draw the Line*. New York: Penguin Books, 1983.

Heller, Steven, and Gail Anderson. *The Savage Mirror: The Art of Contemporary Caricature*. New York: Watson-Guptill, 1993.

Henry, William A., III. "The Sit-Down Comics." *Washington Journal Review* (October 1982), 22–28.

Herman, Edward S. *The Great Society Dictionary*. Philadelphia: Philadelphia Resistance, 1968.

Hess, Stephen, and Milton Kaplan. *The Ungentlemanly Art*. 1968. New York: Macmillan, 1975.

Hess, Stephen, and Sandy Northrop. *Drawn & Quartered: The History of American Political Cartoons*. Montgomery, Ala.: Elliott and Clark, 1996.

Hill, Draper, ed. *Fashionable Contrasts: 100 Caricatures by James Gillray*. London: Phaidon, 1966.

———. *Mr. Gillray, the Caricaturist*. London: Phaidon, 1965.

———. *The Satirical Etchings of James Gillray*. New York: Dover, 1976.

———. "The United States' First Black Editorial Cartoonist?" *AAEC Notebook* (Spring 1991), 16–18.

———. "What Fools These Mortals Be! A Study of the Work of Joseph Keppler, Founder of Puck." Thesis, Harvard College, 1957.

Hillier, Bevis. *Cartoons and Caricatures*. New York: Dutton, 1979.

Hoff, Syd. *Editorial and Political Cartooning*. New York: Stravon Educational Press, 1976.

Hohenberg, John, ed. *The Pulitzer Prize Story*. 1959. New York: Columbia University Press, 1980.

Horwitz, Elinor Lander. *The Bird, the Banner, and Uncle Sam: Images of America in Folk and Popular Arts*. Philadelphia and New York: J. B. Lippincott, 1976.

Huck, Gary, and Mike Konapacki. *Them: More Labor Cartoons*. Chicago: C. H. Kerr, 1991.

Human Rights as Seen by the Leading Cartoonists. New York: CartoonMedia International, 1993.

Huot, Leland, and Alfred Powers. *Homer Davenport of Silverton*. Bingen, Wash.: West Shore Press, 1973.

"I Feel I Should Warn You . . .": Historic Preservation Cartoons. Ed. Terry B. Morton. Washington, [D.C.]: Preservation Press, 1975.

Impressions of Mr. Sam: A Cartoon Profile. Ed. H. G. Dulaney and Edward Hake Phillips. Bonham, Tex.: Sam Rayburn Foundation, 1987.

Ivey, Jim. *U.S. History in Cartoons: The Civil War Through WWII*. Longwood, Fla.: International Media Systems, 1979.

Jirousek, Carolyn S. *Provocative Pens: Four Cleveland Cartoonists, 1900–1975*. Cleveland, Ohio: Cleveland Artists Foundation, 1992.

Johnson, Gerald W. *The Lines Are Drawn*. New York: J. B. Lippincott, 1958.

Johnson, Kenneth M., comp. *The Sting of the Wasp*. San Francisco: Book Club of California, 1967.

Johnson, Malcolm. *David Claypool Johnston, American Graphic Humorist, 1798–1865; Catalog*. Lunenburg, Vt.: Stinehour Press, 1970.

Keen, Sam. *Faces of the Enemy*. San Francisco: Harper and Row, 1986.

Keller, Morton. *The Art and Politics of Thomas Nast*. New York: Oxford University Press, 1968.

Kelly, Selby. *Pogo Files for Pogophiles*. Richfield, Minn.: Spring Hollow Books, 1992.

Ketchum, Alton. *Uncle Sam: The Man and the Legend*. New York: Hill and Wang, 1959. Abridged ed. Chicago: National Association of Realtors, 1975.

King, Nancy. *A Cartoon History of United States Foreign Policy from 1945 to the Present*. New York: Pharos Books, 1991.

Kinnaird, Clark, ed. *Rube Goldberg vs. the Machine Age*. New York: Hastings House, 1968.

Kirby, Rollin. *Highlights*. New York: William Farquahr Payson, 1931.

LBJ Political Cartoons. Austin, Tex.: Lyndon Baines Johnson Library and Museum, 1987.

Lendt, David L. *Ding: The Life of Jay Norwood Darling*. 1979. Ames: Iowa State University Press, 1989.

Levin, Martin. *Five Boyhoods: Howard Lindsay, Harry Golden, Walt Kelly, William K. Zinsser and John Updike*. Garden City, N.Y.: Doubleday, 1962.

Library Company of Philadelphia. *Made in America: Printmaking, 1760–1860; An Exhibition of Original Prints from the Collections of the Library Company of*

Philadelphia and the Historical Society of Pennsylvania, April–June, 1973. Philadelphia: [Library Company of Philadelphia], 1973.

"The Limits of Caricature." *The Nation* 3 (July 19, 1866), 55.

Long, Scott. *"Hey! Hey! LBJ! Or He Went Away and Left the Faucet Running."* [Minneapolis: Ken Sorenson Print, 1969.]

Lozowick, Louis. *William Gropper*. Philadelphia: Art Alliance Press; London: Associated University Presses, 1983.

Lucie-Smith, Edward. *The Art of Caricature*. Ithaca, N.Y.: Cornell University Press; London: Orbis, 1981.

Lurie, Ranan R. *Nixon-Rated Cartoons*. 1973. New York: Quadrangle, 1974.

Lynch, John Gilbert Bohun. *A History of Caricature*. 1927. Detroit: Gale Research, 1974.

Lynx, J. J., ed. *The Pen Is Mightier: The Story of the War in Cartoons*. [London]: Lindsay Drummond, 1946.

MacNelly, Jeff. *The Election That Was—MacNelly at His Best*. New York: Newspaperbooks, 1977.

Malcolm, James P. *An Historical Sketch of the Art of Caricaturing*. London: Longman, Hurst, Rees, Orme, and Brown, 1813.

Manning, Reg. *Little Itchy Itchy, and Other Cartoons*. New York: J. J. Augustin, 1944.

Marlette, Doug. *Faux Bubba*. New York: Times Books, 1993.

Marschall, Rick. "The Truth about Al Capp." *Cartoonist Profiles* (March 1978), 10–20.

Marylanders in Cartoon. Baltimore: [S.n.], 1906.

Marzio, Peter. *The Men and Machines of American Journalism*. [Washington, D.C.]: National Museum of History and Technology, the Smithsonian Institution, [1973?].

———. *Rube Goldberg*. New York: Harper and Row, 1973.

Matthews, Albert. *Uncle Sam*. Worcester, Mass.: Davis Press, 1908.

Matthews, Roy T., and Peter Mellini. *In "Vanity Fair."* London: Scolar Press; Berkeley: University of California Press, 1982.

Mauldin, Bill. *A Sort of Saga*. 1949. New York: Bantam, [1950].

Maurice, Arthur Bartlett, ed. *How They Draw Prohibition*. New York: Association against the Prohibition Amendment, 1930.

Maurice, Arthur Bartlett, and Frederick Taber Cooper. *The History of the Nineteenth Century in Caricature*. New York: Dodd, Mead, 1904.

McCanse, Ralph Alan. *Titans and Kewpies: The Life and Art of Rose O'Neill*. New York: Vantage, 1968.

McCutcheon, John T. *Drawn from Memory*. Indianapolis: Bobbs-Merrill, 1950.

———. *T. R. in Cartoons*. Chicago: McClurg, 1910.

McDougall, Walt. *This Is the Life!* New York: A. A. Knopf, 1926.

Melville, Annette. *Special Collections in the Library of Congress*. Washington, D.C.: Library of Congress, 1980.

Messner, Elmer. *The War in Cartoons*. [Rochester, N.Y.]: Rochester Times-Union, [1946?].

Morgan, Matt, et al. *The American War: Cartoons by Matt Morgan and Other English Artists*. London: Chatto and Windus, 1874.

The Mother of All—Defeats, Retreats & Miscalculations. Port Chester, N.Y.: Sportomatic, 1991.

Mother of All Windbags. New York: Nantier-Beall-Minoustchine, 1991.

Mott, Frank Luther. *American Journalism*. 1941. 3rd ed. New York: Macmillan, 1962.

Murrell, William. *A History of American Graphic Humor*. New York: Whitney Museum of American Art. 2 vols. 1933 and 1938.

———. "The Rise and Fall of Cartoon Symbols." *The American Scholar* 4 (Summer 1935), 306–15.

Museum of Graphic Art. *American Printmaking, the First 150 Years*. Washington, D.C.: Smithsonian Institution Press, [1969].

Nast, Thomas. *Thomas Nast: Cartoons and Illustrations; With Text by Thomas Nast St. Hill*. New York: Dover, 1974.

The National Campaign to Stop the MX. *MX Cartoon Book*. Washington, D.C.: National Campaign to Stop the MX, [198?].

The National Cartoonists Society. *President Eisenhower's Cartoon Book*. New York: F. Fell, 1956.

The National Union Catalog of Manuscript Collections. Washington, D.C.: Library of Congress, 1959/1961–1991/1993.

Neely, Mark E. *The Confederate Image: Prints of the Lost Cause*. Chapel Hill: University of North Carolina Press, 1987.

Nelan, Charles. *Cartoons of Our War with Spain*. New York: F. A. Stokes, 1898.

Nelson, Roy Paul. *Comic Art and Caricature*. Chicago: Contemporary Books, 1975.

Nevins, Allan, and Frank Weitenkampf. *A Century of Political Cartoons*. 1944. New York: Octagon Books, 1975.

New York Metropolitan Museum of Art. *Paul Revere, a Picture Book*. New York: Metropolitan Museum, 1944.

Newspaper Cartoonists' Association of Michigan. *A Gallery of Pen Sketches in Black and White of Our Michigan Friends "As We See 'Em."* Detroit: W. Graham Printing, 1905.

The 1970s, Best Political Cartoons of the Decade. Ed. Jerry Robinson. New York: McGraw-Hill, 1981.

1989 Festival of Cartoon Art. Columbus: Ohio State University Libraries, 1989.

North, Joseph. *Robert Minor*. New York: International, 1956.

Oliphant, Patrick. *Oliphant's Presidents: Twenty-five Years of Caricature*. Text by Wendy Wick Reaves. Kansas City, Mo.: Andrews and McMeel, 1990.

Orr, Carey. *1952 Cartoons from the Chicago Tribune*. Chicago: Tribune, 1952.

Osborn, Robert Chesley. *Osborn on Osborn*. New Haven, Conn.: Ticknor and Fields, 1982.

———. *War Is No Damn Good!* Garden City, N.Y.: Doubleday, 1946.

Paine, Albert Bigelow. *Th. Nast: His Period and His Pictures*. 1904. New York: B. Blom, 1971.

Papritz, Carew, and Russ Tremayane, eds. *100 Watts: The James Watt Memorial Cartoon Collection*. Auburn, Wash.: Khyber Press, 1983.

———. *Reagancomics*. Seattle: Khyber Press, 1984.

Parton, James. *Caricature and Other Comic Art*. 1878. New York: Harper and Row, 1969.

Paul Revere: Artisan, Businessman, and Patriot—the Man behind the Myth. Boston: Paul Revere Memorial Association, 1988.

Penn, Arthur. "The Growth of Caricature." *The Critic* (February 25, 1882), 49–50.

Peters, Harry T. *America on Stone*. 1931. New York: Arno Press, 1976.

———. *Currier and Ives, Printmakers to the American People*. 2 vols. 1929–1931. New York: Arno Press, 1976.

Peters, Mike. *The Nixon Chronicles*. Dayton, Ohio: Lorenz Press, 1976.

———. *Win One for the Geezer*. New York: Bantam Books, 1982.

Philippe, Robert. *Political Graphics: Art as a Weapon*. New York: Abbeville Press, 1982.

The Pillory of the Press. [West Lafayette, Ind.: The Gallery, 1979].

Political Cartooning in Florida 1901–1987. Tallahassee: Museum of Florida History, 1987.

Political Satire '84. Tallahassee: Fine Arts Gallery, Florida State University, 1984.

Pork Roast: 250 Feminist Cartoons. An Exhibition Curated by Avis Lang Rosenberg, Sponsored by UBC Fine Arts Gallery, Vancouver, B.C., Canada, April, 1981. Vancouver, B.C.: University of British Columbia, Fine Arts Gallery, 1981.

Powell, Dwane. *The Reagan Chronicles*. Chapel Hill, N.C.: Algonquin Books, 1987.

Powell, Dwane, and Jesse Helms. *100 Proof Pure Old Jess*. [Raleigh, N.C.: Insider], 1993.

Press, Charles. *The Political Cartoon*. Rutherford, N.J.: Fairleigh Dickinson University Press, 1981.

Pulling Our Own Strings. Ed. Gloria Kaufman and Mary Kay Blakely. Bloomington: Indiana University Press, 1980.

Raemaekers, Louis. *America in the War*. New York: Century, 1918.

———. *Raemaekers' Cartoon History of the War*. New York, Century, 1918–1919.

Rajski, Raymond B., comp. *A Nation Grieved; The Kennedy Assassination in Editorial Cartoons*. Rutland, Vt.: C.E. Tuttle, 1967.

Reaves, Wendy Wick. *Oliphant's Presidents*. Kansas City, Mo.: Andrews and McMeel, 1994.

Regan, Colm. *Thin Black Lines: Political Cartoons & Development Education*. Written and comp. by Colm Regan, Scott Sinclair, and Martyn Turner. Birmingham: Development Education Centre, 1988.

Reid, Albert T. *Albert T. Reid's Sketchbook; Fads, Foibles & Politics: 1896–1908*. Comp. John W. Ripley and Robert W. Richmond. Topeka, Kans.: Shawnee County Historical Society, 1971.

Reilly, Bernard, Jr. *American Political Prints, 1766–1876: A Catalog of the Collections in the Library of Congress*. Boston: G. K. Hall, 1991.

———. *Drawings of Nature and Circumstance*. Washington, D.C.: The Library, 1979.

Rising Up Angry. *Living in the U.S.A.* Chicago: Rising Up Angry, 1975.

Robbins, Trina. *A Century of Women Cartoonists*. Northampton, Mass.: Kitchen Sink Press, 1993.

Robinson, Boardman. *Cartoons on the War*. New York: E. P. Dutton, 1915.

Robinson, Jerry. *The 1970s: Best Political Cartoons of the Decade*. New York: McGraw Hill, 1980.

Robinson, Jerry, and Jens Robinson. *OD'd on O. J.* New York: Universe, 1995.

Rogers, William Garland. *Mightier than the Sword*. New York: Harcourt, Brace, and World, 1969.

Rosenblum, Sig, and Charles Antin, eds. *LBJ Lampooned; Cartoon Criticism of Lyndon B. Johnson*. New York: Cobble Hill Press, 1968.

———. *LBJ Political Cartoons: The Public Years: An Exhibition at the Lyndon Baines Johnson Library and Museum, November 7, 1987-February 28, 1988*. Austin, Tex.: The Lyndon Baines Johnson Library and Museum, 1987.

Roxas, Cynthia, and Joaquin Arevalo Jr. *A History of Komiks of the Philippines and Other Countries*. Quezon City: Islas Filipinas, 1984.

St. John, Bruce. *John Sloan*. New York: Praeger, 1971.

Salisbury, Harrison. *The Indignant Years*. New York: Crown/Arno Press, 1973.

Salon International de la Caricature. International Salon of Cartoons. Montreal: International Pavilion of Humour, Man and His World. 1965-? Later issues published as *Pavilion of Humour of Man and His World*.

Salzman, Ed, and Ann Leigh Brown, eds. *The Cartoon History of California Politics*. Sacramento: California Journal Press, 1978.

Sanders, Bill. *Run for the Oval Room . . . They Can't Corner Us There!* Milwaukee, Wis.: Alpha Press, 1974.

Schreiner, Dave. *Kitchen Sink Press: The First 25 Years*. Northampton, Mass.: Kitchen Sink Press, 1994.

A Selection of Drawings from the Worker, 1924–1960. New York: Worker, [1961?].

Serio, Anne Marie. *Political Cartoons in the 1848 Election Campaign*. Washington, D.C.: Smithsonian Instituion Press, 1972.

Seymour-Ure, Colin, and Jim Schoff. *David Low*. London: Secker and Warburg, 1985.

Shaw, Albert. *Abraham Lincoln*. New York: Review of Reviews, 1929, 1930.

———. *Abraham Lincoln in Contemporary Caricature*. New York: Review of Reviews, 1901.

———. *A Cartoon History of Roosevelt's Career*. New York: Review of Reviews, 1910.

Sheppard, Alice. *Cartooning for Suffrage*. Albuquerque: University of New Mexico Press, 1993.

Shikes, Ralph E. *The Indignant Eye*. Boston: Beacon Press, 1969.

Shikes, Ralph, and Steven Heller. *The Art of Satire* [New York]: Pratt Graphics Center and Horizon Press, 1984.

Siegel, Mark, ed. *The World according to Evan Mecham*. Mesa, Ariz.: Blue Sky Press, 1987.

Slade, John Eaves. *But I Am Too a Black Cartoonist!—Really!* Dubuque, Iowa: Kendall/Hunt, 1995.

Smith, Henry Ladd. "The Rise and Fall of the Political Cartoon." *Saturday Review* (May 29, 1954), 7+.

Somers, Paul P., Jr. *Editorial Cartooning and Caricature: A Reference Guide*. Westport, Conn.: Greenwood Press, 1998.

Spencer, Dick, III. *Pulitzer Prize Cartoons*. Ames: Iowa State College Press, 1953.

Spiegelman, Art. *The Complete Maus*. CD-ROM. New York: Voyager, 1994.

———. *Maus: A Survivor's Tale*. 2 vols. New York: Pantheon, 1991.

Stars & Swipes. Atlanta: Cox Enterprise, 1988.

The Sting of the Bee. Sacramento: Sacramento Bee, 1982.

Suares, Jean-Claude, comp. *Art of the Times*. New York: Universe Books, 1973.

Szep, Paul Michael. *At This Point in Time*. Boston: Boston Globe, 1973.

Szyk, Arthur. *Ink & Blood*. New York: Heritage Press, 1946.

———. *The New Order*. New York: G. P. Putnam's Sons, 1941.

Thunderer of the Prairies; A Selection of Wartime Editorials and Cartoons, 1941–1944 [Chicago: Tribune], 1944.

Tolbert, Matt. *Read My Lips: The Unofficial Cartoon Biography of George Bush*. Westlake Village, Calif.: Malibu Graphics Publishing Group, 1992.

Toledo Museum of Art. *Catalogue [of] American Political Cartoons of Other Days, 1747–1872*. [Toledo]: The Museum, 1936.

Toles, Tom. *Mr. Gazoo*. New York: Pantheon Books, 1987.

Tower, Samuel A. *Cartoons and Lampoons: The Art of Political Satire*. New York: J. Messner, 1982.

Trever, John. *Freeze*. Albuquerque, N. Mex.: New Mexicans for a Bilateral Nuclear Weapons Freeze, 1982.

———. *Trever's First Strike*. Andover, Mass.: Brick House, 1983.

Trudeau, Garry B. *Doonesbury Dossier*. New York: Holt, Rinehart, and Winston, 1984.

———. *Doonesbury Flashbacks: 25 Years of Serious Fun*. CD-ROM. Novato, Calif.: Mindscape, 1995.

———. *Guilty, Guilty, Guilty!* 1974. Toronto: Bantam Books, 1976.

———. *In Search of Reagan's Brain*. New York: Holt, Rinehart, and Winston, 1981.

Viens, Margaret F. *Never Underestimate: The Life and Career of Margaret Chase Smith through the Eyes of the Political Cartoonist*. Skowhagen, Maine: Northwood University Margaret Chase Smith Library, 1993.

Vinson, J. Chal. *Thomas Nast: Political Cartoonist*. Athens: University of Georgia Press, 1967.

Walsh, William S., ed. *Abraham Lincoln and the London Punch*. New York: Moffat, Yard, 1909.

Walt Kelly: A Retrospective Exhibition to Celebrate the Seventy-fifth Anniversary of His Birth: Philip Sills Exhibit Hall, the Ohio State University Libraries, Columbus, Ohio, August 1–September 9, 1988. [Columbus]: Ohio State University, University Libraries, 1988.

War Cartoons by McCutcheon, Orr, Parrish [and] Somdal. [Chicago]: Tribune, 1942.

Warren, Robert. *Nixon Made Perfectly Clear*. New York: Rodney, 1972.

Was It Worth It? A Collection of International Cartoons about Columbus and His Trip to America. Comp. Michael Ricci and Joseph George Szabo. North Wales, Pa.: WittyWorld, 1992.

Webster, H. T. *The Best of H. T. Webster*. New York: Simon and Schuster, 1953.

Weiss, Harry B. *William Charles, Early Caricaturist, Engraver and Publisher of Children's Books*. New York: New York Public Library, 1932.

Weitenkampf, Frank. "American Cartoonists of Today." *The Century* 85 (February 1913), 540–52.

———. *American Graphic Art*. 1912. New York: Johnson Reprint, 1970.

Wells, Clyde. *The Net Effect, or, If This Is the Bottom Line, What Are You Guys Doing Down There?* Augusta, Ga.: Augusta Chronicle, 1979.

West, Richard Samuel, and Richard B. Freeman, eds. *The Best Political Cartoons of 1978*. Lansdale, Pa.: Puck Press, 1979.

Westin, Alan F. *Getting Angry Six Times a Week*. Boston: Beacon Press, 1979.

———. *Satire on Stone: The Political Cartoon of Joseph Keppler*. Urbana: University of Illinois Press, 1988.

Westwood, H. R. *Modern Caricaturists*. London: L. Dickinson, 1932.

What America Thinks. Chicago: What America Thinks, 1941.

White, Richard Grant. "Caricature and Caricaturists." *Harper's New Monthly Magazine* (April 1862), 586–607.

Wilson, Rufus Rockwell. *Lincoln in Caricature*. New York: G. A. Powers Printing, 1903.

———. *Lincoln in Caricature; 165 Poster Cartoons and Drawings for the Press*. Elmira, N.Y.: Primavera Press, 1945.

A Window on the 1992 Campaign. New York: Princeton Club, 1992.

Wood, Art. *Great Cartoonists and Their Art*. Gretna, La.: Pelican, 1987.

Wuerker, Matt. *Standing Tall in Deep Doo-Doo*. New York: Thunder's Mouth Press, 1992.

Wynn Jones, Michael. *The Cartoon History of the American Revolution*. New York: Putnam, 1975.

———. *The Cartoon History of Great Britain*. 1971. New York: Macmillan, 1973.

Young, Art. *Art Young: His Life and Times*. New York: Sheridan House, 1939.

———. *The Campaign Primer*. Chicago: Socialist Party of the United States, 1920.

———. *The Socialist Primer*. Chicago: Socialist Party of America, 1930.

Zemen, Zbynek. *Heckling Hitler*. Hanover, [N.H.]: University Press of New England, 1987.

Zimmerman, Eugene. *Zim: The Autobiography of Eugene Zimmerman*. Ed. Walter M. Brasch. Selinsgrove, Pa.: Susquehanna University Press, 1988.

Zurier, Rebecca. *Art for the Masses (1911–1917): A Radical Magazine and Its Graphics*. 1985. Philadelphia: Temple University Press, 1988.

ETHNIC MINORITIES

Leslie Lewis

In the latter half of the twentieth century, the term "minorities" as used within the context of the United States generally referred specifically to racial or ethnic minority groups. Defining minority status has evolved into a theoretically complex issue, however, and serious debate about the nature of American society, the role of public policy, the need for social justice, and the purpose of education in shaping American citizens continues. Consequently, while this chapter necessarily focuses on numerous minority groups as they are represented and misrepresented in American popular culture, it also discusses the ways in which our understanding of the concept of "minorities" has changed since its first popular usage in the 1960s.

Definitions of what it means to be a minority are rooted in the idea of a particular racial or ethnic group as a numerical minority constituting a small percentage of the national population. Yet demographic projections suggest that the combined number of ethnic minority group members is so rapidly increasing that the very concept "minority" becomes misleading. For this reason, some scholars suggest that the term itself is outdated and in need of replacement. Further, because the concept "minority" often seems to imply inferiority, members of racial or ethnic minority groups sometimes respond to the word as a pejorative term. This response clearly limits the efficacy of the term in contemporary usage. Nevertheless, only the term "minorities" represents the broad umbrella of ethnic or racial minority group members within the United States with regard to such important classification systems as the Library of Congress subject headings. What follows, then, is a history of the usage of the term, including its relation to the terminology of race and ethnic relations in the United States more generally and a discussion of the standard minority group categories as identified for purposes of public policy: African Americans, Asian Americans, Native Americans, and Hispanics.

HISTORICAL OUTLINE

The earliest term used by social scientists to characterize difference among peoples was "race," which implied biological distinctions that scientists and anthropologists now reject. In an attempt to avoid the biological determinism that racial distinctions imply, Donald Ramsey Young introduced the term "minority" in his 1932 study titled *American Minority Peoples: A Study in Racial and Cultural Conflicts in the United States*. By referring to "minorities of racial or national origin," Young focused attention on the similarities in the experiences of minority peoples based upon their subordinate positions within the overall societal structure but did not provide a precise definition of minority peoples. In his 1945 article "The Problem of Minority Groups," Louis Wirth proposed a definition of the term. According to Wirth, minorities are groups of people "who, because of their physical or cultural characteristics, are singled out from others in the society in which they live for differential and unequal treatment and who therefore regard themselves as objects of collective discrimination" (347). This working definition is still applicable to today's discussions of minority groups, with emphases and refinements of the definition focused on one of the three parts: (1) the physical or cultural characteristics shared by the group; (2) the unequal and discriminatory way that members of the group are treated within the larger society; and (3) the understanding of the group as a self-conscious social unit. Alternatively, other definitions of majority–minority relations focus on group differences in power exclusively and do not restrict the term "minorities" to racial and ethnic groupings or even to groups numerically small in size of membership.

What began as the study of minorities has in recent decades developed into the burgeoning fields of ethnic studies and multiculturalism, which, in turn, have introduced into popular culture many terms and controversies surrounding majority–minority positions and relations. Ethnic and other group-specific studies dominated the movement toward diversity in higher education in the 1970s and 1980s and focused attention on the experiences of various racial and ethnic minority groups, as well as the conceptual distinction between race and ethnicity and the interrelated definitions of terms that mark oppression, such as discrimination, prejudice, and racism. Because ethnic studies is rooted in the social protest movements of the 1950s, 1960s, and 1970s, it often calls into question assimilation, both as ideal and as paradigm for understanding intergroup life in America. In contrast to assimilation are pluralist models of understanding the relation between American identities and group identities. While assimilation de-emphasizes difference, pluralism advocates recognizing, tolerating, and/or celebrating difference. By the late 1970s, advocates of cultural pluralism developed a new model of understanding group-specific dynamics: multiculturalism. Within the realm of educational institutions, advocates for multiculturalism stress the need for curriculum and classroom experiences that reflect the diversity of American society, generally with regard not only to race and ethnicity but also to gender, age, class, sexual orientation, and physical ability.

Controversies surrounding multiculturalism and issues of cultural diversity on college and university campuses have become a significant aspect of American culture more generally. Campus issues surrounding hate speech and speech codes, for example, became major news items in the late 1980s and early 1990s. In this

Attorney General Robert Kennedy speaking to Civil Rights demonstrators in front of the Justice Department in Washington. Courtesy of the Library of Congress

context, neoconservative politicians and critics redefined and popularized the phrase "politically correct" (PC), initially a term used self-critically in socialist, Marxist, and feminist circles. By the 1990s, charges of "PC" came to mean that an individual or organization was acting uncritically and according to an accepted liberal agenda. Backlash against the growing acceptance of the tenets of multiculturalism was evidenced not only through the derisive use of the "PC" charge but also through arguments that claimed that "culture wars" were being waged on college campuses. According to popular authors such as Allan Bloom and E. D. Hirsch, for example, and organizations such as the National Association of Scholars, the multiplicity of cultures and the inclusion of minority points of view threaten American society.

Disagreements about the nature of American society and the relation between minority group and national identities have direct consequences for minority group members. Recent legal challenges and voter referenda concerning affirmative action and the rights of immigrants, in particular, are public policy issues of great consequence. The Civil Rights Act of 1964 and the Voting Rights Act of 1965 were intended to eliminate the formal barriers that had relegated nonwhite racial groups to second-class citizenship. Tied to the 1964 Civil Rights Act was the idea of affirmative action, a phrase first used by President Kennedy in Executive Order 10925 in 1961. Title VII, Section 703 (j) of the 1964 Civil Rights Act bans preference by race, ethnicity, gender, and religion in business and government. President Johnson's Executive Order 11246 (1965), which concerns the enforcement of this ban, specifically interprets acts of nondiscrimination as "affirmative action" that undo discrimination and ensure equal treatment. When the Department of Labor's Office of Federal Contract Compliance was created in 1965 to oversee nondiscrimination and affirmative action with regard to goods and services purchased by the federal government, it specified the minority groups with which it was concerned: Negro, Oriental, American Indian, and Spanish-surnamed American. In the mid-1970s, task forces representative of numerous government agencies, including the Bureau of the Census, the Equal Employment Opportunity Commission, and the Civil Rights Commission, took on the work of standardizing categories for the data collection designed to ensure that racial/ethnic minorities were not being discriminated against and determined that the majority category should be named white, not of Hispanic origin, while the four minority categories should be (1) black, not of Hispanic origin; (2) Hispanic; (3) American Indian or Alaskan Native; and (4) Asian or Pacific Islander.

Affirmative action has been controversial from its inception, and in 1978 the Supreme Court ruled, in *University of California Regents v. Bakke*, that while racial preferences in higher education admissions were legal, racial quotas were not. A series of additional Supreme Court cases in the 1980s clarified and upheld affirmative action, but in 1989 a more conservative Court began to reflect a growing societal reluctance to use race-conscious remedies to overcome past discrimination. In the 1990s, affirmative action began to be dismantled through voter referenda and the federal courts, and the rhetoric of reverse discrimination against white Americans became a common refrain in popular culture. Because there is no clear consensus within American society as to the current degree of discrimination against minorities, there is also no clear consensus about whether or not remedies and what kind of remedies are necessary to end discrimination. Societal confusion is further increased because of shifting demographics. While some white majority group members who fear a loss of dominance claim minority status through arguments that they are victims of reverse racism or discrimination, shifting demographics mean that in some geographical regions in the United States white Americans are becoming a numerical minority, whether or not they are subordinate in terms of societal power. The consequent responses of majority group members who perceive themselves to be losing status seem, in turn, to directly affect public policy with regard to minority group members. In California, for example, Proposition 187, the ballot initiative that denies state-supported health and educational services to undocumented immigrants and their children, is the consequence of a perceived threat to majority members from a growing Mexican and Mexican American population.

Our understanding of the specific minority categories black, Hispanic, Native American, and Asian is shifting for reasons in addition to demographics. In the 1980s, Susie Guillory Phipps, a light- or white-skinned woman with straight black hair and Caucasian features, went to court to get the racial designation on her birth certificate at the Louisiana Bureau of Vital Records changed from "colored" to "white." When Phipps lost her case—the 1970 Louisiana law specified as "colored" anyone with one-thirty-second or more "Negro blood"—the question of racial or minority classification was raised anew. Further, publication of Gregory Howard Williams' 1995 autobiography, *Life on the Color Line*, wherein the Ohio State University School of Law dean describes his upbringing and identity as white until he was ten years of age and black thereafter, at least through high school, also introduces into popular imagination the mutability of racial identity. Golf professional Tiger Woods, billed by sports commentators as the first African American to win the prestigious Masters tournament, quickly claimed his Asian, Caucasian, and American Indian ancestry as well. Woods is just one example of someone whose racial identification cuts across set categories; controversy over the 2000 U.S. Census, with increasing demand for a "multiracial" category, makes clear that many people self-identify in ways that current minority classifications do not adequately reflect.

In tandem with the socially constructed and delineated categories of racial/ethnic classification are the socially defined attitudes and actions of prejudice, discrimination, racism, and ethnocentrism. Prejudice, literally, a prejudging, involves hostility or condescension toward a member of a group specifically because of that group membership. Consequently, prejudice takes its form as attitude or emotion. Discrimination, on the other hand, involves action and is characterized by the unfavorable treatment of individuals because of their group membership. Racism, which might involve both attitude and action, in traditional terms refers to an ideology used to rationalize or justify a racially organized and hierarchical social order. Ethnocentrism is similar to racism in supplying a moral justification for the treatment of others, but ethnocentrism characterizes difference culturally, while racism characterizes difference biologically. Current reflection upon the topic of minorities must take into account the dramatic resurgence of racial and ethnic hostilities and tensions throughout the world, including the United States. In the former Yugoslavia, tensions among Serbs, Croats, Slovenes, Bosnians, Montenegrins, Macedonians, and Albanians have led to one of the most bitter and deadly conflicts among European peoples since World War II. In Rwanda, recent ethnic warfare between the Tutsi and Hutu has been equally brutal. As a consequence of these conflicts in other parts of the world, "ethnic cleansing," a term referring to horrific brutality in the name of ethnocentrism, has entered the popular American vocabulary. At the same time, Americans have been stunned by an increasing number of venomous, ideologically based hate crimes against people of minority status. The murders of James Byrd Jr., an African American in Jasper, Texas, and Matthew Shepard, a gay college student in Wyoming, brought hate crimes to the general attention of the American public, while the murderous rampage by white supremacist Benjamin Smith brought attention to the distorted and racist ideas promoted by members of the Identity Church movement.

While hate crimes and racist ideologies create fissures in American society, detailed understanding of minority identities and cultures helps mend rifts created by ignorance and fear. In this vein and despite the inadequacies of the four recognized racial and ethnic minority classifications, we proceed to a discussion of basic information concerning the representation and misrepresentation of African Americans, Asian Americans, Native Americans, and Hispanics.

African Americans

The largest populations of Africans arrived in the Americas from the early seventeenth century until the middle of the nineteenth century because of the slave trade and certainly as unwilling immigrants. Twentieth-century voluntary emigration from Africa and the Carribean was substantial, however, and during the 1990s approximately 5 percent of the African American population comprised immigrants who had come from other countries since 1970. While differences in culture and history tend to prevent unification among native-born black Americans and more recent immigrants, members of both groups are racially identified as minorities in America.

Africans were among the first explorers of the Americas and often part of expeditions or settlements from Spain and France in the sixteenth and seventeenth centuries. The first Africans arrived in the English North American colonies in 1619 as indentured servants on a Dutch ship, but by the mid-1600s the slave status of Africans was fully institutionalized in colonial law. Estimates of the numbers of Africans brought alive into the Western Hemisphere range from 10 to 15 million; only about 5 percent of that population was brought to North America. Living and working conditions for slaves in the colonies allowed this population to increase rapidly so that by 1860, most of the 3 million enslaved African Americans were American-born. While free black populations have always existed in the Americas, American slavery dominates the history of early African American life because it was an institution unique in human history and designed to dehumanize Africans and convince them of their inferiority. Popular arguments and traditions designed to justify slavery emerged in order to ensure its continuation, with the consequence that many white Americans believed myths about the racial inferiority of black Americans. Despite attempts on the part of slaveholders to deny slaves a human existence, Africans in the Americas developed communities and new cultural practices based on old ways of life.

While slavery was formally ended in 1865, the range of "Jim Crow" laws in the South and other discriminatory practices throughout the United States meant that black Americans continued to be treated as second-class citizens. Because of severe economic, political, and social conditions in the South during the early twentieth century, many black Americans migrated to the North. Between 1900 and 1910, for example, New York City's black population doubled, while during that same period Chicago's increased by over 30 percent. Rising urban racial tensions resulted in race riots, proving that the North was not the land of milk and honey as often characterized by newspapers such as the *Chicago Defender*. Nevertheless, many northern cities became population magnets; New York City attracted so many African American artists, writers, and musicians to its Harlem section during the 1920s and 1930s that the era is known as the Harlem Renaissance. For many black Americans, however, it was the experience of serving in the armed forces during World War II and living outside the racially divided United States that increased expectations when the war ended and people came home. The civil rights movement of the 1950s and 1960s, through boycotts, sit-ins, and other challenges to desegregation laws in the South, along with voter registration drives and other community organizing, finally put an end to legal segregation and second-class citizenship for black Americans.

Today, despite many gains, African Americans remain disadvantaged in terms of social stratification. Statistics that reflect median income, percentage of population below the poverty level, and unemployment rates all show that the general economic condition of black Americans is significantly worse than that of white Americans. Further, while African Americans constitute approximately 12 percent of the U.S. population, they are clearly underrepresented in positions of political and economic power. Institutional racism remains a powerful determinant in the lives of many African Americans, as reflected in rejection rates for mortgage and home improvement loans, disparities between the public education offered in predominantly white and black schools, and the differences in prison sentences for black and white offenders. In the workplace, discrimination persists. In the mid-1990s, for example, several top executives at Texaco, the nation's fourteenth largest corporation, were taped as they discussed black employees in the most pejorative terms. Yet according to most surveys, while the overwhelming majority of African Americans do not believe that black Americans have the same opportunities in the workplace as white Americans, the majority of white respondents do believe that opportunities are the same. This clear difference, by race, in social perception has also been highlighted by varying responses to instances of police brutality and to the jury's verdict in the murder trial of athlete O. J. Simpson.

Myths of racial inferiority stemming from the legacy of slavery also remain with us. While African Americans are stereotyped as natural athletes and entertainers, they are persistently charged with being less intelligent than people of other races. This is partly because majority Americans fail to recognize the cultural biases inherent in their systems. IQ scores have been a regular source of controversy in this regard. In the late 1950s, Audrey Shuey's *The Testing of Negro Intelligence* claimed a native difference in the intelligence of black and white Americans. William B. Shockely and Arthur R. Jensen did the same in the late 1960s. While these findings were thoroughly dispelled in the 1970s, Richard Herrnstein and Charles Murray brought the controversy to recent public attention with the publication of their book *The Bell Curve*, which also makes claims about intellectual inferiority based on race. Herrnstein and Murray's argument was particularly pernicious because it attempted to justify the dismantling of affirmative action and the termination of social programs such as Aid to Families with Dependent Children based on racial inferiority.

Asian Americans

Asian Americans are a diverse category of people, representing at least a dozen groups that differ in nationality, language, history, customs, and beliefs. While, historically, Chinese, Japanese, and Filipinos have been the most prominent Asian groups in the United States, more recent immigrants have come from Korea, Vietnam, Cambodia, and Laos. Currently, Asians are proportionately the nation's fastest growing racial category, and high immigration rates are doubling the number of Asian Americans. For example, population figures jumped from 3.5 million in 1980 to 7.3 million in 1990; in California, a full 10 percent of the population is now Asian. Despite unique backgrounds and histories within the United States, Asians of various nationalities are often treated interchangeably and in general are thought of as the model minority group that has achieved the American Dream

Chinese Dragon, Rock Springs, Wyoming. Courtesy of the Denver Public Library

of upward mobility and socioeconomic success. However, this stereotype and the statistical information from which it is formed disguise great variations among Asian population groups.

Chinese immigration to the United States began during the 1840s as a result of the need for labor in the West, particularly in mining and in building the transcontinental railroad. By 1860, about 9 percent of the population of California was Chinese, but because these immigrants were almost exclusively adult and male, they accounted for approximately 25 percent of the labor force in the state. U.S. law did not allow these workers to become citizens, nor were they allowed to send for a wife or marry an American. Seen as peculiar because of their difference in clothing and hairstyles, these Chinese were stereotyped as suspicious and then as filthy and prone to disease. The Chinese Exclusion Act of 1882 marked the first time that the federal government, responding to popular fear, enacted a human embargo on a nationality of laborers. After the passage of the Exclusion Act and similar later legislation, the Chinese American population did not expand appreciably until the 1960s.

Like the Chinese, the first Japanese came to the United States in the latter part of the nineteenth century as laborers. Most settled in the western states and worked as gardeners or farm laborers. As a consequence of their success as farmers, the 1913 California legislature passed the first law prohibiting noncitizens from owning land and allowed land leases of only three years. While citizenship in the late nineteenth century was nominally extended to black Americans, the U.S. Naturalization Act made it clear that citizenship for immigrants excluded nonwhite people. Because children of immigrants born in the United States are automatically citizens, many Japanese held land in their children's names or collectively through landholding companies. By 1940, there were about 127,000 Japanese in the United States, with almost 75 percent of that population in California. Following Japan's attack on Pearl Harbor and the advent of World War II, all Japanese living on the West Coast, many of them second- or third-generation Americans with as little as one-eighth Japanese ancestry, were routinely rounded up and sent to live in detention camps for the duration of the war. While national security interests were cited as the reason for this treatment, white neighbors of Japanese farmers eagerly took over land that had been confiscated without compensation. Until 1988 the actions of the federal government during World War II toward American citizens of Japanese ancestry were dismissed. In 1988, however, Congress passed a bill offering a formal apology to former detainees for violating their basic civil liberties because of racial prejudice and awarded a payment of $20,000 to each of the surviving Japanese Americans treated in this manner.

Additional East Asian groups came to the United States as a result of U.S. aggression or involvement in overseas wars. When the United States acquired the Philippine Islands from Spain in 1898 after the Spanish-American War, Filipinos came to the United States and to Hawaii as nationals. Because Filipinos were not limited by immigration restrictions until 1935, they replaced the Chinese and Japanese laborers in California and Hawaii who had been excluded by earlier immigration restrictions. Consequently, between 1907 and 1910, approximately 150,000 Filipinos entered the United States and Hawaii. While Filipino immigration was negligible from 1935 until 1965, when the Immigration Act eliminated national quotas, since the 1960s the Filipino population has expanded to 1.4 million in 1990, making the group the second largest in the Asian-Pacific census category. Koreans were also able to enter the United States in large numbers after 1965, although they began to immigrate to the United States through the Refugee Relief Act of 1953 during the Korean War. Like Filipinos, many Koreans were familiar with U.S. culture prior to coming to this country, because of a large American presence, via U.S. troops, in South Korea. Similarly, the end of the Vietnam War in 1975 brought numerous Vietnamese and Cambodians to the United States as political refugees. Between 1975 and 1980 more than 166,000 Vietnamese entered the United States, and that population grew by over 140 percent from 1980 to 1990. As a consequence of U.S. involvement in Laos, approximately 90,000 Hmong now also reside in the United States, primarily in California, Minnesota, and Wisconsin. Recruited by the Central Intelligence Agency (CIA) to fight the North Vietnamese and then systematically killed when Pathet Lao took control of Laos, this group from north of the Plain of Jars comes from a society with no written language, no cash economy, and strong extended family bonds, all of which has made living in the United States a very difficult adjustment.

Native Americans/American Indians

The term "Indian" and most names of major Native American groups are generally terms of convenience used by American settlers of European descent and frequently are corruptions of names that settlers heard used among native peoples. Consequently, in most history books there are no major Indian nations recorded under their own name. For example, the "Navajo" call themselves "Dine," meaning "the People," and the Sioux, named as such by the French, knew themselves as the "Lakota" or "Dakota," names preferred to this day. Even the term "Indian" (*los Indios*, from the Portuguese) is a name representing the ignorance of colonizers who believed that they had found the Asian Indies that they were seeking. Today, most native peoples would rather be known by the tribal or national name that they have given themselves; when generalizations are needed, most prefer "Indian" to "Native American," recognizing the latter as yet another term imposed by others and not of their own determination. Also in question is whether native groups are tribes or nations, with some people viewing the term "tribe" as a distortion that obscures variety and complexity and others viewing it as a pejorative.

The U.S. government officially recognizes over 500 Indian nations, sometimes called tribes, and Alaska Native groups. Further, about 200 distinct languages are still spoken among American Indian peoples in North America. These numbers tell us that the diversity of native peoples present in North America when Europeans colonizers first arrived was extraordinary and that the treatment of these distinct groups of people as categorically similar is erroneous. Nevertheless, native peoples share a common history because of their treatment by European colonizers who wanted their land and share, as well, a common decimation by diseases brought from the European continent, against which they had no immunity. The movement west by white settlers displaced native peoples; entire nations were forcibly relocated, generally to reservations in minimally populated areas without the natural resources to support the farming or grazing practices that had been a traditional way of life for many groups. The Indian Removal Act passed by Congress in 1830, for example, forced Atlantic and Gulf Coast nations such as the Cherokee and midwestern peoples such as the Shawnee to Indian Territory west of the Mississippi River. This forced march is known as the "Trail of Tears," because of the number of people who died of exposure and related causes. By the mid-nineteenth century, however, governmental policy had changed from one of annihilation and expulsion to one of segregation and isolation, and the current-day reservation system was adopted at that time.

One popular misconception is that Indians were bloodthirsty savages, as depicted in many books and movies known as "westerns." In fact, of the quarter of a million settlers who made the journey across the plains to the West Coast between 1840 and 1860, less than 1 percent died at the hands of native inhabitants, and fewer than 400 white settlers and just over 400 American Indians died in all the recorded battles along wagon train routes. Clearly, most of the accounts of Indian massacres are fictitious or greatly exaggerated. On the other hand, white aggression against native peoples was extreme. One of the last military engagements was the massacre at Wounded Knee Creek, in the Dakota Territory. Attempting to round up the last of the Sioux, the U.S. Army intercepted one group and forced them to camp near the Dakota Badlands. In response to conflict while disarming the camp, troops shot many old men, women, and children at close range, killing approximately 300 unarmed people.

According to the 1990 census, there were then almost 2 million Americans of native ancestry, including Eskimo and Aleut populations. Approximately 35 percent lived on reservations or similar tribal lands. The increasing attempt to develop and exploit American Indian resources for external economic gain reflects a policy of internal colonialism, and as a consequence of this economic domination life on reservations remains grim. Poverty levels are high, as are related social problems such as alcoholism, family violence, school failure, homicide, and suicide. Because of the concerted efforts of Indian activists, however, economic status has been improving, and in some recent court cases federal judges have ordered compliance with treaties. One of the earliest and most celebrated cases involving Indian claims against the federal government occurred in 1975, when a federal district judge awarded half the annual salmon catch in Puget Sound to Indian nations that had signed an 1855 treaty with the United States. Since then other Indian nations have also received settlements from states and municipalities through land and other property claims. Economic development on reservations continues, and many changes revolve around recently introduced gambling casinos, which have brought profits in the millions of dollars to poverty-stricken people. This controversial development stems from a 1987 Supreme Court ruling that gambling enterprises on tribal lands are exempt from most state gambling laws and regulations. It remains to be seen, however, just what the overall impact of casinos will be on Indian ways of living.

Latinos/Hispanics/Chicanos

People of Mexican, Puerto Rican, Cuban, Dominican, and South and Central American descent are considered to be "Hispanic," an English term rooted in the Latin place-name *Hispania*, referring to Spain. Many people feel that the alternative term *Latino*, also a collective designation, is preferable to "Hispanic," because it recognizes the Latin American origins of these groups of people, acknowledges a plurality of peoples under its rubric, and is a Spanish-language word. Both terms privilege Spanish heritage over other components of national or cultural identity, however, and are consequently problematic in many cases; Mexican American identity, for example, often emphasizes a culture rooted in an Indian, as well as Spanish, past. For this reason, Mexican Americans often wish to be called *Mexicano* or Chicano (an abbreviation of *Mexicano*) instead of Hispanic or Latino. Within the context of U.S. majority–minority relations, Hispanic/Latino is a classification based neither on race nor on ethnicity but instead on language: people are designated "Hispanic" when they are Spanish speakers or of Spanish-speaking origin.

Of the approximately 23 million people designated as "Hispanic" according to the 1990 census, over 75 percent spoke a language other than English at home, with most speaking Spanish. To some Americans, the existence of such a noticeable population of non-English speakers represents an unwillingness to assimilate and a challenge to the dominance of English (and English speakers). Because population figures note that Hispanics are very quickly becoming the largest minority group in the United States and projections suggest that Hispanics will constitute one-quarter of the total U.S. population by midcentury, Anglo responses to Spanish-language speakers has been intense. While the United States currently has no official language designated, the English-only movement, for example, works toward passing statewide referenda that make English the official language, particularly of states with large Hispanic populations. Other nativistic responses to growing Hispanic populations include California's passage of Proposition 187, which denies schooling and medical care to undocumented workers (sometimes called "illegal aliens") and their children.

Mexican Americans are the largest Hispanic group and the second largest ethnic minority group (after African Americans) in the United States. Approximately 90 percent of the total Mexican American population is concentrated in the western or southwestern states of Texas, New Mexico, Arizona, Colorado, and California. The earliest Mexican American population became such through the annexation of Mexican lands by the United States in the 1840s. When Mexico ceded territory

Young women in ethnic costumes at Cinco de Mayo festival. © Skjold Photographs

as a consequence of U.S. military conquest, the Treaty of Guadalupe Hidalgo promised full citizen rights to those Mexicans who chose not to move south of the new United States/Mexico border. In subsequent years, however, through a series of legal and financial maneuvers, Anglos obtained most of the land previously owned by Mexicans, thus causing the native Mexican population in the United States to become landless and poverty-stricken. As a result of this conquest pattern of subordination, subsequent Mexicans who immigrated to the United States in the early part of the twentieth century were also treated poorly. Immigrants who came to the United States seeking jobs were often blatantly exploited by their employers, particularly as farm labor or migrant workers. Currently, chronic economic problems in Mexico force some Mexicans to enter the United States illegally. The stereotype of the "illegal alien" distorts the history of Mexican labor in the United States, however. Beginning in the 1940s, Mexico provided seasonal labor needed by U.S. agriculture, and through an agreement between Mexico and the United States workers were given temporary permits to work in the fields. Employers became eager for these low-wage workers, and this stimulated the migration of undocumented workers as well. Popular press accounts of undocumented workers entering the United States often distort the phenomenon of migrant labor. For example, some studies suggest that virtually all of the Mexican border-crossers apprehended by the U.S. Immigration and Naturalization Service (INS) are temporary labor migrants with no intention of living in the

United States. These people cross the border so often that they are caught again and again by the INS.

The second largest Hispanic group in the United States is Puerto Ricans, whose population in 1990 was almost 2.3 million, or about 12 percent of the total population of documented Hispanics. Puerto Ricans have a unique relation with the United States because of the history of the island of Puerto Rico, ceded to the United States in 1898 after Spain's defeat in the Spanish-American War. As a consequence, Puerto Ricans were granted U.S. citizenship in 1917, and, as citizens, no restrictions are placed on their immigration to the mainland United States. Puerto Ricans began migrating to the mainland in large numbers primarily after World War II, and approximately two-thirds of the Puerto Rican population in the mainland United States lives in New York City. Puerto Ricans in the early twentieth century were dependent upon small farmers who raised coffee and sugar, among other food crops. U.S. occupation of Puerto Rico forced most small Puerto Rican farmers to sell their lands to U.S. corporations. Corporate interests in Puerto Rico shifted from agriculture to manufacturing in the mid-1900s, however, with the Puerto Rican economy completely dependent upon U.S. corporate interests. Today, as firms seek cheaper labor and fewer tax obligations, island unemployment rates are high, but many Puerto Ricans continue to move to the mainland United States in search of employment opportunities.

Cuban Americans are another group that represents a significant portion of the Hispanic population, and Cubans, like Puerto Ricans, are historically tangled in U.S. military aggression. Some Cubans immigrated to the United States in the second half of the nineteenth century while Cuba was engaged in asserting its independence from Spain. Cuban independence from Spain occurred in 1898 with the help of the United States, which then occupied the island. In 1902, Cuba became a U.S. protectorate, and from 1902 until 1959 Cuba was in effect, but not officially, a colony of the United States. In 1959 the revolution in Cuba brought Fidel Castro to power, and Castro's communism led to a break in diplomatic relations between the United States and Cuba. Between 1959 and 1962 approximately 200,000 Cubans entered the United States, and most were members of Cuba's elite or professional middle class. Because south Florida is just ninety miles from Cuba, large populations of Cubans have settled there, and Miami has been transformed into a major international business and commercial center. While Cubans continued to immigrate to the United States during the 1960s and 1970s, the year 1980 added a sudden influx of 125,000 Cubans to the United States, in what is often referred to as the "Mariel boatlift." While stereotyped images of this group of Cubans focuses on the Mariel refugees as undesirably criminal or mentally ill, this was true of only a very small percentage of the refugees. Some 11 percent of this group of immigrants were professionals, and 71 percent were blue-collar workers. Many, however, were darker-skinned than earlier Cuban immigrants, which no doubt played into American color prejudices. In 1994, when the Cuban government lifted its ban on emigration, approximately 35,000 Cubans left for Florida in small boats and on rafts, which created a crisis in the United States and much disagreement about U.S. immigration policies. While an accord was reached in 1995 regarding the fate of this group of immigrants, negotiations between Cuba and the United States continue. At the end of the 1990s, Cuban Americans numbered over 1.5 million.

REFERENCE WORKS

The burgeoning fields of ethnic studies and multiculturalism offer numerous reference works, including textbooks, focused on new conceptual understandings of American ethnic minority groups and power dynamics in the United States. Joe R. Feagin and Clairece Booher Feagin's *Racial and Ethnic Relations* and Vincent N. Parrillo's *Strangers to These Shores: Race and Ethnic Relations in the United States* are well-written texts that present theoretical perspectives related to the study of racial and ethnic groups, as well as information about various ethnic groups, including minorities. Norman R. Yetman's *Majority and Minority: The Dynamics of Race and Ethnicity in American Life*, a more sophisticated introduction to the field of ethnic studies, includes key essays from the most influential scholars in ethnic studies today, as well as significant contextual information and definitions of terms important to the field. James A. Banks' *Teaching Strategies for Ethnic Studies* contains a wealth of information about multicultural curricula, including annotated bibliographies, resources for teachers and teacher education, and resources for students. Two texts that make implicit arguments for the presentation of ethnic studies as it intertwines with issues of race, class, and gender are Paula Rothenberg's *Race, Class, and Gender in the United States: An Integrated Study* and Anthony Gary Dworkin and Rosalind J. Dworkin's *The Minority Report: An Introduction to Racial, Ethnic, and Gender Relations*.

Reference works that focus on multiculturalism tend to incorporate analysis of racial and ethnic minority groups in a conceptual framework that investigates issues of power and oppression more generally and often includes issues related to gender, sexual orientation, and/or disability in addition to race and ethnicity. *The Encyclopedia of Research on Multicultural Education*, edited by James A. Banks and Cherry A. McGee Banks, is an inclusive, forty-seven-chapter collection of the research to date on the most significant topics related to multicultural education generally, with many such topics, for example, immigration policy and language issues, related to racial and ethnic minorities specifically. Susan Auerbach, editor of the *Encyclopedia of Multiculturalism*, has created a general reference work that examines American history and society through the experience of racial, ethnic, religious, and other marginalized groups often excluded from mainstream American history. This encyclopedia includes brief alphabetical entries on key concepts, people, and events, as well as articles on major subjects. It also includes a variety of visual material, a bibliography, resource directory, and filmography. *The Encyclopedia of Multicultural Education*, edited by Bruce M. Mitchell and Robert E. Salsbury, also offers a broad presentation of the key topics related to multiculturalism, with an emphasis on the terms and theories of multicultural education.

The standard reference work on American ethnic groups more generally is the *Harvard Encyclopedia of American Ethnic Groups*, edited by Stephan A. Thernstrom, Ann Orlov, and Oscar Handlin, which includes entries written by recognized experts on every racial and ethnic group with a presence in the United States. Also of interest is the *Gale Encyclopedia of Multicultural America*, edited by Rudolph J. Vecoli, Judy Galens, Anna J. Sheets, and Robyn V. Young. Covering over 100 ethnic groups, this encyclopedia is written more for the general reader than is the *Harvard Encyclopedia* but includes basic cultural and historical information, as well as immigration statistics.

Collections of material specific to one U.S. racial minority group include *Africana: The Encyclopedia of the African and African American Experience*, edited by Kwame Anthony Appiah and Henry Louis Gates Jr. This encyclopedia was the brainchild of early twentieth-century scholar and activist W.E.B. Du Bois, and thirty-five years after his death it has now been completed by Appiah and Gates. This one-volume encyclopedia includes over 3,500 entries from more than 220 contributors and has been designed to give a broad sense of the contributions of people of African descent in the Americas and in the world. Another scholarly text focused on African American experience is *Black Women in America: An Historical Encyclopedia*, edited by Darlene Clark Hine, Elsa B. Brown and Rosalyn Terborg-Penn. This reference work presents a comprehensive picture of black women in America and includes approximately 800 signed entries ranging from biographical treatments to topical essays, as well as hundreds of photographs never before published. The *Reference Encyclopedia of the American Indian*, edited by Barry T. Klein, approaches its subject quite differently than do Appiah and Gates or Hine et al. Klein's encyclopedia is an information sourcebook, divided into listings of organizations, tribal councils, Indian schools, museums and libraries; an extensive bibliography; and biographical sketches of North American Indians and non-Indians active in Indian affairs. *The Latino Encyclopedia*, edited by Richard Chabran and Rafael Chabran, and *The Asian American Encyclopedia*, edited by Franklin Ng, are both published by Marshall Cavendish and are similar in scope. Both encyclopedias are six-volume sets organized according to traditional encyclopedic format. *The Latino Encyclopedia* includes entries on organizations, history, religion, family life, and art. Entries vary in length from unsigned paragraphs to signed articles with bibliographies and are cross-referenced and listed in italicized Spanish when concepts are not yet part of mainstream American English. The *Asian American Encyclopedia* emphasizes the experience of Asian immigrants and the communities in which they live in the United States and provides basic historical and cultural information about the diverse origins of Asian American peoples. While overviews focus on the six largest groups (Chinese, Filipinos, Japanese, Asian Indians, Koreans, and Vietnamese) other less-known groups such as Hmongs and Pacific Islanders are also included.

HISTORY AND CRITICISM

Ronald Takaki's *A Different Mirror: A History of Multicultural America* is perhaps the most often cited single-text contemporary treatment of minorities in today's America. This readable, popular history brings together the viewpoints of many different racial and ethnic minority groups. Rather than looking at groups in isolation, however, he stresses underlying cultural themes and visions that minority groups have in common. Takaki uses folk songs, memoirs, and other literary forms, along with standard historical sources, to paint a vivid picture of the lives of ordinary people. Bibliographic information also makes this an excellent starting point for additional research. Takaki's *From Different Shores: Perspectives on Race and Ethnicity in America*, on the other hand, is an impressive collection of book excerpts and reprinted essays by renowned scholars that lays the groundwork, both historical and theoretical, for a contemporary understanding of minority group identities and dynamics. *Cultural Diversity in the United States*, edited by Larry L. Naylor, also belongs in the category of significant collections of essays about minority group definitions and dynamics. *Race and Ethnicity in America: Meeting the Challenge in the Twenty-First Century*, edited by Gail E. Thomas, is a collection of essays that focus on very specific issues related to education, health, and employment. For example, one essay by James J. Kemple, Richard J. Murnane, Judith D. Singer, and John B. Willett is titled "Why Are There Fewer and Fewer Black Teachers?" and focuses on statistical information about such things as teaching licenses and test score requirements. Well-regarded journals in the fields of ethnic history and sociology that have published widely read and well-regarded articles concerned with issues of minority status as it pertains to race and ethnicity include the *Journal of American Ethnic History*, *Ethnicity*, the *Journal of Ethnic Studies*, and the *Ethnic Studies Review*. The journal devoted to scholarship pertaining to American ethnic literature is *MELUS*, published by the Society for the Study of Multi-Ethnic Literature of the United States.

Underpinning any specific studies of minority groups are theoretical studies of group identity more generally. The most significant texts in this category include Benedict Anderson, *Imagined Communities: Reflections on the Origin and Spread of Nationalism*, which speculates that people group themselves based on the image of their communion; Clifford Geertz, *The Interpretation of Cultures*, which argues anthropologically for a primordial ethnicity; Harold R. Isaacs, *Idols of the Tribe: Group Identity and Political Change*, which analyzes ethnic identity and its dangers from a cross-national perspective; Werner Sollors, *The Invention of Ethnicity*, which explores constructions of ethnicity as collective fictions; and Milton Gordon, *Assimilation in American Life: The Role of Race, Religion, and National Origins*, which presents a significant theory of assimilation. David A. Hollinger argues in *Postethnic America* that multiracial peoples make ethnic identity more a matter of choice than an intrinsic characteristic. The collection *Beyond Pluralism: The Conception of Groups and Group Identities in America*, edited by Wendy F. Katkin, Ned Landsman, and Andrea Tyree, revisits many mid-twentieth-century arguments about assimilation and pluralism from a late-twentieth-century perspective. Finally, *Beyond Identity Politics: Emerging Social Justice Movements in Communities of Color*, edited by John Anner, suggests ways in which disempowered communities of color might establish significant coalitions by focusing on social justice organizing.

One of the significant developments of the 1990s with regard to minority studies involves the interrogation of whiteness, its construction, and its privilege. To this end, *The Wages of Whiteness: Race and the Making of the American Working Class*, by David R. Roediger, offers a working-class history of the social construction of race, while Matthew Frye Jacobson's *Whiteness of a Different Color: European Immigrants and the Alchemy of Race* presents a history that emphasizes the fluidity of racial categories. In terms of group-specific studies, the most significant are Karen Brodkin's *How Jews Became White Folks and What That Says about Race in America*, which focuses on the reracialization of Jews as white in post–World War II America, and Noel Ignatiev's *How the Irish Became White*, a presentation of Irish American history and the construction of "white" Irish identity in the United States in its relation to African American experience and the construction of "black" identity. Abby L. Ferber's approach to the study of whiteness is to examine the rhetoric of the white supremacist movements of the late twentieth century, and in *White Man Falling: Race, Gender, and White Supremacy* she demonstrates in much different terms just how white identity is constructed and maintained.

Numerous scholars have pointed out the implications of social treatments of racial differences and the depth of the problems in American society caused by racism. In *Race: How Blacks and Whites Think and Feel about the American Obsession*, Studs Terkel offers the very disturbing product of a series of interviews about racism. Jonathan Kozol's *Savage Inequalities: Children in America's Schools*, which focuses on six representative school systems, presents compelling data that show just how different and unequal urban and suburban public schools are. Andrew Hacker, in *Two Nations: Black and White, Separate, Hostile, Unequal*, argues convincingly that the racial divide in the United States is supported by white America's deep-rooted ideas about the inferiority of black Americans. *Race Matters*, by Cornel West, offers essays that interrogate both racial understandings and our understanding of race, establishing a definition of race layered with nuance, while *Color Conscious: The Political Morality of Race*, by K. Anthony Appiah and Amy Gutmann, presents an essay by each author that is critical of the very idea of race. Derrick Bell, however, in *Faces at the Bottom of the Well: The Permanence of Racism* and *And We Are Not Saved: The Elusive Quest for Racial Justice*, argues that the idea of race as it is manifested in racism is a permanent and an indestructible component in U.S. society. bell hooks explores the feelings of powerlessness that black Americans feel in the face of the permanence of racism in her tenth book, *Killing Rage: Ending Racism*, but ultimately offers hope for a world without racism.

Analyses of the positive and negative aspects of affirmative action in public policy are abundant and will no doubt continue to proliferate. Sources for the documentation of specific legal challenges to affirmative action as well as the policy changes designed to meet those challenges and the embroiling controversies surrounding both challenges and changes are best presented by media capable of updating themselves very rapidly. Nevertheless, several sources of information are worth mentioning here. Enduring aspects of arguments about affirmative action are represented by Nathan Glazer, who in the mid-1970s in *Affirmative Discrimination: Ethnic Inequality and Public Policy* made a strong case against affirmative action by showing the policy to be, in itself, discriminatory. In his 1997 *We Are All Multiculturalists Now*, however, Glazer very publicly changes his mind and makes the argument that while affirmative action might be bad policy, banning it is worse. Because inequity, particularly in relation to educational opportunity for African Americans, continues to exist and in many ways seems to have gotten worse, Glazer argues, affirmative action is needed to counter the tenacity of racism in U.S. society. Glazer's position in favor of affirmative action with regard to higher education admissions policy is supported by William G. Bowen and Derek Curtis Bok, who presented *The Shape of the River: Long-Term Consequences of Considering Race in College and University Admissions*, a careful analysis of data on the experiences of black and white students at twenty-eight selective colleges and universities. Bowen, former president of Princeton University, and Bok, former president of Harvard University, strongly endorse the policy and practice of preferential admissions and argue for the educational value of student diversity at the most prestigious colleges and universities and for the importance to the nation of increasing the numbers of highly educated African Americans.

Issues pertaining to ethnic and racial minorities are particularly connected to institutions of higher education and through many avenues other than affirmative action policy. Curricular questions addressed by the fields of ethnic studies and multiculturalism have been revisited by scholars calling for a more traditional curriculum. Allan Bloom, in *The Closing of the American Mind: How Higher Education Has Failed Democracy and Impoverished the Souls of Today's Students*, and E. D. Hirsch, in *Cultural Literacy: What Every American Needs to Know*, began the popular call for a shared knowledge that centers around the exclusive, yet traditional, Euro-American canon. Dinesh D'Souza, in *Illiberal Education: The Politics of Race and Sex on Campus*, attempts to document what he sees as the cultural revolution taking place within U.S. colleges and universities in order to argue that this revolution will have dangerous consequences for American society. Two well-regarded responses to these charges that universities are pursuing the wrong educational path are Henry Louis Gates Jr.'s *Loose Canons: Notes on the Culture Wars* and Gerald Graff's *Beyond the Culture Wars: How Teaching the Conflicts Can Revitalize American Education*. *Loose Canons* is a collection of Gates' essays that makes a strong case for education that seeks to understand the diversity of human culture by studying more than the canonical literature of the Western tradition. *Beyond the Culture Wars*, on the other hand, posits that since there are deeply disputed ideas of what should constitute education, contemporary education must include the teaching of these disputes.

Two collections that lay the groundwork for the teaching of multiculturalism are David Theo Goldberg's *Multiculturalism: A Critical Reader* and Avery F. Gordon and Christopher Newfield's *Mapping Multiculturalism*. Both collections offer a selection of scholarly essays whose breadth is impressive and offer, as well, key bibliographic information. *Teaching for Diversity and Social Justice: A Sourcebook*, edited by Maurianne Adams, Lee Anne Bell, and Pat Griffin, does not take up the arguments about multiculturalism but rather offers practical ways to teach about racism, sexism, and heterosexism for the purpose of furthering the cause of social justice. Other collections central to the teaching of diversity focus specifically on the lived experiences of women of color. Two classic texts are *All the Women Are White, All the Blacks Are Men, but Some of Us Are Brave: Black Women's Studies*, edited by Gloria T. Hull, Patricia Bell Scott, and Barbara Smith, and *This Bridge Called My Back: Writings by Radical Women of Color*, edited by Cherrié Moraga and Gloria Anzaldúa.

In the field of African American studies, two recent anthologies of literature represent the literary and, more generally, the intellectual history of African America. *The Norton Anthology of African American Literature*, edited by Henry Louis Gates Jr. and Nellie Y. McKay, offers an impressive collection of African American writing from 1746 to the present, addresses the vernacular tradition in print and, with a companion compact disc, provides significant editorial introductions to both writers and literary or historical periods and includes a substantial selected bibliography for each writer included. *Call and Response: The Riverside Anthology of the African American Tradition*, edited by Bernard W. Bell et al., is just as comprehensive, although perhaps less grounded by scholarly apparatus.

The best one-volume African American history text is John Hope Franklin and

Alfred A. Moss Jr.'s *From Slavery to Freedom: A History of African Americans*. Paula Giddings, in *When and Where I Enter: The Impact of Black Women on Race and Sex in America*, and Dorothy Sterling, in *We Are Your Sisters: Black Women in the Nineteenth Century*, have both written excellent histories of African American women's experiences in the United States. For a history of racism in the United States as it pertains to the misconceptions held by Europeans and Euro-Americans about people of African descent, see Winthrop Jordan's landmark study *White over Black: American Attitudes toward the Negro, 1550–1812* or the more readable *The White Man's Burden: Historical Origins of Racism in the United States*.

Molefi Asante's *Afrocentricity* and *The Afrocentric Idea* offer radical critiques of Eurocentric models of knowledge and posit ways of understanding African American and African diasporic experience as an extension of African history and culture. Paul Gilroy, in *The Black Atlantic: Modernity and Double Consciousness*, explores the theoretical implications of a diasporic, rather than nationalistic, model of black experience. The multivolume, scholarly project of Martin Bernal's, *Black Athena: The Afroasiatic Roots of Classical Civilization*, rewrites our understanding of African influences on early Greek civilization. Significant journals in the field of African American or African diasporic studies include *Journal of Black Studies*, *Journal of Negro History*, *The Black Scholar*, *Phylon*, and *Black Renaissance/Renaissance Noir*.

The burgeoning field of African American literary scholarship is led by Henry Louis Gates Jr., whose critical study *The Signifying Monkey: A Theory of Afro-American Literary Criticism* explores the relation between the African American vernacular and literary traditions. Houston A. Baker Jr.'s critical work, particularly *Blues, Ideology, and Afro-American Literature: A Vernacular Theory*, also explores the vernacular as a way to establish the culturally specific aspects of African American literature and culture. Other significant studies of African American literature include Robert B. Stepto, *From behind the Veil: A Study of Afro-American Narrative*, Hazel Carby, *Reconstructing Womanhood: The Emergence of the Afro-American Woman Novelist* and *Race Men*, and the collection of essays edited by Marjorie Pryse and Hortense Spillers, *Conjuring: Black Women, Fiction, and the Literary Tradition*. Finally, Geneva Smitherman's *Talkin and Testifyin: The Language of Black America* offers a very readable history and linguistic analysis of what has alternatively been called the Black English Vernacular, African American English, and Ebonics. The two most significant journals in the field of African American literary studies are *Callaloo* and the *African American Review* (formerly *Black American Literature Forum*).

American Indian studies has been shaped by the scholarship of Vine Deloria Jr. and Paula Gunn Allen, among others. Deloria's *Custer Died for Your Sins: An Indian Manifesto*, first published in 1969, exposed the facts of U.S. government policies and Euro-American attitudes toward native peoples to the general reading public. His *American Indian Policy in the Twentieth Century* is a more scholarly treatment of similar issues, while *Red Earth, White Lies: Native Americans and the Myth of Scientific Fact* examines modern science as it relates to American Indian oral history. *Spirit and Reason: The Vine Deloria, Jr., Reader*, edited by Barbara Deloria, Kristen Foehner, and Sam Scinta, collects Deloria's writings on political and legal issues.

Paula Gunn Allen's *The Sacred Hoop: Recovering the Feminine in American Indian Traditions* is a pioneering study of the role of women in American Indian tradition.

Her collection *Spider Woman's Granddaughters: Traditional Tales and Contemporary Writing by Native American Women* is a mix of traditional tales, short stories, and biographical writings. Allen has also edited *Studies in American Indian Literature: Critical Essays and Course Designs*, published by the Modern Language Association.

More current studies in American Indian history include *American Holocaust: Columbus, Christianity, and the Conquest of the Americas*, by David Stannard, which documents the full extent of the destruction of Native American civilizations through European and Euro-American conquest; *The Ghost Dance: Ethnohistory and Revitalization*, by Alice Beck Kehoe, which focuses on the religious practices of Plains Indians; and *American Indian Children at School, 1850–1930*, by Michael C. Coleman, which documents American attempts to assimilate Indians through education at boarding schools.

Killing the White Man's Indian: Reinventing Native Americans at the End of the Twentieth Century by Fergus M. Bordewich and *Dressing in Feathers: The Construction of the Indian in American Popular Culture*, edited by S. Elizabeth Bird, both analyze and deconstruct the image of the Indian in popular culture. *American Indian Poetry: An Anthology of Songs and Chants*, edited by George W. Cronyn and first published in 1918, presents oral verse from many Indian nations of the United States. Arnold Krupat's *The Voice in the Margin: Native American Literature and the Canon* views American Indian literature in its relation to traditional Western literature.

Important journals in the field of American Indian studies include *American Indian Quarterly*, published by the Southwestern American Indian Society, *American Indian Culture and Research Journal*, associated with American Indian Studies at UCLA, and *Wicazo Sa Review*, from Indian studies at Eastern Washington University.

Asian American history is well represented by Ronald Takaki's *Strangers from a Different Shore: A History of Asian Americans*, which includes oral testimony and vivid personal recollection. *Asian Americans: An Interpretive History*, by Sucheng Chan, part of the Twayne Immigrant Heritage of America Series, includes significant information for the newcomer to Asian American studies, including terminology, a list of films about Asian American experience, a chronology, and an extensive bibliography.

Joann Faung Jean Lee, in *Asian Americans: Oral Histories of First to Fourth Generation Americans from China, the Philippines, Japan, India, the Pacific Islands, Vietnam and Cambodia* adds to the complexity of Asian American experience with her documentation of peoples from so many different backgrounds and cultures. Other autobiographical treatments of Asian American experience include *Under Western Eyes: Personal Essays from Asian America*, edited by Garrett Hongo, and *Turning Japanese: Memoirs of a Sansei*, by David Mura.

The State of Asian America: Activism and Resistance in the 1990s, edited by Karin Aguilar-San Juan, addresses the grassroots political movements of the Asian and Pacific Islander American community, while Pyong Gap Min's collection, *Asian Americans: Contemporary Trends and Issues*, takes a social science approach to the issues and obstacles facing different groups of Asian Americans. *Making Waves: An Anthology of Writings by and about Asian American Women*, edited by Diane Yen-Mei Wong and Emilya Cachapero, is the most widely regarded Asian American women's studies text, and in popular culture studies Darrell Y. Hamamoto's *Mon-*

itored Peril: Asian Americans and the Politics of TV Representation stands out as an exemplary exploration of the stereotyping of Asian Americans in the mass media.

Asian American literary anthologies include *The Big Aiiieeeee!: An Anthology of Chinese-American and Japanese-American Literature*, edited by Jeffery Paul Chan, Frank Chin, Shawn Wong, and Lawson F. Inada; *Charlie Chan Is Dead: An Anthology of Contemporary Asian American Fiction*, edited by Jessica Hagedorn; and *Asian American Literature: A Brief Introduction and Anthology*, edited by Shawn Wong. Critical texts that focus on Asian American literature include Elaine H. Kim's groundbreaking study *Asian American Literature: An Introduction to the Writings and Their Social Context* and *Reading Asian American Literature: From Necesssity to Extravagance*, by Sau-Ling Cynthia Wong, which establishes an intertextuality of Asian American literature through the motifs of food, doubles, mobility, and play. Also significant to literary studies is the collection of essays edited by Shirley Geok-Lin Lim and Amy Ling titled *Reading the Literatures of Asian America*.

The topic of education within Asian American communities is treated in *The Asian American Educational Experience: A Sourcebook for Teachers and Students*, edited by Don T. Nakanishi and Tina Yamano Nishida. Well-regarded journals in the field of Asian American studies include *Amerasia Journal*, affiliated with the UCLA Asian American Studies Center and the Yale Asian American Students Association, and the *Asian American Review*, affiliated with Asian American Studies at the University of California, Berkeley.

The field of Chicano/a studies has developed substantially in recent years, and Rudolfo A. Anaya and Francisco Lomeli's collection *Aztlan: Essays on the Chicano Homeland* offers a good conceptual starting place for an investigation into Chicano/a studies. Rodolfo Acuña, in *Occupied America: A History of Chicanos*, an important contribution to the new Chicano history, examines the nature of Spanish and Indian cultures as they merged and then collided with U.S. expansionist efforts. *Mexican Americans, American Mexicans: From Conquistadors to Chicanos* by Matt S. Meier and Feliciano Ribera is also a very readable history of the relation between the United States, Mexico, and their peoples with regard to migration, annexation, and immigration issues.

Chicano! The History of the Mexican American Civil Rights Movement, by Francisco A. Rosales, which was published in conjunction with the four-part Public Broadcasting Service series of the same title, focuses on the more recent history of the 1965–1975 Mexican American civil rights movement. *Sometimes There Is No Other Side: Chicanos and the Myth of Equality*, by Rodolfo Acuña, examines the current controversy surrounding minority inclusion in higher education, while *Rethinking the Borderlands: Between Chicano Culture and Legal Discourse*, by Carl Scott Gutierrez-Jones, offers a more theoretical approach to race studies. In a collection from the National Association for Chicano Studies editorial committee, Teresa Cordova, chair, *Chicana Voices: Intersections of Class, Race, and Gender* offers a very substantial set of essays focused on various inequalities within Chicano/a experience. *When Jesus Came, the Corn Mothers Went Away: Marriage, Sexuality, and Power in New Mexico, 1500–1846*, written by Ramón A. Guitiérrez, also focuses on issues of gender in its presentation of the history of the Spanish conquest of New Mexico.

Chicana Feminist Thought: The Basic Historical Writings, edited by Alma M. Garcia and Maria T. Garcia, presents significant documents from early Chicana feminist activists. Gloria Anzaldúa, one of the founders of Chicana feminist thought, in *Borderlands/La Frontera* presents some of the most strikingly original essays in American literary history. Ana Castillo also develops ideas presented by early Chicana feminists and in *Massacre of the Dreamers: Essays on Xicanisma* furthers the argument about the need for an Amerindian (female) rootedness in Chicano/a and American life. *Home Girls: Chicana Literary Voices*, by Alvina E. Quintana, analyzes the literary production of many important Chicana writers, including Gloria Anzaldúa and Ana Castillo.

Divided Borders: Essays on Puerto Rican Identity, by Juan Flores, is a significant treatment of Puerto Rican culture and identity, particularly as it extends to Puerto Ricans living in New York. The anthology *Boricuas: Influential Puerto Rican Writings*, edited by Roberto Santiago, extends popular understanding of Puerto Rican experience by showcasing a variety of Puerto Rican literature.

In Latino studies more generally, *Challenging Fronteras: Structuring Latina and Latino Lives in the U.S.: An Anthology of Readings*, edited by Mary Romero, Pierrette Hondagneu-Sotelo, and Vilma Ortiz, presents Latino/as as the fastest growing racial group in the United States, soon to outnumber African Americans, and offers a challenge to the black–white paradigm of studies in race relations. Journals significant to Latino/Hispanic or Chicano studies include the *Latino Studies Journal* and the *Journal of Hispanic Policy*, formerly the *Journal of Hispanic Politics*, sponsored by the Hispanic Student Caucus of the John F. Kennedy School of Government at Harvard University.

BIBLIOGRAPHY

Books and Articles

Acuña, Rodolfo. *Occupied America: A History of Chicanos*. New York: Harper and Row, 1981.

———. *Sometimes There Is No Other Side: Chicanos and the Myth of Equality*. Notre Dame: University of Notre Dame Press, 1998.

Adams, Maurianne, Lee Anne Bell, and Pat Griffin, eds. *Teaching for Diversity and Social Justice: A Sourcebook*. New York: Routledge, 1997.

Aguilar-San Juan, Karin, ed. *The State of Asian America: Activism and Resistance in the 1990s*. Boston: South End Press, 1993.

Allen, Paula Gunn. *The Sacred Hoop: Recovering the Feminine in American Indian Traditions*. Boston: Beacon Press, 1986.

———. *Spider Woman's Granddaughters: Traditional Tales and Contemporary Writings by Native American Women*. Boston: Beacon Press, 1989.

———. *Studies in American Indian Literature: Critical Essays and Course Designs*. New York: Modern Language Association, 1983.

Anaya, Rudolfo A. and Francisco Lomeli, eds. *Aztlan: Essays on the Chicano Homeland*. Albuquerque: University of New Mexico Press, 1991.

Anderson, Benedict R. O'G. *Imagined Communities: Reflections on the Origin and Spread of Nationalism*. New York: Verso, 1983.

Anner, John, ed. *Beyond Identity Politics: Emerging Social Justice Movements in Communities of Color*. Boston, South End Press, 1986.

Anzaldúa, Gloria. *Borderlands/La Frontera*. San Francisco: Aunt Lute, 1987.

Appiah, Kwame Anthony, and Henry Louis Gates Jr., eds. *Africana: The Encyclo-*

pedia of the African and African American Experience. New York: Basic Civitas Books, 1999.

Appiah, K. Anthony, and Amy Gutmann. *Color Conscious: The Political Morality of Race*. Princeton, N.J.: Princeton University Press, 1998.

Asante, Molefi K. *Afrocentricity*. Trenton, N.J.: Africa World Press, 1988.

———. *The Afrocentric Idea*. Philadelphia: Temple University Press, 1998.

Auerbach, Susan, ed. *Encyclopedia of Multiculturalism*. New York: Marshall Cavendish, 1994.

Baker, Houston A., Jr. *Blues, Ideology, and Afro-American Literature: A Vernacular Theory*. Chicago: University of Chicago Press, 1984.

Banks, James A. *Teaching Strategies for Ethnic Studies*. 6th ed. Boston: Allyn and Bacon, 1997.

Banks, James, and Cherry A. McGee Banks, eds. *Encyclopedia of Research on Multicultural Education*. New York: Macmillan, 1995.

Bell, Bernard W., et al., eds. *Call and Response: The Riverside Anthology of the African American Literary Tradition*. Boston: Houghton Mifflin, 1997.

Bell, Derrick A. *And We Are Not Saved: The Elusive Quest for Racial Justice*. New York: Basic Books, 1987.

———. *Faces at the Bottom of the Well: The Permanence of Racism*. New York: Basic Books, 1992.

Bernal, Martin. *Black Athena: The Afroasiatic Roots of Classical Civilization*. Vol. 1: *The Fabrication of Ancient Greece, 1785–1985*. New Brunswick, N.J.: Rutgers University Press, 1987.

———. *Black Athena: The Afroasiatic Roots of Classical Civilization*. Vol. 2: *The Archaeological and Documentary Evidence*. New Brunswick, N.J.: Rutgers University Press, 1991.

Bird, S. Elizabeth, ed. *Dressing in Feathers: The Construction of the Indian in American Popular Culture*. Boulder, Colo.: Westview Press, 1996.

Bloom, Allan David. *The Closing of the American Mind: How Higher Education Has Failed Democracy and Impoverished the Souls of Today's Students*. New York: Simon and Schuster, 1987.

Bordewich, Fergus M. *Killing the White Man's Indian: Reinventing Native Americans at the End of the Twentieth Century*. New York: Doubleday, 1996.

Bowen, William G., and Derek Curtis Bok. *The Shape of the River: Long-Term Consequences of Considering Race in College and University Admissions*. Princeton, N.J.: Princeton University Press, 1998.

Brodkin, Karen. *How Jews Became White Folks and What That Says about Race in America*. New Brunswick, N.J.: Rutgers University Press, 1998.

Carby, Hazel. *Race Men*. Cambridge, Mass.: Harvard University Press, 1998.

———. *Reconstructing Womanhood: The Emergence of the Afro-American Women Novelist*. New York: Oxford University Press, 1995.

Castillo, Ana. *Massacre of the Dreamers: Essays on Xicanisma*. Albuquerque: University of New Mexico Press, 1994.

Chabran, Richard, and Rafael Chabran, eds. *The Latino Encyclopedia*. New York: Marshall Cavendish, 1995.

Chan, Jeffrey Paul, Frank Chin, Shawn Wong, and Lawson F. Inada, eds. *The Big Aiiieeeee!: An Anthology of Chinese-American and Japanese-American Literature*. New York: Meridian Books, 1991.

Chan, Sucheng. *Asian Americans: An Interpretive History*. Boston: Twayne Press, 1991.

Coleman, Michael C. *American Indian Children at School, 1850–1930*. Jackson: University Press of Mississippi, 1993.

Cordova, Teresa, ed. *Chicana Voices: Intersections of Class, Race, and Gender*. Austin: University of Texas at Austin, 1986.

Cronyn, George W., ed. *American Indian Poetry: An Anthology of Songs and Chants*. New York: Liveright, 1970.

Deloria, Barbara, Kristen Foehner, and Sam Scinta, eds. *Spirit and Reason: The Vine Deloria, Jr., Reader*. Golden, Colo.: Fulcrum Press, 1999.

Deloria, Vine, Jr. *American Indian Policy in the Twentieth Century*. Norman: University of Oklahoma Press, 1985.

———. *Custer Died for Your Sins: An Indian Manifesto*. New York: Macmillan, 1969.

———. *Red Earth, White Lies: Native Americans and the Myth of Scientific Fact*. New York: Scribner, 1995.

D'Souza, Dinesh. *Illiberal Education: The Politics of Race and Sex on Campus*. New York: Free Press, 1991.

Dworkin, Anthony Gary, and Rosalind J. Dworkin, eds. *The Minority Report: An Introduction to Racial, Ethnic, and Gender Relations*. 3rd ed. Fort Worth, Tex.: Harcourt Brace College, 1999.

Feagin, Joe R., and Clairece Booher Feagin. *Racial and Ethnic Relations*. 6th ed. Upper Saddle River, N.J.: Prentice-Hall, 1999.

Ferber, Abby L. *White Man Falling: Race, Gender, and White Supremacy*. Lanham, Md.: Rowman and Littlefield, 1998.

Flores, Juan. *Divided Borders: Essays on Puerto Rican Identity*. Houston: Arte Publico Press, 1993.

Franklin, John Hope, and Alfred A. Moss Jr. *From Slavery to Freedom: A History of African Americans*. 8th ed. Boston: McGraw-Hill, 1999.

Garcia, Alma M., and Maria T. Garcia, eds. *Chicana Feminist Thought: The Basic Historical Writings*. New York: Routledge, 1997.

Gates, Henry Louis, Jr. *Loose Canons: Notes on the Culture Wars*. New York: Oxford University Press, 1993.

———. *The Signifying Monkey: A Theory of Afro-American Literary Criticism*. New York: Oxford University Press, 1988.

Gates, Henry Louis, Jr., and Nellie Y. McKay, eds. *The Norton Anthology of African American Literature*. New York: Norton, 1996.

Geertz, Clifford. *The Interpretation of Cultures: Selected Essays*. New York: Basic Books, 1973.

Giddings, Paula. *When and Where I Enter: The Impact of Black Women on Race and Sex in America*. New York: William Morrow, 1984.

Gilroy, Paul. *The Black Atlantic: Modernity and Double Consciousness*. Cambridge: Harvard University Press, 1993.

Glazer, Nathan. *Affirmative Discrimination: Ethnic Inequality and Public Policy*. New York: Basic Books, 1975.

———. *We Are All Multiculturalists Now*. Cambridge: Harvard University Press, 1997.

Glazer, Nathan, and Daniel Patrick Moynihan. *Beyond the Melting Pot: The Negroes,*

Puerto Ricans, Jews, Italians and Irish of New York City. Cambridge: MIT Press and Harvard University Press, 1963.
Goldberg, David Theo, ed. *Multiculturalism: A Critical Reader*. New York: Blackwell, 1995.
Gordon, Avery F., and Christopher Newfield, eds. *Mapping Multiculturalism*. Minneapolis: University of Minnesota Press, 1996.
Gordon, Milton Myron. *Assimilation in American Life: The Role of Race, Religion, and National Origins*. New York: Oxford University Press, 1964.
Graff, Gerald. *Beyond the Culture Wars: How Teaching the Conflicts Can Revitalize American Education*. New York: Norton, 1992.
Guitiérrez, Ramón A. *When Jesus Came, the Corn Mothers Went Away: Marriage, Sexuality, and Power in New Mexico, 1500–1846*. Stanford, Calif.: Stanford University Press, 1991.
Gutierrez-Jones, Carl Scott. *Rethinking the Borderlands: Between Chicano Culture and Legal Discourse*. Berkeley: University of California Press, 1995.
Hacker, Andrew. *Two Nations: Black and White, Separate, Hostile, Unequal*. New York: Ballantine, 1995.
Hagedorn, Jessica, ed. *Charlie Chan Is Dead: An Anthology of Contemporary Asian American Fiction*. New York: Penguin, 1993.
Hamamoto, Darrell Y. *Monitored Peril: Asian Americans and the Politics of TV Representation*. Minneapolis: University of Minnesota Press, 1994.
Herrnstein, Richard J., and Charles A. Murray. *The Bell Curve*. New York: Free Press, 1994.
Hine, Darlene Clark, Elsa Barkley Brown, and Rosalyn Terborg-Penn. *Black Women in America: An Historical Encyclopedia*. New York: Carlson, 1993.
Hirsch, E. D., Jr. *Cultural Literacy: What Every American Needs to Know*. Boston: Houghton Mifflin, 1987.
Hollinger, David A. *Postethnic America*. New York: Basic Books, 1995.
Hongo, Garrett, ed. *Under Western Eyes: Personal Essays from Asian America*. New York: Anchor, 1995.
hooks, bell. *Killing Rage: Ending Racism*. New York: H. Holt, 1995.
Hull, Gloria T., Patricia Bell Scott, and Barbara Smith, eds. *All the Women Are White, All the Blacks Are Men, but Some of Us Are Brave: Black Women's Studies*. New York: Feminist Press, 1982.
Ignatiev, Noel. *How the Irish Became White*. New York: Routledge, 1995.
Isaacs, Harold Robert. *Idols of the Tribe: Group Identity and Political Change*. New York: Harper and Row, 1975.
Jacobson, Matthew Frye. *Whiteness of a Different Color: European Immigrants and the Alchemy of Race*. Cambridge: Harvard University Press, 1998.
Jordan, Winthrop D. *The White Man's Burden: Historical Origins of Racism in the United States*. New York: Oxford University Press, 1974.
———. *White over Black: American Attitudes toward the Negro, 1550–1812*. Chapel Hill: University of North Carolina Press, 1968.
Juan, Karin Aguilar-San, ed. *The State of Asian America: Activism and Resistance in the 1990s*. Boston: South End Press, 1994.
Katkin, Wendy F., Ned Landsman, and Andrea Tyree, eds. *Beyond Pluralism: The Conception of Groups and Group Identities in America*. Urbana: University of Illinois Press, 1998.

Kehoe, Alice Beck. *The Ghost Dance: Ethnohistory and Revitalization*. New York: Holt Rinehart, and Winston, 1989.

Kim, Elain H. *Asian American Literature: An Introduction to the Writings and Their Social Context*. Philadelphia: Temple University Press, 1982.

Klein, Barry T., ed. *Reference Encyclopedia of the American Indian*. Nyack, N.Y.: Todd, 1998.

Kozol, Jonathan. *Savage Inequalities: Children in America's Schools*. New York: Harper, 1992.

Krupat, Arnold. *The Voice in the Margin: Native American Literature and the Canon*. Berkeley: University of California Press, 1989.

Lee, Joann Faung Jean. *Asian Americans: Oral Histories of First to Fourth Generation Americans from China, the Philippines, Japan, India, the Pacific Islands, Vietnam and Cambodia*. New York: New Press, 1992.

Lim, Shirley Geok-Lin, and Amy Ling, eds. *Reading the Literatures of Asian America*. Philadelphia: Temple University Press, 1992.

Meier, Matt S., and Feliciano Ribera. *Mexican Americans, American Mexicans: From Conquistadors to Chicanos*. New York: Hill and Wang, 1993.

Min, Pyong Gap, ed. *Asian Americans: Contemporary Trends and Issues*. Thousand Oaks, Calif.: Sage Press, 1995.

Mitchell, Bruce M., and Robert E. Salsbury. *The Encyclopedia of Multicultural Education*. Westport, Conn.: Greenwood Press, 1999.

Moraga, Cherrié and Gloria Anzaldúa, eds. *This Bridge Called My Back: Writings by Radical Women of Color*. New York: Kitchen Table: Women of Color Press, 1983.

Mura, David. *Turning Japanese: Memoirs of a Sansei*. New York: Atlantic Monthly Press, 1991.

Nakanishi, Don T., and Tina Yamano Nishida, eds. *The Asian American Educational Experience: A Sourcebook for Teachers and Students*. New York: Routledge, 1995.

Naylor, Larry L., ed. *Cultural Diversity in the United States*. Westport, Conn.: Bergin and Garvey, 1997.

Ng, Franklin, ed. *The Asian American Encyclopedia*. New York: Marshall Cavendish, 1995.

Parillo, Vincent N., ed. *Strangers to These Shores: Race and Ethnic Relations in the United States*. 5th ed. Boston: Allyn and Bacon, 1997.

Pryse, Marjorie, and Hortense Spillers, eds. *Conjuring: Black Women, Fiction, and the Literary Tradition*. Bloomington: Indiana University Press, 1985.

Quintana, Alvina E. *Home Girls: Chicana Literary Voices*. Philadelphia: Temple University Press, 1996.

Roediger, David R. *The Wages of Whiteness: Race and the Making of the American Working Class*. London: Verso, 1998.

Romero, Mary, Pierrette Hondagneu-Sotelo, and Vilma Ortiz, eds. *Challenging Fronteras: Structuring Latina and Latino Lives in the U.S.: An Anthology of Readings*. New York: Routledge, 1997.

Rosales, Francisco A. *Chicano!: The History of the Mexican American Civil Rights Movement*. Houston, Tex.: Arte Publico Press, 1996.

Rothenberg, Paula S., ed. *Race, Class, and Gender in the United States: An Integrated Study*. 3rd ed. New York: St. Martin's Press, 1995.

Santiago, Roberto. *Boricuas: Influential Puerto Rican Writings—An Anthology*. New York: One World, 1995.
Shuey, Audrey. *The Testing of Negro Intelligence*. New York: Social Science Press, 1969.
Smitherman, Geneva. *Talkin and Testifyin: The Language of Black America*. Boston: Houghton Mifflin, 1977.
Sollors, Werner, ed. *The Invention of Ethnicity*. New York: Oxford University Press, 1989.
———. *Multilingual America: Transnationalism, Ethnicity, and the Languages of American Literature*. New York: New York University Press, 1998.
Stannard, David E. *American Holocaust: Columbus, Christianity, and the Conquest of the Americas*. New York: Oxford University Press, 1992.
Stepto, Robert B. *From behind the Veil: A Study of Afro-American Narrative*. Champaign: University of Illinois Press, 1991.
Sterling, Dorothy, ed. *We Are Your Sisters: Black Women in the Nineteenth Century*. New York: W. W. Norton, 1984.
Takaki, Ronald T. *A Different Mirror: A History of Multicultural America*. Boston: Little, Brown, 1993.
———. *Strangers from a Different Shore: A History of Asian Americans*. Boston: Little, Brown, 1989.
———, ed. *From Different Shores: Perspectives on Race and Ethnicity in America*. 2nd ed. New York: Oxford University Press, 1994.
Terkel, Studs. *Race: How Blacks and Whites Think and Feel about the American Obsession*. New York: Anchor, 1993.
Thernstrom, Stephan, Ann Orlov, and Oscar Handlin, eds. *Harvard Encyclopedia of American Ethnic Groups*. Cambridge: Harvard University Press, 1980.
Thomas, Gail E., ed. *Race and Ethnicity in America: Meeting the Challenge in the Twenty-First Century*. Washington, D.C.: Taylor and Francis, 1995.
Vecoli, Rudolph J., Judy Galens, Anna J. Sheets, and Robyn V. Young. *Gale Encyclopedia of Multicultural America*. Detroit: Gale Research, 1995.
Velie, Alan R., ed. *American Indian Literature: An Anthology*. Norman: University of Oklahoma Press, 1991.
West, Cornel. *Race Matters*. Boston: Beacon Press, 1993.
Williams, Gregory Howard. *Life on the Color Line: The True Story of a White Boy Who Discovered He Was Black*. New York: Dutton, 1995.
Wirth, Louis. "The Problem of Minority Groups." In *The Science of Man in the World Crisis*, ed. Ralph Linton. New York: Columbia University Press, 1945, 347–72.
Wong, Diane Yen-Mei, and Emilya Cachapero, eds. *Making Waves: An Anthology of Writings by and about Asian American Women*. Boston: Beacon Press, 1989.
Wong, Sau-Ling Cynthia. *Reading Asian American Literature: From Necessity to Extravagance*. Princeton N.J.: Princeton University Press, 1993.
Wong, Shawn, ed. *Asian American Literature: A Brief Introduction and Anthology*. New York: HarperCollins, 1996.
Yetman, Norman R., ed. *Majority and Minority: The Dynamics of Race and Ethnicity in American Life*. 6th ed. Boston: Allyn and Bacon, 1999.
Young, Donald Ramsey. *American Minority Peoples: A Study in Racial and Cultural Conflicts in the United States*. New York: Harper, 1932.

Periodicals

African American Review. Terre Haute: English Department, Indiana State University, 1992– . Formerly *Black American Literature Forum*, 1976–1991.

Amerasia Journal. Los Angeles: Asian American Studies Center Publication, 1971– .

American Indian Culture and Research Journal. Los Angeles: American Indian Culture and Research Center, University of California, 1974– .

American Indian Quarterly. Hurst, Tex.: Southwestern American Indian Society, 1974– .

Asian American Review. Berkeley: Asian American Studies, Department of Ethnic Studies, University of California, 1974– .

Black Renaissanace/Renaissance Noir. Bloomington: Indiana University Press, 1996– .

The Black Scholar. Oakland, Calif.: Black World Foundation, 1969– .

Callaloo. Baltimore: Johns Hopkins University Press, 1986– , formerly Baton Rouge, La., 1976–1986.

Ethnicity: The Magazine for All America. Los Angeles: Upfront Communications, 1995– .

Ethnic Studies Review. Tempe, Ariz.: National Association of Ethnic Studies, 1996– .

Journal of American Ethnic History. New Brunswick, N.J.: Transaction Periodicals Consortium, 1981.

Journal of Asian American Studies. Baltimore: Johns Hopkins University Press for the Association of Asian American Studies, 1998– .

Journal of Black Studies. Beverly Hills, Calif.: Sage, 1970– .

Journal of Ethnic Studies. Bellingham: Western Washington State College, 1973– .

Journal of Hispanic Policy. Cambridge: Hispanic Student Caucus of the John F. Kennedy School of Government at Harvard University, 1987– . Formerly *Journal of Hispanic Politics*, 1985–1987.

Journal of Negro History. Washington, D.C.: Association for the Study of Negro Life and History, 1916.

Latino Studies Journal. Chicago: Center for Latino Research, DePaul University, 1990– .

MELUS. Los Angeles: Society for the Study of Multi-Ethnic Literature of the United States, 1974– .

Phylon. Atlanta: Atlanta University, 1940– .

Wicazo Sa Review. Cheney: Indian Studies at Eastern Washington University, 1985– .

FANTASY

Roger Schlobin

Since this chapter was first written over a decade ago, the state of fantasy has changed dramatically in four ways. In general, some of this change is the result of the unqualified and continuing success of the International Association for the Fantastic in the Arts with its annual conference, proceedings, and *Journal of the Fantastic in the Arts*. Even more significantly, the Internet is beginning to change access to fantasy literature and its resources just as it has changed modern life.

First, primary and secondary bibliographies have been revolutionized now that Locus Publications maintains a massive on-line database, *The Locus Index to Science Fiction (1984–1977)*, with annual updates* (cf. Brown). (An asterisk indicates that an associated Web site is listed in the Bibliography.)

Second, John Clute, Peter Nichols, and David Langford maintain a "Corrigenda" to *The Encyclopedia of Fantasy** that includes additions and corrections. Hopefully, this effort will begin a trend of up-to-date reference works and eliminate the frequently long wait for revised editions.

Third, the University of Michigan's fantasy and science-fiction "Electronic Library,"* under the direction of Eric S. Rabkin, addresses, in part, the difficulty of locating out-of-print texts that has long plagued fantasy. The selection is limited by copyrights and by the exclusion of individual short stories, but its gathering of primary texts from throughout the Internet makes it an invaluable resource. The ephemeral availability of classroom resources may be slightly alleviated by the entry of such publishers as Oxford University Press and Tom Shippey's admirable *The Oxford Book of Fantasy Stories*, but this work does not replace the passing (and lost alternatives) of such notable anthologies as Kenneth H. Boyer and Robert J. Zahorski's *Fantastic Imagination* and Gary Wilkins' *A Treasury of Fantasy*, which included the full texts of George MacDonald's *Phantastes* and William Morris' *The Wood beyond the World*. Occasionally, Robert H. Silverberg and Martin H. Greenberg's *The Fantasy Hall of Fame* is offered through the Science Fiction Book Club.*

Is it any wonder that when teachers of fantasy gather to discuss the canon, the conversation often turns not to what is appropriate but to what is available?

Fourth, both the International Association for the Fantastic in the Arts* and the nascent Science Fiction, Utopian and Fantastic Literature discussion group* of the Modern Language Association maintain Internet discussion groups ("list-servs") through which scholars and teachers can exchange information and submit queries.

Amid all the innovations in modern technology, fantasy literature still continues to struggle for its rightful place in the general literary and scholarly community. This persists despite such early observations as E. M. Forster's identification of fantasy as

> something that cuts across them [aspects of the novel] like a bar of light, that is intimately connected with them at one place and patiently illumines all the problems, and at another place shoots over or through them as if they did not exist. (74)

Forster might have just as easily agreed with George MacDonald, who identified fantasy as the "richest source of human creativity" (2), for it dwells at the heart of all human endeavor, be it highly creative or lowly everyday. It may not be real in any measurable sense, but it is among the most potent of thought processes.

In a few ways, it is clear why it has always been powerful and popular but has not drawn larger intellectual and scholarly acceptance (see Schlobin, "Scholarship"). The development of Western European culture has frequently been inhospitable to the make-believe that so often is associated with fantasy. Certainly, religion, one of the richest indications of the human faculty to create what is not empirically real, has long been antithetical to any other fanciful constructs. Moreover, in the modern period, the pursuit of the pragmatic and the scientific has not encouraged "escapist excursions" into worlds that cannot be.

For some time, fantasy had some small, token attention, but there are strong indications that this is changing. Occasionally, the Science Fiction Research Association* (established in 1970) would allow the parent fantasy to visit with its younger child. The Modern Language Association (MLA) and its regional associations, the Popular Culture Association, the American Studies Association, and the National Council of Teachers of English, do regularly include sessions. Beginning in 1997, through the efforts of Tom Moylan and Kenneth Roemer, among others, an attempt has been made to invigorate the MLA through the Science Fiction, Utopian and Fantastic Literature discussion group.* It was not until 1980 that fantasy had its own gathering: the International Conference for the Fantastic in the Arts.* This conference was further enhanced in 1983 and 1984 with the formation of the International Association for the Fantastic in the Arts, which assumed control of the conference. Finally, fantasy had its own home, and its varied forms and approaches have dramatically flourished in this interdisciplinary and intercultural environment. Each year the conference is bigger and its presentations more wide-ranging and imposing.

In addition, a number of nonacademic groups and conferences focus on fantasy. The World Fantasy Conference has gathered together fantasy fans from throughout the world and, despite its continued inability to distinguish between fantasy

The Princess Bride, 1987. © The Del Valle Archive

and horror, has been honoring writers and holding meetings since 1975. The British Fantasy Society* has been doing much the same thing on a smaller scale since 1972, and *Locus*, the "newspaper of science fiction," began polling the year's best fantasy novel in 1977. Even the World Science Fiction Conference began recognizing "Grand Masters of Fantasy" with the Gandalf Award in 1974 and added a second Gandalf for best fantasy novel in 1978 (Mallet and Reginald).

The future of fantasy's popular tradition and the International Association for the Fantastic in the Arts are fulfilling their promises. Beginning in 1988, *The Journal of the Fantastic in the Arts (JFA)** became the first scholarly journal to focus exclusively on the field. It regularly publishes wide-ranging essays that cross international boundaries and various media. *Paradoxa** occasionally focuses on the fantastic, but it is far more eclectic than *JFA* and includes romance, westerns, science fiction, and numerous other forms under the rubric of "paraliterature." *Mythlore*,* long exclusively devoted to the British Inklings, has broadened its scope somewhat and occasionally includes essays on American authors. The *CLF Newsletter** is, perhaps, eccentric but deserves watching. At one time, the *Fantasy Review* surveyed much of the activity in the field, but it unfortunately ceased publication in August 1987. Robert A. Collins and Robert Latham continued the valuable work of *Fantasy Review* in book form via the *Science Fiction and Fantasy Book Review*

Annuals for four years. In addition, there have been special fantasy issues of more generally oriented scholarly journals. At this juncture, all looks generative, and no one can guess just how much more extensive it all may become.

HISTORICAL OUTLINE

Fantasy does not yield well to historical or national perspective. It is so elemental, so timeless, and so pervasive that its enormity overpowers thought. Even the smaller realm of American fantasy is a difficult task. Brian Attebery examines the years from Washington Irving (1819) to Ursula K. Le Guin (1972) in his insightful survey *The Fantasy Tradition in American Literature*. Ann Swinfen's *In Defence of Fantasy* adds coverage of British and American fantasy since 1945. However, these two efforts hardly make a dent. In fact, to date, there are only three book-length studies of the British tradition: Stephen Prickett's *Victorian Fantasy*, Tobin Siebers' *The Romantic Fantastic*, and Karen Patricia Smith's *The Fabulous Realm*. Most scholars avoid the historical approach and opt for the theoretical, aesthetic, or thematic. This may be because fantasy is varied, immune to time and place, and multicultural. In just the American tradition alone, for example, William Burroughs' *Naked Lunch* (1959) has been characterized as "pornographic" and banned. Fantasy made its contribution to World War II in Theodore Pratt's *Mr. Limpet* (1942) and came back from war in Gore Vidal's *Kalki* (1978). Don Marquis' *Archy and Mehitabel* (1927) delightfully wandered into the American office and the animal kingdom, and the Second Coming arrived on a construction site in Charles Sailor's *The Second Son* (1979). Fantasy combined with utopia in Austin Tappan Wright's *Islandia* (1942) and presented confounding mysteries in John Dickson Carr's *The Burning Court* (1937), Fritz Leiber's collegiate *Conjure Wife* (1952), and Dean R. Koontz's spoof *The Haunted Earth* (1973). Gordon R. Dickson combined the epic and romance traditions (sword and sorcery) with the burlesque in *The Dragon and the George* (1976) and its numerous sequels. Many fantasies draw upon folktales and mythologies from all nationalities; for example, Patricia Wrightson travels as far as Australia for the Aborigine mythology of *The Ice Is Coming* (1977), *The Dark Bright Water* (1978), and *Journey behind the Wind* (1981), and Charles G. Finney combined numerous traditions and Arizona in *The Circus of Dr. Lao* (1935). Lest anyone think fantasy nontopical, the free lifestyles of the 1960s found expression in Peter S. Beagle's urban "Lila the Werewolf" (1971) and Richard Brautigan's *Trout Fishing in America* (1967), and the absurd was greeted in Philip Roth's *The Breast* (1972; with due respect to Kafka and Woody Allen). Randall Garrett has deconstructed fantasy in his Lord Darcy mysteries. In short, American writers have had home and the world upon which to draw—and they have.

The early stirrings of American fantasy literature have yet to be explored at length. Thomas Hooker's *The Soul's Preparation* (1632), Anne Bradstreet's *The Tenth Muse* (1650), Increase Mather's *Remarkable Providences* (1684), Cotton Mather's *Wonders of the Invisible World* (1693), Benjamin Franklin's *Poor Richard's Almanac* (1732), and Thomas Paine's *Common Sense* (1776) have remained safe from the "fantastic perspective" for the time being. However, scrutiny will one day reveal both the bright and dark fantasies of the Puritans, the Revolutionaries, and the Founding Fathers. Certainly, the early settlers brought their own folk traditions, fairy tales, literary traditions, and magic with them from the "Old

World." Yet as much as Thanksgiving, Manifest Destiny, the American West, and baseball distinguish the American character, its fantasy is largely indistinguishable from the rest of the world's in most senses, except for locale and age. This commonality is undoubtedly due to the United States' polyglot nature and the fact that even its repressed minorities maintained the fantasy privilege (see Bowen; Garber and Paleo). One example of this is the essentially similar treatment of the "most beautiful girl in the world" theme that is common to the widely separated (in time and place) excursions of America's *The Princess Bride* (1973) by William Goldman and Britain's *Zuleika Dobson* (1911) by Max Beerbohm.

Most commentators agree that modern fantasy arises in America much as it did in England. It comes primarily from the Romantic tradition (just as horror arises from the Gothic, and science fiction from the empirical). However, while the first "modern" fantasy in Britain, Sara Coleridge's *Phastasmion* (which was billed as fairy tale), did not appear until 1837, the roots of the American tradition began earlier with the American Romanticists: Washington Irving's *The Sketch Book of Geoffrey Crayon, Gent.* (1819–1820) and *Tales of a Traveller* (1824), the latter with its obvious debt to the Brothers Grimm, Nathaniel Hawthorne's *Twice-Told Tales* (1837), and Edgar Allan Poe's *The Narrative of Arthur Gordon Pym* (1838) and *Tales of the Grotesque and Arabesque* (1840). They were quickly followed by such noteworthy works as Herman Melville's *The Confidence-Man* (1857) and Oliver Wendell Holmes' *Elsie Venner* (1861). Mark I. West's *Before Oz: Juvenile Fantasy Stories from Nineteenth-Century America*, despite its subtitle, is one of the most convincing illustrations of the strength of the American tradition. As these varied works illustrate, American fantasy had already manifested itself in many ways, and its continuing history includes both well-known authors and lesser-known cult ones.

Yet to say that fantasy was widespread and enormously popular in the American literary tradition prior to the late nineteenth and early twentieth centuries would be a mistake. As the century turned, however, both recognized literature and its disreputable pulp relations forever branded the American character. While Brian Attebery sees Mark Twain's *A Connecticut Yankee in King Arthur's Court* (1889) as a demonstration of "the strong hostility between [pragmatic] American thought and pure fantasy" (*The Fantasy Tradition*, 79), it and the posthumously published *The Mysterious Stranger* (1916) actually demonstrate the strong antagonism between authority and virtue that is typical of much fantasy. More importantly, they mark the opening of floodgates. L. Frank Baum's Oz books (1900–1920) and his many imitators, Edgar Rice Burroughs' Mars/Barsoom series (1917–1964), and James Branch Cabell's twenty-volume biography of Manuel (1919–1923) demonstrate an ongoing American fascination that continues to this day.

Curiously, the twentieth century continued a sharp division within fantasy. At one time, fantasy was considered fairy tales and children's fare and was set against "real, adult" literature (and still is in some circles). Beginning in the early 1920s, another chasm appears between "serious" and "pulp" literatures. On one hand are respectable, accepted works: Ben Hecht's *Fantazius Mallare* (1922) and *The Kingdom of Evil* (1924); Thorne Smith's humorous and satiric Topper books (1926, 1932); John Erskine's *Adam and Eve* (1927); Thornton Wilder's *The Skin of Our Teeth* (1942); James Thurber's *The White Deer* (1945), *The 13 Clocks* (1950), and *The Wonderful O* (1957); John Collier's *Fancies and Goodnights* (1951); John Up-

Nathaniel Hawthorne. Courtesy of the Library of Congress

dike's *The Centaur* (1963); Thomas Tryon's *The Other* (1971); John Barth's *Giles Goat-Boy* (1966) and *Chimera* (1972); Robert Coover's *The Universal Baseball Association, Inc.* (1968); Donald Barthelme's *The Dead Father* (1975) and *The King* (1990); John Crowley's *Little, Big* (1981); and Ken Kalfus' short-story collection *Thirst* (1998), besides those mentioned earlier.

On the other hand, buried in those yellowed magazines and paperbacks were works that were making "sword and sorcery" and "fantasy" household words in places far away from the intellectuals and college faculties. These included Abraham Merritt's *The Ship of Ishtar* (1927), L. Sprague de Camp and Fletcher Pratt's Incomplete Enchanter series (1941–1960), Robert E. Howard's *Conan the Conqueror* (1950), Poul Anderson's *The Broken Sword* (1954), H. P. Lovecraft's *The Dream-Quest of Unknown Kadath* (1955), Fritz Leiber's *Two Sought Adventure* (1957), Andre Norton's Witch World series (1963–), Ray Bradbury's *Something Wicked This Way Comes* (1962), and Isaac Asimov's Azazel short stories (1982–1988). In addition, DAW Books enjoyed success with an annual series called *The Year's Best Fantasy Stories. The Year's Best Fantasy*, edited by Ellen Datlow and Terri Windling, continues this tradition under the St. Martin's Press imprint (1988–).

However, it's clear that even this "subliterary" tradition is finding respectability. These works and many like them have found their ways into college classrooms, and Stephen R. Donaldson's *Chronicles of Thomas Covenant the Unbeliever* (1977–1983), Terry Brooks' *The Sword of Shannara* (1977), and Piers Anthony's pun-ridden Xanth books (1977–) have appeared with prominence in the *New York*

Times Best-Seller List (not to mention the successes of Stephen King's horror fiction).

Much seems to be coming together for fantasy as it lives in the American consciousness. Its long and varied tradition is finding a far greater home than many may have imagined but one that others have foreseen.

BIBLIOGRAPHIES OF BIBLIOGRAPHIES AND SECONDARY RESOURCES

In a class by itself is John Clute and John Grant's recent *The Encyclopedia of Fantasy*.* While there are many better sources for author information, it is probably one of the two most valuable volumes in the field. Filled with entries on various publications, terms (superseding Wolfe's *Critical Terms for Science Fiction and Fantasy*), notable people, publishers, genres, theories, and media, it is easily the quickest and handiest of the one-stop desk references.

In addition to Clute and Grant as an essential tool, the "beginning place" for any serious exploration in this realm is Michael Burgess' annotated *Reference Guide to Science Fiction, Fantasy, and Horror*. It is far and away the best bibliography of bibliographies and an invaluable research guide.

Historically and up until 1972, fantasy scholars had to be content with the scattered and unsystematic listing of scholarship in the "Prose Fiction" sections of the annual bibliographies of *PMLA*. In 1972, however, when the late Thomas D. Clareson (the longtime editor of the journal *Extrapolation*) published *Science Fiction Criticism: An Annotated Checklist*, he inspired the beginning of science fiction's and fantasy's annual secondary bibliography, "The Year's Scholarship in Science Fiction, Fantasy, and Horror Scholarship." Conceived in 1975 by Roger C. Schlobin and Marshall B. Tymn and continued by Tymn and a team of scholars following Schlobin's retirement from the project in 1980, this essential tool has appeared in a variety of forms: within the pages of *Extrapolation*, as separate monographs, and in two book-length accumulations. Originally just devoted to fantasy and science-fiction scholarship and with an emphasis on literature, it expanded over the years to include the horror genre and other media (i.e., film). It is well divided into categories and is indexed and annotated. Beginning in 1984 and up until its demise in 1988, however, the annotations have become occasional (due to its increasing size), making it somewhat less valuable. Any slack that might have existed with its termination has been taken up by the energetic Hal W. Hall's *Science Fiction Index: Criticism: An Index to English Language Books and Articles about Science Fiction and Fantasy* and *Science Fiction and Fantasy Reference Index* (see the International Association for the Fantastic in the Arts'* Web site for current listings). Hall lists various publications (i.e., amateur magazines, book reviews, etc.) that were not included in "The Year's Scholarship." He has amplified this with his very worthwhile accumulations, the *Science Fiction and Fantasy Reference Index* and its supplement.

REFERENCES: PRIMARY

The early years of primary book lists, checklists, and bibliographies were distinguished by the highly energetic efforts of selfless and frequently ignored pioneers. Bradford Day, E. F. Bleiler, R. Reginald, and Donald H. Tuck gave valuable direction and resources to fields that were frequently ignored by traditional scholars. Their contributions ensured that fantasy research survived its early dark ages.

However, early primary bibliography suffered from an indiscriminate approach that often tossed fantasy literature into too large a pile, and these early efforts mirror the early and continuing difficulty with definition. Some of this was cleared up with the publication of Roger C. Schlobin's *The Literature of Fantasy: A Comprehensive, Annotated Bibliography of Modern Fantasy Fiction*. To date, it is the authoritative list of fantasy fiction from 1837 to 1979; however, it should be supplemented. The best of these are Marshall B. Tymn, Kenneth J. Zahorski, and Robert H. Boyer's *Fantasy Literature: A Core Collection and Reference Guide*—which has longer annotations but significantly less coverage—and Neil Barron's *Fantasy Literature* (see later). The two unannotated bibliographies that include more titles are L. W. Currey's *Science Fiction and Fantasy Authors* and R. Reginald's *Science Fiction and Fantasy Literature*. Also, while its nonselectivity harks back to the pioneering days of bibliographies of fantastic fiction, E. F. Bleiler's *The Guide to Supernatural Fiction* is a treasure trove of titles, many not mentioned elsewhere, with valuable annotations. Another similarly unusual bibliography, without which any discussion of fantasy bibliography would be incomplete (and significantly less entertaining), is George Locke's *A Spectrum of Fantasy*. This eccentric and enjoyable compilation will be a pleasure for any avid pursuer of the unusual and the arcane. Neil Barron's *Fantasy and Horror: A Critical and Historical Guide to Literature, Illustration, Film, TV, Radio, Internet* supersedes his *Fantasy Literature* and may add to these resources, although its coverage is limited to authors with at least two relevant publications. The *Locus Index** (Brown) is, by far, the best source for raw information, including such items as ISBN and cover artists. The serious scholar will also not ignore "fan" sites on the World Wide Web, most notably, the *SCI-Finder** and *The Linköping Science Fiction & Fantasy Archive*.*

More current than the preceding printed texts, if less specific, are two extraordinarily large compilations. Neil Barron's *What Fantastic Fiction Do I Read Next?* lists over 4,800 titles published in an eight-year period beginning in the late 1980s. It includes valuable indexes and summarizes each title and identifies its genre. David Pringle et al.'s *St. James Guide to Fantasy Writers* is a massive collection of author overviews by noted scholars that nicely complements the individual book emphasis of Frank N. Magill's five-volume *Survey of Modern Fantasy Literature* (see later). The preeminent bibliographies of short stories in anthologies are William G. Contento's CD-ROM *Index to Science Fiction Anthologies and Collections** and Michael Ashley and William Contento's *The Supernatural Index*. Hal Hall's ongoing *Science Fiction and Fantasy Book Review Index* admirably covers this often neglected area. A specialized source that is particularly helpful for its emphasis on multiculturalism is Gary Bowen's *DeColores: A Bibliography of Speculative Fiction by People of Color*,* which cites the works of Jewish, Native American, Eastern European, Latino, Caribbean, and African authors.

Among some of the more controversial and fun primary bibliographies are works like James Cawthorn and Michael Moorcock's *Fantasy: The Hundred Best Books* (also see Pringle, *Modern*). Such compilations are always selective and draw considerable debate.

Those primarily interested in children's and young adults' fantasy should consult Ruth Nadelman Lynn's *Fantasy Literature for Children and Young Adults*. Some may find its categories questionable and its annotations too brief, but its coverage of this important part of fantasy's literary tradition is extensive. Researchers will find any of the bibliographies previously listed valuable. However, Diana Waggoner's *The Hills of Faraway* and Betty Rosenberg's *Genreflecting* (which includes a section on fantasy) should be ignored for the flawed and inaccurate compilations they are.

For a variety of reasons, many types of literature that have caught the popular taste, like fantasy, are filled with authors who use pseudonyms. While many of the bibliographies listed here do include these, there are so many that specialized studies are often very helpful. The best and most current of these is Susannah Bates' *The Pendex*, which can be supplemented with James A. Rock's *Who Goes There*.

Lastly, for those very serious fantasy mavens, librarians, and scholars who would like to do their own, original research, Michael Burgess' *A Guide to Science Fiction and Fantasy in the Library of Congress Classification Scheme* is helpful.

BIOGRAPHICAL AND BIBLIOGRAPHICAL CRITICAL GUIDES

Among the more valuable tools that are available are those that seek to survey large blocks of authors, works, or all of fantasy. These frequently provide extraordinarily helpful introductions (when they are done well). They offer biographical information, critical commentary of varying length and depth, and bibliographic detail. In addition to David Pringle's *St. James Guide to Fantasy Writers*, E. F. Bleiler's two-volume tome *Supernatural Fiction Writers: Fantasy and Horror* is worthy of note. Arranged by a combination of nationality and chronology, its essays survey a significant number of authors (from Apuleius to Roger Zelazny, with stress on British and American) and are written by scholars of varying distinction. While some have found it interesting for the authors omitted as much as for those included, the essays do provide valuable insights and information. Of a considerably briefer nature (although with more author coverage) than Bleiler's *Supernatural Fiction Writers*, Mike Ashley's alphabetical *Who's Who in Horror and Fantasy Literature* contains 400 short biobibliographic entries with very brief critical commentary.

HISTORY AND CRITICISM

The history and criticism of fantasy have been growing rapidly in the past decade as fantasy receives far more attention than ever before. However, while fantasy theory, in general, and the British branch, in particular, have prospered, American treatments have not, perhaps because, in a worldwide context that stretches from Gilgamesh to yesterday, the American portion is small. Also, much of American literature is already placed in traditional categories; for example, it is not unusual to read or hear discussions of Nathaniel Hawthorne and Edgar Allan Poe that do not even allude to the concept of fantasy. The only major book-length study that does focus specifically on American fantasy is Brian Attebery's *The Fantasy Tradition in American Literature from Irving to Le Guin*. Drawing heavily on fantasy's popular folk origin, fairy tales, and legends and on the American development of its own fairyland, Attebery ranges intelligently among such seemingly dissimilar authors as Edgar Allan Poe, Nathaniel Hawthorne, Herman Melville, L. Frank Baum, Ray Bradbury, James Thurber, and H. P. Lovecraft. His landmark study has offered challenges to American literature scholars that are still largely unmet. For example, the aforementioned early American literature is untouched.

In general, the nature of fantasy still has not surrendered to definition by a single scholar. Among newer attempts using postmodern, critical techniques that were first introduced by Lance Olsen is his *The Ellipse of Uncertainty*. Brian Attebery's *Strategies of Fantasy*, which applies some of the approaches of Gerard Genette, Seymour Chapman, and Mikhail Bakhtin, has gained recognition for its premise that fantasy is defined best within the shifting parameters of a "fuzzy set." Attebery, as in his earlier *The Fantasy Tradition*, uses almost exclusively American authors to demonstrate his theory (e.g., Ursula K. Le Guin, Gene Wolfe, John Crowley, Diana Wynne Jones, and Suzette Haden Elgin). Drawing on similar theoretical sources, Neil Cornwall's *The Literary Fantastic* also draws heavily on Hume, Rabkin, Jackson, Todorov, and Brook-Rose and stresses the uncanny and horrific in his more international approach, although he does include brief discussions of Americans Toni Morrison and Edgar Allan Poe. Yuan Yuan's *The Discourse of Fantasy*, which focuses on the postmodern concept of "text," is undeniably the most theoretical of the studies cited here and focuses almost exclusively on non-American authors, as does Lucie Armitt's *Theorising the Fantastic*. Richard Mathews, in his *Fantasy*, includes chapters on Robert E. Howard and Ursula K. Le Guin in his overview of the evolution of fantasy. Curiously, none of the postmodern studies address "literature of exhaustion" authors, whose work seems to cry out for such attention, such as Jack Vance or Tim Powers. Kath Filmer's *Skepticism and Hope in Twentieth Century Fantasy Literature* is more traditional than the aforementioned and concentrates on how fantasy "speaks" religion. While Filmer is primarily interested in British authors, she does include chapters on Ursula K. Le Guin, Russell Hoban, and "Some American Fables."

One of the interesting constellations that have emerged in recent years is the focus on the female protagonist. Beginning with Carl B. Yoke's pioneering "Slaying the Dragon Within: Andre Norton's Female Heroes" and followed by Amy J. Ransom's *The Feminine as Fantastic in the Conte Fantastique*, which examines exclusively nineteenth-century French literature and uses the theories of Todorov and Jackson, four book-length studies with American focus are particularly interesting because they explore, in whole or part, the trickster in the form of the female "picara." Anne K. Kaler's historical and wide-ranging *The Picara: From Hera to Fantasy Heroine* is often more descriptive than critical, but it does include discussions of the use of this important and previously neglected character by such women writers as Suzy McKee Charnas, Marion Zimmer Bradley, Phyllis Ann Karr, Pamela Sargent, Sharon Green, Elizabeth Lynn, Jo Clayton, Janet Morris, Joanna Russ, Sherri S. Tepper, Jane Yolen, Tanith Lee, and Ann Maxwell. Oddly, Marilyn Jurich's *Scheherazade's Sisters*, Lori Landay's *Madcaps, Screwballs and Con Women*, and Sherrie A. Innes' *Tough Girls* do not cite Yoke, Ransom, or Kaler. Jurich concentrates on the female trickster primarily in folklore and feminist revision literature. Landay's historical approach begins with nineteenth-century lit-

Conan the Barbarian, 1982. © The Del Valle Archive

erature by women and concludes with contemporary television and cinema with an emphasis on mass culture. Innes concentrates on female warriors, from *Charlie's Angels* to *Xena*, in popular culture on television and in films and comic books with notable chapters on women in science fiction and postapocalypse media. Of related interest is Charlotte Spivack's *Merlin's Daughters*, which is a feminist revisioning of the wizard, hero, and dragon archetypes in such American authors as Andre Norton, Susan Cooper, Ursula K. Le Guin, Katherine Kurtz, Patricia McKillip, Gillian Bradshaw, and Marion Zimmer Bradley, as well as British writers.

Two older collaborative efforts have made valiant and significant tries at the entire genre. The well-received *The Aesthetics of Fantasy Literature and Art*, edited by Schlobin, attempts to survey fantasy in both literature and art with a series of essays by the major scholars in the field. Its discussions of such varied aspects as the fantasy reader-response, lost-race fantasy, fantasy book illustration, high fantasy, children's fantasy, utopian fantasy, and fantasy's relationships with earlier traditions attempt to provide a primer to the genre.

The five-volume *Survey of Modern Fantasy Literature*, edited by Frank Magill, takes a different approach, and its strong critical essays are arranged by titles (with author and title indexes). While it suffers from an annoying inability to distinguish between fantasy and horror, its 500 entries, especially the general ones in volume 5, are a vast compendium of useful and easy-to-use information that covers authors from a variety of nationalities as well as extensively treats American and British ones.

However, the potentially most valuable source is the continuing proceedings of the International Conference for the Fantastic in the Arts. Published under varying titles and with varying editors by Greenwood Press, these volumes reflect the vast scope and vitality of the International Association for the Fantastic in the Arts, the sponsoring organization. In fact, the interdisciplinary and cross-cultural contents of these volumes, both present and forthcoming, defy any attempt at classification and will long be rich sources for understanding fantasy and the fantastic in all media. A similar effort, although reflecting only a single event, is the far less expansive *Bridges to Fantasy*, edited by George E. Slusser, Eric S. Rabkin, and Robert Scholes, which is the proceedings of the one J. Lloyd Eaton Conference that focused, in part, on fantasy.

Among those earlier scholars who have not been daunted by the challenges that fantasy presents to the single mind, five are still highly regarded and cited frequently (for a valuable overview of fantasy theory, see Gary K. Wolfe's "Contemporary Theories of Fantasy," in Magill, vol. 5, 2220–2234). W. R. Irwin's *The Game of the Impossible: A Rhetoric of Fantasy* is formidable in its literary and philosophical approach. It draws heavily on Victorian and modern literary thought to comment significantly on the intellectual nature of fantasy, especially as it relates to the conspiratorial bond that fantasy demands during the reader's engagement with the authors and their fictions. Colin N. Manlove's *The Impulse of Fantasy Literature* and *Modern Fantasy: Five Studies* contain some of the most clearly conceived and sensitive reactions to modern fantasy. Many of the guidelines that he establishes have become almost "givens" among fantasy scholars and are especially valuable for the insight that they provide into the Romantic and Gothic modes of thought and the nineteenth- and twentieth-century British fantasists (Charles Kingsley, George MacDonald, C. S. Lewis, J.R.R. Tolkien, and Mervyn Peake). Eric S. Rabkin's *The Fantastic in Literature* has been among the most popular of the major examinations of modern fantasy, perhaps because it is among the most readable. His approach is sociological in nature and ranges widely among such topics as fairy tales, optical illusions, mysteries, Henry James, and wish fulfillment. While the nature of the reversal of reality that Rabkin discusses has come under attack in recent years, *The Fantastic in Literature* is still considered by some to be one of the touchstones. Tzvetan Todorov's *The Fantastic: A Structural Approach to a Literary Genre* is among those works that serious students of fantasy return to again and again to discuss. Its often complicated approach to the rhetorical tactics of fantasy and the response to it (which Todorov calls "hesitation") appear to many to identify too general a technique, one that does not identify fantasy specifically enough. Still, it would be hard to measure the pervasive influence that Todorov's work has had on modern critical thought. Kathryn Hume's *Fantasy and Mimesis: Responses to Reality in Western Literature* is helpful and insightful. Deftly building on earlier research and paying valuable attention to the reader–text relationship, Hume places fantasy within the long literary tradition to which it belongs and shows extensive parallels with representations of reality and nonreality within many historical contexts.

There are a number of other studies worthy of note. Christine Brook-Rose's *A Rhetoric of the Unreal: Studies in Narrative and Structure, Especially the Fantastic* works from Todorov's earlier study and extends it further into the areas of structuralism, poststructuralism, formalism, and the nature of literary reality. Rosemary Jackson is another follower of Todorov and her Freudian and psychoanalytic *Fantasy: The Literature of Subversion* seeks to specifically define fantasy as a distinct historical and didactic form of narrative with strong thematic identifications. T. E. Apter's *Fantasy Literature: An Approach to Reality* also takes a psychoanalytic approach and contends that fantasy, rather than distorting or hiding reality, actually exposes it. It is particularly valuable for its discussions of Joseph Conrad and Nathaniel Hawthorne. All of these studies, like most that seriously explore fantasy, impress with their range and their disregard for traditional literary classifications.

Among the studies of fantasy, some focus on special topics. For example, Raymond H. Thompson extensively illustrates the ample use of one of the Western world's major legends in combination with fantasy in *The Return from Avalon: A Study of the Arthurian Legend in Modern Fiction*, and Don D. Elgin brings a modern concern to the forefront in *The Comedy of the Fantastic: Ecological Perspectives on the Fantasy Novel.* Hazel Beasley Pierce demonstrates the aforementioned ability of fantasy to shine across the entire spectrum of literary genres and perspectives in *A Literary Symbiosis: Science Fiction/Fantasy Mystery*, as does Eric Garber and Lyn Paleo's *Uranian Worlds*, Keith L. Justice's *Science Fiction, Fantasy, and Horror Reference: An Annotated Bibliography of Works about Literature and Film*, Robert E. Weinberg's *A Biographical Dictionary of Science-Fiction and Fantasy Artists*, Patrick D. Murphy's *Staging the Impossible: The Fantastic Mood in Modern Drama*, Scott E. Green's *Contemporary Science Fiction, Fantasy, and Horror Poetry*, and Patrick D. Murphy's and Vernon Hyles' *The Poetic Fantastic: Studies in an Evolving Genre.*

In *Fantasists on Fantasy: A Collection of Critical Reflections by Eighteen Masters of the Art*, editors Robert H. Boyer and Kenneth J. Zahorski take a different approach from that of any of the aforementioned works. They have selected important discussions of the art by the artists themselves. While each of these authors frequently demonstrates that there is a marked difference between doing something and understanding what's being done, it is nonetheless enlightening and revealing to discover what George MacDonald, G. K. Chesterton, H. P. Lovecraft, Sir Herbert Read, James Thurber, J.R.R. Tolkien, August Derleth, C. S. Lewis, Félix Martí-Ibáñez, Peter S. Beagle, Lloyd Alexander, Andre Norton, Jane Langton, Ursula K. Le Guin, Mollie Hunter, Katherine Kurtz, Michael Moorcock, and Susan Cooper think of fantasy literature and what they were trying to do in their own creative moments. It is, for example, intriguing to contrast the authors' views with those of a more intellectual (and perhaps more objective) approach, such as Colin Wilson's *The Strength to Dream: Literature and the Imagination.*

One specialized area in which fantasy has received extensive attention is children's literature. This is expected; fantasy has always been associated with the reading affections of the young (it's one of the major misapprehensions and prejudices). For example, even though Bruno Bettelheim's *The Uses of Enchantment: The Meaning and Importance of Fairy Tales* was probably intended for a different audience, its Freudian approach and excursions into the internal psychology of children and their most-loved stories are popular among students of fantasy. C. W. Sullivan III's essay on children's fantasy is a useful introduction to it and its scholarship (cf. Butts 97–111). More specifically related to children's fantasy literature (as is Ruth Nadelman Lynn's bibliography, discussed earlier) are Cathi Dunn MacRae's *Presenting Young Adult Fantasy Fiction* and Jane Yolen's *Touch Magic*. MacRae's is a literary study. Yolen's series of light essays is, like Bettelheim's study, more intended toward understanding children's reactions, yet it, too, addresses issues of fantasy and its literature that are at the bedrock of the development of human culture. This trend of examining the childhood mind and discovering things about fantasy is continued in the conversational *Pipers at the Gates of Dawn: The Wisdom of Children's Literature*, by Jonathan Cott, in its explorations of the creative processes of "Dr. Seuss," Maurice Sendak, William Steig, Astrid Lindgren, Chinua Achebe, and P. L. Travers. Considering that fantasy is one of the most elemental of human characteristics, none of the discoveries about fantasy through children's fantasy fiction should amaze. This point is further amplified and stressed by Marion Lochhead's *The Renaissance of Wonder in Children's Literature*, which is a unified discussion of children's literature, George MacDonald and other nineteenth-century writers, C. S. Lewis, J.R.R. Tolkien, and, most significantly, Celtic mythology. However, it would be interesting to know what the reactions of such traditional scholars of children's literature, fantasy, and psychology would be to Jack Zipes' *Breaking the Magic Spell: Radical Theories of Folk & Fairy Tales*. This valuable historical study, after carefully exploring the generative nature of folktales and fairy tales, moves into the current day and discusses their modern subversion to materialism and marketing.

One of the more striking contrasts in the consideration of the scholarly efforts to explore fantasy is how much the older, amateur efforts pale in comparison. Once thought to be important critical contributions, little is heard anymore of Lin Carter's *Imaginary Worlds: The Art of Fantasy* (whose Ballantine Adult Fantasy series gave the genre a strong popular boost during the 1970s) or L. Sprague de Camp's *Literary Swordsmen and Sorcerers: The Makers of Heroic Fantasy*. There might be some error in neglecting such works, however, because they frequently do provide historical insights that are unavailable elsewhere.

STUDIES AND BIBLIOGRAPHIES OF SINGLE AUTHORS

Individual author studies present a quandary. In many ways, they reflect the popular taste; there are more studies of J.R.R. Tolkien and the Inklings (Charles Williams and C. S. Lewis, especially) than almost the entire remaining corpus of fantasy scholarship. Add the numerous articles written on Ursula K. Le Guin, who, in given years, was the longest author entry in "The Year's Scholarship in Science Fiction, Fantasy and Horror Scholarship," and the preponderance of a few authors is overwhelming.

At present, author bibliographies and studies are infrequently scattered among numerous professional publishers. Occasional volumes appear within various Twayne series (see Griffith, Hettinga, Lindskold, Mikkelsen, Rahn, and Reid) as well as volumes from varied sources, such as William A. Senior's laudable *Stephen R. Donaldson's Chronicles of Thomas Covenant*. The fan press right now is considerably more active, especially Galactic Central's* bibliographies by Phil

Stephensen-Payne and Gordon Benson Jr., which can be very helpful. The Starmont Reader's Guides to Contemporary Science-Fiction, Fantasy, and Horror Authors (series' editor Roger C. Schlobin) was the largest of the continuing examinations of these three genres' authors. However, it ceased active publication in 1992, although many of its titles are available from Borgo Press,* and volumes are occasionally added. The following will be of interest to the student of fantasy: Gary K. Wolfe's *David Lindsay*, Brian Murphy's *C. S. Lewis*, Lahna Diskin's *Theodore Sturgeon*, Michael R. Collings' *Piers Anthony*, Mary T. Brizzi's *Philip José Farmer*, Rosemary Arbur's *Marion Zimmer Bradley*, Carl B. Yoke's *Roger Zelazny*, William Touponce's *Ray Bradbury*, Marc A. Cerasini and Charles Hoffman's *Robert E. Howard*, Ronald Foust's *A. Merritt*, and Kenneth Zahorski's *Peter Beagle*. Greenwood Press' Contributions to the Study of Science Fiction and Fantasy* (series' editors Donald Palumbo and C. W. Sullivan III) is now larger than the Starmont series, but its volumes are more thematic in nature. This is the series that also contains the Proceedings of the International Conference for the Fantastic in the Arts. Another series in which fantasy titles occasionally did appear was Writers of the 21st Century (Joseph D. Olander and Martin Harry Greenberg, general editors). Olander and Greenberg have edited *Ursula K. Le Guin*, and Tim Underwood and Chuck Miller have guest-edited *Jack Vance*. Sadly, the G. K. Hall series of author bibliographies, once edited by L. W. Currey and Marshall B. Tymn, is also defunct. However, there were a number of valuable titles released: Kenneth J. Zahorski and Robert H. Boyer's *Lloyd Alexander*, *Evangeline Walton Ensley*, *Kenneth Morris*, Lahna F. Diskin's *Theodore Sturgeon*, Roger C. Schlobin's and Irene R. Harrison's *Andre Norton* (now superseded by the 1994 edition), and Joseph L. Sanders' *Roger Zelazny*.

LIBRARY COLLECTIONS

Because of fantasy's unrecognized nature among traditional library categories and because of the tendency to lump it together with science fiction, some significant collections remain unrecognized. Hal W. Hall's *Science/Fiction Collections: Fantasy, Supernatural & Weird Tales* did much to give details of the recognized collections, but it is now dated and should be supplemented by Lee Ash's *Subject Collections* and Joanna M. Zakalik's *Directory of Special Libraries and Information Centers*. Well-known repositories include the Merril Collection* (formerly the Spaced Out Library) in Montreal, the very impressive L. W. Currey Collection at the University of Texas at Austin,* and the J. Lloyd Eaton Collection at the University of California at Riverside.* A query of working scholars on the International Association for the Fantastic in the Arts listserv yielded the following additional recommendations: the Marion E. Wade Collection of the Inklings at Wheaton College, the Science Fiction Foundation at the University of Liverpool,* the Lilly Library at Indiana University,* the Graham Collection at the University of Sydney,* the Paskow Collection at Temple University,* the University of Louisville's* large Edgar Rice Burroughs' collection, Boston University's Asimov collection (Green), and Bowling Green University.* However, due to the sometimes uneven reporting, the good researcher should check libraries even when nothing is supposed to be there.

PERIODICALS

Prior to the publication of Marshall B. Tymn and Mike Ashley's *Science Fiction, Fantasy, and Weird Fiction Magazines*, trying to discover the numerous magazines that have existed since the pulp explosions of the 1920s and 1930s involved searching out a large stack of separate volumes (many of them quite rare). Tymn and Ashley's 970-page monster gathers together the efforts of a number of scholars to describe and highlight the contents of 660 international magazines by category with citations of indexes to their contents.

Recently, Locus Publications has made the contents of numerous magazines available through Stephen T. Miller and William G. Contento's Science Fiction, Fantasy, & Weird Fiction Magazine Index (1890–1997)* via Internet subscription or on CD-ROM. This very important reference fills a void.

BIBLIOGRAPHY

Anderson, Anita Loreta, ed. *Hidden Places Secret Words: An Anthology of Fantasy Poetry*. Stafford, Va.: Northwoods, 1980.

Apter, T. E. *Fantasy Literature: An Approach to Reality*. Bloomington: Indiana University Press, 1982.

Arbur, Rosemary. *Marion Zimmer Bradley: A Reader's Guide*. Mercer Island, Wash.: Starmont, 1985. Distributed by Borgo Press.

Armitt, Lucie. *Theorising the Fantastic (Interrogating Texts)*. London: Edward Arnold, 1996.

Ash, Lee. *Subject Collections*. New York: Bowker, 1993.

Ashley, Michael, ed. *The Mammoth Book of Comic Fantasy*. New York: Carroll and Graf, 1998.

———. *Who's Who in Horror and Fantasy Literature*. London: Elm Tree, 1977; New York: Taplinger, 1978.

———. *The Random House Book of Fantasy Stories*. New York: Random, 1997.

Ashley, Michael, and William G. Contento. *The Supernatural Index: A Listing of Fantasy, Supernatural, Occult, Weird, and Horror Anthologies*. Westport, Conn.: Greenwood, 1995.

Attebery, Brian. *The Fantasy Tradition in American Literature from Irving to Le Guin*. Bloomington: Indiana University Press, 1980.

———. *Strategies of Fantasy*. Bloomington: Indiana University Press, 1992.

Barr, Marlene, Richard Law, and Ruth Salvaggio. *Suzy McKee Charnas, Joan Vinge, Octavia Butler: A Reader's Guide*. Mercer Island, Wash.: Starmont, 1986. Distributed by Borgo Press.

Barron, Neil, ed. *Fantasy and Horror: A Critical and Historical Guide to Literature, Illustration, Film, TV, Radio, Internet*. Metuchen, N.J.: Scarecrow, 1999. This is an enlarged and revised edition of Barron's *Fantasy Literature*.

———, ed. *Fantasy Literature: A Readers Guide*. New York: Garland, 1990.

———. *What Fantastic Fiction Do I Read Next?: A Reader's Guide to Recent Fantasy, Horror and Science Fiction*. Detroit: Gale, 1998.

Bates, Susannah. *The Pendex: An Index to Pen Names and House Names in Fantastic, Thriller, and Series Literature*. New York and London: Garland, 1981.

Becker, Allienne R., ed. *Visions of the Fantastic: Selected Essays from the Fifteenth*

International Conference on the Fantastic in the Arts. Contributions to the Study of Science Fiction and Fantasy No. 68. Westport, Conn.: Greenwood, 1996.

Benson, Gordon, Jr. *Jack Williamson: Child and Father of Wonder: A Working Bibliography*. 2nd ed. Albuquerque: Galactic Central, 1985.

———. *Manly Wade Wellman: The Gentleman from Chapel Hill: A Memorial Working Bibliography*. 3rd ed. Albuquerque: Galactic Central, 1987.

Benson, Gordon, Jr., and Phil Stephenson-Payne. *Fritz Leiber: Sardonic Swordsman: A Working Bibliography*. 2nd ed. Leeds, West Yorkshire and Albuquerque: Galactic Central, 1990.

———. *Gordon Dickson: First Dorsai: A Working Bibliography*. 4th ed. Leeds, West Yorkshire and Albuquerque: Galactic Central, 1990.

———. *Philip José Farmer: Good-Natured Ground Breaker: A Working Bibliography*. 2nd ed. Leeds, West Yorkshire, and Albuquerque: Galactic Central, 1990.

Bettelheim, Bruno. *The Uses of Enchantment: The Meaning and Importance of Fairy Tales*. New York: Knopf, 1976.

Bleiler, E. F. *The Checklist of Science-Fiction & Supernatural Fiction*. Glen Rock, N.J.: Firebell, 1978. Supersedes *The Checklist of Fantastic Literature: A Bibliography of Fantasy, Weird and Science Fiction Books Published in the English Language*. 1948. Reprint. 1972.

———. *The Guide to Supernatural Fiction: A Full Description of 1,775 Books from 1750 to 1960, including Ghost Stories, Weird Fiction, Stories of Supernatural Horror, Fantasy, Gothic Novels, Occult Fiction, and Similar Literature with Author, Title, and Motif Indexes*. Kent, Ohio: Kent State University Press, 1983.

———, ed. *Supernatural Fiction Writers: Fantasy and Horror*. 2 vols. New York: Charles Scribner's Sons, 1985.

Bowen, Gary. *DeColores: A Bibliography of Speculative Fiction by People of Color*. <http://www.netgsi.com/~fcowboy/sf.html>.

Bowling Green University <http://www.bgsu.edu/colleges/library/pcl/pcl9.html>.

Boyer, Robert H., and Kenneth J. Zahorski, eds. *Fantasists on Fantasy: A Collection of Critical Reflections by Eighteen Masters of the Art*. New York: Avon, 1984.

———. *The Fantastic Imagination: An Anthology of High Fantasy*. 2 vols. New York: Avon, 1977, 1978.

British Fantasy Society <http://www.geocities.com/SoHo/6859/index.htm>.

Brizzi, Mary T. *Philip José Farmer: A Reader's Guide*. Mercer Island, Wash.: Starmont, 1980. Distributed by Borgo Press.

Brook-Rose, Christine. *A Rhetoric of the Unreal: Studies in Narrative and Structure, Especially the Fantastic*. Cambridge: Cambridge University Press, 1981.

Brown, Charles N. *The Locus Index to Science Fiction (1984–1977)*. CD-ROM. San Bernardino, Calif.: Locus, 1998. <www.sff.net/locus>.

———. *Science Fiction, Fantasy, and Horror 1984*. Oakland, Calif.: Locus, 1984.

———. *Science Fiction in Print, 1985, a Comprehensive Bibliography of Books and Short Fiction Published in the English Language*. Oakland, Calif.: Locus, 1986.

Brown, Charles N., and William G. Contento. *The Locus Index to Science Fiction: 1998*. <www.sff.net/locus>.

———. *Science Fiction in Print, 1986: A Comprehensive Bibliography of Books and Short Fiction Published in the English Language.* Oakland, Calif.: Locus, 1987.

———. *Science Fiction, Fantasy and Horror, 1987: A Comprehensive Bibliography of Books and Short Fiction Published in the English Language.* Oakland, Calif.: Locus, 1988.

———. *Science Fiction, Fantasy and Horror, 1988: A Comprehensive Bibliography of Books and Short Fiction Published in the English Language.* Oakland, Calif.: Locus, 1989.

———. *Science Fiction, Fantasy and Horror, 1989: A Comprehensive Bibliography of Books and Short Fiction Published in the English Language.* Oakland, Calif.: Locus, 1990.

———. *Science Fiction, Fantasy and Horror, 1990: A Comprehensive Bibliography of Books and Short Fiction Published in the English Language.* Oakland, Calif.: Locus, 1991.

———. *Science Fiction, Fantasy, and Horror: 1991.* Oakland, Calif.: Locus, 1992.

Burgess, Michael (also see R. Reginald below). *A Guide to Science Fiction and Fantasy in the Library of Congress Classification Scheme.* 2nd rev. ed. San Bernardino, Calif.: Borgo, 1988.

———. *Reference Guide to Science Fiction, Fantasy, and Horror.* Englewood, Colo.: Libraries Unlimited, 1992.

Butts, Dennis, ed. *Stories and Societies: Children's Literature in the Social Context.* London: Macmillan, 1992.

Cannady, Marilyn. *Bigger than Life: The Creator of Doc Savage.* Bowling Green, Ohio: Bowling Green University Popular Press, 1990.

Carter, Lin. *Imaginary Worlds: The Art of Fantasy.* New York: Ballantine, 1973.

Cawthorn, James, and Michael Moorcock. *Fantasy: The Hundred Best Books.* New York: Carroll and Graf, 1988.

Cerasini, Marc, and Charles Hoffman. *Robert E. Howard: A Reader's Guide.* Mercer Island, Wash.: Starmont, 1987. Distributed by Borgo Press.

Chalker, Jack L., and Mark Owings. *The Science Fantasy Publishers: A Critical and Bibliographic History.* Rev. ed. Westminster, Md.: Mirage, 1992.

———. *The Science Fantasy Publishers: Supplement One, July 1991–June 1992.* Westminster, Md.: Mirage, 1992.

Clareson, Thomas D. *Science Fiction Criticism: An Annotated Checklist.* Kent, Ohio: Kent State University Press, 1972.

Clarke, Boden, and Mary A. Burgess. *The Work of Katherine Kurtz: An Annotated Bibliography & Guide.* San Bernardino, Calif.: Borgo, 1993.

Clute, John, and John Grant et al., eds. *The Encyclopedia of Fantasy.* New York: St. Martin's, 1997. "Corrigenda" <http://www.dcs.gla.ac.uk/SF-Archives/Misc/fec.html>, maintained by David Langford.

Collings, Michael R. *Piers Anthony: A Reader's Guide.* Mercer Island, Wash.: Starmont, 1984. Distributed by Borgo Press.

———, ed. *Reflections on the Fantastic: Selected Essays from the Fourth International Conference on the Fantastic in the Arts.* Contributions to the Study of Science Fiction and Fantasy No. 24. Westport, Conn.: Greenwood, 1986.

Collins, Robert A., and Robert Latham, eds. *Science Fiction and Fantasy Book Review Annual 1988.* Westport, Conn., and London: Meckler, 1988.

———. *Science Fiction and Fantasy Book Review Annual 1989*. Westport, Conn., and London: Meckler, 1990.

———. *Science Fiction and Fantasy Book Review Annual 1990*. Westport, Conn.: Greenwood, 1990.

———. *Science Fiction and Fantasy Book Review Annual 1991*. Westport, Conn.: Greenwood, 1994.

Collins, Robert A., and Howard D. Pearce, eds. *The Scope of the Fantastic: Selected Essays from the First International Conference on the Fantastic in Literature and Film*. 2 vols. Contributions to the Study of Science Fiction and Fantasy No. 11. Westport, Conn.: Greenwood, 1985.

Contento, William G. *Index to Science Fiction Anthologies and Collections*. Boston: G. K. Hall, 1978.

———. *Index to Science Fiction Anthologies and Collections 1977–1983*. Boston: G. K. Hall, 1984.

———. *Index to Science Fiction Anthologies and Collections* [prior to 1984]. Combined ed. CD-ROM. San Bernardino, Calif.: Locus, 1998. <www.sff.net/locus>.

Cornwell, Neil. *The Literary Fantastic: From Gothic to Postmodernism*. New York: Harvester Wheatfield, 1990.

Cott, Jonathan. *Pipers at the Gates of Dawn: The Wisdom of Children's Literature*. New York: Random House, 1981.

Cottrill, Tim, Martin H. Greenberg, and Charles G. Waugh. *Science Fiction and Fantasy Series and Sequels: A Bibliography*. Vol. 1: *Books*. New York: Garland, 1986.

Coyle, William, ed. *Aspects of Fantasy: Selected Essays from the Second International Conference on the Fantastic in Literature and Film*. Contributions to the Study of Science Fiction and Fantasy No. 19. Westport, Conn.: Greenwood, 1986.

Currey, L. W. *Science Fiction and Fantasy Authors: A Bibliography of First Printings of Their Fiction and Selected Nonfiction*. Boston: G. K. Hall, 1979.

Day, Bradford. *The Checklist of Fantastic Literature in Paperback Books*. Denver and New York: Science Fiction and Fantasy, 1965. Reprint. New York: Arno, 1975.

———. *The Supplemental Checklist of Fantastic Literature*. Denver and New York: Science Fiction and Fantasy. 1963. Reprint. New York: Arno, 1975. Rev. ed. Hillsville, Va.: Author, 1994.

De Camp, L. Sprague. *Literary Swordsmen and Sorcerers: The Makers of Heroic Fantasy*. Sauk City, Wis.: Arkham, 1976.

Diskin, Lahna. *Theodore Sturgeon*. Mercer Island, Wash.: Starmont, 1981.

Dozois, Gardner, ed. *Modern Classics of Fantasy*. New York: St. Martin's, 1997.

Egoff, Sheila A. *Worlds Within: Children's Fantasy from the Middle Ages to Today*. Chicago and London: ALA, 1988.

Elgin, Don D. *The Comedy of the Fantastic: Ecological Perspectives on the Fantasy Novel*. Westport, Conn.: Greenwood, 1985.

Filmer[-Davies], Kath, ed. *Twentieth-Century Fantasists: Essay on Culture, Society and Belief in Twentieth-Century Mythopoeic Literature*. New York: St. Martin's, 1992.

———. *Skepticism and Hope in Twentieth Century Fantasy Literature*. Bowling Green, Ohio: Bowling Green University Popular Press, 1992.

Forster, E. M. *Aspects of the Novel and Related Writings*. 1927. Reprint. London: Edward Arnold, 1974.

Foust, Ronald. *A. Merritt: A Reader's Guide*. Mercer Island, Wash.: Starmont, 1989. Distributed by Borgo Press.

Frane, Jeff. *Fritz Leiber: A Reader's Guide*. Mercer Island, Wash.: Starmont, 1980. Distributed by Borgo Press.

Franson, Donald, and Howard DeVore. *A History of the Hugo, Nebula, and International Fantasy Awards*. Rev. ed. Dearborn, Mich.: Misfit, 1985.

Galactic Central Publications <http://ourworld.compuserve.com/homepages/philsp/>.

Garber, Eric, and Lyn Paleo. *Uranian Worlds: A Guide to Alternate Sexuality in Science Fiction, Fantasy, and Horror*. 2nd ed. Boston: G. K. Hall, 1990.

Goldberg, Lee, et al. *The Dreamweavers: Interviews with Fantasy Filmmakers of the 1980s*. Jefferson, N.C.: McFarland, 1995.

Gonzales, Doreen. *Madeleine L'Engle: Author of* A Wrinkle in Time. New York: Dillon, 1991.

Gordon, Joan. *Gene Wolfe: A Reader's Guide*. Mercer Island, Wash.: Starmont, 1986. Distributed by Borgo Press.

Goss, Elliott. *Mere Creatures: A Study of Modern Fantasy Tales for Children*. Toronto: University of Toronto Press, 1988.

Graham Collection. University of Sydney <http://www.library.usyd.edu.au/Services/Libraries/Rare/index.html#scie>

Green, Scott E. *Contemporary Science Fiction, Fantasy, and Horror Poetry: A Resource Guide and Biographical Dictionary*. Westport, Conn.: Greenwood, 1989.

———. *Isaac Asimov: An Annotated Bibliography of the Asimov Collection at Boston University*. Westport, Conn.: Greenwood, 1995.

Greenwood Press Contributions to the Study of Science Fiction and Fantasy <http://info.greenwood.com/cgi-bin/getidx.pl?SUBJECT=subjLTSF>.

Griffith, John. *Charlotte's Web: A Pig's Salvation*. Masterwork Studies 128. New York: Twayne, 1993.

Haas, Robert, ed. *Culture of the Fantastic: Selected Essays from the Sixteenth International Conference on the Fantastic in the Arts*. Contributions to the Study of Science Fiction and Fantasy. Westport, Conn.: Greenwood, forthcoming.

Hall, Hal W., ed. *Science Fiction and Fantasy Reference Index 1878–1985: Author Entries; Subject Entries*. Detroit: Gale, 1987.

———. *Science Fiction and Fantasy Reference Index 1985–1991: An International Author and Subject Index to History and Criticism*. Englewood, Colo.: Libraries Unlimited, 1993.

———. *Science Fiction and Fantasy Reference Index 1992–1995: An International Subject and Author Index to History and Criticism*. Englewood, Colo.: Libraries Unlimited, 1997.

———. *Science Fiction and Fantasy Book Review Index, 1980–1984*. Detroit: Gale, 1985.

———. *Science Fiction and Fantasy Book Review Index 1970–1990*. 20 vols. Bryan, Tex: SFFBRI, 1971–1994. Title varies: early volumes titled *Science Fiction Book Review Index*. [1970–1984 annuals cumulated in *Science Fiction and Fantasy Book Review Index 1980–1984*].

———. *Science/Fiction Collections: Fantasy, Supernatural & Weird Tales*. New York: Haworth, 1983.

———. *Science Fiction Index: Criticism: An Index to English Language Books and Articles about Science Fiction and Fantasy*. Bryan, Tex.: Privately printed, 1980.

Hartwell, David G., with Kathryn Kramer, comps. *Masterpieces of Fantasy and Enchantment*. New York: St. Martin's, 1988.

———. *Masterpieces of Fantasy and Wonder*. Garden City, N.Y.: Doubleday, 1989.

Hatfield, Len, ed. *Theorizing the Fantastic: Selected Essays from the Seventeenth International Conference on the Fantastic in the Arts*. Contributions to the Study of Science Fiction and Fantasy. Westport, Conn.: Greenwood, forthcoming.

Herron, Don, ed. *The Dark Barbarian: The Writings of Robert E. Howard*. Westport, Conn.: Greenwood, 1985.

Hettinga, Donald R. *Presenting Madeleine L'Engle*. Young Adults Authors 622. New York: Macmillan and Twayne, 1993.

Hewett, Jerry, and Daryl F. Mallett. *The Work of Jack Vance: An Annotated Bibliography and Guide*. San Bernardino, Calif.: Borgo Press; Lancaster, Pa.: Underwood-Miller, 1994.

Hokenson, Jan, and Howard Pearce, eds. *Forms of the Fantastic: Selected Essays from the Third International Conference on the Fantastic in Literature and Film*. Contributions to the Study of Science Fiction and Fantasy No. 20. Westport, Conn.: Greenwood, 1986.

Holte, James Craig, ed. *The Fantastic Vampire: Selected Essays from the Eighteenth International Conference on the Fantastic in the Arts*. Contributions to the Study of Science Fiction and Fantasy. Westport, Conn.: Greenwood, 2000.

Hume, Kathryn. *Fantasy and Mimesis: Responses to Reality in Western Literature*. New York: Methuen, 1984.

Innes, Sherrie A. *Tough Girls: Women Warriors and Wonder Women in Popular Culture*. Philadelphia: University of Pennsylvania Press, 1998.

International Association for the Fantastic in the Arts. <http://ebbs.english.vt.edu/iafa/iafa.home.html>.

Irwin, W. R. *The Game of the Impossible: A Rhetoric of Fantasy*. Urbana: University of Illinois Press, 1976.

J. Lloyd Eaton Collection. University of California at Riverside <http://lib-www.ucr.edu/spec_coll/eaton.html>.

Jackson, Rosemary. *Fantasy: The Literature of Subversion*. New York: Methuen, 1981.

Jellybaby's Anthology: Poetry for Fantasy Lovers (or, Fantasy for Poetry Lovers). [Ed. Sharon Davis] <http://www.geocities.com/Area51/2184/index.html>.

Jurich, Marilyn. *Scheherazade's Sisters*. Westport, Conn.: Greenwood Press, 1998.

Justice, Keith L. *Science Fiction, Fantasy, and Horror Reference: An Annotated Bibliography of Works about Literature and Film*. Jefferson, N.C.: McFarland, 1989.

Kaler, Anne K. *The Picara: From Hera to Fantasy Heroine*. Bowling Green, Ohio: Bowling Green University Popular Press, 1991.

Kennard, Jean E. *Number and Nightmare: Forms of Fantasy in Contemporary Fiction*. Hamden, Conn.: Archon/Shoe String, 1975.

Ketterer, David, ed. *Flashes of the Fantastic: Selected Essays from the Nineteenth International Conference on the Fantastic in the Arts*. Contributions to the Study of Science Fiction and Fantasy. Westport, Conn.: Greenwood, 2001.

Krueger, Kenneth J., ed. *Starbound! Poems of Science-Fiction, Fantasy, and Terror*. Buffalo, N.Y.: Pegasus, 1954.

Kuznets, Lois Rostow. *When Toys Come Alive: Narratives of Animation, Metamorphosis, and Development*. New Haven, Conn., and London: Yale University Press, 1994.

The L. W. Currey Collection. University of Texas at Austin <http://www.lib.utexas.edu/Libs/HRC/HRHRC/book.html>.

Landay, Lori. *Madcaps, Screwballs and Con Women: The Female Trickster in American Culture*. Philadelphia: University of Pennsylvania Press, 1998.

Langford, Michele K., ed. *Contours of the Fantastic: Selected Essays from the Eighth International Conference on the Fantastic in the Arts*. Contributions to the Study of Science Fiction and Fantasy No. 41. Westport, Conn.: Greenwood, 1990.

Latham, Robert A., and Robert A. Collins, eds. *Modes of the Fantastic: Selected Essays from the Twelfth International Conference on the Fantastic in the Arts*. Contributions to the Study of Science Fiction and Fantasy No. 66. Westport, Conn.: Greenwood, 1995.

Lilly Library. Indiana University <http://www.indiana.edu/~liblilly/llhours.html>.

Lindskold, Jane M. *Roger Zelazny*. United States Author Series 640. New York: Twayne, 1993.

The Linköping Science Fiction & Fantasy Archive. <http://sf.www.lysator.liu.se:80/sf_archive/sf_main.html>.

Lochhead, Marion. *The Renaissance of Wonder in Children's Literature*. Edinburgh: Canongate, 1977.

Locke, George. *A Spectrum of Fantasy: The Bibliography and Biography of a Collection of Fantastic Literature*. Upper Tooting, London: Ferret Fantasy, 1980.

———. *A Spectrum of Fantasy, Volume II: Acquistions to a Collection of Fantastic Literature, 1980–1993, Together with Additional Notes on Titles Covered in the First Volume*. London: Ferrett Fantasy, 1994.

Lynn, Ruth Nadelman. *Fantasy Literature for Children and Young Adults: An Annotated Bibliography*. 4th ed. New York and London: R. R. Bowker, 1995.

MacDonald, George. "The Imagination, Its Functions and Its Culture." In *The Imagination and Other Essays*. Boston: Lothrop, 1883.

MacNee, Marie J. *Science Fiction, Fantasy and Horror Writers*. 2 vols. Detroit, Mich.: Gale, 1995.

MacRae, Cathi Dunn. *Presenting Young Adult Fantasy Fiction*. United States Authors 699. New York: Twayne, 1998.

Magill, Frank N., ed. *Survey of Modern Fantasy Literature*. 5 vols. Englewood, N.J.: Salem, 1983.

Mallett, Daryl F., and Robert Reginald. *Reginald's Science Fiction and Fantasy Awards: A Comprehensive Guide to the Awards and Their Winners*. 3rd rev. ed. San Bernardino, Calif.: Borgo, 1993.

Manlove, C. N. *Christian Fantasy: 1200 to the Present*. Notre Dame: Notre Dame University Press, 1992.

———. *The Impulse of Fantasy Literature*. Kent, Ohio: Kent State University Press, 1983.

———. *Modern Fantasy: Five Studies*. Cambridge: Cambridge University Press, 1975.

Mathews, Richard. *Fantasy: The Liberation of Imagination*. Studies in Literary Themes and Genres 16. New York: Twayne/Simon and Schuster, 1997.

McGhan, Barry. *Sciencefiction and Fantasy Pseudonyms*. Dearborn, Mich.: Misfit Press, 1976.

Merril Collection of Science Fiction, Speculation and Fantasy (formerly the Spaced Out Library) <http://www.tpl.toronto.on.ca/merril/home.htm>.

Mikkelsen, Nina. *Susan Cooper*. United States Author Series 696. New York: Twayne/Prentice-Hall, 1998.

Miller, Stephan T., and William Contento. *Science Fiction, Fantasy, & Weird Fiction Magazine Index (1890–1997)*. CD-ROM. San Bernardino, Calif.: Locus, 1998. <http://www.sff.net/chkist/0chklst.htm>.

Molson, Francis J. *Children's Fantasy: A Reader's Guide*. Mercer Island, Wash.: Starmont, 1989. Distributed by Borgo Press.

Morrison, Michael A., ed. *Trajectories of the Fantastic: Selected Essays from the Fourteenth International Conference on the Fantastic in the Arts*. Contributions to the Study of Science Fiction and Fantasy No. 70. Westport, Conn.: Greenwood, 1997.

Morse, Donald E., ed. *The Fantastic in World Literature and the Arts: Selected Essays from the Fifth International Conference on the Fantastic in the Arts*. Contributions to the Study of Science Fiction and Fantasy No. 28. Westport, Conn.: Greenwood, 1987.

Morse, Donald E., Marshall B. Tymn, and Csilla Bertha, eds. *The Celebration of the Fantastic: Selected Papers from the Tenth Anniversary International Conference on the Fantastic in the Arts*. Contributions to the Study of Science Fiction and Fantasy No. 49. Westport, Conn.: Greenwood, 1992.

Murphy, Brian. *C. S. Lewis*. Mercer Island, Wash: Starmont, 1983.

Murphy, Patrick D., ed. *Staging the Impossible: The Fantastic Mood in Modern Drama*. Westport, Conn.: Greenwood, 1992.

Murphy, Patrick D., and Vernon Hyles, eds. *The Poetic Fantastic: Studies in an Evolving Genre*. Westport, Conn.: Greenwood, 1989.

Nikolajeva, Maria. *The Magic Code: The Use of Magical Patterns in Fantasy for Children*. Stockholm: Almqvist and Wiksell, 1988.

Olander, Joseph D., and Martin Harry Greenberg, eds. *Ursula K. Le Guin*. New York: Taplinger, 1979.

Olsen, Lance. *The Ellipse of Uncertainty: An Introduction to Postmodern Fantasy*. Westport, Conn.: Greenwood Press, 1987.

Palumbo, Donald, ed. *Erotic Universe: Sexuality and Fantastic Literature*. Westport, Conn.: Greenwood, 1986.

———. *Eros in the Mind's Eye: Sexuality and the Fantastic in Art and Film*. Westport, Conn.: Greenwood, 1986.

———. *Spectrum of the Fantastic: Selected Essays from the Sixth International Conference on the Fantastic in the Arts*. Contributions to the Study of Science Fiction and Fantasy No. 31. Westport, Conn.: Greenwood, 1988.

Paskow Collection. Temple University <http://www.library.temple.edu/speccoll/sfc.htm>.

Pierce, Hazel Beasley. *A Literary Symbiosis: Science Fiction/Fantasy Mystery*. Westport, Conn.: Greenwood, 1983.

Price, Robert M. *Lin Carter: A Look behind His Imaginary Worlds*. Mercer Island, Wash.: Starmont, 1992. Distributed by Borgo Press.

Prickett, Stephen. *Victorian Fantasy*. Bloomington: Indiana University Press, 1979.

Pringle, David. *Modern Fantasy: The Hundred Best Novels: An English-Language Selection*. London: Grafton, 1988.

Pringle, David, et al., eds. *St. James Guide to Fantasy Writers*. New York: St. James [Gale], 1996.

Rabkin, Eric S. *The Fantastic in Literature*. Princeton, N.J.: Princeton University Press, 1976.

Rahn, Suzanne. *The Wizard of Oz*. Masterwork Studies 167. New York: Twayne, 1998.

Ransom, Amy J. *The Feminine as Fantastic in the Conte Fantastique: Visions of the Other*. The Age of Romanticism and Revolution 16. New York: Peter Lang, 1995.

Reginald, R[obert], pseud. [Michael Burgess]. *Science Fiction and Fantasy Literature: A Checklist, 1700–1974 with Contemporary Science Fiction Authors II*. 2 vols. Detroit: Gale, 1979.

———, ed. *Science Fiction and Fantasy Literature: 1975–91: Supplement*. Detroit: Gale, 1992.

———. *Stella Nova: The Contemporary Science Fiction Authors*. Los Angeles: Unicorn and Son, 1970. Reprint as *Contemporary Science Fiction Authors: First Edition*. New York: Arno, 1975.

Reid, Suzanne Elizabeth. *Presenting Ursula K. Le Guin*. United States Authors 677. New York: Twayne, 1997.

Riley, Michael O. *Oz and Beyond: The Fantasy World of L. Frank Baum*. Lawrence: University Press of Kansas, 1998.

Rock, James A. *Who Goes There: A Listing of Science Fiction and Fantasy Pseudonyms*. Bloomington, Ind.: James A. Rock, 1977.

Rosenberg, Betty. *Genreflecting: A Guide to Reading Interests in Genre Fiction*. Littleton, Colo.: Libraries Unlimited, 1982.

Ruddick, Nicholas, ed. *State of the Fantastic: Studies in the Theory and Practice of Fantastic Literature and Film: Selected Papers from the Eleventh International Conference on the Fantastic in the Arts, 1990*. Contributions to the Study of Science Fiction and Fantasy No. 50. Westport, Conn.: Greenwood, 1992.

Saciuk, Olena H., ed. *The Shape of the Fantastic: Selected Essays from the Seventh International Conference on the Fantastic in the Arts*. Contributions to the Study of Science Fiction and Fantasy No. 39. Westport, Conn.: Greenwood, 1990.

Sanders, Joe [Joseph L.], ed. *Functions of the Fantastic: Selected Essays from the Thirteenth International Conference on the Fantastic in the Arts*. Contributions to the Study of Science Fiction and Fantasy No. 65. Westport, Conn.: Greenwood, 1995.

———. *Roger Zelazny: A Primary and Secondary Bibliography*. Boston: G. K. Hall, 1980.

Schlobin, Roger C., ed. *The Aesthetics of Fantasy Literature and Art*. Notre Dame, Ind.: Notre Dame University Press, 1982.

———. *The Literature of Fantasy: A Comprehensive, Annotated Bibliography of Modern Fantasy Fiction*. New York: Garland, 1981.

———. "The Scholarship of Incidence: The Unfortunate State of Fantasy Scholarship." *Extrapolation* (Winter 1984), 335–39.

Schlobin, Roger C., and Irene R. Harrison. *Andre Norton: A Primary and Secondary Bibliography*. 2nd rev. ed. Framington, Mass.: NESFA Press, 1994.

Schweitzer, Darrell, ed. *Discovering Classic Fantasy Fiction: Essays on the Antecedents of Fantastic Literature*. San Bernardino, Calif.: Borgo, 1996.

The Science Fiction Book Club <www.sfbc.com>.

The Science Fiction Foundation. University of Liverpool. <http://www.liv.ac.uk/~asawyer/sffchome.html>.

The Science Fiction Research Association. <http://www.uwm.edu/~sands/sfra/scifi.htm>.

Science Fiction, Utopian and Fantastic Literature discussion group (Modern Language Association) <http://www.uwm.edu/~sands/sfuf/home.htm>.

SCI-Finder <http://www.sf-fantasy.com/fdauthr.htm>.

Searles, Baird, Beth Meacham, and Michael Franklin. *A Reader's Guide to Fantasy*. New York: Avon, 1982.

Senior, W[illiam] A. *Stephen R. Donaldson's Chronicles of Thomas Covenant: Variations on the Fantasy Tradition*. Kent, Ohio: Kent State University Press, 1995.

Shippey, Tom, ed. *The Oxford Book of Fantasy Stories*. Oxford and New York: Oxford University Press, 1994.

Siebers, Tobin. *The Romantic Fantastic*. Ithaca, N.Y.: Cornell University Press, 1984.

Silverberg, Robert, and Martin H. Greenberg, comps. *The Fantasy Hall of Fame*. New York: Arbor, 1983.

Slusser, George E., Eric S. Rabkin, and Robert Scholes, eds. *Bridges to Fantasy*. Carbondale: Southern Illinois University Press, 1982.

Smith, Karen Patricia. *The Fabulous Realm: A Literary-Historical Approach to British Fantasy*. Metuchen, N.J., and London: Scarecrow, 1993.

Spivack, Charlotte. *Merlin's Daughters: Contemporary Women Writers of Fantasy*. Contributions to the Study of Science Fiction and Fantasy No. 23. Westport, Conn.: Greenwood, 1987.

Starmont Reader's Guides <http://www.borgopress.com/seriesfr.htm>.

Stephensen-Payne, Phil[ip Andrew]. *C. J. Cherryh: Citizen of the Universe: A Working Bibliography*. Leeds, West Yorkshire, and Albuquerque: Galactic Central, 1992.

———. *James Blish: Author Mirabilis: A Working Bibliography*. Leeds, West Yorkshire, and Albuquerque: Galactic Central, 1996.

———. *Piers Anthony: Biblio of an Ogre: A Working Bibliography*. Leeds, West Yorkshire, and Albuquerque: Galactic Central, 1990.

———. *Roger Zelazny: Master of Amber: A Working Bibliography*. Leeds, West Yorkshire, and Albuquerque: Galactic Central, 1991.

Stephensen-Payne, Phil[ip Andrew], and Gordon Benson Jr. *Jack Vance: A Fan-*

tasmic Imagination: A Working Bibliography. 2nd ed. Leeds, West Yorkshire, and Albuquerque: Galactic Central, 1990.

———. *John Brunner: Shockwave Writer: A Working Bibliography*. 3rd ed. Leeds, West Yorkshire, and Albuquerque: Galactic Central, 1989.

———. *Poul Anderson: Myth-Master and Wonder Weaver: A Working Bibliography*. 5th ed. Leeds, West Yorkshire, and Albuquerque: Galactic Central, 1989.

Sullivan, C. W., III, ed. *The Dark Fantastic: Selected Essays from the Ninth International Conference on the Fantastic in the Arts*. Contributions to the Study of Science Fiction and Fantasy No. 71. Westport, Conn.: Greenwood, 1997.

Swinfen, Ann. *In Defence of Fantasy: A Study of the Genre in English and American Literature since 1945*. Boston: Routledge and Kegan Paul, 1984.

Thompson, Raymond H. *The Return from Avalon: A Study of the Arthurian Legend in Modern Fiction*. Westport, Conn.: Greenwood, 1985.

Todorov, Tzvetan. *The Fantastic: A Structural Approach to a Literary Genre*. 1970. Reprint and trans. Richard Howard. Ithaca, N.Y.: Cornell University Press, 1973.

Touponce, William E. *Naming the Unnamable: Ray Bradbury and the Fantastic after Freud*. 2nd rev. ed. San Bernardino, Calif.: Starmont, 1997. Distributed by Borgo Press.

———. *Ray Bradbury and the Poetics of Reverie: Gaston, Bachelard, Wolfgang Iser, and the Reader's Response to Fantastic Literature*. I. O. Evans Studies in the Philosophy of Literature and the Criticism of Literature 32. San Bernardino, Calif.: Borgo, 1997.

———. *Ray Bradbury: A Reader's Guide*. Mercer Island, Wash.: Starmont, 1989. Distributed by Borgo Press.

Tuck, Donald H. *The Encyclopedia of Science Fiction and Fantasy through 1968*. 3 vols. Chicago: Advent, 1974, 1978, 1983.

Tymn, Marshall B., and Mike Ashley, eds. *Science Fiction, Fantasy, and Weird Fiction Magazines*. Westport, Conn.: Greenwood, 1985.

Tymn, Marshall B., Kenneth J. Zahorski, and Robert H. Boyer. *Fantasy Literature: A Core Collection and Reference Guide*. New York: Bowker, 1979.

Tymn, Marshall B., et al. *The Year's Scholarship in Science Fiction, Fantasy and Horror Literature 1974–1988*. In various forms: separate cumulations (1972–1975 and 1976–1979) and individual books from Kent State University Press, annuals in *Extrapolation* (1975–1979, 1983–1988), and *The Journal of the Fantastic in the Arts* (1990). Earlier title: "The Year's Scholarship in Science Fiction and Fantasy."

Underwood, Tim, and Chuck Miller, eds. *Jack Vance*. New York: Taplinger, 1980.

University of Louisville (Edgar Rice Burroughs) <http://www.louisville.edu/library/ekstrom/special/rarebook.html>.

University of Michigan's fantasy and science-fiction "Electronic Library" <http://www.umich.edu/~umfandsf/other/etext.html>.

Waggoner, Diana. *The Hills of Faraway: A Guide to Fantasy*. New York: Atheneum, 1978.

Weinberg, Robert E., ed. *A Biographical Dictionary of Science-Fiction and Fantasy Artists*. Westport, Conn.: Greenwood, 1988.

Wells, Stuart W., III, comp. *The Science Fiction and Heroic Fantasy Author Index*. Duluth, Minn.: Purple Unicorn, 1978.

West, Mark I., ed. *Before Oz: Juvenile Fantasy Stories from Nineteenth-Century America*. Hamden, Conn.: Archon, 1989.

Wilkins, Gary, ed. *A Treasury of Fantasy: Heroic Adventures in Imaginary Lands*. New York: Avenel, 1981.

Wilson, Colin. *The Strength to Dream: Literature and the Imagination*. Boston: Houghton Mifflin, 1962. Reprint. Westport, Conn.: Greenwood, 1973.

Wolfe, Gary K. *Critical Terms for Science Fiction and Fantasy: A Glossary and Guide to Scholarship*. Westport, Conn.: Greenwood, 1986.

———. *David Lindsay*. Mercer Island, Wash.: Starmont, 1982.

Yoke, Carl B. *Roger Zelazny: A Reader's Guide*. Mercer Island, Wash.: Starmont, 1979. Distributed by Borgo Press.

———. "Slaying the Dragon Within: Andre Norton's Female Heroes." *Journal of the Fantastic in the Arts* 4:3 (1991), 79–93.

Yolen, Jane. *Touch Magic: Fantasy, Faerie and Folklore in the Literature of Childhood*. New York: Philomel, 1981.

Yuan, Yuan. *The Discourse of Fantasy: Theoretical and Fictional Perspectives*. [Montrose], Colo.: Hollowbrook, 1995.

Zahorski, Kenneth J. *Peter Beagle: A Reader's Guide*. Mercer Island, Wash.: Starmont, 1988. Distributed by Borgo Press.

Zahorski, Kenneth J., and Robert H. Boyer. *Lloyd Alexander, Evangeline Walton Ensley, Kenneth Morris: A Primary and Secondary Bibliography*. Boston: G. K. Hall, 1981.

Zakalik, Joanna M. *Directory of Special Libraries and Information Centers*. Detroit: Gale Research, 1994.

Ziolkowski, Theodore. *Disenchanted Images: A Literary Iconology*. Princeton, N.J.: Princeton University Press, 1977.

Zipes, Jack. *Breaking the Magic Spell: Radical Theories of Folk & Fairy Tales*. Austin: University of Texas Press, 1979.

JOURNALS

CLF Newsletter (annually). 1995– . Dan Pearlman, ed., Department of English, University of Rhode Island, Kingston, R.I. 02881.

Fantasy Review (monthly). June 1978–October 1981, Paul C. Allen, ed.; November 1981–August 1987, Robert A. Collins, ed. Florida Atlantic University, 500 NW. 20th St., Boca Raton, Fla. 33431.

Journal of the Fantastic in the Arts (quarterly). 1988– . Submissions: Roger C. Schlobin, ed., 1915 David Drive, Chesterton, Ind. 46304–3011. <ebbs.english.vt.edu/iafa/jfa/jfa.html>.

Mythlore (quarterly). 1969– . Submissions and subscriptions: P.O. Box 6707, Altadena, Calif. 91003. <http://www.mythsoc.org/mythlore.html>.

Paradoxa (triennially or quarterly). 1995– . David Willingham, ed., P.O. Box 2237, Vashon Island, Wash. 98070. <www.accessone.com/~paradoxa>.

SPECIAL FANTASY ISSUES (OF NONFANTASY JOURNALS)

Children's Literature Association Quarterly 12.1 (Spring 1987).
Extrapolation (Spring 1987).
Kansas Quarterly 16.3 (1984).
Mosiac (Winter 1977).

INTERNET WEB SITES

Bowling Green University <http://www.bgsu.edu/colleges/library/pcl/pcl9.html>.

British Fantasy Society <http://www.geocities.com/SoHo/6859/index.htm>.

The Encyclopedia of Science Fiction. Ed. John Clute and Peter Nicholls <http://www.dcs.gla.ac.uk/SF-Archives/Misc/sfec.html>.

Galactic Central Publications <http://ourworld.compuserve.com/homepages/philsp/>.

Graham Collection. University of Sydney. <http://www.library.usyd.edu.au/Services/Libraries/Rare/index.html#scie>

Greenwood Press Contributions to the Study of Science Fiction and Fantasy. <http://info.greenwood.com/cgi-bin/getidx.pl?SUBJECT=subjLTSF>.

International Association for the Fantastic in the Arts. <http://ebbs.english.vt.edu/iafa/iafa.home.html>.

J. Lloyd Eaton Collection. University of California at Riverside <http://lib-www.ucr.edu/spec_coll/eaton.html>.

The L. W. Currey Collection. University of Texas at Austin <http://www.lib.utexas.edu/Libs/HRC/HRHRC/book.html>.

Lilly Library. Indiana University <http://www.indiana.edu/~liblilly/llhours.html>.

The Linköping Science Fiction & Fantasy Archive <http://sf.www.lysator.liu.se:80/sf_archive/sf_main.html>.

Merril Collection of Science Fiction, Speculation and Fantasy (formerly the Spaced Out Library) <http://www.tpl.toronto.on.ca/merril/home.htm>.

Paskow Collection. Temple University <http://www.library.temple.edu/speccoll/sfc.htm>.

The Science Fiction Book Club <www.sfbc.com>.

The Science Fiction Foundation. University of Liverpool <http://www.liv.ac.uk/~asawyer/sffchome.html>.

The Science Fiction Research Association <http://www.uwm.edu/~sands/sfra/scifi.htm>.

Science Fiction, Utopian and Fantastic Literature discussion group (Modern Language Association) <http://www.uwm.edu/~sands/sfuf/home.htm>.

SCI-Finder <http://www.sf-fantasy.com/fdauthr.htm>.

Starmont Reader's Guides <http://www.borgopress.com/seriesfr.htm>.

University of Louisville (Edgar Rice Burroughs) <http://www.louisville.edu/library/ekstrom/special/rarebook.html>.

University of Michigan's fantasy and science-fiction "Electronic Library" <http://www.umich.edu/~umfandsf/other/etext.html>.

FASHION

Patricia A. Cunningham and
Joseph Hancock

Fashion is distracting, intriguing, and demanding. We admire it, buy it, store it, wear it, and finally discard it. We identify ourselves with it and judge others by it. Fashion reflects our economy and technology and politics, as well as our pastimes, professions, and taste. As such, fashion is a sensitive barometer of popular culture. We define fashion as the clothing styles that are most popular at a particular period of time and place with a group of people, large or small. The elements of fashion that are of most interest for popular culture studies are its changing character and meanings. The most remarkable aspect of fashion in recent years has been the acceleration of change. Its significance lies in its reflection of American culture and society. While, in the past, fashion was most often viewed as frivolous, today the subject engages the public, academics, and the media with equal intensity.

The term "fashion" is derived from the Latin *factio*, a making, and in its pure definition refers to the make, form, or shape of a thing or the current style or mode of speech, conduct, apparel, and so on. A few basic fashion terms are presented in the context of "apparel," but the same concepts apply to many other components of the environment such as furniture, appliances, wall coverings, window treatments, decorative accessories, and automobiles. First, there is the concept of "style." In relation to apparel, a style refers to a garment with particular features or characteristics that distinguish it from other garments of the same type. A style may or may not be popular at any given time, and its distinctive features do not change. For example, bell-bottom jeans may or may not be popular at a given time, but the shape of the flared legs distinguishes the bell-bottom style from pegged or tapered jeans. The style or styles that are accepted or popular at a particular time in a particular place are called "fashions." Acceptance or nonacceptance implies change, and the way in which fashion changes is explained as the "fashion cycle."

Styles of dress that become the mode are products of the apparel industry, which with the rise of a consumer culture grew by leaps and bounds after the mid-1900s. Before the 1960s, the fashion industry could dictate what people wore. Since then, however, Americans have shown an increasing interest in expressing their individuality. The second half of the twentieth century also saw the rise of men's fashion and an interest in dressing correctly on the job, at first in suits and toward the end of the century in casual work dress. Advice books on how to dress continue to sell well. A proliferation of styles on the market allows people to engage in expressive dressing, whether to denote individuality, affiliation, status, gender, or life style. This new twist on the function of clothing has increased the academic concern for fashion, especially with scholars of history, culture studies, media, and the arts. An interest in examining everyday life, issues of gender, and material culture also increased the attention given to fashion. The vintage clothing market likewise broadened the field of fashion for creative dressing and for collectors. The media aided fashion with the transformation of designers into celebrities. Indeed, the study of fashion has itself become fashionable and recognized as rich territory for the study of American popular culture.

This chapter focuses largely on literature, visual and material sources related to fashion, and approaches to its study published since the late 1980s. Particular attention is paid to changes in the industry and new avenues for examining fashion history, its social and cultural meanings, and significance for Americans, including the influence of Europe and Asia on American fashion.

HISTORICAL OUTLINE

As an entity of popular culture, fashion is both an economic and a cultural phenomenon. The production and consumption of fashionable dress have become central to the American economy. Scholars study the growth of the fashion industry and its impact on the economy. They also examine fashion and its relationship to the social, aesthetic, political, and cultural aspects of American life. The changes that have occurred in the industry and the ramifications for American culture are made clear in the *End of Fashion* (2000) by Teri Agins.

If consumption of apparel and fashion can be viewed as the backbone of the American economic system in the twenty-first century, then the ways of dressing or how Americans use clothing and fashion must be viewed as important to the American way of life. A grasp, then, of how fashion functions at all levels of society leads to greater understanding of American popular culture in general.

Three innovations crucial in the history of the American fashion business emerged—the sewing machine, graded paper patterns, and standardized sizes. An early one-thread, chain-stitch sewing machine was patented by Barthelemy Thimonnier in 1830. This was followed by a two-thread machine invented by American Walter Hunt and a hand-run machine by Elias Howe patented in 1846. Isaac Singer developed the foot treadle in 1859 and began to produce sewing machines. Soon they were used in the home by seamstresses, in the production of military uniforms, and in the mass production of men's apparel. Graded or sized paper patterns appeared in the 1860s in two rival fashion magazines. Mr. and Mrs. Ebenezer Butterick introduced paper patterns in 1863 in their magazine *Metropolitan* (later, the *Delineator*). Rival Ellen Demorest published her line of paper patterns in the *Mirror of Fashion*. Both Demorest and the Buttericks enjoyed tremendous

Picnic attire, Manitou Springs, Colorado, ca. 1885.
Courtesy of the Denver Public Library

success. Patterns were used not only by individual homemakers but also by clothing manufacturers. The need for army uniforms during the Civil War stimulated development of mass production in another way. Clothing factories were founded to produce uniforms, and specifications for standardization of sizes were adopted. The elements of customer demand, fabric supply, sewing machines, graded patterns, and standardized sizes were now in place.

As the middle class prospered, more people had the income and leisure time to become interested in fashionable clothing. Although dolls dressed in Paris fashions were sent to the United States as early as the mid-eighteenth century, the proliferation of nineteenth-century popular magazines introduced American consumers to the latest fashions. In addition to black-and-white or color fashion plates, these magazines included needlework, knitting, and crocheting instructions as well as house plans, fiction, music, editorials, society news, and advice. Three early publications were *Graham's Magazine* (1826–1858), *Godey's Lady's Book* (1830–1898), and *Peterson's Magazine* (1842–1898). To these were added the *Metropolitan* (the *Delineator*), *Mirror of Fashion*, the *Woman's Home Companion*, *Pictorial Review*, *Queen of Fashion* (*McCall's*), and *Burton's Gentlemen's Magazine*. Several fashion magazines started in the nineteenth century are still providing American consumers with fashion ideas—*McCall's*, *Ladies' Home Journal*, *Harper's Bazaar*, and *Vogue*.

In addition to the increase in fashion communication, another nineteenth-century fashion industry trend must be mentioned—the recognition of individual European fashion designers. Since the thirteenth century, French royalty had been the fashion trendsetters for Europe. Fashions were created by anonymous tailors and dressmakers, known as the couture, whose identities were carefully guarded by their wealthy clients. The first recognized designer was Rose Bertin, dressmaker to Queen Marie Antoinette. A second early designer was Louis Hippolyte Leroy, official dressmaker to Napoleon's wives, Josephine and then Marie-Louise. The nineteenth century brought the decline of royal fashion dominance and the rise of modern couture, founded by Charles Frederick Worth. Worth, who is considered the first successful independent fashion designer, established his own business in Paris in 1860 and attracted many prominent, wealthy clients, including Empress Eugenie and her court. His success inspired others such as Paquin, Madame Cheruit, Jacques Doucet, Redfern, the Callot sisters, and Jeanne Lanvin, and by the end of the century, Paris couture was a well-established industry.

A highlight of the early-twentieth-century fashion industry was the public acceptance of ready-to-wear clothing and the recognition of individual American fashion designers. As improvements were made in textile and apparel manufacturing technology, the quality of ready-to-wear garments improved, and slowly ready-made clothing overcame its lower-class stigma. Consumers, especially women working outside the home, recognized ready-to-wear clothing as a great convenience.

Fashion has become a subject of interest in the twenty-first century for a number of reasons. The industry—manufacturing, stores, mail order, promotion—has seen enormous growth. We are in an era of mass fashion. University programs now train students for the fashion industry, and faculty in many fields engage in scholarship about the social and cultural meanings of fashion. The media have drawn a great deal of attention to fashion by reporting on various fashion events and fashionable people. Fashion history continues to engage the public with opportunities to see and read about past fashion and, for some, to wear vintage fashion.

With the rise of fashion in the mid-twentieth century, the business of fashion became a subject of study at universities and colleges. Academic programs with focus on the fashion industry provide curricula in merchandising and marketing, product development, or design. In these programs students are taught the business of fashion, as well as fashion as a social, historic, cultural, and aesthetic phenomenon. In the 1960s and 1970s, in order to train students for the growing fashion industry, many departments of clothing and textiles restructured their programs to focus on fashion merchandising and/or design.

The pervasiveness of fashion also wooed more scholars from other fields to examine its meanings. Consequently, today researchers in theater, history, sociology, psychology, English, business, consumer science, geography, women's studies, anthropology, art history, semiotics, popular culture, American studies, cultural studies, and, of course, fashion interpret its meanings. Thus, scholarship on fashion can be found in the arts and humanities, as well as the social sciences, with a wide range of topics.

Fashion has a wide reach. Consequently, symposia, conferences, and publications of professional societies in the fields just referred to frequently include studies on fashion and dress. The Costume Society of America, the Textile Society of America, and the International Textile and Apparel Association devote considerable space to the subject. The Popular Culture Association has an area, "Clothing, Appearance and the Body," with a lively exchange of ideas occurring at yearly conferences. Changes in approaches to the study of fashion have been seen in the rise of interest in material culture, in cultural studies and theory development, and in women's studies, as well as in popular culture and everyday life. Each approach offers its own interpretation of fashion.

Scholarship on fashion takes two avenues: studies that critique the meanings and functions of current fashion and historical studies that interpret meanings of past fashion. The contemporary approach examines the behavior of individuals and groups, as well as the dynamics of fashion change and consumer behavior, especially the influence and uses of advertising. These works offer theories regarding identity, meaning, or change. The new literature of cultural studies expands on the earlier work of John Flügel, Herbert Blumer, Irving Goffman, Dick Hebdige, and Roland Barthes. New studies in this category include Diana Crane's *Fashion and Its Social Agendas: Class, Gender and Identity*, Malcolm Barnard's *Fashion as Communication*, and essays in the journal *Fashion Theory: The Journal of Dress, Body & Culture*.

The rise of interest in material culture studies and a renewed interest in museum exhibitions have aided the advancement of historical scholarship on fashion. Fashion history continues to intrigue scholars, interpreters, collectors and reenactors, who interpret the past through the examination of dress, who bring to light past producers of fashion, or who reinterpret the meanings of dress in paintings. The turn of the millennium brought forth an interest in various aspects of twentieth-century dress and questions about the future of fashion. Scholars have examined the economics and cultural implications of fashion in the last century and the relationship of fashion to such topics as art, beauty, technology, movies, advertising, war, and a changing middle class.

An interest in fashion has been driven, in part, by interests of the media (television, film, magazines, and newspapers), the World Wide Web, and enduring forms of entertainment including museum exhibitions, sporting events, historical reenactments, and music venues, all of which often provide some element or link to fashion. There are increasing reports in the press about fashion and fashionable people, and the names of designers and models have become household words. Stores increasingly include an entertainment element in their design, for example, in Niketown. The fashion mall itself has become a major site for entertainment and is planned, or in some cases redesigned, with recreation and amusement in mind.

The Fashion Industry

In *The End of Fashion* Teri Agins offers insight into the giants of the American industry—Tommy Hilfiger, Ralph Lauren, and Donna Karan, among others. She notes that American mass fashion tends to look alike, but, then, American industry has always been about mass fashion. The industry did not really come into its own until after World War II, and then the emphasis was on ready-to-wear, not couture. In the beginning Americans barely recognized the names of American designers; they knew French designers only by name. All that has changed. Advertising campaigns have aided the interest in fashion; even the controversy over Calvin Klein ads increased visibility. Technology has allowed people to shop from home. They can order fashion items from television shopping channels, or, if they have a computer, they can log onto the many e-commerce sites on the World Wide Web. We cannot escape fashion. The history of the development of the American fashion industry is insightfully discussed by Caroline Rennolds Milbank in *New York Fashion*. A more specific interpretation of New York fashion is found in Sandra Buckland's " 'We Publish Fashions Because They Are News': The *New York Times* 1940 through 1945."

Collecting and Exhibiting Fashion

Major American museums, such as the Metropolitan Museum of Art, Los Angeles County Museum, the Brooklyn Museum, and Boston Museum of Fine Art and historical societies have a long history of collecting and exhibiting fashion. Fashion exhibitions are a major draw for visitors. Individuals can relate to clothing from the past, and the exhibitions often influence designers. While always entertaining, the tone of exhibitions has become more instructive, delving into the relationships of fashion to society and culture. The mission is to educate the public. Two outstanding exhibitions and catalogs that influenced how we think about fashion and that served as models for future fashion exhibitions were Claudia Kidwell and Margaret C. Christman's *Suiting Everyone* and Kidwell and Valerie Steele's *Men and Women: Dressing the Part* at the Smithsonian's Museum of American History. Other insightful exhibition catalogs include The Metropolitan Museum of Art, *Versace* (1997) by Richard Martin and *Cubism and Fashion* (1998) and *Infra-Apparel* (1993) by Richard Martin and Harold Koda; Cincinnati Museum of Art, *With Grace and Favour* (1993) by Charles Thieme; the Philadelphia Museum of Art, *Best Dressed: Fashion from the Birth of Couture to Today* (1997) by Dilys E. Blum and H. Kristina Haugland; Chicago Historical Society, *Fitting In: Four Generations of College Life* (1991) and *Becoming American Women: Clothing and the Jewish Immigrant Experience, 1880–1920* (1994) by Barbara Schreier. Examples of instructive university exhibition catalogs are the Fashion Institute of Technology's *Fashion and Surrealism* (1987) by Richard Martin, *Jocks and Nerds: Men's Style in the Twentieth Century* (1989) and *Splash: A History of Swimwear* (1990) by Richard Martin and Harold Koda; Ohio State University's *Fashioning the Future: Our Future from Our Past* (1996) by Patricia A. Cunningham and Gayle Strege; Kent State University's *Toledo/Toledo* (2000) edited by Alix Browne and Anne Bissonette for the exhibition *Isabel and Ruben Toledo: A Marriage of Art and Fashion*, and *Collection by Design: A Paper Doll History of Costume 1750–1900 from the Kent State University* (1999) by Norma Lu Meehan and Jean Druesedow for the exhibition *Posing for Paper Dolls: Fashion from 1750 to 1900* (2001).

Nostalgia plays an important role in fashion, not only in adapting historic styles of dress for contemporary fashion (which occurred with increasing acceleration in the last quarter of the twentieth century) but in the resurgence of collectors of vintage dress. For some, it is a consuming passion. The used clothing market is a thriving business, not just for collectors but for people wanting to save money, especially on children's clothing. The discovery of a couture dress for pennies is worth the effort of the hunt. Vintage dealers and collectors have come into their own in recent years. The major auction houses regularly feature vintage clothing, and a museum may even install an exhibition around a collector, as was done at the Fashion Institute of Technology by Richard Martin and Harold Koda with *Flair: Fashion Collected by Tina Chow* (1992).

Interest in preserving fashion collections has been given support through museum associations, the National Endowment of the Arts, National Endowment for the Humanities, and similar state organizations. A recent reference work on conservation is Miranda Howard Haddock's *Darning the Wear of Time: Survey and Annotated Bibliography of Periodical Literature of Costume Conservation, Restoration, and Documentation Published in English 1980–1996.*

REFERENCE WORKS

There is a vast amount of literature related to the subject of fashion. Since most libraries are now computerized, it is necessary to be precise in looking up subjects. Use the Library of Congress subject headings and follow the advice on the terminal for finding sources using specific words. The subject of fashion may be found under clothing and dress, costume, or apparel and under specific articles of dress, such as hats, shoes, or swimming suits. Many university libraries offer guides for finding subjects and provide access to many resources on the Internet, including abstracts and indexes of books and journal articles.

Basic tools for research on the subject of fashion include encyclopedias and dictionaries of fashion, textile and apparel indexes, and specialized bibliographies. Recently published works include Valerie Oliver's *Fashion and Costume in American Popular Culture: A Reference Guide* (1996), which offers both an index and bibliographic information. Source books include *20th-Century Fashion: The Complete Sourcebook* by John Peacock (1993) and *Fashion Source Book* by Amy de la Haye and Valerie Mendes (1988). Encyclopedias include *The St. James Fashion Encyclopedia: A Survey of Style from 1945 to the Present*, edited by Richard Martin; Jack Cassin-Scott's *The Illustrated Encyclopaedia of Costume and Fashion: From 1066 to the Present*; Doreen Yarwood's *The Encyclopedia of World Costume* (1986); the reprinted *Historical Encyclopedia of Costumes* by Albert Racinet; Georgina O'Hara Callan's *The Encyclopedia of Fashion* (1986); and O. E. Schoeffler and William Gale's *Esquire's Encyclopedia of 20th Century Men's Fashions. The American Fabrics Encyclopedia of Textiles* also continues to serve as a useful guide regarding textiles. For understanding the language of fashion, recent additions to fashion dictionaries include *Costume Language: A Dictionary of Dress Terms* (1994) by Stephanie Davies; Charlotte Calasibetta's *Fairchild's Dictionary of Fashion* (1998); and Ruben Toledo's *Style Dictionary* (1996). Mary Brooks Picken's *A Dictionary of Costume and Fashion* was again reprinted in 1999. For menswear, see *A Dictionary of Men's Wear* by William Baker. Older terms would be found in George Linton's *The Modern Textile and Apparel Dictionary*, which offers a section on "Fashion and Style," and R. Turner Wilcox's *The Dictionary of Costume*. A more specific guide to eighteenth-century dress is Suzanne Gousse's *Costume in New France from 1740 to 1760: A Visual Dictionary* (1999).

Sources for designers include *The Fashion Guide* (1989–1994); *Who's Who in Fashion* (1996) by Anne Stegemeyer; *McDowell's Directory of Twentieth-Century Fashion* (1985) by Colin McDowell; the useful, but somewhat dated, *World of Fashion: People, Places, Resources* (1976) by Eleanor Lambert; *Contemporary Fashion* (1995), edited by Richard Martin; *The Thames and Hudson Dictionary of Fashion and*

Fashion Designers (1998) by Georgina O'Hara Callan; *Dictionnaire de la Mode au XXe Siècle* (1996) by Bruno De Remaury; and *Die Modedesigner. Ein Lexikon von Armani bis Yamamoto* (1998) by Ingrid Loschek. Other useful guides are *Icons of Fashion: The 20th Century*, edited by Gerda Buxbaum, and *The Fashion Book* (1998).

While Internet sources allow researchers to compile lists of recent publications, these Web sources often do not include earlier books and articles critical of fashion history. It is necessary, therefore, to consult reference works in print. Standard bibliographies for fashion are the recently reprinted (1991) *Bibliographie générale du costume et de la mode* by René Colas and *Katalog der Lipperheideschen Kostümbibliothek*. The Costume Society of America's *Bibliography* 1974–1983 lists works published during the late twentieth century. Two English publications, *The Selected Bibliography of Clothing Sources* and *Costume: A General Bibliography* by Pegaret Anthony and Janet Arnold, offer a broader scope of books and articles on fashion. Geitel Winakor's *Economics of Textiles and Clothing: A Bibliography* would also provide sources for the historian. Hilaire Hiler and Meyer Hiler's *Bibliography of Costume: A Dictionary Catalog of About Eight Thousand Books and Periodicals* also remains a useful guide for the historian.

Many indexes provide references to articles, books, and illustrations of fashion. Most indexes have a Web site, and recent studies can be accessed through these. The Costume Society of America Web site (CostumeSocietyAmerica.com) lists current books, as well as articles published in *Dress*. *The Clothing Index: An Index to Periodical Literature, January 1970–December 1979*, edited by Sandra S. Hutton, surveys fifteen other indexes and abstracts plus twenty-one journals. A second *Clothing Index* includes sources for 1980–1984; the *Clothing Index* continues as a CD-ROM to 1995. Standard index sources for fashion are *America: History and Life*, *Arts Index*, *Business Periodicals Index*, *Industrial Arts Index* (now *Applied Science & Technology Index*), *Artbibliographies Modern*, *Bibliography of the History of Art* (formerly, *RILA*), *International Bibliography of Periodical Literature*, *Reader's Guide to Periodical Literature*, *Social Sciences Index*, *Arts and Humanities Citation Index*, *Historical Abstracts*, *Humanities Index*, and *New York Times Index*. Again, many of these are available on the World Wide Web.

Assessing Artifacts: Collections and Museums

Access to fashion artifacts (clothing, accessories, and textiles) is especially important for scholars interested in a material culture approach. Most museums allow researchers access to garments. It is, however, necessary for the researcher to contact a museum or collection in advance to make an appointment to examine artifacts. Guidance to museum collections is available in a number of publications. Consult the *Costume Society of America 2002 Membership Directory* and *Textile, Costume, and Doll Collections in the United States and Canada* by Pieter Bach. Eleanor Lambert's *World of Fashion* contains listings for European and American costume collections. Cecil Lubbell's *Textile Collections of the World*, vol. 1, has references to collections in the United States and Canada, vol. 2 for the United Kingdom and Ireland, and vol. 3 for France. The *International Directory of Historical Clothing* by Irene Huenefeld lists collections in the United States, Canada, and Europe.

Many museums with fashion collections also have useful libraries and archival materials as well. While not a general rule, many art museums collect couture or

Factory worker at sewing machine. Courtesy of the Library of Congress

high-fashion garments and ethnic dress, while historical societies collect fashion that reflects their cities or region. University collections often collect artifacts that reveal the changing fashion styles over a long period of time. Pattern archives are increasingly important. The Betty Williams pattern collection is housed at the Fashion Institute of Technology. The Kevin Seligman Collection is archived at Los Angeles County Museum. Joy Emery has developed a computer list of all known patterns at the University of Rhode Island.

HISTORY AND CRITICISM

The Business of Fashion: Merchandising, Visual Display, Marketing, Designers

Trade publications are aimed at insiders in the fashion industry: manufacturers, retail buyers, wholesalers, store managers, and so on. They incorporate news of the industry, trends, market research, and classified ads and advertisements. Two major newspapers are *Women's Wear Daily* and *Daily News Record*. Various segments of the industry have their own publications; these include *Textile World*, *Accessories*, *Advertising Age*, *Footwear News*, *Hosiery News*, *Stores*, and *Visual Merchandising and Store Design*.

Works that would help in understanding various aspects of the fashion industry include *The Fashion Business: Theory, Practice, Image* (2000), edited by Nicola White and Ian Griffiths; Jay and Ellen Diamond's *The World of Fashion* (1997); Leslie

Burns and Nancy Bryant's *The Business of Fashion: Designing, Manufacturing, and Marketing* (1997); Elaine Stone's *Fashion Merchandising* (1991); Mary Francis Drake's *Retail Fashion Promotion and Advertising* (1992); Jo Dingeman's *Mastering Fashion Styling* (1999); and Evelyn Brannon's *Fashion Forecasting*; *The Weir/Wolfe Report* likewise would give insight into the forecasting process. Politicized issues related to labor and manufacturing are considered in *Social Responsibility in the Global Market: Fair Trade of Cultural Products* (1999) by Mary Littrell and Marsha Dickson. Other texts offering insight into problems or concerns of the fashion industry include Sara Gay Forden's *The House of Gucci: A Sensational Story of Murder, Madness, Glamour, and Greed* (2000) and Colin McDowell's *The Designer Scam* (1994). Designers themselves offer advice and their own views on the world of fashion. Examples are Michaele Vollbrach, *Nothing Sacred: Cartoons and Comments* (2000) and Tommy Hilfiger and Daniel Keeps, *All American: A Style Book* (1997).

Histories of the fashion industry and the involvement of women are Susan Benson's *Counter Cultures* (1986), *The Politics of Women's Work: The Paris Garment Trades, 1750–1915* by Judith G. Coffin (1996), Jeanne Boydston's *Home and Work: Housework, Wages and the Ideology of Labor in the Early Republic* (1990), *Dress, Culture and Commerce* by Beverly Lemire (1997), and Nicola White, *Reconstructing Italian Fashion: America and the Development of the Italian Fashion Industry* (2000).

The artful display of fashion in stores and illustrations and photographs in magazines are a necessary and sometimes entertaining aspect of marketing. Simon Doonan tells the story of the development of the art in *Confessions of a Window Dresser: Tales from a Life in Fashion* (1998). Practical advice appears in Mary Portas' *Windows: The Art of Retail Display* (1999). In *The Art of Selling: A History of Visual Merchandising*, an Ohio State University exhibition and catalog, Gayle Strege explores the relationship of window dressing, culture, and art. Interest in the history of fashion illustration and photography is seen in the many reprints of illustrators' work, such as Paul Erté, *Erté's Fashion Designs: 210 Illustrations from Harper's Bazaar, 1918–1932* (1981); Julian Robinson, *The Golden Age of Style* (art deco) (1976); Joanne Olian, *Authentic French Fashions of the Twenties: 413 Costume Designs from L'Art et La Mode* (1990); and Carol Belanger Grafton, *Fashions of the Thirties: 476 Authentic Copyright-free Illustrations* (1993). More recent is *Gordon Conway: Fashioning a New Woman* (1997) by Raye Virginia Allen, and the catalog of the exhibition *Reality and Interpretation: 20th Century Clothing and Illustration: Riffe Gallery [Columbus, OH], April 26–July 9, 2000*, as well as Antonio Lopez's *Antonio: 60, 70, 80: Three Decades of Fashion Illustration* (1995). Laird Borrelli's *Stylishly Drawn: Contemporary Fashion Illustration* (2000) offers a current view of the subject.

An understanding of fashion photography can enlighten opinions about fashion. *Lisa Fonssagrives: Three Decades of Classic Fashion Photography* (1996), edited by David Seidner, celebrates that model's successes. A historic view is provided by Elizabeth Owen in *Fashion in Photographs, 1920–1940*, Katrina Rolley's *Fashion in Photographs, 1900–1920*, and, for a more recent view, Paul Jobling's *Fashion Spreads: Word and Image in Fashion Photography since 1980*. *Melvin Sokolsky: Seeing Fashion* by the photographer provides a personal view, while contemporary works *Fashion in Motion* by Esther Haase, *Fashion Images De Mode 4*, edited by Lisa Lovatt-Smith, and *Runway* by photographer Larry Fink are instructional and entertaining.

Books about fashion designers (not autobiographies) range from encyclopedic, comprehensive biographies to coffee-table picture books. More inclusive studies include Caroline Rennolds Milbank's *Couture, the Great Designers* and *New York Fashion*; Valerie Steele's *Women of Fashion*; and Diana DeMarly's *The History of Haute Couture* (1980). Others include Maria Costantino's *Designers* and the *Height of Fashion*, edited by Lisa Eisner and Roman Alonso. Numerous books that accompany fashion exhibitions, like Richard Martin and Harold Koda's *Haute Couture*, and *Christian Dior* for the Metropolitan Museum of Art, likewise offer comprehensive and instructive views. While there are almost too many to mention, recent ones include *Giorgio Armani* by Germano Celant and Harold Koda, Solomon R. Guggenheim Museum, and *Best Dressed: Fashion from the Birth of Couture to Today* by Dilys Blum and H. Kristina Haugland, Philadelphia Museum of Art.

Interest in earlier twentieth-century designers is apparent with the publication of studies like Betty Kirke's *Madeleine Vionnet*; Guillermo de Osma's *Fortuny: Mariano Fortuny; His Life and Work*; *Claire McCardell: Redefining Modernism* by Kohle Yohannan and Nancy Wolfe; *Elsa Schiaparelli* by François Baudot; *Charles James* by Richard Martin; *Balenciaga* by Marie-Andree Jouve; and *Chanel* by Francois Baudot. There are several books on Dior, besides Richard Martin's *Christian Dior*. They are Nigel Cawthorne's *The New Look: The Dior Revolution* and Marie France Pochna's *Christian Dior: The Man Who Made the World Look New*. Books about more recent American designers include *Halston: An American Original* by Elaine Gross and Fied Rottman and *The Rudi Gernreich Book* by Peggy Moffitt.

As contemporary designers take on celebrity status and to secure their place in fashion history, books about them and by them have proliferated. Recent works on designers, some of whom are deserving of a retrospective view, include *Ruben Toledo, Isabel Toledo* by Ruben Toledo; *Ralph Lauren: The Man behind the Mystique* by Jeffrey A. Trachtenberg; *Obsession: The Lives and Times of Calvin Klein* by Steven S. Gaines; *Todd Oldham: Without Boundaries* by Todd Oldham; *Issey Miyake & Miyake Design Studio* by Issey Miyake; *In My Own Fashion: An Autobiography* by Oleg Cassini; *Pucci: A Renaissance in Fashion* by Shirley Kennedy; *Christian Lacroix* by Francois Baudot; *Diane: A Signature Life* by Diane Von Furstenburg and Linda Bird Franke; *Valentino* and *Scassi* by Bernadine Morris; and *Yves Saint Laurent* by Yves Saint Laurent.

History

Scholars continue to investigate past fashions. Indeed, historical scholarship on fashion saw a steady increase in the late twentieth century. Texts include new general histories of dress, many books on the twentieth century, guides to fashion in various decades, and insightful studies of specific types of clothing such as dress reform garments, lingerie, accessories, and swim wear. Scholars have examined the role of women in design and manufacturing and their part in the development of the department store. Although the subject is far removed from twenty-first-century fashion, two of the most important books written regarding fabric and clothing are Elizabeth Barber's *Women's Work: The First 20,000 Years: Women, Cloth, and Society in Early Times* and *Prehistoric Textiles: The Development of Cloth in the Neolithic and Bronze Ages*. Barber's explorations provide a model for research on women's history, especially regarding their roles in the business of "making fashion."

There are several popular general costume history textbooks: Phyllis Tortora and Keith Eubank's *Survey of Historic Costume*; Blanche Payne, Geitel Winakor, and Jane Farrell-Beck's *History of Costume, From Ancient Mesopotamia through the Twentieth Century*; and Douglas Russell's *Costume History and Style*. Although not a textbook, university professors often assign *20,000 Years of Fashion: The History of Costume and Personal Adornment* by Francois Boucher. Classics in the field are Millia Davenport's *The Book of Costume* and James Laver's *Costume and Fashion: A Concise History*, John Peacock's *The Chronicle of Western Costume: Complete in Colour with More than 1000 Illustrations from the Ancient World to the Late Twentieth Century* (1991), Karen Baclawski's *The Guide to Historic Costume* (1995), Joan Nunn's *Fashion in Costume, 1200–2000* (2000), and Margaret Knight's *Fashion through the Ages* (1998) (juvenile literature).

A new approach to history is offered by Elizabeth Wilson in *Adorned in Dreams: Fashion and Modernity*, Christopher Breward in *The Culture of Fashion: A New History of Fashionable Dress*, and a 2000 imprint, Ulrich Lehmann's *Tigersprung: Fashion in Modernity*. A recent brief overview is offered by Anna Buruma with *Fashions of the Past* (1999). Lynn Schnurnberger's *Let There Be Clothes: 40,000 Years of Fashion* (1991) offers a unique historical view. Texts that cover several decades of Western dress are Elizabeth Wilson and Lou Taylor, *Through the Looking Glass: A History of Dress from 1860 to the Present Day* (1989), and Natalie Rothstein, *Four Hundred Years of Fashion* (1997). Brief surveys include Andrew Tucker's *Fashion: A Crash Course* and Gertrud Lehnert's *Fashion* (1999).

Many studies reexamine the past to provide a fresh assessment, others raise questions about the relationship of fashion to art, music, or film, and still others raise gender issues or take a philosophical stance. Interest in beauty culture is examined in Kate De Castelbajac's *The Face of the Century: 100 Years of Makeup and Style* (1995), Kate Mulvey's *Decades of Beauty* (1998), Joseph Hansen and Evelyn Reed's *Cosmetics, Fashions, and the Exploitations of Women* (1986), and Kathy Peiss' *Hope in a Jar*. While not strictly a book about fashion, Cynthia Kierner's *Beyond the Household: Women's Place in the Early South, 1700–1835* (1998) considers fashion and women's role.

Costume historians rely largely on paintings, sculpture, and other art forms as well as actual garments to accurately illustrate clothing worn before the age of photography. Yet, the reliability of this method remains in question. An insightful solution to some of the problems regarding interpretations of dress in paintings appears in Claudia Kidwell's "Are Those Clothes Real?: Transforming the Way Eighteenth-Century Portraits Are Studied" (*Dress* 1997). Kidwell was responding to the publication *John Singleton Copley in America* by Carrie Rebora et al., in which contributors offer conflicting accounts of fashion. Anne Hollander's *Seeing through Clothes* provides insights into fashion and art. Many costume history books of necessity examine fashion history through art. Recent studies include Jane Ashelford, *The Art of Dress: Clothes and Society, 1500–1914* (1996), and Aileen Ribeiro's *The Art of Dress: Fashion in England and France 1750–1820* (1995).

Extant garments also can be problematic because alteration of clothing was such a common practice. Sources that discuss the make or cut of actual garments are rare. Good examples for the cut of fashionable eighteenth-century American and European dress are Linda Baumgarten, John Watson, and Florine Carr, *Costume Close Up: Clothing Construction and Pattern, 1750–1790* (2000); Meredith Wright

Godey's Lady's Book, 1875. Courtesy of the Library of Congress

and Nancy Rexford, *Everyday Dress of Rural America 1783–1800: With Instructions and Patterns* (1992); Avril Hart, Susan North, and Richard Davis, *Fashion in Detail: From the 17th and 18th Centuries* (1998); and Sharon Ann Burnston, *Fitting & Proper* (1998). Janet Arnold's books are highly valued classics for accurate period patterns.

Books on nineteenth-century fashion that draw on photographs rather than paintings include Alison Gernsheim, *Victorian and Edwardian Fashion: A Photographic Survey*, and Joan Severa's award-winning *Dressed for the Photographer: Ordinary Americans and Fashion, 1840–1900* (1997). Two books that focus on nineteenth-century women's lives are Cynthia Cooper's *Magnificent Entertainments: Fancy Dress Balls of Canada's Governors General 1876–1898* (1997) and Nancy Isenberg's *Sex and Citizenship in Antebellum America* (1998). Mary Blanchard's *Oscar Wilde's America* offers a critical view of the counterculture in the Gilded Age.

General twentieth-century texts include Valerie Mendes and Amy de la Haye's *20th Century Fashion* (1999); Kate Mulvey and Melissa Richards, *Decades of Beauty: The Changing Image of Women, 1890s–1990s*; Francois Baudot, *Fashion, the Twentieth Century* (1999); John Peacock's *20th-Century Fashion: The Complete Sourcebook* (1993); David Bond's *The Guinness Guide to 20th Century Fashion* (1988); Prudence Glynn's *In Fashion: Dress in the Twentieth Century* (1978); Gerda Buxbaum, *Icons of Fashion: The 20th Century* (1999); Elizabeth Ewing, *History of Twentieth Century*

Fashion (1992); Jane Mulvagh, *Vogue History of 20th Century Fashion* (1988); Linda Watson, *Vogue: Twentieth Century Fashion* (1999); Anne Tyrrell's *Changing Trends in Fashion: Patterns of the Twentieth Century, 1900–1970* (1986); and Maggie P. Murray, *Changing Styles in Fashion* (1989).

A number of scholars offer interpretive views of twentieth-century fashion during a decade: John Peacock, *The 1920s* (1997); Ruth Countryman and Elizabeth Weiss Hopper, *Women's Wear of the 1920's: With Complete Patterns* (1998); Jacqueline Herald, *Fashions of a Decade: The 1920s*; Maria Costantino, *Fashions of a Decade: The 1930s*; Julian Robinson, *Fashion in the 40's* (1980); John Peacock, *The 1940s* (1998); Colin McDowell, *Forties Fashion and the New Look* (1997); Lauren Welker, *Fabulous '50s Fashions* (1984); Joel Lobenthal, *Radical Rags: Fashion of the Sixties* (1990); Barbara Bernard's earlier *Fashion in the 60's* (1978); Kennedy Fraser, *The Fashionable Mind: Reflections on Fashion, 1970–1983* (1985); *Fashions of a Decade: The 1970s* by Jacqueline Herald; Vicky Carnegy's *Fashions of a Decade: The 1980s*; and Colin McDowell, *Fashion Today* (2000).

Twentieth-century books that consider more than one decade are Jean Darnell, *Victorian to Vamp: Women's Clothing 1900–1929* (2000); Deirdre Clancy, *Costume since 1945: Couture, Street Style, and Anti-Fashion* (1996); and Valerie Steele's *Fifty Years of Fashion: New Look to Now* (1997).

The future of fashion is constantly being reassessed. The turn of the millennium saw a number of new publications, as have the turn of decades and the year 1984. Examples include Trudy Schlachter, *Millennium Mode: Fashion Forecasts from 40 Top Designers* (1999); Lucille Khornak, *Fashion 2001* (1982); Stephen Gan and Alix Browne, *Visionaire's Fashion 2001: Designers of the New Avant-Garde* (1999); and Stephen Gan, *Visionaire's Fashion 2000: Designers at the Turn of the Millennium* (1997). See also Gwendolyn O'Neal's "Fashioning Future Fashion" in *Fashioning the Future: Our Future from Our Past.*

The changing styles of underwear and the use of underwear as fashionable outerwear continue to attract scholars. Nora Waugh's *Corsets and Crinolines* (1981) is a classic. Newer texts are Beatrice Fontanel, *Support and Seduction: A History of Corsets and Bras* (1997); Gilles Neret, *1000 Dessous: A History of Lingerie* (1998); Farid Chenoune, *Beneath It All: A Century of French Lingerie* (2000); and Karoline Newman, Gillian Proctor and Karen Bressler, *A Century of Lingerie* (1998).

The literature of hats, shoes, gloves, purses, and more instructs us on the formalities of the past. *Women's Shoes in America, 1795–1930* (2000) by Nancy Rexford sets a scholarly standard. A number of new pictorial works offer archival images: Judy Johnson's *French Fashion Plates of the Romantic Era in Full Color* (1991) and Carol B. Grafton's two studies, *Shoes, Hats and Fashion Accessories: A Pictorial Archive 1850–1940: 2,020 Illustrations* (1998) and *Victorian Fashions: A Pictorial Archive* (1999). Two general works for the twentieth century are John Peacock, *Fashion Accessories: The Complete 20th Century Sourcebook* (2000), and Joanne Ball, *The Art of Fashion Accessories: A Twentieth Century Retrospective* (1993). *Shoes: A Celebration of Pumps, Sandals, Slippers, & More* by Linda O'Keefe (1996) was a bestseller. *Bags: A Lexicon of Style* by Valerie Steele and Laird Borrelli (1999) accompanied an exhibition at the Fashion Institute of Technology, as did Steele's *Shoes, a Lexicon of Style* (1999).

In the 1990s a number of books appeared about men's fashion: John Harvey's *Men in Black* (1995); Farid Chenoune, *A History of Men's Fashion* (1993); Christopher Breward, *The Hidden Consumer: Masculinities, Fashion and City Life, 1860–1914* (1999); Colin McDowell, *The Man of Fashion: Peacock Males and Perfect Gentlemen* (1997); Anne Hollander, *Sex and Suits* (1995); Lloyd Boston, *Men of Color: Fashion, History, Fundamentals* (1998); and Maria Costantino, *Men's Fashion in the Twentieth Century: From Frock Coats to Intelligent Fibres* (1997).

The vintage market continues to appeal to many consumers. Useful books include Tiffany Dubin and Ann Berman, *Vintage Style: Buying and Wearing Classic Vintage Clothes* (2000); Tracy Tolkein, *Dressing Up Vintage* (2000); Frances Grimble and Deborah Kuhn, *After a Fashion: How to Reproduce, Restore, and Wear Vintage Styles* (1998); Diane McGee, *A Passion for Fashion: Antique, Collectible, and Retro Clothes* (1987); and Cynthia Giles, *The Official Identification and Price Guide to Vintage Clothing* (1989).

Many current books and exhibition catalogs offer critiques based on specific fashion styles, textiles, influences, or regions. These include Linda Arthur, *Aloha Attire: Hawaiian Dress in the Twentieth Century* (1999); Amy Edelman, *The Little Black Dress* (1997); Susannah Handley, *Nylon: The Story of a Fashion Revolution* (1999); Nigel Cawthorne, *Key Moments in Fashion* (1998); *Making Waves: Swimsuits and the Undressing of America* (1989) by Lena Lencek and Gideon Bosker; Valerie Mendes, *Dressed in Black* (2000); Richard Martin, *Khaki: Cut from the Original Cloth* (1999); Amy de la Haye and Cathie Dingwall, *Surfers, Soulies, Skinheads & Skaters: Subcultural Style from the Forties to the Nineties* (1996); and Ted Polhemus, *Diesel: World Wide Wear* (1998) and *Streetstyle* (1994).

The question, Is fashion art? continues to inspire exhibitions and authors. New studies include *Art/fashion*, an exhibition catalog (1996) that offers a twentieth-century perspective; *Addressing the Century: 100 Years of Art & Fashion* (1998); and *Art and Fashion* by Florence Muller (2000).

Media focus on Hollywood stars, rock stars, and highly placed public figures in many respects canonized them as fashion icons. A number of books explore the relationship of the fashion world to Hollywood. Marsha Hunt provides a first-person account of her fashion experience in *The Way We Wore: Styles of the 1930s and '40s and Our World since Then* (1993). Other interpretations are offered by Patty Fox, *Star Style: Hollywood Legends as Fashion Icons* (1999), and Sarah Berry, *Screen Style: Fashion and Femininity in 1930s Hollywood* (2000). More critical views appear in *Fabrications: Costume and the Female Body*, edited by Jane Gaines and Charlotte Herzog (1990), and *Undressing Cinema: Clothing and Identity in the Movies*, in which Stella Bruzzi examines the propensity of movies to depend on clothing for discourse in films. Additional studies are an anthology, *Zoot Suits and Second-Hand Dresses* (1988), edited by Angela McRobbie, which contains an eclectic mix of writings on music style and fashion, and *Rock Style: How Fashion Moves to Music* (1999) by Tommy Hilfiger and Anthony Decurtis, which accompanied an exhibition of the same name at the Metropolitan Museum of Art. The influence of punk style and music is explored in Vivienne Westwood's biography, *Vivienne Westwood: An Unfashionable Life* by Jane Mulvagh (1999).

Some highly visible public figures have become true icons of fashion. Books written about these women are Kathleen Craughwell-Varda, *Looking for Jackie: American Fashion Icons* (1999); Oleg Cassini, *A Thousand Days of Magic: Dressing Jackie Kennedy for the White House* (1995); Davina Hanmer, *Diana, the Fashion*

Princess (1984); and Jayne Fincher, *Debrett's Illustrated Fashion Guide—The Princess of Wales* (1989).

Theory and Criticism: Culture, Sex, the Body, and Identity

Fashion criticism has become an area of study capturing the attention of many fashion historians, textile and clothing academics, and cultural critics. The bibliographical list is endless and continues to grow and develop on a daily basis. Researchers and practitioners of various disciplines and occupations have become "fashion authorities" detailing their knowledge about the culture of fashion. During the last decade, an influx of fashion research focused on postmodernism, *new* culture, sex, and the body. Fashion history is no longer just clothing and the *rag* industry but is also an extension of individuality, multiculturalism, consumerism, and sexuality. Fashion is examined for its contextual and inherent meaning. For an understanding of fashion and meaning, Alison Lurie's *The Language of Clothes*, Ruth Rubinstein's *Dress Codes: Meanings and Messages in American Culture*, and George Sproles and Leslie Davis Burns, *Changing Appearances: Understanding Dress in Contemporary Society*, present the processes in the social context. Fashion is given multi-interpreted meaning based upon personal experiences and the interpretations of researchers. One only has to peruse issues of *Fashion Theory: The Journal of Dress, Body & Culture* to see the various interpretations of the words "fashion," "style," and "dress." This journal presents fashion in a cultural critical context allowing for a postmodern presentation and interpretation of the word "fashion."

Fashion cultural criticism takes some of its theoretical foundations from history, psychology, sociology, and philosophy. To understand the terminology associated with cultural criticism, *The Columbia Dictionary of Modern Literary and Cultural Criticism* is an excellent guide. Because cultural criticism challenges our current social understandings of what we know as truth, researchers must have a basic understanding of current Western European ideals. For those intrigued by fashion and cultural criticism, it is necessary to start with the theoretical foundations and current issues in the clothing and textiles discipline. For a basic notion of the psychological and sociological aspects of fashion, Michael Solomon's *The Psychology of Fashion*; Juliet Ash and Elizabeth Wilson's *Chic Thrills: A Fashion Reader*; and Susan Kaiser's *The Social Psychology of Clothing: Symbolic Appearances in Context* are places to begin. Each of these works gives basic theoretical foundations for tying dress and fashion to psychological and sociological theories. New interpretations and theories about fashion and culture appear in Roland Barthes' *The Fashion System*; Gilles Lipovetsky's *The Empire of Fashion*; and Alison Gills' "Deconstruction Fashion: The Making of Unfinished, Decomposing and Reassembled Clothes." Many researchers take the postmodern approach to their writings on fashion and cultural criticism. For an introduction to postmodern theories on fashion, first consult Mike Featherstone's *Consumer Culture and Postmodernism* and Marcia Morgado's "Coming to Terms with Postmodern: Theories and Concepts of Contemporary Culture and Their Implications for Apparel Scholars" for a basic understanding of the concept.

Prior to the 1970s, culture, gender, sex, identity, and the body were not discussed as explicitly as they are today. Now, an entire book series by Berg is dedicated to these topics. Berg's titles include Helen Bradley Foster's *"New Raiments of Self": African American Clothing in the Antebellum South*; Claudine Griggs' *S/he: Changing Sex and Changing Clothes*; Michaele Thurgood Haynes' *Dressing Up Debutantes: Pageantry and Glitz in Texas*; Anne Brydon and Sandra Niessen's *Consuming Fashion: Adorning the Transnational Body*; Dani Cavallaro and Alexandra Warwick's *Fashioning the Frame: Boundaries, Dress and the Body*; Judith M. Perani and Norma H. Wolff's *Cloth, Dress, and Art Patronage in Africa*; Linda Boynton Arthur's *Religion, Dress and the Body*; Fadwa El-Guindi's *Veil: Modesty, Privacy and Resistance*; Thomas S. Abler's *Hinterland Warriors and Military Dress: European Empires and Exotic Uniforms*; Linda Welters' *Folk Dress in Europe and Anatolia: Beliefs about Protection and Fertility*; Kim K. P. Johnson and Sharron J. Lennon's *Appearance and Power*; Barbara Burman's *The Culture of Sewing*; Annette Lynch's *Dress, Gender and Cultural Change*; Antonia Young's *Women Who Become Men*; and Paul Jobling's *Fashion Spreads*.

In *Fashion Spreads*, Jobling forces us to look at the evolution of sex and gender through the eyes of fashion advertising. He investigates how fashion photography used in ads has changed during the 1980s to the present. His postmodern historical perspective reintroduces how specific issues (in his book, fashion advertising) are neglected. Others who examine current changes in fashion advertising and marketing are Teri Agins in *The End of Fashion*, Matthew Debord in "Texture and Taboo: The Tyranny of Texture and Ease in the J. Crew Catalog," and Katherine Wallerstein in "Thinness and Other Refusals in Contemporary Fashion Advertisements."

Women's issues concerning gender and fashion changed during the 1990s. Efrat Tseelon's book *The Masque of Femininity* explores the construction of femininity in relation to clothing. Other publications that critique the relationship of women to beauty and fashion include Alison Guy, Eileen Green, and Maura Banim's *Through the Wardrobe*, Kate Ince's *Orlan*, and Joanne Entwistle's *Dress, Bodies and Business: Fashioning Women at Work*.

During the 1990s, men's fashion was recognized as a valuable topic, not only for fashion historians but also for cultural critics. Works such as Christopher Breward's *The Culture of Fashion* and *The Hidden Consumer: Masculinities, Fashion and City Life 1860–1914*, John Harvey's *Men in Black*, Anne Hollander's *Sex and Suits*, Sean Nixon's *Hard Looks*, Colin McDowell's *The Man of Fashion*, Richard Martin and Harold Koda's *Jocks and Nerds*, Farid Chenoune's *A History of Men's Fashion*, Lloyd Boston's *Men of Color*, and David Mussleton's *Inside Subculture* allowed readers to see men playing a contributing role in fashion change and consumption. These books verify that there has always been men's fashion. Men are and have been active participants in the history of consuming and adorning new styles of fashionable clothing. While some of these publications focus strictly on Western European ideals of fashion history, like McDowell's *The Man of Fashion*, others address thought-provoking issues concerning ethnicity and fashion style (Boston's *Men of Color*).

Ethnicity has become another key topic for cultural studies. Fashion research focusing on ethnicity has revealed that many previous textiles and clothing studies take an ethnocentric perspective. Not all Americans accept the aesthetic prescribed by mass fashion. Gwendolyn O'Neal in "African-American Aesthetic of Dress:

Current Manifestations" and Carol Tulloch in her book *The Birth of Cool: Dress Culture of the African Diaspora* reveal the uniqueness of African American fashion.

Fashion researchers are also addressing historically risqué concepts and misunderstood stereotyped subcultural groups, which were once perceived as unethical, "not normal," or taboo. In *Vested Interests: Cross-Dressing & Cultural Anxiety*, Marjorie Garbor discusses the notions of fetish fashion with regard to the male-to-female cross-dresser. More recently, works by Gayle Fischer, Claudine Griggs, and Antonia Young examine issues concerning the female-to-male cross-dresser, as well as transgendered subjectivities. Another publication by Valerie Steele called *Fetish: Fashion, Sex & Power* gazes into the world of black leather, fetish corsets, and sadomasochism. All of these academicians examined marginalized, but important, groups from both personal and outside perspectives, relating the importance of fashion for social identification within specific cultural boundaries.

Homosexuals are another group that has been identified as important for fashion cultural studies. While some past researchers have "dabbled" in fashion and homosexuality, recent publications are more serious and comprehensive. Shaun Cole's book *"Don We Now Our Gay Apparel": Gay Men's Dress in the Twentieth Century* has been instrumental in revealing how gay men's fashion has influenced mainstream dress. An earlier publication edited by Daniel Wardlow, *Gays, Lesbians, and Consumer Behavior: Theory, Practice and Research Issues in Marketing*, examines consumer culture and homosexuals.

Anthologies and Reprints

A number of instructive anthologies related to fashion theory and history have been published since the late 1980s. *Dress and Popular Culture* (1991) and *Dress in American Culture* (1993), edited by Patricia Cunningham and Susan Voso Lab, offer insights into meanings of everyday dress worn in America. *Defining Dress: Dress as Object, Meaning, and Identity* (1999), edited by Amy de la Haye and Elizabeth Wilson, appears in the series Studies in Material Culture (Britain). All aspects of the business of fashion are included in *The Style Engine: Spectacle, Identity, Design, and Business: How the Fashion Industry Uses Style to Create Wealth*, edited by Giannino Malossi (1998). The Berg series of books includes several anthologies. Examples related to fashion include Ruth Barnes and Joanne Eicher's *Dress and Gender: Making and Meaning*; Joanne Eicher, *Dress and Ethnicity: Change across Space and Time*; and Anne Brydon and Sandra Niessen's *Consuming Fashion: Adorning the Transnational Body*.

R. L. Shep's reprints reveal the long-standing interest in men's fashion and in guides to early etiquette. See *Federalist & Regency Costume, 1790–1819, Regency Etiquette: The Mirror of Graces (1811), Late Victorian Costume (1820s), Late Victorian Women's Tailoring (1890s), The Great War: Styles and Patterns from the 1910s*, and *Shirts and Men's Haberdashery, 1840s–1920s*. A renewed interest in fashion saw reprints of Alison Lurie, *Language of Clothes* (2000), and Anne Hollander's *Seeing through Clothes* (1993). Dover Publications has reprinted many early fashion books, including Douglas Gorsline's *What People Wore: 1,800 Illustrations from Ancient Times to the Early Twentieth Century America* (1994), George Lepape's *French Fashion Plates in Full Color from the Gazette du Bon Ton* (1979), Kristina Harris' *The Home Pattern Company 1914 Fashions Catalog* (1995), Stella Blum's *Victorian Fash-*

ions and Costumes from Harper's Bazaar, 1867–1890 (1975), Florence Leniston and Joanne Olian's *Le Mode Illustree: Fashion Plates in Full Color* (1997), *Jordan Marsh Illustrated Catalog of 1891* (1991), Stella Blum's *Fashions and Costumes from Godey's Lady's Book* (1985), Braun and Schneider's *Historic Costume in Pictures* (1975), Priscilla Harris Dalrymple's *American Victorian Costume in Early Photographs* (1991), Herbert Norris' *Medieval Costume and Fashion* (1999), Houston's *Medieval Costume in England and France: the 13th, 14th and 15th Centuries* (1996), and Norris' *Tudor Costume and Fashion* (1997).

Theatre Arts Books likewise includes fashion in its reprint series, many on the cut of clothing and costuming for the theater such as *The Cut of Women's Clothes, 1600–1930* by Norah Waugh. In 1999 Drama Publishers reprinted Bonnie Ambrose's *The Little Corset Book: A Workbook on Period Underwear.*

Researching Fashion: Sources and Journals

In addition to the books listed here, research on fashion history draws on a variety of primary and secondary sources. These might include written information found in public records, census records, diaries, letters, and account books, as well as fashion advertisements and text in magazines and store catalogs. Novels often reveal period opinions and biases. Visual images and illustrations are found in these sources and in paintings and professional photographic archives and family scrapbooks. Lists of early American magazines may be found in Mott's *A History of American Magazines.* Frequently used magazines include *Godey's Lady's Book, Peterson's Magazine*, *Harper's Bazaar*, *Vogue*, and *Burton's Gentleman's Magazine.* Depending on the research question, mail-order catalogs from Sears and Roebuck, Montgomery Ward, and L.L. Bean are valuable sources. Other sources are maps, patents, and insurance records. See the section on Museums and Collections regarding access to extant garments. For insight into a material culture approach to research on fashion, see Thomas Schlereth, *Material Culture Studies in America* (1982), especially Fleming's essay on method. See also Kenneth Ames et al., *Material Culture: A Research Guide* (1985).

Scholarly journals that publish articles on various aspects of the fashion industry, design, and fashion history are *Dress*, the journal of the Costume Society of America; the *Clothing and Textiles Research Journal*, published by the International Textile and Apparel Association; *Family and Consumer Science Research Journal*, formerly *HERJ*; *Costume Research Journal* (*CRJ*) (formerly *Cutter's Research Journal*); *Costume Arts Digest*; *Ars Textrina*; and on-line, *Journal of Textile and Apparel Technology and Management.* Three English journals, *Costume*, *Journal of Design History*, and *Textile History*, likewise publish articles on fashion. In addition, articles on fashion also occasionally appear in the *Journal of Popular Culture*, *Journal of American Culture*, *Journal of American Studies*, *American History Review*, *Journal of Women's History*, and *Signs.*

Some recent articles in *Dress* characteristic of the current discourse on fashion are Christina Waugh, " 'Well-Cut through the Body': Fitted Clothing in Twelfth-Century Europe" (1999); Joan Sullivan, "In Pursuit of Legitimacy: Home Economists and the Hoover Apron in World War I" (1999); Kimberly Crisman, " 'The Upholstery of Life': Clothing and Character in the Novels of Edith Wharton" (1998); and Elizabeth Ann Coleman, "Jessie Franklin Turner: A Flight Path for

Early Modern American Fashion" (1998); Claudia Brush Kidwell, "Are Those Clothes Real? Transforming the Way Eighteenth-Century Portraits Are Studied" (1997); Linda Welters, "Dress as Souvenir: Piña Cloth in the Nineteenth Century" (1997); Patricia C. Warner, "Clothing as Barrier: American Women in the Olympics, 1900–1920" (1997); Sophie White, "Dress in French Colonial Louisiana, 1699–1769: The Evidence from Notarial Sources" (1997); and Laurel Wilson, "The Cowboy: Real and Imagined" (1996).

BIBLIOGRAPHY

Reference Works

America: History and Life. Santa Barbara, Calif., 1964– .

American Fabrics and Fashions Magazine, ed. *American Fabrics Encyclopedia of Textiles*. 3rd ed. Englewood Cliffs, N.J.: Prentice-Hall, 1980.

American Home Economics Association. *Aesthetics and Clothing: An Annotated Bibliography*. Washington, D.C.: American Home Economics Association, 1972.

Anthony, Pegaret, and Janet Arnold. *Costume: A General Bibliography*. London: Costume Society of England, 1977.

Applied Science & Technology Index. New York.

Artbibliographies Modern. Santa Barbara, Calif.: American Bibliographical Center, 1969– .

Arts and Humanities Citation Index. Philadelphia: Institute for Scientific Information, 1976– .

Arts Index. New York: H. W. Wilson, 1930– .

Bibliography of the History of Art. Santa Monica, Calif., 1973– .

Business Periodicals Index. New York: W. H. Wilson, 1958– .

Calasibetta, Charlotte Mankey. *Essential Terms of Fashion: A Collection of Definitions*. New York: Fairchild, 1986.

———. *Fairchild's Dictionary of Fashion*. New York: Fairchild Books, 1998.

Callan, Georgina O'Hara. *The Encylopedia of Fashion*. New York: Harry N. Abrams, 1986.

———. *The Thames and Hudson Dictionary of Fashion and Fashion Designers*. London: Thames and Hudson, 1998.

Cassin-Scott, Jack. *The Illustrated Encyclopedia of Costume and Fashion: From 1066 to the Present*. London: Studio-Vista, 1994.

Childers, Joseph, and Gary Hentzi, eds. *The Columbia Dictionary of Modern Literary Criticism*. New York: Columbia University Press, 1995.

Clothing Terms and Definitions. 3rd ed. London: Clothing and Footwear Institute, 1983.

Colas, René. *Bibliographie générale du costume et de la mode*. Genève: Slatkine Reprints; Paris: Libr. Gaspa, 1991.

Costume Society of America. *Bibliography*. New York: Costume Society of America, 1974–1983.

Costume Society of America 2002 Membership Directory. Earleville, Md., 2002.

Davies, Stephanie Curtis. *Costume Language: A Dictionary of Dress Terms*. Malvern: Cressrelles, 1994.

De Remaury, Bruno. *Dictionnaire de la Mode au XXe Siècle*. Paris: Editions du Regard, 1996.

The Fashion Book. London: Phaidon, 1998.

The Fashion Guide: International Designer Directory. New York: Fashion Guide International, 1989– .

Gousse, Suzanne. *Costume in New France from 1740 to 1760: A Visual Dictionary*. Chambly, Quebec: Fleur de Lyse, 1997.

Haddock, Miranda Howard. *Darning the Wear of Time: Survey and Annotated Bibliography of Periodical Literature of Costume Conservation, Restoration, and Documentation Published in English 1980–1996*. New York: Rowman and Littlefield, 1996.

Hiler, Hilaire, and Meyer Hiler. *Bibliography of Costume: A Dictionary Catalog of About Eight Thousand Books and Periodicals*. New York: H. W. Wilson, 1939.

Historical Abstracts. Santa Barbara, Calif.: American Bibliographical Center, 1955– .

Huenefeld, Irene Pennington. *International Directory of Historical Clothing*. Metuchen, N.J.: Scarecrow Press, 1967.

Humanities Index. New York: H. W. Wilson, 1975– .

Hutton, Sandra S., ed. *The Clothing and Textiles Arts Index: An Index to Periodical Literature, 1980–1984*. Monument, Colo.: Sandra S. Hutton, 1986.

———. *The Clothing Index: An Index to Periodical Literature, January 1970–December 1979*. Lincoln, Nebr.: Micro Control Systems, 1982.

International Bibliography of Periodical Literature. Osnabruck, Germany, 1964– .

Lambert, Eleanor. *World of Fashion: People, Places, Resources*. New York: R.R. Bowker, 1976.

Linton, George Edward. *The Modern Textile and Apparel Dictionary*. 4th ed. Plainfield, N.J: Textile Book Service, 1973.

Loschek, Ingrid. *Die Modedesigner. Ein Lexikon von Armani bis Yamamoto* (1998).

Lubbell, Cecil. *Textile Collections of the World*. Vol. 1: *United States and Canada*. New York: Van Nostrand Reinhold, 1976.

———. *Textile Collections of the World*. Vol. 2: *United Kingdom and Ireland*. New York: Van Nostrand Reinhold, 1976.

———. *Textile Collections of the World*. Vol. 3: *France*. New York: Van Nostrand Reinhold, 1976.

Martin, Richard. *Contemporary Fashion*. New York: St. James Press, 1995.

———, ed. *The St. James Fashion Encyclopedia: A Survey of Style from 1945 to the Present*. New York: Visible Ink, 1996.

McDowell, Colin. *McDowell's Directory of Twentieth-Century Fashion*. Englewood Cliffs, N.J.: Prentice-Hall, 1985.

Neinholdt, Eva, and Gretel Wagner-Neumann. *Katalog der Lipperdheideschen Kostumebibliothek*. Berlin: Mann, 1965.

New York Times Index. New York: New York Times, 1851– .

O'Hara, Georgina. *The Encyclopedia of Fashion*. New York: H. N. Abrams, 1986.

Oliver, Valerie Burnham. *Fashion and Costume in American Popular Culture: A Reference Guide*. Westport, Conn.: Greenwood Press, 1996.

Picken, Mary Brooks. *A Dictionary of Costume and Fashion: Historic and Modern: With Over 950 Illustrations*. Mineola, N.Y.: Dover, 1999.

Racinet, Albert. *The Historical Encyclopedia of Costumes*. New York: Facts on File, 1988.

Readers' Guide to Periodical Literature. New York: H. W. Wilson, 1900– .

Schoeffler, O. E., and William Gale. *Esquire's Encyclopedia of 20th Century Men's Fashions*. New York: McGraw-Hill, 1973.

The Selected Bibliography of Clothing Sources: Compiled according to the Structure of the Clothing Examinations of the Clothing Footwear Institute. London: Clothing and Footwear Institute, 1980.

Social Sciences Index. New York: H. W. Wilson, 1975– .

Stegemeyer, Anne. *Who's Who in Fashion*. New York: Fairchild Publications, 1996.

Toledo, Ruben. *Style Dictionary*. New York: Abbeville Press, 1996.

United Nations Industrial Development Organization. *Information Sources on the Clothing Industry*. New York: United Nations, 1974.

U.S. Department of Commerce. International Trade Administration. *Sources of Statistical Data: Textiles and Apparel, 1980*. Washington, D.C.: Government Printing Office, July 1981.

Wilcox, R. Turner. *The Dictionary of Costume*. New York: Macmillan, 1986.

Winakor, T. Geitel. *Economics of Textiles and Clothing: A Bibliography*. Ames: Iowa State University, 1980.

Yarwood, Doreen. *The Encyclopedia of World Costume*. New York: Bonanza Books, 1986.

Books and Articles

Abler, Thomas S. *Hinterland Warriors and Military Dress: European Empires and Exotic Uniforms*. New York: Berg, 1999.

Agins, Teri. *The End of Fashion: How Marketing Changed the Clothing Business Forever*. New York: First Quill, 2000.

Alcega, Juan de. *Tailor's Pattern Book, 1589*. Bedford, England: Ruth Bean, 1979.

Allen, Raye Virginia. *Gordon Conway: Fashioning a New Woman*. American Studies Series. Austin: University of Texas Press, 1997.

Ambrose, Bonnie Holt. *The Little Corset Book: A Workbook on Period Underwear*. Reprint. New York: Drama, 1999.

Ames, Kenneth, et al. *Material Culture: A Research Guide*. Lawrence: University Press of Kansas, 1985.

Armstrong, Helen Joseph. *Pattern Making for Fashion Design*. New York: Harper and Row, 1987.

Arnold, Janet. *A Handbook of Costume*. London: Macmillan, 1973.

———. *Patterns of Fashion: The Cut and Construction of Clothing for Men and Women, 1560 to 1620*. New York: Macmillan, 1985.

———. *Patterns of Fashion: Englishwomen's Dresses & Their Construction*. London: Macmillan, 1977.

Arthur, Linda Boynton. *Aloha Attire: Hawaiian Dress in the Twentieth Century*. New York: Schiffer, 1999.

———. *Religion, Dress and the Body*. New York: Berg, 1999.

Ash, Juliet, and Elizabeth Wilson, eds. *Chic Thrills: A Fashion Reader*. Berkeley: University of California Press, 1993.

Ashelford, Jane. *The Art of Dress: Clothes and Society, 1500–1914*. New York: Harry N. Abrams, 1996.

Avedon, Richard. *Avedon-Photographs, 1947–1977*. New York: Farrar, Straus, and Giroux, 1978.

Bach, Peter, ed. *Textile, Costume, and Doll Collections in the United States and Canada*. Lopez, Wash.: R. L. Shep, 1981.

Baclawski, Karen. *The Guide to Historic Costume*. London: B. T. Batsford, 1995.

Bailey, David, and Martin Harrison. *Shots of Style: Great Fashion Photographs*. London: Victoria and Albert Museum, 1985.

Baker, Lillian. *100 Years of Collectible Jewelry, 1850–1950*. Paducah, Ky.: Collector Books, 1978.

Baker, William Henry. *A Dictionary of Men's Wear*. Cleveland: W. H. Baker, 1908.

Ball, Joanne Dubbs. *The Art of Fashion Accessories: A Twentieth Century Retrospective*. West Chester, Pa.: Schiffer, 1993.

Balmain, Pierre. *My Years and Seasons*. London: Cassell, 1964.

Banner, Lois W. *American Beauty*. New York: Knopf, 1983.

Barber, E.J.W. *Prehistoric Textiles: The Development of Cloth in the Neolithic and Bronze Ages with Special Reference to the Aegean*. Princeton, N.J.: Princeton University Press, 1991.

———. *Women's Work: The First 20,000 Years: Women, Cloth and Society in Early Times*. New York: W. W. Norton, 1994.

Barnard, Malcolm. *Fashion as Communication*. London: Routledge, 1996.

Barnes, Ruth, and Joanne B. Eicher. *Dress and Gender: Making and Meaning*. New York: Berg, 1993.

Barthes, Roland. *Elements of Semiology*. Berkeley: University of California Press, 1964.

———. *The Fashion System*. Berkeley: University of California Press, 1967.

Barton, Lucy. *Historic Costume for the Stage*. Boston: Walter H. Baker, 1938.

Batterberry, Michael, and Ariane Batterberry. *Mirror, Mirror: A Social History of Fashion*. New York: Holt, Rinehart, and Winston, 1977.

Baudot, Francois. *Chanel*. New York: Vendome Press, 1996.

———. *Christian Lacroix*. New York: Universe, 1997.

———. *Elsa Schiaparelli*. New York: Universe, 1997.

———. *Fashion, the Twentieth Century*. New York: Universe Press, 1999.

Baumgarten, Linda, John Watson, and Florine Carr. *Costume Close Up: Clothing Construction and Pattern, 1750–1790*. New York: Costume and Fashion Press, 2000.

Beaton, Cecil Walter Hardy. *The Glass of Fashion*. London: Cassell, 1989.

Benson, Susan. *Counter Cultures: Saleswomen, Managers, and Customers in American Department Stores, 1890–1940*. Urbana: University of Illinois Press, 1986.

Benstock, Shari, and Suzanne Ferriss, eds. *On Fashion*. New Brunswick, N.J.: Rutgers University Press, 1994.

Berge, Pierre, and Grace Mirabella. *Yves Saint Laurent*. New York: Vendome Press, 1996.

Berger, Vicki L. "Fashion." In *Handbook of American Popular Culture*, ed. M. Thomas Inge. Westport, Conn.: Greenwood Press, 1989, 417–43.

Bernard, Barbara. *Fashion in the 60's*. New York: St. Martin's Press, 1978.
Berry, Sarah. *Screen Style: Fashion and Femininity in 1930s Hollywood*. Minneapolis: University of Minnesota Press, 2000.
Berstein, Leonard S. *"How's Business?" "Don't Ask": Tales from the Garment Center*. New York: Saturday Review Press, 1974.
Biennele di Firenze. *Art/Fashion*. Ed. Germano Celant. New York: Art, 1997.
Black, J. Anderson, and Madge Garland. *A History of Fashion*. New York: William Morrow, 1975.
Blanchard, Mary Warner. *Oscar Wilde's America: Counterculture in the Gilded Age*. New Haven, Conn.: Yale University Press, 1998.
Blau, Herbert. *Nothing in Itself: Complexions of Fashion*. Bloomington: Indiana University Press, 1999.
Blum, Dilys E., and H. Kristina Haugland. *Best Dressed: Fashion from the Birth of Couture to Today*. Philadelphia Museum of Art Store, 1997.
Blum, Stella, comp. *Victorian Fashions and Costumes from Harper's Bazaar 1867–1890*. New York: Dover, 1975.
———. *Ackermann's Costume Plates: Women's Fashions in England 1818–1820*. New York: Dover, 1979.
———. *Fashions and Costumes from Godey's Lady's Book*. Reprint. New York: Dover, 1985.
Blumer, Herbert. "Fashion: From Class Differentiation to Collective Selection." *Sociological Quarterly* 10 (1969): 275–91.
Bonami, Francesco, Maria Luisa Frisa, and Stefano Tonchi, eds. *Uniform: Order and Disorder*. Milano: Charta, 2000.
Bond, David. *The Guinness Guide to 20th Century Fashion*. Enfield, Middlesex, England: Guinness, 1988.
Borrelli, Laird. *Stylishly Drawn: Contemporary Fashion Illustration*. New York: Harry N. Abrams, 2000.
Boston, Lloyd. *Men of Color: Fashion, History, Fundamentals*. New York: Artisan, 1998.
Boucher, Francois Leon Louis. *20,000 Years of Fashion: The History of Costume and Personal Adornment*. New York: Harry N. Abrams, 1987.
Boydston, Jeanne. *Home and Work: Housework, Wages, and the Ideology of Labor in the Early Republic*. New York Oxford University Press, 1990.
Brannon, Evelyn L. *Fashion Forecasting*. New York: Fairchild, 2000.
Braun and Schneider. *Historic Costume in Pictures*. 2d ed. New York: Dover, 1975.
Breward, Christopher. *The Culture of Fashion: A New History of Fashionable Dress*. Manchester: University of Manchester Press, 1995.
———. *The Hidden Consumer: Masculinities, Fashion and City Life 1860–1914*. Manchester: University of Manchester Press, 1999.
Brockman, Helen L. *The Theory of Fashion Design*. New York: Wiley, 1965.
Browne, Alix, and Anne Bissonnette, eds. *Toledo/Toledo*. New York: Vissionnaire, 2000.
Bruzzi, Stella. *Undressing Cinema: Clothing and Identity in the Movies*. London: Routledge, 1997.
Brydon, Anne, and Sandra Niessen. *Consuming Fashion: Adorning the Transnational Body*. New York: Berg, 1998.

Buck, Anne. "Clothes in Fact and Fiction, 1825–1865." *Costume* 17 (1983), 89–104.

———. *Victorian Costume and Costume Accessories*. New York: Thomas Nelson, 1961.

Buckland, Sandra. " 'We Publish Fashions Because They Are News': The *New York Times* 1940 through 1945." *Dress* (1998), 33–41.

Burman, Barbara. *The Culture of Sewing*. New York: Berg, 1999.

Burns, Leslie Davis, and Nancy O. Bryant. *The Business of Fashion: Designing, Manufacturing, and Marketing*. New York: Fairchild, 1997.

Burnston, Sharon Ann. *Fitting & Proper: 18th Century Clothing from the Collection of the Chester County Historical Society*. Texarcana, Tex.: Scurlock, 1998.

Buruma, Anna. *Fashions of the Past*. London: Collins and Brown, 1999.

Buttolph, Angela, Alice Mackrell, Richard Martin, Melanie Rickey, and Judith Watt. *The Fashion Book*. London: Phaidon Press, 1998.

Buxbaum, Gerda. *Icons of Fashion: The 20th Century*. New York: Prestel, 1999.

Carillo, Loretta. "Fashion." In *Concise Histories of American Popular Culture*, ed. M. Thomas Inge. Westport, Conn.: Greenwood Press, 1982, 129–35.

Carnegy, Vicky. *Fashions of a Decade: The 1980s*. New York: Facts on File, 1990.

Carter, Ernestine. *20th Century Fashion: A Scrapbook, 1900 to Today*. London: E. Methuen, 1975.

Cash, Patrick, and Irene Cumming Kleeberg, eds. *The Buyer's Manual*. New York: National Retail Merchants Association, 1979.

Cassini, Oleg. *In My Own Fashion: An Autobiography*. New York: Pocket Books, 1990.

———. *A Thousand Days of Magic: Dressing Jackie Kennedy for the White House*. New York: Rizzoli, 1995.

Cavallaro, Dani, and Alexandra Warwick. *Fashioning the Frame: Boundaries, Dress and the Body*. New York: Berg, 1998.

Cawthorne, Nigel. *Key Moments in Fashion: The Evolution of Style*. London: Hamlyn, 1998.

———. *The New Look: The Dior Revolution*. London: Hamlyn Reed International Books, 1996.

Celant, Germano, and Harold Koda, eds. *Giorgio Armani*. New York: Guggenheim Museum and Abrams, 2000.

Celebrating Seventh: New York Fashion Designers. Houston Museum of Fine Art. Houston, Tex.: The Museum, 1996.

Charles-Roux, Edmonde. *Chanel and Her World*. London: Weidenfeld and Nicolson, 1981.

Chenoune, Farid. *Beneath It All: A Century of French Lingerie*. New York: Rizzoli, 2000.

———. *A History of Men's Fashion*. Paris: Flammarion, 1993.

Clancy, Deirdre. *Costume since 1945: Couture, Street Style, and Anti-Fashion*. New York: Drama, 1996.

Cobrin, Harry A. *The Men's Clothing Industry: Colonial through Modern Times*. New York: Fairchild, 1970.

Coffin, Judith G. *The Politics of Women's Work: The Paris Garment Trades, 1750–1915*. Princeton, N.J.: Princeton University Press, 1996.

Cohn, David Lewis. *The Good Old Days: A History of American Morals and Manners as Seen through the Sears, Roebuck Catalogs 1905 to the Present*. New York: Simon and Schuster, 1940.

Cole, Shaun. *"Don We Now Our Gay Apparel": Gay Men's Dress in the Twentieth Century*. New York: Berg, 2000.

Coleman, Dorothy Smith. "Fashion Dolls/Fashionable Dolls." *Dress* 3 (1977), 18.

Coleman, Elizabeth Ann. "Jessie Franklin Turner: A Flight Path for Early Modern American Fashion." *Dress* (1998), 58–64.

Cook, Pam. *Fashioning the Nation: Costume and Identity in British Cinema*. London: British Film Institute, 1996.

Cooper, Cynthia. *Magnificent Entertainments: Fancy Dress Balls of Canada's Governors General 1876–1898*. Fredricton, N.B.: Goose Lane Editions and the Canadian Museum of Civilization, 1997.

Costantino, Maria. *Designers*. London: Batsford, 1997.

———. *Fashions of a Decade: The 1930s*. New York: Chrysalis Books, 1991.

———. *Men's Fashion in the Twentieth Century: From Frock Coats to Intelligent Fibres*. London: Batsford, 1997.

Countryman, Ruth, and Elizabeth Weiss Hopper. *Women's Wear of the 1920's: With Complete Patterns*. New York: Players Press, 1998.

Craik, Jennifer. *The Face of Fashion: Cultural Studies in Fashion*. New York: Routledge, 1994.

Crane, Diana. *Fashion and Its Social Agendas: Class, Gender, and Identity*. Chicago: University of Chicago Press, 2000.

Craughwell-Varda, Kathleen. *Looking for Jackie: American Fashion Icons*. New York: Hearst Books, 1999.

Crawford, Morris De Camp. *One World of Fashion*. New York: Fairchild, 1946.

———. *The Ways of Fashion*. New York: Fairchild, 1948.

Crisman, Kimberly. " 'The Upholstery of Life': Clothing and Character in the Novels of Edith Wharton." *Dress* (1998), 17–32.

Cullerton, Brenda, Richard Martin, and Harold Koda. *Geoffrey Beene: The Anatomy of His Work*. New York: Harry N. Abrams, 1995.

Cunningham, Patricia A. "Classical Revivals in Dress." In *Fashioning the Future: Our Future from Our Past*. Columbus, Ohio: Costume and Textiles Collection, 1996, 3–11.

———. *Reforming Fashion, 1850–1914: Politics, Health, and Art*. Columbus, Ohio: Historic Costume and Textile Collection, 2000.

———. "To Be Healthy, Artistic, and Correct: Alternatives to the Fashionable Ideal." In *With Grace and Favour* by Charles Thieme. Cincinnati: Cincinnati Art Museum, 1993, 14–25.

Cunningham, Patricia A., and Susan V. Lab, eds. *Dress and Popular Culture*. Bowling Green, Ohio: Popular Press, 1991.

———. *Dress in American Culture*. Bowling Green, Ohio: Popular Press, 1993.

Cunningham, Patricia A., and Gayle Strege. *Fashioning the Future: Our Future from Our Past*. Columbus: Department of Consumer and Textile Sciences, Ohio State University, 1996.

Dalrymple, Priscilla Harris. *American Victorian Costume in Early Photographs*. New York: Dover, 1991.

Damhorst, Mary Lynn, Kimberly Miller, and Susan O. Michelman. *The Meaning of Dress*. New York: Fairchild, 1999.

Darnell, Paula Jean. *Victorian to Vamp: Woman's Clothing 1900–1929*. New York: Fabric Fancies, 2000.

Davenport, Millia. *The Book of Costume*. New York: Crown, 1948.

Davis, Fred. *Fashion, Culture and Identity*. Chicago: University of Chicago Press, 1992.

Davis, Marian L. *Visual Design in Dress*. 2nd ed. Englewood Cliffs, N.J.: Prentice-Hall, 1987.

Debord, Matthew. "Texture and Taboo: The Tyranny of Texture and Ease in the J. Crew Catalog." *Fashion Theory: The Journal of Dress, Body and Culture* 1.3 (1997), 261–78.

De Castelbajac, Kate. *The Face of the Century: 100 Years of Makeup and Style*. New York: Rizzoli, 1995.

De Givry, Valerie. *Art & Mode: Inspiration Artistique des Createurs de Mode*. Paris: Regard, 1998.

De la Haye, Amy and Cathie Dingwall. *Surfers, Soulies, Skinheads, and Skaters: Subcultural Style From the Forties to the Nineties*. Woodstock N.Y.: Overlook Press, 1996.

De la Haye, Amy and Valerie Mendes. *Fashion Source Book*. London: Macdonald Orbis, 1988.

De la Haye, Amy and Elizabeth Wilson, eds. *Defining Dress: Dress as Object, Meaning, and Identity*. Manchester, UK: Manchester University Press, 1999.

DeLong, Marilyn Revell. *The Way We Look: A Framework for Visual Analysis of Dress*. Ames: Iowa State University Press, 1987.

DeMarly, Diana. *The History of Haute Couture, 1850–1950*. New York: Holmes and Meier, 1980.

DePaola, Helena, and Carol Stewart Mueller. *Marketing Today's Fashion*. 2nd ed. Englewood Cliffs, N.J.: Prentice-Hall, 1986.

Dewey, Melvil. *Dewey Decimal Classification and Relative Index*. 9th ed. New York: Forest Press, 1965.

Diamond, Jay. *Fashion Advertising and Promotion*. New York: Fairchild, 1999.

Diamond, Jay, and Ellen Diamond. *The World of Fashion*. New York: Fairchild, 1997.

Dickerson, Kitty G. "Imported versus U.S.-Produced Apparel: Consumer Views and Buying Patterns." *Home Economics Research Journal* 10 (March 1982), 241–52.

Dillon, Linda S. "Business Dress for Women Corporate Professionals." *Home Economics Research Journal* 9 (December 1980), 124–29.

Dingeman, Jo. *Mastering Fashion Styling*. Houndmills, England: Macmillan, 1999.

Dolan, Maryanne. *Vintage Clothing, 1880–1960: Identification and Value Guide*. Florence, Ala.: Books Americana, 1984.

Dolce & Gabbana. *10 Years of Dolce & Gabbana*. New York: Holt, Rinehart, and Winston, 1977.

Doonan, Simon. *Confessions of a Window Dresser: Tales from a Life in Fashion*. New York: Penguin Studio, 1998.

Downey, Lynn, Jill Novack Lynch, and Kathleen McDonough. *This Is a Pair of Levi's Jeans: The Official History of the Levi's Brand.* San Francisco: Levi Strauss, 1995.

Drake, Mary Frances. *Retail Fashion Promotion and Advertising.* New York: Macmillan, 1992.

Dries Van Noten: Shape, Print, and Fabric (Cutting Edge). New York: Watson-Guptill, 1999.

Druesedow, Jean. *In-Style: Celebrating Fifty Years of the Costume Institute.* New York: Metropolitan Museum of Art, 1987.

Dubin, Tiffany, and Ann E. Berman. *Vintage Style: Buying and Wearing Classic Vintage Clothes.* New York: HarperCollins, 2000.

Earle, Alice Morse. *Two Centuries of Costume in America: 1620–1820.* 1903. Reprint. 2 vols. New York: Dover, 1970.

Edelman, Amy Holman. *The Little Black Dress.* New York: Simon and Schuster Editions, 1997.

Eicher, Joanne B. *Dress and Ethnicity: Change across Space and Time.* New York: Berg, 1995.

Eicher, Joanne B., Sandra Lee Evenson, and Hazel A. Lutz. *The Visible Self: Global Perspectives on Dress, Culture and Society.* New York: Fairchild, 2000.

Eisner, Lisa and Roman Alonso, eds. *Height of Fashion.* New York: Greybull Press, 2000.

El-Guindi, Fadwa. *Veil: Modesty, Privacy and Resistance.* New York: Berg, 1999.

Elvish, Andrew William. "Death Becomes Her: The Death Aesthetic in/as Fashion Advertising." Master's Thesis, Concordia University, Quebec, 1997.

Entwistle, Joanne. *Dress, Bodies and Business: Fashioning Women at Work.* New York: Berg, 2001.

Erté, Paul. *Erté's Fashion Designs: 210 Illustrations from Harper's Bazaar, 1918–1932.* New York: Dover, 1981.

Etherington-Smith, Meredith. *Patou.* New York: St. Martin's/Marek, 1983.

Ewing, Elizabeth. *History of Twentieth Century Fashion.* Lanham, Md.: Barnes and Noble Books, 1992.

Fabric of Fashion. Houston, Tex.: Museum of Fine Arts, 1994.

Fairchild, John. *The Fashionable Savages.* Garden City, N.Y.: Doubleday, 1965.

Farber, Robert. *Professional Fashion Photography.* Garden City, N.Y.: American Photographic Book, 1978.

Featherstone, Mike. *Consumer Culture and Postmodernism.* London: Sage, 1991.

Fetterman, Nelma Irene. "A Bibliometric Analysis of Clothing Literature with Implications for Information Storage and Retrieval." Ph.D. diss., Ohio State University, 1977.

Filene, Adele, and Polly Willman. *The Costume Society of America Bibliography: 1974/1979.* N.p.: Costume Society of America, n.d.

Fincher, Jayne. *Debrett's Illustrated Fashion Guide—The Princess of Wales.* Devon: Webb and Bower, 1989.

Fink, Larry. *Runway.* New York: Power House Books, 2000.

Finkel, Alicia. *Romantic Stages: Set and Costume Design in Victorian England.* New York: McFarland, 1996.

Finlayson, Ian. *Denim: An American Legend.* New York: Simon and Schuster, 1990.

Fischer, Gayle V. *Pantaloons & Power: A Nineteenth-Century Dress Reform in the United States*. Kent, Ohio: Kent State University Press, 2001.

Flügel, John Carl. *The Psychology of Clothes*. London: Hogarth Press, 1930.

Folse, Nancy McCarthy, and Marilyn Henrion. *Careers in the Fashion Industry: What the Jobs Are and How to Get Them*. New York: Harper and Row, 1981.

Fontanel, Beatrice. Trans. Willard Wood. *Support and Seduction: A History of Corsets and Bras*. New York: Harry N. Abrams, 1997.

Forden, Sara Gay. *The House of Gucci: A Sensational Story of Murder, Madness, Glamour, and Greed*. New York: William Morrow, 2000.

Foster, Helen Bradley. *"New Raiments of Self": African American Clothing in the Antebellum South*. New York: Berg, 1997.

Fox, Patty. *Star Style: Hollywood Legends as Fashion Icons*. Santa Monica, Calif.: Angel City Press, 1999.

Fraser, Kennedy. *The Fashionable Mind: Reflections on Fashion, 1970–1983*. Boston: D. R. Godine, 1985.

Furstenburg, Diane Von, and Linda Bird Franke. *Diane: A Signature Life*. New York: Simon and Schuster, 1998.

Gaines, Jane, and Charlotte Herzog, eds. *Fabrications: Costume and the Female Body*. New York: Routledge, 1990.

Gaines, Steven S. *Obsession: The Lives and Times of Calvin Klein*. New York: Carol, 1994.

Gan, Stephen. *Visionaire's Fashion 2000: Designers at the Turn of the Millennium*. London: Laurence King, 1997.

Gan, Stephen, and Alix Browne. *Visionaire's Fashion 2001: Designers of the New Avant-Garde*. New York: Universe, 1999.

Garbor, Marjorie. *Vested Interests: Cross-Dressing & Cultural Anxiety*. New York: HarperCollins, 1993.

Gernsheim, Alison. *Victorian and Edwardian Fashion: A Photographic Survey*. New York: Dover, 1982.

Giles, Cynthia. *The Official Identification and Price Guide to Vintage Clothing*. New York: House of Collectibles, 1989.

Gill, Alison. "Deconstruction Fashion: The Making of Unfinished, Decomposing and Re-assembled Clothes." *Fashion Theory: The Journal of Dress, Body & Culture* 2: 1 (1998), 25–49.

Glynn, Prudence. *In Fashion: Dress in the Twentieth Century*. New York: Oxford University Press, 1978.

Goffman, Erving. *The Presentation of Self in Everyday Life*. Garden City, N.Y.: Doubleday, 1959.

Gold, Annalee *90 Years of Fashion*. New York: Fairchild, 1991.

———. *One World of Fashion*. New York: Fairchild, 1987.

Gorsline, Douglas W. *A History of Fashion: A Visual Survey of Costume from Ancient Times*. London: Batsford, 1993.

———. *What People Wore: 1,800 Illustrations from Ancient Times to the Early Twentieth Century*. Reprint. New York: Dover, 1994.

Grafton, Carol Belanger. *Fashions of the Thirties: 476 Authentic Copyright-Free Illustrations*. New York: Dover, 1993.

———. *Shoes, Hats and Fashion Accessories: A Pictorial Archive, 1850–1940*. Mineola, N.Y.: Dover, 1998.

———. *Victorian Fashions: A Pictorial Archive*. Mineola, N.Y.: Dover, 1999.

Griggs, Claudine. *S/he: Changing Sex and Changing Clothes*. New York: Berg, 1998.

Grimble, Frances, ed. *The Edwardian Modiste: 85 Authentic Patterns with Instructions, Fashion Plates, and Period Sewing Techniques*. New York: Lavolta Press, 1997.

———. *The Voice of Fashion: 79 Turn-of-the Century Patterns with Instructions and Fashion Plates*. New York: Lavolta Press, 1998.

Grimble, Frances, and Deborah Kuhn. *After a Fashion: How to Reproduce, Restore, and Wear Vintage Styles*. New York: Lavolta Press, 1998.

Gross, Elaine, and Fred Rottman. *Halston: An American Original*. New York: HarperCollins, 1999.

Guy, Alison, Eileen Green, and Maura Banim. *Through the Wardrobe*. New York: Berg, 2000.

Haase, Esther. *Fashion in Motion*. London: Edition Stemmle, 2000.

Handley, Susannah. *Nylon: The Story of a Fashion Revolution: A Celebration of Design from Art Silk to Nylon and Thinking Fibres*. Baltimore: Johns Hopkins University Press, 1999.

Hanmer, Davina. *Diana, the Fashion Princess*. New York: Holt, Rinehart, and Winston, 1984.

Hansen, Joseph, and Evelyn Reed. *Cosmetics, Fashions, and the Exploitation of Women*. New York: Pathfinders Press, 1986.

Harris, Alice. *The White T*. New York: Harper Collins, 1996.

Harris, Kristina. *The Home Pattern Company 1914 Fashions Catalog: The Home Pattern Company*. Reprint. New York: Dover, 1995.

Hart, Avril, Susan North, and Richard Davis. *Fashion in Detail: From the 17th and 18th Centuries*. New York: Rizzoli, 1998.

Harvey, John. *Men in Black*. Chicago: University of Chicago Press, 1995.

Haynes, Michaele Thurgood. *Dressing Up Debutantes: Pageantry and Glitz in Texas*. New York: Berg, 1998.

Hebdige, Dick. *Subculture: The Meaning of Style*. London: Methuen, 1979.

Herald, Jacqueline. *Fashions of a Decade: The 1920s*. New York: Facts on File, 1991.

———. *Fashions of a Decade: The 1970s*. New York: Facts on File, 1992.

Hilfiger, Tommy, and Anthony Decurtis. *Rock Style: How Fashion Moves to Music*. New York: Universe, 1999.

Hilfiger, Tommy, and David Keeps. *All American: A Style Book*. New York: Universe, 1997.

Hodgman, Ann. *A Day in the Life of a Fashion Designer*. Mahwah, N.J.: Troll Associates, 1988.

Hollander, Anne. *Seeing through Clothes*. Reprint. Berkeley: University of California Press, 1993.

———. *Sex and Suits: The Evolution of Modern Dress*. New York: Kodansha International, 1995.

Houston, Mary G. *Medieval Costume in England and France: The 13th, 14th and 15th Centuries*. Reprint. New York: Dover, 1996.

Howell, Georgina. *In Vogue: 75 Years of Style*. London: Condé Nast Books, 1991.

Hunt, Marsha. *The Way We Wore: Styles of the 1930s and '40s and Our World since Then*. Fallbrook, Calif.: Fallbrook, 1993.

Ince, Kate. *Orlan: Millennial Female*. New York: Berg, 2000.

Isenberg, Nancy. *Sex and Citizenship in Antebellum America*. Chapel Hill: University of North Carolina Press, 1998.

Jaffe, Hilde, and Nurie Relis. *Draping for Fashion Design*. Reston, Va.: Reston, 1973.

Jarnow, Jeannette A., Miriam Guerrciro, and Beatrice Judelle. *Inside the Fashion Business: Text and Readings*. 4th ed. New York: Macmillan, 1987.

Jobling, Paul. *Fashion Spreads: Word and Image in Fashion Photography since 1980*. New York: Berg, 1999.

Johnson, Judy M., ed. *French Fashion Plates of the Romantic Era in Full Color: 120 Plates from "Petit Courrier des Dames," 1830–34*. New York: Dover, 1991.

Johnson, Kim K. P. and Sharron J. Lennon. *Appearance and Power*. New York: Berg, 1999.

Jordan Marsh, Co. *Jordan Marsh Illustrated Catalog of 1891 [Abridged]*. Reprint. New York: Dover, 1991.

Joseph, Nathan. *Uniforms and Nonuniforms: Communication through Clothing*. New York: Greenwood Press, 1986.

Jouve, Marie-Andree. *Balenciaga (Universe of Fashion)*. New York: Universe, 1997.

Judelle, Beatrice. *The Fashion Buyer's Job*. New York: National Retail Merchants Association, 1971.

Kaiser, Susan. *The Social Psychology of Clothing: Symbolic Appearances in Context*. 2nd ed. New York: Macmillan, 1990.

Kean, Rita C. "Perceived Importance of Selected Skills to a Group of Discount Store Buyers." *Clothing and Textiles Research Journal* 4 (Fall 1985), 31–37.

Kefgen, Mary, and Phyllis Touchie-Specht. *Individuality in Clothing Selection and Personal Appearance: A Guide for the Consumer*. 4th ed. New York: Macmillan, 1986.

Kelley, Eleanor, David Blouin, Rose Glee, Sarah Sweat, and Lydia Arledge. "Career Appearance: Perceptions of University Students and Recruiters Who Visit Their Campuses." *Home Economics Research Journal* 10 (March 1982), 253–63.

Kennedy, Shirley. *Pucci: A Renaissance in Fashion*. New York: Abbeville Press, 1991.

Kennett, Frances. *The Collector's Book of Fashion*. New York: Crown, 1983.

Khornak, Lucille. *Fashion 2001*. New York: Viking Press, 1982.

Kidwell, Claudia Brush. " 'Are Those Clothes Real?': Transforming the Way Eighteenth-Century Portraits are Studied." *Dress* (1997), 3–15.

———. *Cutting a Fashionable Fit: Dressmakers' Drafting Systems in the United States*. Washington, D.C.: Smithsonian Institution Press, 1979.

———. *Women's Bathing and Swimming Costume in the United States*. Washington, D.C.: Smithsonian Institution Press, 1968.

Kidwell, Claudia Brush, and Margaret C. Christman. *Suiting Everyone: The Democratization of Clothing in America*. Washington D.C.: Smithsonian Institution Press, 1974.

Kidwell, Claudia Brush and Valerie Steele, eds. *Men and Women: Dressing the Part*. Washington D.C.: Smithsonian Institution Press, 1989.

Kierner, Cynthia. *Beyond the Household: Women's Place in the Early South, 1700–1835*. Ithaca, N.Y.: Cornell University Press, 1998.

Kim, Minja, and Holly Schrank. "Fashion Leadership among Korean Women." *Home Economics Research Journal* 10 (March 1982), 227–34.

Kirke, Betty. *Madeleine Vionnet*. San Francisco: Chronicle Books, 1998.

Kleeberg, Irene C., and Patrick Cash, eds. *The Management of Fashion Merchandising: A Symposium*. New York: National Retail Merchants Association, 1977.

Knight, Margaret J. *Fashion through the Ages: From Overcoats to Petticoats*. Ringwood, Victoria, Canada: Viking, 1998.

Kohler, Karl. *A History of Costume*. London: G. G. Harrap, 1928.

Kopp, Ernestine, Vittorina Rolfo, Beatrice Zelin, and Lee Gross. *Designing Apparel through the Flat Pattern*. Rev. 5th ed. New York: Fairchild, 1982.

Koren, Leonard. *New Fashion Japan*. New York: Kodansha International, 1984.

Langner, Lawrence. *The Importance of Wearing Clothes*. New York: Hastings House, 1959.

Laver, James. *Costume and Fashion: A Concise History*. New York: Thames and Hudson, 1995.

———. *Costume in Antiquity*. New York: Clarkson N. Potter, 1964.

———. *Modesty in Dress: An Inquiry into the Fundamentals of Fashion*. Boston: Houghton Mifflin, 1969.

Lawford, Valentine. *Horst: His Work and His World*. New York: Alfred A. Knopf, 1984.

Lee, Sara Tomerlin. *American Fashion: The Life and Lines of Adrian, Mainbocher, McCardell, Morell, and Trigere*. New York: Quadrangle/New York Times, 1975.

Lehmann, Urich. *Tigersprung: Fashion in Modernity*. Cambridge: MIT Press, 2000.

Lehnert, Gertrud. *Fashion*. London: L. King, 1999.

Lemire, Beverly. *Dress, Culture and Commerce: The English Clothing Trade before the Factory, 1660–1800*. New York: St. Martin's Press, 1997.

Lencek, Lena, and Gideon Bosker. *Making Waves: Swimsuits and the Undressing of America*. San Francisco: Chronicle Books, 1989.

Leniston, Florence, and Joanne Olian, eds. *La Mode Ilustree: Fashion Plates in Full Color*. Reprint. New York: Dover, 1997.

Lepape, George. *French Fashion Plates in Full Color from the Gazette du Bon Ton (1912–1925): 58 Illustrations of Styles by Paul Poiret, Worth, Paquin and Others*. Reprint. New York: Dover, 1979.

Ley, Sandra. *Fashion for Everyone: The Story of Ready-to-Wear, 1870–1970's*. New York: Scribner's, 1975.

Linton, George Edward. *The Modern Textile and Apparel Dictionary*. 4th ed. Plainfield, N.J.: Textile Book Service, 1973.

Lipovetsky, Gilles. *The Empire of Fashion: Dressing Modern Democracy*. Princeton, N.J.: Princeton University Press, 1987.

Little, David. *Vintage Denim*. Salt Lake City: Gibbs-Smith, 1996.

Littrell, Mary, and Marsha Dickson. *Social Responsibility in the Global Market: Fair Trade of Cultural Products*. Thousand Oaks, Calif.: Sage, 1999.

Lloyd, Valerie. *Tile Art of Vogue Photographic Covers: Fifty Years of Fashion and Design*. New York: Harmony Books, 1986.

Lobenthal, Joel. *Radical Rags: Fashion of the Sixties*. New York: Abbeville Press, 1990.
Lopez, Antonio. *Antonio: 60, 70, 80: Three Decades of Fashion Illustration*. London: Thames and Hudson, 1995.
Los Angeles County Museum of Art. *An Elegant Art: Fashion and Fantasy in the Eighteenth Century*. New York: Harry N. Abrams, 1983.
———. *Fabric and Fashion: Twenty Years of Costume Council Gifts*. Los Angeles: Los Angeles County Museum of Art, 1974.
Lovatt-Smith, Lisa, ed. *Fashion Images De Mode 4*. London: Steidl, 1999.
Lurie, Alison. *The Language of Clothes*. 1981. Reprint. New York: Henry Holt, 2000.
Lynam, Ruth. *Couture: An Illustrated History of the Great Paris Designers and Their Creations*. Garden City, N.Y.: Doubleday, 1972.
Lynch, Annette. *Dress, Gender and Cultural Change*. New York: Berg, 1999.
Madsen, Axel. *Living for Design: The Yves Saint Laurent Story*. New York: Delacorte Press, 1979.
Malossi, Giannino, ed. *The Style Engine: Spectacle, Identity, Design, and Business: How the Fashion Industry Uses Style to Create Wealth*. New York: Monacelli Press, 1998.
Martin, Richard. *Charles James*. New York: Universe, 1999.
———. *Fashion and Surrealism*. New York: Rizzoli, 1987.
———. *Khaki: Cut from the Original Cloth*. Santa Fe, N. Mex.: Tondo, 1999.
———. *Versace*. New York: Universe Publishing, 1997.
Martin, Richard, and Harold Koda. *Christian Dior*. New York: Metropolitan Museum of Art, 1997.
———. *Cubism and Fashion*. New York: Metropolitan Museum of Art and H. N. Abrams, 1998.
———. *Flair: Fashion Collected by Tina Chow*. New York: Rizzoli, 1992.
———. *Giorgio Armani: Images of Man*. New York: Rizzoli, 1990.
———. *Haute Couture*. New York: Metropolitan Museum of Art, 1996.
———. *The Historical Mode: Fashion and Art in the 1980s*. New York: Rizzoli, 1989.
———. *Infra-Apparel*. New York: Metropolitan Museum of Art, 1993.
———. *Jocks and Nerds: Men's Style in the Twentieth Century*. New York: Rizzoli, 1989.
———. *Splash: A History of Swimwear*. New York: Rizzoli, 1990.
Martin, Richard, and Grace Mirabella. *Versace*. New York: Vendome, 1997.
McCracken, Grant. *Culture and Consumption*. Bloomington: Indiana University Press, 1990.
McDowell, Colin. *The Designer Scam*. London: Hutchinson, 1994.
———. *Fashion Today*. New York: Phaidon Press, 2000.
———. *Forties Fashion and the New Look*. London: Bloomsbury, 1997.
———. *Galliano*. New York: Rizzoli, 1997.
———. *The Literary Companion to Fashion*. London: Sinclair-Stevenson, 1995.
———. *The Man of Fashion: Peacock Males and Perfect Gentlemen*. London: Thames and Hudson, 1997.
———. *Manolo Blahnik*. New York: HarperCollins, 2000.
McGee, Diane. *A Passion for Fashion: Antique, Collectible, and Retro Clothes*. Omaha, Nebr.: Simmons-Boardman Books, 1987.

McKelvey, Kathryn. *Fashion Source Book*. Cambridge, Mass.: Blackwell Science, 1996.
McRobbie, Angela, ed. *Zoot Suits and Second-Hand Dresses: An Anthology of Fashion and Film*. Boston: Unwin Hyman, 1988.
Meehan, Norma Lu, and Jean Druesedow. *Collection by Design: A Paper Doll History of Costume 1750–1900*. Lubbock: Texas Tech University Press, 1999.
Meij, Letse, ed. *Haute Couture & Pret-A-Porter: Mode 1750–2000*. New York: Waanders, 1999.
Mendes, Valerie D. *Dressed in Black*. New York: Harry N. Abrams, 2000.
Mendes, Valerie D. and Amy de la Haye. *20th Century Fashion*. London: Thames and Hudson, 1999.
Milbank, Caroline R. *Couture, the Great Designers*. New York: Stewart, Tabori, and Chang, 1985.
———. *New York Fashion: The Evolution of American Style*. New York: Harry N. Abrams, 1989.
Miyake, Issey. *Issey Miyake & Miyake Design Studio, 1970–1985*. Tokyo: Obunsha, 1985.
Moffitt, Peggy. *The Rudi Gernreich Book*. New York: Rizzoli, 1991.
Molloy, John T. *Dress for Success*. New York: Warner Books, 1975.
———. *The Woman's Dress for Success Book*. New York: Warner Books, 1977.
Mona Bismark, Cistrobal Balenciaga, Cecil Beaton. Paris: Mona Bismark Foundation, 1994.
Monro, Isabel Stevenson, and Dorothy E. Cook. *Costume Index: A Subject Guide to Plates and to Illustrated Text*. New York: H. W. Wilson, 1937.
Monroe, Isabel Stevenson, and Kate M. Monro. *Costume Index Supplement*. New York: H. W. Wilson, 1957.
Morgado, Marcia A. "Coming to Terms with Postmodern: Theories and Concepts of Contemporary Culture and Their Implications for Apparel Scholars." *Clothing and Textiles Research Journal* 14.1 (1996), 41–53.
Morris, Bernadine. *Scassi: A Cut Above*. New York: Rizzoli, 1996.
———. *Valentino (The Universe of Fashion)*. New York: Vendome Press, 1996.
Mott, Frank Luther. *A History of American Magazines*. 5 vols. Cambridge: Harvard University Press, 1930–1968.
Muggleton, David. *Inside Subculture: The Postmodern Meaning of Style*. New York: Berg, 2000.
Muller, Florence. *Art and Fashion*. London: Thames and Hudson, 2000.
Mulvagh, Jane. *Vivienne Westwood: An Unfashionable Life*. London: HarperCollins, 1999.
———. *Vogue History of 20th Century Fashion*. New York: Viking, 1988.
Mulvey, Kate. *Decades of Beauty, The Changing Image of Women, 1890s–1990s*. New York: Facts on File, 1998.
Municchi, Anna. *Furs for Men*. Modena: Zanfi Editori, 1988.
Murray, Maggie Pexton. *Changing Styles in Fashion: Who, What, Why*. New York: Fairchild, 1989.
National Geographic Society. *National Geographic Index: 1888–1946*. Washington, D.C.: National Geographic Society, 1967.
———. *National Geographic Index: 1947–1976*. Washington, D.C.: National Geographic Society, 1977.

Neret, Gilles. *1000 Dessous: A History of Lingerie/Eine Geschichte Der Reizwasche/ Histoire de la Lingerie*. New York: Taschen, 1998.

Nevinson, John Lea. *Origin and Early History of Fashion Plate*. Washington, D.C.: Smithsonian Institution Press, 1967.

Newman, Karoline, Gillian Proctor, and Karen Bressler. *A Century of Lingerie*. Edison, N.J.: Chartwell, 1998.

Newton, Stella Mary. *Health, Art and Reason: Dress Reformers of the Nineteenth Century*. London: J. Murray, 1974.

A New Wave in Fashion: Three Japanese Designers. Phoenix: Arizona Costume Institute of the Phoenix Art Museum, 1983.

Nicholson, Kathleen. *WWD Century: One Hundred Years of Fashion*. New York: Fairchild, 1998.

Nickerson, Camilla, and Neville Wakefield, eds. *Fashion Photography of the Nineties*. New York: Scalo, 1996.

Nixon, Sean. *Hard Looks: Masculinities, Spectatorship and Contemporary Consumption*. New York: St. Martin's Press, 1996.

Nordquist, Barbara K. "International Trade in Textiles and Clothing: Implications for the Future." *Clothing and Textiles Research Journal* 3 (Spring 1985), 35–39.

Norris, Herbert. *Medieval Costume and Fashion*. Reprint. New York: Dover, 1999.

———. *Tudor Costume and Fashion*. Mineola, N.Y.: Dover, 1997.

Nunn, Joan. *Fashion in Costume, 1200–2000*. Chicago: New Amsterdam Book, 2000.

Nystrom, Paul Henry. *Economics in Fashion*. New York: Ronald Press, 1928.

O'Keefe, Linda. *Shoes: A Celebration of Pumps, Sandals, Slippers & More*. New York: Workman, 1996.

Oldham, Todd. *Todd Oldham: Without Boundaries*. New York: Universe, 1997.

Olian, Joanne, ed. *Authentic French Fashions of the Twenties: 413 Costume Designs from L'Art et La Mode*. New York: Dover, 1990.

O'Neal, Gwendolyn. "Fashioning Future Fashion." In *Fashioning the Future: Our Future from Our Past*. Columbus: Department of Consumer and Textile Sciences, Ohio State University, 1996.

Osma, Guillermo de. *Fortuny: Mariano Fortuny, His Life and Work*. New York: Rizzoli, 1980.

Owen, Elizabeth. *Fashion in Photographs, 1920–1940*. London: Batsford, 1993.

Packard, Sidney. *The Fashion Business: Dynamics and Careers*. New York: Holt, Rinehart, and Winston, 1983.

———. *Strategies and Tactics in Fashion Marketing: Selected Readings*. New York: Fairchild, 1982.

Packard, Sidney, and Abraham Raine. *Consumer Behavior and Fashion Marketing*. 2nd ed. Dubuque, Iowa: Kendall/Hunt, 1979.

Packard, Sidney, Arthur A. Winters, and Nathan Axelrod. *Fashion Buying and Merchandising*. 2nd ed. New York: Fairchild, 1983.

Packer, William. *Fashion Drawings in Vogue*. New York: Coward-McCann, 1983.

Paoletti, Jo B. "Clothes Make the Boy, 1869–1910." *Dress* 9 (1983), 16–20.

Parmal, Pamela A. *Geoffery Beene*. Providence: Museum of Art, Rhode Island School of Design, 1997.

Parsons, Frank Alvah. *The Psychology of Dress*. New York: Doubleday, 1920.

Payne, Blanche. *History of Costume from the Ancient Egyptians to the Twentieth Century*. New York: Harper and Row, 1965.

Payne, Blanche, Geitel Winakor and Jane Farrell-Beck. *The History of Costume: From Ancient Mesopotamia through the Twentieth Century*. New York: HarperCollins, 1991.

Peacock, John. *The Chronicle of Western Costume: Complete in Colour with More than 1000 Illustrations from the Ancient World to the Late Twentieth Century*. London: Thames and Hudson, 1991.

———. *Fashion Accessories: The Complete 20th Century Sourcebook*. New York: Thames and Hudson, 2000.

———. *The 1940s*. New York: Thames and Hudson, 1998.

———. *The 1920s*. London: Thames and Hudson, 1997.

———. *20th-Century Fashion: The Complete Sourcebook*. London: Thames and Hudson, 1993.

Peiss, Kathy. *Hope in a Jar: The Making of America's Beauty Culture*. New York: Owl Books, 1999.

Penn, Irving. *Inventive Paris Clothes, 1909–1939: A Photographic Essay*. New York: Viking Press, 1977.

Perani, Judith M., and Norma H. Wolff. *Cloth, Dress and Art Patronage in Africa*. New York: Berg, 1999.

Perna, Rita. *Fashion Forecasting: A Mystery or a Method?* New York: Fairchild, 1987.

Phillips, Pamela M., Ellye Bloom, and John D. Mattingly. *Fashion Sales Promotion: The Selling behind the Selling*. New York: Wiley, 1985.

Pochna, Marie France. *Christian Dior: The Man Who Made the World Look New*. New York: Arcade, 1996.

Poiret, Paul. *My First Fifty Years*. London: V. Gollancz, 1931.

Polhemus, Ted. *Diesel: World Wide Wear*. New York: Watson-Guptill, 1998.

———. *Streetstyle: From Sidewalk to Catwalk*. New York: Thames and Hudson, 1994.

———. *Style Surfing: What to Wear in the 3rd Millennium*. New York: Thames and Hudson, 1996.

Portas, Mary. *Windows: The Art of Retail Display*. London: Thames and Hudson, 1999.

Powell, Jeanne, and Carol Foley. *Pattern Making*. Englewood Cliffs, N.J.: Prentice-Hall, 1987.

Quick, Harriet. *Catwalking: A History of the Fashion Model*. Edison, N.J.: Wellfleet Press, 1997.

Randall, Robert. *Fashion Photography: A Guide for the Beginner*. Englewood Cliffs, N.J.: Prentice-Hall, 1984.

Reality and Interpretation: 20th Century Clothing and Illustration. Columbus: Ohio Arts Council, 2000.

Rebora, Carrie, et al. *John Singleton Copley in America*. New York: Metropolitan Museum of Art, 1995.

Rexford, Nancy. *Women's Shoes in America, 1795–1930*. Kent, Ohio: Kent State University Press, 2000.

Rhodes, Zandra, and Anne Knight. *The Art of Zandra Rhodes*. Boston: Houghton Mifflin, 1985.

Ribeiro, Aileen. *The Art of Dress: Fashion in England and France 1750–1820*. New Haven, Conn.: Yale University Press, 1995.

———. *Dress and Morality*. New York: Holmes and Meier, 1986.

RILA: International Repertory of the Literature of Art. Williamston, Maine: Clark Art Institute, 1973– .

Riley, Robert. *The Fashion Makers*. New York: Crown, 1968.

Roach, Mary Ellen, and Joanne B. Eicher. *The Visible Self Perspectives on Dress*. Englewood Cliffs, N.J.: Prentice-Hall, 1973.

Roach-Higgins, Mary E., Joanne B. Eicher, and Kim K. Johnson, eds. *Dress and Identity*. New York: Fairchild, 1995.

Robertson, Helie. *Esprit, the Making of an Image*. San Francisco: Esprit, 1985.

Robinson, Julian. *Fashion in the 40's*. New York: St. Martin's Press, 1980.

———. *The Golden Age of Style*. New York: Gallery Books, 1976.

Roche, Daniel. *The Culture of Clothing: Dress and Fashion in the Ancien Regime*. Cambridge: Cambridge University Press, 1994.

Rogers, Dorothy S., and Lynda R. Gamans. *Fashion: A Marketing Approach*. New York: Holt, Rinehart, and Winston, 1983.

Rolley, Katrina. *Fashion in Photographs, 1900–1920*. New York: B. T. Batsford, 1992.

Rosencranz, Mary Lou. *Clothing Concepts: A Social-Psychological Approach*. New York: Macmillan, 1972.

Roshco, Bernard. *The Rag Race*. New York: Funk and Wagnalls, 1963.

Rothstein, Natalie. *Four Hundred Years of Fashion*. New York: Trafalgar Square, 1997.

Rouse, Elizabeth. *Understanding Fashion*. New York: Sherian House, 1989.

Rubinstein, Ruth P. *Dress Codes: Meanings and Messages in American Culture*. Boulder, Colo.: Westview Press, 1995.

Rudofsky, Bernard. *Are Clothes Modern? An Essay on Contemporary Apparel*. Chicago: P. Throbald, 1947.

Russell, Douglas. *Costume History and Style*. Englewood Cliffs, N.J.: Prentice-Hall, 1983.

Ryan, Mary Shaw. *Clothing: A Study in Human Behavior*. New York: Holt, Rinehart, and Winston, 1966.

Saint Laurent, Yves. *Yves St. Laurent: Images of Design 1958–1988*. New York: Knopf, 1988.

Sanderson, Elizabeth. "The Edinburgh Milliners, 1720–1820." *Costume* 20 (1986), 18–28.

Schefer, Dorothy. *What Is Beauty?: New Definitions from the Fashion Vanguard*. New York: Universe, 1997.

Schlachter, Trudy. *Millennium Mode: Fashion Forecasts from 40 Top Designers*. New York: Rizzoli, 1999.

Schlereth, Thomas J. *Material Culture Studies in America*. Nashville, Tenn.: American Association for State and Local History, 1982.

Schnurnberger, Lynn. *Let There Be Clothes: 40,000 Years of Fashion*. New York: Workman, 1991.

Schrank, Holly L., Alan L. Sugawara, and Minja Kim. "Comparison of Korean and American Fashion Leaders." *Home Economics Research Journal* 10 (March 1982), 235–40.

Schreier, Barbara. *Becoming American Women: Clothing and the Jewish Immigrant Experience, 1880–1920*. Chicago: Chicago Historical Society, 1994.

———. *Fitting In: Four Generations of College Life*. Chicago: Chicago Historical Society, 1991.

Sears, Roebuck and Co. *The 1897 Sears, Roebuck Catalogue*. New York: Chelsea House, 1968.

———. *The 1902 Sears, Roebuck Catalogue*. New York: Bounty Books, 1969.

Segal, Marvin E. *From Rags to Riches: Success in Apparel Retailing*. New York: Wiley, 1982.

Seidner, David, ed. *Lisa Fonssagrives: Three Decades of Classic Fashion Photography*. New York: Vendome Press, 1996.

Setnik, Linda. *Victorian Costume for Ladies*. New York: Schiffer, 2000.

Severa, Joan L. *Dressed for the Photographer: Ordinary Americans and Fashion, 1840–1900*. Kent, Ohio: Kent State University Press, 1997.

Severn, Bill. *The Long and Short of It: Five Thousand Years of Fun and Fury over Hair*. New York: David McKay, 1971.

Shelden, Martha G. *Design through Draping*. Minneapolis: Burgess, 1967.

Silverman, K. "Fragments of a Fashionable Discourse." In *On Fashion*, ed. S. Bernstock and S. Ferriss. New Brunswick, N.J.: Rutgers University Press, 1994, 183–96.

Skinner, Tina. *Fashionable Clothing from the Sears Catalogs: Early 1980s*. Atglen, Pa.: Schiffer, 1999.

Sokolsky, Melvin. *Melvin Sokolsky: Seeing Fashion*. New York: Arena, 2000.

Solomon, Michael, R. *The Psychology of Fashion*. Lexington, Mass.: Lexington Books, 1985.

Sozzani, Franca, and Luca Stoppini. *Valentino Fashion Photocopy Manual 1960–00; Valentino's Red Book*. New York: Rizzoli, 2001.

Spitzer, Harry, and F. Richard Schwartz. *Inside Retail Sales Promotion and Advertising*. New York: Harper and Row, 1982.

Sproles, George B., and Leslie Davis Burns. *Changing Appearances: Understanding Dress in Contemporary Society*. New York: Fairchild, 1994.

Stamper, Anita A., Sue H. Sharp, and Linda B. Donnell. *Evaluating Apparel Quality*. New York: Fairchild, 1986.

Sternquist, Brenda, and Bonnie Davis. "Store Status and Country of Origin as Information Cues: Consumer's Perception of Sweater Price and Quality." *Home Economics Research Journal* 15 (December 1986), 124–31.

Steele, Valerie. *Fetish: Fashion, Sex & Power*. New York: Oxford University Press, 1996.

———. *Fifty Years of Fashion: New Look to Now*. New York: Yale University Press, 1997.

———. *Shoes: A Lexicon of Style*. New York: Rizzoli, 1999.

———. *Women of Fashion: 20th Century Designers*. New York: Rizzoli, 1991.

Steele, Valerie, and Laird Borrelli. *Bags: A Lexicon of Style*. New York: Rizzoli, 1999.

Stone, Elaine. *Fashion Merchandising: An Introduction*. 5th ed. New York: Glencoe, 1994.

Storm, Penny. *Functions of Dress: Tool of Culture and the Individual*. Englewood Cliffs, N.J.: Prentice-Hall, 1987.

Stowell, Donald, and Erin Wertenberger. *A Century of Fashion 1865–1965*. Chicago: Encyclopedia Britannica, 1987.

Strege, Gayle. *The Art of Selling: A History of Visual Merchandising*. Columbus: Ohio State University Historic Costume and Textiles Collection, 1999.

———. *The Dynamics of Fashion*. New York: Fairchild, 1999.

———. "Historicism in Fashionable Dress." In *Fashioning the Future, Our Future from Our Past*. Columbus: Ohio State University Historic Costume and Textiles Collection, 1996.

Sullivan, Joan. "In Pursuit of Legitimacy: Home Economists and the Hoover Apron of World War I." *Dress* (1999), 31–46.

Swain, Margaret. "The Patchwork Dressing Gown." *Costume* 18 (1984), 59–65.

Tarrant, Naomi E. *Collecting Costume: The Care and Display of Clothes and Accessories*. London: G. Allen and Unwin, 1983.

Tate, Sharon Lee. *Inside Fashion Design*. 2nd ed. New York: Harper and Row, 1984.

Tate, Sharon Lee, and Mona Shafer Edwards. *The Complete Book of Fashion Illustration*. 2nd ed. New York: Harper and Row, 1987.

Thackara, John. *Design after Modernism: Beyond the Object*. New York: Thames and Hudson, 1988.

Thames, Bill. *Drawing Fashion*. New York: McGraw-Hill, 1985.

Thieme, Charles. *With Grace & Favour: Victorian & Edwardian Fashion in America*. Cincinnati, Ohio: Cincinnati Art Museum, 1993.

Tobias, Tobi, and Chesley McLaren. *Obsessed by Dress*. New York: Beacon Press, 2000.

Toledo, Ruben. *Ruben Toledo, Isabel Toledo*. New York: Visionnaire, 2000.

Tolkein, Tracy. *Dressing Up Vintage*. New York: Rizzoli, 2000.

Tortora, Phyllis, and Keith Eubank. *Survey of Historic Costume: A History of Western Dress*. 2nd ed. New York: Fairchild, 1994.

Trachtenberg, Jeffrey A. *Ralph Lauren: The Man behind the Mystique*. Boston: Little, Brown, 1988.

Traliey, Jane, ed. *Harper's Bazaar: 100 Years of the American Female*. New York: Random House, 1967.

Trautman, Patricia. *Clothing America: A Bibliography and Location Index of Nineteenth Century American Pattern Drawing Systems*. Brooklyn, N.Y.: Costume Society of America, 1987.

Tseelon, Efrat. *The Masque of Femininity*. London: Sage, 1995.

Tucker, Andrew. *Fashion: A Crash Course*. New York: Watson-Guptill, 2000.

———. *The London Fashion Book*. New York: Rizzoli, 1998.

Tulloch, Carol. *The Birth of Cool: Dress Culture of the African Disapora*. London: Berg, 2002.

Turner, Lowri. *Gianni Versace: Fashion's Last Emperor*. London: Essential, 1997.

Tyrrell, Anne V. *Changing Trends in Fashion: Patterns of the Twentieth Century, 1900–1970*. London: Batsford, 1986.

Vecchio, Walter, and Robert Riley. *The Fashion Makers: A Photographic Record*. New York: Crown, 1968.

Vecellio, Cesare. *Vecellio's Renaissance Costume Book*. New York: Dover, 1977.

Vogue Company. *Vogue: 100th Anniversary Special*. New York: Vogue, 1992.

Vollbrach, Michaele. *Nothing Sacred: Cartoons and Comments*. New York: Rizzoli, 2000.

Vreeland, Diana. *D.V.* Ed. George Plimpton and Christopher Hemphill. New York: Knopf, 1984.

Walker, Catherine. *Catherine Walker*. New York: Universe, 1998.

Wallach, Anne. "Fashions and Underfashions: Two Hundred Years of Attitudes and Underwear as Seen in Contemporary Paper Dolls." *Dress* 5 (1979), 49–62.

Wallerstein, Katherine. "Thinness and Other Refusals in Contemporary Fashion Advertisments." *Fashion Theory: The Journal of Dress, Body and Culture* 2: 2 (1998), 129–50.

Wardlow, Daniel L., ed. *Gays, Lesbians, and Consumer Behavior: Theory, Practice and Research Issues in Marketing*. New York: Haworth Press, 1996.

Warner, Patricia C. "Clothing as Barrier: American Women in the Olympics, 1900–1920." *Dress* (1997), 55–68.

Warwick, Edward, Henry C. Pitz, and Alexander Wyckoff. *Early American Dress: The Colonial and Revolutionary Periods*. New York: Bonanza, 1965.

Watkins, Susan M. *Clothing: The Portable Environment*. Ames: Iowa State University Press, 1984.

Watson, Linda. *Vogue: Twentieth Century Fashion*. London: Carlton, 1999.

Waugh, Christina. " 'Well-Cut through the Body': Fitted Clothing in Twelfth-Century Europe." *Dress* (1999), 3–16.

Waugh, Norah. *Corsets and Crinolines*. New York: Theatre Arts Books, 1981.

———. *The Cut of Women's Clothes, 1600–1930*. New York: Theatre Arts Books, 1994.

Welker, Lauren. *Fabulous '50s Fashions*. Cumberland, Md.: Hobby House Press, 1984.

Welters, Linda. "Dress as Souvenir: Piña Cloth in the Nineteenth Century." *Dress* (1997), 16–26.

———. *Folk Dress in Europe and Anatolia: Beliefs about Protection and Fertility*. New York: Berg, 1999.

Westby, Barbara M. *Sears List of Subject Headings*. 10th ed. New York: H. W. Wilson, 1972.

White, Emily, ed. *Fashion 85: The Must-Have Book for Fashion Insiders*. New York: St. Martin's Press, 1994.

White, Nicola. *Reconstructing Italian Fashion: America and the Development of the Italian Fashion Industry*. New York: New York University Press, 2000.

White, Nicola, and Ian Griffiths, eds. *The Fashion Business: Theory, Practice, Image*. New York: Berg, 2000.

White, Palmer. *Elsa Schiaparelli: Empress of Paris Fashion*. New York: Rizzoli, 1986.

White, Sophie. "Dress in French Colonial Louisiana, 1699–1769: The Evidence from Notarial Sources." *Dress* 24 (1997), 69–75.

Wilcox, R. Turner. *The Dictionary of Costume*. New York: Scribner's, 1969.

———. *Five Centuries of American Costume*. New York: Scribner's, 1963.

———. *The Mode in Costume*. New York: Scribner's, 1958.

———. *The Mode in Hats and Headdress*. New York: Scribner's, 1948.

Willman, Polly. *The Costume Society of America Bibliography: 1983*. 3rd ed. New York: Costume Society of America, n.d.

Wilson, Elizabeth. *Adorned in Dreams: Fashion and Modernity*. London: Virago, 1985.
Wilson, Elizabeth, and Lou Taylor. *Through the Looking Glass: A History of Dress from 1860 to the Present Day*. London: BBC Books, 1989.
Wilson, Laurel. "The Cowboy: Real and Imagined." *Dress* (1996), 3–15.
Wingate, Isabel B., ed. *Fairchild's Dictionary of Textiles*. 6th ed. New York: Fairchild, 1979.
Winter, Janet. *Elizabethan Costuming*. 2d ed. New York: Other Times Productions, 1991.
Winters, Arthur A., and Stanley Goodman. *Fashion Advertising and Promotion*. 6th ed. New York: Fairchild, 1984.
Wollen, Peter, and Fiona Bradley, eds. *Addressing the Century: 100 Years of Art and Fashion*. London: Hayward Gallery, 1998.
Women's Wear Daily. *The Changing American Woman: 200 Years of American Fashion*. New York: Fairchild, 1976.
Wood, Barry James. *Show Windows: Seventy-five Years of the Art of Display*. New York: Congdon and Weed, 1982.
Worrell, Estelle Ansley. *Children's Costume in America 1607–1910*. New York: Scribner's, 1980.
———. *Early American Costume*. Harrisburg, Pa.: Stackpole, 1975.
Wright, Meredith, and Nancy Rexford. *Everyday Dress of Rural America 1783–1800: With Instructions and Patterns*. New York: Dover, 1992.
Yarwood, Doreen. *Fashion in the Western World, 1500–1990*. New York: Drama Book, 1992.
Yohannan, Kohle and Nancy Wolfe. *Claire McCardell: Redefining Modernism*. London: Harry N. Abrams, 1998.
Young, Antonia. *Women Who Become Men*. New York: Berg, 2000.
Zdaty, Steven. *Hairstyles and Fashion: A Hairdresser's History of Paris, 1910–1920*. New York: Berg, 1999.

Periodicals

Accessories. Norwalk, Conn., 1908– .
Advertising Age. Chicago, 1930– .
American Fabrics and Fashion. New York, 1946– .
American History Review. Washington, D.C., 1895– .
Apparel Executive. New York, 1964–1972.
Ars Textrina. Winnipeg, 1983– .
Bobbin Magazine. Columbia, S.C., 1959– .
Bride's Magazine. New York, 1934– .
Burton's Gentlemen's Magazine. Philadelphia, 1837–1840.
California Apparel News. Los Angeles, 1945– .
Chain Store Age: General Merchandise Trends. New York, 1925– .
Clothing and Textiles Research Journal. Monument, Colo., 1982– .
Connoisseur. New York, 1901– .
Cosmopolitan. New York, 1886– .
Costume. London, 1967/1968– .

Costume Research Journal (CRJ), formerly *Cutter's Research Journal*. Syracuse, N.Y., 2000– .
Daily News Record. New York, 1892– .
Delineator. New York, 1873–1937.
Dress. New York, 1975– .
Ebony. Chicago, 1945– .
Elle. New York, 1985– .
Esquire. New York, 1933– .
Essence. New York, 1970– .
Family Circle. New York, 1932– .
Family and Consumer Science Research Journal, formerly *HERJ*. Washington, D.C., 1972– .
Fashion Images de Mode. Göttingen, 1996– .
Fashion Theory. Oxford, 1997– .
FemmeLines. New York, 1957– .
Footwear News. New York, 1945– .
Gazette du Bon Ton. Paris, 1912–1925.
Gentlemen's Quarterly. New York, 1957– .
Godey's Lady's Book. Philadelphia, 1830–1898.
Good Housekeeping. New York, 1885– .
Graham's Magazine. Philadelphia, 1826–1858.
Harper's Bazaar. New York, 1867– .
Home Economics Research Journal. Washington, D.C., 1972– .
Hosiery News. Charlotte, N.C., 1921– .
Ingenue. Dunellen, N.J., 1959–1973.
Journal of American Culture. Bowling Green, Ohio, 1978– .
Journal of American Studies. London, 1989– .
Journal of Design History. Oxford, 1988– .
Journal of Popular Culture. Bowling Green, Ohio, 1967– .
Journal of Textile and Apparel Technology and Management. Raleigh, 2000– .
Journal of Women's History. Bloomington, Ind., 1989– .
Knitting Times. New York, 1833– .
Ladies' Home Journal. Des Moines, 1893– .
M: The Civilized Man. New York, 1983– .
Mademoiselle. New York, 1935– .
MascuLines. New York, 1957– .
McCall's. New York, 1870– .
Metropolitan. New York, 1868–1875.
Metropolitan Fashions. New York, 1873–1901.
Mirror of Fashion. New York, 1840–1850, 1853–1855.
Modern Bride. New York, 1949– .
New Ingenue. New York, 1973– .
New York Times Magazine. New York, 1896– .
Peterson's Magazine. Philadelphia, 1842–1898.
Pictorial Review. New York, 1899–1939.
Playboy. Chicago, 1953– .
Queen of Fashion. New York, 1870–1879.
Redbook. New York, 1903– .

Sears, Roebuck Catalog. Chicago, 1891– .
Seventeen. New York, 1944– .
Signs: Journal of Women in Culture and Society. Chicago, 1976– .
Sports Illustrated. New York, 1954– .
Stores. New York, 1912– .
Textile History. Guildford, England, 1968– .
Textile World. Atlanta, 1892.
Town and Country. New York, 1846– .
Visual Merchandising and Store Design. Cincinnati, 1922– .
Vogue. New York, 1892– .
W. New York, 1971– .
Weir/Wolfe Report. New York, 1998– .
Woman's Day. New York, 1937– .
Woman's Home Companion. Springfield, Ohio, 1873–1957.
Women's Wear Daily. New York, 1892– .

High school prom, 1947. Courtesy of Temple University Library, Urban Archives

Hippies, 1968. © Bettmann/CORBIS

Flapper, ca. 1935. Photo by Harry M. Rhoads. Courtesy of the Denver Public Library

Scene from the film *Hairspray*, 1988. © The Del Valle Archive

Teens in front of school in Denver, 2001. Photo by Liz Kincaid

"Grunge" girl. © Painet

"Raver" kids. Photo by Brian St. John (www.oneiromancer.org)

Heavy metal kids. © Painet

Punk kids. © Richard Olivier/CORBIS

FILM

Robert P. Holtzclaw and
Robert A. Armour

Cinema's first one hundred years have been a period of amazing growth in terms of technology, artistry, and economics. From those tentative, flickering initial images in the late nineteenth century to the multi-million dollar budgets and extravagant special effects of some movies today, the industry has moved into a central position in American popular culture. While the advent of television, among other factors, has led to a decrease in the number of people attending theaters each week, television has conversely increased public exposure to movies through video and DVD accessibility, cable and satellite movie channels, etc. It seems unlikely that the industry will ever return to the late 1940s attendance levels of 60 million movie tickets weekly, but estimates for 2001 indicate that each week an average of 18 million people went to a movie, and this figure includes only those attending theaters as opposed to renting videos or choosing other stay-at-home options. These figures, coupled with the billions of dollars in budgets and receipts worldwide, cement the film industry's dual identity as big business and as a primary source for the public's leisure activity and entertainment.

The number of people writing about film has grown exponentially as well, and cinema studies courses and programs are now commonplace at many colleges and even some high schools. These classes approach the movies from a variety of angles, including historical, aesthetic, and theoretical fields of study. In keeping with the concurrent development of film as a source for entertainment and as a field for scholarly study, books and articles and journals and Web sites devoted to the movies have been introduced at a sometimes frantic pace, with offerings for both the casual movie fan and those more interested in the cinema as an academic pursuit. A seemingly endless procession of new material continues to enter the marketplace, and the problem becomes one of wading through the mass of material to find good scholarly help when studying film. Students and others interested in film from a critical perspective can often have difficulty assessing the value or relevance of all that is out there, from reviews in the daily paper or monthly magazine to scholarly treatises on a particular director, movement, or thematic concern.

As with any other area of popular culture, the books published on film appeal to a wide variety of audiences. Many are intended for the popular audience and are written quickly without much film analysis. This chapter will focus on the more serious type whose facts and judgments can more generally be considered reliable; occasional reference will be made to more popular books when they have proved to be especially well done or unique. In this brief survey of film study materials, books are the primary focus. There are, of course, thousands of useful articles, but in this limited space all that can be done is to direct the reader to indexes of journals. The emphasis here—by limitation of space and purpose—is on American film and on books readily available in this country in English.

HISTORICAL OUTLINE

What follows in this history section is an attempt to highlight some of the key events, films, and artists of the first hundred years plus of cinema. The Reference Works section which comes after this history will direct interested readers and scholars to some of the many books and articles about these important elements of film; these books and articles also provide information about many other directors, performers, and movies not mentioned here due to the necessities of space. Thus, while this account must gloss over or omit some significant elements of the art form, it has been constructed to provide a useful introduction to the sprawling history of American film.

The movie now generally regarded as the "first film" has the rather undignified title of *Fred Ott's Sneeze*. Thomas Edison filmed his assistant, the now famous Mr. Ott, as he sneezed, and then he copyrighted the very short movie on January 7, 1894 (its copyright title is *Record of a Sneeze*). What is now considered the first public, theatrical showing of films was to come more than a year later, thousands of miles away.

The date was December 28, 1895. The place was the basement of a café in Paris. The audience was the first public one to pay its way to watch movies, paying to be fascinated by moving images of a baby eating his meal, workers leaving a factory, and a train rushing into a station. The scenes were taken from ordinary life, but the experience was far from ordinary. This event was produced by the Lumière brothers, but the technology that led to this moment had been the result of the imagination and persistence of many inventors, in both Europe and America.

Edward Muybridge in 1877 had discovered that sequential still photographs of a horse running could be placed in a series and "projected" in such a manner as to make the photographic image of the horse appear to actually be running. In New Jersey in the late 1880s Thomas Edison and his crew led by William Dickson developed the idea of putting photographs on a single piece of continuous film, and George Eastman supplied the film. For projection Edison decided on the Kinetoscope, a peephole machine through which the film could be shown to one person at a time. Several creative inventors worked on the idea of a projector, but it was finally the Lumière brothers who were able to adapt Edison's ideas and develop the first practical means of allowing many people to view a movie simultaneously. The history of this new art form was then to be written in light.

Once the photographic technology had been developed, the next stage was to decide what to do with it. Obviously audiences could not long be enthralled by shots of a baby eating and would demand more. The Lumières, Edison, rivals at American Mutoscope and Biograph Co., as well as others, attempted to expand the cinematic subject matter; but it was another Frenchman, George Méliès, who first achieved any success at telling a story with film. He was a magician who used the medium as part of his act, but in the process he began to develop plot as well as action. His most famous film was *A Trip to the Moon* (1902), which depicted a fanciful space voyage.

In order to develop a narrative process for film, the filmmaker had to learn to manipulate both space and time, to change them, and to move characters and action within them. What Méliès had started, Edison and his new director of production continued. Edwin S. Porter learned how to use dissolves and cuts between shots to indicate changes in time and/or space; the result was films such as *The Great Train Robbery* (1903). This Western, shot in the wilds of New Jersey, told the complete story of a train robbery, the chase of the bandits, and their eventual defeat in a gunfight with the posse. Cross-cutting allowed Porter to show activities of both the posse and the bandits that were supposed to take place simultaneously, a technique new to audiences at the time. Some audience members would even cower in terror when one of the bandits pointed his pistol directly at the camera and fired.

Businessmen began to realize the financial potential for movies. While movies were first shown as part of vaudeville and other forms of entertainment, they soon became the featured attraction themselves. By 1905 the first nickelodeon had opened in Pittsburgh, where customers each paid a nickel to see a program of a half dozen short films. The opening of theaters completed the elements necessary for an industry: product, technology, producer, purchaser, and distributor.

In 1907, a would-be playwright came to Edison with a filmscript for sale. Edison did not like the script, but he hired its author, David Wark Griffith, as an actor. Griffith needed money and accepted the job. Thus began the career of the man who would help turn this entertainment into an art. Soon, he began making films himself. His tastes in plots were melodramatic, but his interests in technique were both innovative and scientific. Guided by his cameraman, Billy Bitzer, he began to experiment with editing and shots, finding the inspiration for many ideas of cinematic technique in the sentimental novels and poems of nineteenth-century literature. Gradually he persuaded both audiences and company bosses to accept the idea of a more complicated plot told in a lengthier movie. The result was the first major, long film. In 1915, after a then unprecedented amount of time in production, Griffith released *The Birth of a Nation*, a story of the South during the Civil War and Reconstruction. The racial overtones of the film caused considerable controversy, but the power of the images and the timing of the editing created a work of art whose aesthetic excellence is not questioned. In response to the criticism of his racial views, the next year Griffith directed *Intolerance*, which interwove four history-spanning stories of intolerance into a single film. Griffith was to continue as one of America's leading directors until audiences began to lose their taste for melodrama, and other directors had learned his methods. He was responsible for launching the careers of several directors, such as Raoul Walsh, and numerous actors, such as Lillian and Dorothy Gish, Mary Pickford, and H. B. Walthall.

While Griffith was learning how to get the most from screen actors, Thomas Ince was polishing the art of telling a story efficiently. In the early 1900s, he directed a few films (*Civilization*, 1916, is the best known), but he quickly turned his attention to production, leaving the details of directing to others under his close supervision. His talent was for organization, and today he is credited with establishing the model for the studio system. Film is truly a collaborative art, and Ince learned how to bring the talents of many different people into a system that produced polished films, without the individualizing touches found in those films of Griffith or others who worked outside the strict studio system.

One man who learned his trade from Griffith was Mack Sennett. Sennett worked for Griffith for a few years as a director and writer, but his interests were more in comedy than in melodrama. In 1912 he broke away and began to work for an independent company, Keystone. Here he learned to merge the methods of stage slapstick comedy with the techniques of film; the results included the Keystone Kops, Ben Turpin, and Charlie Chaplin. Sennett's films used only the barest plot outline as a frame for comic gags that were improvised and shot quickly. From the Sennett method, Charlie Chaplin developed his own technique and character. He began making shorts under the direction of Sennett, but in 1915 he left and joined with Essanay Studios, which agreed to let him write and direct his own films at a then enormous salary. Here he fleshed out his tramp character; one of his first films for Essanay was *The Tramp* (1915). He continued making films that combined his own comic sense and acrobatic movements with social commentary and along with Mary Pickford became one of the cinema's first "stars." Later he made features, such as *The Gold Rush* (1925) and *Modern Times* (1936), which are still considered to be among the medium's finest blends of comedy, pathos, and commentary. While Sennett and Chaplin helped inaugurate this period of great film comedy, other performers of the time have equally enduring legacies. Buster Keaton combined a deadpan demeanor (he was sometimes called "The Great Stoneface") with remarkable physical dexterity and flawless comedic timing. He too began making shorts, but soon was directing and starring in features, such as *Sherlock Jr.* (1924), which falls between short- and feature-length, and *The General* (1926). Many of his movies feature incredibly complex and dangerous stunts, which he performed himself, and a compelling mixture of physical comedy and character development. Harold Lloyd (*The Freshman*, 1925) and Harry Langdon (*The Strong Man*, 1926) also created comic characters that demonstrated their originators' individuality and imagination. Many of these films hold up well even today in terms of comedic value and filmmaking prowess.

From these ingredients came the studio system and the star system. Movie-going audiences created a need for a great number of films, and small companies were unable to meet the demand. Adolph Zukor at Paramount and Marcus Loew, Louis B. Mayer, and Irving Thalberg at Metro-Goldwyn-Mayer quickly learned the means of applying American business methods to this new industry. They bought out their competition and eventually controlled film production, distribution, and exhibition. Even the actors and directors got into the act as Chaplin, Griffith, Pickford, and Douglas Fairbanks joined forces to create United Artists, intended at first to distribute the various productions of its founders. Later it too became a major studio, along with Columbia, Fox, Warners, and others.

With the studios came the stars. The public hungered for new heroes and new sex symbols, and the studios were quick to give the public what it wanted. Along with the stars who had been established in the early 1900s came the new generation of the 1920s: Rudolph Valentino, Gloria Swanson, Clara Bow. The stars soon became components of the American social fabric, and the public followed their affairs, marriages, and extravagant lives with keen interest. This was the stuff Hollywood was made of. Fortunately there were behind these stars creative directors, such as Cecil B. DeMille, Eric von Stroheim, and Henry King, who were able to mold the talents of the stars into some worthwhile movies.

During the 1920s American films dominated the worldwide industry, but they were greatly influenced and enhanced by developments and personalities from Europe. The Russians Sergei Eisenstein (*Potemkin*, 1925) and V. I. Pudovkin (*Mother*, 1926) were especially influential in their understanding of montage (the relationship of the images to each other and the meaning that results through editing). Additionally, American interest in fantasy was influenced both directly and indirectly by *The Cabinet of Dr. Caligari* (1919), directed by the German Robert Wiene, and *Destiny* (1921), directed by an Austrian working in Germany, Fritz Lang. Some Europeans came to America to make films, including some of those just mentioned, as well as other prominent directors such as Ernst Lubitsch, Victor Seastrom, and F.W. Murnau. The influence of all these films and filmmakers on American cinema was profound; they left their strong stylistic, thematic and narrative impressions on what came to be known as the Hollywood movie, an influence that continues to this day.

Technological developments during these early years would sometimes affect the movies in noticeable ways, with the biggest change of all affecting not what was seen, but what could be heard. The coming of sound to cinema both enhanced the possibilities of the art form for some and caused problems (even ended careers) for others. The story surrounding the advent of sound is a complex and complicated one. The idea of connecting sound to visuals had been around from the earliest days; Edison had in fact entered the movie business because he was searching for visuals to go with the phonograph he was already marketing. Converting the movie technology to sound was expensive. Despite development of the necessary technology (most notably in this country by Lee de Forest), the industry was reluctant to invest in the change. In the mid-1920s Western Electric developed a method for putting the sound on a disk that could be roughly synchronized with the film. None of the big studios could be convinced to try it, but Warner Brothers was about to be forced out of business by the other, larger companies. It had little to lose and decided to take the risk. For a year Warner distributed a program with short sound films of slight interest, but on October 6, 1927, it premiered *The Jazz Singer* with Al Jolson. Sound was used to help tell the story, and the public loved it. Quickly, Warner established its financial base, and other studios rushed to imitate it; but problems developed. Studios had to reequip themselves. The camera, which had been struggling to free itself and discover new methods of expression, found itself immobilized in a large box. Actors had to learn to speak to their audiences, and exhibitors had to invest in sound projectors and speakers. Certain vocally challenged actors saw their careers vanish once audiences heard their squawks or strong accents, and others were reduced to pantomime performances while more pleasingly voiced performers delivered the lines off-screen. Later, Hollywood movies such as *Singin' in the Rain* (1952) and *Sunset Boulevard* (1950) dealt with both the comic and more tragic elements of Hollywood's adjustment to sound. Once the initial problems were overcome, however, the industry moved on and the marriage of sound with visuals became a natural extension of the art.

The period between the coming of sound and World War II was dominated by the studios. They controlled the production—including story, the role of the directors, and the selection of actors, distribution, and exhibition (they owned their own theaters). In the 1930s America went to the movies; by the end of the decade some 80 million people saw a movie every week. The studios provided them with the means to live out their fantasies, find heroes, and escape from the Depression.

One factor directly affecting the films of the 1920s and 1930s was censorship. Hollywood movies had become rather open for the time in their allusions to sex and sin, and the scandals in the private lives of some stars (Fatty Arbuckle and Wallace Reid, among others) shocked the public even as it hungered for the salacious details. Fear of government intervention and of offending the public to a mortal (for the industry) degree led the studios to move toward censoring themselves. In 1922 they established their own regulatory organization, officially named the Motion Picture Producers and Distributors of America, under the directorship of Will Hays, former postmaster-general. The MPPDA was more commonly known as the Hays Office, and initially it was little more than an informal advisor. As pressure due to the aforementioned scandals and other concerns increased, however, Hays became more active and in the early 1930s his office announced a strict code for on-screen activities and language. The results stifled creativity in some instances, but the ostensible moral tastes of the public, and the ever watchful government, were satisfied.

The stars during this era captured the public's imagination as at no other time in American popular culture; Fred Astaire and Ginger Rogers, Jean Harlow, Clark Gable and Vivien Leigh, Edward G. Robinson, and Marlene Dietrich were among those bringing talent, glamour, and intrigue to the growing industry and its eager public. Musicals, melodramas, and gangster films were among the genres that helped define this era of cinema through their artistry and their popularity with audiences. Meanwhile, film comedians maintained and expanded upon the traditions of their silent predecessors: Charlie Chaplin continued to make movies and was joined by the Marx Brothers, Mae West, and W. C. Fields. All these performers combined physical comedy, or slapstick, with verbal wit and indelibly individual screen personalities.

At the same time, directors had to find a path through the maze created by the studios, the Hays Office, and the stars. They had to bring all these divergent elements together to make movies. Men such as John Ford and Howard Hawks created their own visions of America and discovered methods of capturing the American myth on film. Hawks, in particular, directed classic movies in a number of genres during his long career. Beginning in the 1930s he helped to cement the popularity and continuing legacy of the "screwball comedy" with such artistic and critical triumphs as *Bringing Up Baby* (1938) and *His Girl Friday* (1940). Later he moved with great success into other genres as well, including detective/noir (*The*

Big Sleep, 1946), the musical (*Gentlemen Prefer Blondes*, 1953), and the western (*Rio Bravo*, 1959).

Many of the directors of the period were immigrants. Some have been mentioned previously, but listed here are some of the most prominent, along with one movie that might be said to represent key elements of their work (although each director has many other movies, and facets to his career, than can be represented by a single title). This wave of foreign-born directors who helped shape the style and narrative of mid-century Hollywood includes Josef von Sternberg (*The Scarlet Empress*, 1934), Fritz Lang (*The Big Heat*, 1953), Otto Preminger (*The Moon Is Blue*, 1953) and Frank Capra, who moved to America when he was quite young (*It's a Wonderful Life*, 1946). The most famous of this group of directors is undoubtedly the British transplant Alfred Hitchcock, whose name has become synonymous with suspense to even the most casual moviegoer, thanks to a string of influential films including *Notorious* (1946), *Rear Window* (1954), and *Psycho* (1960). Each of these directors brought elements of his own upbringing and personal worldview to a series of cinematic treatments of the flaws and virtues of America and its people.

Perhaps those considerations were most masterfully expressed in a work that came at the end of the prewar period, *Citizen Kane* (1941), Orson Welles' feature-film directorial debut. This landmark movie is regarded by many, even today, as the fullest encapsulation of the capabilities of cinema in terms of artistry, narrative, and thematic excellence.

World War II changed the industry yet again. Many residents of Hollywood took time off to participate in the war effort. Some of the aforementioned directors, including John Ford and Frank Capra, made films for the government. Others, like Fritz Lang, continued to make commercial films, but they were propaganda-oriented and helped build morale. The stars went to the battle areas to entertain the troops. Even studio space was commandeered to produce war documentaries, and war films became a dominant genre.

After the war the rate of change accelerated, not always to the benefit of the industry. Anti-trust suits broke up the large studio conglomerates and forced them to sell their theaters, and television began to keep the potential audience at home. The film industry responded by attempting to tinker with the medium's modes of presentation in hopes of recapturing the somewhat distracted public's interest in movies. Among the innovations, for better or worse, were 3-D movies, CinemaScope, Technicolor, and other fads involving movie-related aromas and theater seats that moved or tingled at narratively appropriate times. Some of these attempts died merciful deaths, while others continue in some form today and have been joined by quadraphonic sound, sensurround, holographic images, and continual advances in special effects.

This industry response to competition from television and other threats to the box-office receipts has not been limited to technological changes, however. Moviemakers have also loosened up their Hays Office-era subject matter restrictions as well, although a ratings system is in place to, at least theoretically, provide guidance to the public in terms of the degree to which a movie incorporates sex, violence, language, or other potential concerns. Until the advent of cable television, movies had the advantage of being able to offer more in these somewhat taboo areas than could their network competitors, but that line has blurred since

Scene from the film *Poltergeist*, 1982. © The Del Valle Archive

HBO, Cinemax, and assorted specialty channels have eliminated the traditional television restrictions on nudity, language, and other "adult" issues.

The 1960s and 1970s are, in retrospect, watershed decades in the changing face of the American movie industry. As the major Hollywood studios began to lose their domination of the film business (in part because of the anti-trust decisions) and turned their attention to television production, independent producers and directors moved to increasingly prominent positions in the world of film. Often these new filmmakers would arrange financing on their own rather than through an established production company, and then make the movie and either distribute through the networks originally established by the Hollywood companies or through new distribution avenues as well.

Stanley Kubrick, Woody Allen, Robert Altman, Arthur Penn, Martin Scorsese, and Francis Ford Coppola are among the most significant directors to emerge during these decades. All have demonstrated a certain independence of subject and method, and all have, to varying degrees, seen some of their works meet with financial and critical success while others languished in one or both areas. It may still be too early to assess career legacies for any of these artists, but all will certainly merit some consideration in film histories for many decades to come.

Kubrick directed (and sometimes wrote or produced as well) a series of startling films in the 1960s and 1970s that continue to be discussed and debated today. Among the most prominent are *Dr. Strangelove* (1963), *2001: A Space Odyssey* (1969), and *A Clockwork Orange* (1971). Other, later works such as *Full Metal Jacket* (1987) and his final film, *Eyes Wide Shut* (he died just before its 2000 release) also have drawn considerable attention, comprised of both admiration and scorn. Kubrick's style can often be marked by excess, as he seemingly intentionally provokes reaction through his cinematography, narrative approach, and even subject matter.

Among the most prolific major directors since the demise of the studio era, Woody Allen has directed (and usually written and often starred in) an average of at least a film a year since the mid-1960s. Allen has crafted his own screen persona as one that varies little from film to film, and his settings and general thematic preoccupations often are carried from movie to movie as well. In a career this long there have been arcs, however, and periods of bleak, depressing narratives followed by runs of comedy, nostalgia, or whimsy. He has few equals in terms of sustaining a career and gaining a devoted audience along with a great degree of artistic freedom. Among the movies most useful in getting a sense of the director (from a very long and somewhat varied list of options) are *Bananas* (1971), *Annie Hall* (1977), and *Radio Days* (1987).

Robert Altman has drifted in and out of industry and public favor since the early 1970s, yet he has continued to work steadily, holding true to his artistic visions and working hard at times just to secure financing to get his movies made. In the 1970s he was, at times, a celebrated success with such movies as *M*A*S*H* (1970) and *Nashville* (1975). A master at the seamless interweaving of multiple narratives, he kept a lower profile through the 1980s (not always by choice) as he worked on smaller films, including a series of filmed adaptations of modern plays. *The Player* (1992) was a scathing indictment of some elements of the movie industry itself that brought him renewed attention and acclaim, and he followed it with another multi-storyline commentary on elements of the American experience, *Short Cuts* (1993). He continues in the new century with his recent financial and critical success *Gosford Park* (2001), for which he has received directing nominations and awards from several critics' groups.

Arthur Penn is best known for one movie, but through it he has had immeasurable influence on a number of subsequent directors and individual films. *Bonnie and Clyde* (1967) is considered by many critics and film historians to herald the beginning of a new American cinema through its mix of dazzling cinematic style, violence, comedy, and even contemporary social commentary. The movie was attacked by a majority of critics upon its initial release, but it was a movie that demanded further consideration. Eventually *Bonnie and Clyde* was named Best Film of the Year by many of the critics who had originally criticized it, and this reappraisal even led *Time* magazine to take the unprecedented action of offering a public retraction of its own initial negative review. Penn continued to work and even received an Academy Award nomination for his next film, *Alice's Restaurant*, but nothing has matched the bravado and attention generated by his breakthrough film.

The dark visions of Martin Scorsese's America were first introduced to critics and audiences with an under-the-radar film that gained most of its attention in retrospect, after later works caused viewers to look back and take notice. Since then, *Mean Streets* (1973) has only increased in recognition and stature within the industry, seen as the opening act of a challenging and at times brilliant career. *Alice Doesn't Live Here Anymore* (1974) was a step toward lasting recognition, and then *Taxi Driver* (1976) polarized critics but caused everyone to take notice of the director and the stories he had to tell. Scorsese kicked off the 1980s with a movie that many scholars now see as the decade's finest by any director, *Raging Bull*, which he soon followed with another tour-de-force starring Robert De Niro, *The King of Comedy* (1983). Both movies dealt with the negative effects of fame and celebrity, both on those who achieve them and on the masses who seem at times to crave them. Scorsese stirred up even more controversy (while also receiving an Oscar nomination) for *The Last Temptation of Christ* (1988), and he began the 1990s as he had started the previous decade, with another movie that has, over time, gained in critical importance and stature—*Goodfellas*.

Finally among this group of the "new breed" of American directors, Francis Ford Coppola has worked with success as both a director and producer, while overseeing a number of critical/financial failures as well. Coppola has expended a great deal of effort in the creation of his own variation of the studio system, drawing on what he sees as the advantages of such an operation while trying to avoid its more artistically oppressive tendencies. He, like Penn, is most closely associated with a single film title—*The Godfather*, which won Best Picture Oscars for both the original (1972) and *Part Two* (1974)—but he has also made several other much discussed films, including *The Conversation* (1974) and *Apocalypse Now* (1979). And, since then, he has continued to direct at times and produce at times, with mixed results but with his place in film history assured.

All six men, then, first came to prominence in the 1960s–1970s with their roles as directors of some of the era's most important and accomplished films. Most are still working, and all have seen both great success and massive indifference in terms of reactions to their subsequent work. This overview is not exhaustive—many other directors and many other important movies from the period are worthy of exploration—but a working knowledge of these six careers provides a solid overview of some of the most significant work in American cinema during a time of societal, artistic, and industry upheaval.

Which brings us to the 1980s and beyond. Despite some popular and critical sentiment to the contrary, the past twenty years of American cinema have not been a vast wasteland of special effects and epic tales, with commercial concerns completely quashing any attempts at narrative, thematic, or artistic risk-taking. But, to be sure, such a dismal view is reflective of some major elements of the industry, as bottom-line financial concerns have made the high-stakes game of movie financing into a dangerous venture with the potential for huge rewards or huge losses. Despite that fact, however, great movies and exciting artists have emerged, and individual films and careers are being shaped right now that will be discussed in future accounts of the history of the medium. We are still too close, in time, to know for certain which trends will bubble to the top and be most apparent to future scholars. Some directors may have yet to make their marks, perhaps prompting another look at earlier works, and some movies may yet develop a coalition of critical attention years after their release, as has happened many times in the past. For now, though, what follows are some key elements of the recent history of film, even as the passage of time has yet to rewrite it.

Oliver Stone is another director whose work has polarized critics and audiences throughout his career. He began his career as a scriptwriter for such brutal movies as *Midnight Express* (1978) and *Scarface* (1983), and has since forged a directorial career with such challenging, confrontational movies as *Platoon* (1986), which won the Academy Award for Best Picture of the Year, *Wall Street* (1987), and *Born on the Fourth of July* (1989). Media attention and controversy may have peaked (for now at least) with the one-two punch of *JFK* (1991) and *Natural Born Killers* (1994). The former did receive some favorable reviews but also an outpouring of criticism, even outside the traditional film press, for its conspiratorial take on the Kennedy assassination. And the latter has been a party to several lawsuits while being blamed, in general, for its depiction (some would say glorification) of violence. Stone's own pronouncements and demeanor in many interviews have not helped his public image, as he is at times overly defensive about his work, seemingly embracing his right to express his views through his movies while simultaneously denouncing those who express their views of the works he creates. There is little doubt, however, that he can be an immensely gifted stylist and storyteller, and his passion burns through in every film he creates, sometimes to the advantage of the movie itself, while other times less so.

Representing the array of film types and visions at work in the era, one can swing from the intensity of Oliver Stone to what seems to be the other extreme, at least on the surface—the films of John Hughes. Enormously popular during his mid-1980s string of hits, Hughes mined a familiar genre—the teen film—but updated it and made it his own, to the degree that even today, a new movie may be described as "John Hughes-like" and audiences know exactly what is being suggested. Hughes' successes—*Sixteen Candles* (1984), *The Breakfast Club* (1985), and *Ferris Bueller's Day Off* (1986)—serve as a trilogy of sorts that captures a particular time and age in a manner that has come to define the period and the type of film. Nothing in his career thus far suggests the range of Stone, nor the controversy and excess, but chances are his work will also be remembered, albeit for different reasons, as a representation of its era.

Like Oliver Stone, director Spike Lee has often served as a lightning rod for intense praise and scorn, both from film critics and the moviegoing public. Lee has emerged as the most prominent African American director in film history (a much shorter film history than that afforded white directors, to be sure), and he has shown a range of style and technique while continuing to develop his core thematic concerns, most notably connected to perceptions and attitudes on both sides of a perceived black-white racial divide. Lee emerged with *She's Gotta Have It* (1986), a quick-shoot, low-budget independent feature that landed him some attention, as well as his first taste of split critical reaction. The divide intensified with several of his subsequent films: Some see him as a gifted stylist not afraid to tackle important issues in uncompromising ways, while others observe an iconoclastic, even shrill theme to many of his movies. Among the most discussed of his works are *School Daze* (1988), *Do the Right Thing* (1989), an explosive film about racial tensions on one hot summer day in Brooklyn, and *Jungle Fever* (1991), which is concerned with the romance between an African American man and an Italian American woman. The parallels to Stone are perhaps most direct when Stone's *JFK* is compared to Lee's biographical film *Malcolm X* (1992). Released the year after the Stone film, it too ignited public debate and led to more discussion of the way movies can shape or question public perception of important events. And, like Stone, Lee has a sometimes combative relationship with the press and with critics who question some elements of his work.

A major figure when the cinematic history of this period is written (and quite likely a large influence for years to come) is producer/director Steven Spielberg. Spielberg has been a guiding force for some of the biggest blockbusters of the past twenty to thirty years, serving as producer, director, or both of such "event" movies as *Jaws* (1975), *Close Encounters of the Third Kind* (1977), *Raiders of the Lost Ark* (1981), *E.T.* (1982), *Who Framed Roger Rabbit?* (1988), and *Jurassic Park* (1993). There have also been a few critical/box-office duds along the way, but even that does not diminish the cultural significance (not to mention financial success) of the list above. And there is another side to Spielberg's work as well, as he has also directed what might be termed an alternate series of movies that move away from large-scale effects and tell more personal, more painful stories, yet still with the identifiable Spielberg touch. These include *The Color Purple* (1985), *Schindler's List* (1993), for which he won the Best Director and Best Picture Oscars, *Amistad* (1997), and *Saving Private Ryan* (1998).

Any discussion of Spielberg can quite logically be linked to the equally successful career of his sometimes associate, George Lucas. Lucas's spot in film history is assured simply from his work with the *Star Wars* films (beginning in 1977) and, with Spielberg, the *Raiders of the Lost Ark* series. Additionally, he has played a large role in the revolutionary advancements in special effects of the past few years, due to his establishment of the Industrial Light and Magic studios. Lucas has yet to demonstrate Spielberg's desire to tackle more emotionally heavy material, but individually and in tandem the two are key players in the recent course of American film history.

Although he had a career before 1997, director James Cameron cemented his spot in any history of late twentieth-century film (to the delight of some and the chagrin of others) with *Titanic* (1997). The film's enormous budget, along with reports of troubles during the shooting, led many to predict an epic critical and financial disaster. Critical reaction was mixed (though not wholly negative), but the movie tied a record by winning 11 Academy Awards (including Best Picture) and, most astoundingly, amassed more that $300 million in North American box-office receipts and more than $1 billion worldwide. Cameron also wrote the movie's script, mixing the story of the ship's disastrous voyage with his own created narrative about a lower-class male passenger and an upper-class female passenger. Whatever its merits and flaws, the fact that it attracted so many viewers (including many who returned to see it time and again) makes it a cultural artifact as well as an important component of any account of American cinema.

Even though many of the aforementioned directors are seemingly still in the primes of their careers, it might be said that even a newer wave of filmmakers has emerged in the last ten years. This is not based solely on age, but on an even more identifiable independent spirit in terms of such movie basics as narrative and stylistic conventions. Among the most notable in this regard, Quentin Tarantino has managed to forge a style so identifiable that his name has become an adjective to describe a type of movie (much like John Hughes, although they have little else in common). *Reservoir Dogs* (1992), Tarantino's first film, merged independent film characteristics with more traditional studio genre traits, bringing in the director's own quirky vision (and extreme violence) to a sort of B-movie caper story told hundreds of times in pictures thirty to forty years ago. The movie was not a big success, but it got him noticed. The attention then escalated dramatically with *Pulp Fiction* (1994), another crime caper of sorts, told with a disjointed narrative structure and a visual (and audio) style that played with innovation and convention in fresh ways. The movie divided audiences and critics alike, but it did break through to mainstream audiences and put Tarantino into the general public's film awareness. In many ways, *Pulp Fiction* sealed the independent filmmaker's move into the main current of the motion picture industry (and the movie's nomination for a Best Picture Oscar didn't hurt either). Tarantino followed his success with another crime caper, *Jackie Brown* (1997), and his narrative and stylistic techniques have become a model for many aspiring directors and writers.

The brother team of Joel and Ethan Coen also debuted with their own twisted spin on a crime drama, *Blood Simple* (1984). In both this film and their more recent *The Man Who Wasn't There* (2001), the producer/director team plays with some of the narrative and stylistic conventions of film noir, concurrently paying tribute through homage while also tweaking some of the conventions into a more self-reflexive take on the genre itself. In the seventeen years between these two movies, the Coens have put their own mark on other genres in a series of quirky films including the kidnap comedy *Raising Arizona* (1987), the gangster throwback *Miller's Crossing* (1990), the Cannes-winning movie business tale *Barton Fink* (1991), and one of their biggest commercial and critical successes to date, the crime thriller/character study *Fargo* (1996). The Coens remain fearless in their willingness to tackle odd subjects, through unusual stylistic techniques, sometimes at a creaking pace, and though their movies lack the unity of subject matter that identifies some directors as auteurs, there is an underlying thematic resonance, as well as an ironic appreciation for traditional Hollywood genres, that do mark a Coen Brothers film.

David Lynch, though older than both Tarantino and the Coens, may be the most unconventional of the group. He served notice of both his eccentricity and his talent with his debut, *Eraserhead* (1976), a surreal account of alienation with a strong stylistic voice of its own. The more mainstream (in style, anyway) *The Elephant Man* (1980) followed, and although it was based on a true story it still shared many of the narrative and thematic attributes of his debut film. Even more surreal and at least equally disturbing was *Blue Velvet* (1986), a stylish and decadent look at the rotting core beneath the veneer of a typical small town. This film, in tandem with Lynch's much discussed television series *Twin Peaks* and the feature film *Wild at Heart* (1990), came to identify the director most clearly in public perception as a stylistically skillful but narratively almost impenetrable storyteller. What a surprise, then, to see *The Straight Story* (1999), yet another unusual narrative but one told with a much more conventional cinematic style. With *Mulholland Drive* (2001) the director is back to his trademark mix of dreamlike imagery and complex, at times unfathomable, narrative twists, and the movie has won him critical acclaim as well as some Best Director honors.

Even a cursory look at the key directors and producers and other creatively prominent individuals throughout the history of American cinema will reveal the extreme predominance of white males in all decision-making areas of the industry. Slowly but noticeably the creative avenues are opening a little wider to women and blacks, so that perhaps a subsequent history of film might feature more than Spike Lee and no females in a survey of the most important directors of the industry.

As far back as the 1920s and 1930s a market existed for "black cinema" as a viable commercial enterprise, although it operated on the fringes of the industry and opportunities for black directors and producers within the studio system were extremely rare. Oscar Micheaux was a pioneer in this area, as he produced, directed, edited and even distributed more than thirty-five feature films to primarily black audiences from approximately 1920 to 1948. In later years, directors such as Gordon Parks (*The Learning Tree*, 1969; *Shaft*, 1971) and Melvin Van Peebles

Movie poster for *House of Usher*, 1960. © The Del Valle Archive

(*Sweet Sweetback's Baadasssss Song*, 1971) achieved a measure of mainstream success and recognition. Spike Lee's work has helped open doors for a new generation of black filmmakers in an environment that affords them greater opportunity to work "within" the system. Among the new directors, John Singleton (*Boyz N the Hood*, 1991) is among the most promising in terms of artistic, critical, and possible commercial success.

Women directors, too, have long been shut out of the inside track in Hollywood, although, again, a few were able to work and sustain careers even in the earlier days of the studio system. Among the most prominent pre-1980 are Dorothy Arzner (*Merrily We Go to Hell*, 1932; *Dance Girl Dance*, 1940) and actress/director Ida Lupino (*The Trouble with Angels*, 1966). Additionally, female screenwriters were able to find a modicum of work in the early years of cinema, including a long and distinguished career from Frances Marion, the Academy-Award-winning screenwriter of *The Big House* (1930) and *The Champ* (1931). Fast-forwarding to the 1970s and 1980s, the industry finally found a place for a small group of women in the directorial ranks, and many new careers are now being built, film by film, by a slowly but steadily increasing number of women. Based on past success and potential for the future, some of the names to know include Amy Heckerling (*Fast Times at Ridgemont High*, 1982), Susan Seidelman (*Desperately Seeking Susan*, 1985), Martha Coolidge (*Rambling Rose*, 1991), Nancy Savoca (*Dogfight*, 1991), Agnieszka Holland (several well-received foreign-language films, followed by *Washington Square*, 1997), Penny Marshall (*Big*, 1988; *A League of Their Own*, 1992), and Kasi Lemmons (*Eve's Bayou*, 1997). The degree to which these women, and others, will be able to sustain careers has yet to be determined, dependent on the factors that affect any director's career as well as some additional gender-based considerations that the industry continues to work through.

One additional group finally making some headway into cinema mainstream is the assortment of young directors and producers dealing with gay and lesbian subject matter as the central focus or as a significant element of their films. After years of only underground gay-themed movies (and the occasional camp or victim-centered Hollywood treatment), the past two decades have seen critical attention and some success for such artists as Todd Haynes (*Poison*, 1991), producer Christine Vachon (*Go Fish*, 1994; *Kids*, 1995), Kimberly Peirce (*Boys Don't Cry*, 1999), and Gus van Sant (*My Own Private Idaho*, 1991), among others, and a growing scholarly interest in the study of film from what is sometimes called the "queer theory" perspective.

Any attempt to summarize the varied and complex history of film and to highlight the most significant of the many thousands of American movies and directors and stars will, by necessity, be incomplete. Some important people and movies have been omitted, but the preceding is an attempt to acquaint the interested reader and budding film scholar with a general overview of the development of the industry and some of the many key figures and movies within it.

What follows, now, is a similarly incomplete but still representative account of some of the thousands of books and other resources in which one may read about film history, theory, individual performers and directors, and individual movies. Each reference work mentioned here will most likely direct readers to still other works, thus revealing more of the vast array of materials available for study.

REFERENCE WORKS

A valuable collection of general reference books that cover a great number of film topics has been published. None is complete in itself, and all contain numerous errors, but they can be used for quick and easy reference as long as detailed criticism or analysis is not needed.

Four books compete as encyclopedias of film. The oldest is Roger Manvell's *The International Encyclopedia of Film*. It contains brief essays on film directors, important films, significant actors, and recurring cinematic themes. Where possible, a book or two on the entry will be mentioned as bibliography. *The Filmgoer's Companion*, edited by Leslie Halliwell, is updated periodically, but, aside from the occasional brief discussion of a theme, consists almost entirely of filmographies of film figures. *The Oxford Companion to Film*, edited by Liz-Anne Bawden, is flawed, but it can be perceptive and generally accurate. Perhaps its most disappointing feature is its limited filmographies of the major figures. Ephraim Katz's *The Film Encyclopedia* keeps its errors to a minimum. It gives brief entries on directors, actors, and others, and its definitions of film terms are quite useful.

One important general reference is the annual *International Film Guide* published in London under the general editorship of Peter Cowie. This book is an odd collection of film information from reviews to lists of film societies to a survey of film production in countries around the world. It is sometimes difficult to find what one is looking for, but the search can also be fun when the reader stumbles upon some information that was not part of the original quest.

A vital and sometimes vexing component of film research and study involves finding the factual background data for films, such as year and studio of release, production crew credits, and casting (particularly for minor roles). Particularly when a film is not available for video or DVD screening (and a surprising though slowly decreasing number of movies remain unreleased for home viewing), a researcher or film buff must depend on reference guides. Richard Dimmitt began such a work, *A Title Guide to the Talkies*, which has been continued by Andrew Aros. This collection lists titles, dates, distributors, and source material for each film's narrative, but includes little else. In a series of volumes, the Library of Congress has published a complete list of all the films that have been copyrighted. These volumes also include date of release, length, and producer credits for each film. One particularly useful feature of this reference is its inclusion of television commercials and short films, which are often difficult to date or verify from other sources. A similar work is sponsored by the American Film Institute, called *The AFI Catalogue of Motion Pictures*. Each decade is covered in a separate volume, with every movie from the decade listed with credits, date, and plot summary. The volumes also feature extensive indexes. The first two volumes to be released covered 1921–1930 (edited by Kenneth W. Munden) and 1961–1970 (Richard Krasfur), and others have followed suit. Selected short films, newsreels, and feature articles are included as well.

Frank Magill's *Cinema Annual* and *Survey of Cinema* are also useful reference works for gathering information about individual films. Magill's books are not exhaustive—they do not summarize every movie released in a particular year—but they provide basic cast information as well as lengthier discussion (a mix of summary and critical reaction) of the included movies. The writing and critical level of books in the series is appropriate for secondary school and undergraduate students, as well as the general public. Given their intended role as basic guides to the most significant films of each year, the scholarship is sound and reliable while generally avoiding controversy. Some volumes of the annual also include brief descriptions of books on film published during the year, as well as brief interviews with filmmakers of note that year.

For film scholars wishing to view a movie on celluloid rather than video or DVD (either for aesthetic reasons or because the movie is not available in the more common formats), James Limbacher's *Feature Films on 8mm and 16mm* provides information on renters and sellers of individual films, as well as the movies' running times and brief credits.

Bibliographies of published material about film are central to film study as they lead researchers to articles and books on specific movies, artists, and theories. Finding magazine and journal articles is often among the more challenging tasks for a researcher, although the task has been made somewhat easier with the help of indexes and data available online. A number of bibliographic guides exist in print as well, but it is best to consult several, since any one individually is likely to feature omissions of some key articles or references. The number of possible sources for articles is simply too vast for any single index to cover reliably. Peter Bukalski's *Film Research* is a solid general bibliographic tool; it is a selected critical bibliography with some limited annotation. Similar is *The Film Book Bibliography* by Jack C. Ellis, Charles Derry, and Sharon Kern. Robert Armour in *Film: A Reference Guide* covers fewer books than do some of the others, but his bibliography is in essay form and somewhat more descriptive. A more recent and more exhaustive source for consultation is George Rehrauer's *The Macmillan Film Bibliography*. In two volumes he lists and annotates thousands of books on film, including his own recommendations for the most useful.

Harold Leonard's *The Film Index*, first published in 1941, was for years the major bibliography of articles (as opposed to books) on film. It covers the silent period in most detail, but also includes articles written into the mid-1930s. To fill the gap between Leonard and the present day, three different bibliographies may be useful to scholars and researchers. Perhaps the most valuable is *The New Film Index*, edited by Richard Dyer MacCann and Edward W. Perry. They have included the articles listed in standard annual journal indexes, such as *The Readers' Guide*, and then in addition have fully indexed thirty-eight of the major film journals in English. MacCann and Perry have brought their bibliography to 1970, at which point several annual bibliographies have begun. The *Humanities Index* and *Readers' Guide to Periodical Literature* both list numerous articles on film; in each the reader must look under "moving pictures" to find the bulk of the entries. They are especially valuable in locating reviews.

Two major annual indexes to periodical articles are now being published. Vincent Aceto, Jane Graves, and Fred Silva have begun their annual bibliography *Film Literature Index*, which covers 126 journals fully and another 150 non-film journals selectively. Unfortunately there is no annotation of the entries. Karen Jones is the general editor of the *International Index to Film Periodicals*, which covers fewer journals than the *Film Literature Index* but does include a few journals not indexed by the latter. The *International Index*'s brief annotations are helpful. The researcher would do well to consult both indexes.

Literally thousands of Web sites now exist which are devoted to particular genres, stars, directors, and movies. Most movies have their own "offiicial" Web sites, along with many fan-developed ancillary sites. Conducting a Web search for most any figure from film history, even those considered somewhat obscure, will likely reveal sites that contain biographical, and bibliographical, information about the person and where a researcher can look for more information. Among the most useful general film Web sites, the Internet Movie DataBase (imdb.com) can be a one-stop source for an amazing array of information on cast listings, reviews, plot summaries, and other facts for thousands of movies. From information provided at imdb, scholars can follow the Web trail to numerous other sites and indexes about an individual star or movie. The very act of research itself has been revolutionized by the advent of the Internet, and this site is an excellent starting point for almost any area of movie research.

The most convenient print guide to the numerous periodicals containing articles on film is a recent publication of the American Film Institute called *Factfile: Film and Television Periodicals in English*, edited by Diana Elsas. This volume lists eighty-two journals that deal primarily with film, or television, or both, and gives a brief annotation of each. The list includes the scholarly journals, such as *Film Quarterly* or *Cinema Journal*, technical ones, such as *American Cinematographer*, and popular ones, such as *American Film*, the organ of the AFI. The researcher should be aware that while many of the journals are of general interest, others appeal to the special interests of readers. For instance, *Literature/Film Quarterly* devotes its space to articles on feature films that have some connection with works of literature. *Media and Methods* is directed at the secondary school teacher, and *Film Culture* is concerned with the independent filmmaker. The list in *Factfile* is not complete and does not include the many periodicals that, though not primarily film journals, frequently publish articles on film, but it contains the basic journals and is an excellent checklist. Other checklists may be found in the bibliographies mentioned earlier in this chapter, but unlike the AFI *Factfile*, they all lack annotation and do not include subscription information.

One final reference book will prove valuable for the film fan, the student, and the scholar alike. *Film Facts* by Cobbett Steinberg is a collection of useful and not so useful information about the movies. It covers the economics of the industry, lists of popular films and stars, ten-best lists from numerous sources, and catalogs of awards and festivals.

RESEARCH COLLECTIONS

In dealing with archives that house film materials, the researcher is faced with some libraries that collect films and others that collect film-related materials. Locating the film itself may be one of the most difficult problems for the researcher. Most of the early nitrate films have been destroyed for one reason or another, often because the film stock itself is unstable. The researcher can depend on only five centers in this country for major and expensive efforts to preserve the early films: the Library of Congress and the American Film Institute in Washington, the Museum of Modern Art in New York, Eastman House in Rochester, and the University of California at Los Angeles Film and Television Archive. Each of these archives is collecting, preserving and holding films and does a first-rate job of maintaining our film heritage, but there are problems. The work is costly and time-consuming. Not all films are held in viewable prints, and the archives have not yet been able to publish an index of their holdings. There are additionally several other libraries with sizable collections of films, and the researcher should not overlook local sources.

Aside from the films themselves, film-related material might include film scripts, stills, journals, books, costumes, and fugitive materials, such as letters and posters. All of the archives mentioned with film collections also have some film-related material, but the best collections of related material are at the Library and Museum of the Performing Arts (a branch of the New York Public Library at Lincoln Center) and the Theater Arts Library at the University of California at Los Angeles.

Whether the researcher is looking for films or film-related materials, he or she would do best to write to the archives to inquire whether they have the necessary material before making the effort to visit the archives themselves. Security is understandably tight at these centers, and the researcher should take proper identification and should be prepared to demonstrate the seriousness of his or her research.

Among the best general surveys of libraries that house film collections and service film scholars is *Film Study Collections* by Nancy Allen. This book is a guide to the development of the collections by librarians and their use by researchers. For the librarian, Allen describes collection development, both retrospective and current, selecting periodicals, and evaluating both published materials and non-print materials. For the scholar and film fan, Allen describes the use and location of film scripts, bookstores and film memorabilia dealers, major U.S. archives, reference services, and the holdings in film study of many important libraries. She even provides a chapter of basic library instruction for those who do not know how to use a library. This important book should be in every private and public collection.

A general guide to the archives can be found in the *North American Film and Video Directory* by Olga S. Weber. This guide lists the archives and their locations and approximate sizes, but its value is limited. It lists only archives with film collections and does not describe the holdings or distinguish between significant holdings and minor ones.

Finally, it might be noted that while the distributors of films do not maintain research collections, they are usually most helpful to the researcher. Most are happy to work with researchers. Some of their better catalogs are useful sources of information, and the people in charge of collections for the companies are often knowledgeable and helpful.

HISTORY AND CRITICISM

One of the most popular aspects of film study is concerned with the personalities of the people involved in the industry. Perhaps the actors and actresses attract the most attention, but directors and other members of the production team have their devoted followers too. In a guide as short as this one, it is impossible to list individually all the books that have appeared on movie people. The researcher can consult the Web sites (or card catalogs) for most any good library and find a large number of books and collected articles about significant individuals both in front of and behind the camera. These works may well lead the researcher to other sources of information as well.

Mel Schuster has written two books, *Motion Picture Performers* and *Motion Picture Directors*, that list magazine and periodical articles. These guides list articles on both the personalities and their cinematic contributions from the turn of the century to the early 1970s.

David Thomson's book, *A Biographical Dictionary of Film*, also covers both directors and actors, but he provides different information. His book consists of short essays on the major figures. Most essays include a filmography, brief critical comments, and a selective bibliography.

Information about the actors can be found in other works. Richard Dimmitt has edited *An Actor Guide to the Talkies*, which covers movies between 1949 and 1964. He surveys some 8,000 features and lists the actors for each, but he does not list the role played by each actor, a serious handicap. Evelyn Mack Truitt has also listed actors in *Who Was Who on Screen*. Arranged by actor rather than by film, this guide gives all of an actor's films and dates.

David Quinland has published two useful guides to actors. His *Illustrated Directory of Film Stars* and *The Illustrated Directory of Film Character Actors* include capsule descriptions as well as evaluations and filmographies.

Directors are the subjects of several research guides. James Robert Parish and Michael R. Pitts have edited *Film Directors: A Guide to Their American Films*. Included are the feature films, with dates and company, for approximately 520 directors. Georges Sadoul's *Dictionary of Filmmakers* is even more inclusive. This book contains about 1,000 entries for directors, screen-writers, and others on the production side of the industry, but no actors.

A valuable collection of critical essays on numerous directors serves as a good general introduction to directors' work. *Great Film Directors: A Critical Anthology* is edited by Leo Braudy and Morris Dickstein. They have included three or four scholarly essays each on Ingmar Bergman, Frank Capra, Fritz Lang, D. W. Griffith, and nineteen more. A second book, in two volumes, with essays on major directors is *American Directors* by Jean-Pierre Coursodon and Pierre Sauvage. In this case they have only a single essay on each director, but the essays are informative and interesting. One of the most thorough books of this type is the two-volume *World Film Directors* (1890–1945 and 1945–1985), edited by John Wakeman. As the title suggests this reference work includes many directors working outside of America, and overall it is a thorough and clear collection of essays and filmographies about directors both famous and more obscure.

A reference guide to screenwriters has been published jointly by the Academy of Motion Pictures and the Writers' Guild of America. *Who Wrote the Movie and What Else Did He Write?* is extensive for the period 1936 through 1969. Included are both film title and writer's indexes. Larry Langman's *A Guide to American Screenwriters: The Sound Era, 1929–1982* lists the complete works of American screenwriters. Its two volumes cover over 5,000 writers and their films.

A number of variations of the generic screenplay are now being published. A shooting script is written before the film is shot and is the outline for what is going to happen. The cutting continuity is the written record of what has been shot and obviously is made after the film is finished. The shooting script tells what the screenwriter felt should be included. The cutting continuity tells what the director and the editor actually left in. And, finally, a shot analysis is a more detailed cutting continuity. The researcher needs to know which he/she is dealing with since a shooting script may indicate a scene that was never included in the final film and a cutting continuity may not demonstrate the screenwriter's intentions at all.

There are two checklists of published screenplays in print. Both are needed, as neither is inclusive, and neither makes a distinction between shooting scripts, cutting continuities, and shot analysis. Howard Poteet's *Published Radio, Television and Film Scripts: A Bibliography* lists some 668 film scripts (some are different versions of the same film script). Clifford McCarty's *Published Screenplays: A Checklist* lists the scripts for only 388 films, but he gives slightly more information than does Poteet about each entry. McCarty includes production company, date, director, author of the screenplay, original source, and the bibliographical data for the published screenplay. Through both of these sources the researcher can locate most of the screenplays that have so far been published. Additionally, Web sites such as the aforementioned imdb.com and even a retailer such as amazon.com can provide information on the print availability of a particular script.

Another variation of the screenplay that is gaining in popularity is the frame blowup continuity treatment. These books give frame enlargements from key shots in the film, and the researcher can almost "read a film." Among the most impressive of these works (from an older, classic film) is *The Complete Greed*, by Herman Weinberg, which combines frame blowups with the screenplay. Such treatments are more common with recent films.

Numerous book-length attempts to trace the history of film have been published through the years, some attempting to cover everything while others focus on a genre, or a decade, or some other organizing principle. Especially considering its relatively young age (when compared to other art forms), the history of film is very well-documented, but there remains much confusion about many of the details in the early development of film, in part because at the beginning so few people took this new form of entertainment seriously.

One of the earliest attempts at writing the history of the medium came from an Englishman, Paul Rotha, in what is now a respected classic, *The Film—Till Now*. The book first was published in 1930, but in the mid-1960s Richard Griffith brought it up to date. It is thorough, complete, and long, and it looks at film critically and theoretically, as well as historically. In 1939, Lewis Jacobs wrote the first general history of real importance to deal primarily with the American cinema. *The Rise of the American Film* emphasizes the industry but manages to cover a great number of films and their makers.

In the post-World War II period, Arthur Knight contributed *The Liveliest Art: A Panoramic History of the Movies*, which first came out in 1957. Though dated now, the book is still readable and reliable. It is valuable but too short to make any claim at completeness.

Most recently there have been several attempts at writing a good general history. Highly regarded is Gerald Mast's *A Short History of the Movies* (with, in later editions, revisions and updates by Bruce F. Kawin). This balanced and perceptive book is among the most useful of its type on the market. His format is rather

Scene from *Tarzan, the Ape Man*, 1932. The Kobol Collection.

standard for one-volume histories of film, but his research is thorough and his writing reasonably lively.

Thomas Bohn and Richard Stromgren have written *Light and Shadows*, which is also a solid general history. Their book is valuable, especially in the modern period, on which they have an excellent chapter on the influence of television on movies. John Fell's *A History of Films* and David Cook's A *History of Narrative Film* are also solid and valuable works. One of the more recent large-scale attempts to convey the development of the medium is Robert Sklar's *Film: An International History of the Medium*. As the title suggests it is worldwide in scope, and Sklar is particularly adept at placing the various international developments in film in context with one another and with broader historical events of the time. Yet another quality work (among the many which were released around the time of the movies' 100th birthday) is *Cinema: The First Hundred Years* by David Shipman. This is something of a coffee-table book, large in size and full of pictures, but it also provides useful commentary and information about other sources for those wishing to learn more about a particular event. A similarly successful century-spanning account is Robyn Karney's *Chronicle of the Cinema*. By necessity many of these books contain much of the same information, but different emphases and omissions, as well as variations in approach and writing style, will lead different scholars to find some more useful than others. Overall, however, all of these books are written by competent scholars and provide basic histories of the American film and, in some instances, the cinemas of other countries.

And finally, Eric Rhode's massive book, *A History of the Cinema from Its Origins to 1970*, is a large-scale effort at writing a world history of the movies. He also devotes chapters to the European cinematic contributions and developments, with more international general focus than many of the aforementioned histories. The book is not as readable as Mast's, in particular, but on the international scene it is unsurpassed in the period it covers.

Then there are books that do not record a general history, but do focus on a particular period, such as the silent era. Firsthand accounts, such as *When the Movies Were Young* by Linda Arvidson, who was Mrs. D. W. Griffith, and *The Movies, Mr. Griffith, and Me* by Lillian Gish have the natural flaws of any history written by the subjective participants, but the freshness and familiarity make such books excellent places to begin a study of the early days of the art.

Kevin Brownlow's *The Parade's Gone By* makes a similar contribution. In this case a scholar has interviewed the most important directors of the silent era and has intermingled their remarks with his own deliberate insights. This is oral history interpreted by a scholar without the biases of participation in the events that become that history. While Brownlow intermingled his thoughts with the words of the directors, George Pratt has written his history of the era, *Spellbound in Darkness*, by combining his commentary with reviews of the films as they were seen by critics contemporary with the films. The book is at times hard to follow, but Pratt is a competent scholar, and the reviews chronicle an art form and the culture that spawned it.

Naturally, latter-day scholars are writing histories of the silent era without including the primary material found in Brownlow or Pratt. D. J. Wenden's short book, *The Birth of the Movies*, takes the medium to the coming of sound; and Harry Geduld's *The Birth of the Talkies* is actually a study of the efforts of the industry to develop a sound system. He starts with Edison and takes the reader through the early stages of sound technology that eventually led to "You ain't heard nuthin' yet."

An important anthology on the early silent era is *Film Before Griffith*, edited by John Fell. The essays in this volume cover the development of the industry from the early 1890s until about 1908 and present readers with history too often neglected in the brief histories mentioned above. The most complete history of early film is *American Silent Film* by William K. Everson. This is a thoroughly scholarly study of film from the beginnings to the coming of sound. Much has been uncovered about the earliest years since this book was written, but it still remains among the most useful general survey of the period. Another valuable book is the American Film Institute-sponsored *The American Film Heritage*, edited by Tom Shales and others. It includes essays by scholars on films, filmmakers, studios, and themes of the silent era. Often the essay subject is little known to the general public, and the book becomes part of the AFI's effort at rediscovering the lost heritage of the medium.

Other eras in film history have received similar attention. Books such as Andrew Bergman's *We're in the Money*, about the Depression, and Penelope Houston's *The Contemporary Cinema, 1945–1963* devote themselves to particular periods and manage to provide more detail than can be found in books which attempt to cover the entire range of film history.

Some of the histories concentrate on the role Hollywood has played in the development of American culture. Hortense Powdermaker was one of the first to take an anthropological look at Hollywood in her book *Hollywood: The Dream Factory*. The book is a bit dated now, but it has set standards for a particular method of considering the medium. The American Film Institute sponsored a book by Garth Jowett that is a general history with an emphasis on Hollywood and its impact. Jowett includes much history of the controversies originated by Hollywood and is especially detailed on the problems of censorship. A delightful book for the fan of the popular film, edited by Todd McCarthy and Charles Flynn, is entitled *Kings of the B's*. The focus of the book is on the many minor directors who worked within the Hollywood system to produce countless movies that may be aesthetically insignificant but culturally powerful. In addition to history and criticism, the book includes a valuable filmography for 325 directors who are given scant attention in other histories.

Tino Balio's *The American Film Industry* is an anthology of essays on the industry that made the movies. Some of these essays were written by actual industry participants, and others by scholars on the outside looking in. The mix of perspectives is interesting in and of itself, and the book is among the best so far in the emerging area of research into the practices of the industry. The book is historically organized around the chronological period of the subject of each essay.

And there is a large group of books concentrating on single studios and their roles within the Hollywood industry. Studies such as Charles Higham's *Warner Brothers* and Rochelle Larkin's *Hail Columbia* explore the inner workings of a studio and the escapades of the moguls who made it successful.

The area of film criticism is large, diverse, and eclectic, but perhaps the best critical research tools can be divided into smaller categories. Many of the best can be considered introductions to film. The fact that a book is intended as an introduction to the subject and was published for the many students who may be taking their first film course should not suggest that the book is necessarily superficial. In fact, a number of them delve deeply into the aesthetics of the medium. One of the earliest scholars to publish an introduction was Lewis Jacobs in his anthology *Introduction to the Art of the Movies*. This book is a collection of essays on image, movement, time and space, color, and sound—standard topics to be covered in an introductory text.

During the 1960s a number of introductions came out, and several have remained highly regarded. Ernest Lindgren's *The Art of the Film* has sections on mechanics, techniques, and criticism. *The Film Experience* by Roy Huss and Norman Silverstein deals with continuity, rhythm, structure, image, and point of view.

Of the film texts first introduced in the 1970s, Louis Giannetti's *Understanding Movies* has proved to be among the most durable. Now in its ninth edition (as of 2002), the book addresses film from the perspectives of picture, movement, editing, sound, drama, literature, and theory. A somewhat similar book, *Critical Focus: An Introduction to Film*, is by Richard Blumenberg, a teacher and scholar with some experience as a filmmaker. After an introduction that defines the medium and relates it to the other arts, Blumenberg devotes sections to the narrative film, the documentary, and the experimental film.

Elements of Film by Lee R. Bobker is perhaps the best of the introductions in the area of technique. None of the others explains the technical side of the art in prose as easy to understand. Of the anthologies that serve as introductions to film theory, one of the best is *Film Theory and Criticism: Introductory Readings* (edited, in its most recent edition, by Leo Braudy and Marshall Cohen). A judicious selection of essays makes this a useful introduction to the topic, and the text's subtopics (including reality, language, theory, literature and film, genre, artists, and audience) cover a wide range of film criticism. Other theory-based works that may prove helpful to scholars and interested filmgoers include Robert Stam's *Film Theory: An Introduction* and a book edited by John Hill and Pamela Church Gibson, *Film Studies: Critical Approaches*. One area that has received less attention in book-length critical assessments is the aesthetics of the short film, but David Sohn's *Film: The Critical Eye* is useful in this regard. Although his discussion is concerned primarily with movies distributed by Pyramid Films, his general points are worth consideration in any research or writing about short films.

Other potentially worthwhile texts for those interested in reading and writing about film include James Monaco's *How to Read a Film*, which covers a full range of film studies from technique to history, and George Wead and George Lellis's *Film: Form and Function*, on Hollywood and the alternatives to the Hollywood traditions. This introduction to film also discusses movie techniques. For an example of an introduction to film studies which mixes close analysis of films and filmmakers with history and technical understanding, the reader might consult Lewis Jacobs's *The Emergence of Film Art: The Evolution and Development of the Motion Picture as an Art, from 1900 to the Present*. And, in a final grouping of relatively recent texts which bring useful information and approaches to the study of film, these stand out (some are new, while others are updated editions of older works): Bernard Dick's *Anatomy of a Film*, William Phillips's *Film: An Introduction*, Joseph Boggs and Dennis Petrie's *The Art of Watching Films*, and Richard Beck Peacock's *The Art of Moviemaking: Script to Screen*. As film studies continues to develop and expand as an area of academic enterprise, the number of new books and revised editions expands rapidly as well. Clarity, balance, and a sense of contributing something new to the field are worthwhile standards for evaluating the steady stream of new material.

Most of the introductions to film study discussed previously are based on the writings of film theorists whose work is earlier and more complex. Once the students have passed the need for the introductions, they will find the work of the theorists challenging and fascinating. As early as 1915 the poet Vachel Lindsay published a curious book that was part theory and part encomium on what was then a new art form. In fact his title, *The Art of the Moving Picture*, would have surprised many people who would not have called this entertainment form an art.

Much of the early theory was developed by Russian artists, some of whom learned their lessons by watching films made by Americans who wrote little about the theory. Sergei Eisenstein (*The Film Sense*, *Film Form*, and *Film Essays and a Lecture*) and V. I. Pudovkin (*Film Technique and Film Acting*) were directors who, through their writings, helped to establish the language of film criticism while at the same time coming to an understanding of how film works.

They were followed by French and German filmmakers and theorists. Of the French, Bela Balazs was also a director; his *Theory of the Film* was a summary of his thoughts on the use of the camera and editing. André Bazin was not a director but a mentor of the directors who make up the French New Wave and editor of *Cahiers du Cinema*, the most important French cinema journal. *What Is Cinema?*

contains a sample of his extensive criticism. Siegfried Kracauer was a German who came to America to escape the Nazis. His book, *Theory of Film*, is basically a general theory with an emphasis on acting, sound, and music. The book, however, does range into many areas, including a notable chapter on the film and the novel. Most recently, important film theory has again been coming from France, where the theory of semiotics has been developed. The semiotics of film is a linguistic approach to the study of film in which visuals are seen as signs between the sender and viewer. Among the leading proponents of this theory is Christian Metz, whose book *Film Language* is the easiest of his works to understand, but the beginner should be warned that semiotics is not a simple approach to film.

There are several anthologies of essays that attempt to give an overview of film criticism. Richard Dyer MacCann's *Film: A Montage of Theories* is well known. His essays are by the best-known writers of film theory from Eisenstein to Bergman and cover the nature of film, film and the other arts, the reality of film, and the future of the medium. More recent is *The Major Film Theories* by J. Dudley Andrew. This book analyzes the work of the major theorists, who are separated into three broad groups: the formative tradition, realist film theory, and contemporary French film theory. MacCann covers more theorists, but Andrew is more up to date.

One of the types of film criticism that both scholars and film viewers have found most useful is the study of film genre, although there is some debate over the meaning of the word *genre* when applied to film. As far as this essay is concerned, *genre* will refer simply to film types, without much regard for the important scholarly debate over definition. It is admitted that "fantasy" may well overlap with "Western" and that "comedy" or "film noir" may not be a genre at all, but there is not space enough here to resolve that controversy. It does, however, make for interesting reading in and of itself.

Many books deal with the broad concept of film genre. *Beyond Formula* by Stanley J. Solomon devotes a chapter each to many of the important genres: Western, musical, horror, crime, detective, and war. Each chapter begins with a general discussion of the genre and its characteristics. It then discusses in depth seven or eight feature-length films of the genre. *American Film Genres* by Stuart M. Kaminsky begins with an intelligent essay on film genre, then moves to a discussion of genres that can productively be compared to one another, followed by sections on literary adaptations of genre, horror and science fiction, musicals, comedy, and genre directors (such as Donald Siegel and John Ford). *Film Genre: Theory and Criticism* opens with six essays on the theory of genre. The editor, Barry K. Grant, has selected essays on several major genres: screwball comedy, disaster, epic, gangster, horror, musical, sports, Western, and science fiction. *Hollywood Genres* by Thomas Schatz is yet another useful discussion of broader genre theory and its application to some particular genres.

The guides to fantasy films, including horror films and science fiction, are numerous. Walt Lee in the *Reference Guide to Fantastic Films* packs a lot of information about horror, science fiction, and fantasy films into a short space. He includes data about the cast, director, running time, source and type of fantasy, and a brief bibliography for each film. Less complete but valuable is a checklist compiled by Donald C. Willis, *Horror and Science Fiction Films*. He has included some 4,400 titles and has given a one-sentence plot description, lacking in Lee.

The Science Fiction Film Source Book by David Wingrove contains a brief history of the genre, a chronology of important science fiction films, and a survey of films and serials. Roy Huss and T. J. Ross have concentrated on the horror film alone in their book *Focus on the Horror Film*, an anthology of essays on gothic horror, monster terror, and the psychological thriller. And Carlos Clarens does not overwhelm the excellent text of *An Illustrated History of the Horror Film* with too many photos. *The Horror Film Handbook* by Alan Frank gives credits and brief synopses for important horror films. *The Aurum Film Encyclopedia: Horror*, edited by Phil Hardy and others, arranges its discussion by decades. It too gives credits and a brief history of horror film production. A special type of horror film is covered in James Ursini and Alain Silver's *The Vampire Film*, but *In Search of Dracula*, by Raymond T. McNally and Radu Florescu is more reliable even though its chief focus is not on films.

The standard book on the Western, by George N. Fenin and William K. Everson, is simply titled *The Western*. It traces the history of the genre, discusses the major films and even many of the minor ones, and includes enough photographs to stir memories of Saturday afternoons of long ago sitting in small theaters, munching popcorn, and watching heroes on beautiful horses. An excellent reference guide to study about the Western is *Western Films: An Annotated Critical Bibliography* by John G. Nachbar. This book, with both author and subject indexes, includes an intelligent and scholarly introduction and useful annotations. Phil Hardy has also edited *The Aurum Film Encyclopedia: The Western*. It includes an overview essay on the genre and a decade-by-decade survey of the important Western films.

One of the most useful guides to the gangster pictures is *The Great Gangster Pictures* by James Robert Parish and Michael R. Pitts. This book is basically an index to the credits, distributors, and running times of the movies in this genre, but an introductory essay on the history of the genre and brief critical comments about the individual films raise it beyond the level of an index. Related to the gangster genre is the moody, stylistically daring group of films known as film noir. Even as the debate rages about whether or not these films can be classified as a genre, many books continue to come out that group them as a basis for discussion from stylistic, narrative, and gender-based analyses.

John Kobal's *Gotta Sing, Gotta Dance* is a popular history of the musicals; it is a good place to begin the study of that genre and has been joined in the last few years by several other valuable assessments.

Comedy is a diverse and complex genre, if in fact it is a genre at all. The books on the movie comedies are numerous, and it is most difficult to select one or two as the point at which one might begin a study. Gerald Mast's *The Comic Mind* is a major study with an emphasis on the silent comedians. As with most of Mast's work, this book is both theoretical and historical. Walter Kerr in *The Silent Clowns* presents a historically oriented study of the greats.

The serials that many may remember from those Saturday afternoons of youth are well represented and studied in *Continued Next Week: A History of the Moving Picture Serial* by Kalton C. Lahue. This excellent history is complemented by an extensive appendix that includes credits and other data about the serials. Ken Weiss and Ed Goodgold have indexed the serials in *To Be Continued*.

Several books deal with the narrative in film. John Fell's excellent *Film and the*

Narrative Tradition traces the development of cinematic narrative in the early years of the medium. He looks back to nineteenth-century art forms for the source of film narrative. In *Narration in Light: Studies in Cinematic Point of View*, George M. Wilson discusses the narrative and narrators of major filmmakers such as Alfred Hitchcock and Josef von Sternberg. And David Bordwell's *Narration in the Fiction Film* also discusses theories of cinematic story telling. He analyzes the Hollywood narrative tradition, experimental films, and the European modernist films.

The history of work in documentary film is ably recorded in both *Non-fiction Film* by Richard Meran Barsam and *Documentary: A History of the Non-fiction Film* by Erik Barnouw. Both are solid, but the latter especially emphasizes the images and themes of the documentaries rather than the personalities.

Two anthologies have selected essays on the theory of the documentary as well as the history. *The Documentary Tradition*, edited by Lewis Jacobs, contains essays on the leading films and filmmakers from *Nanook* to *Woodstock*. Arranged according to the decades of the films studied, the essays also include general theory. Another of Barsam's books is *Nonfiction Film: Theory and Criticism*. This anthology includes essays on the idea of the documentary, its history, its artists, and its films.

Finally, Roy Levin's *Documentary Explorations* is a series of interviews with the major makers of documentary films. Included are Frederick Wiseman and Richard Leacock, among others.

One of the most important, but often overlooked, areas of film production is the experimental film. This area is difficult to define, even difficult to name. Whether it goes by the term *experimental film*, or *underground film*, *independent film*, it is concerned with the efforts of the filmmaker to expand the impact and technology of the medium. The basic study of the experimental film is by Sheldon Renan, *An Introduction to the American Underground Film*. This important book contains definition, history, and theory as well as studies of the important filmmakers and films. The appendix includes an excellent list of significant experimental films and an all too brief bibliography.

The history of the underground movement is told in two good books: *Underground Film: A Critical History* by Parker Tyler and *Experimental Cinema* by David Curtis. The latter book emphasizes the economic aspect of the experimental films, an important subject since these films are rarely shown in big money markets.

Two interesting anthologies of essays on the experimental film have been published. Gregory Battcock edited *The New American Cinema*, which includes essays by critics, such as Andrew Sarris, and filmmakers, such as Stan VanDerBeck and Stan Brakhage. P. Adams Sitney's *Film Culture Reader* is a collection of the most important essays from the journal that bills itself as "America's Independent Motion Picture Magazine." The essays give history and criticism, but the emphasis is on theory.

The best study of the technology of the experimental film is *Expanded Cinema*. This outstanding book by Gene Youngblood begins with a difficult but sound discussion of the nature of the experimental film and its effect on audiences. The first chapter is as much sociology as film criticism. His second and third chapters deal with the theory and cosmic consciousness of this type of film, and the latter part of the book considers in depth the technology of the major attempts at expanding the limits of the medium.

Another area of cinema study that has been written about extensively is the relationship that exists between film and the other arts—literature, theater, music, dance, even architecture—perhaps because, to a large extent, film is a synthesis of the arts. A good general introduction can be found in an anthology edited by T. J. Ross, *Film and the Liberal Arts*. The essays here compare and contrast film with literature, the visual arts, and music. An index to the relationship is *Filmed Books and Plays, 1928–1983* by A.G.S. Enser. The book contains indexes to the authors, films, and changes in original titles. It is by no means complete, but it is a good place to begin the study of the relationship between film and novels and the theater. That relationship between film and the theater is further explored by Nicholas Vardac in *Stage to Screen*, a study of theatrical method from David Garrick to D. W. Griffith; and critics, filmmakers, and playwrights have commented on that relationship in *Focus on Film and Theatre*, edited by James Hurt.

Perhaps the best known of the books dealing with the relationship between literature and film is George Bluestone's *Novels into Film*. He begins with a theoretical essay and then analyzes several major adaptations, such as *The Grapes of Wrath* and *The Ox Bow Incident*. Overall the book provides a good introduction to the relationship, but it is more limited in scope than its title and first chapter suggest. More valuable as introduction because it is more general and more theoretical is Robert Richardson's *Literature and Film*. Richardson has a good background in both media, and the result is a basic resource. His is one of the few books to pay much attention to the relationship between poetry and film, as most books concentrate on fiction or theater. Other studies abound, such as Geoffrey Wagner's thought-provoking (at times it is just provoking) *The Novel and the Cinema* and John Harrington's anthology *Literature and/as Film*. Only two volumes appeared in a series of books dealing with the adaptation of short stories into film under the general editorship of Gerald Barrett and Thomas Erskine. Titles included "An Occurrence at Owl Creek Bridge" and "The Rocking-Horse Winner." Each of the volumes is introduced by a solid essay on the problems and nature of adaptation. Fred Marcus has published a book called *Short Story/Short Film* that will be very useful to the researcher working with the shorter material. He gives the story, a story board, and film continuity, as well as analysis.

In the last few years, more critical attention has finally been paid to the role played by women and minorities in film and their image as portrayed by the films. For instance, books analyzing the depiction of women on the screen have been written by Marjorie Rosen (*Popcorn Venus*), Molly Haskell (*From Reverence to Rape*), and Joan Mellon (*Women and Their Sexuality in the New Film*). These books all combine history with criticism. Reference guides to women in film include a valuable book by Sharon Smith, *Women Who Make Movies*. Her brief essay on each filmmaker analyzes the woman's career and mentions her most important films. Bonnie Dawson's book *Women's Films in Print* is an annotated guide to some 800 films by women. A brief bibliography for each film is included when possible. Kaye Sullivan, in *Films for, by, and About Women*, provides brief descriptions of features and shorts that have women as either their subjects or creators. Louise Heck-Rabi writes on some of the best-known women filmmakers in *Women Filmmakers: A Critical Reception*. She deals with the critical reputations of eleven filmmakers, including Maya Deren, Mai Zetterling, and Shirley Clarke. And finally, in *Women and Film: Both Sides of the Camera*, E. Ann Kaplan compares the view of women in the classical Hollywood tradition, which was dominated by men, with that of the independent feminist filmmakers, which clearly has a new perspective.

Among the critical works dealing with African Americans and film, several have been historical surveys mixed with a bit of analysis. Donald Bogle calls his *Toms, Coons, Mulattoes, Mammies, and Blacks* an "interpretative history of blacks in American films." Lindsay Patterson has edited an anthology of essays that considers both the image of the black in film and the black's role in the film industry. His *Black Films and Film-makers* is notable for its contributors as well as its subject. Daniel Leab in *From Sambo to Superspade* demonstrates the progress—or more accurately the lack of progress—of the black screen image from *Birth of a Nation* to *Shaft*. The most scholarly of the critical histories of the black on the screen is by Thomas Cripps. *Slow Fade to Black* is an excellent study of the black in American film from 1900 to 1942. The reference guides to blacks and film, however, are somewhat less satisfactory. Anne Powers has published *Blacks in American Movies: A Selected Bibliography*. This book is fair but uneven and at times pedestrian. It includes both an author and subject index, as well as an occasional brief annotation. Richard Maynard has written a guide for teachers who wish to use films about blacks in the classroom. *The Black Man on Film: Racial Stereotyping* includes essays and a practical filmography; its chief weakness lies in its brevity. Two filmographies provide reference materials for those who wish to identify films presenting a black perspective: *The Afro-American Cinematic Experience: An Annotated Bibliography and Filmography* by Marshall Hyatt and *Frame by Frame: A Black Filmography* by Phyllis Rauch Klotman. Each includes films not listed in the other, so both should be consulted. Additionally, the aforementioned imdb.com and other Web sites are useful trails to follow as one seeks sources in this area.

A popular form of film criticism is the interview; the current expression for this device is *oral history*, history recorded through the actual words of the men and women who made history. Film and comics are probably the only art forms so far whose entire history can be recorded in this manner. This is the method and virtue of Kevin Brownlow's *The Parade's Gone By*, mentioned earlier in this essay. Other interviews with movie people abound, but most often they are published in journals and must be discovered through the various guides to periodicals. Some few have been published in book form. Director Cameron Crowe's book-length series of interviews with Billy Wilder is one recent example of the continuation of this valuable type of research and preservation.

For some years now the American Film Institute has been publishing the written record of interviews held by the staff and students at the AFI West Coast facility. Many movie makers, directors, actors, and others have talked informally with the students and staff, and the results have been transcribed. The transcriptions were first published separately in a journal, *Dialogue on Film*; more recently they have been included as the centerfold of *American Film*. The AFI says that they have an additional 300 interviews that will not be published, but are on file at their offices on both coasts.

The first important published book of interviews was probably that of Andrew Sarris, *Interviews with Film Directors*. He reprints interviews with forty directors, most of which were conducted by people other than himself. He believes that the results support his theory about the importance of the role of the director in the movie-making process. He has been followed by others interested chiefly in directors. Eric Sherman and Martin Rubin, in *The Director's Event*, interviewed Peter Bogdanovich, Samuel Fuller, Abraham Polonsky, Budd Boetticher, and Arthur Penn. Charles Thomas Samuels interviewed no Americans, but in *Encountering Directors* he has recorded interviews with filmmakers, such as Alfred Hitchcock and Ingmar Bergman, who have been especially influential in this country. And in *The Men Who Made the Movies*, Richard Schickel gives the transcripts of his televised interviews with Frank Capra, George Cukor, Howard Hawks, Alfred Hitchcock, Vincente Minnelli, King Vidor, Raoul Walsh, and William Wellman.

Probably the form of criticism most people see most often is the movie review published in the daily newspaper or monthly magazine. Naturally reviews serve a different purpose than does the in-depth scholarly article, but the review can provide the researcher with valuable material. It can suggest the public reaction to the film at the time it was released; it can cite needed data about the production of the film. For many films in many libraries the review may be the only printed material available. *Readers' Guide* and the *Humanities Index* both list reviews under "Moving Picture Plays" for the year in which the review appeared.

Stephen Bowles's *Index to Critical Film Reviews in British and American Film Periodicals* is a three-volume guide to the reviews published in thirty-one journals. It is useful but the list of journals is not complete. The critic, rather than the journal, becomes the emphasis for Richard Heinzkill in *Film Criticism: An Index to Critics' Anthologies*. A number of the better critics, such as Andrew Sarris, Pauline Kael, and John Simon, have had their reviews, originally published in periodicals, collected and published in book form. Heinzkill has indexed the work of twenty-seven such reviewers, and through his list it is possible to begin the study of either films or critics.

There are a few books that reprint reviews from a number of critics. *The New York Times Film Reviews, 1913–1980* is a massive eight-volume collection of all the film reviews published in the *Times*. Included are the reviews of Bosley Crowther, Vincent Canby, Frank S. Nugent, and others. Reviews from *Variety* have also been collected in a multivolume set: *Variety Film Reviews, 1907–1980*. Both the *New York Times* and *Variety* sets are well indexed. Stanley Kauffman, with Bruce Henstell, has edited a book of reviews: *American Film Criticism* is a collection of one or two reviews of many of the important films from the beginning to *Citizen Kane*. *American Film Directors*, edited by Stanley Hochman, is a collection of excerpted reviews of the important films of major American directors. Among the growing group of book-length collections by individual reviewers, interested readers would be well-served by seeking out collections by James Agee and Pauline Kael, among others. *Roger Ebert's Book of Film* is a collection of writings from a variety of authors, gathered by the well-known newspaper and television critic. Sections of the book include review excerpts, as well as sections on going to the movies, movie stars, the business of film, and other concerns.

This essay is not intended as a how-to guide to making movies, but some knowledge of technique is essential to the critic. The critic must know what each of the persons involved in the process does even if he or she does not want to make a film personally.

First, a critic must develop a vocabulary of technical terms. Raymond Spottiswoode's *A Grammar of the Film* discusses the art of film production and helps with definition of the terms. It is now somewhat old and hard to read, but useful.

More up to date is *An Illustrated Glossary of Film Terms* by Harry Geduld and Ronald Gottesman. The definitions are brief, and even complicated matters are not discussed in depth, but as a guide it does what it is supposed to.

The entire process of film production is given an overview in several books. John Quick and Tom La Bare have written a *Handbook of Film Production*, which is an easy method of studying all the work that goes into the production of a film. More ambitious are two volumes sponsored by the American Film Institute. Eric Sherman in *Directing the Film* covers in depth the contribution of the directors, while Donald Chase considers the rest of the collaborators in *Filmmaking: The Collaborative Art*. There are many other books that deal with the individual contributions of members of the production team, but these general guides are a good place to begin.

Some of the best film criticism is that written about a single film, but space here does not permit a list of the books on single films any more than it permits lists of books on individual actors or directors. The researchers should consult the card catalog at the local library or search through the bibliographies mentioned earlier in this essay. The researcher should be aware that there is a large range of types of books about individual films—some are historic, others technical, some analytic.

The range of books on film is large, and this bibliographic essay is by necessity highly selective. As the moviegoing audience has become better educated, the demand for intelligent books to provide background and interpretation has increased. This list can only point in the direction of the appropriate books and offer the encouragement that many of these works, and countless others, can enhance the experience of watching and writing about the movies themselves. Fred Ott could have never dreamed his sneeze would lead to this.

BIBLIOGRAPHY

Books

Aceto, Vincent J., Jane Graves, and Fred Silva. *Film Literature Index*. Albany, NY: Filmdex. Annual.

Allen, Nancy. *Film Study Collections*. New York: Frederick Ungar, 1979.

Andrew, J. Dudley. *The Major Film Theories*. New York: Oxford University Press, 1976.

Anobile, Richard J. *Casablanca*. New York: Universe Books, 1974.

———. *The General*. New York: Universe Books, 1975.

Armour, Robert A. *Film: A Reference Guide*. Westport, CT: Greenwood Press, 1980.

Aros, Andrew. *A Title Guide to the Talkies, 1964 Through 1974*. Metuchen, NJ: Scarecrow Press, 1977.

Arvidson, Linda. *When the Movies Were Young*. New York: Benjamin Blom, 1968.

Balazs, Bela. *Theory of the Film*. New York: Arno Press, 1972.

Balio, Tino, ed. *The American Film Industry*. Madison: University of Wisconsin Press, 1985.

Barnouw, Erik. *Documentary: A History of the Non-fiction Film*. New York: Oxford University Press, 1983.

Barrett, Gerald R., and Thomas L. Erskine. *From Fiction into Film: Ambrose Bierce's "An Occurrence at Owl Creek Bridge."* Encino, CA: Dickenson, 1973.

———. *From Fiction to Film: D. H. Lawrence's "The Rocking-Horse Winner."* Encino, CA: Dickenson, 1974.

Barsam, Richard Meran. *Nonfiction Film*. New York: E. P. Dutton, 1973.

———, ed. *Nonfiction Film: Theory and Criticism*. New York: E. P. Dutton, 1976.

Battcock, Gregory, ed. *The New American Cinema*. New York: E. P. Dutton, 1967.

Bawden, Liz-Anne. *The Oxford Companion to Film*. New York: Oxford University Press, 1976.

Bazin, André. *What Is Cinema?* Berkeley: University of California Press, 1967.

Bergman, Andrew. *We're in the Money*. New York: New York University Press, 1971.

Bluestone, George. *Novels into Film*. Berkeley: University of California Press, 1957.

Blumenberg, Richard. *Critical Focus: An Introduction to Film*. Belmont, CA: Wadsworth, 1975.

Bobker, Lee R. *Elements of Film*. New York: Harcourt, Brace and World, 1979.

Boggs, Joseph, and Dennis W. Petrie. *The Art of Watching Films*. 5th ed. Mountain View, CA: Mayfield, 2000.

Bogle, Donald. *Toms, Coons, Mulattoes, Mammies, and Blacks*. New York: Viking, 1973.

Bohn, Thomas W., and Richard L. Stromgren. *Light and Shadows*. Port Washington, NY: Alfred Publishing, 1975.

Bordwell, David. *Narration in the Fiction Film*. Madison: Wisconsin University Press, 1985.

Bowles, Stephen B. *Index to Critical Film Reviews in British and American Film Periodicals*. 3 vols. New York: Burt Franklin, 1979.

Braudy, Leo, and Marshall Cohen, eds. *Film Theory and Criticism*. 5th ed. New York: Oxford University Press, 1999.

Braudy, Leo, and Morris Dickstein. *Great Film Directors: A Critical Anthology*. New York: Oxford University Press, 1981.

Brownlow, Kevin. *The Parade's Gone By*. Berkeley: University of California Press, 1976.

Bukalski, Peter J. *Film Research: A Critical Bibliography*. Boston: G. K. Hall, 1972.

Catalogue of Copyright Entries: Motion Pictures. 4 vols. Washington, DC: Library of Congress, 1951, 1953, 1960, 1971.

Chase, Donald. *Filmmaking: The Collaborative Art*. Boston: Little, Brown, 1975.

Clarens, Carlos. *An Illustrated History of the Horror Film*. New York: Capricorn Books, 1967.

Cook, David A. *A History of Narrative Film*. 3rd ed. New York: W. W. Norton, 1996.

Coursodon, Jean-Pierre, and Pierre Sauvage. *American Directors*. New York: McGraw-Hill, 1983.

Cowie, Peter, ed. *International Film Guide*. London: Tantivy. Annual.

Cripps, Thomas. *Slow Fade to Black*. New York: Oxford University Press, 1977.

Crowe, Cameron. *Conversations with Wilder*. New York: Knopf, 2001.

Curtis, David. *Experimental Cinema*. New York: Dell, 1971.

Dawson, Bonnie. *Women's Films in Print*. San Francisco: Booklegger Press, 1975.

DeNitto, Dennis, and William Herman. *Film and the Critical Eye*. New York: Macmillan, 1975.

Dick, Bernard. *Anatomy of Film*. Boston: Bedford/St. Martin's, 2002.

Dickinson, Thorold. *A Discovery of Cinema*. New York: Oxford University Press, 1971.

Dimmitt, Richard Betrand. *An Actor Guide to the Talkies, 1949–1964*. Metuchen, NJ: Scarecrow Press, 1967–1968.

———. *A Title Guide to the Talkies, 1927–1963*. Metuchen, NJ: Scarecrow Press, 1965.

Ebert, Roger. *Roger Ebert's Book of Film*. New York: Norton, 1997.

Eisenstein, Sergei. *Film Essays and a Lecture*. New York: Praeger, 1970.

———. *Film Form*. New York: Harcourt, Brace and World, 1949.

———. *The Film Sense*. New York: Harcourt, Brace and World, 1947.

Ellis, Jack C., Charles Derry, and Sharon Kern. *The Film Book Bibliography, 1940–1975*. Metuchen, NJ: Scarecrow Press, 1979.

Elsas, Diana, ed. *Factfile: Film and Television Periodicals in English*. Washington, DC: American Film Institute, 1977.

Enser, A.G.S. *Filmed Books and Plays, 1928–1983*. Aldershot, Eng.: Gower, 1985.

Everson, William K. *American Silent Film*. New York: Oxford University Press, 1978.

Fell, John L. *Film and the Narrative Tradition*. Norman: Oklahoma University Press, 1986.

———. *Film: An Introduction*. New York: Praeger, 1975.

———. *A History of Films*. New York: Holt, Rinehart and Winston, 1979.

———, ed. *Film Before Griffith*. Berkeley: University of California Press, 1983.

Fenin, George N., and William K. Everson. *The Western*. New York: Orion, 1962.

Frank, Alan. *The Horror Film Handbook*. Totowa, NJ: Barnes and Noble, 1982.

Friar, Ralph F., and Natasha A. Friar. *The Only Good Indian . . . The Hollywood Gospel*. New York: Drama Book Specialists, 1972.

Geduld, Harry M. *The Birth of the Talkies*. Bloomington: University of Indiana Press, 1975.

Geduld, Harry M., and Ronald Gottesman. *An Illustrated Glossary of Film Terms*. New York: Holt, Rinehart and Winston, 1973.

Giannetti, Louis D. *Understanding Movies*. 9th ed. Upper Saddle River, NJ: Prentice-Hall, 2002.

Gish, Lillian. *The Movies, Mr. Griffith, and Me*. Englewood Cliffs, NJ: Prentice-Hall, 1969.

Grant, Barry K., ed. *Film Genre: Theory and Criticism*. Metuchen, NJ: Scarecrow Press, 1977.

Halliwell, Leslie. *The Filmgoer's Companion*. New York: Granada, 1977.

Hardy, Phil. *The Aurum Film Encyclopedia: The Western*. London: Aurum, 1983.

Hardy, Phil, et al. *The Aurum Film Encyclopedia: Horror*. London: Aurum, 1985.

Harrington, John. *Literature and/as Film*. Englewood Cliffs, NJ: Prentice-Hall, 1977.

Haskell, Molly. *From Reverence to Rape*. New York: Holt, Rinehart and Winston, 1974.

Heck-Rabi, Louise. *Women Filmmakers: A Critical Reception*. Metuchen, NJ: Scarecrow Press, 1984.

Heinzkill, Richard. *Film Criticism: An Index to Critics' Anthologies*. Metuchen, NJ: Scarecrow Press, 1975.

Higham, Charles. *Warner Brothers*. New York: Scribner's, 1975.

Hill, John, and Pamela Church Gibson. *Film Studies: Critical Approaches*. New York: Oxford University Press, 2000.

Hochman, Stanley, ed. *American Film Directors*. New York: Frederick Ungar, 1974.

Houston, Penelope. *The Contemporary Cinema, 1945–1963*. Baltimore: Penguin Books, 1963.

Humanities Index. New York: H. W. Wilson. Annual.

Hurt, James, ed. *Focus on Film and Theatre*. Englewood Cliffs, NJ: Prentice-Hall, 1974.

Huss, Roy, and T. J. Ross, eds. *Focus on the Horror Film*. Englewood Cliffs, NJ: Prentice-Hall, 1972.

Huss, Roy, and Norman Silverstein. *The Film Experience*. New York: Dell, 1969.

Hyatt, Marshall. *The Afro-American Cinematic Experience: An Annotated Bibliography and Filmography*. Wilmington, DE: Scholarly Resources, 1983.

Jacobs, Lewis, ed. *The Documentary Tradition*. New York: W. W. Norton, 1979.

———. *The Emergence of Film Art: The Evolution and Development of the Motion Picture as an Art, from 1900 to the Present*. New York: W. W. Norton, 1979.

———. *Introduction to the Art of the Movies*. New York: Noonday Press, 1960.

———. *The Movies as Medium*. New York: Hippocrene, 1973.

———. *The Rise of the American Film*. New York: Teachers College Press, 1968.

Jones, Karen. *International Index to Film Periodicals*. New York: St. Martin's Press. Annual.

Jowett, Garth. *Film: The Democratic Art*. Boston: Little, Brown, 1976.

Kaminsky, Stuart M. *American Film Genres: Approaches to a Critical Theory of Popular Film*. New York: Dell, 1974.

Kaplan, Ann E. *Women and Film: Both Sides of the Camera*. New York: Methuen, 1983.

Karney, Robyn. *Chronicle of the Cinema*. New York: DK Publishing, 1997.

Katz, Ephraim. *The Film Encyclopedia*. New York: Crowell, 1979.

Katz, John Stuart, ed. *Perspectives on the Study of Film*. Boston: Little, Brown, 1971.

Kauffman, Stanley, with Bruce Henstell, eds. *American Film Criticism*. Westport, CT: Greenwood Press, 1979.

Kawin, Bruce. *How Movies Work*. New York: Macmillan, 1987.

Kerr, Walter. *The Silent Clowns*. New York: Alfred A. Knopf, 1979.

Klotman, Phyllis Rauch. *Frame by Frame: A Black Filmography*. Bloomington: Indiana University Press, 1979.

Knight, Arthur. *The Liveliest Art: A Panoramic History of the Movies*. New York: New American Library, 1979.

Kobal, John. *Gotta Sing, Gotta Dance*. New York: Kamlyn, 1971.

Kracauer, Siegfried. *Theory of Film*. New York: Oxford University Press, 1960.

Krafsur, Richard, ed. *The American Film Institute Catalogue of Motion Pictures: Feature Films, 1961–1970*. New York: R. R. Bowker, 1976.

Lahue, Kalton C. *Continued Next Week: A History of the Moving Picture Serial*. Norman: University of Oklahoma Press, 1964.

Langman, Larry. *A Guide to American Screenwriters: The Sound Era, 1929–1982*. 2 vols. New York: Garland, 1984.

Larkin, Rochelle. *Hail Columbia*. New Rochelle, NY: Arlington House, 1975.
Leab, Daniel J. *From Sambo to Superspade*. Boston: Houghton Mifflin, 1975.
Lee, Walt. *Reference Guide to Fantastic Films: Science Fiction, Fantasy and Horror*. Los Angeles: Chelsea-Lee Books, 1974.
Leonard, Harold. *The Film Index: A Bibliography*. New York: Arno Press, 1970.
Levin, G. Roy. *Documentary Explorations*. Garden City, NY: Doubleday-Anchor, 1971.
Limbacher, James. *Feature Films on 8mm and 16mm*. New York: R. R. Bowker, 1985.
Lindgren, Ernest. *The Art of the Film*. New York: Macmillan, 1963.
Lindsay, Vachel. *The Art of the Moving Picture*. New York: Liveright, 1970.
MacCann, Richard Dyer, ed. *Film: A Montage of Theories*. New York: E. P. Dutton, 1966.
MacCann, Richard Dyer, and Edward S. Perry. *The New Film Index*. New York: E. P. Dutton, 1975.
Magill, Frank N. *Magill's Cinema Annual, 1986: A Survey of the Films of 1985*. Englewood Cliffs, NJ: Salem Press, 1986.
Magill's Survey of Cinema: English Language Films. Englewood Cliffs, NJ: Salem Press, 1980, 1981.
Magill's Survey of Cinema: Foreign Language Films. Englewood Cliffs, NJ: Salem Press, 1985.
Manchel, Frank. *Film Study: A Resource Guide*. Rutherford, NJ: Fairleigh Dickinson University Press, 1973.
Manvell, Roger, ed. *The International Encyclopedia of Film*. New York: Crown, 1972.
Marcus, Fred H. *Short Story/Short Film*. Englewood Cliffs, NJ: Prentice-Hall, 1977.
Martin, Leonard. *The Great Movie Shorts*. New York: Crown, 1972.
Mast, Gerald. *The Comic Mind*. Chicago: University of Chicago Press, 1979.
Mast, Gerald, and Bruce F. Kawin. *A Short History of the Movies*. 5th ed. New York: Macmillan, 1992.
Maynard, Richard. *The Black Man on Film: Racial Stereotyping*. Rochelle Park, NJ: Hayden, 1974.
———. *The Celluloid Curriculum*. Rochelle Park, NJ: Hayden, 1971.
McCarthy, Todd, and Charles Flynn. *Kings of the B's*. New York: E. P. Dutton, 1975.
McCarty, Clifford. *Published Screenplays: A Checklist*. Kent, OH: Kent State University Press, 1971.
McNally, Raymond T., and Radu Florescu. *In Search of Dracula*. New York: Galahad Books, 1972.
Mellon, Joan. *Women and Their Sexuality in the New Film*. New York: Dell, 1973.
Metz, Christian. *Film Language*. New York: Oxford University Press, 1974.
Monaco, James. *How to Read a Film*. New York: Oxford University Press, 1981.
Munden, Kenneth W., ed. *The American Film Institute Catalogue of Motion Pictures Produced in the United States, Feature Films, 1921–1930*. New York: R. R. Bowker, 1971.
Nachbar, John G. *Western Films: An Annotated Critical Bibliography*. New York: Garland, 1975.

The New York Times Film Reviews, 1913–1980. 8 vols. New York: New York Times Arno Press, 1970.

Niver, Kemp R. *Motion Pictures from the Library of Congress Paper Print Collection, 1894–1912*. Berkeley: University of California Press, 1967.

Parish, James Robert, and Michael R. Pitts. *Film Directors: A Guide to Their American Films*. Metuchen, NJ: Scarecrow Press, 1974.

———. *The Great Gangster Pictures*. Metuchen, NJ: Scarecrow Press, 1976.

Patterson, Lindsay, ed. *Black Films and Film-makers*. New York: Dodd, Mead, 1975.

Peacock, Richard Beck. *The Art of Moviemaking: Script to Screen*. Upper Saddle River, NJ: Prentice-Hall, 2001.

Phillips, William H. *Film: An Introduction*. Boston: Bedford/St. Martin's, 2002.

Poteet, G. Howard, ed. *The Complete Guide to Film Study*. Urbana, IL: National Council of Teachers of English, 1972.

———. *Published Radio, Television, and Film Scripts: A Bibliography*. Troy, NY: Whitson Publishing, 1975.

Powdermaker, Hortense. *Hollywood: The Dream Factory*. Salem, NH: Ayer, 1979.

Powers, Anne. *Blacks in American Movies: A Selected Bibliography*. Metuchen, NJ: Scarecrow Press, 1974.

Pratt, George C. *Spellbound in Darkness*. Greenwich, CT: New York Graphic Society, 1973.

Pudovkin, V. I. *Film Technique and Film Acting*. New York: Grove Press, 1970.

Quick, John, and Tom La Bare. *Handbook of Film Production*. New York: Maemman, 1972.

Quinland, David. *The Illustrated Directory of Film Character Actors*. London: B. T. Batsford, 1985.

———. *Quinland's Illustrated Directory of Film Stars*. London: B. T. Batsford, 1986.

Readers' Guide to Periodical Literature. New York: H. W. Wilson. Annual.

Rehrauer, George. *The Macmillan Film Bibliography*. 2 vols. New York: Macmillan, 1982.

Renan, Sheldon. *An Introduction to the American Underground Film*. New York: E. P. Dutton, 1967.

Rhode, Eric. *A History of the Cinema from Its Origins to 1970*. New York: Da Capo Press, 1985.

Richardson, Robert. *Literature and Film*. New York: Garland, 1985.

Rosen, Marjorie. *Popcorn Venus*. New York: Avon, 1974.

Ross, T. J. *Film and the Liberal Arts*. New York: Holt, Rinehart and Winston, 1970.

Rotha, Paul, with Richard Griffith. *The Film—Till Now*. London: Spring Books, 1967.

Sadoul, Georges. *Dictionary of Filmmakers*. Berkeley: University of California Press, 1972.

———. *Dictionary of Films*. Berkeley: University of California Press, 1965, 1972.

Samuels, Charles Thomas. *Encountering Directors*. New York: Capricorn, 1972.

Sarris, Andrew. *Interviews with Film Directors*. New York: Avon, 1967.

Schatz, Thomas. *Hollywood Genres*. New York: McGraw-Hill, 1981.

Schickel, Richard. *The Men Who Made the Movies*. New York: Atheneum, 1975.

Schuster, Mel. *Motion Picture Directors: A Bibliography of Magazine and Periodical Articles, 1900–1972*. Metuchen, NJ: Scarecrow Press, 1973.

———. *Motion Picture Performers: A Bibliography of Magazine and Periodical Articles 1900–1969*. Metuchen, NJ: Scarecrow Press, 1971.

Shales, Tom, et al. *The American Film Heritage*. Washington, DC: Acropolis Books, 1972.

Sherman, Eric. *Directing the Film*. Boston: Little, Brown, 1976.

Sherman, Eric, and Martin Rubin. *The Director's Event*. New York: New American Library, 1969.

Shipman, David. *Cinema: The First Hundred Years*. New York: St. Martin's Press, 1993.

Sitney, P. Adams, ed. *Film Culture Reader*. New York: Praeger, 1970.

Sklar, Robert. *Film: An International History of the Medium*. Upper Saddle River, NJ: Prentice-Hall, 2002.

Smith, Sharon. *Women Who Make Movies*. New York: Hopkins and Blake, 1975.

Sohn, David A. *Film: The Critical Eye*. Dayton, OH: Pflaum, 1970.

Solomon, Stanley J. *Beyond Formula*. New York: Harcourt Brace Jovanovich, 1976.

Spottiswoode, Raymond. *A Grammar of the Film*. Berkeley: University of California Press, 1969.

Stam, Robert. *Film Theory: An Introduction*. Malden, MA: Blackwell, 2000.

Steinberg, Cobbett S. *Film Facts*. New York: Facts on File, 1980.

Sullivan, Kaye. *Films for, by, and About Women*. Metuchen, NJ: Scarecrow Press, 1980.

Thomson, David. *A Biographical Dictionary of Film*. New York: William Morrow, 1976.

Truitt, Evelyn Mack. *Who Was Who on Screen*. New York: R. R. Bowker, 1984.

Tyler, Parker. *Underground Film: A Critical History*. New York: Grove Press, 1969.

Ursini, James, and Alain Silver. *The Vampire Film*. Cranbury, NJ: A. S. Barnes, 1975.

Vardac, A. Nicholas. *Stage to Screen*. New York: Ayer, 1968.

Variety Film Reviews, 1907–1980. New York: Garland, 1983.

Wagner, Geoffrey. *The Novel and the Cinema*. Rutherford, NJ: Fairleigh Dickinson University Press, 1975.

Wakeman, John, ed. *World Film Directors, 1890–1945*. New York: Wilson, 1987.

———. *World Film Directors, 1945–1985*. New York: Wilson, 1988.

Walls, Howard Lamarr. *Motion Pictures, 1894–1912: Identified from the Records of the U.S. Copyright Office*. Washington, DC: Library of Congress, 1953.

Wead, George, and George Lellis. *Film: Form and Function*. Boston: Houghton Mifflin, 1981.

Weber, Olga S. *North American Film and Video Directory*. New York: R. R. Bowker, 1976.

Weinberg, Herman G. *The Complete Greed*. New York: Arno Press, 1972.

Weiss, Ken, and Ed Goodgold. *To Be Continued*. New York: Crown, 1972.

Wenden, D. J. *The Birth of the Movies*. New York: E. P. Dutton, 1974.

Who Wrote the Movie and What Else Did He Write? Los Angeles: Academy of Motion Picture Arts and Sciences and Writers' Guild of America, 1970.

Willis, Donald C. *Horror and Science Fiction Films: A Checklist*. Metuchen, NJ: Scarecrow Press, 1972.

Wilson, George M. *Narration in Light: Studies in Cinematic Point of View*. Baltimore: Johns Hopkins University Press, 1986.
Wingrove, David. *The Science Fiction Film Source Book*. London: Longman, 1985.
Youngblood, Gene. *Expanded Cinema*. New York: E. P. Dutton, 1970.

Periodicals

American Cinematographer, Los Angeles, 1919– .
American Film. Washington, D.C., 1975– .
Cinema Journal. Philadelphia, 1961– .
Dialogue on Film. Beverly Hills, Calif., 1972–1975.
Film Culture. New York, 1962– .
Film Quarterly. Berkeley, Calif., 1945– .
Literature/Film Quarterly. Salisbury, Md., 1973– .
Media and Methods. Philadelphia, 1965– .

Regal movie theater, Chicago, 1941. Courtesy of the Library of Congress

"Theater Row" in Denver. Photo by Harry M. Rhoads. Courtesy of the Denver Public Library

In front of a Chicago movie theater, 1941. Courtesy of the Library of Congress

Rafael Theater, San Francisco. © Painet

Mann's Chinese Theater, Hollywood, California. © Painet

Ornate Los Angeles Theater with movie marquee. © Nik Wheeler/CORBIS

FOODWAYS

Sara Lewis Dunne

Interest in American foodways has exploded over the last ten years, growing from the narrowly focused research of anthropologists and folklorists into an important element in popular culture research. Since 1995, the "Food" section of the national Popular Culture Association conference has expanded from one section of four papers to multiple sections spread over several days. Regional popular culture associations are likewise devoting whole sessions to the subject of food and foodways. The July 9, 1999, issue of *The Chronicle of Higher Education* featured a lengthy article, "A Place at the Table," in which its author, Jennifer J. Ruark, writes about the increasing popularity of food studies as a scholarly pursuit. She cites the doctoral program in food studies at New York University as evidence of the growing, "if hard-fought," legitimacy of this scholarship. There is also a new scholarly journal, *Gastronomica*, which focuses on food and culture. Because food has become one of the foci of popular culture research and cultural studies research generally, the term "foodways" has expanded to cover not just regional or ethnic cooking and cuisine or regional food festivals but the treatment of food and eating in popular media, film, and fiction and the increased importance of "fast food" as an element of American culture. Apart from scholarly interests, many Americans have an increasing interest in food and food writing.

HISTORICAL OUTLINE

Charles Camp's invaluable book *American Foodways* (1989) traces the background of foodways research in America. W. K. McNeil, author of Camp's introductory chapter, cites Lafcadio Hearn as one of the first writers to chronicle American foodways in *La Cuisine Creole*, published in 1885, the result of Hearn's seven-year stay in New Orleans. McNeil also cites *The Journal of American Folklore* as another valuable, if sporadic, source of foodways scholarship, but few books devoted solely to food practices of specific American populations or specific American foods were produced until the 1980s, and even then, a multidisciplinary approach was rare. The folklorist Don Yoder is credited by McNeil with spurring interest in food scholarship since 1970, the year of the first International Symposium on Ethnological Food Research, held in Sweden and attended by Yoder, who had already published three important articles on American ethnic foodways. Yoder urged research into ethnic foodways, which were being replaced by more generic, nonregional "American" foodways—fast food in particular. Consequently, much of the foodways research for the 1970s focused on ethnic and regional cooking and eating.

Before the rise of professional folklorists beginning in the 1960s, McNeil claims that American foodways research had been the domain of anthropologists but that folklorists, particularly students of Yoder, have since assumed a dominant role in foodways research. Camp notes that the term "foodways" has come to replace the term "folkways," partly because research has expanded from a narrowly focused emphasis on food choices, to a broader interest in food as both divider and joiner of cultural groups. The folklorist "changes the definition of the things being studied from objects (food) to behaviors" (25).

The scholar of popular culture, taking cues from the anthropologist and the folklorist, expands research from ethnic interests to broader cultural and artistic interests, asking not just what actual people eat (and why they eat it) but also what fictional characters eat—in film, on television, in novels and short stories, in print and other advertising—and what the food practices observed in popular media show us about American culture or the culture that produced the artifact. How are our national concerns mirrored not just in actual food practices but in our popular images of those practices? Foodways scholarship has made the shift from anthropological studies of "folk" foodways and some historical and literary studies of elite foodways (e.g., medieval scholars' studies of royal banquets or Latin scholars' studies of Trimalchio's famous dinner in *The Satyricon*) to focus on the buying, cooking, and eating of America's masses as well as the ways in which mass foodways are both reflected in and influenced by popular art forms: television, film, music, print advertising—in short, popular culture.

Numerous magazines are now devoted to food and cooking: *Gourmet*, *Bon Appetit*, *Food and Wine*, *Cooking Light*, *Chile Pepper*, *Vegetarian Times*, *Saveur*, *Cuisine*, *Coffee Journal*, *Cookbook Digest*, *Veggie Life*, and *Weight Watchers*, to name only some. For those with an interest in foodways from the past, there is *Food History News*. There is also now the Food TV Network, which runs cooking shows, restaurant reviews, food game shows, and related food-centered programs, twenty-four hours a day. There are "food stars" and "star chefs" featured on this network and on other televised programs on both regular network and cable stations, all of which testify to America's interest in food as both sustenance and entertainment.

In America, food is also arguably our most accessible avenue for exploring other cultures, although what we find is sometimes a bogus kind of culture invented for American consumers in ethnic restaurants: Chinese fortune cookies, for example, or Paul Prudhomme's blackened fish. Even so, our exposure to various kinds of ethnic food does provide at least some means of broadening our cultural perspectives and, we hope, lessening our suspicions about "the other." Chinese, Mexican, Thai, soul food, Cajun, Tex-Mex, Japanese, Middle Eastern, Greek, southwestern,

Chef Paul Prudhomme. © Painet

Polynesian, and Italian restaurants can be found in small-town America as well as in larger cities where even more exotic Afghan, Argentinean, Brazilian, Caribbean, Cuban, Ethiopian, French, German, Hungarian, Indian, Irish, Korean, kosher, Lebanese, Malaysian, Moroccan, Nigerian, Russian, Spanish, Vietnamese, "and other" restaurants feed Americans daily. Opening ethnic restaurants is often the immigrant family's entrée into American capitalism; for their customers, buying food is buying culture, all questions of "authenticity" aside.

Recent popular films, both American and international, also attest to Americans' near-obsession with food. The *Godfather* series, for example, has often been noted for its lingering shots of Italian American food, as have other films with Italian American themes or subthemes: *Goodfellas*, *Moonstruck*, *Radio Days*, *Big Night*. Chinese export films have often focused on food—*Tampopo*, *The Wedding Banquet*, and *Eat, Drink, Man, Woman*, to name only three. The Baltimore films of Barry Levinson chronicle the assimilation of a Russian Jewish family, and part of their assimilation eventually includes diner food and TV dinners. The recent African American film *Soul Food* parallels the breakup of an African American family's life with the cessation of family dinners where bonds are cemented and problems are solved. Americans are, clearly, interested not just in food and eating but also in popular art forms focused on those concerns.

REFERENCE WORKS

A valuable source of information on food itself, as well as cooking, is Harold McGee's *On Food and Cooking: The Science and Lore of the Kitchen*. McGee explains the chemical makeup of foods and the chemical processes that determine results in the cooking process. This is a valuable source of information for the researcher seeking knowledge about how foods are processed before purchase and changes in farming and processing techniques. There are interesting historical anecdotes as well, including brief accounts of eating trends associated with various foods.

A volume more focused on food history is Maguelonne Toussaint-Samat's *History of Food*, translated from the French by Anthea Bell in 1992. Toussaint-Samat begins this study with "Collecting, Gathering, Hunting" and moves on through the histories of meat, cereals, oils, dairy products, wine, fish, poultry, salt, sugar, spices, vegetables, fruits, and preserved foods. Included are historic illustrations and quotes from fiction and nonfiction writings about food and eating. Probably because its author is French, the food practices of Europe are given greater emphasis than those of the New World, a focus that may limit the usefulness of this book to those researching more recent foodways or North/South American foodways. The "Chronology of Dietary Progress" near the volume's end, however, provides a quick reference for food scholars, beginning with the Australopithecus hunters of 2,000,000 B.C. and ending with the discovery of vitamins in 1912 in Poland. A similar volume, *Food, A Culinary History from Antiquity to the Present*, was translated from the Italian by a group of translators and edited by Albert Sonnenfeld. This is a large collection of essays that deals principally with the history of food and cooking techniques but also the history of foodways, taste, and eating. The volume's concluding essay offers a European perspective on American fast food.

James Trager's *The Food Chronology*, 1995 winner of the International Association of Cooking Professionals (IACP) Julia Child Cookbook award for Best Food Reference book, is subtitled *A Food Lover's Compendium of Events and Anecdotes, from Prehistory to the Present*. Trager provides symbols for the entries to indicate what area of research might be best served by the information contained. They include political events, food availability, social justice/human rights, exploration, economics, mergers, grocery stores and supermarkets, transportation, food technology, science, medicine, religion, education, communications, food writing, various art forms, everyday life, seafood, animal husbandry, agriculture, nutrition, consumer protection, food brands, beverages, restaurants, and population. The entries are arranged chronologically and begin with "prehistory" and end in 1995 with the information, labeled with the symbol for "beverages," that the U.S. Supreme Court had ruled that a brewer could list a beer's alcoholic content on its label, overturning a long-standing ban on this information. The previous ban was judged a violation of the First Amendment. There are black-and-white illustrations and photographs, for example, a lithograph of ice cutters in New England, preparing to ship their product to "the Southern states and even to India" in 1846, and from 1966, a photograph of a jar of Taster's Choice freeze-dried coffee. Trager's entries are brief but useful for the researcher who needs a starting point. There is an exhaustive index but no formal bibliography; instead, for each year, next to the food-writing icon (shaped like a fountain pen nib), Trager lists the major food books under the categories of nonfiction, fiction, and cookbooks and offers short blurbs about many of the books.

Two recent works with even larger scope are *The Cambridge World History of Food*, edited by Kenneth F. Kiple and Kriemhild Conee Ornelas, nearly 2,000 pages in two volumes, and *The Oxford Companion to Food* by Alan Davidson. The Cambridge history covers not only the history of food practices but also some of the nutritional and health implications of eating patterns. The shift from hunting and gathering to farming brought with it, according to reviewer and novelist John Lanchester, a decrease in human size and health and an increase in anemia and infant mortality caused by the decreased consumption of meat. The mass cultivation of grains likewise affected human development adversely. Rice, wheat, and corn, when they form the basis of a diet, can inhibit human growth, vitamin activity, and iron absorption. Farming also led to the development of communities and the sharing of diseases and parasites between humans and animals, caused by contact with waste products. The intimate connections between food and illness are heavily emphasized in the *Cambridge History* perhaps because its editors began work on it while completing a previous companion volume, *The Cambridge History of Human Disease*. Like the other *Oxford Companions*, the *Oxford Companion to Food* is set up in dictionary form but is about half the length of the *Cambridge* work. Reviewers have noted that it seems to focus somewhat less on the strictly scientific approach to its subject and is rather more readable, displaying at times a "deadpan wit" not found in the other Cambridge volumes. Reviewer Lanchester comments that both volumes attest that "food has finally and irrefutably become an intellectually reputable object of study" (171).

HISTORY AND CRITICISM

One of several food history books is Reay Tannehill's *Food in History*, first published in 1973, with a second edition out in 1988. This book differs from the two European food histories cited earlier in that its reach seems less wide and the author draws many more examples from American history. Tannehill's chapter on "The Americas" begins with Columbus' voyage to, and return from, the Caribbean and the consequent transportation of corn from the New World to the old. Tomatoes, sweet and hot peppers, avocados, various starch beans, peanuts, chocolate, turkeys, potatoes, and tapioca were likewise transported back to the Old World by explorers in Mexico and Latin America and incorporated into European cuisines. Two new cooking techniques also presented themselves to new European settlers in America: the clambake (using a dug pit lined with hot stones) and the barbecue.

As Europeans settled America, their traditional dishes were adapted to available food supplies. According to Tannehill, the English brought us "apple pie; the Dutch, cookies (*koekjes*), coleslaw (*kool*: cabbage, and *sla*: salad) and waffles; and the Germans, sauerkraut." European recipes were quickly adapted to American game: possums, raccoons, buffalo, woodchuck, and bear. Later, African slaves would bring their foods and cooking techniques: okra, black-eyed peas, chitterlings, greens cooked with ham hocks. Most historians of American food agree that the great abundance of meat, fish, and fowl as ready food sources along with a great preference for sweets in any form marked American cuisine from its beginnings. As new waves of immigrants arrived, however, foodways altered, sometimes subtly and sometimes obviously. Reviews of the following comprehensive studies reveal many of the details of America's food history.

In *Perfection Salad*, Laura Shapiro, an editor for *Newsweek*, traces the history of the "domestic science" movement in America that, she writes, was an effort to give women "access to the modern world, the world of science, technology, and rationality" (9) through the applications of scientific principles and methods to cooking and housekeeping. An unfortunate by-product of this movement was the eradication of much traditional native and immigrant cooking and the introduction of products such as Crisco, praised for its lack of taste or odor. She cites a white sauce made with Crisco (introduced in 1911) as a "food substance from which virtually everything had been stripped except a certain number of nutrients and the color white. Only a cuisine molded by technology could prosper on such developments, and it prospered very well" (215). Shapiro's book is valuable as a history of an aspect of popular culture but also as an illustration of a method of analyzing humans—women in particular—and their relations to both cooking and eating food. In the time period with which she begins, early in the twentieth century, women seemed determined to disguise food as something else, decorating it with sauces, candied violets, gelatin, or garnishes. At her book's end, she cites the alarming recent rise in eating disorders among young women and the still-problematic, often disguised and distant relation that many women have to food. Although Shapiro does not cite Roland Barthes, the French structuralist critic, in her eleven-page bibliography, clearly she and Barthes both rely on binary coding (Is the food plain or decorated? Disguised or undisguised? Is it a food preferred by women or men, adults or children?) in their analytical methodologies.

Another seminal work in the history of American food is Harvey Levenstein's *Revolution at the Table*. Levenstein, a historian whose previous work had focused on labor unions in the United States and Mexico, turned his attentions to American foodways and the ways in which they changed between 1880 and 1930. Prior to 1880, Americans consumed large quantities of meat and starch—sweets in particular—and negligible amounts of fresh produce, fruits, or spices, unless the spices were part of a sweetened dessert. Levenstein quotes several nineteenth-century British and European travelers to America who were shocked by the huge amounts of meat consumed by middle- and upper-middle-class Americans. The opening of the West served chiefly to increase the amount of beef served on these Americans' dinner, lunch, and breakfast tables. Working-class Americans also ate great quantities of beef, potatoes, cabbage, and sweets if they lived in the East or Midwest and corn and pork if they lived in the South. The expansion of railways made changes in the American diet possible, and food reformers such as William Sylvester Graham, Horace Fletcher, and John Harvey Kellogg encouraged Americans to eat less meat, chew their food longer, and eat more grains, vegetables, and yogurt. Alcoholism among working-class men was attributed to "bad cooking at home" (99), and overuse of spices and garlic—common to the cuisine of Central, Eastern, and Southern Europe—was also thought to encourage alcoholism (104). The European immigrants' preference for rich mixtures of foods and flavors in soups, stews, goulashes, and pasta sauces was therefore seen by food reformers as not only un-American but dangerous. In addition to the domestic science movement and several national nutrition campaigns, Levenstein cites two forces that did much to "Americanize" the foodways of immigrants: the school-lunch program and the military. In the period that Levenstein covers, Americans also learned that the quality of their food mattered as much as the quantity and that even middle-class Americans might be classified as "malnourished" because their food intake did not include a balance of vitamins and minerals. Levenstein asserts that "by the time of the Great Depression, the basic ideas of the Newer Nutrition—that vitamins and minerals were essential to stimulating growth, protecting good health, and even prolonging life—prevailed in middle-class America" (160). This volume has no separate bibliography, but the chapter notes are extensive and provide a large variety of scholarly and popular primary and secondary sources of information. A thorough index is provided.

Levenstein's second food book, *The Paradox of Plenty*, picks up where the first one leaves off, in the 1930s. Its title refers to the paradox in America "that hunger, breadlines, and food banks can exist in a land of such agricultural abundance" (viii). In addition to hunger produced by the Great Depression and other instances of widespread poverty, Levenstein addresses the great popularity of dieting in America even during times of economic hardship and ongoing concerns about the purity or heartiness of American food. During the hard years of the depression, Americans were still concerned with vitamins and with the quality of the foods that they ate, so much so that numerous crusaders and reformers railed against the large food-processing corporations and urged them to fortify their products with vitamins and minerals. By the early 1940s thiamin deficiency was seen as the cause of "depression and mental weakness and despair" (22), and it was rumored that thiamin starvation was Hitler's secret weapon in occupied countries. Levenstein sums up the foodways of the 1930s and 1940s by contrasting public attitudes about starvation: that in the 1930s many Americans were physically—and sometimes obviously—starved but that by the end of the 1940s, they feared a kind of invisible starvation because of fears about the nutrients removed from their food through processing. These fears receded somewhat during World War II but resurfaced several decades later.

Another concern with American food was highlighted by Rachel Carson's *Silent Spring*, published first in 1962 as a series of articles in *The New Yorker*. Carson's now-famous exposé of chemical industrial waste that leached into American crops, poultry, fish, and cattle and pork led to interest in organic food in the late 1960s and, perhaps naturally, to vegetarianism as both a spiritual and health practice. Many books about the dangers of mass-produced, processed foods appeared in the 1970s, some of them in response to Ralph Nader's reports on the dangers of hot dogs and hamburgers; probably the best-selling of those books was Frances Moore Lappé's *Diet for a Small Planet*, in which she encourages readers to "eat low on the food chain." Levenstein compares the vegetarian and organic-food movements of the 1970s to William Sylvester Graham's nineteenth-century attempts to encourage Americans to eat less meat and more whole grains; Levenstein's comparison reminds readers of the cyclical nature of foodways.

The natural-foods/vegetarian movement also had its detractors. One counter-movement to the organic-natural-vegetarian food movement was the feminist movement, primarily because the former regularly cast women in the role of cooks and caregivers or, in Levenstein's words, "because it still reflected traditional ideas about the division of labor" (186). Another deterrent to the vegetarian/organic diet, with its emphasis on dairy products and eggs, was the U.S. Senate's Nutrition Committee's push for "negative nutrition" after research showed that Americans ate too much cholesterol, fat, sugar, and salt. In 1979, the surgeon general recommended that to prevent disease, Americans should eat "more fish, poultry, complex carbohydrates, and legumes" (208) and less salt, sugar, saturated fat, and cholesterol. At the same time, Americans saw the rise of interest in gourmet cooking and restaurant dining. The 1980s, when the baby boomers reached adulthood and began to explore the world at large, saw a large increase in interest in international cuisine. Levenstein remarks that the "former countercultures and New Leftists who had rejoined the mainstream [brought] with them their reverence for the artisanal and a disdain for foods that were not fresh, natural, and 'authentic' " (219). The scares about fat and cholesterol led Americans to favor food prepared simply, without fatty sauces, and "fresh, raw, or barely cooked vegetables were esteemed as never before" (220).

Regional American cooking also rose in esteem and popularity in the 1980s, evidenced by the popularity of Cajun, New England, southwest, California, Tex-Mex, southern, and soul and the related foods, cookbooks, and television cooking shows. (The first edition of Richard Schweid's *Hot Peppers*, out in 1987, is a fine example of new interest in regional food.) Processed foods such as condensed soups, processed cheese, Jell-O, canned foods, and many frozen foods lost popularity, while imported foods, raw foods, and pasta all gained ascendancy. Another aspect of the paradox of America's plenty is that fast food—hamburgers, tacos, fried chicken, sandwiches, pizza, any food that could be eaten while moving—kept pace in popularity with Americans' interests in "gourmet" food. Americans continued in the 1980s to be concerned with body image (women in particular) and diet. In 1981, Stouffers brought out Lean Cuisine, frozen dinners that were lower in calories and fat than the old TV dinners of the 1950s. Being both "rich" and "thin" seem to have been driving forces in America long before "Babe" Paley made being both famous, so that by the time the Reagans moved into the White House, Nancy Reagan, according to Levenstein, seemed the literal embodiment of that American paradox. Nancy Reagan was interested in the food served in the White House, instructing White House chef Henry Haller to "make the platters fancier, the color combinations more striking, and the portions smaller" (237).

The late 1980s and early 1990s also saw Americans become suspicious, for the first time, of a long-standing favorite meat: beef. Levenstein remarks that the image of the benevolent Elsie, Borden's icon, or Carnation's "contented cows" altered so that Americans saw instead, "hundreds of pounds of life-threatening cholesterol production" (252), which, as Francis Lappe had warned in the early 1970s, ate more than they produced, contributed to global warming and the greenhouse effect and, because of Americans' devotion to fast food, were partly responsible for the destruction of the Brazilian rain forests to make room for cattle ranches. Levenstein does not address "mad cow" disease because *Paradox of Plenty*'s publication predates it, nor does he take on the issue of growth hormones in beef and other American meat and poultry, the central factor in Ruth Little Ozecki's novel *My Year of Meats*. He does hope, in the end, that Americans may someday be able to "have their good food and eat it too" (255).

Another food scholar who has produced a pair of important works is Margaret Visser, author of *Much Depends on Dinner* and *The Rituals of Dinner*. Visser, a literary scholar, takes her headnote for the first volume from Lord Byron's *Don Juan*: "Since Eve ate apples, much depends on dinner." Its lengthy subtitle is *The Extraordinary History and Mythology, Allure and Obsessions, Perils, Taboos, of an Ordinary Meal.* The "ordinary meal" that she uses as the organizing principle of the book consists of buttered corn with salt, chicken, rice, and lettuce dressed with olive oil and lemon juice, with ice cream for dessert. Visser's approach is more inclusive than that of many other food scholars in that she includes, in addition to history and nutritional information, theoretical perspectives that might help a writer who is searching for a suitable approach toward a subject. For example, in the chapter about lettuce, she describes a kind of binary coding, used also by Mary Douglas and Roland Barthes. Visser writes about the "Hippocratic complex," which sees food in terms of "a series of diametrically opposing principles: up and down, light and dark, male and female, hot and cold, dry and wet. . . . Harmony and balance must be found between these opposites" (197). Lettuce, therefore, is seen as dark, female, cold, and wet. It is valuable for food scholars to see how theoretical approaches may be used in addition to historical and scientific ones. *The Rituals of Dinner* is another reader-friendly volume that explains "[t]he origins, evolution, eccentricities, and meaning of table manners" (title page). This volume has proven useful to writers analyzing works of popular culture (e.g., film) in which food is consumed in group settings. She explores the definition of pollution in a succinct and provocative way: "matter out of place" (301).

Raymond Sokolov's *Why We Eat What We Eat* concentrates on the relation of "New World" foods to "Old World" cooking and eating patterns and the importation of European farming and growing practices onto American soil. Sokolov carries on a running argument with the idea of "authenticity" and points out repeatedly the influences that are exerted on all cooking and eating patterns. When considering the concept of "authentically French" cuisine, he writes, "There never was a time when French food had a Platonic essence. A continuous record of recipes going back to the Middle Ages shows a dynamic, evolving process—not immutable granite traditions. Authenticity is yesterday's orthodoxy" (95).

Gerry Schremp, a reporter for *Life* magazine, editor of a Time-Life cookbook series *The Good Cook* and text editor of their *Foods of the World* series, covers fads in foods in *Kitchen Culture: Fifty Years of Food Fads*. Her book contains many vintage photographs from the 1940s and later decades and is a good source of information about such popular culture phenomena as cooking shows on television, which began with Dione Lucas' show *To a Queen's Taste* in 1947. She also covers magazines devoted more or less exclusively to food, the earliest of which she cites is *Gourmet*, which began publication in 1941, followed fourteen years later by *Bon Appetit* and by *Food and Wine* in 1978. She also includes brief entries on well-known chefs and food and cooking critics, beginning with Duncan Hines, who first published *Adventures in Good Eating* in 1936 as a guide for travelers and gave his seal of approval to select restaurants and hotels and, eventually, to a line of food products put out by Proctor and Gamble. There is a brief entry on Chuck Williams, founder of Williams-Sonoma cookware stores and several other spin-off businesses. Famous chefs, such as Alice Waters and Paul Bocuse, are pictured as well as the well-known food writer M.F.K. Fisher. Schremp also treats such kitchen equipment as microwaves, electric skillets, and Tupperware. Schremp's brief articles provide time frames and starting points for researchers. Her bibli-

A madrigal dinner staged in Yosemite National Park, 1999. Courtesy Yosemite Concession Services Corp.

ography is helpfully divided into "General Reading," "Cookbooks," and "Newspapers and Magazines."

Sylvia Lovgren's *Fashionable Foods: Seven Decades of Food Fads*, more than twice as long as Schremp's at more than 450 pages, covers the territory previously treated by Shapiro as well as Schremp, but she also fills in the gaps left between those two volumes, roughly the 1920s and 1930s. Unlike Harvey Levenstein and Laura Shapiro, Lovgren does not theorize deeply about the culture that produced the food, and, unlike Schremp, she does not cover so many ancillary fields as television, cooking equipment, and marketing. She sticks, primarily, to the popularity of various dishes during the seven decades that she considers. Lovgren acknowledges Shapiro's work and begins her chapter on the food fads of the 1920s with a section on salads in which the ingredients are disguised as something else (a tomato and canned pineapple as a water lily, for instance) or some sweet ingredient might be added. Her candidate for the "worst salad of the twenties" is banana and popcorn salad, consisting of a split banana laid over lettuce leaves, with popcorn and dabs of mayonnaise scattered over. This book contains numerous recipes, which should be valuable to a food or nutrition researcher. The text is interspersed with boxes containing unusual recipes (such as the one for banana-popcorn salad), information about food trends, and sometimes photographs of kitchen arrangements or appliances.

In *We Are What We Eat: Ethnic Food and the Making of Americans*, Donna R. Gabaccia takes up a theme introduced by Laura Shapiro and elaborated on by Harvey Levenstein: efforts to "Americanize" the foodways of European, Caribbean, Asian, African, and "other" immigrants. Like Shapiro and Levenstein, she traces the efforts of New England food reformers such as Ellen Richards, Fannie Farmer, and other "domestic scientists" to convince early-twentieth-century European immigrants to give up the foodways of their ancestors—mixing ingredients together in one pot, for example—and adopt the bland cuisine of New England. In her chapter "Food Fights and American Values," she relates that many early dieticians tried to persuade immigrant cooks that their native foods were unhealthy. "For example, they attempted to persuade Mexicans to reduce their use of tomato and pepper" on the premise that tomatoes and peppers were hard to digest and damaging to the kidneys and that "Hungarian, Polish, and Jewish children [should be kept] from eating dill pickles [with their supposedly negative impact on the urinary tract]" (128). Spicy foods favored by European immigrants were thought to lead to overly emotional behavior, and the grade A eggs and prime cuts of meat that Jewish mothers fed their children kept their young ones from learning self-denial (128). Levenstein and Gabaccia both quote an early social worker's notes that one Italian family was "still eating spaghetti, not yet assimilated." Also like Levenstein, Gabaccia considers the impact that the New Left, "hippies," and, later, "Yuppies" exerted on American foodways from the 1960s to the millennium and credits them with renewed interest in and appreciation of ethnic foods and the 1980s craze for "gourmet" foods. In a departure from several food-writing predecessors, she credits these same groups with America's growing and thriving wine industry, mentioning that after Prohibition and the depression, American wine was perceived as fit mostly for "immigrants, bohemians, and winos" (212). Beginning in the 1960s, however, American vintners began to market their product—more often than not varietal mixtures sold in jugs—to college-age buyers, the same consumers of ethnic peasant cuisine. When these consumers matured and earned more disposable income, they became the target market for the more sophisticated wines produced by American vineyards. College-educated consumers who had traveled to Europe or other continents were also not content with processed versions of ethnic foods—canned spaghetti, for instance, or Chef Boyardee ravioli—and now deemed unprocessed, freshly made ethnic foods as a way to protest "American cultural imperialism" (213). Gabaccia also traces the development of vegetarianism and, unlike some of her predecessors, mentions not just counterculture vegetarians but Jewish vegetarians as well, citing Jonathan Wolf's kosher recipes for holiday foods. Connected to the interest in the 1980s with gourmet food was the beginning of "nouvelle" or "fusion" cuisine, sometimes seen as happy combinations of varied cultures, sometimes as a violation of the "rules of good taste and culinary laws" (216).

Gabaccia's book includes a chapter on local cookbooks and the great interest in them spurred by the corresponding interest in ethnic foodways during the 1970s and 1980s. In addition, as succeeding generations of Americans drifted in time from their immigrant ancestors, interest in the foodways of their grandparents and great-grandparents grew. Two examples that she cites are *From Generation to Generation*, put out by Dallas' Temple Emanu-El sisterhood in 1992, and *The Black Family Reunion Cookbook*, produced by the National Council of Negro Women in

1991. She also delves into the relatively recent practice (in most of America) of ethnic food festivals as ways to attract attention and dollars to a community, stating, "Before the 1970s, larger-scale festivals rarely focused specifically on ethnic foods" (189). She goes on to discuss several communities and their food festivals and celebrations but, curiously, makes no mention of the numerous (and historically long-standing) food festivals of Louisiana, focusing instead on San Antonio, other Texas communities, and some locations in the Midwest. Another aspect of ethnic food in America that she writes about is the more recent wave of immigrants from the Caribbean, from India, from various African nations, and from the Pacific Rim. The rising popularity of bodegas in New York is part of this new appreciation of ethnicity, as is the proliferation of fresh-produce markets run, primarily, by Asians.

Donna Gabaccia concludes her study of American foodways with a short chapter called "Sources," in which she explains her methodology. Hers is a "culturally sensitive yet essentially materialist and economic view of American eating" (235). She cites helpful written sources as well as the locations of her case studies, choosing Charleston, Minneapolis-St. Paul, New York, San Antonio, and San Francisco as representative of the regional and ethnic diversity of American foods. She does admit regret at having ignored the foodways of Louisiana. She helpfully outlines avenues for further research and cites libraries and helpful sources of information. There is no bibliography per se, but her notes are extensive enough to help a new researcher.

Another volume with an extensive bibliography—seventeen pages in close type, to be exact—is *Consuming Geographies: We Are Where We Eat*, by David Bell and Gill Valentine. This work is centered on British eating habits, but many of the social, ethnic, and other issues are to be found in most modern cultures. The authors divide the book into chapters about the body, home, community, city, region, and nation and end it with global concerns about food. There are numerous interviews with individuals who are asked questions about their eating attitudes and practices. "Food as Popular Culture" is a subsection of the introductory chapter, and the authors touch on food magazines and television shows. They point out the "luscious center-folds" of food as "gastro-porn—seductive but unobtainable and artificially, stereotypically perfect" in magazines and similar pictures of food on television and in film.

The question of whether American food is, indeed, cuisine is addressed by Leslie Brenner in *American Appetite: The Coming of Age of a Cuisine*. Brenner previously published books on wine and food and has extensive magazine publications and was the 1996 winner of the James Beard Foundation Journalism Award for Magazine Feature Writing. This book's title clearly asserts that American food has risen to the level of cuisine, but Brenner found that in researching this book, she would be called on to defend the idea. She claims, "Whether or not what has happened to food in this country has been a revolution, in the lives of a generation of individual cooks there has been an awakening, a moment when a gastronomic light bulb switched on, and a heretofore uncharted world of cuisine became illuminated" (4). She traces the influences toward this "food enlightenment" back to the victory gardens that Americans were encouraged to plant during World War II, when both the metal for cans and canned foods were needed for the war effort. Americans who had grown up on canned food learned how much better fresh produce tasted, and, although many of them would succumb to frozen TV dinners in the 1950s and McDonald's in the 1950s and 1960s, the seeds of a taste revolution had been planted. Another influencing factor in the 1960s was the ease of foreign travel and the increase in college education and its sometimes attendant heightening of cultural awareness. Brenner parallels the post–World War II interest in modern jazz, abstract expressionist painting, modern architecture, and modernist literature with a new seriousness about food, in spite of the "Jell-O and luau mind-set" of the suburbs (39). She describes the growing restaurant scene on both coasts, citing New York's Forum of the Twelve Caesars, which opened in 1957, and Aware Inn, which opened in Los Angeles, also in 1957. Their cuisine now strikes us as amusingly retro—beef stroganoff, for example, or flaming partridge—but Brenner quotes reviews and first-person interviews with diners who remembered the food as refreshingly different and exciting.

Brenner also cites the heavy influence of French cooks and French culture on American food and American popular culture; the movie *To Catch a Thief*, which came out in 1955, "went a long way in popularizing Francophilia" (42). James Beard preceded Julia Child as a dominant food force, and his contributions to *Gourmet* magazine, which had begun publication in 1941, helped ensure its popularity as a source of information for the gourmands of the late 1950s. Interest in French food and wines paved a welcoming path for Julia Child and her television cooking and created a ready market for *Gourmet* reader Chuck Williams' growing business in French cookware. Williams' store in Sonoma, California, began as a hardware store, but a trip to France in 1952 and a later trip in 1958 helped Williams realize that his true passion was cookware rather than hardware. The eventual result was, of course, the Williams-Sonoma empire, which eventually expanded into businesses specializing in dishes, containers, storage goods, and gardening products. The Kennedy White House also did its part to popularize both French culture and French food, hiring French chef Rene Verdon, whose elaborate seasonal menus were reported on the front page of the April 7, 1961, *New York Times* by *Times*' food writer Craig Claiborne. Brenner spends most of Chapter 3 on the influence of Julia Child's cookbooks and television shows on American cooking and eating and ends it by saying, "The performing cook trend that Julia started on her show in 1963 has mushroomed enormously in the three decades since," and she cites a cover headline from the September 22, 1997, *U.S. News and World Report*: " 'How Julia Invented Modern Life' " (78–79).

Changes in U.S. immigration policy have also helped contribute to American cuisine. Brenner describes immigration laws previous to 1965 as "xenophobic" and devotes a chapter to sketching the connection between immigration laws and waves of immigrants who have all added their touches to American foodways. The Immigration Act of 1965, which went into effect in 1968, served to reverse the quotas on non-Northern European immigrants, and "since then millions have come from China, Hong Kong, Taiwan, Japan, Korea, Thailand, Eastern Europe, the Philippines, India, Pakistan, the Middle East, Africa, Mexico, the Caribbean, and Central and South America, bringing their foodways along with them" (99). Food magazines have reflected this change and have also helped ensure Americans' growing familiarity with ingredients once thought to be unobtainable. For many years, the term "Chinese cooking" was synonymous with "Cantonese cooking," but by the 1980s many Americans, because of exposure either here or on mainland

China, could distinguish among several varieties of Chinese cooking, branching out to restaurants that specialize in the cuisine of Szechuan and Hunan provinces. Italian cooking also rose in prestige as Americans began to distinguish among kinds of olive oil, brands of Parmigiano Reggiano cheese, and vintage Chiantis. Brenner includes upscale Mexican, Thai, Indian, Middle Eastern, North African, Cuban and Caribbean, and Vietnamese cuisines and spends several paragraphs on "fusion" cuisine, a blend of Eastern and Western ingredients and cooking techniques. She concludes this chapter by describing a dish served "[a]t San Francisco's Aqua [restaurant] . . . steamed littleneck clams and shiitake tortellini with spicy Thai coconut broth and basil chiffonnade" (119), a dish that exhibits culinary influences from Japan, Italy, Thailand, France, and America.

Brenner devotes as much space to the career of Alice Waters as she does to Julia Child. Alice Waters is a major figure in the development of "California cuisine," a kind of backlash against French cuisine that Waters and other California chefs had been schooled in and had produced early in their careers. Founded in 1972, Chez Panisse, Waters' famous Berkeley, California, restaurant, obviously grew from French roots, but California cuisine, which came to be near the end of the 1970s, celebrated local ingredients without apology for their not being "French." Brenner quotes Waters on her decision to print her restaurant's menus in English rather than French: " 'There was a point when we had to stop in French because we were saying 'huitres de Bodega Bay.' And it seemed so foolish—why don't we just say 'Bodega Bay oysters?' " (142). California cuisine depended on fresh local ingredients and innovative recipes. It coincided with "nouvelle cuisine" in France, a similar move away from classic, but rather tired, recipes and presentations, and "cuisine minceur," a French food movement credited to Michel Guerard, a French spa chef who used less butter and cream and, again, more fresh ingredients. Cuisine minceur was intended as food for those who wanted to lose weight, and it inspired what was called "spa food" in America.

California cuisine also was greatly influenced by Italian cooking, especially the food practices of northern Italy, with its emphasis on fresh produce, choice olive oils, and high-quality vinegars. In the 1980s California wines also saw an upturn in quality and reputation. Another restaurant trend developed also—the concept of "plating" food or decorating a plain white over-sized plate with food and sauces drizzled in interesting patterns, a trend that still continues twenty years later throughout the country in restaurants of varying degrees of pretentiousness. Out of the California cuisine phenomenon came also the concept of the star chef, Alice Waters being but one, in company with Jeremiah Towers, Mark Miller, and Wolfgang Puck. In terms of popular culture, this avenue to fame—the chef as icon—is an interesting development aided, no doubt, by the popularity of food magazines mentioned earlier—*Gourmet*, *Bon Appetit*, *Saveur*, *Cooks*, *Food and Wine*—and the popularity of the weekly food column in midsize newspaper markets and restaurant review columns in larger markets.

In spite of all the celebration of American cuisine and California cuisine, however, Brenner observes that food, for many Americans, is more a matter of style than of taste and that restaurants are more places to be seen than to enjoy what we eat. She attributes our inability to truly savor good food partly to our Puritan heritage but also says that "we find it difficult to slow down long enough to relish [good food]" (165), echoing sentiments expressed earlier by French and Italian

Crayfish festival in New Orleans, 1999. Photo by Paul McGuirk

food scholars. She does, happily, consider food films as an offshoot of America's interest in cuisine as well as some novels and nonfiction food-centered works.

Two writers who disagree with Brenner and have little good to say about American cuisine or Julia Child (or about numerous other food writers, including fellow *Times* food writer Ruth Reichl) are John L. Hess and Karen Hess, restaurant reviewers and food critics for the *New York Times*. *The Taste of America* bemoans most of the food trends described by other writers. Their first two chapters are titled "Rape of the Palate" and "Onward and Downward." In spite of this volume's gloomy tone, however, it concludes with an extensive and excellent bibliography, divided by historical periods.

At the opposite end of the food-scholarship spectrum from questions about cuisine, Americans, Canadians, and no doubt many others have recently evinced interest in an area of food study called "Nutraceuticals" by some and "functional foods, phytonutrients, or phytofoods" by others. This idea is not new, of course, as we have seen in the writings of Harvey Levenstein and other food historians. Much of the information on it, however, is disseminated through the relatively new source of the World Wide Web. One source quotes Dr. Morton Walker, author of *Secrets of Long Life*, who claims,

> Nutritionally high-powered foods aren't new to the natural products industry—we have been selling nutrition-rich foods such as whole grains, lecithin, brewer's yeast and soy products for over 60 years. What is new about these foods, however, is science's added knowledge about the disease-preventing components they contain. Stephen de Felice, M.D., director of New York's Foundation for Innovation in Medicine, is credited with first use of the term "nutraceutical." It describes specific chemical compounds found in foods that may prevent disease. Phytochemical is a more recent evolution of the term that emphasizes the plant source of most of these protective, disease-preventing compounds.

Again, we are reminded of the cyclical nature of our culture's interest in food as medicine.

ANTHOLOGIES

An anthology of food writing that has been used as a classroom text for courses in food discourse is Lilly Golden's *A Literary Feast*, a collection of primarily fiction, including Isak Dineson's "Babette's Feast," "The Dead" by James Joyce, Isaac Bashevis Singer's "Short Friday," and, among the nonfictional works, Betty Fussell's superbly written "On Murdering Eels and Laundering Swine." An anthology of secondary food writing and critical articles is *Cooking by the Book*, edited by Mary Anne Schofield. Among the collected articles and essays about food in/and literature is one of the seminal nonanthropological works about food, Susan J. Leonardi's "Recipes for Reading: Pasta Salad, Lobster a la Riseholm, Key Lime Pie." This volume concludes with a bibliographic piece by Karen Madeira, "Cultural Meaning and Use of Food: A Selective Bibliography (1973–1987)." *Granta*, a British magazine, published *Food: The Vital Stuff* in 1995, and it contains, among other writings, an excerpt from John Lanchester's food novel *The Debt to Pleasure*, in which the narrator defines and describes the British culinary term "stodge." The appearance of this volume was one of many indicators of the importance of food as a scholarly and literary topic.

Food and Culture, a Reader, edited by Carole Counihan and Penny Van Esterik, contains four sections of writings about food—eating, fasting, the body and culture, and the political economy of food. Many food scholars and writers are included: M.F.K. Fisher, Margaret Mead, Roland Barthes, Claude Levi-Strauss, Mary Douglas, Anna Freud, Susan Bordo, Stephen Mennell, Sidney Mintz, and Frances Moore Lappe, among them. This is a multidisciplinary approach to the subject of food and culture and represents a wide spectrum of knowledge and opinion. Both early and later scholars are represented so that a beginning scholar can see in this work some of the writers who have undertaken the task of exploring the intensely complex relation between food and culture.

Eating Culture, edited by Ron Scapp and Brian Seitz, is a less comprehensive showing of food scholarship but offers more information and more examples of eating as art and eating in art. A comment from this work's introduction neatly summarizes the editors' philosophy: "Eating is seldom merely about destination or purpose. Eating is largely about creation and self-creation, and about the production and reproduction of human life." Eating as a part of the larger consumer culture is also considered in this book, in Joanne Finkelstein's chapter "Dining Out: The Hyperreality of Appetite." Finkelstein avers, "Two institutions that have blatantly promoted consumerism are the department store and the restaurant" (207). Two of the chapters explore the idea of "gastroporn" touched on in other works, Marianna Beck's "Only Food" and Alphonso Lingis' "Appetite." This collection is varied and probably more useful to an experienced food writer than to a novice.

Food: An Oxford Anthology, edited by Brigid Allen, is divided into several parts, some of which concern literary characters and their relations to food and eating, and some of which concern real people. Nathaniel Hawthorne's notebooks, for instance, are quoted, as are numerous other works of both nonfiction and fiction. There is a sizable representation of British poetry—Keats' "The Eve of St. Agnes," for example—as well as standard British food writing, as exemplified by Sir John Evelyn. Brief writings about eating, buying, preparing, and serving food are included. This work is very likely more useful to a literary scholar than any other researcher, but the selections do provide a broad sampling of food writing past and present, in fiction and nonfiction.

In the nonfiction category is *Best Food Writing 2000*, edited by Holly Hughes, part of the Best Writing Series. It contains selections of book, magazine, newspaper, newsletter, and Internet prose about food. Included is the work of John Thorne, author of both *Outlaw Cook* and *Serious Pig*. Magazine writer Jeffrey Steingargen and *Gourmet* editor Ruth Reichl are also included as are Calvin Trillin and novelist and screenwriter Jim Harrison.

BIBLIOGRAPHY

Most of the previously discussed and reviewed books include bibliographies that serve as starting points for most scholars, but several recent bibliographic sources should also be mentioned here. One is a bibliographic essay from the March–April 1997 issue of *Nutrition Today*, from which the following list of bibliographies is taken:

Camp, Charles. "Food in American Culture: A Bibliographic Essay." *Journal of American Culture* (1979), 559–70.

———. "Foodways in Everyday Life." *American Quarterly* (1982), 278–89.

Food and Nutrition Bibliography: Compiled from Data Provided by the National Agricultural Library. U.S. Department of Agriculture. 11th ed. Phoenix: Oryx, 1984.

Freedman, R. L. *Human Food Uses: A Cross-Cultural, Comprehensive Annotated Bibliography*. Westport, Conn.: Greenwood, 1981.

Grivetti, L. E. "Cultural Nutrition: Anthropological and Geographical Themes." *Annual Review of Nutrition* (1981), 47–68.

Grivetti, L. E., S. J. Lamprecht, H. J. Rocke, and A. Waterman. "Threads of Cultural Nutrition: Arts and Humanities." *Progressive Food Nutritional Science* 11 (1987), 249–306.

Mennell, Stephen, Anne Murcott, and A. H. van Otterloo. "The Sociology of Food: Eating, Diet and Culture." *Current Sociology* 40 (1992), 1–152.

Newman, J. M. *Melting Pot: An Annotated Bibliography and Guide to Food and Nu-*

trition Information for Ethnic Groups in America. 2nd ed. New York: Garland, 1993.

Schveibinz, M. *Cultural Perspectives on Food and Nutrition*. Beltsville, Md.: National Agricultural Library, 1994.

Wilson, C. S. "Food: Custom and Nurture—An Annotated Bibliography on Sociocultural and Biocultural Aspects of Nutrition." *Journal of Nutrition Education* 11, suppl. 1 (1979), 211–263.

A newer source that is updated often is Gary Allen's *Resource Guide for Food Writers*. It includes food interest and information organizations and their addresses, food publications, and Web sites. Allen includes sources, food-related library collections, organizations, Internet news groups, periodicals, interview techniques, culinary reference works, writing guides, recipe formatting, food-writing courses and conferences, and techniques on getting works published.

Books and Articles

Allen, Brigid, ed. *Food: An Oxford Anthology*. Oxford: Oxford University Press, 1994.

Allen, Gary. *Resource Guide for Food Writers*. New York: Routledge, 1999.

The American Heritage Cookbook and Illustrated History of American Eating and Drinking. New York: American Heritage, 1964.

Anderson, Jay Allan. "Scholarship on Contemporary American Folk Foodways." *Ethnologia Europaea* 5 (1971), 56–63.

Andrews, Jean. *Peppers: The Domesticated Capsicums*. Austin: University of Texas Press, 1984.

Barber, Edith M. "The Development of the American Food Pattern." *Journal of the American Dietetic Association* 24 (July 1948), 586–91.

Barthes, Roland. *Mythologies*. Trans. Annette Lavers. New York: Hill and Wang, 1972.

———. "Toward a Pyschosociology of Contemporary Food Consumption." In *European Diet from Pre-Industrial to Modern Times*, ed. Elborg Forster and Robert Forster. New York: Harper and Row, 1975, 47–59.

Beard, James A. *James Beard's American Cookery*. Boston: Little, Brown, 1972.

Bell, David, and Gill Valentine. *Consuming Geographies: We Are Where We Eat*. New York: Routledge, 1997.

Bennet, John. "Food and Culture in Southern Illinois." *American Sociological Review* 7 (October 1942), 645–60.

———. "An Interpretation of the Scope and Implications of Social Scientific Research in Human Subsistence." *American Anthropologist* 48 (October 1946), 553–73.

Biester, Charlotte Elizabeth. *Some Factors in the Development of American Cookbooks*. Field Study Number 2. Ann Arbor, Mich.: University Microfilms, 1950.

Bourke, John Gregory. "The Folk Foods of the Rio Grande Valley and of Northern Mexico." *Journal of American Folklore* 8 (January–March 1895), 41–75.

Brenner, Leslie. *American Appetite: The Coming of Age of a Cuisine*. New York: Avon, 1999.

Brown, Bob, and Eleanor Parker. *Culinary Americana: 1860–1960*. New York: Roving Eye Press, 1961.

Brown, Dale. *American Cooking*. New York: Time, 1968.

———. *American Cooking: The Northwest*. New York: Time, 1970.

Brown, Linda Keller, and Kay Mussell, eds. *Ethnic and Regional Foodways in the United States: The Performance of Group Identity*. Knoxville: University of Tennessee Press, 1984.

Burton, Thomas G., and Ambrose N. Manning. *Folk Methods of Preserving and Processing Food*. East Tennessee University Monograph Series, No. 3. Johnson City, Tenn.: Institute of Regional Studies, 1966, 27–31.

Camp, Charles. *American Foodways: What, When, Why and How We Eat In America*. Little Rock, Ark.: August House, 1989.

Carson, Jane. *Colonial Virginia Cookery*. Williamsburg, Va.: Colonial Williamsburg, 1968.

Carson, Rachel. *Silent Spring*. New York: Houghton Mifflin, 1993.

Cassell, B. "Jewish Dietary Laws and Food Customs." *Public Health Nursing* 32 (November 1940), 685–87.

Chang, B. "Some Dietary Beliefs in Chinese Folk Culture." *Journal of the American Dietetic Association* 65 (October 1974), 463–68.

Claiborne, Craig. *The New York Times Guide to Dining Out in New York*. Rev. ed. New York: Atheneum, 1968.

Clark, Faith, ed. *Symposium III: The Changing Patterns of Consumption of Food*. International Congress of Food Science and Technology. Proceedings of the Congress Symposia, 1962. Vol. 5. New York: Gordon and Breach Science, 1967, 159–254.

Collin, Richard. *New Orleans Restaurant Guide*. New Orleans: Strether and Swann, 1977.

———. *New Orleans Underground Gourmet*. New Orleans: Strether and Swann, 1973.

———. *The Pleasures of Seafood*. New York: Holt, Rinehart, and Winston, 1977.

Committee on Food Habits, National Research Council. *Manual for the Study of Food Habits*. Bulletin of the National Research Council No. 111. Washington, D.C.: National Research Council, 1945.

———. *The Problem of Changing Food Habits*. Bulletin of the National Research Council No. 108. Washington, D.C.: National Research Council, 1943.

Counihan, Carole, and Penny Van Esterik, eds. *Food and Culture, a Reader*. New York: Routledge, 1997.

Cummings, Richard Osborn. *The American and His Food: A History of Food Habits in the United States*. Chicago: University of Chicago Press, 1940.

Cussler, Margaret, and Mary Louise De Give. *Twixt the Cup and the Lip: Psychological and Socio-cultural Factors Affecting Food Habits*. New York: Twayne, 1952.

Davidson, Alan. *The Oxford Companion to Food*. Oxford: Oxford University Press, 1999.

Dickins, Dorothy. "Changing Pattern of Food Preparation of Small Town Families in Mississippi." *Mississippi Agricultural Experimental Station Bulletin* 415 (1945), 1–56.

Dickson, Paul. *Chow: A Cook's Tour of Military Food*. New York: New American Library, 1978.

Dodson, R. "Tortilla Making." *In the Shadow of History*. Texas Folklore Society Publications No. 15 (1939), 1–18.

Douglas, Mary. "The Abomination of Leviticus." *Purity and Danger*. New York: Praeger, 1966, 41–57.

———. "Deciphering a Meal." In *Myth, Symbol, and Culture*, ed. Clifford Geertz. New York: W. W. Norton, 1971, 61–81.

———, ed. *Food in the Social Order: Studies of Food and Festivities in Three American Communities*. New York: Russell Sage Foundation, 1984.

Feibleman, Peter S., and the Editors of Time-Life Books. *American Cooking: Creole and Acadian*. New York: Time, 1971.

Gabaccia, Donna R. *We Are What We Eat: Ethnic Food and the Making of Americans*. Cambridge: Harvard University Press, 1998.

Glaser, Milton, and Jerome Snyder. *The Underground Gourmet*. Rev. ed. New York: Simon and Schuster, 1970.

Golden, Lilly, ed. *A Literary Feast*. New York: Atlantic Monthly Press, 1993.

Granta, ed. *Food: The Vital Stuff*. London: Granta Books, 1995.

Greene, Gael. *Bite*. New York: W. W. Norton, 1971.

Harris, Marvin. *Cows, Pigs, Wars, and Witches: The Riddles of Culture*. New York: Random House, 1974.

Hess, John L., and Karen Hess. *The Taste of America*. Urbana: University of Illinois Press, 2000.

Hines, Duncan. *Adventures in Good Eating*. Bowling Green, Ky.: Adventures in Good Eating Inc., 1936.

Hirshorn, Paul, and Steven Isenour. *White Towers*. Cambridge: MIT Press, 1979.

Hughes, Holly, ed. *Best Food Writing 2000*. New York: Marlowe, 2000.

Humphery, N. D. "Some Dietary and Health Practices of Detroit Mexicans." *Journal of American Folklore* 58 (July 1945), 255–58.

Jones, Michael Owens, Bruce Giuliano, and Roberta Krell, eds. *Foodways and Eating Habits: Directions for Research*. Los Angeles: California Folklore Society, 1981.

Jordan, G. L. *Changing Food Habits in Relation to Land Utilization in the United States*. Carbondale: University of Illinois Press, 1933.

Kiple, Kenneth F., and Kriemhild Conee Ornelas. *The Cambridge World History of Food*. Cambridge: Cambridge University Press, 2000.

Kroc, Ray. *Grinding It Out: The Making of McDonald's*. Chicago: Henry Regnery, 1977.

Lanchester, John. "The History of Food." *The New Yorker* (November 27, 2000), 170–73.

Langdon, Philip. *Orange Roof, Golden Arches: The Architecture of American Chain Restaurants*. New York: Alfred A. Knopf, 1986.

Lappé, Frances M. *Diet for a Small Planet*. New York: Ballantine, 1976.

Lasky, Michael S. *The Complete Junk Food Book*. New York: McGraw-Hill, 1977.

Leach, Edmund. "Cooking." In *Culture and Communication*. New York: Cambridge University Press, 1976, 60–61.

Le Gros, Clark F. "Human Food Habits as Determining the Basic Patterns of Economic and Social Life." *Nutrition* 22 (January 1966), 134–45.

Leonard, Jonathan Norton, and the Editors of Time-Life Books. *American Cooking: New England*. New York: Time, 1970.

———. *American Cooking: The Great West*. New York: Time, 1971.

Levenstein, Harvey. *The Paradox of Plenty*. Oxford: Oxford University Press, 1993.

———. *Revolution at the Table*. Oxford: Oxford University Press, 1988.

Lévi-Strauss, Claude. "The Culinary Triangle." *Partisan Review* 33 (Fall 1966), 586–95.

Lincoln, Waldo. *American Cookery Books, 1742–1860*. Worcester, Mass.: American Antiquarian Society, 1954.

Loeb, M. B. "The Social Functions of Food Habits." *Journal of Applied Nutrition* 4 (1951), 227–29.

Lovgren, Sylvia. *Fashionable Foods: Seven Decades of Food Fads*. New York: Macmillan, 1995.

Lowenberg, M. E. "Socio-Cultural Basis of Food Habits." *Food Technology* 24 (1970), 27–32.

Massachusetts State Department of Health. *The Food of Working Women in Boston*. Studies in Economic Relations of Women, Vol. 10. Boston: Women's Educational and Industrial Union, Department of Research, 1917.

McGee, Harold. *On Food and Cooking: The Science and Lore of the Kitchen*. New York: Macmillan, 1983.

Mead, Margaret. "The Challenges of Cross-Cultural Research." *Journal of the American Dietetic Association* 45 (December 1964), 413–14.

———. "Dietary Pattern and Food Habits." *Journal of the American Dietetic Association* 19 (January 1943), 1–5.

———. *Food Habits Research: Problems of the 1960's*. Washington, D.C.: National Research Council, 1964.

Moser, Ada M. *Farm Family Diets in the Lower Coastal Plain of South Carolina*. Bulletin 319. South Carolina Agricultural Experimental Station, 1939.

———. *Food Habits of South Carolina Farm Families*. Bulletin 343. South Carolina Agricultural Experimental Station, 1942.

Newall, Venetia. "Selected Jamaican Foodways in Homeland and in England." In *Folklore Today*, ed. Linda Degh, Henry Glassie, and Felix J. Oinas. Bloomington: Indiana University Press, 1976, 369–77.

Niehoff, Artur H. "Food Habits and Cultural Patterns." *Food Science and Society*. New York: Nutrition Foundation, 1969, 42–52.

Ozecki, Ruth L. *My Year of Meats*. New York: Viking, 1999.

Patten, Mauguerite. *Books for Cooks: Bibliography of Cookery*. New York: Bowker, 1975.

Paz, Octavio. "Eroticism and Gastrostrophy." *Daedalus* 101 (Fall 1972), 67–85.

Phillips, Doris E., and Mary A. Bass. "Food Preservation Practices of Selected Homemakers in East Tennessee." *Ecology of Food and Nutrition* 5 (Winter 1976), 26–39.

Pyke, Magnus. *Food and Society*. London: John Murray, 1968.

———. "The Influence of American Food and Food Technology in Europe." In *Superculture: American Popular Culture and Europe*, ed. C.W.E. Bigsby. Bowling Green, Ohio: Bowling Green University Popular Press, 1975, 83–95.

Read, R. B. *The San Francisco Underground Gourmet*. New York: Simon and Schuster, 1969.

Root, Waverly. *The Food of France*. New York: Alfred A. Knopf, 1958.
Root, Waverly, and Richard de Rochement. *Eating in America: A History*. New York: William Morrow, 1976.
Ruark, Jennifer J. "A Place at the Table." *Chronicle of Higher Education*, July 9, 1999, A17–A19.
Sachett, Marjorie. "Folk Recipes as a Measure of Intercultural Penetration." *Journal of American Folklore* 85 (January–March 1972), 77–91.
Sakr, A. H. "Dietary Regulation and Food Habits of Muslims." *Journal of the American Dietetic Association* 58 (February 1971), 123–26.
Scapp, Ron, and Brian Seitz, eds. *Eating Culture*. Albany: SUNY Press, 1998.
Schofield, Mary Anne, ed. *Cooking by the Book: Food in Literature and Culture*. Bowling Green, Ohio: Bowling Green State University Popular Press, 1989.
Schremp, Gerry. *Kitchen Culture: Fifty Years of Food Fads*. New York: Pharos Books, 1991.
Schweid, Richard. *Hot Peppers*. Rev. ed. Chapel Hill: University of North Carolina Press, 1999.
Shapiro, Laura. *Perfection Salad*. New York: Farrar, 1986.
Shenton, James Patrick, et al. *American Cooking: The Melting Pot*. New York: Time, 1971.
Shorett, Alice, and Murray Morgan. *The Pike Place Market: People, Politics, and Produce*. Seattle: Pacific Search Press, 1982.
Sokolov, Raymond. *Why We Eat What We Eat*. New York: Summit, 1991.
Sonnenfeld, Albert, ed. *Food: A Culinary History from Antiquity to Present*. Trans. Clarissa Botsford et al. New York: Columbia University Press, 1999.
Sorre, Max. "The Geography of Diet." In *Readings in Cultural Geography*, ed. Philip L. Wagner and Marvin W. Mikesell. Chicago: University of Chicago Press, 1962, 445–56.
Stamets, John. *Portrait of a Market: Photographs of Seattle's Pike Place Market*. Seattle: Real Comet Press, 1987.
Steinberg, Sally Levitt. *The Donut Book*. New York: Alfred A. Knopf, 1987.
Stern, Jane, and Michael Stern. *Roadfood*. New York: Random House, 1977.
Tannehill, Reay. *Food in History*. 2nd ed. New York: Crown, 1988.
Todhunter, E. N. "The History of Food Patterns in the U.S.A." *Proceedings of the Third International Congress on Dietetics*. New York: Nutrition Foundation, 1961.
Toussaint-Samat, Maguelonne. *History of Food*. Trans. Anthea Bell. Cambridge: Blackwell, 1992.
Trager, James. *The Food Chronology*. New York: Henry Holt, 1995.
Trillin, Calvin. *Alice, Let's Eat*. New York: Random House, 1978.
———. *American Fried*. New York: Penguin Books, 1975.
———. *Third Helpings*. New Haven, Conn., and New York: Ticknor and Fields, 1983.
Trulson, M. R. "The American Diet: Past and Present." *American Journal of Clinical Nutrition* 7 (January–February 1959), 91–97.
U.S. Department of Agriculture. *Experimental Station Record*. Washington, D.C.: U.S. Department of Agriculture, 1889.
U.S. Department of Health, Education, and Welfare. *Cumulated Index Medicus*.

Washington D.C.: National Institutes of Health, Public Health Service, 1959– .

Vance, Rupert B. "Climate, Diet, and Human Adequacy." *Human Geography of the South*. Chapel Hill: University of North Carolina Press, 1932, 411–41.

Vehling, Joseph Dommers. *America's Table*. Chicago: Hostends, 1950.

Viorst, Judith, and Milton Viorst. *The Washington, DC Underground Gourmet*. New York: Simon and Schuster, 1970.

Visser, Margaret. *Much Depends on Dinner*. New York: Grove, 1986.

———. *The Rituals of Dinner*. New York: Grove, 1991.

Walker, Morton. *Secrets of Long Life*. Old Greenwich, Conn.: Devin-Adair, 1984.

Walter, Eugene. *American Cooking: Southern Style*. New York: Time, 1971.

Weaver, William Woys, ed. *A Quaker Woman's Cookbook: The Domestic Cookery of Elizabeth Ellicott Lea*. Philadelphia: University of Pennsylvania Press, 1982.

Welsch, Roger. "We Are What We Eat: Omaha Food as Symbol." *Keystone Folklore Quarterly* 16 (Winter 1971), 165–70.

Wilson, Christine S. "Food Habits: A Selected Annotated Bibliography." *Journal of Nutrition Education* 5 (January–March 1973), suppl. 1, 36–72.

Wilson, Jose. *American Cooking: The Eastern Heartland*. New York: Time, 1971.

Yoder, Don. "Folk Cookery." In *Folklore and Folklife: An Introduction*, ed. Richard M. Dorson. Chicago: University of Chicago Press, 1972, 325–50.

———. "Historical Sources for American Foodways Research and Plans for an American Foodways Archive." *Pennsylvania Folklife* 20 (Spring 1971), 16–29.

———. "Sauerkraut in the Pennsylvania Folk Culture." *Pennsylvania Folklife* 12 (Summer 1961), 56–59.

———. "Schnitz in the Pennsylvania Folk Culture." *Pennsylvania Folklife* 12 (Fall 1961), 56–59.

Magazines

Bon Appetit. Los Angeles, 1955– .

Chile Pepper. Albuquerque, N. Mex., 1990– .

Coffee Journal. Minneapolis, 1995– .

Cookbook Digest. New York, 1968– .

Cooking Light. Birmingham, Ala., 1999– .

Cuisine. Santa Barbara, Calif., 1970– .

The Digest. Philadelphia, 1977– .

Ecology of Food and Nutrition. London, 1971– .

Food and Foodways. London, 1986– .

Food and Wine. New York, 1997– .

Gourmet. New York, 1941– .

International Review of Food and Wine. New York, 1958– .

Natural History. New York, 1900– .

The New Yorker. New York, 1924– .

Nutrition Abstracts and Reviews. Boston, 1942– .

Vegetarian Times. New York, 1978– .

Veggie Life. Concord, Calif., 1993– .

Weight Watchers. New York, 1968– .

Journals, Periodicals

American Journal of Clinical Nutrition. New York, 1954– .
British Journal of Nutrition. Cambridge, England and Chicago, 1947– .
Food History News. Isleboro, Maine, 1989– .
Food Research. Champaign, Ill., 1936– .
Gastronomica. Berkeley, Calif., 2001– .
Journal of Agricultural and Food Chemistry. Columbus, Ohio, 1996– .
Journal of American Dietetic Association. Chicago, 1925– .
Journal of Applied Nutrition. La Habra, Calif., 1953– .
Journal of Food Science: An Official Publication of the Institute of Food Technologists. Chicago, 1961– .
Journal of Nutrition Education. Philadelphia, 1969– .
Proceedings of the Nutrition Society. Cambridge, England, 1944– .

GAMES AND TOYS

Bernard Mergen

This chapter, written twenty years ago and updated a decade later, is here completely revised in the light of significant new research on the subjects. Games and toys and the larger topic of play have been studied by anthropologists, folklorists, psychologists, and historians for over a century, and there is general agreement that these activities are significant in both shaping and explaining individual personality and cultures. While games and toys are not limited to childhood, in our society the things connoted by these terms are usually associated with children's activities, with the prefix "adult" attached to games and toys that are not primarily meant for minors. On the other hand, as Jac Remise has pointed out, most toys are made by adults to appeal and sell to other adults. When is a miniature a toy, and when is it a collectible? When is throwing a ball a game, and when is it a sport? Purpose and context can help make some useful distinctions, but the study of games and toys quickly leads to related subjects such as leisure, child development, education, sport, and recreation. Indeed, it is difficult to abstract games and toys from the study of work, recreation, leisure, sports, and play.

Games may be subdivided into many categories, physical skill, strategy, and chance being the most obvious. Most games involve some combination of the three, and, more often than not, some kind of competition is involved between teams, players, or an individual with self. Competition may be the key element in distinguishing between games and play since most definitions of play emphasize process rather than any specific activity. As Stephen Miller has written: "There are goals in play, but these are of less importance in themselves than as embodiments of the process involved in obtaining them. Process in play is not streamlined toward dealing with goals in the shortest possible way, but is voluntarily elaborated, complicated, in various patterned ways" (97) All games are played, but not all play is a game. Similarly, all toys are played with, but not all play involves toys. Toys may be thought of as props in activities that may involve skill, competition, chance, imitation, fantasy, entertainment, or even doing nothing.

HISTORICAL OUTLINE

The games and toys of colonial children were those of their European, African, and Native American ancestors. Paintings and engravings by Pieter Breughel, Jacob Cats, and other Dutch artists show children playing tag, blindman's buff, jump rope, and leapfrog. They also depict a variety of stilts, hoops, tops, dolls, kites, and musical instruments. The sixteenth- and seventeenth-century child had a rich assortment of playthings, and there is no reason to suppose that the colonial child did not share in this abundance. Neither the rigors of frontier life nor the strictness of New England Puritanism could eliminate games and toys.

Prosperity and changing values brought even greater variety to the toy market in the eighteenth century. Benjamin Franklin recalled buying imported toys in Boston in 1713, and English, German, and American potters made miniature dishes and tea sets in increasing quantities. The earliest surviving dollhouse, now in the collection of the Van Cortlandt Museum in New York City, is believed to date from 1774. If we extend the definition of toys, as Dorothy Howard does, then potentially any object such as a stick or a broken dish found in an attic or an abandoned well could have been a child's plaything. Children of the wealthy had silver whistles and bells, which are often shown in eighteenth-century portraits. Pottery cradles made in England also found their way to the colonies, where they were sold for christening and birthday presents.

Older children and adults played with ivory or hardwood "cup and ball" toys, in which the object was to catch the ball in the cup or on the point of the handle that fitted into a small hole in the ball. Battledore and shuttlecock were popular outdoor games, as were marbles and ball games. Each game had its season; marbles came first, in the early spring, followed by kites, tops, and hoops. In New York, the sequence was slightly different, according to the adage "Top-time's gone, kite-time's come, and April Fool's day will soon be here." Ball games—rudimentary forms of soccer and baseball—were played on holidays. According to William Wells Newell, "In Boston, *Fast-day* (the first Thursday of April) was particularly devoted to this sport. In England, the playing of ball at Easter-tide seems to have been a custom of the festival, inherited probably from pre-Christian ages. Football was a regular amusement on the afternoon of a New England Thanksgiving" (176). Bowling, handball, and hockey were other forms of ball games in seventeenth- and eighteenth-century America.

Indoor games of the same period included backgammon, chess, billiards, and various card games. As early as 1775, the *Pennsylvania Packet* advertised a card game to teach geography, but the heyday of educational card and board games was in the nineteenth century. The appearance of animals in many eighteenth-century family portraits suggests that pets were important elements in children's play. Dogs, cats, birds, squirrels, lambs, and even deer were part of the domestic scene. Samuel Goodrich described another pastime of late-eighteenth-century boys: "During my youthful days I found the penknife a source of great amusement, even instruction. Many a long winter evening, many a dull, drizzly day . . . have I spent in great ecstasy making candlerods or some other simple article of household goods, for my mother, or in perfecting toys for myself and my young friends" (*Recollections of a Lifetime* [New York: Miller, Orton, and Mulligan, 1856], vol. 1, 92).

Action figures from the early 1980s. Courtesy of Gary Cross

A generation later, Edward Everett Hale grew up with

> an infinite variety of amusements—almost everything we wanted for purposes of manufacture or invention. Whalebone, spiral springs, pulleys and catgut, for perpetual motion or locomotive carriages, rollers and planks for floats . . . good blocks for building, carpenter's tools, a work-bench, and printing materials. . . . When we became chemists we might have sulfuric acid, nitric acid, litmus paper, or whatever we desired, so our allowance would stand it. I was not more than seven years old when I burned off my eyebrows by igniting gun-powder with my burning glass. (*A New England Boyhood* [Boston: Little, Brown, 1964], 45)

The 1830s and 1840s witnessed the birth of the American toy and game industry. William S. Tower, a carpenter in South Hingham, Massachusetts, organized a guild of toy makers in the late 1830s, and Franklin Peal exhibited a small steam locomotive made by Matthias Baldwin at the Peale family's Philadelphia museum. For the next forty years, wooden and metal toys were usually produced as a sideline by craftsmen engaged in cabinetmaking or tool manufacturing.

Paper toys and games were developed by stationers and lithographers. The titles of some board and card games echo the concerns of the period. In 1843, W. & B. Ives of Salem, Massachusetts, issued a highly moralistic board game, "The Mansion of Happiness," intended to teach young Americans to practice the virtues of industry, honesty, and sobriety. The following year introduced "The Game of Pope or Pagan or the Missionary Campaign or the Siege of the Stronghold of Satan by the Christian Army." By the 1860s, moralism began to be replaced by current events and an emphasis on material success. Milton Bradley's tremendously popular "The Checkered Game of Life," which appeared in 1860, alternated squares printed with "wealth," "happiness," "industry," and "ambition," with others labeled "gambling," "poverty," "jail," and "suicide."

In 1868, according to McClinton, four games of war and patriotism were packaged together under the title "The Union Games" (227). Anagrams, puzzles, zoetropes (a slotted revolving drum that gives the viewer the sense of moving pictures), and conversation cards gained in popularity through the 1860s. Conversation cards, with printed questions such as "Have you ever been in love?" and "What is your favorite food?" were intended to enliven the "cold and ceremonious" social gatherings that European travelers often found in the United States. The McLoughlin Brothers' catalog of 1867 lists seven kinds of conversation cards, including "Loves and Likes," "Comical Conversation Cards," "Conversations on Marriage," and "Quizzical Questions and Quaint Replies." Another type of game involving dialogue is illustrated by "Japhet Jenkins and Sally Jones visit to Boston," copyrighted in 1867. In this game, cards with brief sentences are shuffled and dealt to the players, who take turns reading them and filling in blanks in a book that tells the adventures of a pair of country bumpkins visiting the city.

In 1883, sixteen-year-old George S. Parker invented his first game, the "Game of Banking." Subsequent games also reflected the concerns of the Gilded Age. "The Game of Moneta: or Money Makes Money" appeared in the Montgomery Ward catalog of 1889, and a "Game of Business" came out in 1895. One of the most popular games of the period was marketed by the Crandalls in 1889 under the name "Pigs in Clover." This puzzle required the player to maneuver four marbles through a maze into a cardboard enclosure. Hundreds of thousands were sold, and the game seems to have been especially popular in Washington, D.C., where the symbolism of the spoils system was obvious. Political election games appeared regularly in the late nineteenth century, and an interesting study could be done by comparing the "Centennial Presidential Game" of 1876 with the "Presidential Election" game of 1892, "Politics" of the 1950s, and "Bigwig" in 1973.

Games and toys were inspired by every conceivable event. The Chicago Columbian Exposition of 1893 was commemorated in games, puzzles, and building blocks. "Sherlock Holmes" and "The Amusing Game of Innocence Abroad" profited from the popularity of the books that preceded them. "White Squadron Picture Puzzles" helped to make the names of the warships *Baltimore*, *Chicago*, and *Monterey* familiar to American children. The 1886 catalog of sporting goods and games sold by the Peck & Snyder Company lists chess, checkers, lotto, dominoes, Parcheesi, cards, bagatelle, cribbage, tetotums or spinning dice, and dice, as well as a board game called "The Monopolist." "On the board," the catalog reads, "the great struggle between Capital and Labor can be fought out to the satisfaction of all parties, and, if the players are successful, they can break the Monopolist, and become Monopolists themselves." Again, it would be instructive to compare this game with the well-known Parker Brothers game "Monopoly," introduced in 1935. Robert H. Canary's essay on "Monopoly" and the 1950s "Game of Life" and James M. Hughes' comparison of "Monopoly" and "The Cities Game" are suggestive beginnings. The "Class Struggle" game, marketed in 1978 by political science professor Bertell Ollman, offers still another point of comparison.

The plethora of games in the twentieth century reveals much about American culture. Since most of these games involve elements of chance as well as strategy, they may reflect a growing uncertainty about the future and the desire to prepare individuals "to endure bad times in the hope of brighter futures." This is the hypothesis advanced by J. M. Roberts and Brian Sutton-Smith in their work on "Child Training and Game Involvement" in non-Western societies. Luck has always played a significant, if neglected, role in American thought, and a study of gambling games, especially among children, would be revealing. The problem, of course, is that like other illegal activities, few records exist that describe gambling games. One of the few comes from Stewart Culin, an anthropologist and museum curator, who described "Street Games of Boys in Brooklyn, New York" in 1891. Culin found a game that the boys called "Pictures," which was played by shooting the cards found in cigarette packages toward a wall, the winner being the boy whose card landed nearest the wall. The winner then threw all the cards into the air and kept the ones that fell faceup. Culin's ten-year-old informant claimed to be ignorant of the related game—penny pitching. "It was regarded among his associates as a vulgar game, and only practiced by bootblacks and boys of the lowest class, such as compose the 'gangs' that are a well-known feature of street life among the boys of our cities" (234–35).

There are many other kinds of toys that parallel adult activities. Toy models of steam engines, trains, telegraphs, telephones, washing machines, automobiles, and airplanes appeared soon after their introduction in the adult world. In some cases, an inventor seems to have no clear purpose and tries out his invention in toy form. Edison put one of his early phonograph cylinders in a "Talking Doll" in 1890. Dollhouses and dollhouse furniture are obvious examples of toys that follow the fashion and changes in technology. Building materials are another example. In 1901, a British inventor, Frank Hornby, patented a set of construction materials made of thin strips of metal with perforations for nuts and bolts. His "Mechanics Made Easy," or "Meccano," was soon copied in the United States as "Erector" sets, allowing American children to build skyscraper skeletons to mirror those outside their bedroom windows. Charles Pajeau's 1914 patent for "Tinkertoys" followed the same general idea of building in outline, but his colorful rods, knobs, and pulleys seem closer to the abstract forms of the Armory Show than to the cantilever of the Queensboro Bridge. Pajeau may also have borrowed his idea from Friedrich Froebel, whose rods, strings, and balls inspired the young Frank Lloyd Wright in 1876.

More often, the power of toys to mold the habits and talents of children fails. During World War I, Edward Hurley, chairman of the U.S. Shipping Board, decided that Americans should learn the value of the merchant marine and persuaded the Ives Toy Manufacturing Company to make a copy of the standard merchant ship being constructed by the Emergency Fleet Corporation. In his letter to the company, Hurley wrote:

> It is none too early to begin waking Americans to the importance of ships, putting ships and the sea into their daily thought and work, and making ships appeal to the imagination of everybody in the country. We want to reach the children as well as the grown-ups, and, in this connection knowing how closely toys follow popular interest and what an educative value they have, it has been in my mind to have this great new national interest before the men who invent and design your goods. (*Emergency Fleet News*, January 1, 1919: 9)

When the Ives catalog for 1919 appeared, the advertising copy echoed Hurley's patriotic note: A boy "can get thoroughly interested in the great game of commerce and the big Merchant marine of his country. He can talk it, play it and interest his chums in it. . . . Who knows but what it may lead them into the big business of transportation by sea that is going to play such a wonderful part in the future world trade of the United States?" (Schroeder, 232). The ironic end to this effort to build support for an American merchant marine was the bankruptcy of the Ives Company in 1929, a collapse that Ives' accountants attributed in part to poor sales of the toy merchant fleet.

Turning from toys to games played without equipment, the historical record is strongest for the years since 1883, when folklorists, psychologists, and anthropologists first began to study children's play systematically. In that year, William Wells Newell, linguist, poet, and folklorist, published *Games and Songs of American Children*. This collection of almost 200 folk songs and counting-out rhymes, clapping and ring games, and tag and guessing games gives us a sense of the complexity and formality of games in the 1870s. Few adults or children today would be willing to memorize the long poem "Knights of Spain," which accompanied a popular kissing game. Some songs, such as the familiar "Barbara Allen," were used to circumvent the religious ban on dancing. As the ballad was sung, couples kept time with slow movements without changing place. Newell's research showed that most American games and songs had British and European origins. He was impressed by the conservatism of the children in preserving these games, but he was also afraid that increased immigration, urbanization, and industrialization were destroying traditional games.

There is some evidence that cities did make play difficult. In 1892, Washington, D.C., passed an ordinance that declared it unlawful

> for any person or persons to play the game of football, or any other game with a ball, in any of the streets, avenues, or alleys in the cities of Washington and Georgetown; nor shall it be lawful for any person or persons to play the game of bandy, shindy, or any other game by which a ball, stone, or other substance is struck or propelled by any stick, cane, or other substance in any street, avenue, or alley. (U.S. Department of Labor, Children's Bureau, *Facilities for Children's Play in the District of Columbia* [Washington, D.C.: Government Printing Office, 1917], 68)

In the same year, Helen and Robert Lynd tell us, Muncie, Indiana, made it illegal to pitch quoits or coins, to play cricket, bandy, cat, townball, or any other game of public amusement, or to discharge a gun, pistol, or firearm on Sunday. Both laws tell us a great deal about the play life of small cities and towns and about the kinds of games and where they were played. Whether the motive was a reformist hope that play could be regulated in school yards and playgrounds or a conservative desire to maintain fundamental religious values, the 1890s and the early twentieth century saw numerous efforts to redefine games and play.

Observers unanimously agreed that most children were "doing nothing" and wasting their time when they were not working. A survey in Milwaukee, Wisconsin, in 1911 put the percentages at 19 percent working, 31 percent playing, and 50 percent doing nothing on a typical November day (*The Playground* 6 [May 1912], 51). A similar survey in Cleveland, Ohio, on June 23, 1913, found 10 percent working, 50 percent playing, and 40 percent of the city's children doing nothing (George Johnson, *Education through Recreation* [Cleveland: Survey Committee of the Cleveland Foundation, 1916], 49). Of those who were playing, 43 percent were described as "just fooling." Doing nothing and just fooling were categories that included breaking windows, chalking suggestive words on buildings, standing around on corners, fighting, looking at pictures of women in tights on billboards, stealing, and gambling with dice, cards, buttons, marbles, and beer bottle tags. Joseph Lee, Luther Gulick, Henry Curtis, and others sought to improve opportunities for urban recreation under the supervision of professional playground directors. The founding of the Playground Association in 1906 and the publication the following year of the first issue of *The Playground* (now *Parks and Recreation*) mark the beginnings of highly organized children's games and play in the United States.

Typical of the way in which traditional games were appropriated by the recreation movement is a list published in the *Seventh Annual Report of the Department of Playgrounds* of Washington, D.C., in 1918. Games were divided into "Low Organized Games," "High Organized Games," "Quiet Games," "Races," "Relay," and "Memory and Sense Games." An example of each included "Prisoners Base," "Basketball," "Boiler Burst," "Wheelbarrow," "All up Indian Club," and "Ghosts." Early surveys of games and play suggest that there have been important changes in game preferences among American children. For example, T. R. Croswell, who studied about 2,000 schoolchildren in Worcester, Massachusetts, in 1896, found only 4 of 1,000 boys playing cowboys and Indians and only 2 who mentioned playing with toy soldiers. Girls' game preferences seem to have changed more than boys' in the past century, with many more girls playing games that were played exclusively by boys in the past, such as leapfrog and red rover. Boys and girls now play few singing and dialogue games such as those recorded by Newell, and many of the rhymes that were recited with those games are now used in jump rope.

Brian Sutton-Smith argues that children's play has become more sophisticated and that fantasy play and games involving the manipulation of symbols have been encouraged by middle-class parents. Playground planners in the United States have tried to introduce "Adventure Playgrounds," in which children are encouraged to organize and develop their own games and to build their own play structures. A new vocabulary has entered the playground movement: "loose parts," "ambiguity," "flexibility," "diversity," "change," and "open-endedness." The contemporary student of games is faced with a bewildering variety of theories and an equally confusing body of raw data. Games, toys, and play serve many functions,

Dollhouse, ca. 1935. Photo by Harry M. Rhoads. Courtesy of the Denver Public Library

not the least of which is to help cope with a chaotic, violent, and even dangerous world. We should not be surprised to find much that is shocking in play, but we must try to understand what is actually going on, rather than impose preconceived definitions of what play is and what it is not. We must try to discover what games and toys mean to the players. For that, we may well begin with ourselves.

The 1980s saw the commercial development of home computer games, the cultural impact of which is difficult to measure. Two things seem clear, however: first, these games will continue to compete for the free time of the players, thereby reducing time for other activities, and second, children as young as six can learn to play games on the computer, so that a new generation is growing up that is completely at ease with electronic games that were formerly played on boards. They are also playing more sophisticated interactive games that further encourage solitary play. Children under seven are being introduced to electronic learning aids such as Speak & Spell, Sesame Street, and Whiz Kid, but the favorite toys continue to be action figures such as GI Joe, robots like the Transformers, baby dolls like the Cabbage Patch Kids, and fashion dolls such as Barbie. The popularity of weapons such as Laser Tag and Phasor Force Guns has sparked renewed debate among psychiatrists and child development experts.

In the 1990s Mattel continued to find ways to keep Barbie at the top of the list of best-selling toys, while Transformers and Power Rangers surrendered their place in the toy box to Teenage Mutant Ninja Turtles and various movie spin-off action figures. In an unpublished survey of more than 1,000 children ages three to eight living the Delaware Valley in 1993, Nintendo video games ranked first on a list of favorite games and toys, followed closely by Monopoly and Monopoly Jr., hide-and-seek, Candy Land, Barbie, and baseball. A much smaller sample of boys and girls ages fourteen to sixteen in Washington, D.C., in 1991 found that watching television, video and board games, and talking were the three most popular activities done for "fun." Such surveys strongly suggest more continuity than change in the patterns of children's play.

Nevertheless, a University of Michigan survey of 3,600 families with children revealed that children ages three to five spent over thirteen hours a week watching television, seventeen hours playing, and twenty hours in nursery or preschool, while children nine to twelve spent about the same amount of time watching television, almost forty hours in school, and only eight hours and forty-four minutes playing (*Washington Post*, November 9, 1998: A2). As children's lives are increasingly structured, they have less time for games and toys.

REFERENCE WORKS

Since definitions of games, toys, and play vary widely, this section lists several kinds of reference material. First and most basic are bibliographies that list primary and secondary works on games and play. For games in general, including those used in education and by the military, the most complete bibliography is still *The Study of Games*, edited by Elliott M. Avedon and Brian Sutton-Smith. Their book is also an anthology of articles on the historical, anthropological, and folkloristic aspects of games. Joseph M. Hawes and N. Ray Hiner's *American Childhood: A Research Guide and Historical Handbook* is also a good place to begin research.

Child's Play, edited by R. E. Herron and Brian Sutton-Smith, is an anthology with a bibliography of over 700 items on the theory of play and on psychological studies of children's play. It should be supplemented with Helen B. Schwartzman's *Transformations: The Anthropology of Children's Play*. Schwartzman's bibliography of over 750 items combines both psychological and anthropological studies and includes publications through 1976. Simon Bronner's annotated edition of *American Children's Folklore* contains hundreds of examples of jokes, songs, games, and handmade toys and an extensive bibliography. Elliott West places play and games in the context of home, work, and community in *Growing Up in Twentieth-Century America*. His bibliographies are organized by decade. Geographically limited but broad in its contents and beautifully illustrated with photographs and drawings, Edward Abernethy's *Texas Toys and Games* is a pleasure to read.

The most complete reference work on children's games and toys to date is *Children's Folklore: A Source Book*, edited by Brian Sutton-Smith and others. Fourteen chapters cover such subjects as school yard games, summer camp activities, and handmade playthings. A glossary, index, and bibliography of almost 1,000 items enhance the usefulness of the volume. There is still no bibliography on American toys. The distinction between reference works and general histories of toys and dolls is not clear. Most of the historical accounts of toys, as contrasted with histories of the toy industry, are little more than chronologies of technological change. The latest and best is Richard O'Brien's *The Story of American Toys: From the Puritans to the Present.* Among those books that are basically catalogs of different types of toys and games, *The Collector's Encyclopedia of Dolls* by Dorothy, Elizabeth, and Evelyn Coleman ranks high. Leslie Daiken's *Children's Toys throughout the Ages* is typical of an older, collector's approach to the subject, but it is useful for its discussion of various definitions of toys. Daiken's *World of Toys: A Guide to the Principal Public and Private Collections in Great Britain* is also a useful starting place for the study of eighteenth- and nineteenth-century toys, especially since the United States imported a great many British and European toys.

For this country, a basic reference work is still Louis Hertz's 1947 guide, *The Handbook of Old American Toys*, which has a brief introduction to such topics as classification, identification, materials, and terminology. Hertz arranges his study by tin toys, cast iron, clockwork, wooden, steam, banks, cannon, cap pistols, musical toys, electric toys, trains, toy household equipment, games, wheel toys, and dolls. His more recent book, *The Toy Collector*, has useful chapters on research as well as a guide to manufacturers and to identification marks. Another excellent work is Katharine McClinton's *Antiques of American Childhood*, a guide that expands the definition of toy to include children's costumes, buttons, furniture, dishes, and needlework. Specialized reference works include Cecil Chandler's *Toys and Dolls Made in Occupied Japan*; Kenny Harman's *Comic Strip Toys*; Gwen White's *Toys and Dolls: Marks and Labels*; Cecil Gibson's *A History of British Dinky Toys: Model Car and Vehicle Issues, 1934–1964*; and Linda Hannas' *The English Jigsaw Puzzle, 1760–1890, with a Descriptive Check-list of Puzzles in the Museums of Great Britain and the Author's Collection.* Fred Ferretti's *The Great American Marble Book* contains color illustrations of dozens of different kinds of marbles and the games played with them. Ferretti's *The Great Amerian Book of Sidewalk, Stoop, Dirt, Curb, and Alley Games* is less successful because it only touches on each kind of game. A more satisfying collection is Alan Milberg's *Street Games.* Although they are not reference books in the usual sense, the Ferretti and Milberg books provide 1970s comparisons to the great collections of Douglas, Gomme, Newell, and the Opies.

Newell's classic *Games and Songs of American Children* has been cited, but the British provide the most comprehensive game surveys. *The Traditional Games of England, Scotland, and Ireland* by Alice Gomme, *London Street Games* by Norman Douglas, and *Children's Games in Street and Playground* by Iona and Peter Opie supply a detailed history of British games of the past century. Roger D. Abrahams' *Jump-Rope Rhymes: A Dictionary*, Bessie Jones and Bess Lomax Hawes' *Step It Down: Games, Plays, Songs and Stories from the Afro-American Heritage*, and Paul G. Brewster's *American Nonsinging Games* are the only American surveys since Newell that attempt a wide sample of selected types of play, although Mary and Herbert Knapp provide a useful beginning in *One Potato, Two Potato . . . The Secret Education of American Children*, while Simon Bronner's book mentioned earlier continues their effort. Brian Sutton-Smith's *A History of Children's Play: New Zealand, 1840–1950* offers an inventory of play from another transplanted English society.

Perhaps the most useful reference works for the student of games and toys are still the catalogs of the toy manufacturers and retailers and their trade publications. Some of the catalogs have been reprinted. *The Wonderful World of Toys, Games and Dolls*, edited by Joseph J. Schroeder Jr., contains reprints from the catalogs of F.A.O. Schwartz, Montgomery Ward, Marshall Field, and other stores from 1862 to 1930. By far the most important trade journal is *Playthings*, which has been published monthly since 1903. Each issue has articles on toy manufacturing and advertising from most of the large firms. Other trade journals include *Toy World*, which was published in San Francisco in the 1920s and which merged with *Toys and Novelties* (now *Toys*) in 1936. For the German toy industry, *Das Spielzeug*, published in Bamberg, provides trade information.

There are also several magazines and newspapers published by and for collectors; *Antique Toy World* and *Collectibles Monthly* are good examples. These publications are useful for discovering private collections, and they often contain articles on toy and doll manufacturers. There are three published censuses of toy manufacturers—one in 1927, one in 1931, and another in 1940. The Department of Commerce also sponsored two studies of the international toy business—Jeannette M. Calvin's *International Trade in Toys* in 1926 and E. D. Schutrumpf's *World Trade in Toys* in 1939. Both volumes contain detailed statistics on exports and imports of toys in all industrialized countries.

RESEARCH COLLECTIONS

Almost every museum and historical society has a collection of games, toys, and dolls that is used for an annual Christmas display. Students of games and toys should always begin research with a visit to their local museum. The next step would be to identify private collectors and collections. There are, however, a number of museums throughout the country with large and growing collections of toys. The following cannot claim to be a complete list of all the significant doll and toy collections, but it is a sample of museums that have reported collections. The museums are listed with current address, telephone number, and E-mail when available. Researchers should always write in advance to the institution that they wish to visit, so that the curator has time to assemble relevant materials.

The Atlanta Historical Society (130 W. Paces Ferry Road., NW, Atlanta, Ga. 30305–1366, telephone 404-814–4000, Web site: www.atlhist.org) has a few items relating to nineteenth- and twentieth-century children's play. The Atwater Kent Museum (15 South Seventh Street, Philadelphia 19106, telephone 215–922–3031) has a small collection of eighteenth-, nineteenth-, and twentieth-century dolls, as well as some iron toys and some blocks and board games. The Barnum Museum (820 Main Street, Bridgeport, Conn. 06604, telephone 203–331–1104) has a core collection of toys that it used to create several large exhibitions in the 1990s. A small, uncataloged collection of dolls, dollhouse furnishings, board games, trucks, and cars is available by appointment at the Chicago Historical Society (Clark Street at North Avenue, Chicago 60614, telephone 312–642–4600, Web site: www.chicagohs.org). The Children's Museum (30th Street and North Meridian, Indianapolis 46208, telephone 317–924–5431, Web site: www.childrensmuseum.org) is one of the largest and most comprehensive children's museums in the country. It has educational programs and exhibits of many kinds, and a permanent exhibit of toys opened in December 1978. The museum owns a well-documented collection of over 1,000 toy cars from the 1950s and has one of the largest toy train collections in the country.

Colonial Williamsburg (P.O. Box 1776, Williamsburg, Va. 23187–1776, telephone 804–229–1000, Web site: www.history.com) has a number of games and toys. There is no catalog, but there are files available to scholars for research by appointment. The Colorado Historical Society (The Colorado Heritage Center, 1300 Broadway, Denver 80203, telephone 303–866–3682) has a good collection of toys, including household items, board games, guns, ships, toy soldiers, cowboys, Indians, and badges. A collection of about 200 dolls and a few toys may be examined in the Daughters of the American Revolution Museum (1776 D Street, NW, Washington, D.C. 20006, telephone 202–829–3241). The Delaware Toy & Miniature Museum (P.O. Box 4053, Route 141, Wilmingon, Del. telephone 302–427–8697, Web site: www.thomes.net/toys/) has a collection of over 100 dollhouses and toys by Bliss, Hubley, Ives, Gilbert, McLoughlin, and others. The Peabody Essex Museum (E. India Square, Salem, Mass. 01970, telephone 508–745–1876, Website: www.pem.org) has dolls, dollhouses, trains, and cast-iron wagons. An illustrated book, *Dolls and Toys at the Essex Institute* by Madeline and Richard Merrill, describes the collection. Greenfield Village and Henry Ford Museum (20900 Oakwood Boulevard, Dearborn, Mich. 48124, telephone 313–271–1620) has over 4,000 dolls and doll-related items, 2,500 toys, and 760 games. The Maryland Historical Society (201 West Monument Street, Baltimore 21201, telephone 410–846–0813) has a large and varied toy collection, including some outstanding dollhouses reflecting the architectural styles of the state. The Mercer Musem of the Bucks County Historical Society (Pine Street, Doylestown, Pa. 18901, telephone 215–345–0210, Web site: www.libertynet.org/~bchs) has a small collection accessible by appointment with the curator. Among the animals, banks, blocks, dolls, dollhouses, games, puppets, rocking horses, tops, and wagons is a coffin made for a doll owned by Ella Good of Solesbury, Pennsylvania.

The National Farm Toy Museum (1110 16th Avenue, SE, Dyersville, Iowa 52040, telephone 319–875–2727, Web site: www.reww.com/dyversville) is described by its name. A small collection of dolls, both homemade and commercial, a football game played with marbles, and a number of games taken from comic strips may be found at the Nevada Historical Society (1650 North Virginia Street, Reno 89503, telephone 702–688–1191). The Museum of International Folk Art, a division of the Museum of New Mexico (Box 2087, Santa Fe 87503, telephone 505–827–6350), has a few contemporary toys. The Newport Historical Society (82 Touro Street, Newport, R.I. 02840, telephone 401–846–0813) has a limited number of toys but a large collection of doll and furnished dollhouses. One of the best collections of dollhouses may be found in the Museum of the City of New York (1220 Fifth Avenue, New York 10029, telephone 212–534–1672, Web site: www.mcny.org).

A few blocks away, the New York Historical Society (170 Central Park West at 77th Street, New York 10024, telephone 212–477–9753, Web site: www.NYHistory.org) has an extensive collection of nineteenth-century carved animals by Wilhelm Schimmel; a peddler's cart dated 1884 with miniature pots and pans; a walking doll patented in 1862 and sold under the name "Autoperipatetikos"; circus toys, including ball-jointed wooden animals, from Albert Schoenhut's 1892

Boys playing "Snap the Whip." Engraving after a painting by Winslow Homer, 1873. Courtesy of the Library of Congress

"Humpty Dumpty Circus"; and tin toys from George W. Brown of Forestville, Connecticut, made in 1856. Old Salem (Box F, Salem Station, Winston-Salem, N.C. 27108, telephone 910–721–7300, Web site: www.oldsalem.org) has late eighteenth- and nineteenth-century toys, games, dolls, and books that are displayed in a Boys' School Museum. Old Sturbridge Village (Old Sturbridge Village Road, Sturbridge, Mass. 01566) has 400 or 500 toys, games, dolls, and dolls' tea sets exhibited in its buildings.

The Please Touch Museum (210 N. 21st Street, Philadelphia 19103, telephone 215–963–0667, Web site: www.libertynet.org/~pleastch) has created a Childlife Center to collect toys, children's clothing and furniture and the archival records of organizations dealing with children and children's play, particularly in the Delaware Valley. In 1992–1993 the staff of the museum collected data on the games and toy preferences of over 1,000 children ages three to seven in the region. A major acquisition was the Child Development Association (CDA) Consortium archives. The CDA was founded in 1972 to assess the competence of child-care personnel and to grant credentials to persons assessed as competent. The records cover the years 1971 to 1985 and are being supplemented by an oral history project. With the cooperation of the Toy Manufacturers' Association, the museum has annually received examples of the ten best-selling toys in all the major toy categories since 1982. For historical depth the museum acquired a collection of more than 400 objects from a Quaker family in Kennett Square, Pennsylvania, the toys and playthings of three generations from the 1880s to the 1950s. The Savery-Taylor-Frysinger Collection is unique in its range of objects and documentation.

The Seattle Historical Society (749 N. 175th Street, P.O. Box 7171, Seattle 98133, telephone 206–542–7111) has a collection of over 2,000 dolls, several hundred toys and games, and several hundred books on marionettes and puppetry. A large collection of marionettes, as well as doll furniture, building blocks, mechanical toys, models, banks, stuffed toys, and games, is exhibited in the Toy Shop at the Shelburne Museum (U.S. Rt. 7, P.O. Box 10, Shelburne, Vt. 05482, telephone 802–985–3346, Web site: www.shelburnemuseum.org). Shelburne also has several hundred dolls in its variety unit and a small, but good, research library.

Both the National Museum of American History and the National Museum of Natural History of the Smithsonian Institution (Washington, D.C. 20560, telephone 202–357–2700, Web site: www.si.edu) have collections relating to games and toys. In the former, the Division of Cultural History has "Little Golden Books," games, and toys including the Sears, Roebuck Collection of cast-iron toys. Some interesting material on nineteenth-century games and toys may be gleaned from the 1,700 lithographs in the Harry T. Peters "America on Stone" Collection. The Archives Center in the Museum of American History contains the millions of items in the Warshaw Collection of Business Americana, some of which relate to games and toys. The ethnographic collections of the Natural History Museum contain games and toys from around the world. Genre paintings and portraits often contain data on games and toys, and the collections of the National Gallery of Art, the National Portrait Gallery, and the National Museum of American Art should all be consulted. The library in the National Museum of American Art houses the Inventory of American Painting executed before 1914, a computerized index of 175,000 paintings in public and private collections throughout the country. There are several entries under the subject classification "Sports and Games." The staff of the Office of Folklife Studies, which organizes the annual Festival of American Folklife, has gathered considerable material on games and children's lore. Tapes, videotapes, and publications are available. The National Air and Space Museum, which has organized exhibitions on both "Star Trek" and "Star Wars," and the Museum of African Art, which has an extensive collection of African games, can provide information on toys and games in their respective areas of specialization.

Also in Washington, four other institutions have valuable information on games and toys. The Library of Congress (Washington, D.C. 20540, telephone 202–707–5000, Web site: www.loc.gov), through its rare book collections and folk music division and in its vast holdings of prints, photographs, and film, contains an unequaled store of material on games and toys. Within the Prints and Photographs Division, for example, the Farm Security Administration and Office of War Information photographs of America in the 1930s and 1940s and the Frances Benjamin Johnston, Theodore Horydczak, and George Grantham Bain collections are especially rich on play, games, and toys in the period 1890–1945. The Copyright Division of the Library of Congress should also be consulted, as should the Patent Office (Jefferson Davis Highway, Arlington, Va. 20231). Another good source for pictures of games and toys is the Audio-Visual Division of the National Archives and Records Administration (Archives II, College Park, Md.). Here, for example, you can find the Helen Levitt photographs of children's chalk drawings on the streets of New York in 1936, the files of the Environmental Protection Agency's Documerica project in the 1970s, and thousands of feet of motion picture film of children's activities in the years 1914–1934 taken by cameramen for the Ford Motor Company.

A large collection of games and toys is owned by the Society for the Preservation of New England Antiquities (Harrison Gray Otis House, 141 Cambridge Street, Boston 02114, telephone 617–227–3956). Possibly the best collection of dolls and toys in the nation is at the Margaret Woodbury Strong Museum (1 Manhattan Square, Rochester, N.Y. 14618, telephone 716–263–2700, Web site: www.strongmuseum.org). Here one can see many of the 25,000 dolls, 600 dollhouses, and thousands of models, miniatures, toys, and playing cards that the museum owns. The Toy Hall of Fame, located at the A. C. Gilbert Discovery Village (116 Marion Street, NE, Salem, Oreg. 97301, telephone 503–316–3485) opened in 1998. It has an interesting Web site (www.acgilbert.org) that provides histories of the first ten toys placed on display—Barbie, Etch-a-Sketch, Teddy Bear, Monopoly, Erector Set, Frisbee, Tinker Toys, Playdough, Crayola Crayons, and Legos. A Toy & Miniature Museum of Kansas City (5235 Oak Street, Kansas City, Mo. 64112, telephone 816–333–2055, Web site: www.umkc.edu/tmm) was founded in 1982 in a house at the University of Missouri-Kansas City. It has twenty-four rooms of dolls, dollhouses, antique miniatures, farm toys, toy theaters, and other toys and miniatures.

The Washington Dolls' House and Toy Museum (5236 44th Street, NW, Washington, D.C. 20015, telephone 202–244–0024) is a small, private museum founded by Flora Gill Jacobs, author of several books on dollhouses and furniture. Jacobs has a small, but excellent, collection of Schoenhut animals, including a circus, a Theodore Roosevelt safari, a Bliss village, and some games. An elaborate dollhouse made in Puebla, Mexico, in the early twentieth century provides an interesting contrast to the houses made north of the Rio Grande. Another important research collection may be found at the Western Kentucky University Folklore, Folklife, and Oral History Archive (Bowling Green, Ky. 42101, telephone 502–745–6434). The archive contains material on play, games, toys, and toy making.

Perhaps the finest collection of paper dolls in the United States can be found in the library of the Winterthur Museum (Winterthur, Del. 19735, telephone 302–888–4701, Web site: www.winterthur.org). The Maxine Waldron Collection of Children's Books and Paper Toys contains hundreds of items, mostly American but with some English and European paper dolls, games, peep shows, panoramas, paper soldiers, valentines, and Christmas cards and decorations. Among the rare items are the "Protean Figure of Metamorphic Costumes," published by S. and J. Fuller in 1811; "Flora, the Game of Flowers"; "Newton's New Game of Virtue Rewarded and Vice Punished"; and the paper dolls "Lady of New York," "The Virtuous Girl," "Jenny Lind," "Little Henry," and "Ellen, or the Naughty Girl Reclaimed." Some of the other games, dolls, and toys in Winterthur's collections may be seen in the rooms of the museum. The State Historical Society of Wisconsin (30 N. Carroll Street, Madison 53706, telephone 608–264–6575, Web site: www.wisc.edu/shs-archives/) has a large collection of children's toys and games dating from the 1850s to the present. An annual Christmas exhibit, emphasizing playthings of Wisconsin children, displays some of the society's material. Yesteryears Doll & Toy Museum (Main and River Streets, P.O. Box 609, Sandwich,

Mass. 02563, telephone 508–888–1711) is a small private collection open to the public.

HISTORY AND CRITICISM

Games and toys have drawn the attention of four kinds of writers—hobbyists and collectors, who are usually interested in a fairly narrow aspect of the subject; moralists, who select examples from children's play to make points about the corruption of society; anthropologists and psychologists, who use games and toys to study human development; and historians, who have attempted to make the subject a respectable part of social and cultural history. Among the first of the serious collectors was Louis Hertz, whose numerous books have been cited throughout this chapter. One of his best contributions to the history of toys is *Messrs. Ives of Bridgeport*, a study of the Ives Manufacturing Company's sixty years of toy making. Another pioneer collector who has written well-researched books on dollhouses is Flora Gill Jacobs. Her illustrations and text reveal a number of interesting details about the relation of dollhouses to the "larger" world, including the fact that a California bungalow dollhouse appeared in 1920, a doll's swimming pool in 1928, and a Frank Lloyd Wright-style house in 1936. Wooden furniture was rapidly replaced by metal after 1922, when Tootsietoy began to produce doll furniture for the mass market, and metal was challenged by plastic after 1946.

The Story of American Toys by Richard O'Brien and *Toys in America* by Inez and Marshall McClintock fall between a collector's reference work and a historian's interpretive survey. Although the McClintocks suspected "that toys might give some insight into our entire society; [and] that the amount of play, the number and nature of toys might reveal a great deal about any stage of our history," they stick to descriptive narrative history and fail to prove "that toys and games were indeed accurate mirrors of the adult world." The same may be said of Jac Remise and Jean Fondin's *The Golden Age of Toys*, which was first published in Switzerland in 1967. The beautiful photographs, many in color, compensate for the lack of interpretation in the text. Patrick Murray's *Toys*, Charles Best's *Cast Iron Toy Pistols, 1870–1940: A Collector's Guide*, Betty Cadbury's *Playthings, Past*, David Pressland's *The Art of the Tin Toy*, D. W. Gould, *The Top: Universal Toy, Enduring Pastime*, George Malko, *The One and Only Yo-Yo Book*, and John O'Dell and Richard Loehl, *The Great Depression Era Book of Fun* are all good examples of the excellent work done by curators and collectors in recent years.

Ever since 1882, when Herbert Spencer proclaimed the "gospel of relaxation," moralists and social critics have used games and play to argue that society is in desperate need of reform. The 1950s was a decade of debate among sociologists and social critics about the proper uses of leisure. In France, both Roland Barthes and Roger Caillois published on the meaning of toys and games. Barthes, in *Mythologies*, saw toys as microcosms of the materialism of the adult world, while Caillois took a more detached stance in *Les Jeux et les hommes*, published in English as *Man, Play, and Games*. Nevertheless, Caillois moralizes about the loss of courtesy in competitive games and the corruption of masks into uniforms in contemporary society. This kind of criticism continued in the 1970s in an interesting variety of forms.

Frank and Theresa Caplan, owners of Creative Playthings from 1944 to 1966, expounded on *The Power of Play*. The Caplans drew on an impressive range of authorities from Cicero to Piaget but often overstated their case and frequently expressed a regrettable ethnocentricism:

> We believe the Mexican, Asiatic, and Indian child for whom there is no lively play during early childhood loses the ability to create imaginary situations. An examination of the play materials of these cultures shows them to be made of clay, papier-mâché, and flimsy wood, none of which lend themselves to active use . . . Introduce the rubber or vinyl doll, building blocks, and other unbreakable toys, and we maintain that the innate playfulness of these children would quickly be given active support.

Two years earlier, in 1971, Edward M. Swartz had attacked the toy industry for unsafe toys and deceptive advertising. *Toys That Don't Care* follows Ralph Nader and other consumer advocates in finding considerable hazards in the marketplace. The industry lashed back with a moralist of its own. Marvin Kaye, former editor of *Toys*, wrote *A Toy Is Born* as a partial refutation of Swartz. Most of Kaye's book consists of brief chapters on well-known manufacturers—Lionel, Parker Brothers, Lesney, and others. Many readers will be touched by nostalgia when they read about the invention of Silly Putty at General Electric in 1945, Wham-O's first Frisbee in 1956, and Hasbro's GI Joe of 1963, but few will be convinced by Kaye's defense of the toy industry's social conscience even after the passage of the Child Protection and Toy Safety Act of 1969.

A spate of books on the toy industry has appeared since 1990, some critical, others exculpatory. In *Toyland: The High-Stakes Game of the Toy Industry* Sydney Stern and Ted Schoenhaus were the first to call attention to the toy industry's decision to develop toys that look good on the tube and the subsequent bitter competition among toy manufacturers. Stephen Kline, a professor of communications, studied the impact of television advertising on children's play by both analyzing the ads and observing children playing. In *Out of the Garden: Toys, TV, and Children's Culture in the Age of Marketing* he concludes that by linking toys to stories and marketing toys through movies and programs that feature the toys as characters, children's culture is becoming more divided by gender and more limited to learning rules for role-playing. Ellen Seiter, author of *Sold Separately: Parents & Children in a Consumer Culture*, is also a professor of communications. She used her own children to study the effects of televised toy marketing and comes to less fearful conclusions. For Seiter, the major effect of the ads is to produce anxiety in parents, rather than reduce children to stereotyped behavior. She also has a clever chapter on the physical layout of Toys "R" Us stores, founded in 1957 by Charles Lazarus, and their classification of toy categories.

Historian Gary Cross surveys changes in the kind of toys manufactured in the twentieth century and some of the ways in which they have been marketed in his book *Kids' Stuff*. Like Kline, Cross is convinced that television toys are having a negative impact on children's culture and further separating children from their parents, but he is unable to offer any convincing evidence because his sources are chiefly trade journals and newsmagazines. Cross' negative attitudes toward the toy industry may be contrasted with those of industry spokesmen such as Dan S. Acuff and Robert H. Reiher, whose *What Kids Buy and Why* is addressed to potential product developers and advertisers. Based on a handful of psychological studies, the book is full of questionable generalizations about children's behavior, but its very naïveté reveals the weaknesses of the industry in attempting to manipulate its customers. A virtue of the book is its broad definition of the kid market, which includes toys, games, sporting goods, foods, software, publications, clothing, personal hygiene items, animation and entertainment programs on television, electronic games, and even educational software. Scholars often miss the significance of individual marketing strategies when they fail to consider that the industry sees toys in the context of total daily life.

G. Wayne Miller, a journalist and novelist, tells the story of the Hasbro toy company and its archrival Mattel with verve in *Toy Wars: The Epic Struggle between G.I. Joe, Barbie and the Companies That Make Them*. Hasbro, established in 1922, bought many older toy and game manufactures such as Playskool, Milton Bradley, and Tonka, which already owned Parker Brothers and Kenner, and Mattel, founded in 1944, grew rapidly after the success of Barbie in the 1960s, taking over Hot Wheels and Cabbage Patch dolls. Neither company was quite prepared for the enormous impact of video games, the subject of David Sheff's lively *Game Over: How Nintendo Zapped an American Industry, Captured Your Dollars, and Enslaved Your Children* and Michael Hayes and Stuart Disney's more sober economic analysis, *Games War: Video Games—A Business Review*, which carries the story to 1995. Justine Cassell and Henry Jenkins explore the impact of computer games on young women in *From Barbie® to Mortal Kombat: Gender and Computer Games*.

Scholarly studies of computer and video games are just emerging. Theresa Escobedo studied two boys and two girls ages four and five as they drew pictures using computer graphics. She concludes that the children used the computers for two types of play, "transformation of objects for constructive purposes and transformation of objects for imaginary play," following other researchers who have compared the computer to a sand castle and a paintbrush (135). Synthia Slowikowski looked at Nintendo in the context of family life and discovered that children as young as eight used the games in ways unintended by the manufacturer. One group of children created what they called "fake Nintendo" by building a television set from cardbard boxes and drawing their own stories on paper attached to the "screen." The children decided that they preferred the fake to the real Nintendo.

The third group of game and toy scholars is the social scientists. Beginning with G. Stanley Hall's studies in the 1880s, an impressive body of literature has developed. These are usefully summarized in Susanna Miller's *The Psychology of Play*. Among the major theorists in child development, Erik Erikson is the most readable. His *Childhood and Society* has influenced research in half a dozen fields in the past thirty years. Erikson's insistence on the opportunity for children to develop their imaginations through play has done much to make the study of play respectable. He has summarized these beliefs in *Toys and Reasons*, which takes its title from a line by William Blake: "The child's toys and the old man's reasons are the fruits of the two seasons." Jean Piaget has gone further than Erikson in arguing that play is essential for the development of adult intelligence. Throughout his work but especially in *Play, Dreams and Imitation in Childhood*, Piaget reduces play to a function of thought and limits the role of play in creativity and innovation. This role is restored in Jerome Singer's *The Child's World of Make-*

Believe: Experimental Studies of Imaginative Play. The importance of fantasy is recognized by Jerome S. Bruner in several important studies and by Catherine Garvey in her book *Play*. Another attempt to synthesize several theories of play is Mihaly Csikszentmihalyi's *Beyond Boredom and Anxiety: The Experience of Play in Work and Games*. Although his work is confined to adult behavior, Csikszentmihalyi's idea that play is a state between boredom and anxiety has applications to children's activities as well.

A note should be added on the application of psychological theories by playground planners and landscape architects. Beginning with Marjorie Allen's *Planning for Play* in 1969, a large number of books and articles have argued the necessity of including children in the planning process and making basic materials such as water, dirt, and wood available in playgrounds. Although playgrounds are still seen as a place where children should learn, the arrangement of equipment and the supervision tend to be much less didactic than in the past. This trend may be followed in M. Paul Friedberg's *Play and Interplay: A Manifesto for New Design in Urban Recreational Environment*, Paul Hogan's *Playgrounds for Free*, and Richard Dattner's *Design for Play*. For a vividly illustrated history of how children actually play in a city, see Amanda Dargan and Steven Zeitlin's *City Play*.

Brian Sutton-Smith's *The Ambiguity of Play* is a magnificent synthesis of psychological, biological, anthropological, philosophical, and literary theories of play. His approach identifies seven rhetorics of play: (1) play as progress, the belief that children develop and learn from games, toys, and play; (2) play as fate, that all games are determined by luck and chance; (3) play as power, involving contests to establish group leadership; (4) play as identity, a way of finding a place in a community; (5) play as imagination, creativity, and innovation; (6) play as self-actualization, fun, escape; and (7) play as frivolity, the carnivalesque. He is skeptical of the progressive rhetoric and believes that play has more to do with waiting then preparing. Ultimately, he argues, play is like evolution, a way for organisms, both human and animal, to adapt to variations in their environments. Perhaps this is also a rhetoric of progress, but not toward a specific goal. Toys for Sutton-Smith are simply the things that children use symbolically, their meanings always mediated by the child's imagination.

Examples of ethnographies of children's lives and games include Roger G. Barker and Herbert F. Wright's *One Boy's Day: A Specimen Record of Behavior*, a minute-by-minute record of a seven-year-old midwestern boy on April 26, 1949. The description, gathered by observers, parents, and teachers, illustrates the difficulty of labeling any particular activity as "play." Diana Kelly-Byrne's *A Child's Play Life* is a record of her play with a seven-year-old girl over a year's time in the 1970s. This precocious child read Judy Blume, C. S. Lewis, and J. R. Tolkien, watched *Wonder Woman* and *Mork and Mindy*, and shared her fantasy play with stuffed animals with Kelly-Byrne, leading her to define play as "paraguise," a combination of paradox and disguise.

An interesting description of children playing at school may be found in Sue Parrott's "Games Children Play: Ethnography of a Second-Grade Recess." Robyn Holmes has studied kindergarten children's definitions of play and toys. They identify four activities as play: (1) games, including tag, hide-and-seek, checkers, Candyland, and tic-tac-toe; (2) "not a game," which involves pretend play such as house, cops and robbers, and teacher; (3) building and making things; and (4) action figures and dolls, including Barbie. Toys were anything played with and grouped into categories such as riding toys, props for playing house, stuffed animals, puppets, and puzzles. Linda Hughes contributes to a better understanding of the social context for play in her ethnographic studies of games such as "four-square." The players, ages seven to twelve, distinguished among "real rules," which include both regular rules and part-rules involving special "slams" and "spins"; "rules that are not *really* rules," involving speed, intensity, and variants of the basic game; and "rules that are not rules," involving fancy moves, tricks, and coded communication. Hughes' insights into the importance of the rule-making and -breaking process in games have wide implications for the study of play.

Accounts of play in other cultures offer useful comparisons. *Six Cultures: Studies of Child Rearing*, edited by Beatrice B. Whiting, contains data on the Nyansongo of Kenya, the Rajputs of India, the Taira of Okinawa, the Mixtecans of Mexico, the Tarong of the Philippines, and "the New Englanders of Orchard Town"; but all the ethnographies are disappointingly sketchy on play. Mexican children's games are well covered by Cecila Gil de Partearroyo's *Links into Past: A Folkloric Study of Mexican Children Relative to Their Singing Games*, while Dorothy Howard's *Pedro of Tonalá* provides details of the play of an eleven-year-old boy near Guadalajara in 1963. Herbert Berry III and John Roberts provide a link between psychological and anthropological theories in their "Infant Socialization and Games of Chance," a cross-cultural study.

Historians, too, may trace their interest in games and toys back to the nineteenth century. E. B. Tylor, the British anthropologist, published "The History of Games" in *The Fortnightly Review* in 1879, and Alice Morse Earle anticipated the revival of interest in the seventeenth and eighteenth centuries in 1899 with her *Child Life in Colonial Days*. The rediscovery of play in the 1880s left little time for stocktaking, however, and it is not until the 1920s and 1930s that historical studies began to appear. Clarence Rainwater published his history of playground reform, *The Play Movement in the United States: A Study of Community Recreation*, in 1922. At the end of the 1930s, Foster Rhea Dulles completed *America Learns to Play*, which is chiefly concerned with adult play but which still provides the only comprehensive history of games and sports in this country.

Although it was not published in English until after his death, *Homo Ludens: A Study of the Play Element in Culture*, by Johan Huizinga, first appeared in 1938. *Homo Ludens* remains today one of the great studies of play. Huizinga's chapter titles—"The Play-Concept as Expressed in Language," "Play and Contest as Civilizing Functions," "Play and Law," "Play and War," "Play and Knowing"—suggest that he, too, thought that play was didactic, but his definition of play as "a voluntary activity or occupation executed with certain fixed limits of time and place, according to rules freely accepted but absolutely binding, having its aim in itself and accompanied by a feeling of tension, joy and the consciousness that it is 'different' from 'ordinary life,' " obviates any specific goal in play. Writing at a time when Hitler's uniformed Nazis were staging their pageants of conquest, Huizinga was critical of the corruption of play that he observed in their rituals, yet he was convinced that civilization arose in play. *Homo Ludens* remains a rich and subtle cultural history from which all students of games, toys, and play can profit.

Since 1960, historians of childhood and children's play have been influenced by Philippe Ariés' *Centuries of Childhood*. Ariés' chapter on the games and toys of the

French court in the seventeenth and eighteenth centuries is interesting, but his thesis that a period of childhood did not exist at that time has limited value for American historians. There is good evidence that our colonial ancestors did recognize several stages of childhood and youth, as Ross Beales shows in his essay "In Search of the Historical Child: Miniature Adulthood and Youth in Colonial New England." J. H. Plumb has done work on the history of childhood in England, while in the United States, the major work on games and play has been done by Brian Sutton-Smith. Many of his pioneering articles have been reprinted in his *The Folkgames of Children*. From the historical standpoint, special attention should be given the essay that he coauthored with B. G. Rosenberg, "Sixty Years of Historical Change in the Game Preferences of American Children." Sutton-Smith's *Toys as Culture* (1986) is a thorough discussion of the multiple meanings of toys and playthings. Sutton-Smith explores the paradox of the toy in the family context, in which an adult gives a toy to a child with the message, "Here is a trivial object that shows that I love you, now go and play with it by yourself and try to learn something from it."

Beginning in the early 1970s, a number of scholars began to place games and play in the context of cultural history. Bernard Mergen's *Play and Playthings* attempts to organize a variety of materials by psychologists, anthropologists, educators, and historians on children's play. He has developed his ideas further in three essays, one on children's play as remembered in autobiographies, another on the material culture of childhood, and one on recent changes in children's game and toy preferences. Dominick Cavallo's *Muscles and Morals: Organized Playgrounds and Urban Reform, 1880–1920* provides a good overview of the organization and motivation of the early playground advocates. Dorothy Howard's beautiful and insightful autobiography, *Dorothy's World: Childhood in Sabine Bottom 1902–1910*, adds information on rural child life. Cary Goodman's *Choosing Sides: Playground and Street Life on the Lower East Side* and David Nasaw's *Children of the City: At Work and at Play* fill in many details of immigrant child life in New York City in the early twentieth century. Gary Alan Fine has written on the possibilities of approaching children's games through folklore.

Miriam Formanek-Brunell's *Made to Play House: Dolls and the Commercialization of American Girlhood, 1830–1930* adds significantly to our understanding of doll play as a form of socialization and the business of manufacturing and retailing dolls. Her book is especially good on the struggles of women doll designers and manufacturers. Rodris Roth, a curator at the Smithsonian's National Museum of American History, has located twenty-five scrapbooks made by young women in the 1890s and early 1900s that were used as paper dollhouses. Her analysis of these scrapbook houses illustrates the complex interrelationships between doll play and the emerging consumer culture.

A fascinating study of more than 100 women and their dolls by Dorothy Washburn concludes that while most women consider their doll play as training for motherhood, a view that they share with doll retailers and some scholars, their definitions of doll were significantly narrower. "The only figures considered to be dolls must look and feel like real people. For doll players, dolls have soft bodies, hair that can be combed, and realistic body and facial proportions" (118). Some stuffed animals may attain doll status, but Barbie is in a category by herself, a conclusion also reached by Robyn Holmes. Washburn's doll players further classified dolls as baby dolls, including Cabbage Patch dolls and some stuffed animals; little-girl dolls, including paper dolls; and display dolls, who are often in ethnic or ceremonial costumes or who represent specific fairy tale characters. The style of play changed with each category. Washburn's observation that linguistic labels, even those used by the doll players themselves, fail to capture the conceptual ambivalence that the objects have for the different players indicates that games and toys as well as dolls need to be studied in the broadest possible contexts. Two unusual readings of Barbie may be found in Billy Boy, *Barbie: Her Life and Times* and Erica Rand, *Barbie's Queer Accessories.*

An interesting study of the ways in which dolls and toys have been used in children's fiction, television, and movies is *When Toys Come Alive* by Lois Rostow Kuznets. Her subtle readings of stories whose characters have been made into dolls and toys raise questions about the meaning of "real" and the ways in which children may manipulate their playthings to interpret the secret world that surrounds them. The success of the movie *Toy Story* in 1995 raises other issues about the miniature and the fantastic. Gillian Avery's illustrated history of American children's books from 1621 to 1922, *Behold the Child*, provides a good overview of the sources for some fantasy play. R. Gordon Kelly has interpreted the cultural meanings of children's magazines.

Doll play in the nineteenth century has been studied by Marilyn Ferris Motz. The ways that children incorporate toys and stories into their own fictional creations have been studied by Sutton-Smith, *The Folkstories of Children*, and by Greta Fein, in "Toys and Stories." Robin C. Moore's *Childhood's Domain: Play and Place in Child Development* focuses on spaces where children play as well as on the objects they play with. Four periodicals (some no longer published) contain reports on games and toys from various perspectives: *Children's Folklore Newsletter*, *Children's Environment Quarterly*, *Play and Culture*, and the *ITRA Newsletter*.

For further comparisons with the history of games and toys in other countries, a half-dozen studies are available. Karl Ewald Fritzsch's *An Illustrated History of Toys* is especially good on German toy production. *A History of Toys* by Lady Antonia Fraser presents a popular survey. Closer to home, Musée de Quebec's *Le Jouet dans l'univers de l'enfant, 1800–1925*, Robert-Lionel Séguin's *Les Jouets anciens du Quebec*, and Harry Symons' *Playthings of Yesterday: Harry Symons Introduces the Percy Band Collection* offer some basic information on the history of Canadian toys. Séguin's book suggests that toys in Quebec and the northeastern United States are basically similar but that the Quebecois had some unusual folk toys such as the *pite* or *tapecul*—a narrow sled with a vertical post in the middle and a handle for sledding or skiing standing up. South of the border, *Los Juegos Infantiles en las Escuelas Rurales* by Ramón Garcia Ruiz is an older study that still has much merit, while Francisco Javier Hernández's *El Juguete Popular en México: Estudio de interpretacion* is a scholarly monograph on toys from the pre-Hispanic period to the present. Aida Reboredo's *Jugar es un Acto Politico* is a critique of the ideological domination of Third World countries by the toy industry of the United States. The author, a Mexican sociologist, also presents some interesting evidence on the ways in which toys are perceived by children in her country.

ANTHOLOGIES AND REPRINTS

The anthologies by Elliott Avedon and Brian Sutton-Smith and by R. E. Herron and Sutton-Smith have already been mentioned. A wealth of material is reprinted in *A Children's Game Anthology: Studies in Folklore and Anthropology*. For recent scholarship in psychology, see Jerome Bruner, Alosin Jolly, and Kathy Sylva. Curiously, Robert H. Bremner et al.'s three-volume anthology, *Children and Youth in America: A Documentary History*, has nothing on games or toys. *The Children's Culture Reader*, edited by Henry Jenkins, has a few chapters on games and toys, notably the essay by Miriam Formanek-Brunell.

BIBLIOGRAPHY

Books and Articles

Abernethy, Francis Edward. *Texas Toys and Games*. Dallas: Southern Methodist University Press, 1989.

Abrahams, Roger D. *Jump-Rope Rhymes: A Dictionary*. Austin: University of Texas Press, 1969.

Acuff, Dan S., and Robert H. Reiher. *What Kids Buy and Why: The Psychology of Marketing to Kids*. New York: Free Press, 1997.

Allen, Marjorie. *Planning for Play*. Cambridge: MIT Press, 1969.

Almqvist, Brigitta. "Age and Gender Differences in Children's Christmas Requests." *Play & Culture* 2: 1 (February 1989), 2–19.

Ariés, Philippe. *Centuries of Childhood*. New York: Alfred A. Knopf, 1962.

Avedon, Elliott M., and Brian Sutton-Smith, eds. *The Study of Games*. New York: Wiley, 1971.

Avery, Gillian. *Behold the Child: American Children and Their Books 1621–1922*. Baltimore: Johns Hopkins University Press, 1994.

Barenholtz, Bernard, and Inez McClintock. *American Antique Toys, 1830–1900*. New York: Harry N. Abrams, 1986.

Barker, Roger G., and Herbert F. Wright. *One Boy's Day: A Specimen Record of Behavior*. New York: Harper, 1951.

Barnett, L. A., and Gary Chick. "Chips off the Ol' Block: Parents' Leisure and Their Children's Play." *The Journal of Leisure Research* 18 (1986), 266–83.

Barthes, Roland. *Mythologies*. New York: Hill and Wang, 1972.

Beales, Ross W. "In Search of the Historical Child: Miniature Adulthood and Youth in Colonial New England." *American Quarterly* 27 (October 1975), 379–98.

Berry, Herbert, III, and John Roberts. "Infant Socialization and Games of Chance." *Ethnology* 2 (July 1972), 296–308.

Best, Charles W. *Cast Iron Toy Pistols, 1870–1940: A Collector's Guide*. Englewood, Colo.: Rocky Mountain Arms and Antiques, 1973.

Boy, Billy. *Barbie: Her Life and Times*. New York: Crown, 1987.

Bremner, Robert H., et al., eds. *Children and Youth in America: A Documentary History*. 3 vols. Cambridge: Harvard University Press, 1970.

Brewster, Paul G. *American Nonsinging Games*. Norman: University of Oklahoma Press, 1953.

———. *Children's Games and Rhymes*. Chapel Hill: University of North Carolina Press, 1952.

Bronner, Simon J. *American Children's Folklore*. Little Rock, Ark.: August House, 1988.

Bruner, Jerome S., Alosin Jolly, and Kathy Sylva, eds. *Play—Its Role in Development and Evolution*. New York: Basic Books, 1976.

Burns, Thomas A. "The *Game of Life*: Idealism, Reality, and Fantasy in the Nineteenth- and Twentieth-Century Versions of a Milton Bradley Game." *The Canadian Review of American Studies* 9 (Spring 1978), 50–83.

Cadbury, Betty. *Playthings Past*. Newton Abbot, England: David and Charles, 1976.

Caillois, Roger. *Man, Play, and Games*. London: Thames and Hudson, 1962.

Calvert, Karin. *Children in the House: The Material Culture of Early Childhood, 1600–1900*. Boston: Northeastern University Press, 1992.

Calvin, Jeannette M., comp. *International Trade in Toys*. Washington, D.C.: Government Printing Office, 1926.

Canary, Robert H. "Playing the Game of *Life*." *Journal of Popular Culture* 1 (Spring 1968), 427–32.

Caplan, Frank, and Theresa Caplan. *The Power of Play*. Garden City, N.Y.: Anchor Press/Doubleday, 1973.

Cassell, Justine, and Henry Jenkins, eds. *From Barbie® to Mortal Kombat: Gender and Computer Games*. Boston: Northeastern University Press, 1998.

Cavallo, Dominick. *Muscles and Morals: Organized Playgrounds and Urban Reform, 1880–1920*. Philadelphia: University of Pennsylvania Press, 1981.

Champlin, John D., and Arthur E. Bostwick. *The Young Folks' Cyclopaedia of Games and Sports*. New York: H. Holt, 1890.

Chandler, Cecil. *Toys and Dolls Made in Occupied Japan*. Houston: Chandler's Discriminating Junk, 1973.

A Children's Game Anthology: Studies in Folklore and Anthropology. New York: Arno Press, 1976.

Coleman, Dorothy S., Elizabeth A. Coleman, and Evelyn J. Coleman. *The Collector's Encyclopedia of Dolls*. New York: Crown, 1968.

Cross, Gary. *Kids' Stuff: Toys and the Changing World of American Childhood*. Cambridge: Harvard University Press, 1997.

Croswell, T. R. "Amusements of Worcester School Children." *Pedagogical Seminary* 6 (September 1899), 314–71.

Csikszentmihalyi, Mihaly. *Beyond Boredom and Anxiety: The Experience of Play in Work and Games*. San Francisco: Jossey-Bass, 1975.

Culin, Stewart. "Street Games of Boys in Brooklyn, New York." *Journal of American Folklore* 4 (July–September 1891), 221–37.

Daiken, Leslie. *Children's Toys Throughout the Ages*. London: Batsford, 1953.

———. *World of Toys: A Guide to the Principal Public and Private Collections in Great Britain*. Kent: Lambarde Press, 1963.

Dargan, Amanda, and Steven Zeitlin. *City Play*. New Brunswick, N.J.: Rutgers University Press, 1990.

Dattner, Richard. *Design for Play*. Cambridge: MIT Press, 1974.

Douglas, Norman. *London Street Games*. London: St. Catherine Press, 1916.

Dulles, Foster Rhea. *America Learns to Play*. New York: Appleton-Century, 1940.

Earle, Alice Morse. *Child Life in Colonial Days*. New York: Macmillan, 1899.

Erikson, Erik. *Childhood and Society*. New York: W. W. Norton, 1950.
———. *Toys and Reasons*. New York: W. W. Norton, 1977.
Escobedo, Theresa H. "Play in a New Medium: Children's Talk and Graphics at Computers." *Play & Culture* 5:2 (May 1992), 120–40.
Fein, Greta G. "Toys and Stories." In *The Future of Play Theory*, ed. Anthony D. Pellegrini. Albany: State University of New York Press, 1995, 151–64.
Ferretti, Fred. *The Great American Book of Sidewalk, Stoop, Dirt, Curb, and Alley Games*. New York: Workman, 1975.
———. *The Great American Marble Book*. New York: Workman, 1973.
Fine, Gary Alan. "Children and Their Culture: Exploring Newell's Paradox." *Western Folklore* 39 (July 1980), 170–83.
Formanek-Brunell, Miriam. *Made to Play House: Dolls and the Commercialization of American Girlhood, 1830–1930*. New Haven, Conn.: Yale University Press, 1993; Baltimore: Johns Hopkins University Press, paperback, 1998.
Fraser, Antonia. *A History of Toys*. New York: Spring Books, 1972.
Friedberg, M. Paul. *Play and Interplay: A Manifesto for New Design in Urban Recreational Environment*. New York: Macmillan, 1970.
Fritzsch, Karl Ewald. *An Illustrated History of Toys*. Leipzig: Edition Leipzig, 1968.
Garvey, Catherine. *Play*. Cambridge: Harvard University Press, 1977.
Gibson, Cecil. *A History of British Dinky Toys: Model Car and Vehicle Issues, 1934–1964*. Hemel Hempstead: Model Aeronautical Press, 1966.
Gil de Partearroyo, Cecilia. *Links into Past: A Folkloric Study of Mexican Children Relative to Their Singing Games*. Mexico, D.F.: Editorial Jus, 1953.
Gomme, Alice. *The Traditional Games of England, Scotland, and Ireland*. 2 vols. London: D. Nutt, 1894–1898.
Goodman, Cary. *Choosing Sides: Playground and Street Life on the Lower East Side*. New York: Schocken Books, 1979.
Gould, D. W. *The Top: Universal Toy, Enduring Pastime*. New York: Clarkson Potter, 1973.
Grover, Kathryn, ed. *Hard at Play: Leisure in America, 1840–1940*. Amherst and Rochester: University of Massachusetts Press and Strong Museum, 1992.
Hall, G. Stanley. "The Contents of Children's Minds." *Princeton Review* 2 (May 1883), 249–72.
Hannas, Linda. *The English Jigsaw Puzzle, 1760–1890, with a Descriptive Check-list of Puzzles in the Museums of Great Britain and the Author's Collection*. London: Wayland, 1972.
Harman, Kenny. *Comic Strip Toys*. Des Moines, Iowa: Wallace-Homestead Books, 1975.
Hawes, Joseph M., and N. Ray Hiner, eds. *American Childhood: A Research Guide and Historical Handbook*. Westport, Conn.: Greenwood Press, 1985.
Hayes, Michael, and Stuart Disney. *Games War: Video Games—A Business Review*. London: Bowerdean, 1995.
Hernández, Francisco Javier. *El Juguete Popular en México: Estudio de interpretacion*. Mexico, D.F.: Ediciones Mexicanas, 1950.
Herron, R. E., and Brian Sutton-Smith, eds. *Child's Play*. New York: Wiley, 1971.
Hertz, Louis. *The Handbook of Old American Toys*. Wethersfield, Conn.: Mark Haber, 1947.
———. *Messrs. Ives of Bridgeport*. Wethersfield, Conn.: Mark Haber, 1950.

———. *The Toy Collector*. New York: Funk and Wagnalls, 1969.

Hogan, Paul. *Playgrounds for Free*. Cambridge: MIT Press, 1974.

Holmes, Robyn M. "Categories of Play: A Kindergartner's View." *Play & Culture* 4:1 (February 1991), 43–50.

Howard, Dorothy. *Dorothy's World: Childhood in Sabine Bottom 1902–1910*. New York: Prentice-Hall, 1977.

———. *Pedro of Tonalá*. Roswell, N. Mex.: Hall-Poorbaugh Press, 1989.

Hughes, James M. "A Tale of Two Games: An Image of the City." *Journal of Popular Culture* 6 (Fall 1972), 357–62.

Hughes, Linda A. "A Conceptual Framework for the Study of Children's Gaming." *Play & Culture* 4:3 (August 1991), 284–300.

———. "Foursquare: A Glossary and 'Native' Taxonomy of Game Rules." *Play & Culture* 2:2 (May 1989), 103–36.

Huizinga, Johan. *Homo Ludens: A Study of the Play Element in Culture*. London: Routledge and Kegan Paul, 1949.

Jacobs, Flora Gill. *Dolls' Houses in America: Historic Preservation in Miniature*. New York: Scribner's, 1974.

Jenkins, Henry, ed. *The Children's Culture Reader*. New York: New York University Press, 1998.

Johnson, J. E., J. F. Christie, and T. D. Yawkey. *Play and Early Childhood Development*. Glenview, Ill.: Scott, Foresman, 1987.

Jones, Bessie, and Bess Lomax Hawes. *Step It Down: Games, Plays, Songs and Stories from the Afro-American Heritage*. New York: Harper and Row, 1972.

Kaye, Marvin. *A Toy Is Born*. New York: Stein and Day, 1973.

Kelly, R. Gordon, ed. *Children's Periodicals of the United States*. Westport, Conn.: Greenwood Press, 1984.

Kelly-Byrne, Diana. *A Child's Play Life*. New York: Teacher's College Press, 1989.

King, Nancy R. "See Baby Play: Play as Depicted in Elementary School Readers, 1900–1959." *Play & Culture* 4:2 (May 1991), 100–107.

Kline, Stephen. *Out of the Garden: Toys, TV, and Children's Culture in the Age of Marketing*. New York: Verso, 1993.

Knapp, Mary, and Herbert Knapp. *One Potato, Two Potato . . . The Secret Education of American Children*. New York: W. W. Norton, 1976.

Kuznets, Lois Rostow. *When Toys Come Alive: Narratives of Animation, Metamorphosis, and Development*. New Haven, Conn.: Yale University Press, 1994.

Malko, George. *The One and Only Yo-Yo Book*. New York: Avon, 1978.

McClintock, Inez, and Marshall McClintock. *Toys in America*. Washington, D.C.: Public Affairs Press, 1961.

McClinton, Katharine. *Antiques of American Childhood*. New York: Bramhall House, 1970.

McGhee, Zach. "A Study of the Play Life of Some South Carolina Children." *Pedagogical Seminary* 7 (December 1900), 459–78.

Mechling, Jay. "Sacred and Profane Play in the Boy Scouts of America." In *Play and Culture*, ed. Helen B. Schwartzman. West Point, N.Y.: Leisure Press, 1980, 206–13.

Mergen, Bernard. "Children's Play in American Autobiographies, 1820–1914." In *Hard at Play: Leisure in America, 1840–1940*, ed. Kathryn Grover. Amherst and Rochester: University of Massachusetts Press and Strong Museum, 1992, 161–187.

———. "Made, Bought, and Stolen: Toys and the Culture of Childhood." In *Small Worlds: Children and Adolescents in America, 1850–1950*, ed. Elliott West and Paula Petrik. Lawrence: University Press of Kansas, 1992, 86–106, 334–339.

———. "Ninety-five Years of Historical Change in the Game Preferences of American Children." *Play & Culture* 4:3 (August 1991), 272–283.

———. *Play and Playthings: A Reference Guide*. Westport, Conn.: Greenwood Press, 1982.

Merrill, Madeline and Richard. *Dolls and Toys at the Essex Institute*. Salem, Mass.: Essex Institute, 1976.

Milberg, Alan. *Street Games*. New York: McGraw-Hill, 1976.

Miller, G. Wayne. *Toy Wars: The Epic Struggle between G.I. Joe, Barbie and the Companies That Make Them*. New York: Times Books, 1998.

Miller, Stephen. "Ends, Means, and Galumphing: Some Leitmotifs of Play." *American Anthropologist* 75 (February 1973), 87–98.

Miller, Susanna. *The Psychology of Play*. New York: Pelican Books, 1968.

Moore, Robin. *Childhood's Domain: Play and Place in Child Development*. London: Croom Helm, 1986.

Motz, Marilyn Ferris. "Maternal Virgin: The Girl and Her Doll in Nineteenth-Century America." In *Objects of Special Devotion: Fetishism in Popular Culture*, ed. Ray Browne. Bowling Green, Ohio: Bowling Green State University Popular Press, 1982, 54–69.

Murray, Patrick. *Toys*. London: Studio Vista, 1968.

Musée de Québec. *Le Jouet dans l'univers de l'enfant, 1800–1925*. Québec: Musé de Québec, 1977.

Nasaw, David. *Children of the City: At Work and at Play*. Garden City, N.Y.: Doubleday, 1985.

Newell, William Wells. *Games and Songs of American Children*. New York: Harper and Brothers, 1883.

O'Brien, Richard. *The Story of American Toys: From the Puritans to the Present*. New York: Abbeville Press, 1990.

O'Dell, John, and Richard Loehl. *The Great Depression Era Book of Fun*. New York: Harper and Row, 1981.

Opie, Iona, and Peter Opie. *Children's Games in Street and Playground*. Oxford: Clarendon Press, 1969.

Page, Hilary Fisher. *Toys in Wartime*. London: G. Allen and Unwin, 1942.

Parrott, Sue. "Games Children Play: Ethnography of a Second-Grade Recess." In *The Cultural Experience: Ethnography in Complex Society*, ed. James Spradley and David McCurdy. Chicago: Science Research Associates, 1976, 207–19.

Petrik, Paula. "The House That Parcheesi Built: Selchow & Righter Company." *Business History Review* 60 (Autumn 1986), 410–37.

Piaget, Jean. *Play, Dreams and Imitation in Childhood*. New York: W. W. Norton, 1962.

Plumb, J. H. "The New World of Children in Eighteenth-Century England." *Past and Present* 67 (May 1975), 64–93.

Pressland, David. *The Art of the Tin Toy*. New York: Crown, 1976.

Rainwater, Clarence. *The Play Movement in the United States: A Study of Community Recreation*. Chicago: University of Chicago Press, 1922.

Rand, Erica. *Barbie's Queer Accessories*. Durham, N.C.: Duke University Press, 1995.

Reboredo, Aida. *Jugar es un Acto Politico. El jugete industrial: Recurso de dominacion*. Mexico, D.F.: Nueva Imagen, 1983.

Remise, Jac, and Jean Fondin. *The Golden Age of Toys*. Greenwich, Conn.: New York Graphic Society, 1967.

Roberts, J. M., M. J. Arth, and R. R. Bush. "Games in Culture." *American Anthropologist* 61 (1959), 597–605.

Roberts, J. M., and Brian Sutton-Smith. "Child Training and Game Involvement." *Ethnology* 1 (1962), 166–85.

Rosenberg, B. G., and Brian Sutton-Smith. "Sixty Years of Historical Change in the Game Preferences of American Children." *Journal of American Folklore* 74 (January–March 1961), 17–46.

Roth, Rodris. "Scrapbook Houses: A Late Nineteenth-Century Children's View of the American Home." In *The American Home: Material Culture, Domestic Space, and Family Life*, ed. Eleanor McD. Thompson. Winterthur, Del., and Hanover, N.H.: Winterthur Museum and University Press of New England, 1998, 301–23.

Ruiz, Ramón Garcia. *Los Juegos Infantiles en las Escuelas Rurales*. Mexico City: El Nacional, 1938.

Schroeder, Joseph J., Jr., ed. *The Wonderful World of Toys, Games and Dolls*. Northfield, Ill.: Digest Books, 1971.

Schutrumpf, E. D. *World Trade in Toys*. Washington, D.C.: Government Printing Office, 1939.

Schwartzman, Helen B. *Transformations: The Anthropology of Children's Play*. New York: Plenum Press, 1978.

Séguin, Robert-Lionel. *Les Jouets anciens du Quebec*. Montreal: Lemeac, 1969.

Seiter, Ellen. *Sold Separately: Parents & Children in a Consumer Culture*. New Brunswick, N.J.: Rutgers University Press, 1993.

Sheff, David. *Game Over: How Nintendo Zapped an American Industry, Captured Your Dollars, and Enslaved Your Children*. New York: Random House, 1993.

Singer, Jerome L. *The Child's World of Make-Believe: Experimental Studies of Imaginative Play*. New York: Academic Press, 1973.

Slowikowski, Synthia S. "The Culture of Nintendo: Another Look." *The Journal of Play Theory & Research* 1:1 (1993), 1–16.

Stern, Sydney Ladensohn, and Ted Schoenhaus. *Toyland: The High-Stakes Game of the Toy Industry*. Chicago: Contemporary Books, 1990.

Sutton-Smith, Brian. *The Ambiguity of Play*. Cambridge: Harvard University Press, 1997.

———. *The Folkgames of Children*. Austin: Published for the American Folklore Society by the University of Texas, 1972.

———. *The Folkstories of Children*. Philadelphia: University of Pennsylvania Press, 1981.

———. *A History of Children's Play: New Zealand, 1840–1950*. Philadelphia: University of Pennsylvania Press, 1981.

———. *Toys as Culture*. New York: Gardner Press, 1986.

Sutton-Smith, Brian, Jay Mechling, Thomas W. Johnson, and Felicia R. McMahon, eds. *Children's Folklore: A Source Book*. New York: Garland Press, 1995.

Swartz, Edward M. *Toys That Don't Care*. Boston: Gambit, 1971.

Symons, Harry. *Playthings of Yesterday: Harry Symons Introduces the Percy Band Collection*. Toronto: Ryerson Press, 1963.

Tylor, E. B. "The History of Games." *The Fortnightly Review* 31 (n.s. 25) (1879), 735–47.

U.S. Bureau of Census. *Census of Manufacturers: 1927. Carriages and Sleds, Children's Toys, Games, and Playground Equipment, Sporting and Athletic Goods, Not including Firearms or Ammunition*. Washington, D.C.: Government Printing Office, 1929.

———. *Census of Manufacturers: 1931*. Washington, D.C.: Government Printing Office, 1931.

———. *Sixteenth Census of the United States 1940. Manufacturers: 1939. Toys and Sporting and Athletic Goods*. Washington, D.C.: Government Printing Office, 1941.

Washburn, Dorothy K. "Getting Ready: Doll Play and Real Life in American Culture, 1900–1980." In *American Material Culture: The Shape of the Field*, ed. Ann Smart Martin and J. Ritchie Garrison. Winterthur, Del., and Knoxville, Tenn.: Winterthur Museum and University of Tennessee Press, 1997, 105–34.

West, Elliott. *Growing Up in Twentieth-Century America: A History and Reference Guide*. Westport, Conn.: Greenwood, 1996.

West, Elliott, and Paula Petrik, eds. *Small Worlds: Children & Adolescents in America, 1850–1950*. Lawrence: University Press of Kansas, 1992.

White, Gwen. *Toys and Dolls: Marks and Labels*. Newton, Mass.: L. T. Branford, 1975.

Whiting, Beatrice B., ed. *Six Cultures: Studies of Child Rearing*. New York: Wiley, 1963.

Willson's Canadian Toy, Notion and Stationery Directory. Toronto: Willson's Directories, 1956.

Yoffie, Lea Rachel Clara. "Three Generations of Children's Singing Games in St. Louis." *Journal of American Folklore* 60 (January–March 1947), 1–151.

Periodicals

Antique Toy World. Chicago, 1970– .

Children's Environment Quarterly. New York, 1984–?.

Children's Folklore Newsletter. Greenville, N.C., 1978– .

Collectibles Monthly. York, Pa., 1977– .

The Doll Reader. Riverdale, Md., 1973– .

ITRA Newsletter (International Toy Research Association). Halmstad, Sweden, 1997– .

Play and Culture. Champaign, Ill., 1988–1992.

The Playground. New York, 1907–1915; Cooperstown, N.Y., 1916–1923; Greenwich, Conn., 1923–1924; New York, 1924–1929; *Playground and Recreation*, New York, 1929–1930; *Recreation*, New York, 1931–1965; *Parks and Recreation*, Arlington, Va., 1966– .

Play Theory & Research. Champaign, Ill., 1993.
Playthings. New York, 1903– .
Das Spielzeug. Bamberg, Germany, 1909– .
TASP Newsletter. Logan, Utah (place varies), 1975– .
Toy and Hobby World. New York, 1963– .
Toys and Novelties. Chicago, 1909–1972.

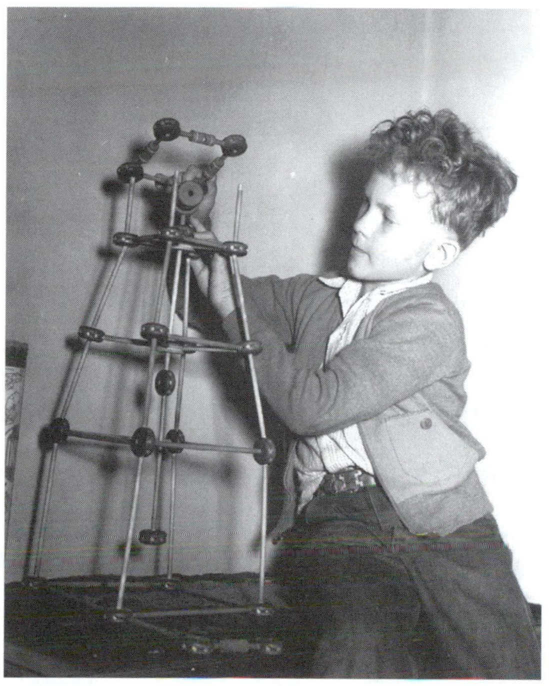

Boy playing with Tinker Toys, 1942. Photo by Arthur Rothstein. Courtesy of the Library of Congress

Boys playing cards in Washington, 1935. Courtesy of the Library of Congress

Boys playing stickball in rural Colorado, 1912. Courtesy of the Denver Public Library

Little League baseball. © Skjold Photographs

Hula hooping at the Minnesota State Fair. © Skjold Photographs

Playing checkers. © Painet

Playing a video game. © Painet

Playing with Barbie dolls. © Painet

Skateboarding. © Skjold Photographs

Singers perform at *Pokémon the Movie 2000* premiere. © Reuters NewMedia Inc./CORBIS

GARDENING

Patsy Hammontree

The term "garden" is an inclusive one. It applies to both ornamental gardens and vegetable gardens. In American culture, however, a reference to a garden means a vegetable garden. If someone inquires about a person's garden, the inquirer does not have a mental image of japonica and wisteria but of neat rows of tomatoes, beans, and corn. Although ornamentals provide fragrance and beauty, vegetables can provide both of those and good health as well.

Gardening is so much a part of American culture that it has its own folk heroes, individuals as diverse as Johnny Appleseed, Luther Burbank, George Washington Carver, and Ewell Gibbons. It also has its own folklore. Often novice gardeners are discouraged by well-meaning lore passed on by experienced gardeners. The information ranges from too scientific to too sophisticated. Even a book such as *A Creative Step-by-Step Guide to Fruit and Vegetables* by Peter Blackburne-Maze, which purports to enlighten beginning gardeners, is intimidating. The book's color pictures of perfect vegetables and its sophisticated gardening vocabulary (advice on constructing a "U-cordon") make growing such beautiful edibles seem out of reach to a neophyte gardener.

Gardeners are in love with seeds and soil. Gardening is a recurrent topic in their conversations. They analyze methods of planting and share gardening advice. In autumn they ask, "Has your garden been plowed for the dormant season?" In winter, they ponder over selections in early seed catalogs. In the early spring, they talk about tilling the soil and applying the fertilizer suited to soil type. Then they impatiently wait until weather permits them to set the seeds.

Although there is a plethora of information about gardening, there is a fundamental gardening pattern that has not changed through the ages. If ancestors could return to the contemporary world, they would be much in awe of strange, modern inventions. If they walked outside and caught sight of the vegetable garden, however, they would see something quite familiar. A cursory overview would not reveal certain innovations such as hybrid plants and genetically altered plants, but the garden itself would be hardly different from a garden planted centuries ago. Most modern gardening methods enhance gardening, but they do not alter the basic pattern of planting a garden.

Developments such as biointensive and ecological methods gardening with hydroponics and installing individual plant covers to guard against late frost have been useful. Researchers and writers often have effective advice, but to show their own innovative abilities, they (or their editors) use titles that diminish the article's credibility. During the sexual revolution of the 1970s, an *American Home* essay was entitled "Today's Vegetable Turn-On" (Powers). Other writers publish with the belief that gardeners are attracted by a comic play on words. Examples are "Great Hoe-Down," "Beat the Southern Broccoli Blues" (Pleasant), "Meet the Hotheads: Growing Lettuce in the South" (Pleasant) and "Laugh at Food Prices—Hoe! Hoe! Hoe!" (Tilling). Only in popular culture could essays survive with such titles.

Gardening's place in popular culture is firmly established by a Duane Newcomb gardening book. The Trail-R-Club of America commissioned Newcomb to write the *Mobile Home Gardening Guide*. If owners of travel trailers—a conveyance that by its nature seems contradictory to planting a garden—are so addicted to gardening that they plant where they are parked, gardening has truly permeated American culture.

Gardening is especially suited to Americans. It encourages American individualism and self-reliance, and it allows for creativity. Despite space constraints, gardeners devise a suitable plan. They plant a container garden, design a postage-stamp garden, or plant vertically, using trellises. If there is no space restriction, they might fill an acre with traditional rows of vegetables, relying on companion planting to deter insects. There is no limit to a gardener's ingenuity for growing vegetables.

Gardening is a challenge. It appeals to the American desire to compete. Indeed, growing a garden is one of the culture's major competitive sports. The competition can be serious or frivolous. The foremost challenge that a gardener faces is competing with the elements, unpredictable weather conditions. Either excessive rain or lack of rain can destroy a garden. Hailstorms can beat plants into the ground, and strong winds can bend and break them. Such forces are beyond the gardener's control, but the contest is in developing ways to divert the power of an uncontrollable aggressor.

A gardener also competes with plant disease and with the insect world. Insects are insidious creatures that outdate humankind. They have developed incredible survival abilities. They can become immune to the best of chemical insecticides and thwart a passionate ecological gardener's efforts to defeat such persistent adversaries. Plant disease is equally destructive to a garden. A blight appears without warning and withers a healthy plant. The war is constant, but a gardener takes pleasure in winning limited battles.

Gardeners also compete with themselves. Gardening is generally thought of as humankind working with nature. In reality, it is humankind working against nature. A garden is not natural. Its order and plan go against the chaos that nature desires. Gardeners must have stamina to struggle against efforts of nature to retake the garden and to fill the space with weeds. Gardeners struggle against the temptation to abandon the garden to let it return to chaos. If gardeners endure and bring the vegetables to fruition, they compete with their previous year's record. They also compete with other growers to produce the best vegetables.

Gardening's competitive spirit is encouraged by the culture. For example, a *Southern Living* article challenged, "Get a Jump on Spring," reflecting people's race against nature (Steadman). Competition is endorsed officially by organizations that in the autumn hand out prizes at regional and state fairs for the largest tomato, watermelon, or pumpkin. In 1975, *Sunset Magazine* conducted a contest for the best garden in the Pacific Northwest. Fourteen hundred people entered (Chan and Gill). Four-H Clubs and similar young people's groups engender competition by giving awards, even scholarships for those who excel in gardening. In the children's book *Growing Up Green*, the authors endorse competition with chapter titles such as "Pumpkin Derby" and "Bean Olympics" (Skelsey and Huckaby).

There are many reasons that individuals garden. At one time, gardening was not a choice but a necessity. People planted a garden to have food. In contemporary culture, however, gardening is a choice, not an imperative. Most gardeners grow for pleasure. Whatever factor causes them to garden, they garden in large numbers.

In 1994, the *New York Times* reported that gardening had become the nation's number one hobby. Citing more recent statistics, in 1997 the Home Gardening Television network released the following information: "Americans spend 50 billion dollars annually on gardening related items. Two out of five Americans are gardeners, 78 million people—an increase of thirty percent between 1993 and 1996. Gardening has been the number one hobby for the last fifteen years" (Mullen).

Gardening connects humankind with Mother Earth, evoking the mystery of life and death. A seed is buried, and the earth gives back life. Even though a gardener knows the science of what happens, the process retains something of the mystical. The connection between planting and an abstract, unseen force is as old as gardening itself. Many Native American cultures paid homage to the corn god, acknowledging the unity between an unknown power and the growing process. Modern cultures do not conduct formal rituals to express an abstract belief, but gardeners have their private superstitions. Plowing and planting by the moon and the stars join the modern to the ancient. There is something biblical in humankind's mysterious connection to the soil—to the dust from which we came and the dust to which we will return.

HISTORICAL OUTLINE

Gardening in the Americas began with the indigenous people in North, Central, and South America. Three of the most popular garden items in the United States are native to this part of the world. Maize, the American Indian name for corn, came from the North American Indians. From the Mayan Indians in southern Mexico and Central America came the fruit-bearing plant tomatl or xtomatl—known today as tomato (Hendrickson). The pre-Incan Indians of the Andes Mountains grew edible tubers called papas, the potato (Carefoot and Sprott).

New methods of gardening came to North America when English settlers, beginning with the Pilgrims, brought European seeds and cultivation methods with them. The settlers, however, soon adopted many of the native plants for their own gardens. Growing foods for harvest began long before their arrival.

Gardening has a long ancestry. It reaches back to the people of the Middle East, where the first plots of what can be called cultivations appeared. According to Anthony Huxley in *An Illustrated History of Gardening*, "The earliest cultivators seem to have lived around Jerico in Palestine about 8000 B.C." The cultivation of such plots apparently evolved both from the wild grains that grew in the area and from seeds and pits casually spat out or dropped by persons having eaten wild fruits. These seeds eventually reappeared as trees, growing within the areas of habitation and leading finally to selected planting of grains and fruit trees as well as seeds collected from wild plants. Gardens then moved throughout the Middle East and eventually to Europe through Greece. Huxley approximates the dates for organized cultivation in Greece at sometime pre-6000 B.C.; in Egypt and Crete, 5000 B.C.; in China, 5000 B.C.; and in South America, 25000 B.C.

In *The Perfect Vegetable and Herb Garden*, Roy Genders remarks that, though using very primitive cultivation methods, the Egyptians had highly productive vegetable gardens. Genders provides the following list of Egyptian food-producing plants: almond, barley, broad bean, cabbage, chicory, dates, endive, figs, garlic, grapes, leeks, lettuce, melons, olives, onions, peas, radishes, shallots, watercress, and wheat. Genders points out that only two significant food crops were not grown by the Egyptians: rice and potatoes. Rice, which must grow with its roots submerged in water, originated in Asia. The potato is a native South American food, unknown to the Egyptians.

Gardening moved into Europe through Greece and then into Rome. The Romans left evidence of having advanced gardening methods, due in part to their technical skills. Huxley states, "By the second century B.C. [the Romans] had developed farming, market gardening, and decorative gardening to new levels." He contends that the Romans "laid the foundations of gardening ideals."

During the Middle Ages, gardening was essentially nonexistent among the populace, being maintained primarily by monks within the monasteries. Edward Hyams reports in *A History of Gardens and Gardening* that the monks who founded monasteries adopted the Roman idea of having gardening academies. They also followed the Roman practice of establishing agriculture estates, which were self-supporting. The estates grew a wide variety of plants and used multiple gardening methods. Gardening taught monks the importance of cultivation for the temporal life and connected them to the spiritual through the mystery of birth, growth, and death. Thus, the gardening provided both food for the soul and sustenance for the body.

Hyams suggests that the vegetable gardens of monasteries owe a debt to St. Benedict, who placed great stock in both the discipline and the intrinsic self-sufficiency associated with a garden. He credits the monasteries with having improved gardening techniques during the Middle Ages as well as preserving plants and herbs that might otherwise have been lost. Hyams also notes that the monks' interest in gardening raised the surrounding communities' awareness of the importance of growing food. He remarks, "The advancement of gardening in the eleventh and twelfth centuries in Europe was not solely in ecclesiastical hands. Secular lords were soon learning the worth of a garden from observing the benefits of the monks' gardens." By having gardens planted within the castle walls, the upper classes enjoyed certain foods for themselves. As was customary in the feudal social structure, the needs of the titled and wealthy were met with little, if any, regard for the needs of the general populace. The lower classes, however, benefited to a minimal degree from the castle's gardens, depending in part upon benevolence of the person in charge of the castle's food preparation.

Further, even though gardening was restricted primarily to monasteries and within the castle grounds, the cultivation of gardening became commonplace knowledge, showing the populace the possibility—and the advantage—of growing a variety of food (Genders). In *The Canterbury Tales*, Chaucer gives evidence of bulbous plants being popular among the general population. In his description of the Summoner, Chaucer writes, "Well loved he garlic and onions and the leek."

During the Renaissance, gardening emphasis shifted to the ornamental rather than the practical. Although vegetable gardens did not disappear among the general populace, high culture dictated that an elaborately designed flower garden should be a prominent part of a landowner's estate. Since artistic flower gardens required more attention and financial support than the general public could provide, large gardens were restricted to the wealthy (Huxley).

England's enthusiasm for ornamental gardens, however, was severely curtailed during the eleven years of Oliver Cromwell's conservative rule. In the Commonwealth years, Cromwell, a Puritan of utilitarian bent, stressed growing for nourishment, not growing for aesthetics. With the restoration of Charles II to the British throne, elaborate ornamental gardens once more moved to the forefront. Though luxury gardens were again politically correct, vegetable gardens maintained a steady popularity throughout the period. They thrived due to individual choice, not because of governmental sanction.

The British took their interest in gardening with them to the American colonies, where it was put to good use. The earliest settlers in North America were largely Puritans, adhering to the same utilitarian philosophy of Oliver Cromwell, but, in reality, they had little choice. Conditions demanded cultivation of the land as a means of survival.

The English, followed by the Dutch and the Swedes, came prepared to grow food crops. They brought seeds with them, and, depending upon the weather conditions, they began cultivation. Households had both a kitchen garden and an herb garden. As an indication of the early Americans' interests in cultivation, three prominent Americans—Washington, Jefferson, and Franklin—wrote a great deal about gardening. Jefferson's gardening books are still popular. More than a decade ago, Robert Baron edited a version of *The Garden and Farm Books of Thomas Jefferson*.

Unlike the English and other Europeans in the Americas, the Spanish were more interested in finding precious metals than in creating communities. Their armies and their camp followers subsisted on provisions carried with them, supplemented by what they appropriated from the natives. A mobile group, the Spanish explorers did not place value on planting and growing food. Nevertheless, in the earliest Spanish settlement in St. Augustine, Florida, the houses had garden plots beside them. According to Huxley, garden cultivation in Spanish territories was done by the priests who came after the soldiers and built missions. From those early gardens planted by the Spanish came citrus trees and selected fruit

Poster from the Work Projects Administration, ca. 1942. Courtesy of the Library of Congress

trees, peaches in particular. We are indebted to those early gardens for most of our citrus groves as well as peach orchards (Huxley).

Natives, although traditionally thought of as strictly hunters and gathers, were growing food long before pilgrims arrived. In *The Story of Gardening*, Richardson Wright comments on the Indians' cultivation habits and remarks that they "were not given to gardening finely." He goes on to list the varied composition of their gardens. They grew maize (two varieties), beans, pumpkins, squash, groundnut, and Jerusalem artichoke. They also included wild onions. They grew sunflowers for oil, tobacco for smoking, and gourds for containers. A look at the contents of the Indian garden reveals a great similarity to contemporary choices in planting.

From the seventeenth through the nineteenth centuries, North American gardening moved with the frontier as settlers relocated and created new gardens in new home clearings. Gardening methods tended to follow the pattern of the country from which immigrants came. Cultivation of gardens was an absolute necessity. Families could not survive on wild game, fruits, nuts, berries, and beef jerky.

Conditions that settlers faced as they established homes across the continent were frequently not conducive to successful cultivation. Yet, families sometimes had to settle in less than ideal areas because of circumstances. Some pioneers even established settlements in the inhospitable Rocky Mountains. Gardening was not then—and is not now—a simple task in the high desert. Difficulties of cultivation in mountainous areas has been a recurring topic for analysis and advice.

As America became urbanized, many found gardening less inviting, preferring instead to buy foods from a produce market, but growing vegetables has never lost its appeal for large numbers of Americans. Even urban dwellers within the boundaries of large cities find ways to cultivate gardens. Space is limited on most urban lots. To encourage interested gardeners, Duane Newcomb explained in *The Postage Stamp Garden Book* varied ways to get the best results from small space. Newcomb's book *The Apartment Farmer: The Hassle-Free Way to Grow Vegetables Indoors, on Balconies, Patios, Roofs, and in Small Yards* is even more encouraging to growers.

In many large cities, there are spaces for rent either for a single garden plot or for public community gardening. Most persons who wish to garden can satisfy themselves. Mary Lee Coe's *Growing with Community Gardening* describes the wide-ranging interest in shared garden space. In the 1970s emphasis on ecological movements inspired biointensive gardening. The biointensive method had many dedicated participants in California. John Jeavons in *How to Grow More Vegetables* writes of an experiment that began in northern California in 1972. He states, "The Common Ground Garden was started in 1972 to find the agricultural techniques that would make food raising by small farmers and gardeners more efficient. We have come to call the result 'mini-gardening.' Mini-Farms can flourish in non-agricultural areas such as mountainous regions, arid areas, and in and around urban centers. Food can be produced where people live." The first Common Ground Garden was located in Palo Alto, California, provided by Landal Institute, Sausalito, California. It is still in existence under the direction of Yvonne Savio, who is also coordinator of the master gardener program at the University of California in Los Angeles.

Container gardening has also become increasingly popular for gardeners with limited space, but traditionally the types of plants have had restrictions. Michael MacCasky suggests a variety of possibilities in *Gardening for Dummies*. He lists carrots, red- and green-leaf lettuces, dwarf or cherry tomatoes, peppers, and radishes. He also suggests herbs, traditional container plants. *The Creative Container Garden* by Elaine Stevens, is informative but is concerned largely with ornamental plants.

The most recent publication in the "Dummies" series is an incentive for all small-space gardeners. *Container Gardening for Dummies*, by Bill Marken of National Gardening Association, expands possibilities for both ornamentals and edibles. Among the seventeen vegetables that Marken lists are such unexpected plants as peas and corn. The variety of vegetables to be grown in containers is a far cry from the longtime favorite container vegetable, the patio tomato. Recent information on gardening in containers diminishes the lure of the single patio tomato. New methods promise an entire patio garden instead.

Gardening, either container or traditional, seems to be an activity in a vacuum, unaffected by outside factors. Yet, some scholars have shown that gardening reflects social, political, and economic movements. In 1934, Richardson Wright, looking at gardening in a larger perspective in the *Story of Gardening*, remarked: "It would be interesting to trace the effect of political and religious upheavals in the world's gardening." He referred specifically to the Russian collective farms, a method imposed by the political beliefs of Soviet Union, and he noted the political and religious connection to gardening in England during the Commonwealth era.

Political, social, and economic issues have also affected the planting of gardens in the United States. To a large extent, in both the nineteenth and twentieth centuries the economic and military history of the United States is also the history of gardening.

During the American Civil War, gardening came to a virtual halt in the South. Even if it had been possible to obtain seeds and fertilizer, conditions certainly did not permit gardening. During the southern Reconstruction period, however, gardens once again became a mainstay for families.

Postwar southern agriculture as an economic power was in remission, but individuals in seemingly impossible situations managed to till enough soil for a family garden. One of *Gone with the Wind*'s famous scenes shows Scarlett O'Hara standing at the back of what remains of her ravaged family home after battles had raged. She lifts a turnip, raising it to the sky, and vows never again to be hungry. The soil's promise is both physical and spiritual.

Though the backyard garden has not always been looked upon as a savior as in Scarlett O'Hara's case, it has long been a source of pleasure. Gardens have contributed to the United States' retention of pastoral quality—in part because gardens are the nation's lingering connection to its agricultural past. As America moved increasingly toward being an industrial nation, the country became more compartmentalized and consumerized.

Nevertheless, the desire to garden has remained active—even in unorthodox circumstances. For example, in a 1911 issue of *Survey*, the article "Garden Plots of the Bridge Builder" shows the recreational preference of a group of steelworkers who spent their working hours handling inanimate objects but heard the siren call and turned to gardening as a satisfying pastime.

The intrinsic value of gardens became apparent when gardening was a choice, not a necessity. Once individuals could purchase foodstuffs instead of being compelled to raise for themselves what they ate, gardening began to take on recreational characteristics. National circumstances in the twentieth century, however, sometimes moved gardening from recreation to utilitarian function. The garden's importance has often increased or decreased in relation to broader environmental circumstances.

In 1915, World War I created a need for increased food production. Defense officials turned to the public for help, asking it to plant home gardens. The gardens were given special status by labeling them "Defense Gardens." The official call for home gardens aroused a strong sense of nationalism. Adolph Kruhm, known for early-twentieth-century gardening publications, wrote in *Home Vegetable Gardening from A to Z*: "April 15, 1917 will go down as one of the most momentous days in American history quite apart from the fact that it marked our entrance into the World War. It will be remembered by gardeners throughout the land as the day when the President asked every citizen to recognize the importance of home gardening as a means to help feed the world."

President Woodrow Wilson called for 10,000 gardens each year. From 1915 until the end of the war in 1918, people responded, and publication of gardening advice greatly increased. The public became unified in support of the war effort. But at the end of the conflict, gardening once again became an individual's choice. The surge of gardening periodicals receded as gardening resumed a less urgent role.

The Great Depression, economic disaster of the 1930s, marked another trauma in the country, and again gardening became a focus. The listings in *Readers Guide to Periodical Literature* show that gardening advice increased by more than 60 percent during the depression era in an effort to encourage people to grow food. There is no record, however, of the extent to which people put the advice to use. Although many might have wanted to garden, they simply did not have the money to buy seed or fertilizer for cultivation. There is evidence, however, of elective gardening during the period. In his popular-history narrative *The Glory and the Dream*, William Manchester mentions that the Bonus Army, which marched on Washington in 1932, cultivated small garden plots during the period that they camped out in the city. Like the steelworkers in the early part of the century, these men, camped in the midst of concrete and chaos, chose to mark their waiting time in Washington by cultivating a garden. Their gardens had a larger purpose than growing food, however. Primarily, they provided recreational diversion for the Bonus Army members. They also made a political statement, indicating that the strikers were willing to wait for a response from the government for as long as it takes a garden to mature. Before the gardens came to fruition, however, the protesters were evicted from their squatters lots and removed from the city.

In 1941, another national crisis again channeled the nation's energies into food production. At the beginning of World War II, the call went out from the Roosevelt administration to utilize all possible space into what were this time called "Victory Gardens." In the introduction to Charles Nissley's 1942 *Home Vegetable Gardening*, William H. Martin offered cautionary remarks, providing insight into the emotional reaction to gardening during World War I. Martin remarked, "We should avoid the mistakes of the First World War when the home owner was urged to plow up his lawn, his flower beds, and even his tennis court to grow vegetables. In too many cases, such ventures were dismal failures from the standpoint of the production of food-stuffs." What Martin does not acknowledge, however, is the psychological benefit of such a venture. Even if a food production quota was not met during the Defense Garden period of World War I, the participating citizens considered themselves as contributors to the war effort. Between 1942 and 1945, Victory Gardens achieved the same result. Indeed, the enthusiasm and support with which the call for Victory Gardens was answered reveal the country's intense patriotism.

Periodicals carried rousing challenges to American nationalism. The article titles indicate the optimism with which gardeners approached the venture. For instance, a 1942 issue of the *Rotarian* carried an article by G. T. Donoguhe, "Put That Dirt to Work!" In a 1943 issue of the *Christian Science Monitor* E. M. Eaton's article stressed to the reader: "They Haven't Rationed Your Own Back Yard." Eaton adopted just the right tone to inspire patriotic Americans. Generating further interest in participation was D. W. Bailey's "Make Your First Line of Defense in the Back Yard" in a 1942 issue of *House Beautiful*. Through gardening, Americans could believe that they had some control over their existence, even though unpredictability enveloped most of the world. In the last year of the war, some members of the military, like the bridge builders and members of the Bonus Army before them, found sustenance for body and spirit in gardening. In a 1945 *Better Homes & Gardens* article, the title "G.I.s Garden around the World" indicates the appeal of a garden to soldiers who created small gardens when stationed behind the battle lines (Ford).

As the country went through transition after World War II, growing vegetables was left largely to commercial food producers. The building boom of the late 1940s had a momentum that pushed other activities aside. New homes did not advertise gardening space as a marketing device. Buyers readily bought available houses. The new homeowners' consuming interest was in modern, efficient home appliances available for the first time in half a decade. The postwar years of the 1940s and the 1950s reflected little interest in the pastoral aspect of living. Interest in technological advancements increased; consequently, gardening receded as a dominant activity on a national level; it did not disappear, however. Many Americans continued their enthusiasm for gardening as a family recreation.

The Korean War in the mid-1950s was not a national trauma that evoked a surge of patriotism. There was no unified national home-front effort as had been the case in World War I and World War II. Although the battles on the Korean peninsula were very grim and bloody for the participants, Americans as a whole pushed the war into the background of their lives. Most Americans continued to enjoy the prosperity of the period. Gardening, always popular, was a pleasurable end in itself, not a duty to country.

The decade of the 1960s, however, became the counterpoint to technology as a new romanticism swept the country. Once again gardening reflected the country's social and political changes. Rebelling against both American involvement in the Vietnam War and the technological emphasis of American culture, large numbers of Americans created a new value system. Much popular sentiment turned toward preservation—both of human lives and of environment. There were no Victory or Defense Gardens to mark the conflict in Southeast Asia, but there were gardens planted as a show of faith in fundamental American values. One of the social battle cries of the period was that individuals should live off the land—just as the pioneers had done.

Two distinct gardening philosophies emerged early in the 1960s: the chemical and the organic. Organic gardening became the watchword for a new generation of cultivators. Ecological concerns dominated, giving rise to many publications offering information and advice on how to grow vegetables without using insecticides and herbicides. Though technology was, on the whole, loudly denounced, technical skills did introduce two new methods of growing plants: solar power and hydroponic gardening. Both methods were embraced by the ecology-minded Americans. In this instance, technology was working to the good, providing a natural means to grow food. Three new terms—"organiculture," "biointensive gardening," and "sustainable agriculture"—denoting an antitechnology and antichemical philosophy began to appear in gardening publications. Moreover, new publications devoted to organic gardening became available.

A frontier spirit emerged as popular interest focused on self-sufficiency. Unquestionably, the country was in the midst of another romantic movement, and one of its major manifestations was a kind of spiritualism related to vegetable gardening. Indicating the mood of those who had rediscovered the soil is M. A. Roche's essay "Happiness Is a Thing Called Vegetable Gardening," printed in *Flower Grower*, but happiness could come to the novitiates only if they practiced organic gardening.

Emerging as a shaman of the new gardening religion was Robert Rodale, prolific writer who also founded the Rodale Press, Emmaus, Pennsylvania, which began publishing *Organic Gardening & Farming*, a monthly periodical that later became

Rodale's Organic Gardening. The publication addressed the efficacy of organic gardening in articles such as one by M. C. Goldman, "Organic Gardeners Grow 'Em Big!" The Rodale Press also publishes books and has been a major source of information on vegetable gardening for those adhering to the organiculture. The press' success attests to the power of this new movement in the history of vegetable gardening.

In fact, the ecological movement essentially took control of gardening in the 1960s and 1970s and remained prominent throughout the remainder of the century. The obsession with protecting the environment turned into a religious fervor to purify everything, even the digestive system. Robert Rodale's 1978 article "Holistic Gardening" in *Organic Gardening & Farming* reflects both the movement away from mainstream gardening techniques and an increased sense of mission about the practice.

Emphasis on ecological gardening gave new life to companion planting. It was promoted as a natural way to protect plants from insects. French gardeners have grown vegetables, fruit, flowers, and aromatics together since medieval gardens. According to Louisa Jones in *The Art of French Vegetable Gardening*, they have done so for both pleasure and profit. A revised version of Louise Riotte's *Carrots Love Tomatoes* points out that "mixed plantings give better control than a monoculture." She also notes that plants work well together—not only to deter insects but also to staunch plant disease.

Not all Americans are enthusiastic supporters of companion planting, even gardening specialists. Barbara Damrosch, author of *The Garden Primer*, considers alternative planting to be stronger in reputation than in fact, stating, "I don't know how many of the assertions have been proven successful." But she adds that she does "scatter plenty of onions and marigolds throughout the garden just in case." For most ecologically minded gardeners, however, the idea of companion planting is strongly held and is practiced faithfully. At the end of the 1990s, Rodale Press published another book on the subject: *Great Garden Companions: A Planting System for a Beautiful, Chemical-Free Vegetable Garden*. The book provides the most current methods for pairing vegetables (Cunningham).

A significant offshoot of gardening evangelism has been a movement by some to preserve food flavor. Increasing numbers of flavorless fresh fruits and vegetables are presented for public consumption. The mass agricultural endeavors of farms in the warm climates grow foods to ship to winter-bound states. Technological advancements in shipping have meant that fruits and vegetables once available only within a limited growing period are now available year-round. Availability, however, has not meant flavor. Instead, in many cases flavor has disappeared.

Tomatoes, for example, are for sale every month of the year—if the purchaser does not mind a taste similar to styrofoam. In *The Great American Tomato Book*, Robert Hendrickson shows that concern over the loss of tomato flavor reached the nation's legislative body. He cites an example of Representative James A. Burke of Massachusetts, who demonstrated the intractability of what he describes as one of the "rocklike store-bought spheres." In an Agriculture Subcommittee hearing, Representative Burke—in support of his assertion that such objects do not deserve to be called tomatoes—dropped a "shipped tomato" on a table and watched it bounce off. The fall did not even break the tomato's skin. Shipped tomatoes, like many other fruits and vegetables, are now grown for stability in transportation, not for flavor. Strawberries also are now available throughout the year. They travel well, and they are a magnificent size, but in taste they resemble apples more than strawberries. Though green onions can now be had the year-round, the consumer often bites into a hollow stalk, virtually devoid of the onion's once-familiar pungent taste.

More and more growers have turned to vegetable and fruit seeds that not only hold up through distance shipping but also boast a long shelf life in the grocery. Foodstuffs have become more important for longevity than for flavor. Drawing public attention to vegetable barbarism has been a beneficial side effect of popular interest in ecology. By taking note of a serious loss of flavor in foods, the ecology-minded alerted the general population to the gradual extinction of many seeds that produce succulent fruits and vegetables. The seeds for many such plants are in some cases lost forever. To prevent further loss, interested people formed organizations to collect and preserve what is now known as "heirloom vegetables." Even the business community recognized the movement. For example, S. D. Atchison wrote an essay for *Business Week* entitled "Growing Food with That Ol' Time Flavor." Eliot Tozer's article in *Modern Maturity*, "Heirloom Seeds: The New Collectibles," reached the Americans who knew firsthand how vegetables once tasted. He hoped that these individuals might be able to provide badly needed help in saving seeds of heirloom plants. Many older Americans who have gardened all their lives, particularly residents in rural areas, continue to save seeds from the slowly disappearing plants.

Flavor in food is somewhat subjective, but there is general agreement regarding the flavor distinction in tomatoes grown in one's garden and tomatoes shipped to groceries in winter months. Vanishing flavor in tomatoes—and in many other fruits and vegetables—is a warning of something ominous happening. The seeds of fruits and vegetables long valued for their flavor and their quality are becoming extinct. Once they are gone, they will not be recoverable. Precious seeds often vanish because of human carelessness in storing and in planting. For example, a flavorful bean known as the blue ribbon has virtually disappeared. The seeds have become intermixed with other bean seeds and have lost their distinctness.

Sometimes seeds disappear through the deaths of those who were keepers and users of the seeds. Surviving family members often fail to understand the importance of keeping the seeds. With the loss of these historically significant seeds, we lose something that can never be replaced. Historic preservation, which has become important in American culture, means more than restoration of historic buildings. Preserving heirloom seeds is also a part of our heritage.

Seeds are such small, seemingly insignificant objects that their historical connections are often overlooked, but, in reality, seeds are the earliest evidence of the beginning of cultivation culture, that is, agriculture. According to Kent Whealey, executive director of the Seed Savers Exchange, "The seeds planted each year by gardeners and farmers are living links in an unbroken chain reaching back into antiquity." He adds, "We cannot possibly comprehend the magnitude of the history contained in these seeds in terms of what has gone before and what may potentially come after our brief involvement." The Seed Savers Exchange, established by Kent and Diane Whealey in 1975, is making a contribution of inestimable value to gardening and to posterity.

Diane Whealey's grandfather annually planted seeds long kept by his family.

Lithograph of Johnny Appleseed (John Chapman). Courtesy of the Library of Congress

Indeed, his parents had brought the seeds from Bavaria when they immigrated to northeast Iowa in the 1800s. At the time of the elderly man's death, Kent and Diane realized that they must assume the responsibility of saving the family seed collections. The fact that her grandfather had planted seeds that had been preserved for a century aroused Diane and Kent's respect for seed preservation. They began seeking information, and they also contacted other families in the area to learn whether they, too, had kept seeds for planting over an extended period. In the course of his research, Whealey discovered theories of prominent geneticists—Jack Harlan, Garrison Wilkes, and Erna Bennett. These botanists warned of dangers inherent in allowing long-preserved seeds to disappear. They referred to the very real "catastrophic potential of genetic erosion." The scientists also warned of the potential for "increasing epidemics and infestations if the breeding material for food crops of the future continues to die out at such a rapid and alarming rate" (Whealey).

Alerted to such possible dangers, the Whealeys set about protecting seeds that were in danger of disappearing forever. Many such heirloom seeds came to the United States with the surge of immigrants in the nineteenth century. The Whealeys discovered that most of the descendants of those families had carefully preserved the seeds of their ancestors and continued to plant them annually. There are particular areas of the country in which families had often saved seeds for more than a century. The most likely families to have preserved seeds have farms in the relative isolation of the Ozarks, the Smoky Mountains, and the Appalachian Mountains. The same is true of insular families such as the Mennonites, the Amish, and the Native Americans. These peoples have kept seeds for generations.

Even though there were seeds in existence, there was no central system to catalog the collections. Often only the families themselves knew of the seeds. The Whealeys began to systemize seed saving. In 1986, they established a 170-acre Heritage Farm, where permanent collections of the seeds are preserved. Much like a museum, the farm has samples available for people to examine. The Seed Savers Exchange publishes an annual catalog of all the seeds available through the exchange. When the network began in 1975, according to Whealey, "[I]t consisted of twenty-nine members offering a few dozen varieties through a six page newsletter. Now," he added, "there are 1,000 'listed members' offering nearly 12,000 rare varieties through the current four hundred page Seed Savers Yearbook, sent to 8,000 gardeners." Whealey reports, "Each summer 3,000 visitors tour nine large Preservation Gardens and the Historic Orchard." In 1992, Seed Savers Exchange (SSE) organized Seed Savers International to preserve seeds from farms and families in rapidly changing Eastern Europe.

A factor in the United States that almost guarantees the vanishing of heirloom seeds is the rapid disappearance of family farms. Economic conditions cause the children of farmers to seek their livelihood elsewhere. Once the third or fourth generations leave the land, the heirloom seeds are lost—usually forever. Corporations—factory farms that often buy the old family farms—have no interest in saving seeds for the sake of the flavor. They are concerned with seeds that grow vegetables for high volume results and for shipping stamina.

The matter of disappearing seeds is of much broader significance than just to the family farmer. It affects the food supply of everyone. Sue Stickland's *Heirloom Vegetables: A Home Gardener's Guide to Finding and Growing Vegetables from the Past*, with superior photographs by David Cavagnaro, offers a wealth of information for persons interested in heirloom vegetables. The book also includes a list of seed suppliers. Popular interest in heirloom vegetables greatly increased during the last decades of the twentieth century. The number of subscribers to the Seed Savers Exchange newsletter and the volume of visitors to the Heritage Farm indicate the popularity of seed preservation.

American emphasis on a healthy lifestyle since the 1980s has been a significant factor in stimulating and maintaining an interest in gardening. To have ready access to fresh vegetables rich in nutrition, people plant their own gardens. Herb gardens have also gained wider popularity as a contributor to flavorful and healthy meals. Herbs, one of the constants in growing foodstuffs, appeared in the earliest forms of humankind's gardens. For centuries, much of the preparation of edible foods depended on herbs. Because most meat consumed was wild game, herbs helped overcome the strong flavor. Herb specialist Lesley Bremness states, "The use of herbs in cooking features as far back as the first century cookbook written by the Roman epicure, Apicius."

During the last quarter of the twentieth century, a U.S. obsession with cooking foods untainted by fats and sodium made herbs again a valued ingredient. Herbs effectively season both meats and vegetables, providing flavor and eliminating the need for salt or other potentially unhealthy seasonings.

In addition to using herbs for seasoning foods, certain cultures have made herbs intrinsic to medicines, while others have incorporated herbs into religious ceremonies. The Middle East, Asia, and Europe grew herbs for multiple purposes. The author of *Herbs* writes, "Many of the earliest writings are about herbs, which were important in ceremony, magic, and medicine. Babylonian clay tablets from 3000 B.C. illustrate medical treatments." The tablets also record the Babylonians' having imported herbs from other countries. Bremness discusses other historical cultures, stating, "Egyptian writings dating from 1550 B.C. contain medical prescriptions and notes on the aromatic and cosmetic uses of herbs."

At the end of the twentieth century, as nontraditional medical treatments gained in popularity, much of the American culture embraced herbs for their healing factors. Botanicals that were not grown in a traditional herb garden became greatly valued for medicinal properties. An index of their popularity is the degree of scorn that they received from pharmaceutical and health specialists. *New York Times* health and science writer Jane Brody stated that at the end of the 1990s, some 70 million Americans used various types of botanical treatments. Skeptical of the highly touted herbals, Brody observed wryly, "Whatever it is you may seek—a memory boost, weight loss, stress relief, immune enhancement, mood elevation, sexual stimulation or therapy for your ailing heart, there is a herb being sold as the 'natural drug-free' answer to your prayers."

Botanicals for medicinal purposes have long been used in other countries. They reached a phenomenal height in the United States during the last decade of the twentieth century. According to a survey in *Consumer Reports*, in 1997 Americans spent an estimated $12 billion for nontraditional medicines, including herbs, vitamins, and minerals. Sales of such products increased almost 30 percent between 1995 and 1997 ("Herbal"). People increasingly turned to "physiomedicalists," who united botany and medicine (Bremness).

Of the literally thousands of herbal medicines, one of the most revered is the root of the ginseng plant as an alleged source of energy. Another major seller, ginkgo biloba, from the ginkgo tree, supposedly sharpens memory and alertness by stimulating blood circulation in the brain. Also dominant in sales, echinacea, from the cone flower, is reputed to immunize and promote general well-being during the cold and flu season. Another significant seller has been Saint-John's-wort. A plant long familiar to Europeans, it allegedly alleviates depression. Most botanical users consider herbs healthier than refined pharmaceuticals. Few pharmacists and physicians agree. Larry Sasich, a pharmacist and an analyst at the Public Citizen Health Research Group, stated, "This stuff has become the snake oil of the 1990s." Sasich expresses a commonly held opinion of many physicians and pharmacists ("Herbal").

A newcomer in the healing pantheon has had minimal attention among the general public. By the end of the twentieth century, however, vegetables as healers gained status. Traditional table edibles have not been widely considered to have medicinal properties. Medical herbalists, however, have identified healing elements possible in commonplace vegetables. In 1998, Anne McIntyre, the former director of the National Institute of Medical Herbalists, published *The Good Health Garden: Growing and Using Healing Foods*. McIntyre refers to the vegetable garden as a "healing garden." *The Good Health Garden* provides directions for preparing specific remedies. Included is a graphic treatment chart to direct users to appropriate vegetables for particular ailments. As a sample, one of McIntyre's remedies is a "decoction of potato peelings," which reduces high blood pressure. First in preparation is to "boil the potato skins." In the liquid, one must put "raw potato juice from three or four organic potatoes." Next, "add honey, carrot, and lemon juice to taste," and, of course, consume the mixture. According to McIntyre, the decoction will also help "both stomach ulcers and arthritis." Many health-conscious individuals turned to the alternative healing methods and grew gardens for a medical supplement as well as a source of food.

Many gardeners believe that gardens provide healing for the psyche as well as the body. In fact, the idea of psychic healing has historically been associated with gardening. In *1,001 Old-Time Garden Tips*, Roger Yepsen mentions that gardeners have long used their "green spaces" as a means to counteract stress. He remarks, "Gardening magazines of the late 1800s ran statistics to show that only ministers had longer average life spans" than gardeners. He added, "These [statistics] confirmed the centuries-old belief that plants have special powers to relieve ills of the body and mind. It wasn't even necessary to make a tea or special potion to enjoy this cure; you could simply wear a garland of an aromatic plant, or lie down in the garden and inhale" (Yepsen).

A number of authors have promoted the therapeutic dimensions of gardening. In *Modern Home Gardening*, authors Clyde Calvin and Donald Knutson note, "Gardeners universally find pleasure in working with the soil and plants and this involvement with nature reduces pressures and tensions." Other researchers make a direct connection. An issue of *Science Digest* features an article entitled "Hortitherapy," uniting therapy and botany. *Parks and Conservation*, a pamphlet of the U.S. Parks System, includes an article on "Man's Psychic Need for Nature" (Stainbrooke). In *Organic Gardening & Farming* writer John Wellencamp recommends: "Just Plough Your Problems into the Garden."

John Heinerman, medical anthropologist, has worked with folk healers as well as traditional physicians and scientists to identify psychic healing powers of plants. In a revised expanded version of *Heinerman's New Encyclopedia of Fruits and Vegetables*, Heinerman contends, "Potatoes should figure frequently in the diets of those who may be experiencing mental and emotional instabilities of some sort as a reasonable precaution against potential suicide." Heinerman makes clear that serotonin, derived from the potatoes, causes the difference. He remarks, "Once a particular amino acid reaches the area of the brain, sufficient serotonin can be produced, which helps to lower depression and anxiety somewhat."

Heinerman contends that corn and wheat also contribute to psychological healing, noting that the aroma of freshly baked bread has a therapeutic effect. He cites as evidence a case at the Utah State Hospital in Provo concerning a woman in deep depression. After being assigned to assist the baker in the hospital kitchen, the patient's mental and emotional state began to improve. When her therapists asked about the improvement, she told them that the aroma of the freshly baked loaves exhilarated her.

A sampling of other book and periodical selections indicates the extent to which gardening has been considered emotionally and mentally beneficial. In "Gardening Is Good for Your Mental Health," an article in *Flower and Garden*, author Donna

Bickley suggests that the quiet setting of a garden provides an opportunity for one to restore oneself. She adds that gardening also satisfies a need to achieve tangible results from labor invested, that is, a sense of accomplishment. A collection edited by Diane Relf entitled *The Role of Horticulture in Human Well Being and Social Development* advances a concept that gardening contributes to social interaction as well as to physical and emotional strengths.

Green Prints, a quarterly journal, joins in the discourse on gardening's abstract benefits. *Green Prints* was first published in 1990 by Pat Stone, who also serves as editor. Rather than being a "how-to" gardening periodical, it reflects on the deeper meaning of gardens and explores the source of their allure. Pat Stone looks at the soul of gardening. Stone has characterized the journal as a publication that provides humorous accounts of gardeners' experiences—both successful and sterile—in reaching a truce with plants. The journal is compatible with discussions of gardening and the human psyche.

Although not promoted as being a national therapeutic, gardening has always increased in the United States at times of national tension. During the high inflation of the late 1970s, many people began to cultivate gardens. They did not indicate that they turned to gardening as a means of therapy, but the gardening perhaps had psychological as well as economic benefits. Their concrete reason for gardening during the period was the exorbitant prices of food. In addition to inspiring individual backyard gardens, high inflation caused community gardening to markedly increase. This upsurge in community gardening brought about the formal founding of the National Gardening Association, a nonprofit, member-supported organization that established offices in Burlington, Vermont. The association also publishes a gardening journal.

Initially, the association focused on helping villages and cities organize and operate community gardens. Its bimonthly periodical, *Gardens for All*, began in 1972, when the organization was founded, but in 1978 it changed into *National Gardening*. The journal identifies itself as a source of general advice for "food and flower gardening enthusiasts." It also specifies that it is a "non-profit education and information organization that promotes the benefits of gardening." The periodical gives information useful to gardeners throughout the United States. It has a wide circulation.

One of National Gardening Association's expanded services has been to provide classroom materials. The editors publish the *Growing Ideas Newsletter* to promote combined ecology and gardening. They also publish *GrowLab* and *Growing Science Inquiry*. The association makes funds available for young people's garden projects through Youth Garden Grants. The value of arousing youngsters' interest in gardening is strategic to a gardening community for the future.

The adult gardening population has recognized a need to interest young people in gardening. There is a variety of juvenile and adolescent gardening books on the market designed to create excitement about planting and growing. The following titles reflect the tone that the authors and publishers adopt as a means to generate enthusiasm among juveniles: *Ready, Set, Grow!: A Kid's Guide to Gardening*, by Rebecca Hershey (1995); *Plant a Garden in Your Sneakers!: Fun and Outrageous Planting Projects for All Seasons* by Diane L. Burns and Jill Burns (1998); *My First Garden Book*, provided by N. K. Lawn and Garden Company, Chattanooga (1991); *Little Green Thumbs* by Mary Van Hage, Bettina Paterson, and Lucy

Tizard (1996); *Let's Get Growing: Twenty-Five Quick and Easy Gardening Projects for Kids* by Joel Rapp (1992); *Let's Go Gardening: A Young Person's Guide to the Garden* by Ursula Kruger (1996); and *Dinner from Dirt: Ten Meals Kids Can Grow and Cook* by Emily Scott and Catherine Duffy (1998). These titles are only a few of those available.

At one time gardening books were written primarily about gardening in the North and the East. The information was based upon soil texture, climate, and spring and fall freeze dates of that area. The advice was largely ineffectual in other regions of the country. In the past two decades, more emphasis has been placed on regional growing needs in both books and periodicals. *Pacific Horticulture*, for example, deals with gardening in the special climate of the Pacific Northwest. A state such as Texas, however, is so diverse in soil type and climate that periodicals and books often focus on Texas alone. The bimonthly *Texas Gardener: The Magazine for Texas Gardeners by Texas Gardeners* gives information for gardening in both coastal and arid sections of the state. *Commonsense Vegetable Gardening for the South* by William D. Adams and Thomas LeRoy is an effective book for the Southeast. Its most insightful characteristic is addressing the wide diversity of the South instead of viewing it as a monolith. The book marks distinctions in pests and diseases, the multiple soil types, and the differing freeze dates in the region. There are considerable differences between the mid-South, the Deep South, and the varied regions of the Florida peninsula. Of great help to gardeners is the conversion chart, showing how to convert the amounts listed for large areas to the appropriate measurement for small gardeners. The chart makes clear how to convert tons per acre to pounds per 100 square feet. *Commonsense* also provides a glossary for gardeners who might be unfamiliar with particular terms. The book has a first-rate appendix listing additional sources of information such as the State Horticulture Extension Service Offices.

Desert terrain requires very specialized cultivation practices. A book devoted to desert gardening is *Plants for Dry Climates: How to Select, Grow, and Enjoy* by Mary Duffield (1998). Periodical articles such as "Desert Gardening" in *Flower and Garden* discuss gardening in the dry areas around Phoenix, Arizona, and other environmentally unfriendly regions of the Southwest (Cook 65). High desert cultivation differs from that in the low desert. Julie Weinberg's *Growing Food in the High Desert* offers useful information, as does *Rocky Mountain Gardener*, a quarterly journal published in Gunnison, Colorado. *National Gardening* is consistently a dependable source for specialized information. *Sunset Magazine* publishes regional editions, including one for the Central West in which "How Three Bountiful Colorado Gardens Solved Mountain Problems" appeared. The essay explains how food production can thrive in a fundamentally hostile environment.

Bookstore shelves have an abundance of gardening books and gardening periodicals. With their eye-pleasing color photographs, many of these books make growing and harvesting vegetables an irresistible endeavor. There are also many how-to books for persons desiring instructions in gardening. In the last decades of the twentieth century, however, written material had competition. Television programming, videocassette recorders, and the Internet became pervasive in dispersing gardening information.

The communications industry entered the gardening milieu through various routes. Network television's morning news and information programs—*Today*,

Good Morning America, and *CBS This Morning*—have featured gardening specialists to discuss planting and growing methods for both edibles and ornamentals. Since networks respond to public interest, producers would have quickly dropped the segment if audience response had not been strong.

For two decades PBS has broadcast the popular *The Victory Garden*, one of the first gardening shows. Not the least of popular gardening influences has been Martha Stewart, a woman who appeared out of the mists of her garden in Connecticut to permeate television. In addition to her syndicated television program, *Martha Stewart*, for several years she had a segment on NBC's *Today Show*. Later she became a feature on *CBS This Morning*. At the same time, her syndicated program is broadcast on stations throughout the country. She covers decorating and cooking as well as gardening. Her thirty-minute broadcast generates considerable response from viewers. Florists and nursery employees report that after a weekly broadcast, optimistic customers come to retail shops to buy plants and other materials in an attempt to duplicate Martha's creations.

Indicative of the program's popularity, Martha Stewart's broadcast has had imitators. *Better Homes and Gardens* has produced a syndicated weekly show modeled after Martha Stewart's production. *B. Smith with Style* is another similar home and garden show in syndication. Indeed, B. Smith has referred to herself as "the black Martha Stewart." Most local news and information programs feature short gardening segments, particularly during the growing season. But the greatest media example of gardening's popularity has been the Home & Garden Television network.

On December 30, 1994, HGTV, the Home & Garden Television network, began its cable broadcast with 70 percent original programming. The network, owned by E.W. Scripps Company, operated through its subsidiary Scripps Howard Broadcasting Company. HGTV soon became a major part of the growing communications industry, offering twenty-four-hour programming, seven days a week. HGTV was the first network to devote twenty-four hours a day to home and gardening topics. Its launch audience was 6.5 million households ("Home").

HGTV programs offer information in four primary areas: how to remodel homes, how to decorate homes, how to grow gardens, and how to do home-repair jobs. The network's stated goal is "to give people the ideas to make the most of their life at home." The network describes itself as being "designed to appeal to all ages and lifestyles." In reality, the network comes close to doing exactly that (Thomas).

To television analysts, a network devoted entirely to what they viewed as a limited topic seemed a hazardous undertaking. The founders of the network, however, were confident that their investment was creatively and economically well placed. Within a short period, they proved themselves correct. The number of cable companies adding the network to its lineup and the number of individual viewers increased steadily.

Six months after the channel began broadcasting, a newspaper writer assigned the network's immediate popularity a rational justification. She wrote, "Baby boomers are now into gardening, joining green-thumbers of all ages who have made gardening America's favorite pastime, spending twenty-two billion [dollars] annually on the hobby." The reporter was tardy in coming to that awareness.

HGTV's founders and investors had those statistics firmly in hand when they laid the groundwork for such a network (Mullen).

The network's original objective was to reach a niche audience, but the audience turned out to be much broader than planners expected (Thomas). Within a year, the cable channel realized the diversity of its audience. Indeed, in audience surveys the network discovered that it had many male viewers. They had expected primarily a female audience (Mullen).

A reporter commenting on the home and garden network's phenomenal success remarked, "The new Home and Garden Television network [is] intent on becoming the MTV of the boomer generation." In 1996, little more than a year after its initial broadcast, the network reached 14 million households in the United States. Joe Ruggiero, host of two shows on HGTV, said, "It's addictive, much as MTV was for music enthusiasts." Like the reporter, Ruggiero draws a parallel to MTV (Mullen).

By 1997, Home & Garden's subscriber base had increased to 22 million homes, almost one out of three cable homes, more than a triple increase in viewers. These statistics indicate the popularity of home and garden topics. One concrete measurement of a channel's popularity is the advertising. Merchandisers are eager to advertise only if there is a large audience. According to the network information, since its first broadcast, HGTV's list of national advertisers has grown from 40 to nearly 700.

Despite the surveys, which showed a high level of viewers, HGTV wanted its own validation of audience depth. To that end, the network chose an in-house method to measure viewer numbers. Ken Lowe, HGTV founder, president, and chief executive officer (CEO), remarked, "One recent Saturday morning [in 1997], the network aired its first viewer call-in show. We purposely didn't promote it at all. HGTV experts took questions on everything, including gardening, interior decorating and rebuilding. The response was ten thousand calls in two hours" (Mullen).

Concurrently, HGTV broadcast its Internet address for the first time. The network's file server jammed with 50,000 E-mail queries from forty-seven states. The network had its proof (Mansfield). One viewer's simple criterion for evaluating the channel offers insight into the network's success. The viewer explained, "They'll tell you . . . how deep to plant a tomato" (Stefansky). The HGTV network exists as testimony to the popular interest in gardening and varied home topics.

As VCR usage worked its way throughout the culture, gardening videos began to appear on the market. The British Broadcasting Corporation in conjunction with Turner Broadcasting System (Atlanta) released six videocassettes, David Attenborough's *The Private Life of Plants: A Natural History of Plant Behavior*. Each videocassette is fifty minutes in length. The titles are (1) *Branching Out*, (2) *Putting Down Roots*, (3) *The Birds and the Bees*, (4) *Plant Politics*, (5) *Living Together*, and (6) *It's a Jungle Out There*. Persons familiar with Attenborough's style from PBS programming can anticipate the tone of the videos.

Other more practical how-to videotapes were marketed. *Gardening by Video* became available, offering advice on design and growing techniques for both vegetables and ornamentals. Also covered through the videos were methods of planting and growing particular plants along with information on controlling insects. A list of video catalogs is included (Otis).

The Victory Garden Vegetable Video, featuring information from PBS' "Victory Garden" broadcast, is available. The one-hour color video explains thirty-one projects. Garden Way Publishing sells a set of audiotapes, step-by-step cassettes, packaged with printed material for review. Titles include such challenges as *Grow the Best Tomatoes* and *Grow 15 Herbs for the Kitchen*. Garden master Dave Schaefer narrates the thirty-minute tapes. Other tapes and videos are available through catalogs and bookstores and on the Internet.

Of greater significance to gardening, however, is the increasing use of computers. A variety of publications began promoting computer use in the mid-1980s. The February 1984 issue of *Mechanics Illustrated* features an article by Barris Benn entitled "Use a Computer Service to Increase Your Garden Harvest." Clyde Faris published "Gardening by Computer" in a 1986 *Saturday Evening Post* issue.

The Internet has brought gardeners a treasury of sources and has created a sea change in gardening research—both scholarly and practical. Bob Boufford, gardening expert and computer authority, commented, "The Internet has forever changed the 'landscape' of gardening information. A gardener is no longer limited to the local library, a few gardening magazines, and the monthly garden club meeting for new tips." He points out that a "vast dynamic body of information is just a few mouse clicks away."

By the end of the decade, many writers and researchers connected computers and gardeners. One of the most effective books is Bob Boufford's *The Gardener's Computer Companion*. Published in paperback, the book has a CD-ROM fastened in its binding for the purchaser's further edification.

Boufford clarifies how a computer is compatible with a garden. He takes a potential computer buyer through specific steps in what to look for in a computer and how to buy one. Then he explains the computer's assets and includes information about the Internet. One of the advantages that the author lists is that through the Internet, a person can see the diagram of plants and gardens as well as images of, in his words, "gardens in all their splendor." One chapter is devoted to ways to develop a garden with software, describing how to organize information in what he calls a "garden data tool shed." Boufford's sense of humor makes routine material interesting.

The Gardener's Computer Companion encourages the gardener to take the computer to the garden. The author advises the gardener to "take or refer to notes as you check out your garden, to keep track of the watering, or to take notes as you visit other gardens." He suggests that a gardener can even use a portable computer to keep an eye on the garden without having to go outside. He exclaims, "Imagine watching your home garden grow while you work at your desk."

Boufford includes an extensive directory listing names and addresses of companies and products mentioned in the book. He also provides a list of Internet Web sites. This book is invaluable for serious gardeners who understand the advantages of the Internet, and it will encourage computer-shy gardeners to be more innovative. Even a dilettante gardener who can use a computer will enjoy the Boufford book.

The Internet provides specific sources for traditional gardeners, and it also provides gardening information targeted for differing lifestyles. For example, individuals looking for a peaceful environment can find information in *Land*, an Oregon periodical that states that it is for "folks wanting to live at a slower pace in harmony with the earth and Mother Nature."

Serving as a kind of marriage broker, the Internet lists an organization called Singles in Agriculture, boasting 1,200 members. The national organization began in 1984 in Pearl City, Illinois, and provides "opportunities for friendship between unmarried rural people." Since the organization's beginning, there have been 300 marriages of people who met through the group. The Internet explains how to join the group and how to receive a newsletter.

Individuals with alternative lifestyles are also provided for, as the following titles indicate: *Gardening Variety Dykes: Lesbian Traditions in Gardening* (1994). There is information for people who defy regulations to grow plants of their choice: *How to Grow the Finest Marijuana Indoors under Lights*. For people who are elderly and handicapped, the Internet gives sources to enlighten one on possibilities for gardening no matter the handicap: *The Able Gardener, Overcoming Barriers of Age and Physical Limitations*. Gardeners with special religious commitments can consult *Plants of the Bible and How to Grow Them*, or *Planting a Bible Garden*. For ethnic specialties, the Internet lists The *Mexican Kitchen Garden* (1998). These titles are only a sampling. The brief list can be supplemented from the *Agricultural Index*.

Though modern techniques have dominated gardening research, not everybody uses the Internet. There is still an abundance of reading material directed at a specific audience. According to *Publishers Weekly*, baby boomers are the engine moving gardening book sales. There is an increase in nontraditional gardening books, rather than the familiar "how-to" books. New books are more philosophical, exploring humankind's link to nature. The primary readers are the proverbial baby boomers, and they have been conditioned to assume responsibility for protection of the environment. The country was still in the "age of ecology" at the end of the century. In 1998, however, resistance to the ecological movement emerged.

When philosophical movements become dominant, a countermovement is inevitable. The biointensive, organic, ecological theme in gardening philosophy has held sway for a quarter of a century. In the "age of ecology," most publications emphasize the importance of treating all elements of the environment with care. Although there has always been some resistance to environmentalists' efforts, ecology as a theme has dominated books and periodicals. One of the strongest statements against nature's right to be unrestricted is Cooper Rutledge's book *Backyard Battle Plan*. Rutledge objects to what have become "politically correct" environmental attitudes.

Of major concern to him is the unchecked animal population, allowed to multiply in the misplaced belief that destroying part of the population is an assault on nature. He is dismayed at the romanticizing of wild animals, turning them into gentle characters of fiction, perhaps a movement that began innocently with Bambi and has been perpetuated by the Disney organization and by marketing techniques. As Rutledge sees it, these attitudes bring problems, one of which is the inevitable destruction of backyard gardens as animal populations grow uncontrolled.

Rutledge wants to return to the more certain chemical methods of ridding gardens of pests, both animal and insect. He contends that a green garden is an invitation to lunch to wild animals. He believes that to garden, "One needs a backyard battle plan." During the years of ecological emphasis, Mother Nature took on the image of a benign, positive presence. Rutledge asserts that this personification is wrong, stating, "Mother Nature is a cruel, non religious, non thinking force. She has no compassion, no pity, no love. Things sprout and grow, decay and die. In natural systems, birth and death are as one."

Cooper Rutledge's intention to change attitudes about the efficacy of uncontrolled environmentalism does not come either from a fanatical antiecology group or from a developer who wants to cut the forests and cover the meadows with asphalt. Rutledge is a landscape and forestry professional who is known as a conservationist. He has a number of publications on gardening, conservation, and ecology. His is a voice from within the original ecology movement and is therefore more influential. Rutledge's *Backyard Battle Plan* is a fireball in the night for extreme environmentalists.

Philosophical movements come and go. Experimental methods of gardening gain popularity and then recede in favor. Gardening authorities expound on the multiple benefits of cultivation. Yet, it is not possible to dislodge beliefs about planting that have been held for centuries.

The old *Farmer's Almanac* telling people how to plant with the moon and the stars is still quite popular. Despite advanced scientific explanations of correct planting methods, many people continue to rely on the zodiac. Continued interest in astrological signs inspired a revision of Louise Riotte's *Astrological Gardening*. Riotte provides information on ancient wisdom of successful planting and harvesting by stars and moon. For many persons, there is still something mystical about planting. There is for them a connection between all of nature's elements. It is the age-old link between the ancients and moderns. High technology is not an absolute. Humankind is joined to the universe through a mystery not explainable by science and high technology. Direct contact with the soil and with the elements reaffirms that connection. Gardening is the transmitter.

REFERENCE WORKS

There is minimal bibliographic work available on vegetable gardening. The most thorough index is *Garden Literature: An Index to Periodical Articles and Book Reviews*, edited by Sally Williams. An annual bibliography, *Garden Literature* indexes over 100 journals, newsletters, newspapers, and annuals of interest to gardeners. It covers garden designers, growers and retailers, historians, horticulturists, landscape architects, and preservation. The index also includes book reviews about gardening, horticulture, garden design and history, landscape design and maintenance, and plants. Information is listed through both author and subject index to periodicals.

Garden Literature began publication in 1992 with the following introduction: "The Index includes, on a selective basis, both feature articles and articles in regularly published columns and departments. It includes calendars of events, society membership announcements, letters from readers, and news of an ephemeral nature found in such departments which are not generally indexed" (Williams).

Each entry includes in brackets a description of the article's content beyond what a researcher can infer from the title and the subtitle. The concise annotations provide focus, as the following entry reflects: "RABBITS—relatives of Flopsy, Mopsy, and Cottontail [rabbit evolution]."

The index is comprehensive. Its thoroughness is both an asset and a detriment. There is a vast amount of material in each volume. Using it requires patience and persistence to scan the magnitude of listings for vegetable gardening entries. Nevertheless, the index is invaluable to research in gardening. The enthusiastic response of users is reflected in the following letter to the editor: "I love your index. I even read it in bed, like a novel."

Another bibliography, *The Gardener's Index: Where to Find Information about Gardens and Garden Plants* by Beth Clewis, began publication in 1993 but ceased in 1997. It, too, is a comprehensive index, arranged alphabetically by botanical name with cross-references by common names. The index was unsuccessful because it was too sophisticated for general readers; that is, its listings of scholarly sources are familiar to specialists in gardening but unfamiliar to the generalist who needs adequate identifying information. An anonymous reviewer referred to the index as "well-intentioned but misguided."

The Internet provides indexes such as *Agriculture Literature* and *Gardening Magazines*. Both indexes provide a varied list of sources not restricted to vegetables. Gardening.com (http://gardening.sierrahome.com/) also gives a useful list of sources. Other listings are available.

Most gardening books, particularly the gardening manuals and other how-to books, include bibliographies, but the quality is uneven. Some authors provide carefully detailed information, while others give nothing more than titles and prices of available books and periodicals. The annotated bibliography, *Gardening: A Guide to the Literature*, compiled by Richard T. Isaacson, is helpful. It is not as complete as a researcher might wish, but it is a generally helpful source that a researcher should consult. Author Richard Isaacson states in his introduction that the bibliography is not comprehensive, and he gives a rationale for what he includes and excludes from the index. The book is arranged well, and the annotations are helpful.

The Isaacson book's major drawback for the person interested specifically in vegetable gardening is that the book also includes information on landscape design and ornamental gardening plants—a handicap for the researcher. Isaacson provides a useful list of general gardening periodicals as well as information on libraries that have gardening interests and collections. This book is a major source for work on gardening.

A traditional index, the H. W. Wilson Company's *Readers Guide to Periodical Literature* is unwieldy but useful as a source for gardening articles. The more specialized and technical Wilson index, *The Biological and Agricultural Index*, is equally cumbersome, but another important source for periodical articles. Like the *Readers Guide*, the index leads one to have higher expectations than the located article necessarily provides. Moreover, because this index covers large commercial planting as well as home gardening, the researcher needs to look extra carefully at the titles to avoid fruitless searches. A particular asset is that the index covers articles from some gardening periodicals not available in other sources.

A seemingly unlikely source is *Home Gardening in International Development: What the Literature Shows*. The index was published in 1985 by the League for International Food Education under a grant from the U.S. Agency for International Development. It is designed primarily to give information on gardening projects internationally—many of which receive economic assistance form the United States. There is superfluous material on Asia and Europe, but the annotated bibliography and the inventories of international organizations involved in home gardening include information on U.S. publications and agencies. The book is somewhat confusing in its format, but the extensive appendix rewards a patient researcher.

The Brooklyn Botanic Garden Record, published quarterly, provides a helpful list of recent books, magazines, and articles as well as state experimental station bulletins. The list is selective, but it is annotated.

Richard Nichols' book *Plant Doctor in His Vegetable Garden*, published in 1976, has a useful annotated bibliography. His commentary in the annotation is to the point and gives the researcher a good sense of the quality of the publications. A *Bibliography of Garden Books*, prepared by Richardson Wright in 1943 is, of course, dated. Since some things in gardening never change, however, many of the books listed are useful within restricted needs. Also dated is Paul F. Frese's *100 Best Books for the Gardener's Library*, first published in 1948 and revised in 1952. The provided list is beneficial in research on gardening techniques at the middle of the century.

Gardening encyclopedias, annuals, and handbooks tend to present information in similar ways. Most of them give details about times to plant particular vegetables, identify and illustrate plants, suggest ways to deal with weeds and insects, and recommend gardening tools. They distinguish themselves in part by the quality of illustration as well as by the thoroughness of content. Gardening dictionaries also are similar in naming and defining techniques and in describing plants.

One of the best sources available for the serious researcher is the work by Liberty H. Bailey, a name familiar to most gardening authorities and many generalists. The most current and complete reference to cultivated plants is Bailey's *Hortus Third: A Concise Dictionary of Plants Cultivated in the United States and Canada*. This book is considered the authority on gardening plants by people in diverse fields of study. The plants are arranged alphabetically by genus, including the complete family of the plant, the authorities in the field of study, and botanical terms. This book is thorough, scholarly, and reliable.

The *Vegetable Gardening Encyclopedia* by the editors of *Consumer Guide* is also a first-rate source. The work is exactly what one has come to expect from the Consumer Guide organization, a balanced and fair report. The book is written in simple, easy-to-read language that at the same time does not demean the reader's intelligence. The graphs and charts are easy to comprehend; the illustrations, all in black and white, are clear and useful. Specific calendar information on when the first frost and the last frost can be expected in regions of the United States helps both planters and researchers. Garden pests are identified with illustrations in addition to explanations of their favorite plant food and of the best ways to destroy these insects.

The *Vegetable Gardening Encyclopedia* identifies beneficial insects so that the gardener will not eradicate insect helpers. At the same time, there are suggestions on how to destroy plant-eating insects. Along with recipes at the end of the book, there are canning guides. Additionally, the editors provide a list of state cooper-

Hydroponic lettuce production. © Painet

ative extension service offices. There is practical information on a variety of topics, making the book useful for research. This book gives the researcher a view of the complete cycle of gardening from preparation of ground through preservation of foods for the table.

Time-Life's *The Time-Life Encyclopedia of Gardening* is a multivolume series, with each volume on a different gardening topic, prepared by different editors. The *Vegetables and Fruits* volume is edited by James Underwood Crockett. As is common with Time-Life publications, the books are well illustrated with photographs, graphs, and drawings. Because the books are aimed at a general audience, they are more helpful for beginning gardeners than for research. Another multivolume work, Thomas H. Everett's *The New York Botanical Garden Illustrated Encyclopedia of Horticulture* is invaluable for a researcher. It gives extensive cross-references and details of the ancestry of the plants. The advice on cultivation is intellectually stimulating as well as informative. The book is an excellent source of information for gardeners—either novice or experienced.

A useful source is Donald Wyman's *Wyman's Gardening Encyclopedia*. Because Professor Wyman is himself a gardener, his explanations are presented in an exceptionally clear and informative way. He includes helpful detail on the likelihood of a plant's thriving in differing climate zones. It is an excellent reference for gardeners, and it is useful to researchers as a means to verify information.

The Encyclopedia of Gardening Techniques, edited by Christopher Brickell under the guidance of the Royal Horticulture Society, England, would seem to be of little use to American gardeners. The edition distributed in the United States, however, provides information on climate and growing seasons applicable to American regions. The book is divided into sections with large Arabic numbers denoting distinct points of information on separate vegetables, making details easy to locate. There is an abundance of illustrations done in subdued shades of gray and green. This book is an excellent source of step-by-step guidance on growing plants, and its format makes it helpful for research. The National Gardening Association's *Gardening: The Complete Guide to Growing America's Favorite Fruits and Vegetables* is edited by Genoa Shepley and Anne Eldridge. The pages are filled with glossy color pictures of all aspects of gardening. There are details on every stage of planting and growing vegetables. This book will be of great help to anyone seeking a dependable source. Its handsome presentation makes it a pleasure to browse through. Another useful sourcebook is Joan L. Faust's *The New York Times Book of Vegetable Gardening*. Faust's sense of humor and her thoroughness make this book a pleasant and useful source.

Since most gardening books base their information on northern or eastern planting, it is important to examine handbooks from other regions. An excellent source of information is the *Southern Living Home Garden Handbook: A Month-by-Month Checklist*, edited by H. C. Thompson. The book comes from Oxmoor House, publishers of *Southern Living*. The southern climate creates a need for details not found in other gardening manuals. *Commonsense Vegetable Gardening for the South* by William D. Adams and Thomas LeRoy is also helpful for southern growers. The book provides an appendix for seed catalogs. It gives a truncated list of sources for additional information, addresses for gardening supplies, and low-toxicity pest control sources. It also lists the state extension horticulture offices for the southern states, including Texas.

Vegetables by Roger Phillips and Martyn Rix provides detailed coverage of more than 650 types of vegetables from around the world. Interested gardeners in the United States can grow all of the types listed. *Vegetables* is an excellent introduction to vegetables and vegetable gardening. It describes the important vegetable families, lists tips on cultivation, and names seed suppliers. Its index makes using the book efficient. The bibliography is limited, but the content of the book is thorough.

Whether a believer in chemical gardening or in organic gardening, the gardener must come to terms with weeds. It is impossible to escape weeds, even with sophisticated methods. They are as persistent and pervasive as insects. Nor can research in gardening be complete without an understanding of weeds. A first-rate dictionary-handbook is Mea Allen's *Weeds: The Unbidden Guests in Our Gardens*. This interesting and informative book illustrates and describes weeds and includes a glossary and a good bibliography. Also beneficial for general information is F. F. Rockwell's *10,000 Garden Questions Answered by 20 Experts*. Published in 1959, the book is dated; nevertheless, it contains helpful information.

There are two additional aids for gardeners: almanacs and seed catalogs. At one time, the gardener had only the almanac for advice on weather conditions and the correct times for planting. Popular gardening today has more sophisticated methods. Starwood Calendars publishes regional editions of color calendars. Included in each regional calendar is a U.S. Department of Agriculture map with guidance regarding climate in that zone. Within the last decade a number of regional books have been published, giving specific information for the region's climate, seasonal changes, and dates for freezing weather. The old *Farmer's Almanac* is still useful, however.

Since most seed catalogs are free, gardeners on the mailing lists have easy access. Often, however, a gardener needs information not provided in seed catalogs. Barbara J. Barton has compiled *Gardening by Mail: A Source Book*, a Mariner book published by Houghton Mifflin Company. The revised fifth edition is a reference book for mail-order gardening. It covers the varied sources for seeds, plants, and even worms—for those who want a particular kind of cultivation. Barton also lists the addresses, fax numbers, and E-mail numbers of gardening suppliers.

Additional sources for help are local county agents' offices, the state departments of agriculture, and the U.S. Department of Agriculture. Also useful as a source is the U.S. Government Printing Office, Washington, D.C. 20402. Useful as a source of pamphlets and other material is Garden Resources of Washington (GROW), 1419 V. Street NW, Room 300, Washington, D.C. 20009.

The Internet is one of the newest and most effective methods for compiling gardening information. *The Gardener's Computer Companion* is an expensive, but invaluable, book. In addition to specific information throughout the book, author Bob Boufford includes a White Pages Directory and a Yellow Pages Directory. The White Pages lists the companies and products mentioned in the book or on the CD-ROM that is included in the book. The Yellow Pages is "A Gardener's Internet Pages." The list is, of necessity, selective, but it is invaluable. The book also has a listing of 3-D landscape designs and sources for ordering.

The bibliography in *How to Grow More Vegetables* is detailed and organized by topics for easy access. The author, John Jeavons, has included diverse sources, which will be useful to all types of gardeners. He even lists sources for out-of-print books. The book is worth buying for the bibliography alone. *Gardening for Dummies* by Michael MacCaskey has an appendix useful for both dummies and sophisticates. Barbara Damrosch's *The Garden Primer* includes a superior appendix with sources useful to both ornamental and vegetable gardeners. She lists the names of plant societies of diverse interest.

The preceding list does not attempt to cover the surface of gardening books, but it provides a selective sample for gardening research. An exhaustive annotated list of gardening publications would constitute a volume in itself.

RESEARCH COLLECTIONS

Research in vegetable gardening is not restricted to libraries. While a number of libraries maintain collections on gardening, equally as many botanical gardens and arboretums have book repositories. Additionally, there are experimental farms or living-historical farms and museums open for research.

Traditional library collections are largely in the East, although one important repository is in Cleveland, Ohio, at the Garden Center of Greater Cleveland, Eleanor Squire Library, 11030 East Blvd., Cleveland, Ohio 44106. Since Richard T. Isaacson, compiler of *Gardening: A Guide to the Literature*, is librarian at Eleanor Squire, research work there has an additional advantage.

The Horticultural Society of New York Library on 128 West 57th Street, New York 10019 contains a useful collection of gardening material.

The Smithsonian Institution Libraries are traditional places of research. The Smithsonian Botany Library at 10th and Constitution, Washington, D.C. 20560 offers helpful information. Researchers can find wide-ranging material on plants, including, of course, ornamentals.

A little less orthodox is the Rodale Experiment Station, 33 East Minor Street, Emmaus, Pa. 18049. With the increasing interest in sustainable agriculture, the Rodale organization has become a major center to advance organic gardening. The station maintains a library of almost 15,000 books and bound periodicals. It subscribes to 800 journals and subject files related to its own publications. Researchers can benefit from the library, particularly if the topic is related in any way to organic gardening.

The U.S. Department of Agriculture maintains its National Agriculture Library in Beltsville, Maryland. The library holds the largest collection of documents related to agriculture in the United States. Gardening is only a division of the collection, but the computerized database AGRICOLA offers maximum efficiency in locating particular items. Access to AGRICOLA is available on the Internet. A further benefit is the comprehensive bibliographies, which the library database publishes on an irregular basis. Reference services are available at the library itself from 8:00 to 4:30 P.M. on federal workdays. The library also maintains a Small Grains Collection at the Plant Genetics and Germplasm Institute at the Beltsville site.

RAIN Information and Referral Center, 2278 Northwest Irving Street, Portland, Oreg. 97210 has a small library of 4,000 volumes, but the library is open only three days a week. The center also publishes a bimonthly journal, answers telephone and written inquiries, and conducts workshops. Though the library collection is small, its general services are useful to people in the Northwest. The library is also on the Internet.

Botanical gardens that maintain libraries are as follows: Chicago Botanic Garden Library, P.O. Box 400, Glencoe, Ill. 60022. It is advisable to make a reservation. The Denver Botanic Gardens, 909 York Street, Denver 80206 maintains a research collection and operates an outreach community gardening project. Hunt Institute for Botanical Documentation, Hunt Botanical Library, Carnegie-Mellon University, Pittsburgh 15213 has an extensive botanical history collection. The New York Botanical Gardens Library, Bronx, N.Y. 10458 has the largest North American botanical library. In the Midwest, the Missouri Botanical Garden Library, 4344 Shaw Blvd., St. Louis 63166–0299 is a superior repository of botanical information. The library answers specific inquiries, and its laboratories analyze data. There is an herbarium, which has an excellent collection of tropical plants. These sources are available on the Internet.

Libraries affiliated with arboretums are located in most regions of the country. Harvard University's Arnold Arboretum and Gray Herbarium Libraries, 22 Divinity Avenue, Cambridge 02138 are excellent sources, as is the Farlow Reference Library at Harvard. Both the Minnesota Landscape Arboretum Andersen Horticultural Library, 3675 Arboretum Drive, Chahassen 55317 and the Los Angeles State and County Arboretum Plant Science Library, 301 N. Baldwin Avenue, Arcadia, Calif. 91006 are useful sources for research.

Under the official name PLENTY, an experimental farm—referred to appropriately enough as the Farm—is a working farm on 156 Drakes Lane, Summertown, Tenn. 38483. For a number of years, the communal farm residents, composed of former Californians who settled in the small Tennessee town in the

1960s, were not receptive to researchers, viewing them primarily as curiosity seekers. Now that the organization is established, the residents permit limited observation of their experimental garden methods.

Persons interested in heirloom gardening can gather primary information at the National Seed Storage Laboratory, Fort Collins, Colo. 80521. The facility is a major seed bank in the United States. Another source is Seeds of Change, P.O. Box 15700, Santa Fe, N. Mex. 87506. A third source is Native Seeds/Search, 2509 N. Campbell Avenue # 325, Tucson, Ariz. 85719. The most significant source, however, is the Seed Savers Exchange, 3076 North Winn Road, Decorah, Iowa 52101. The exchange is a nonprofit organization that preserves heirloom varieties. On its 170-acre farm, Heritage Farm, which is open to visitors, 20,000 vegetable varieties are grown organically for seed in Preservation Gardens. Additionally, Heritage Farm grows seed for 700 old-time apples and grapes in Historic Orchard. Flowers and herbs are also grown for seed.

Seed Savers Yearbook publishes names and addresses of over 1,000 members of the organization. Twelve thousand varieties of seeds are available from members. The most recent source of information on heirloom vegetables is Sue Stickland's *Heirloom Vegetables: A Home Gardener's Guide to Finding and Growing Vegetables from the Past*, published by Fireside, Rockefeller Center, 1230 Avenue of the Americas, New York 10020. Kent Whealy, heirloom seed specialist, served as Stickland's consultant. Stickland provides detailed information and includes an extensive list of seed savers, many of whom do a mail-order business.

There are a number of living-historical farms and museums in all regions of the United States. In the Southeast is an interesting, but not greatly publicized, farm museum: the Acadian House Museum, St. Martinville, La. 70582. In the central Atlantic seaboard, the Accokeek Foundation maintains a farm at 3400 Bryant Point Road, Accokeek, Md. 20607. In the Northeast, there is the Howell Living Farm in Titusville, New Jersey.

There are too many of these living museums to list here, but anyone interested can get information from the Association of Living Historical Farms and Museums, c/o The Smithsonian, Washington, D.C.

BIBLIOGRAPHY

Books and Articles

Adams, William D., and Thomas LeRoy. *Commonsense Vegetable Gardening for the South*. Dallas: Taylor, 1995.

Allen, Mea. *Weeds: The Unbidden Guests in Our Gardens*. New York: Viking, 1978.

Atchinson, S. D. "Growing Food with That Ol' Time Flavor." *Business Week* (March 2, 1987), 106.

Bailey, D. W. "Make Your First Line of Defense in the Back Yard." *House Beautiful* 84 (February 1942), 56–57, 97.

Bailey, Liberty H. *Hortus Third: A Concise Dictionary of Plants Cultivated in the United States and Canada*. New York: Macmillan, 1976.

Baron, Robert C. *The Garden and Farm Books of Thomas Jefferson*. Golden, Colo.: Fulcrum, 1988.

Bartholomew, Mel. *Square Foot Gardening*. Emmaus, Pa.: Rodale Press, 1981.

Barton, Barbara J. *Gardening by Mail: A Source Book*. 5th ed. New York: Houghton Mifflin, 1997.

"The Believe-It-or-Not One Day Vegetable Garden." *Sunset Magazine* (March 1987), 88–91.

Benn, Barris. "Use a Computer Service to Increase Your Garden Harvest." *Mechanics Illustrated* 80 (February 1984), 48.

Berrall, Julia S. *The Garden: An Illustrated History*. New York: Viking, 1966.

Bickley, Donna. "Gardening Is Good for Your Mental Health." *Flower and Garden* 34 (March/April 1996), 38.

Blackburne-Maze, Peter. *A Creative Step-by-Step Guide to Fruit and Vegetables*. North Vancouver: Whitecap Books, 1977

Boufford, Bob. *The Gardener's Computer Companion*. San Francisco: No Starch Press, 1998.

Bremness, Lesley. *Herbs*. Pleasantville, N.Y.: Readers Digest Association, 1990.

Brickell, Christopher, ed. *The Encyclopedia of Gardening Techniques*. New York: Exeter Books, 1984.

Brody, Jane. "Natural? Safe? Drug-Free?" *Knoxville News Sentinel*, February 15, 1999: Section B.

Brownrigg, Leslie. *Home Gardening in International Development: What the Literature Shows*. Washington, D.C.: League for International Food Education, 1985.

Burns, Diane L., and Jill A. Burns. *Plant a Garden in Your Sneakers!: Fun and Outrageous Planting Projects for All Seasons*. New York: McGraw-Hill, 1998.

Calvin, Clyde L. and Donald M. Knutson. *Modern Home Gardening*. New York: John Wiley and Son, 1983.

Carefoot, G. L. and E. R. Sprott. *Famine on the Wind: Man's Battle against Plant Disease*. Chicago: Rand McNally, 1981.

Carver, Joseph. *How to Grow the Finest Marijuana Indoors under Lights*. Seattle: Homestead Books, 1996.

Cetron, Marvin, and Owen Davies. *The Gardening of America: Prosperity for the Gardening Business and Landscape Professions into the 21st Century*. Radnor, Pa.: Chilton-Capital Cities/ABC, 1991.

Chan, Peter, with Spencer Gill. *Better Vegetable Gardens the Chinese Way*. Portland, Maine: Graphic Arts Center, 1977.

Clewis, Beth. *The Gardener's Index: Where to Find Information about Gardens and Garden Plants*. New York: Neal-Schuman, 1993.

Coe, Mary Lee. *Growing with Community Gardening*. Woodstock, Vt.: Countryman Press, 1978.

Cook, Rick. "Desert Gardening." *Flower and Garden* 40 (August/September 1996).

Crockett, James Underwood. *Vegetables and Fruits: The Time-Life Encyclopedia of Gardening*. New York: Time-Life Books, 1972.

Cunningham, Sally J. *Great Garden Companions: A Planting System for a Beautiful, Chemical-Free Vegetable Garden*. Emmaus, Pa.: Rodale Press, 1998.

Damrosch, Barbara. *The Garden Primer*. New York: Workman, 1988.

Donoghue, G. T. "Put That Dirt to Work!" *Rotarian* 60 (April 1942), 39.

Duffield, Mary. *Plants for Dry Climates: How to Select, Grow, and Enjoy*. Tucson, Ariz.: Fisher Books, 1998.

Eaton, E. M. "They Haven't Rationed Your Own Back Yard." *Christian Science Monitor Weekly Magazine* (February 1943), 8–9.

Editors of *Consumer Guides. Vegetable Gardening Encyclopedia*. New York: Galahad Books, 1982.

Everett, Thomas. *The New York Botanical Garden Illustrated Encyclopedia of Horticulture*. 10 vols. New York: Garland, 1980–82.

Faris, C. "Gardening by Computer." *Saturday Evening Post* (April 1986), 32.

Faust, Joan L. *The New York Times Book of Vegetable Gardening*. New York: Quadrangle, 1975.

Ford, C. "G.I.s Garden around the World," *Better Homes & Gardens* 23 (February 1945), 23.

Frese, Paul. *100 Best Books for the Gardener's Library*. Norwood, Mass.: Holliston Mills, 1952.

"Garden Plots of the Bridge Builders." *Survey* 26 (May 27, 1911), 323–24.

Genders, Roy. *The Perfect Vegetable and Herb Garden*. New York: Drake, 1972– .

Goldman, M. C. "Organic Gardeners Grow 'Em Big!" *Organic Gardening & Farming* 16 (June 1969), 43–45.

"Great Hoe-Down." *Time*, 105: 5 (May 1975), 63–64.

Hage, Mary Van, Bettina Paterson, and Lucy Tizard. *Little Green Thumbs*. Brookfield, Ct.: Millbrook Press, 1996.

Headrick, Ulysses P. *A History of Horticulture in America to 1860*. New York: Oxford University Press, 1950.

Heinerman, John. *Heinerman's New Encyclopedia of Fruits and Vegetables*. West Nyack, N.J.: Parker, 1995.

Hendrickson, Robert. *The Great American Tomato Book*. New York: Doubleday, 1977.

Hepper, Frank N. *Planting a Bible Garden*. Ada, Mich.: Fleming H. Revell, 1998.

"Herbal Rx: The Promises and Pitfalls." *Consumer Reports* (March 1999), 44–48.

Herd, Meg, and Andrew Elton. *Learn and Play in the Garden*. Hauppage, N.Y.: Barron's Educational Series, 1997.

Hershey, Rebecca. *Ready, Set, Grow!: A Kid's Guide to Gardening*. Reading, Pa.: Addison Wesley Educational, 1995.

"Home Garden TV Goes on the Air Today." *Knoxville News Sentinel*, December 30, 1994, Section E.

"Hortitherapy." *Science Digest* 80 (October 1976), 10.

"How Three Bountiful Colorado Gardens Solved Mountain Problems." *Sunset Magazine* (May 1987), 264–65.

Huxley, Anthony. *An Illustrated History of Gardening*. New York: Paddington Press, 1978.

Hyams, Edward. *A History of Gardens and Gardening*. New York: Praeger, 1971.

Isaacson, Richard T. *Gardening: A Guide to the Literature*. New York: Garland, 1985.

Jabs, Carolyn. *The Heirloom Gardener*. San Franscisco: Sierra Club Books, 1984.

Jeavons, John. *How to Grow More Vegetables*. Berkeley, Calif.: Ten Speed Press, 1995.

Jones, Louisa. *The Art of French Vegetable Gardening*. New York: Artisan, 1995.

Kruger, Ursula. *Let's Go Gardening: A Young Person's Guide to the Garden*. Jersey City, N.J.: Parkwest, 1996.

Kruhm, Adolph. *Home Vegetable Gardening from A to Z*. New York: Doubleday, 1918.

Krutch, Joseph Wood, ed. *The Gardener's World*. New York: Putnam, 1959.

MacCasky, Michael. *Gardening for Dummies*. Chicago: IDG Books Worldwide, 1999.

Manchester, William. *The Glory and the Dream: A Narrative History of America—1932–1972*. Boston: Little, Brown, 1974.

Mansfield, Duncan. "Home and Garden TV Channels into 22 Million Homes." *Roanoke Times & World News*, January 24 1997, Business Section, Metro edition.

Marken, Bill. *Container Gardening for Dummies*. Chicago: IDG Books Worldwide, 1998.

Martin, William H. Introduction in *Home Vegetable Gardening*, by Charles H. Nissley. New Brunswick, N.J.: Rutgers University Press, 1942.

McIntyre, Anne. *The Good Health Garden: Growing and Using Healing Foods*. Pleasantville, N.Y.: Readers Digest Assoc., 1998.

Meeker, John. *The Mexican Kitchen Garden*, Kansas City, Mo.: Andrews and McMeel, 1998.

"Meet the Hotheads: Growing Head Lettuce in the South." *Rodale's Organic Gardening* 35 (January 1988), 36.

Mullen, Betsy P. "I Want My HGTV." *Richmond Times Dispatch*, July 6, 1996, Home Section, City Edition.

My First Garden Book. Chattanooga: N. K. Lawn and Garden, 1991.

Nelson, Jerrod, ed. "Reprints of the Victory Garden Articles." *Horticulture* 54 (July 1976), 25–40.

Newcomb, Duane. *The Apartment Farmer: The Hassle-Free Way to Grow Vegetables Indoors, on Balconies, Patios, Roofs, and in Small Yards*. Los Angeles: J. P. Tarcher, 1976.

———. *Mobile Home Gardening Guide*. Beverly Hills, Calif.: Trail-R-Club of America, 1963.

———. *The Postage Stamp Garden Book: How to Grow All the Food You Can Eat in Very Little Space*. Los Angeles: J. P. Tarcher, 1975.

Nichols, Richard. *Plant Doctor in His Vegetable Garden*. Philadelphia: Running Press, 1976.

Otis, Denise. "Gardening by Video." *House and Garden* 165 (April 1993), 46.

Phillips, Roger, and Martyn Rix. *Vegetables*. New York: Random House, 1994.

Pleasant, B. "Beat the Southern Broccoli Blues." *Rodale's Organic Gardening* 34 (November 1987), 80.

Powers, L. V. "Today's Vegetable Turn-On." *American Home* (March 1973), 86–87.

Rapp, Joel. *Let's Get Growing: Twenty-Five Quick and Easy Gardening Projects for Kids*. New York: Crown, 1992.

Relf, Diane, ed. *The Role of Horticulture in Human Well-Being and Social Development*. Portland, Oregon: Timber Press, 1992.

Reti, Irene, ed. *Garden Variety Dykes: Lesbian Traditions in Gardening*. Santa Cruz, Calif.: HerBooks, 1994.

Riotte, Louise. *Astrological Gardening*. Pownal, Vt.: Storey, 1989.

———. *Carrots Love Tomatoes: Secrets of Companion Planting for Successful Gardening*. Pownal, Vt.: Storey, 1998.

Roche, M. A. "Happiness Is a Thing Called Vegetable Gardening." *Flower Grower* 51 (January 1964), 40–42.

Rockwell, F. F. *10,000 Garden Questions Answered by 20 Experts*. New York: Doubleday, 1959.

Rodale, Robert. "Holistic Gardening." *Organic Gardening & Farming* 25 (May 1978), 36–38.

Rutledge, Cooper. *Backyard Battle Plan*. New York: Penguin, 1998.

Scott, Emily, and Catherine Duffy. *Dinner from Dirt: Ten Meals Kids Can Grow and Cook*. Layton, Utah: Gibbs Smith, 1998.

Shepley, Genoa and Anne Eldridge, eds. *Gardening: The Complete Guide to Growing America's Favorite Fruits and Vegetables*. Reading, Mass.: Addison-Wesley, 1986.

Skelsey, Alice, and Gloria Huckaby. *Growing Up Green: Children & Parents Gardening Together*. New York: Workman, 1973.

Stainbrooke, E. "Man's Psychic Need for Nature." *Parks and Conservation* (September 1973), 22–23.

Steadman, T. "Get a Jump on Spring." *Southern Living* (January 1987), 70–71.

Stefansky, Kris. "Day and Night for Hours on End." *Norfolk Virginia Pilot*, March 23, 1997, Home and Garden Section, Final Edition.

Stevens, Elaine. *The Creative Container Garden*. Berkeley, Calif.: Ten Speed Press, 1995.

Stickland, Sue. *Heirloom Vegetables*. New York: Fireside, 1998.

Swenson, Allan. *Plants of the Bible and How to Grow Them*. New York: Doubleday, 1981.

Thomas, Helen R. "Scripps Will Buy Bagwell/Cintel as Base for Its New Cable Network." *Knoxville News Sentinel*, January 9, 1995, Section B.

Thompson, H. C., ed. *Southern Living Home Garden Handbook: A Month-by-Month Checklist*. Birmingham: Oxmoore House, 1975.

Tilling, T. "Laugh at Food Prices—Hoe! Hoe! Hoe!" *Saturday Evening Post* 254 (May–June 1982), 70–72.

Tozer, Eliot. "Heirloom Seeds: The New Collectibles." *Modern Maturity* 31 (April–May 1988), 24–28.

Weinberg, Julie. *Growing Food in the High Desert*. Santa Fe, N. Mex.: Sunstone Press, 1985.

Wellencamp, J. "Just Plough Your Problems into the Garden." *Organic Gardening & Farming* 25 (January 1978), 158.

Whealy, Kent. Foreword to *Heirloom Vegetables*, by Sue Stickland. New York: Fireside, 1998.

Wilkes, Angela. *Let's Grow a Garden*. New York: D. K., 1997.

Williams, Sally, ed. *Garden Literature: An Index to Periodical Articles and Book Reviews*. Boston: Garden Literature Press, 1999.

Wright, Richardson. *Bibliography of Garden Books*. New York: Saturday Review of Literature, 1943.

———. *The Story of Gardening*. New York: Dover, 1934.

Wyman, Donald. *Wyman's Gardening Encyclopedia*. Rev. New York: Macmillan, 1988.

Yeomans, Kathleen. *The Able Gardener, Overcoming Barriers of Age and Physical Limitations*. Pownal, Vt.: Storey, 1993.
Yepsen, Roger, ed. *1,001 Old-Time Garden Tips*. Emmaus, Pa.: Rodale Press, 1997.

Periodicals

Agricultural Index. New York: H. W. Wilson, 1916–1983.
Avant Gardener. New York, 1968– .
Biological & Agricultural Index. New York: H. W Wilson, 1983– .
Brooklyn Botanic Garden Record. New York, 1945– .
City Harvester. Newark, N.J., 1978– .
Diversity. Arlington, Va., 1982– .
Family Handyman (incorporating *Home Gardening*). New York, 1951– .
Farm and Garden Index. Wooster, Ohio: Bell & Howell Microphoto, 1978– .
Flower and Garden. Kansas City, Kans., 1957– .
Gardening Know-How; Meeting the South's Specific Garden Needs. Gardening Know-How, 225 Ridgeland Avenue, Decatur, Ga. 30030.
Green Prints. Box 1355, Fairview, N.C. 28730.
The Growing Edge. New Moon Publishing, 341 SW 2nd Street, Corvallis, Oreg. 97333.
The Herb Companion. Herb Companion Press, 741 Corporate Circle, Golden, Colo. 80401–0101.
The Herb Quarterly. Long Mountain Press, 223 San Anselmo Ave., San Anselmo, Calif. 94960.
Herbalism: The Journal of the American Botanical Council. P.O. Box 144345, Austin, Tex. 78714–4345.
Kitchen Gardener: The Vegetable and Herb Gardening Journal. Taunton Press, 63 South Main Street, P.O. Box 5506, Newtown, Conn., 06470–5506.
Land. 300 N. Water Street, Silverton, Oreg. 97381.
The Mother Earth News. Henderson, N.C., 1970– .
National Gardening. Burlington, Vt., 1978– .
Pacific Horticulture. P.O. Box 485, Berkeley, Calif. 94701.
Popular Gardening. London, 1950–1970.
Readers Guide to Periodical Literature. New York: H. W. Wilson, 1900–
Rocky Mountain Gardener. Gunnison, Colo., 1989– .
Rodales' Organic Gardening (formerly *ROM Organic Gardening and Farming*). Emmaus, Pa., 1942– .
Singles in Agriculture. P.O. Box 7, Pearl City, Ill. 61062.
Southern Living. Birmingham, Ala., 1966– .
Sunset Magazine. Menlo Park, Calif., 1949– .
Texas Gardener: The Magazine for Texas Gardeners by Texas Gardeners. Suntex Communications, 680713 Woodway Drive, P.O. Box 9005, Waco, Tex. 76714.
Weeds Today. Champaign, Ill., 1937– .

GOTHIC FICTION

Douglass H. Thompson

From its inception, gothic fiction has provided an exemplary instance and wonderfully contentious battleground of the culture wars. Browbeaten by a high literary culture that deplored its excesses yet borrowed constantly from its conventions, the gothic has always been a scene of controversies: religious, aesthetic, scientific, political—in essence, cultural in the broadest and most contested sense of the term. As this literature holds a mirror to the societies that it darkly images, we are often horrified by the picture but unable to resist looking. In the decade since the second edition of the *Handbook of American Popular Culture*, the once-marginalized gothic has finally come into its own with a number of new and important reassessments. Where once upon a time gothic fiction was dismissed as sacrilegious, we now understand its demonic character, which is often uneasily counterbalanced by a shrill morality, as telling representations of religious sectarianism and malaise. Where once the gothic's slender artistic merit was said to consist of its pandering to our lowest desires and fears—a "degrading thirst after outrageous stimulation," to quote Wordsworth's withering estimate of the genre—we now find many studies of gothic elements in canonical writers, yes, obviously enough in Poe and Hawthorne but also in James (who wrote over twenty "ghost stories") and Faulkner and O'Connor and Toni Morrison. Where once-offended moral critics warned against the damage that such fiction would inflict upon the fairer sex, today's feminist criticism has discovered in the gothic a perfect medium to study an encyclopedia of gender concerns, from that obvious gothic staple, the victimization of women, to the socialization of female readers, and, finally, to women writers' creation of a distinctly "female gothic." Where once *Frankenstein* and its brood were read simply as rebels against the orderly cosmos of the Enlightenment, we now see them as heralds of a new scientific understanding, prophetic warnings of where science may lead us, and progenitors of the genre that engages these issues, science fiction. Where once a British critic of the 1790s disparaged the gothic as "the Terrorist System of Novel-Writing," we now recognize his concern as justifiable, for the gothic provides a powerful record of changing political and economic realities and anxieties. Finally, where more than once American culture has struggled to emerge from the daunting influences of its European heritage, the gothic, that always lowly genre on the literary scale, has in many ways provided an idiom that we have made distinctly our own. How important has the gothic become to understanding both high and popular American culture? A recent, much-noticed book, Mark Edmundson's *Nightmare on Main Street: Angels, Sadomasochism, and the Culture of Gothic*, argues nothing less than that the gothic, with its unsteady blend of the lurid, the puritanical, and the commercial, provides *the* trope for understanding contemporary American society. Or, as Angela Carter put it simply, "We live in Gothic times" ("Afterword" to *Fireworks*).

HISTORICAL OUTLINE

When Charles Brockden Brown wrote in his preface to *Edgar Huntly* (1800) that he intended to move beyond "Puerile superstition and exploded manners; Gothic castles and chimeras" to engage "the sympathy of the reader" in new ways (3), he was not so much dismissing the European tradition of gothic novelists as announcing his aim to provide a new, American direction for the genre. To understand the American gothic achievement, we must first turn to the English inventors of the "gothic romance" for an overview of its development and resonant literary conventions.

Horace Walpole's *Castle of Otranto*, subtitled in its second edition (1765) *A Gothic Story*, began the late-eighteenth-century literary craze for things mysterious and medieval. Set in an Italian castle during the Crusades, this "romance" concerns the career of the first of many villain-heroes, Count Manfred, whose attempted crimes against the political and natural order are redressed by weird supernatural interventions and chastisements. A gigantic helmet falls from the heavens to crush the son of the tyrant and prevent his succession; portraits of troubled ancestors spring to life; statues bleed; and a giant torso abruptly appears to prevent the overreaching Count's desperate final measures. To present-day connoisseurs of horror, Walpole's novel may seem a slight thing, with its flat characters, abrupt and artificial supernaturalism, and too tidy moral resolutions (the right heir eventually shows up to marry the Count's intricately persecuted daughter to ensure that all ends well). But in neat terms it provided his followers with many of the essential ingredients for a "gothic romance" (here ably summarized by Victor Sage):

> the "authenticating" pretense that the author is merely the editor of a found manuscript; the setting in medieval and "superstitious" Southern Catholic Europe; the conflation of hero and villain; the decay of primogeniture and of aristocratic rights in general, and the rise of an ambitious bourgeoisie eager to exercise individual freedom in marriage and inheritance; the focus on the victimized, but often defiant, position of women; the use of confined spaces—castles, dungeons, monasteries, and prisons, to symbolize extreme emotional states by labyrinthine incarceration. (82)

Edgar Allan Poe. Courtesy of the Library of Congress

This darkly imagined world both mirrored a period of social change and offered compensation for rationalist and deist insistence on an explainable universe, devoid of the supernatural. In his "Preface" to *Otranto*, Walpole offers his readers an alternative universe because, he argues, "the great resources of fancy have been dammed up by a strict adherence to common life." The gothic tradition in America and everywhere has never quite forgotten his haunted house.

The flood of gothic novels that followed attests to the great, if always somewhat sub rosa and unnerving, popularity of the genre. Accounting, at least in part, for that nervous reception was the fact that many of the earliest gothics were written by women, and women appeared to be their most avid readers. Some writers, like Clara Reeve with her *Old English Baron* (1777), attempted to domesticate and rehabilitate the extravagances of Walpole's vision; others, like Charlotte Dacre with *Zofloya* (1806)—featuring a stunningly villainous heroine—and William Beckford, with his Orientalist *Vathek* (1786), carried the genre into strange and forbidden regions of violence and dark desire. German ballads (especially those of Bürger), plays (Schiller's *Die Räuber*), and novels (Goethe's *Werther*) helped fuel and influence the craze, so much so that the word "gothic" often came to be associated with "Germanic," as in "Visigothic," menacingly foreign, and violent. Forgotten today but most truly indicative of the popular culture then are the hundreds of cheap imitations and chapbooks, charmingly referred to as "shilling shockers." A sampling of titles tells the story: *Romano Castle: Or, The Horrors of the Forest*; *The Midnight Assassin: Or, The Confessions of the Monk Rinaldi*; *The Hor-*

rors of the Secluded Castle: Or, Virtue Triumphant; *The Impenetrable Secret, Find It Out!* (See Frank's *The First Gothics* and Tracy's *The Gothic Novel 1790–1830* for a fuller listing of these "bluebooks.")

Most reviewers of the day were understandably distressed by this dark and ever-growing progeny of Walpole's, and no small pleasure of gothic research is the reading of seriously offended male and moral reviews of this literary phenomenon. A reviewer, possibly Samuel Taylor Coleridge, blasted Lewis' infamous *The Monk* (1796) as a "poison for youth, and a provocative for the debauchee" and, even worse, as a fiction that could "extract pollution from the word of purity and . . . *turn the grace of God into wantonness*" (197). But accompanying official censure of the *genre noir* came an early philosophical investigation into the appeals of terror that would provide an important, if contested, justification for the genre. Edmund Burke's *A Philosophical Enquiry into the Origin of Our Ideas of the Sublime and Beautiful* (1757) explained our irresistible attraction to terrifying scenes in terms of our instinct for self-preservation and defined the sublime in terms of awe, vastness, darkness, solitude, and obscurity. The Unitarian educators and writers John and Anna Laetitia Aikin (later, Barbauld) went a step further, directly praising Walpole and insisting that

> where the agency of invisible beings is introduced, of "forms unseen, and mightier far than we," our imagination, darting forth, explores with rapture the new world which is laid open to its view, and rejoices in the expansion of its powers. Passion and fancy cooperating elevate the soul to its highest pitch; and the pain of terror is lost in amazement. ("On the Pleasure Derived from Objects of Terror" 125)

With this argument comes an aesthetic justification for the gothic that clearly anticipates, in its emphasis on passion and imaginative expansion, the Romantic revolution in literature and the arts on the horizon. This is what continues to make the gothic such a fascinating topic for the study of literary history. As a product of the Enlightenment, it would continue to bear the stamp of strong moral closure, "where the vicious are punished, the virtuous are rewarded, and social and ethical imbalances are tidily corrected" (Napier 10). But in its exploration of irrational states of mind and the sublime and the marvelous, the gothic would become aligned to Romanticism—yet not by the major poets themselves (with the possible exception of Percy Shelley), who continued to disparage these "frantic" novels even as they borrowed from them and relied upon them to distinguish their own higher and more exalted notions of imaginative pleasure. We are finally coming to understand the gothic as a category that importantly helps us rethink the enduring, but surely too tidy, divide between the Ages of Reason and Imagination. Set against, yet uneasily contained by, Enlightenment ideals, allied with, but condescended to by, Romantic ones, the gothic occupied even back then a pivotal position in the culture wars.

As the gothic moved into the volatile 1790s with the stunning and highly controversial success of Matthew Lewis' *The Monk*, it increasingly came to be read, in the spirit of the age, as a "terrorist system of novel-writing." Lewis is rightly and importantly recognized by historians of the gothic as the English writer who most vividly imported the horror conventions of the German *Schauerroman*, with its unapologetic mix of supernaturalism and sex, fascination and disgust. But in its depiction of Ambrosio the Monk's anarchic desires struggling within and against stifling institutional conformity, the novel also uneasily mirrored the spirit of the age. With its conventional depiction of decadent aristocrats set against economically deprived heroines, the gothic formula had from its inception an element of political insurgency. Lewis' monstrously corrupt authority figures meet their just deserts in a mob scene of terrific energy and chaos at the end of the novel, an image that invokes the real Reign of Terror abroad and related anxiety on the home front. Many avowedly "Jacobin" novels of the period also seem to borrow from the gothic in their criticism of the horrors of poverty and political persecution, most importantly William Godwin's *Caleb Williams: Or, Things As They Are* (1794), which exerted an influence upon Charles Brockden Brown, Edgar Allan Poe, and Nathaniel Hawthorne. The novel relates the sufferings of a young workingman, Caleb, whose encyclopedic persecution by an exemplar of Burkean ideals, Falkland, and his infernal agent Gines truly reaches mythic (and gothic) proportions: England itself becomes a prison with no way out for those victimized by an arbitrary judicial and political system. Maurice Lévy in his *Le Roman Gothique Anglais* (1968) was the first critic to underscore the relationship between gothic and political terror, and, as we shall see in the History and Criticism section of this chapter, reading the "politics of the gothic" comes to the forefront in criticism of the 1980s and 1990s.

Godwin's achievement points to another significant factor in the historical development of the gothic. Noting Godwin's hyper-Calvinist upbringing before his turn to "atheistical Jacobinsim," Joel Porte convincingly argues that a "framework of secularized Calvinism" shapes the pattern of pursuit and persecution in the novel. This thesis points to another powerful religious source of gothic terror, one again with particular relevance for the American scene. Where the appeal of the "First Gothics" may be said to lie in the compensation that they provided for an increasingly scientific and deistic age, Porte suggests a contrary, but related, source: the *return* of conservative religious thought to chastise the freethinkers and radicals of the "new age." This element, dubbed the "Protestant as Prometheus" syndrome by James Rieger, has great resonance in the gothic works of the early nineteenth century. One thinks of such haunted figures as Coleridge's Ancient Mariner, Godwin's St. Leon (who finds the secret for immortal life), Byron's Manfred, Shelley's Ahasuerus, Charles Robert Maturin's Melmoth, Mary Shelley's Victor Frankenstein, *and* Brown's Carwin, Melville's Ahab, Washington Irving's student of German philosophy, Hawthorne's Ethan Brown—all are solitary questers and overreachers who meet terrible retribution. The Wandering Jew figure, appearing first in Lewis but later in Godwin, Brown, Shelley, Maturin, and Hawthorne, crystallizes this complex, the man who denies Christ only to be haunted through eternity by the damning knowledge of his sin. This "Prometheus as Protestant" syndrome points to how richly complex a phenomenon the development of the gothic is: from works often considered sacrilegious and from the pens of Romantic radicals come terrifying depictions of "sinners in the hands of an angry God"—a powerful conservative countercurrent to, yet arguably stemming from, the more subversive elements of the genre.

Another powerful countercurrent to the more demonic and overreaching and typically male strains of the gothic imagination can be found in the development of the "female gothic." The powerful name most associated with the genesis of the female gothic is Ann Radcliffe (1764–1823), but many of the first gothics and pulp gothics were written by women for women. These involved plots that invited vicarious identification with heroines thrilled by terrors, besieged by darkly attractive aristocrats, and rescued by virtuous and eligible, but boring, bourgeois heroes. With her virtuosic landscape painting and interspersed poetry, Radcliffe was seen to elevate the female gothic to a new level of art, but we now also read in those landscapes, often swarming with banditti and villainous Mediterranean Counts, an implicit criticism of patriarchy. (For more on the hugely influential feminist reinterpretation of the gothic, see Kay Mussell's version of this chapter in the preceding *Handbook* and the History and Criticism section.)

Radcliffe's Unitarianism led her to be ambivalent about the late-eighteenth-century cult of sensibility. Her heroines often revel in it, but her moral message frequently warns about the perils of a too-refined yearning for the exquisite and the exotic. She thus introduced the convention of the "explained supernatural," in which the spooky goings-on haunting her agitated heroines are explained away—in good rationalist fashion—as natural events and misunderstandings. From Radcliffe's ambivalence stems an enduring critical and historical dichotomy about the gothic, earliest formulated in her posthumously published essay "On the Supernatural in Poetry" (1826): the literature of "terror" versus the literature of "horror." Terror came to be associated with a high literary aesthetic related to the sublime; it demands an active reader, a literary detective of sorts, to distinguish between "real" and "imaginary" presentations of the preternatural; it ruminates reflectively on the pleasures and perils of the otherworldly. Horror, on the other hand, panders to our baser, lower (even animal) instincts; it presents ghastly and ghostly scenes that bewilder waking interpretation; its ultimate goal?—to scare the hell out of us (which, of course, has its own powerful, if cruder, moral function). This distinction came to be crystallized in the obvious contrast between Radcliffe, with her genteel, poetic, rationalist gothic, and Lewis, with his "real" panoply of succubi, devils, taboo sex, and infernal machinery.

American writers would inherit this central, shaping dichotomy, explore and extend many of the other paradoxes shaping the English gothic, and give the gothic a distinctly different national identity. This is the juncture where Charles Brockden Brown occupies an absolutely pivotal place. Brown is pivotal because he both gives a distinctively American cast to virtually all of the gothic crosscurrents from the British tradition and charts a direction for those writers who would follow him. In *Wieland*, *Edgar Huntly*, *Ormond*, and *Arthur Mervyn* (1798–1800), Brown inherits, but richly complicates, the tidy British division between the dynamics of terror and horror. Such characters as Clara Wieland and Edgar Huntly hover in exquisitely prolonged states of uncertainty, unsure as to whether their fears proceed from some otherworldly and irreversible fatality or from some empirical and palpable source of evil—or from their own delusions and madness. Where all British gothic fictions up to this time contained some kind of moral norm or redemptive voice, Brown's fiction sets these voices against one another, interrogating the integrity of their worldviews when faced with inexplicable terror, suggesting, even, that the reductive nature of those moral positions can breed terror. Clara is caught right between the great late-eighteenth-century debate that so decisively shaped the course of the first gothics: her brother Theodore is a

Calvinist fanatic who personifies the sense of religious dread haunting the genre; her love interest, Pleyel, is a Ciceronian rationalist who denies existence of the miraculous. Brown shows how exclusive commitment to either worldview can breed disaster, and some critics have wanted to see him as primarily a "Romantic" critic of religious fanaticism or, contrarily, of sterile rationalism. But Brown's novels also appear to deconstruct Romantic ideals: Edgar Huntly, a man of feeling if there ever was one, enters a nightmare world very much the product of his own sensibility; other critics have seen the first American novelist as expressing, in good Puritan terms, misgivings about the literary imagination itself. Where British writers like Burke and Radcliffe may have wanted to assert a higher imaginative pleasure for the poetics of terror, Brown's stubbornly deny it and look unflinchingly at the darker sides of the American grain.

These unresolved contradictions in Brown's gothic tapped many of the conflicts of the new nation and provided a wellspring for new American directions in the genre. With his scenes of terror taking place at the edge of the wilderness or in cities under plague, Brown moved the gothic from medieval never-never land to closer to home. His "frontier gothic" tapped a ripe source of American horror, early colonial captivity narratives, and set a direction for such later writers as James Fenimore Cooper, Ambrose Bierce, and the lesser-known John Neal, with his paradigmatically frontier gothic *Logan: or, the Mingo Chief.* His "urban gothic" provided a new landscape of terror essential to later nineteenth-century American and British explorations of the darker sides of industrialism. His intricately "psychological gothic" (in essence, where terror is realized as coming from within) drew from and recast typically Calvinist preoccupations with the innateness of evil and set the stage for the achievements of Poe, Hawthorne, and Henry James. With such new, more self-reliant heroines as Clara Weiland and Constantia Dudley, he arguably set a course for a differently American female gothic. Where once Brown was relegated to a minor role in the mainstream of American arts and letters, critics now regard him as providing a crucial counterpoint to the more optimistic, patriotic strains of the national literature, giving us a fallen Eden in place of a new one, revealing the darker underside to the new nation's bright hopes. As regards that enduring American literary dilemma, the search for its own voice beyond the European tradition, we have this irony: Brown succeeded better than most by taking a lesser, more "popular" European genre and remaking it wholly in distinctively American terms, ones that will shape an enduring tradition in our literature that we are just now coming to appreciate—the American gothic.

While Brown's innovations can be seen as setting the stage for a distinctively American version of the literature of terror, another durable strain of the gothic crossed the seas very early on and would have an enduring impact: the Radcliffean and female gothic. Issac Mitchell's *The Asylum; or Alonzo and Melissa, an American Tale Founded on Fact* (1811) easily transplants such Radcliffean staples as the encastled heroine (now in Connecticut) besieged by mysterious torments, the "unfeeling father" forcing her into a marriage against her will, and the artful climax uniting the long-suffering (and now Revolutionary War) hero with his true love. With *Dorval; or The Speculator* (1801) and *Amelia; or The Influence of Virtue* (1802), Sally Wood grafted the formula onto an American stem: substitute an evil land speculator for an Italian count and keep the long-suffering heroine, and the result is a firm stalk for the flowering of the sentimental gothic from the nineteenth century down to present times. The most popular author of the century was E.D.E.N. Southworth, who from 1849 to the 1890s churned out over sixty novels with sentimental gothic themes and tea table morals. Louisa May Alcott, with her anonymously published "tales of sensation," secretly exploited one of the few financially viable niches of the literary marketplace for women, and many women authors have followed. Kay Mussell has closely documented the hugely popular legacy of the Radcliffean formula in American fiction, down to the use of "gothic" to characterize an Ace Books paperback series of "mysteries designed for women readers" in the 1960s and on to the enduringly popular Harlequin romances of today. Yet even in the nineteenth century certain American heroines chafed uneasily against this romance formula. Hester Prynne comes to mind as a powerful exception, and many critics of today regard Charlotte Perkins Gilman's "The Yellow Wallpaper" (1899) as a decisively American unraveling of the nocturnal adventures and happy endings experienced by most heroines of the gothic romance. One thing is for sure: whether used as fantasy to titillate but essentially socialize its female readers *or* to challenge the premises of such fantasies, the Radcliffean legacy in our fiction remains alive and well as a valuable reflection of American women's fears and hopes—and as a commercially successful way for women authors to voice them.

While writers continue to develop American variations on the Radcliffean gothic, two great American writers, Edgar Allan Poe and Nathaniel Hawthorne, would follow the legacy of Brown and decisively alter the course of the European gothic vision with distinctive achievements of their own. Frederick Frank, this age's premier bibliographer on the subject, has drawn a daringly bold contrast between the traditions: "While the English gothic had dealt with physical terror and social horror, the American Gothic would concentrate on mental terror and moral horror" (*Though the Pale Door* xii). Although this formulation surely invites qualification—it is not, for example particularly true of the female gothic, and one can argue that all American gothics provide some kind of social commentary—Frank's sweeping generalization has a provocative value that points toward something uniquely American in the gothic vein. For Poe *is* fundamentally the master of mental terror; his plots lay bare the gothic encounter of the self with barely imaginable horror. Yes, terror *and* horror—although critics praise Poe for his artful plotting, concentrated effect, and teasing ambiguities, he is not afraid to serve up scenes rivaling the worst that the *Schauerroman* can offer: the eye plucking of "The Black Cat"; the too-vivid bodily decomposition of "M. Valdemar"; dental violation (!) in "Berenice." The list could go on. He appeals to the "Imp of the Perverse," sure that his readers cannot resist the vivid enactment of their worst nightmares. With his volatile, agitated narrators and claustrophobic narratives, Poe creates nothing less than an ontological gothic: virtual soliloquies in which the mind confronts and often creates the object that it most fears. This strangely exclusive focus on "mental terror"—Poe *does* seem only incidentally concerned with moral and social dimensions of the gothic—begins a rich heritage of American gothic *tales*, for novels cannot sustain the intensity of the encounter: witness Hawthorne's "The Haunted Mind," James' "The Beast in the Jungle," Lovecraft's "The Outsider." As father of this characteristically American version of the gothic tale, Poe distilled elements of the tradition of terror into its quintessential form.

Hawthorne's career-long engagement with the gothic was more diffuse and varied. With works like *The House of the Seven Gables* (1851)—a distinctly American *Otranto*—and *The Marble Faun* (1862), Hawthorne moved beyond European models in using the gothic genre as a vehicle for complex moral allegory, although one of his favorites, Charles Robert Maturin, pointed the way. He has, indeed, been credited with something called the "Yankee Gothic," nowhere more emphatically than in "The Gray Champion," in which the typically gothic avenging specter turns out to be nothing less than the spirit of Liberty itself. But Hawthorne also used the gothic as a medium to explore the darker conflicts in the national vision. In such tales as "Young Goodman Brown," The Man of Adamant," "Ethan Brand," "The Minister's Black Veil," and "Roger Malvin's Burial," he tapped that frequent source of American terror, Calvinism and Protestant anxiety, to create dark parables exploring the underside of American hope and ambition. With such tales as "The Birthmark" and "Rappaccini's Daughter," Hawthorne brought to perfection tales of the evil scientist, a subgenre whose gothic potential has proved especially fertile for an increasingly industrial and scientific nation.

While the big names of Poe and Hawthorne must loom large in any survey of the American gothic, we should not forget that the gothic flourished, as it had earlier in England, in many cheaper and lowbrow forms, such as literary magazines and dime novels. The master purveyor of cheap gore fiction was John Hovey Robinson (active 1846–1870s), whose garish rip-offs of earlier English goths include one (*Black Ralph, the Forest Fiend!*) that Westernizes the *Rauberroman*. Also noteworthy is George Lippard's *The Lady Annabel; or The Doom of the Poisoner* (1844), an absolute hyperbole of horror effects with something ghoulish or gruesome occurring on every page. In *Through the Pale Door*, a guide to the American gothic, Frederick Frank lists a large sampling of titles from this literary underground of the nineteenth century, including illustrated shockers and tales that play off contemporary events in the young nation's history. These remind us that the American public has always had a taste for the more sensational and visceral versions of the literature of horror.

Although much in the achievement of Poe and even Brown can be regarded as pointing the way to modern literature, two very different writers are acknowledged as transitional figures between the nineteenth- and twentieth-century gothic: Ambrose Bierce and Henry James. As the earlier gothic elements of Poe, Hawthorne, and Melville can be read as providing a dark counterpoint to American transcendentalism, the tales of Bierce, collected in *Tales of Soldiers and Civilians* (1891) and *Can Such Things Be?* (1893), take a fierce and sardonic delight in blowing up such illusions as the nation's Manifest Destiny, domestic tranquillity, and the glory of war. Having fought in the Civil War himself, Bierce conveys the utter horror of the battlefield through such tales as "An Occurrence at Owl Creek" and "One of the Missing," yet what makes all of his stories "Biercean" is a characteristically fierce irony, a dark joke at the expense of not only his victims but the reader as well, who is often left to grope for a sane interpretation among deliberately conflicting perspectives. In ghost stories ranging the gamut from the droll to the dreadful, Henry James also deals frequently with this theme of misperception and toys with the reader's ability to distinguish between real and imagined horror; indeed, one can say that he thematizes the typical gothic experience of uncertainty. Many of his characters, like the Cambridge divinity student of "The Ghostly Rental" or the Prufrockian narrator of "The Private Life," hover in the suspended animation of the "unlived life," unsure as to whether what haunts their consciousness comes from within or from without. On this score, of course, we have the uncertainties of "The Turn of the Screw," which have created a kind of haunted cottage industry, but it is important to note that James' experiments with the psychology and emphemerality of the ghostly spanned his entire career, beginning with "The Romance of Certain Old Clothes" (1868) and ending with the twin masterpieces "The Beast in the Jungle" (1902)—in which John Marcher discovers too late that the beast exists within—and "The Jolly Corner (1902)—in which Spencer Brydon finally must confront and make peace with another kind of beast, the specter of his rejected American self. Although Bierce prefers the grisly to the exquisite reticences of James, both in their own ways add narrative irony and psychological complication to a genre whose usually visceral impact on its readers was ripe for these more typically modernist elements. The wrongfully neglected Gertrude Atherton provides a powerful commingling of these elements in her *The Bell in the Fog and Other Stories* (1905), which shows both a mastery of her contemporaries' wicked irony and a distinctive adaptation of time-honored gothic themes to turn-of-the-century California.

While Atherton's example reminds us that no geographic region of the United States has remained impervious to the gothic—witness the New England ghost stories of Mary Freeman (active 1891–1903), the so-called San Francisco gothic of Emma Dawson and W. C. Morrow (active in the 1890s), and, more recently, Leslie Silko's powerful southwestern gothic—the American South has furnished a haunted moral landscape especially conducive to gothic representation. In the dark fictions of William Faulkner, Flannery O'Connor, and Carson McCullers one persistently finds, beneath the genteel facade, with its emphasis on piety, respectability, honor, and family values, a gnawing and, finally, horrifically intrusive sense of a denied past, carrying with it the stigma of racism, violence, and distorted sexuality. While many of Poe's stories, especially the foundational "The Fall of the House of Usher," and those of William Gilmore Simms (active 1828–1846) point the way, the distinguishing characteristics of southern gothic converge in Faulkner's Yoknapatawpha novels and tales: a brooding sense of the past, often cryptically disclosed from a variety of perspectives, that finally contaminates the present (the bloody Sutpen legacy of *Absalom, Absalom!*); sexual violence and perversion as symptoms of a wider social malaise (the necrophilia of Emily Grierson, the brutal rape of Temple Drake, the devotional nymphomania of Joanna Burden); the horrors of racism, presented so viscerally (see the lynching of Will Mayes in "Dry September" or the mob's castration of Joe Christmas in *Light in August*) that they exceed the worst terrors that the gothic can summon and have made more than one critic edgy about using the term to describe them; and a gallery of real, dry-hearted demons, from the rubbery-eyed Popeye to the white-supremacist Percy Grimm. O'Connor adds to these gothic parables of inverted desire and disintegrating families that powerful religious vision of hers, as once again in good American gothic tradition we find sinners in the hands of an inscrutable deity, who this time excoriates the self-righteous and the "nasty-nice" while reserving his grace, maybe, for the maddened and miscast. McCullers' version of the southern gothic focuses on the seemingly hopeless quest of "lonely hunters" for love in a cruel world warped by their exhausted or misplaced desire; that misplaced desire can erupt into violence, as it does in *Reflections in a Golden Eye* (1941), with its racial murder, tortured homosexuality, and self-mutilation. A. Robert Lee has defined the essence of the southern gothic as a world "shot through with family darkness and a deeply inward sense of the past as burden" (219). Other frequently cited authors exploring this particularly American version of the gothic include Truman Capote, James Purdy, and even James Dickey, with *Deliverance* (1970). Recently, Tony Morrison's *Beloved* (1987) has received increasing attention as a powerful—and gothic—vision of that "horrifically intrusive sense of a denied past," with an insistence that it cannot, should not be denied. Her example has led many critics to reexamine gothic elements in African American depictions of racial horrors (see the African-American gothic in History and Criticism).

As America moved through and beyond the twentieth century, the story of the gothic got a bit murky, as its wide diffusion in many literary and cultural forms made tracing its trajectories a difficult task. One relatively stable genre, the maiden-centered "gothic romance," keeps going strong; in addition to the commercial successes of such writers as Rosemary Rogers and Claire Lorimer, the 1990s saw the first printing and best-seller status of Alcott's *A Long Fatal Love Chase*, a novel deemed too sensational for publication at the time of its creation (1866). Looking beyond these enduring Radcliffean themes and variations, one can rely upon the old distinction between the literatures of horror and of terror to chart two broadly different directions for the recent American gothic. First, beginning with the seminal figure of H. P. Lovecraft, one finds the gothic engagement with literatures of the fantastic, in which the horrors are "real" but assume a mythic presence and intricate coding reminiscent of Beckford and the more extravagant first gothics. On the other hand, one can discern the continuance of a classic line of American tales of terror, whose organizing theme is, as Ann B. Tracy has noted, "the intrusion of the uncanny threat, not into the comfortably long ago and far away, but into the emphatically familiar fabric of our lives" ("Contemporary Gothic" 38). What follows is a provisional scheme built upon this distinction, not so much (heaven and hell forbid) a canon of twentieth-century gothic but a brief exploration of its various formations and deformations.

H. P. Lovecraft (1890–1937) is an important figure for understanding the convergence of time-honored gothic themes and conventions with the mythopoetics of twentieth-century fantasy literature. As his "Supernatural Horror in Fiction" (1927) reveals, he had a keen appreciation for such "first" gothic writers as Walpole, Beckford, Radcliffe, "Monk" Lewis, and Maturin and an equally strong sense of an American tradition of horror descending from Brown, Poe, and Hawthorne. His "weird tales" conjure up many old ghosts from the tradition, from the vampirish reincarnations of "The Thing on the Doorstep," to the Vatekian underworlds of his Cthulhu tales (such as "The Rats in the Wall" and "Entombed with the Pharoahs"), and on to that ghastly parable of identity, "The Outsider," which bears the unmistakable imprint of Poe. Two other key features of Lovecraft's gothic vision include a highly mythologized presentation of evil (those primordial octopoids, the Old Ones of the Cthulhu mythos, with its archetypal book of evil, the *Necronomicon*, that "ghastly soul-symbol of the corpse-eating cult of inaccessible Leng, in Central Asia" ["The Hound" 174]) and the presence of a scholarly detective or antiquarian who wrestles with a cryptic text of ominous import. With their palpable sense of evil and essential pessimism about the ability of human beings to fathom or ward it off, Lovecraft's fictions may belong more in the

Scene from the film *Dunwich Horror*, 1970. © The Del Valle Archive

"horror" category than that of "terror," but surely his is an intricate, mythopoetic horror, one whose mysterious presences of the past haunt the American present and comment indirectly on the American depression and other between-the-wars anxieties.

Lovecraft's fantastic horror fiction has spawned a cult following—best sampled in the pages of the pulp magazine *Weird Tales* (1929–1940)—and, indeed, there is something cultish, both in theme and in reception, of the many writers who have followed him. In a modern world of rampant consumerism and its evil twin skepticism, there seems to be this need for dreaming of primordial beings, secret societies governed by special vocabularies, and parallel universes, even if the dream often turns to nightmare. One can cite among a horde of fantastical gothics Clark Ashton Smith's *The Abominations of Yondo* (1942), which contains tales of deadly alternative universes with direct homage to both Lovecraft and William Beckford; L. Sprague Decamp and Fletcher Pratt's *Castle of Iron* (1950), a kind of Spenserian nightmare filled with metamporphoses and various, multilayered, surreal quests; Gene Wolfe's *The Book of the New Sun* (1967–1975), a "posthistoric" sequence of novels yet rife with stylish medieval horrors and allegory; and Jack Matthews' *Ghostly Populations* (1986), which uses Poe-like narrators usually succumbing to some mysterious, superior force. The best contemporary example of fantastic gothic can be found in the so-called cybergothic of works like William Gibson's *Necromancer* series (beginning in 1984), which imagine a merging of human and artificial intelligence and the promise of a monstrous future (and which, in good cult fashion, have spawned a flood of keys, manifestos, and imitations). These fantastic excursions into gothic horror may seem to provide a darkly exhilarating escape from clichéd modern alienation and postmodern boredom. But they are best read as oblique commentaries on the material nature of those conditions, just as we now read the fantasies of the first gothics within and against Enlightenment ideals and prohibitions. As Richard Kerridge persuasively argues, modern "popular horror fiction" offers, as did the eighteenth-century British gothic, "remedies" that are essentially "conservative, depending not on new attitudes toward the repressed or abject, but on violent confrontation, ritual cleansing, [and] rediscovery of lost heroism and authenticity" (282).

No subgenre of the contemporary horror gothic better typifies this weird conflation of the conservative and the forbidden, the purgatorial and the perverse, than our ongoing resurrection of that most gothic of secret societies, the vampire cult. In the fictions of Chelsea Quinn Yarbro and Anne Rice we find the old bogey just as bloodthirsty and powerful as ever—and just as sexually charged and ambiguous, if now more easily accepted for being so. But today's vampires also appear ridden with a peculiarly modern sense of angst and ennui, as they struggle to survive in a human world that often seems crueler and more capricious than they. Rice's Lestat invites a response that F. W. Murnau's Nosferatu and John Polidori's Lord Ruthven never evoke, our sympathy. Other recent vampire tales, like those of Poppy Z. Brite's *Lost Souls* (1992), tap into today's "changes in the cultural valorization of blood" (Hughes 245), especially anxieties occasioned by the HIV virus. These new adaptations of the vampire myth remind us that no matter how exotic or fantastic the appeals of gothic horror stories, they reflect the cultural values and contradictions of the age in which they are conceived.

What sets apart the line of American tales of terror from their horrific counterparts is just what set apart the earliest American versions of the gothic from their British forebears: a firm setting in the here and now, an "intrusion of the uncanny threat," as Tracy says, into the "familiar fabric of our own lives" (38), and a direct voicing of the anxieties that haunt American ideals of progress, economic well-being, and safety. From Brown to Bierce, Gilman to Morrison, this has been the distinguishing line of what can be regarded as a classic line of the American gothic: the stubborn refusal to mythologize away the sources of terror and the insistence, instead, on discovering the terror within ourselves and our culture. Given this insistence, it is not really surprising to find that some of the best examples in this classic line come from writers who are not considered primarily gothic, as Joyce Carol Oates' recent anthology, *American Gothic Tales* (1996), indicates, with its inclusion of such authors as John Cheever ("The Enormous Radio"), Robert Coover ("In Bed One Night"), Harlan Ellison ("Shattered like a Glass Goblin"), and Raymond Carver ("Little Things"). In concluding this section, I want to focus on some representative works from recent American writers that continue the gothic vision even as they shape and redefine it for our times. (For the reader interested in the broader range of recent gothic canon formations, please refer to the Anthologies and Criticism sections later in this chapter.)

"Gothicism," Oates once said wryly, "is not a literary tradition so much as a fairly realistic assessment of modern life." She thus collapses two terms long opposed in critical understanding and puts a modern spin on what actually has long characterized our American gothic literature: its capacity to illumine contemporary events. A perfect early example of this dark assessment of modern life is Robert Bloch's *Psycho* (1955), a novel that violates its decade's devotion to domestic security by Americanizing a range of gothic themes with a vengeance: the haunted castle now becomes a motel; the chamber of horrors, a shower; the dark villain, a murderous momma's boy. Bloch's interest in documentary technique in such works as "Yours Truly, Jack the Ripper" (1943) and *American Gothic* (1975), both of which reconstruct the careers of actual mass murderers, also testifies to this erstwhile Lovecraftian's interest in the psychology of real horror. Ira Levin's *Rosemary's Baby* (1967) may at first seem an odd choice in this line of more realistic gothics, with its satanic nativity, but it chillingly suggests something rotten at the core of American matrimony and has spawned a following of apocalyptic invasions of family units. Arguably the preeminent writer extending the gothic tradition to explore American loneliness, lost connections, and psychic disintegration is Shirley Jackson. Her crazed households, such as that of the Hallorans in *The Sundial* (1958), Hill House (1959), and the kooky castle of the Blackwoods (*We Have Always Lived in a Castle*, 1962) are truly modern haunted houses, haunted not so much by the old bogeys—although there is just enough suggestion of that—as by American families in various disarrays of warped desire, deadly despair, and exquisite lunacy. Such classic tales as "The Lottery" (1962) and "The Possibility of Evil" (1965) excoriate American moral complacency and hypocrisy. Shirley Jackson's vision of modern America is a darkly tragicomic one, deftly sketched with an often Jamesian sense of unlived or wrongly lived lives. Joyce Carol Oates also explores the thin line between sanity and the abyss in such explosively violent, yet psychologically penetrating, novels as *Them* (1970) and *Mysteries of Winterthurn* (1984). One finds a wide-ranging and wonderful complexity in her reimagining of the gothic consciousness to voice modern terror. Emblematic is "Where Are You Going? Where Have You Been?" (1966), in which the always tenuous dream of American innocence, now represented by a high school Christabel in a world of fast food and even faster sex, succumbs to a hot-rod demon of our collective unconscious.

The master manipulator of that region today remains Stephen King. King and his somewhat more difficult compatriot, Peter Straub (they coauthored *The Talisman*), ably carry the American gothic into the twenty-first century, as their fiction cuts across many categories in the tradition and raises, once again, the question of literary merit. With his encyclopedia of monsters and monstrous machines, vampires, and viruses—perhaps reaching their apex with the protean *It* (1986)—King unabashedly exploits the more stagy side of the literature of horror. But King also clearly belongs in the classic line of terror, as his expanding oeuvre just about always offers telling social commentary on American hopes, banalities, and fears. As Anthony Magistrale has said, the essence of King's terror "has less to do with prehistoric creatures roaming the night or vampires cruising for nourishment. Rather, his deepest terrors are sociopolitical in nature, reflecting our worst fears about vulnerable Western institutions—our governmental bureaucracy, our schools, our communities, our family relationships" (40). Although, like King, Peter Straub has incorporated such ripe sociopolitical terrors as the Vietnam experience into his fiction (see *Koko* and the recent *Throat*), his social commentary seems more oblique, subordinated to creating a really insidious, pervasive sense of evil—usually from an unresolved past—haunting the American scene. The labyrinthine complexity and length of Straub's novels somewhat recall the daunting dimensions of the first English gothics, but his sinister riddles challenge the modern reader to confront the possibility of dark forces within ourselves and our culture.

The huge popularity of King has become something like his stigma, just as it was for such wildly popular first gothic writers as Lewis and Radcliffe. Whatever we make of his or, say, Rice's literary merits, it is worth stressing the obvious, but terribly important, truth from the perspective of cultural studies: the enduring popularity of American gothic fiction attests to its value as an uncanny indicator of social concerns and contradictions. On the one hand, the continuing appeal of the gothic lies in its promise of the miraculous, in its ready offer of an escape from the mundane into a world governed only by the laws of the imagination, however dark it may be. But that darkly imagined world also tells us much about our waking world, and one can be sure that as we enter a new millennium, the specter of the American gothic will be lurking to haunt our national consciousness—and to reveal powerful truths about it.

REFERENCE WORKS

As Victor Frankenstein nears completion of his loathsome task of creating a bride for his lonely monster, a horrid thought gives him pause: what if his grotesque Adam and Eve should propagate "a race of devils . . . who might make the very existence of man a condition precarious and full of terror?" The American bride of the British gothic has, indeed, spawned its own "hideous progeny" of critical studies, discoveries and rediscoveries, canon formations, and occasional nonsense, and few bibliographic enterprises seem to have greater parental affection with the publishing houses, as they appeal to both academic and popular readership. Although recent and radical redefinitions of just what constitutes the American gothic make any survey of the current bibliography on the subject a "precarious" undertaking, a wealth of new reference guides makes tracing the genesis, genealogy, and rearing of the American gothic a less formidable task.

The orthodox procedure for conducting a bibliographic survey would be to begin with reference works containing the broadest treatment of the subject and to work down to more specialized approaches. But because bibliographic material relating to the gothic impinges on so many broad categories (e.g., supernatural, detective, and science fiction), the researcher of American gothic studies would be wise instead to begin with Frederick S. Frank's *Guides to the Gothic* (vol. 1: 1984; 2: 1995; 3: ongoing on-line). These *Guides* present not only a judicious overview of general resources but bibliographical information on specific American authors. The first sections of the *Guides* provide crucial information on "Research and Reference Works" in gothic studies—a bibliography of bibliographies of sorts—that enables a researcher to determine the value and relevance of each cited reference tool. The *Guides* also contain through their national organization of gothic literatures a separate and extensive section on the American gothic, including both "General Histories and Critical Studies" and secondary studies of particular American authors. All entries are incisively annotated and conveniently indexed through both authors and critics.

A number of broader reference guides, in which the gothic appears as a category or genre among others, provide important secondary and primary material. E. F. Bleiler's two-volume *Supernatural Fiction Writers* (1985) offers excellent critical and bibliographical surveys of many gothic writers and periods; volume 2, with such categories as "American Early-Nineteenth Century and Victorian Writers" and "Early American Pulp Writers," provides the focus on a range of American gothic writers, both major and minor. Neil Barron's *Horror Literature: A Reader's Guide* (1990; revised and enlarged in 2000) is also an indispensable aid; its thirteen chapters, written by specialists in the field and each containing that godsend for the researcher, a selective and annotated bibliography on its topic, cover not only the full historical range of the gothic but such items as "General Reference Books" (Barron), "History and Criticism" (Michael A. Morrison), and, especially valuable, "Libraries and Fantasy/Horror Publishing" (Barron). Including "horror" and "gothic fantasy" writers among its 500 alphabetically arranged essay-reviews, Frank N. Magill's *Survey of Modern Fantasy Literature* (1979) furnishes valuable primary and secondary material on a number of American gothic writers. More recent but in many ways less useful is David Pringle's *The St. James Guide to Horror, Ghost & Gothic Writers* (1998), which provides 427 entries of varying quality and less sound critical and bibliographical coverage than guides like Frank's and Barron's.

The student of the gothic might also consult early on for general mooring some recent, encyclopedic approaches to the subject. Marie Mulvey-Roberts' *The Handbook to Gothic Literature* (1998) is a delightful *excursus*, offering insightful and often witty definitions of key gothic terms and studies of individual authors, schools, and periods. Although providing only sporadic bibliography, this primarily British undertaking provides much of interest to American gothicism, including surveys of "American Gothic" (Allan Lloyd Smith), "Contemporary Gothic" (Ann B. Tracy), and "Southern Gothic" (A. Robert Lee). Another primarily British production, edited by David Punter, *A Companion to the Gothic* (1999), offers a fine chapter on "Nineteenth-Century American Gothic" and other entries that explore its dispersal across an entertaining range of media and critical discourses. Clive Bloom's *Gothic Horror: A Reader's Guide from Poe to King and Beyond* (1998) is of little bibliographic value but provides a general critical and theoretical introduction to the subject through its excerpts of a wide range of primary (e.g., from Poe's "Imp of the Perverse" to Stephen King's *Playboy* interview) and secondary material (e.g., Tzetan's Todorov's durable "The Fantastic and the Uncanny").

A number of more specialized reference guides, narrowing mainly primary sources of the gothic to certain topics and periods, reflect the growing diversity of scholarly endeavors in the field. Researchers interested in recent and, especially, popular versions of the gothic should consult Elsa J. Radcliffe's *Gothic Novels of the Twentieth Century: An Annotated Bibliography* (1979) and James Vinson and D. L. Kirkpatrick's *Twentieth Century Romance and Gothic Writers* (1982). Students of the female gothic have three valuable resources: Nina Baym's *Women's Fiction: A Guide to Novels by and about Women in America, 1820–1870* (1978); Lina Mainiero's *American Women Writers: A Critical Reference Guide from Colonial Times to the Present* (1979); and Kay Mussell's *Women's Gothic and Romantic Fiction: A Reference Guide* (1983). Allen Hubin's *The Bibliography of Crime Fiction, 1749–1975* (1979) contains many valuable intersections with gothic texts in regard to this enduring theme of the genre. Those primarily interested in the gothic tale will find some value in Fred Siemon's *Ghost Story Index* (1967), which lists some 2,200 titles from 190 books and anthologies. Michael Burgess' *Reference Guide to Science Fiction, Fantasy, and Horror* (1992) provides extensive information on the rich relationship between science fiction and the gothic, as do Marshall B. Tymn's annual reviews in *Extrapolation*, "This Year's Scholarship in Science Fiction, Fantasy and Horror Literature," and Barron's *Anatomy of Wonder: A Critical Guide to Science Fiction* (1995). Given recent focus on the subject, one would also like to see a bibliographic study of African American literature and its relation to gothic or horror genres. For more detailed information on the scope of specialized reference guides, the researcher would do well to consult the previously mentioned "General Reference Guides" entry in Barron and the "Previous Guides" to the gothic in Frank's annotated bibliographies of criticism.

On-line Web sites, electronic forums, and discussion lists dedicated to the gothic have surely augmented resources available to students of the subject, but the surfer should, like any good gothic hero or heroine, be wary. Typing in "gothic" for a keyword search will lead one to an indecipherable plethora of sites—from nightclubs to necrophilia, from fashion to any number of fetishes—that give a good understanding of the widely usable (and often useless) value of the term in contemporary cyberculture. However, in addition to the previously mentioned *Guide to the Gothic III* of Frank's *The Sickly Taper* web site, two sites stand out among many for their scholarly integrity and take Web researchers to the places where they need to go for information: Voller's *The Literary Gothic Page* and Potter's *Gothic Literature*. A good idea as well is to use the on-line *World Catalog of the Library of Congress* or a database like the *MLA Bibliography On-Line* and limit author or subject searches with the cross-referencing term "gothic." Steven Bruhm maintains a decent, but as yet underused, e-list for the International Gothic Association (ICA), the leading international society in the field, whose Web site is also very much worth consulting. The IGA sponsors a new journal, *Gothic Studies* (1998), the first academic periodical to be dedicated entirely to gothic matters, which contains valuable reviews of recent gothic scholarship.

It may seem unusual to have reserved until last mention the issue of primary gothic bibliographies, usually a starting point for any study of literary reference guides. But guides to primary sources involve arguably the most contested aspect of gothic studies: its canon. Again, the indefatigable Frederick Frank leads the way with his *Through the Pale Door: A Guide to and through the American Gothic* (1990), which offers for its eclectic range of 509 entries plot summaries, information of first and where available reprint editions, research sources, and an index to motifs. Tymn's *Horror Literature: A Core Collection and Reference Guide* (1981) organizes its presentation of the subject into historically defined chapters, offering a critical introduction to the period before itemizing works of particular authors. Even more wide-ranging in its chronicling of primary sources is Bleiler's *A Guide to Supernatural Fiction: A Full Description of 1,775 Books from 1750 to 1960* (1983). (Both Bleiler's aforementioned *Supernatural Fiction Writers* and Barron's *Horror Literature* contain much in the way of primary bibliography.) To track down the location of a specific title, researchers can consult, in addition to *World Cat* (on-line), Lyle H. Wright's *American Fiction* (3 vols.) and Arthur Quinn's *American Fiction: An Historical and Critical Survey* (1965), which contains plot summaries helpful in locating forgotten gothics. Jack Voller's on-line "Gothic Authors" provides perhaps the most promising approach to the compiling of a primary American gothic bibliography, as the changeable nature of the electronic document encourages the kinds of revisions and reflections, additions and deletions appropriate for the charting of this most protean literary phenomenon.

To review: let's say a researcher wants to learn all about H. P. Lovecraft's horror fiction. She first consults Frank's *Guides* and finds, for example in volume 2, fifty-three closely annotated entries, which include descriptions of Joshi's and Blackmore's "authoritative bibliography" on the writer and frequent reference to the periodical *Lovecraft Studies*. That's a good start. For information on Lovecraft in his milieu and an introdution to the range of his work, she then consults Burleson's entry on Lovecraft under "Early American Pulp Writers" in Bleiler's *Supernatural Fiction Writers* (853–59) and Stableford's "Early Modern Horror Fiction, 1897–1949" in Barron (93–159), where she learns a great deal about the "Lovecraft Circle." Bloom's entry on Lovecraft in Mulvey-Roberts offers a brief and lively chapter on his idiosyncratic life and reasons for his reemergent appeal (149–51), and Bloom's own *Gothic Horror* offers excerpts from Lovecraft's "Supernatural Horror in Literature" and a report from "The Los Angeles Science Fiction Society's Symposium on H.P. Lovecraft." Turning from the page to the Web, our intrepid researcher finds through Voller's "Gothic Authors" links to *The H. P. Lovecraft Archive*, maintained by Donovan Loucks and to the Necronomicon Press, the publisher of Lovecraft and other dark fantasy titles. To round out her already growing primary bibliography, the researcher then turns to Frank's *Through the Pale Door*, which contains plot summaries and information on twelve of Lovecraft's most gothic tales (157–64), and to Crawford's "The Modern Masters" (Tymn 276–369). Finally, a tour through *World Cat* on-line with the prudent "limits" added to the search should locate up-to-date information on editions and reprints, manuscript locations, and archival material.

ANTHOLOGIES AND COLLECTIONS

Tracking down an obscure or suspected gothic title can be quite an adventure. Although library collections across the United States contain many gothic titles—from high to low, classic novels to dime novels—this material is rarely cataloged in ways that allow easy or systematic identification of it as "gothic"; indeed, the Library of Congress uses the subject heading "Gothic Revival Literature." The single greatest library collection of early American gothics—the equivalent to the famous Sadleir-Black collection of early British gothic fiction at the University of Virginia—can be found at the American Antiquarian Society of Worcester, Massachusetts. To locate a known title, one should consult the indispensable *World Cat* on-line; to search for the little or unknown, one can look through Quinn's *American Fiction: An Historical and Critical Survey*, which contains plot summaries helpful in locating forgotten gothics. Also helpful in terms of primary bibliography and library holdings of popular fiction are Mussell's pointers in the earlier versions of this essay and Barron's "Libraries and Fantasy/Horror Publishing" in *Horror Literature: A Reader's Guide*.

Without the equivalent of the Arno Press and its republication of many neglected English first gothics, we presently await modern reprints of such important early American gothic writers as Isaac Mitchell, Sally Wood, and John Neal, all of whom could benefit from a scholarly edition. But, somewhat curiously, we have *two* fine new editions each of Southworth's parlor gothic *The Hidden Hand, or, Capitola the Madcap* and Lippard's gore-infested *The Quaker City, or, The Monks of Monk Hall* (the first by Fiedler in 1970). Frank's *Through the Pale Door* lists first editions and, when available (but they are rarely so), reprint editions of many early American gothics awaiting resurrection.

As for anthologies, one can choose from a great number of collections billing themselves as "gothic," but some seem more designed to exploit the commercial potential of the term than to offer the real article (but so it has always been with the marketing of gothic titles). A number of good anthologies house classic American works with their British forebears and offer solid critical introductions to the subject: *The Evil Image: Two Centuries of Gothic Short Fiction and Poetry* (edited by Patricia L. Skarda and Nora Crow Jaffe, 1981); *Great Tales of Terror from Europe and America* (edited by Peter Haining, 1972); *Romantic Gothic Tales, 1790–1840* (edited by G. Richard Thompson, 1979); and *The Penguin Book of Horror Stories* (edited by J. A. Cuddon, 1984). The best and most recent of these multinational compilations is Chris Baldick's *The Oxford Book of Gothic Tales* (1992), which captures the full range from Poe to Oates, canvasses the southern gothic (including Welty), and considers Morrison's *Beloved* "the most outstanding Gothic work of recent years." Of singular importance for American studies is Joyce Carol Oates' fine anthology *American Gothic Tales* (1996), which not only ranges from Brown to such obvious contemporaries as Rice, King, and Straub but makes a provocative case for the inclusion of such writers as Raymond Carver, Robert Coover, and Isaac Bashevis Singer (among others). Also indicative of the widening range of the canon are *The New Gothic* (edited by Bradford Morrow and Patrick McGrath, 1993), whose contributors include Oates, Hawkes, Rendell, Rice, and Straub, and the recent *American Gothic: An Anthology, 1787–1916* (edited by Charles Crow, 1999). One can also widen the descriptor to such terms as "American ghost stories" or "American horror" on such search engines as *World Cat* or amazon.com and find more than enough anthologies and titles to keep one's heart pounding and pulse racing, as they like to say. But do not forget that a number of good gothic anthologies deal with special topics or authors (such as Leon Edel's *The Ghostly Tales of Henry James*). Catherine A. Lundie offers an excellent anthology, *Restless Spirits: Ghost Stories by American Women, 1872–1926* (1996), and Alfred Bendixen similarly presents *Haunted Women: The Best Supernatural Tales by American Women Writers* (1985). *Between Time and Terror* (1995), edited by Robert Weinberg, Stephan Dziemianoqicz, and Martin Greenberg, contains seventeen stories that exemplify the merging of gothicism and science fiction; and Leonard Wolf's *Blood Thirst: 100 Years of Vampire Fiction* (1997) includes such writers as Anne Rice, Edith Wharton, August Derleth, John Cheever, Ray Bradbury, and Stephen King.

HISTORY AND CRITICISM

In Henry James' "The Real Right Thing," the ghost of a great writer, Ashton Doyle ("Immense. But dim. Dark. Dreadful.") returns to haunt the writer who has undertaken his official biography. At first a "mystic assistant" helping the biographer, the ghost soon turns into an admonitory presence to disrupt the telling of his tale because the writer cannot capture the "real right thing" about his achievement. In many ways James' ghost story can stand as a parable about the elusive attempt to write the critical history of the American gothic. Until the 1960s, scholarly narratives of the nation's literary progress rarely include discussion of the dark and the dreadful genre, often exalting the Hawthornian idea of "romance" by isolating the term from its erstwhile modifier "gothic." As studies of the American gothic began in earnest in the 1960s, the diverse findings made it quickly clear that defining "the real right thing" about our nation's gothic literature would prove a daunting task. Ours lacks the relative continuity of the English "First Gothics" (Walpole to Maturin), resists readings in terms of a tradition, and embraces an immense variety of literary forms and subgenres. Yet many critics of today find that the very value of an American gothic lies in the way that it disrupts traditional narratives of the nation's literary progress. We might never be in a position to say the real right thing about such a protean literary phenomenon, but the ghostly—and generic—otherness of the American gothic has finally proved to be a potent admonitory presence in contemporary American criticism. It warns us against the tendency toward "generic essentializing" (Hart 138), underscores the always tenuous nature of a national canon, and provides, in Fiedler's memorable formulation, "a literature of darkness and the grotesque in a land of light and affirmation" (29). Always before a shadowy aspect of our national literary consciousness, the gothic today has finally moved to center stage in our current reexaminations of just what characterizes American culture.

It is not surprising to find that the first literary historians to address the possibility of an American gothic come from abroad. The English critic Edith Birkhead includes a chapter on "American Tales of Terror" in her *The Tale of Terror: A Study of the Gothic Romance* (1921), and the Finn Eino Railo offers an early examination of themes that the American version shares with the British in his *The Haunted Castle: A Study of the Elements of English Romanticism* (1927). Early-twentieth-century criticism in the United States generally concerned itself with defining what was characteristic of the national literature, and the various models of realism and naturalism offered little opportunity for discussion of something as seemingly foreign as the gothic. The rise of the New Criticism hardly helped matters—one assumes that for this school the gothic novel was indeed too loose and baggy a monster—and formalist readings of such writers as Poe and Hawthorne tend to exalt their artistry by suggesting how they transcend the ghostly and romantic parameters of their working materials. A quiet, but important, exception to the general trend was the republication of *Weiland* in 1926, with an introduction by Fred Pattee that examines Brown's conscious reworking of the European gothic tradition. In reading the haunted world of the novel as a dark counterpoint to the Edenic promise of the new nation's hopes, Pattee signaled a direction for studies of the American gothic that remains in progress today. Also noteworthy for its effective examination of early American gothicism is Oral Coad's "The Gothic Element in American Literature before 1835" (1925), which stresses the shaping influence of Radcliffe.

During the 1940s and 1950s various studies of individual authors in gothic terms began to signal a change in the critical fortunes of the genre (for these and all scholarship on the gothicism of particular American writers, the reader is directed to Frank's *Guides to the Gothic*, which usefully annotate gothic-oriented critical monographs—including dissertations—on individual authors). But the landmark

Scene from the 1931 film *Frankenstein*. Kobol Collection/Universal

book noisily marking an end to sober neglect of the gothic impulse is Leslie Fiedler's *Love and Death in the American Novel* (1966). In controversially moving the gothic very near the center of American consciousness and in seeing Brown as foundational, Fiedler links two key concepts that would prove hugely influential in the gothic revival on the horizon: the shaping historical context of Calvinism with a specifically Freudian psychoanalytic critical approach. Because of the Puritan grain, Fiedler argues, many American writers' attempts to deal with sexuality and freedom come contaminated with the fears and horrors of guilt and divine retaliation and richly invite readings of repressed content: "American Gothic identified evil with the id and was therefore conservative at its deepest core" (48). Joel Porte, with his revealingly titled "In the Hands of an Angry God: Religious Terror in Gothic Fiction" (1974), offers an excellent exposition of Fiedler's linking of gothic horror to Protestant anxieties, finding the literature of terror not, as the usual argument goes, sacrilegious but symptomatic "of a profound religious malaise" (47). In her introduction to *American Gothic Tales*, Joyce Carol Oates agrees that "extreme gothic sensibility springs from such paradoxes" of Puritan theology (2). On the other hand, Irving Malin's *New American Gothic* (1962) extends Fiedler's psychoanalytic approach to explore neogothic themes in such recent American writers as O'Connor, Hawkes, and McCullers; and in the line of Fieldler's psychosexual readings, there came a flood of articles reading this or that ghost as this or that character's sublimated something. Finally, criticism began to see something like a workable genre or literary impulse, at least, and better yet, one with a host of rich contradictions (religious, psychological, political) that would powerfully appeal to the emerging schools of postmodern criticism.

The 1980s saw a spate of studies characterized by a diversity of approaches, especially in regard to the idea of an American gothic canon. Donald Ringe's *American Gothic: Imagination and Reason in Nineteenth Century American Fiction* (1982) offers a corrective, if narrow, historical antidote to Fiedler's wide-ranging exuberance, arguing that the high-water mark of the genre occurs in the works of Poe, Hawthorne, and Melville (Ringe is insightful on the American transformation of British conventions). Terry Heller's *The Delights of Terror: An Aesthetics of the Tale of Terror* (1987), with its mix of Todorovan theory and deconstructive strategies, does not quite follow through on its promise to explain the pleasures of terror. But in its summoning a wide range of American authors from Brown to the present, the book is indicative of widening examinations of the topic. Also in the Todorovan line is Allan Lloyd-Smith's *Uncanny American Fiction: Medusa's Face* (1989), which uses his theory of the uncanny to enrich and complicate Freudian readings of the gothic, especially the genre's recurrent stigmatization of women as objects of male fear and desire. Howard Kerr, Charles L. Crow, and John W. Crowley present in *The Haunted Dusk: American Supernatural Fiction, 1820–1920* (1983) a collection of essays that charts the evolution of the ghost story in terms of our "culture's preoccupation with death in an increasingly secular, individualistic, and scientific age" (3). Also emblematic of the expanding range of American gothic studies is Brain Docherty's collection *American Horror Fiction: From Brockden Brown to Stephen King* (1990).

As these and many, many studies of gothic elements in individual authors ranging from Washington Irving to John Irving expanded the definition of the gothic, feminist scholars developed a more coherent and, in many ways, more historically legitimate canon under the heading of the "female gothic." Tracing a lineage from Ann Radcliffe to Mrs. Julia Wood and on through such writers as Charlotte Perkins Gilman, Shirley Jackson, Joyce Carol Oates, *and* the popular Harlequin version of the maiden-centered gothic, these critics found in this literature by women for women a powerful vehicle to study a range of gender concerns. First coined by Ellen Moers in *Literary Women* (1977), the term became widely accepted with the publication of Juliann Fleenor's *The Female Gothic* (1983), a landmark collection of essays that range easily and productively from high to low versions of the gothic. Also important (but mainly concerning English gothicism) is Eugenia De La Motte's *Perils of the Night: A Feminist Study of Nineteenth Century Gothic* (1989). These studies generally argue for a narrower construction of the gothic canon. For example, Kay Mussell's "Gothic Novels" entry in the 1988 *Handbook* contains no mention of Poe or King in making the case that "[b]ecause the American democratic and practical mind was never quite comfortable with the gothic novel of terror, the true heirs of the original gothics can be found in the women's novels of the nineteenth and twentieth centuries" (160). In this chapter under the new title "gothic fiction" I have, of course, provided a broader understanding of the term, and, as we shall see, new historical studies in the 1990s, with their emphasis on the persistently *discomfiting* nature of the gothic "impulse" in American fiction, take sharp exception to Mussell's thesis. But her earlier "Gothic Novels" remains required reading for students of the subject and not only for the more detailed attention that she gives the female gothic. The eminent historian of the gothic,

Maurice Lévy, in recently lamenting the loose use of the term, agrees with feminist scholarship: "For me, Gothic necessarily conjures up images of female innocence engaged in labyrinthine pursuits and threatened by monarchal or baronial lucibricity. . . . 'Gothic' has that special eighteenth-century flavor, which attaches itself to ruined castles and abbeys" (" 'Gothic' " 2). At the dawn of a new millennium, criticism remains very much divided between the gothic as a specifically definable genre and the gothic as a wider literary impulse.

Although one finds an intriguing irony in feminist scholarship, long wary of too narrowly defined canons, insisting on a prescribed range for the gothic, its contributions to an understanding of the gothic are proving rich and varied. One line (Elaine Showalter and Fleenor, among others) stresses the victimization of women in the genre, finding in the entrapped heroine and her sexual persecution powerful indictments of patriarchal social and filial structures. Another line, ably represented by Kay Mussell's *Fantasy and Romance: Contemporary Formulas of Women's Romance Fiction* (1984), stresses how the female gothic socializes its female audience, thrilling them with sexual terror and intrigue but safely returning them to the safety of a bourgeoisie closure. A third and relatively newer line of criticism follows Moers in rereading the ways that the gothic enables expression of female rage and rebellion at the same time that it provides for women a viable and lucrative niche in the literary marketplace. Two provocative studies, Michelle Massè's *In the Name of Love: Women, Masochism, and the Gothic* (1992) and Kathy A. Fedorko's *Gender and Gothic in the Fiction of Edith Wharton* (1995), provide a representative example of these approaches. Few critical theories of the gothic better understand the social and historical reasons for its marginalization, and feminist reading of the gothic romance remains a vital and productive area of interpretation.

It would be hard to argue that the gothic is marginal today. With the advent of cultural criticism and its fierce distrust of privileged critical categories and canons, the gothic has become *the* vehicle for haunting and unsettling the once-accepted narratives of the nation's literary progress. One senses at times that the critical pendulum has, in the gathering momentum of rediscovery and revision, swung a bit too far, but the deep and ever-widening pit of gothic studies seems to have no foreseeable bottom as of this writing.

Louis Gross' slender volume *Redefining the American Gothic* (1989) epitomizes and sets the stage for recent historicist reassessments of the topic. Gross argues that "there is a more central position for the Gothic in American literature than in any other national literature"; he sees the mode as presenting "an alternative vision of American experience" that gives voice to those groups marginalized by the mainstream: women, gays, colonials, and, above all, African Americans as "the most wholly Other voice" in our fiction (2–3). Ladell Payne in *Black Novelists and the Southern Literary Tradition* (1981) was the first to discuss African American use of gothic conventions to depict the real horrors of slavery and racism, and the idea of an "African American gothic," with Morrison's *Beloved* a touchstone, has become a central referent in ongoing cultural redefinitions of the gothic vision. Teresa Goddu insists on restoring the racial dimension to gothic "darkness" in her *Gothic America: Narrative, History, and Nation* (1997); this strategy provides her a governing metaphor to recover the social pathologies too conveniently ignored by interior and psychological readings of the gothic. Goddu's emphasis on how "the gothic disrupts the dream world of national myth with the nightmare of history" (4) also finds varied exposition in a collection of essays edited by Robert K. Martin and Eric Savoy, *American Gothic: New Interventions in a National Narrative* (1998); characteristic of the volume's materialist approach is Ginsburg's "Slavery and the Gothic Horror of Poe's 'The Black Cat.' " Jennifer Schulz and Jeanette Idiart detect "American Gothic Landscapes" from "The New World to Vietnam." Mark Edmundson's ambitious *Nightmare on Main Street: Angels, Sadomasochism, and the Culture of Gothic* (1997) takes these reappraisals the inevitable step further by examining how the libidinal energies of the gothic have permeated the mainstream of American thought. In the contemporary world of O. J., the Stringer show, and slasher films, Edmundson finds "a culture at large that has become suffused with Gothic assumptions, with Gothic characters and plots" (12). Ann Tracy even worries that in a culture so saturated with topics once taboo, the literary genre of the gothic may fall on "hard times," as it has always depended "upon a foil of normalcy, some sane world that can be disrupted" ("Contemporary Gothic" 39). In a reversal that eerily echoes that of many a gothic plot, the critical history of the genre has thus come full circle: what was once the monster of popular culture has left its mark on all culture; what was once marginal has pervaded the majority.

Goddu's call for "localized and sustained readings of the gothic's cultural engagements" (163 n.10) is being answered with a number of studies that place the genre in specific contexts. Steven Bruhm, David Jarraway, and Eric Savoy have followed Eve Kosofsky's discussion of the gothic and homosocial desire with essays on, to use Jarraway's title, "The 'Queer' Contours of American Gothic." Edward J. Ingebretsen's *Maps of Heaven, Maps of Hell: Religious Terror as Memory from the Puritans to Stephen King* (1996) returns to Fiedler's and Porte's theological studies of the gothic with fresh insight. Karen Halttunen's *Murder Most Foul: The Killer and the American Gothic* (1998) extends Davis' earlier study of *Homicide in American Fiction* (1968) in charting the evolving social and religious constructions of the murderer in gothic fiction. Complementing the traditional emphasis on the South as a regional Other ripe for gothic insinuations is Faye Ringel's *New England's Gothic Literature* (1995). Renewed emphasis on the philosophical dimensions of terror and its reception can be found in Dieter Meindl's *American Fiction and the Metaphysics of the Grotesque* (1996) and Jack Voller's excellent *The Supernatural Sublime: The Metaphysics of Terror in Anglo-American Romanticism* (1994). A lively collection of essays studies the idea of a *Frontier Gothic: Terror and Wonder at the Frontier in American Thought* (1993). Sage and Smith's *Modern Gothic: A Reader* (1996) directly addresses the relationship between postmodernism and gothicism and offers among its essays studies on King (by Punter), Morrison, and David Lynch's *Blue Velvet*. Helen Thompson even finds "Gothic Numbers" lurking in that most unexpected of places, *The Federalist No. 10*. Just how elastic can the term and the topic be? Witness Jerry Mills' "Equine Gothic: The Dead Mule as Generic Signifier in Southern Literature of the Twentieth Century" (1996). Really.

One can see how far studies of the American gothic have come since the last printing of the *Handbook*. In the 1974 collection of essays *The Gothic Imagination: Essays in Dark Romanticism*, the editor, G. R. Thompson, felt compelled to note how contributors to the volume had risked their professional reputations in writing on such a dicey topic. Today no such apology need be made, and Marilyn Gaull (editor of *The Wordsworth Circle* and reader, one suspects, of countless submissions about the gothic) has gone so far as to express amazement and chagrin at the ever-widening circle of gothic studies. These proliferating studies have generally undercut the idea of the gothic as a distinct, historically identifiable genre. A lover of pleasure derived from the literature of terror might complain that the persistently materialist approaches to this most immaterial of subjects have deprived the gothic of some of its archaic creepiness. But expansive treatments of the gothic as a literary impulse continue to illumine many dark corners of American literature and culture. From her dark corner, Clara Wieland once summed up the paradoxical insight afforded by the gothic experience: "Those thoughts which we ought not to disclose it is criminal to harbor." Recent and continuing criticism of the American gothic appears intent on full disclosure of just those thoughts.

NOTE

I want to thank Frederick S. Frank, that most generous of gothic sages, for his advice and insight as this chapter progressed and students in my graduate bibliography seminar, whose wrestling with the idea of an American gothic provided much inspiration: Amy Griger, Anne Carson, Teresa Welford, Dawn Yoder, Rachel Pigg, and Roger Smith.

BIBLIOGRAPHY

Books and Articles

Aikin, Anna Laetitia, and John. "On the Pleasure Derived from Objects of Terror, with Sir Bertrand, a Fragment." In *Miscellaneous Pieces in Prose*. London: J. Johnson, 1773.

American Gothic: An Anthology, 1787–1916. Ed. Charles Crow. Malden, Mass.: Blackwell, 1999.

American Gothic: New Interventions in a National Narrative. Ed. Robert K. Martin and Eric Savoy. Iowa City: Iowa University Press, 1998.

American Gothic Tales. Ed. Joyce Carol Oates. New York: Plume/Penguin, 1996.

American Horror Fiction: From Brockden Brown to Stephen King. Ed. Brian Docherty. New York: St. Martin's Press, 1990.

Barron, Neil. *Anatomy of Wonder: A Critical Guide to Science Fiction*. New Providence, N.J.: R. R. Bowker, 1995.

———. *Horror Literature: A Reader's Guide* New York: Garland, 2000.

Baym, Nina. *Women's Fiction: A Guide to Novels by and about Women in America, 1820–1870*. Ithaca, N.Y.: Cornell University Press, 1978.

Between Time and Terror. Ed. Robert Weinberg, Stefan Dziemianoqicz, and Martin Greenberg. New York: Penguin Books, 1995.

Birkhead, Edith. *The Tale of Terror: A Study of the Gothic Romance*. London: Constable, 1921. Reprint. New York: Russell and Russell, 1963.

Bleiler, E. F. *A Guide to Supernatural Fiction: A Full Description of 1,775 Books from 1750 to 1960*. Kent, Ohio: Kent State University Press, 1983.

———. *Supernatural Fiction Writers: Fantasy and Horror*. 2 vols. New York: Scribner's, 1985.

Blood Thirst: 100 Years of Vampire Fiction. Ed. Leonard Wolf. New York: Oxford University Press, 1997.

Bloom, Clive. *Gothic Horror: A Reader's Guide from Poe to King and Beyond*. New York: St. Martin's Press, 1998.

Brown, Charles Brockden. *Edgar Huntly, or, Memoirs of a Sleep-walker*. Ed. Norman S. Grabo. New York: Penguin Books, 1988.

Bruhm, Steven. "Picture This: Stephen King's Queer Gothic." In *A Companion to the Gothic*. Oxford and Malden, Mass.: Blackwell, 2000, 269–80.

Burgess, Michael. *Reference Guide to Science Fiction, Fantasy, and Horror*. Englewood, Colo.: Libraries Unlimited, 1992.

Carter, Angela. *Fireworks*. London: Virago, 1988.

Coad, Oral. "The Gothic Element in American Literature before 1835." *JEGP* 24 (1925), 72–93.

Coleridge, Samuel T. "Review" of *The Monk*. *The Critical Review* (February 1797), 194–200.

Davis, David B. *Homicide in American Fiction, 1798–1860: A Study in Social Values*. Ithaca, N.Y.: Cornell University Press, 1968.

De La Motte, Eugenia. *Perils of the Night: A Feminist Study of Nineteenth Century Gothic*. New York: Oxford University Press, 1989.

Edmundson, Mark. *Nightmare on Main Street: Angels, Sadomasochism, and the Culture of Gothic*. Cambridge: Harvard University Press, 1997.

The Evil Image: Two Centuries of Gothic Short Fiction and Poetry. Ed. Patricia L. Skarda and Nora Crow Jaffe. New York : New American Library, 1981.

Fedorko, Kathy A. *Gender and Gothic in the Fiction of Edith Wharton*. Alabama University Press, 1995.

The Female Gothic. Ed. Juliann Fleenor. Montreal: Eden Press, 1983.

Fiedler, Leslie A. *Love and Death in the American Novel*. New York: Dell, 1966.

Frank, Frederick S. *The First Gothics: A Critical Guide to the English Gothic Novel*. New York: Garland, 1987.

———. *Guide to the Gothic: An Annotated Bibliography of Criticism*. Metuchen, N.J.: Scarecrow Press, 1984.

———. *Guide to the Gothic II: An Annotated Bibliography of Criticism, 1983–1993*. Lanham, Md.: Scarecrow Press, 1995.

———, with Anthony Magistrale. *The Poe Encyclopedia*. Westport, Conn.: Greenwood, 1997.

———. *Through the Pale Door: A Guide to and through the American Gothic*. New York: Greenwood Press, 1990.

Frontier Gothic: Terror and Wonder at the Frontier in American Thought. Ed. David Mogen et al. Rutherford, N.J.: Fairleigh Dickinson University Press, 1993.

Gaull, Marilyn. "The Profession of Romanticism: The Caverns Measureless and the Sunless Sea." *The Wordsworth Circle* 27 (1996), 51–53.

The Ghostly Tales of Henry James. Ed. Leon Edel. New Brunswick, N.J.: Rutgers University Press, 1949.

Goddu, Teresa A. *Gothic America: Narrative, History, and Nation*. New York: Columbia University Press, 1997.

The Gothic Imagination: Essays in Dark Romanticism, ed. G. R. Thompson. Pullman: Washington State University Press, 1974.

Gothic Studies. Ed. Robert Miles. Manchester, England: Manchester University Press, 1998– .

Great Tales of Terror from Europe and America. Ed. Peter Haining. London: Gollancz, 1972.

Gross, Louis. *Redefining the American Gothic*. Ann Arbor, Mich.: UMI Press, 1989.

Halttunen, Karen. *Murder Most Foul: The Killer and the American Gothic*. Cambridge: Harvard University Press, 1998.

Hart, Francis R. "Limits of the Gothic: The Scottish Example." In *Racism in the Eighteenth Century*. Cleveland: Press of Case Western Reserve University, 1973, 137–53.

The Haunted Dusk: American Supernatural Fiction, 1820–1920. Ed. Howard Kerr, John W. Crowley, and Charles L. Crow. Athens: University of Georgia Press, 1983.

Haunted Women: The Best Supernatural Tales by American Women Writers. Ed. Alfred Bendixen. New York: Frederick Ungar, 1985.

Heller, Terry. *The Delights of Terror: An Aesthetics of the Tale of Terror*. Normal: Illinois University Press, 1987.

Hubin, Allen J. *The Bibliography of Crime Fiction, 1749–1975*. Del Mar, Calif.: Publisher's, 1979.

Hughes, William. "Vampire." In *The Handbook to Gothic Literature*, ed. Marie Mulvey-Roberts. New York: New York University Press, 1998, 240–46.

Idiart, Jeannette, and Jennifer Schulz. "American Gothic Landscapes: The New World to Vietnam." In *Spectral Readings: Towards a Gothic Geography*, ed. Glennis Byron and David Punter. New York: St. Martin's, 1999.

Ingebretsen, Edward J. *Maps of Heaven, Maps of Hell: Religious Terror as Memory from the Puritans to Stephen King*. Armonk, N.Y.: M. E. Sharpe, 1996.

The International Gothic Association. n. pag. On-line. Internet. (January 15, 1998) <http://www-sul.stanford.edu/mirrors/romnet/iga/>

Jarraway, David R. " 'Divided Moment' Yet 'One Flesh': The 'Queer' Contours of American Gothic Today." *Gothic Studies* 2: 1 (2000), 90–103.

Kerridge, Richard. "Popular Horror Fiction." In *The Handbook to Gothic Literature*, ed. Marie Mulvey-Roberts. New York: New York University Press, 1998, 281–82.

Lévy, Maurice. " 'Gothic' and the Critical Idiom." In *Gothick Origins and Innovations*, ed. A. L. Smith and Victor Sage. Amsterdam and Atlanta, Ga.: Rodopi Costerus, 1994, 1–15.

———. *Le Roman gothique anglais, 1764–1824*. Toulouse, France: Sciences Humaines de Toulouse, 1968.

Lloyd-Smith, Allan. "Nineteenth Century American Gothic." In *A Companion to the Gothic*. Oxford and Malden, Mass.: Blackwell, 2000, 109–21.

———. *Uncanny American Fiction: Medusa's Face*. New York: St. Martin's Press, 1989.

Lovecraft, H. P. "The Hound." *Weird Tales* 3 (February 1924), 50–52, 78.

———. "Supernatural Horror in Fiction." *The Recluse* 1 (1927), 23–59.

Magill, Frank. *Survey of Modern Fantasy Literature*. 5 vols. Englewood Cliffs, N.J.: Salem Press, 1979.

Magistrale, Anthony. *Landscape of Fear: Stephen King's American Gothic*. Bowling Green, Ohio: Bowling Green Popular University Press, 1988.

Mainiero, Lina. *American Women Writers: A Critical Reference Guide from Colonial Times to the Present*. 4 vols. New York: Frederick Unger, 1979.

Malin, Irving. *New American Gothic*. Carbondale: Southern Illinois Press, 1962.

Massè, Michelle A. *In the Name of Love: Women, Masochism, and the Gothic*. Ithaca, N.Y.: Cornell University Press, 1992.

Meindl, Dieter. *American Fiction and the Metaphysics of the Grotesque*. Columbia: University of Missouri Press, 1996.

Mills, Jerry Leath. "Equine Gothic: The Dead Mule as Generic Signifier in Southern Literature of the Twentieth Century." *Southern Literary Journal* 29 (1996), 2–17.

Moers, Ellen. *Literary Women*. New York: Doubleday, 1977.

Mulvey-Roberts, Marie. *The Handbook to Gothic Literature*. New York: New York University Press, 1998.

Mussell, Kay J. *Fantasy and Romance: Contemporary Formulas of Women's Romance Fiction*. Westport, Conn.: Greenwood Press, 1984.

———. "Gothic Novels." In *Handbook of American Popular Culture*, ed. M. Thomas Inge. Westport, Conn.: Greenwood Press, 1988, 157–169.

———. *Women's Gothic and Romantic Fiction: A Reference Guide*. Westport, Conn.: Greenwood, 1983.

Napier, Elizabeth. *The Failure of the Gothic: Problems of Disjunction in an Eighteenth Century Literary Form*. Oxford: Oxford University Press, 1986.

The New Gothic. Ed. Bradford Morrow and Patrick McGrath. London: Picador, 1993.

The Oxford Book of Gothic Tales. Ed. Chris Baldick. New York: Oxford University Press, 1992.

Pattee, Fred Lewis. "Introduction" to *Wieland*. New York: Harcourt, Brace, 1926. Reprint. Hafner, 1960, ix–xlvi.

Payne, Ladell. *Black Novelists and the Southern Literary Tradition*. Atlanta: Georgia University Press, 1981.

The Penguin Book of Horror Stories. Ed. J. A. Cuddon. Baltimore: Penguin, 1984.

Porte, Joel. "In the Hands of an Angry God: Religious Terror in Gothic Fiction." In *The Gothic Imagination: Essays in Dark Romanticism*, ed. G. R. Thompson. Pullman: Washington State University Press, 1974, 42–64.

Pringle, David, ed. *The St. James Guide to Horror, Ghost & Gothic Writers*. Detroit, New York, Toronto, and London: St. James Press, an Imprint of Gale, 1998.

Punter, David, ed. *A Companion to the Gothic*. Oxford: Blackwell, 1999.

Quinn, Arthur Hobson. *American Fiction: An Historical and Critical Survey*. New York: Appleton-Century-Crofts, 1936, 1965.

Radcliffe, Ann. "On the Supernatural in Poetry." *The New Monthly Magazine* (1826), 145–52.

Radcliffe, Elsa J. *Gothic Novels of the Twentieth Century: An Annotated Bibliography*. Metuchen, N.J.: Scarecrow Press, 1979.

Railo, Eino. *The Haunted Castle: A Study of the Elements of English Romanticism*. London: E. P. Dutton, 1927. Reprint. Humanities Press, 1965.

Restless Spirits: Ghost Stories by American Women, 1872–1926. Ed. Catherine A. Lundie. Amherst: University of Massachusetts Press, 1996.

Rieger, James. *The Mutiny Within: The Heresies of Percy Bysshe Shelley*. New York: George Braziller, 1967.

Ringe, Donald A. *American Gothic: Imagination and Reason in Nineteenth Century American Fiction*. Lexington: Kentucky University Press, 1982.

Ringel, Faye. *New England's Gothic Literature: History and Folklore of the Supernatural from the Seventeenth through the Twentieth Centuries*. Lewiston, Maine: Edwin Mellen, 1995.

Romantic Gothic Tales, 1790–1840. Ed. G. Richard Thompson. New York: Harper and Row, 1979.

Sage, Victor. "Gothic Novels." In *The Handbook to Gothic Literature*, ed. Maries Mulvey-Roberts. New York: New York University Press, 1998, 81–90.

Sage, Victor, and Allan Lloyd-Smith, eds. *Modern Gothic: A Reader*. Manchester, England: Manchester University Press, 1996.

Savoy, Eric. "Spectres of Abjection: The Queer Subject of James's 'The Jolly Corner.' " In *Spectral Readings: Towards a Gothic Geography*, ed. Glennis Byron and David Punter. New York: St. Martin's Press, 1999.

Siemon, Fred. *Ghost Story Index*. San Jose, Calif.: Library Research Assoc., 1967.

St. James Guide to Horror, Ghost & Gothic Writers. Ed. David Pringle. Detroit, New York, Toronto, and London: St. James Press, an Imprint of Gale, 1998.

"The Terrorist System of Novel-Writing." *The Monthly Magazine* (August 1797), 102–4.

Thompson, Helen F. "Gothic Numbers in the New Republic: The Federalist No. 10 and Its Spectral Factions." In *Spectral Readings: Towards a Gothic Geography*, ed. Glennis Byron and David Punter. New York: St. Martin's Press, 1999.

Tracy, Ann B. "Contemporary Gothic." In *The Handbook to Gothic Literature*, ed. Marie Mulvey-Roberts. New York: New York University Press, 1998, 38–39.

———. *The Gothic Novel 1790–1830: Plot Summaries and Index to Motifs*. Lexington: University Press of Kentucky, 1981.

Tymn, Marshall B. *Horror Literature: A Core Collection and Reference Guide*. New York: R. R. Bowker, 1981.

Vinson, James, and D. L. Kirkpatrick. *Twentieth Century Romance and Gothic Writers*. Detroit: Gale, 1982.

Voller, Jack. *The Supernatural Sublime: The Metaphysics of Terror in Anglo-American Romanticism*. Dekalb: Northern Illinois University Press, 1994.

Wright, Lyle H. *American Fiction, 1774–1850*. San Marino, Calif.: Huntington Library, 1939.

———. *American Fiction, 1876–1900*. San Marino, Calif.: Huntington Library, 1963.

———. *American Fiction, 1774–1900*. Louisville, Ky.: Lost Cause, 1970.

Web Sites

Frank, Frederick S. *Guide to the Gothic III. The Sickly Taper*. N. pag. On-line. Internet. (September 1, 2000) <http://www.toolcity.net/~ffrank/>

The International Gothic Association Page. N. pag. On-line. Internet. (September 1, 2000) <http://www-sul.stanford.edu/mirrors/romnet/iga/frmain.htm>

Potter, Franz. *Gothic Literature*. N. pag. On-line. Internet. (September 1, 2000) <http://members.aol.com/iamudolpho/basic.html>

Voller, Jack. *The Literary Gothic Page*. N. pag. On-line. Internet. (September 1, 2000) <http://www.siue.edu/~jvoller/gothic.html>

GRAFFITI

Lisa N. Howorth and Sarah L. Croy

Of all the many overlooked aspects of American urban popular culture, graffiti has become the most difficult manifestation to ignore. A ubiquitous feature of the landscape of most large American cities, graffiti has been embraced by urban and youth cultures around the world in the same way that other phenomena of American popular culture have been: rock and roll, blue jeans, and hamburgers, to list a few notable examples.

For centuries a means of marking one's presence ("I was here") or making a particular scatological, political, sexual, or intellectual statement, graffiti has transcended limitations imposed by the written word and has evolved into a full-blown art. The questions and problems presented by graffiti are many and are of both an aesthetic and a sociological nature. What are the psychological and sociological implications? What are the messages of graffiti, and what does it tell us about the writers? What does it say about society? Are the fantastic and original subway car paintings illuminating the underground transit system of New York City to be considered vandalism or art? If art, is it folk, or is it fine? Is it still graffiti when it is transferred to canvas, sold in a gallery, and hung on a living room wall? The message, medium, and significance of graffiti metamorphose rapidly—practically from year to year and certainly from decade to decade—and it seems barometric in response to other cultural phenomena, such as official campaigns to eradicate it, rock and roll trends, or the climate of the art world.

Traditionally, graffiti has been researched and discussed as an age-old method of simple communication. Psychologists have studied graffiti as a manifestation of certain identifiable patterns in individual human behavior. Sociologists have scrutinized it in search of clues about society—how people view themselves as a part of, or separated from, society and how those views are expressed. Folklorists have examined graffiti for the linguistic evidence that it can provide. Many of these studies, done before the 1940s, have looked at graffiti as the action of individuals in a psychosocial context.

The great significance of graffiti as an important artifact of several subcultures was not investigated until recent years after graffiti had flowered into a popular art with connections to other facets of urban popular culture: dance, music, television, comic books, drugs, and computers. Even more recently graffiti has been given serious consideration as a "high" art and therefore as a marketable commodity.

For the purposes of this chapter, it is useful to discuss graffiti as two forms: graffiti and graffiti art. Graffiti is discussed as the traditional, monochromatic initials, names, and messages found inscribed on tree trunks, in cement, on bridge overpasses, and on the walls of "private" areas such as public rest rooms. Traditional graffiti continues to be common throughout the United States and is not usually associated exclusively with any particular environment.

Graffiti art, however, is strictly an urban phenomenon and is considered here as the colorful spray-painted names, messages, and three-dimensional images that began appearing on walls, subway trains, and handball courts in the mid-1970s. In addition to being a popular urban art form, graffiti art is identified with smaller subcultures, such as the youth and ethnic cultures of a city. Graffiti art is a melting pot of pop influences, drawing images and inspiration from 1960s nostalgia, music, dance, television, comic books, and computer graphics and jargon. Because a good deal of research has already been compiled on traditional graffiti, and because graffiti art is a relatively new phenomenon and the research is scant and ephemeral and involves a variety of media, the greater part of this chapter is devoted to graffiti art.

HISTORICAL OUTLINE

The folklorist Alan Dundes has pointed out that while it is academically acceptable to study graffiti of past cultures, there is something less permissible about scholarly investigations of graffiti in our own time. Since Dundes made this observation, nearly a quarter of a century has elapsed, during which time graffiti in America has evolved into a phenomenon with powerful cultural and sociological implications. Its dimensions as a cultural phenomenon have expanded and metamorphosed from the traditional marking of public surfaces with names and initials to the spectacular street murals featured in *Colors*, the 1988 Dennis Hopper film about gang violence in Los Angeles, and to contemporary works of art offered for sale for thousands of dollars by the prestigious and highly proper auction houses of Sotheby and Christie. Those who are interested in the study of popular culture in America should be very thankful that a handful of "graffiti watchers" has been observing and documenting this ephemeral and rapidly changing phenomenon because it is such a rich source of cultural information, revealing a great deal not only about widely disparate societal groups but also about urban American popular arts.

The history of graffiti is as old as that of humankind. Wherever there have been people and inviting, unmarked surfaces, there have been the scrawled gesticulations signifying ritual, warning, decoration, or simply existence. The word itself, *graffiti*, originates with the Italian verb *graffiare*, meaning "to scratch," an infinitive that might evoke images from lovers' optimistic inscriptions on trees, to the magical beasts adorning the caves of Lascaux. In fact, some who study graffiti view it as having come full circle from the subterranean corridors of prehistoric Europe to the subterranean corridors of modern New York City. What began as a primitive art form evolved and grew in complexity until it was elevated (or reduced) to a neoprimitive high art form.

Written rather than pictorial graffiti has its origins in Western culture with the Greeks, whose common people were the first to learn to write and therefore to express themselves graphically. Many examples exist from the ancient Athenian marketplace. Most are obscene.

The Romans were great graffitists, too, and, interestingly, much of their graffiti dealt with either sexual and scatological subjects or politics and, not infrequently, both in the same inscription. The eruption of Vesuvius in A.D. 79 preserved a great deal of Pompeiian graffiti on a vast array of subjects. Other ancient people who apparently practiced graffiti-writing were the Mayans at Tikal, Guatemala, whose graffiti can be dated between 100 B.C. and A.D. 700, and the Phrygians of what is now central Turkey, whose writings have been dated about 1200 B.C.

Medieval England had its share of graffitists who chose to incise walls, pillars, and floors of churches, monasteries, and dungeons. The Tower of London features quite a few grim inscriptions, some in blood, by those incarcerated within, many awaiting execution. During the earthy eighteenth century there was an incredible flowering of graffiti, inspired by literature and encompassing a variety of themes from love, to admonishments about health and disease. So prevalent and elaborately witty were these English inscriptions that Hurlo Thrumbo was inspired to collect examples found in taverns and inns. He published his anthology, *The Merry-Thought, or The Glass-Window Bog House Miscellany*, in 1731, describing it in his own words as "by persons of the first Rank and Figure in Great Britain; relating to Love, Matrimony, Drunkenness, Sobriety, Ranting, Scandal, Politics, Gaming and many other Subjects, Serious and Comical." This eighteenth-century propensity for graffiti-writing was evidently transplanted in the New World, as Daniel Boone's legendary inscription on a Tennessee tree, "D. Boon Cilled a BAR in THE YEAR 1760," attests. Even earlier examples of colonial graffiti exist at Williamsburg, where the elegant rubbed brick of the Public Records Office bears initials of many FFVs (First Families of Virginia), including Blairs and Carters, leading one to suspect that if we could examine the hold of the *Mayflower*, we would find it to have been liberally inscribed with initials, complaints about seasickness, hopeful religious messages, and griping about less than ideal accommodations.

For two centuries American graffiti adhered closely to traditional subject matter as described by Thrumbo—that is, it mostly had to do with some of the baser aspects of life: drinking, defecating, and politicking. Although ubiquitous in the United States, no serious scholarly attention was granted to graffiti until the twentieth century, when folklorist Allen Walker Read published *Lexical Evidence from Folk Epigraphy in Western North America: A Glossarial Study of the Low Element in the English Vocabulary*. Based on examples that he had gathered in public latrines throughout the western United States and Canada, Read's study examined the linguistic significance of words that occurred frequently in graffiti, such as *bitch*, comparing the colloquial usage with the standard definitions found in dictionaries. Read's pioneering work not only identified graffiti as worthy of serious study but also revealed the interesting discrepancy between the way that words are supposed to be used in American language and the way that people actually use them.

Most traditional American graffiti is very specific in regard to place, time, or situation, but a few examples have become internationally recognized. Such an example is the omnipresent and elusive Kilroy of the mischievous graffiti brag, "Kilroy was here." Kilroy was always depicted as hanging onto and peering over a wall, and he could be drawn very rapidly with a minimal number of marks. The mascot of World War II (military humor and iconography are another understudied area of popular culture), Kilroy's platypus-like visage could be found from the Marshall Islands to the Arc de Triomphe. There is some speculation that Kilroy was born of the old army–air force rivalry, in which he represented the lowly infantry sergeant who could always beat everyone, especially the air force, to any scene. A Freudian interpretation goes so far as to suggest that the Kilroy legend is oedipal in origin, the enemy being the father and the territory occupied by the enemy the mother that Kilroy desires to possess. It seems a little more likely that Kilroy was simply a product of GI humor and bluster, the indomitable American spirit in the face of adversity.

In the post–World War II years, graffiti, like many things in America, began to change slightly in character. In the 1950s, America experienced the rapid growth of its first real culture of youth—a vigorous, vital phenomenon that has had as much to do with the world's image of the United States as anything has. Also occurring in the 1950s were a growing ethnic pride and identity among different racial groups and nationalities. For both these cultures—youth and ethnic—graffiti became a useful medium of communication, especially when the two cultures overlapped. Mexican American gangs, for instance, were first formed in Los Angeles after the war and began to rely on graffiti to mark territories and to propagandize. A rival gang would know better, for instance, than to try to frequent a neighborhood in which "BLOODS" appeared many times. For the first time, graffiti became an expression of groups, not only the individual.

In the late 1960s, graffiti changed again, this time becoming again the medium of the individual, but with a difference. "Tagging," or writing one's initials and street number, became popular in New York City and touched off a graffiti explosion that lasted twenty years. What made tagging different from simple vandalism or initialing was its territorial significance as well as its representation of an even more powerful subculture of youth with little regard for the values and laws of established society. As graffiti proliferated, the subculture developed aesthetic values and standards all its own.

The spark that ignited this graffiti explosion was "TAKI 183." In 1969 New Yorkers began to see the mysterious name and number everywhere. It appeared in subways, on walls along Broadway, at Kennedy International Airport, and in the "bedroom" suburbs of New Jersey and Connecticut. An enterprising *New York Times* reporter finally identified Taki as a teenage Greek immigrant from a blue-collar neighborhood on the edge of Manhattan. His real name was Demetrius, Taki being the Greek diminutive of that name, and his family home was on 183rd Street. Although Taki put his first "tag" or initial on an ice-cream truck in the summer of 1970, he recalled having been inspired as early as 1967 by "JULIO 204," whose tag appeared around their neighborhood. Taki's ambitions were greater than Julio's, and because his job as a messenger took him by subway to all five boroughs of the city, his tag became a sort of neo-Kilroy in the New York City area. Taki is also credited with popularizing the wide Magic Marker as a tagging medium, eventually enabling graffitists to enhance their names with interesting calligraphic effects.

Before long, New York and Philadelphia were covered with a blizzard of graffiti spawned by Taki imitators. Immediately, there were innovations and refinements in technique. In 1972, Super-Kool 223 was one of the first writers to discover that by using spray paint instead of, or in combination with, markers, large areas could be painted very rapidly and draw more attention. Super-Kool purportedly also discovered that by replacing the narrow caps of spray paint cans with "fat caps" from oven cleaner or spray starch, broader or smoother areas could be painted. Distinctly different styles developed. Bronx style was characterized by bubble letters, Brooklyn used a curious, almost ancient Celtic style featuring flourishes and arrows, and Broadway or Manhattan style had long, slim letters and was thought to have been imported from Philadelphia by a writer named Topcat, who claimed to have learned it from Cornbread. Styles merged, resulting in wild style—Brooklyn structured lettering crossed with Manhattan spray techniques.

No surface was spared, but the subway system became the preferred medium for several reasons. Subway trains provided a means of communicating with other writers in distant neighborhoods. The S train, for instance, one of the subway lines preferred by writers, takes four hours to traverse the city from the Bronx to Brooklyn, guaranteeing a very wide audience. Tagging trains could also be very dangerous, and writers found the increased element of risk attractive. Despite the spontaneity of their work, graffiti writers have a studied knowledge of the transit system and know exactly where trains are parked and which trains have the best surfaces for painting.

City authorities became alarmed at the unchecked proliferation of graffiti. On October 10, 1972, the New York City Council unanimously passed a tough antigraffiti bill, which made it unlawful to carry spray paint in a public building. Convictions could carry fines of up to $500 and up to three months in prison. Special compounds were invented to remove graffiti from trains and buildings. By 1973, New York City was spending $10 million a year to combat graffiti without making an appreciable dent. The city even went so far as to implement an attack-dog program, which, not surprisingly, seemed only to stimulate the phenomenon.

As efforts to eradicate graffiti intensified, so did the challenge to create ever more daring and spectacular graffiti tags. Individual writers or "style masters" and gangs or "crews" like the Ex-Vandals, the Independent Writers, and Wanted—the largest group, with seventy members—vied to create the most original and outrageous pieces, further stimulating the frenzy of graffiti activity. One important artistic development was "3D," which added the illusion of mass and depth to a tag. Shading, highlighting, and overlapping letters also enhanced the name, which became less recognizable as a word and more like an abstract or pop art painting. Graffiti grew enormously in size, culminating with the first "top-to-bottom whole car": the ultimate achievement in which the tag covers an entire subway car, windows, doors, and all. In addition to scale and color, composition was carefully planned, as were decorative motifs like stars, clouds, flames, checkerboards, cracks, and polka dots. Writers had also begun incorporating illustrative material like television, cartoon, and comic book characters into their work. Subway graffiti has featured Mickey Mouse, Pluto, Donald Duck, Felix the Cat, Dondi, the Pink Panther, Deputy Dawg, Howard the Duck, the Silver Surfer, the Incredible Hulk, Cheech Wizard, and characters from ZAP comics of the 1960s, most notably R. Crumb's Mr. Natural and Rick Griffin's winged eyeball.

These "style wars," or aesthetic experiments, underscored the difference between graffiti and graffiti art. Graffiti became something more than a way of "watching your name go by," and writers became something more than vandals. An underground subculture had developed with an art form, value system, and language all its own. No longer "toys" or beginners who were proficient only at "tagging," graffiti artists became "bombers" who executed "throw ups," the large-scale works on train exteriors; "downs," a painting or large signature below a train's windows; or "masterpieces," which generally featured an ambitious theme and elaborate technique, like the John Lennon memorial train created by Lady Pink and Iz the Wiz in 1981.

By the 1980s graffiti art had come off the walls and trains and into a number of small, unfashionable galleries like Fashion Moda in the South Bronx. The Times Square Show in 1980 was followed by the New York/New Wave Show in 1981, and before long exclusive SoHo and 57th Street galleries were hanging work by graffiti writers. Graffiti artists were commissioned to paint backdrops for the Twyla Tharp dance troupe and to design nightclubs, Mardi Gras floats, magazine covers, record jackets, billboards, postcards, and upholstery. Graffiti art has inspired textile design, clothing, and jewelry. Major exhibitions of paintings inspired by American graffiti art have been mounted in cities around the world, attracting serious critical attention and making graffiti, like pork bellies, a marketable commodity. In 1985 a painting by a former American graffitist, Jean-Michel Basquiat, commanded $820,900 in a Christie's auction—the same price paid for a DeKooning in the same sale. Another former graffitist, Keith Haring, became an instant celebrity when his neo-neoprimitive, graffiti-inspired work was featured in *People* magazine.

There have been two noticeable developments in graffiti in the past few years, Japanese Anime and "Scratchiti." Japanese Anime, or "Japanamie," is the style of mixing other graffiti styles with characteristics of Japanese animation, the most common of these characteristics being large eyes and low-profile noses. "Scratchiti" is most commonly used on windows of subway trains but can be seen in other areas. It is done by scratching or etching a tag or image on the surface of the glass. It can also be done with acid, by burning an image or tag in the glass.

Nowadays, many of the large cities have legally sanctioned walls or "yards" where graffiti writers can legally display their skills. Unfortunately, since these walls have become accepted and popular in the graffiti community, the pieces that are done on such walls get covered over quickly by other writers wanting space for their own works. This tends to drive away those with the most skill and interest.

Graffiti's evolution illustrates a wild ride on the roller coaster of American culture. Beginning as a monochromatic, personalized scrawling, it metamorphosed into awesome, lush creations bursting with sensuous color, finally becoming a formal art form that we see in galleries today. Do graffitists deserve praise or blame? Are their impulses creative or destructive? Is graffiti art merely a fad, or is it portentous of a direction that art is to take? What are the implications of the

Graffitti in New York. © Painet

change of context—from street and subway to gallery and canvas? Is graffiti art fine or folk?

There is certainly evidence to support the view that it has much in common with what is generally considered to be "high" art. There is a strong and identifiable aesthetic theory in graffiti art. Because it is illegal, it is a radical art, making a social statement and having evolved out of a social condition not unlike American social realism and Mexican mural art of the 1930s. It is not officially acceptable, which is what gives it its vitality. It breaks frontiers and therefore can be seen to have historic precedent in other pioneering American art movements like the Ashcan school and abstract expressionism. There are obvious similarities to pop art, conceptual art, and new realism. Some see graffiti art as being as cataclysmic a development as the frescoes of Giotto. The painter Frank Stella suggests that graffiti artists have something in common with Caravaggio and painters of sixteenth-century Rome, particularly in regard to their rebellion against the spatial confinement of the traditional easel painting. Some see graffiti as having precedent in all of modern abstract painting. In his poetic 1974 essay *The Faith of Graffiti*, Norman Mailer said: "Art had been rolling down the fall-line from Cezanne to Frank Stella, from Gauguin to Mathieu. On such a map, subway graffiti was an alluvial delta, the mud-caked mouth of a hundred painterly streams."

Some graffiti artists have academic backgrounds and seem to have used graffiti as a fertile medium for their art, not without a certain self-consciousness. Keith Haring, with his black-and-white "new wave Aztec" style, is an example. Raised far from the urban ghetto, in Kutztown, Pennsylvania, Haring studied commercial art in Pittsburgh and then spent two years at Manhattan's School of Visual Arts. He has also studied semiotics and lists some of his influences as Aztec art, Pierre Alechinsky, and Jean Dubuffet. He began his graffiti career by scribbling on spaces intended for advertisements on the walls of subway stations.

Some art critics see graffiti art as marking the end of modernist arrogance and elitism and as a reaction against the institutionalized and commercialized art of today, although plenty of graffiti artists are happy to be selling works on canvas. Other critics have refused to envision graffiti art as a positive force in the future of art, however. Robert Hughes predicts that the current art market will soon crash, beginning with a slide brought about by the entrance of graffiti into the art world. Critic Barbara Rose excluded any graffiti art from her important 1979 "crystal ball" exhibition *American Painting: The Eighties.*

Some characteristics of graffiti art as it appears on the street constitute elements frequently used to define "folk art." Quite clearly, graffiti art demonstrates much that is "folk" in urban culture, although folklorists seem reluctant to recognize it as such or to bestow the respectable label of "folk art" upon it. There is certainly a communal aesthetic shared by a group of artists and their audience in graffiti art. Critic Harold Rosenberg has said that "the graffiti in New York subways are probably the largest spontaneous outpouring and group showing of folk art that have ever taken place." There is a tradition in which forms are perfected and passed on, and this transmission is carried out in an apparently informal, but highly systematic, way. Graffiti art relies on words, signs, and images that have universality and that are meant to be taken at face value, like Haring's radiant child or Bill Blast's 1982 masterpiece *Sky's the Limit.* Reviews of graffiti shows are fraught with words like "shamanistic," "primal," "primordial," and "orgiastic." Graffiti art is often reflective of roots in other cultures, such as the work of Basquiat, whose parents are Haitians, or the Hispanic graffiti of the Los Angeles ghetto. Graffiti incorporates the everyday elements of popular culture, drawing imagery and tags from cars (Futura 2000), baseball players (Cey I for Ron Cey), comic strips, drugs, and even computer jargon and graphics. It is vividly decorative, sometimes visionary or surreal, and certainly is a reaction against the stark colorlessness of modern architecture and the bleakness of the ghetto environment. Most graffiti artists are unschooled; sometimes they are self-taught, but more frequently they learn through an informal apprenticeship, during which the tools, techniques, jargon, ritual, and protocol of graffiti are passed along. As artist Futura 2000 has pointed out, "I wouldn't mind going to art school if I could get a scholarship, but it would probably interfere with my work." Regarding the problem of defining folk art, collector Herbert Hemphill has stated, "It seems a waste of time to backtrack into semantics while the art can disappear, undocumented and unappreciated." Certainly, this admonition applies to graffiti art.

It must be said that once graffiti is painted on canvas, hung in galleries, museums, and other legitimate spaces, and bought and sold commercially, it becomes something else. It may or may not be "art," but by breaking with the traditional medium for graffiti—forbidden public surfaces—and by removing the taboo, it no longer is graffiti. It is the vandalism aesthetic that gives graffiti its validity. Once the element of risk is removed and the spontaneity with it, graffiti loses its vitality and its very essence. Painted on buildings and subways, graffiti is an authentic urban folk art, but when it becomes discovered by the galleries and dealers who cater to high culture, its aesthetic is debased.

Will graffiti art endure, and will it have a lasting impact or influence on art or other aspects of American culture? There are already signs that graffiti art has come full circle and is again becoming a method of communicating gang territorial parameters and warnings. But graffiti art has already lasted longer than many art movements, fauvism and impressionism, for instance, and who is to say that the impact of graffiti on art may not be as great? Norman Mailer believed that "the beginning of another millennium of vision" may be vested in graffiti art. As long as cities are stark, impersonal, and oppressive, the creative urge will be stimulated. In 200 or 2,000 years, the questions of labeling or categorizing graffiti as one thing or another will not be as important as what it will be able to tell us about urban dwellers in America in the late twentieth and twenty-first centuries.

REFERENCE WORKS

Because of the underground or avant-garde nature of graffiti, it is a difficult, if not fruitless, topic to approach through general reference works. Entries on traditional graffiti can be found in some general encyclopedias like the *Academic American* and *Encyclopedia Americana*, but even the latest editions make no mention of subway art.

General reference works on social science, psychology, folklore, and art consistently fail to include graffiti at all. To get at information on graffiti, the best approach is through periodical indexes. *Art Index* is notoriously slow to catch on to new trends—before 1980, looking up the word *graffiti* yielded only articles on attic vases and Etruscan art. Other indexes dealing specifically with art are *Arts and Humanities Citation Index*, *Artbibliographies Modern*, and *RILA: Repertoire international de la litterature de l'art*. Among specialized indexes, the Modern Language Association's *MLA International Bibliography of Books and Articles on the Modern Languages and Literatures* includes articles on graffiti in the fourth section, "General Literature and Related Topics," subsection "Folk Literature." *Psychological Abstracts* might yield articles dealing with that aspect of graffiti. The *Readers' Guide* is a good general index, as are some of the machine indexes, like the *Magazine Index* and *Infotrac*; the latter is available on CD-ROM. These indexes are also very useful because they often index publications not indexed elsewhere, like *New York* magazine or *Los Angeles*. Newspapers like the *New York Times* and the *Los Angeles Times* have their own indexes and are extremely rich sources, in the case of graffiti providing a real chronicle of its rise and metamorphosis and efforts to combat it.

The most thorough resource is a Web resource, *Art Crimes*, found at www.graffiti.org. This site is an ideal starting point for those researching any aspect of graffiti. The site showcases numerous artists each month, publishing pictures of their tags and pieces. It also displays pictures of pieces from all around the world. Postings of shows and events in cities of the United States and Europe are updated regularly. The goods and services section contains links to a directory of muralists and designers and links to the on-line merchandise store where you can buy books, videos, and magazine subscriptions. In the sources and information section you can find numerous interviews with graffiti writers, texts of articles, a list of helpful resources, and information on books, videos, and magazines about graffiti. The site also provides links to other graffiti sites. *Art Crimes* is the best place to gain information on the European graffiti scene, which is growing rapidly. This invaluable source strives to keep current with the ever-changing face of graffiti as well as preserve and document the pieces.

Collections of examples of traditional graffiti abound. Most sources represent specific kinds of graffiti relating to feminism, politics, sports, sex, ethnic humor, and so on. Already mentioned is Read's pioneering graffiti glossary. The *Encyclopedia of Graffiti* by Robert Reisner and Lorraine Wechsler includes hundreds of examples of graffiti, organized by subject; most were gathered by the authors. Books by Henry Chalfant and Steven Hager include glossaries of graffiti jargon. Other sources are amusing collections like the books compiled by Richard Hammerstein and Maria Haan dealing with sports-related graffiti in four college athletic conferences.

RESEARCH COLLECTIONS

There is, of course, little archival material available on graffiti, and its very nature precludes its being collectible or preservable. Some of the "alternative art-space" galleries that first showed graffiti-inspired paintings are still going strong, like Fashion Moda in the South Bronx. Another gallery that shows postgraffiti painting is Sidney Janis, at 110 West 57th Street, New York. In a school yard at 106th Street and Park Avenue there is the "Graffiti Hall of Fame," where graffiti artists may paint on ball court walls. In Paris, there is reportedly a graffiti museum under the directorship of Serge Raymond.

HISTORY AND CRITICISM

Studies of graffiti in America are best divided, like the subject itself, into two separate entities: traditional graffiti and graffiti art. Research on traditional graffiti can also be grouped further into studies of its psychological and sociological aspects.

A good place to begin researching graffiti is Robert Reisner's *Graffiti: Two Thousand Years of Wall Writing*. A general history, Reisner's work includes information on the significance of caste and class and graffiti as art and literature, as well as illustrations and a compendium of selected graffiti organized by subject.

It would be impossible to discuss graffiti as a popular art without first consulting some of the standard works on popular culture, such as Russel B. Nye's *The Unembarrassed Muse: The Popular Arts in America*. Herbert J. Gans' *Popular Culture and High Culture* identifies graffiti as a popular art of the last of his five "taste cultures"—the quasifolk low culture. Graffitists are characterized as poor, mostly nonwhite, unskilled, blue-collar workers with little education whose tastes include tabloids, comic books, adventure films, and television soap operas. Graffiti, like other aspects of Gans' quasi-folk low culture, is overwhelmingly a male activity.

The psychological and sociological aspects of graffiti have been well explored and provide a number of intriguing perspectives. A thorough and entertaining examination has been provided by Ernest L. Abel and Barbara E. Buckley in *The Handwriting on the Wall: Toward a Sociology and Psychology of Graffiti*. The authors discuss the history of graffiti and review the many theories about its psychological motivations. Among the various motivational forces that they identify are sex (heterosexual, autosexual, and homosexual), humor, defecation, and, surprisingly, smell. Abel and Buckley define two types of graffiti, public and private, differentiate between male and female graffiti, and also make the shortsighted statement that after its heyday in 1972–1973 graffiti artistry began to disappear.

More specific studies theorize in graphic detail about the psychological inspiration for American graffiti. A landmark study by the folklorist Alan Dundes suggests that with scatological graffiti the motivation "is related to an infantile desire to play with feces and to artistically smear it around." In his paper "Here I Sit—A Study of American Latrinalia," Dundes equates defecation and this "smearing impulse" with writing and coins the term *latrinalia* to describe the inscriptions relating to excretory functions commonly written on the walls of public rest rooms. Another important article is W. J. Gadpaille's "Graffiti: Its Psychodynamic Significance," which concentrates on sexual graffiti. Gadpaille differentiates between male and female graffiti, pointing out a male preoccupation with penis size, and cites statistics from Kinsey that show that most (75 percent) sexual graffiti is homosexual. In "Graffiti: Some Observations and Speculations," Harvey D. Lomas looks at the psychological significance of the wall itself and the need of the graffiti writer to possess or destroy the wall.

Some attempts have been made to study graffiti scientifically. Notably, David Ley and Roman Cybriwsky have written "Urban Graffiti as Territorial Markers," in which they pinpoint occurrences of graffiti on distribution maps in order to delineate the territories of various Philadelphia street gangs. They point out the importance of learning to read the "diagnostic indicators" of the behavioral environment, stating that if "the scholar is unable to interpret the visible, then the invisible meaning of place will be beyond his grasp." Terrance L. Stocker, Linda W. Dutcher, Stephen M. Hargrove, and Edwin A. Cook's "Social Analysis of Graffiti" is a midway report of a study that has analyzed graffiti gathered at three American universities in order to determine specific social attitudes that are evident.

Jill Posener's *Spray It Loud* is a black-and-white photodocumentation of political graffiti. Although British, the book is a good representation of graffiti-writing that has been inspired by contemporary social concerns: nuclear warfare, smoking, and feminism. Posener believes in graffiti as an effective political weapon when it is a complement to other actions such as demonstrations or campaigns.

Other sources document ethnic graffiti, such as Gusmano Cesaretti's *Street Writers: A Guided Tour of Chicano Graffiti*. Cesaretti's photographic essay is accompanied by text in the form of the words of a young Los Angeles *plaquito*, or street writer, who describes the major inspiration for the graffiti of the *cholos* (gang members): their Mexican heritage (Aztec and Spanish) and territorial demarcation.

Much of what is known and remembered about graffiti art in years to come will be due to the spectacular and thorough photodocumentation of Henry Chalfant. In two extraordinary books Chalfant's photographs have captured the sensational artwork that is often literally "here today gone tomorrow." (Five hundred "pieces" that no longer exist were photographed over a five-year period.) To truly understand the visual impact and appeal of graffiti art and its significance as a popular art, one would have to refer to Chalfant's books: *Subway Art* (coauthored with Martha Cooper) and *Spraycan Art* (coauthored with James Prigoff). No other sources represent the dazzling colors and fantastic designs with such fidelity. In *Subway Art* the authors have managed a rapport with graffiti writers that facilitated a revealing glimpse into style, technique, and materials. *Spraycan Art* looks at the phenomenon in the 1980s, recognizing the spread of graffiti art to Europe, Australia, and New Zealand as well as new trends: painting on racquetball courts, computer influences, and the appearance of Japanese comic book characters. Craig Castleman's *Getting Up* provides the other side of the story: interviews with police. Another fascinating and essential source is Steven Hager's *Hip Hop: The Illustrated History of Break Dancing, Rap Music, and Graffiti*, which documents the important connections of graffiti with other urban popular arts. Hager identifies hip-hop as an urban subculture that has created art forms all its own. Included is a great deal of how-to information: how to dress, how to use spray paint appropriately, how to "backspin" records. Richard Goldstein's December 1980 article in the *Village Voice* was the first to link rap music and graffiti.

The first and best source to refer to regarding the aesthetics of graffiti art would be Norman Mailer's landmark essay *The Faith of Graffiti*. Dubbing himself the "Aesthetic Investigator," Mailer endowed graffiti with a number of apocalyptic properties as well as noble historic associations with art from the caves of Lascaux to Giotto, Michelangelo, Picasso, and Pollock. In this essay, Mailer also relates a dream that could have been the inspiration for Keith Haring's subway station work. Most of the thoughtful considerations of graffiti exist as periodical articles. Two very informative ones are Suzi Gablik's "Report from New York: The Graffiti Question," which examines questions posed by graffiti's entrance into the gallery, and Francesca Alinova's "Twenty-First Century Slang," which accepts graffiti as art and scrutinizes the iconography of works on canvas by Keith Haring and others. Cynthia Nadelman's "Graffiti Is a Thing That's Kind of Hard to Explain" is also important. A feisty radical defense is René Ricard's "The Radiant Child." Few current books on contemporary art even mention graffiti, but Edward Lucie-Smith's *American Art Now* and Harold Rosenberg's *Art on the Edge* are two exceptions. Lucie-Smith differentiates between graffiti artists and postgraffiti artists who have made the transition from subway to canvas. In *Working Space*, Frank Stella's collection of Charles Eliot Norton lectures given at Harvard, the painter acknowledges his own interest in and debt to graffiti art by taking the book's title from a "piece" on a New York street. Any researcher wishing to understand the place of postgraffiti art in the contemporary art scene would do very well to consult two invaluable sources: auction catalogs from Sotheby's (980 Madison Avenue, New York 10021) and Christie's (502 Park Avenue, New York 10022–1199). Although few libraries collect them, subscriptions are available and include not only the catalogs, with prices that the art is expected to fetch, but a list of "prices realized," which is sent after the auction occurs.

AUDIOVISUAL RESOURCES

Fortunately, several films exist that either document the graffiti phenomenon or prominently feature graffiti or graffiti writers. Anyone wishing to understand the graffiti art phenomenon must see *Style Wars*, an excellent documentary co-produced by Henry Chalfant in 1984. It is the best single source on the subject and includes interviews with the artists (available through New Day Films in New

Jersey or Tony Silver Films in New York). Based on *Style Wars* and produced in 1985 by Harry Belafonte, *Beat Street* is a 35mm feature film that was responsible for spreading the culture of hip-hop around the United States and the world. Directed in 1983 by Charlie Ahearn, *Wild Style* is a 35mm docudrama on the street culture of hip-hop. Famous graffitists and break dancers like the Rock Steady Crew, Lee Quinones, and Lady Pink are featured. In 1985, Twentieth Century Fox (Interscope Productions) released a mediocre feature film entitled *Turk 182*, in which a young graffiti artist is portrayed unrealistically but sympathetically. In Dennis Hopper's 1988 film *Colors*, several scenes are staged with Los Angeles graffiti art in the background, providing a good look at some excellent examples but unfortunately creating the impression that hip-hop street murals are associated with violent, drug-trafficking youth gangs. Musician Malcolm McLaren's rock video *Buffalo Gals* was shot in front of Bill Blast's 1982 masterpiece *Sky's the Limit*. A television documentary on graffiti, "The Writing on the Wall," was produced by New Jersey Network and aired on New Jersey Educational Television on February 6, 1987. Finally, an audiotape, *Young Graffiti Artists*, in which several graffiti artists were interviewed in 1982, is available from National Public Radio.

BIBLIOGRAPHY

Books and Articles

Abel, Ernest L., and Barbara E. Buckley. *The Handwriting on the Wall: Toward a Sociology and Psychology of Graffiti*. Westport, Conn.: Greenwood Press, 1977.

Academic American Encyclopedia. Danbury, Conn.: Grolier, 1980– .

Alinova, Francesca. "Twenty-First Century Slang." *Flash Art* 114 (November 1983), 23–31, 59.

Artbibliographies Modern. Santa Barbara, Calif.: ABC Clio, 1969– .

Art Index. Bronx, N.Y.: H. W. Wilson, 1929– .

Arts and Humanities Citation Index. Philadelphia: Institute for Scientific Information, 1976– .

Ashbery, John. "Graffiti on Canvas." *Newsweek* 101 (April 18, 1983), 94.

Barnett, Claudia. "The Death of Graffiti: Postmodernism and the New York City Subway." *Studies in Popular Culture* 16 (April 1994), 25–38.

Baudrillard, Jean. "The Ecstasy of Communication." In *The Anti-Aesthetic*, ed. Hal Foster. Port Townsend, Wash.: Bay Press, 1983, 111–25.

Brassai. *Graffiti*. Stuttgart: C. Beiser Verlag, 1960.

Castleman, Craig. *Getting Up: Subway Graffiti in New York*. Cambridge: MIT Press, 1982.

Cesaretti, Gusmano. *Street Writers: A Guided Tour of Chicano Graffiti*. Los Angeles: Acrobat Books, 1975.

Chalfant, Henry, and James Prigoff. *Spraycan Art*. London: Thames and Hudson, 1987.

Cooper, Martha, and Henry Chalfant. *Subway Art*. New York: Holt, Rinehart, and Winston, 1984.

Dundes, Alan. "Here I Sit—A Study of American Latrinalia." *Kroeber Anthropological Society Papers* 34 (Spring 1966), 91–105.
Encyclopedia Americana. Danbury, Conn.: Grolier, 1918– .
"Folk Art Meeting: Calm and Placid on the Surface . . ." *Folklife Center News* (Library of Congress) 7 (January-March 1984), 4–5, 13.
Fried, Frederick. *America's Forgotten Folk Arts*. New York: Pantheon, 1978.
Gablik, Suzi. "Graffiti in Well-Lighted Rooms." *Has Modernism Failed?* New York: Thames and Hudson, 1984, 103–13.
———. "Report from New York: The Graffiti Question." *Art in America* 70 (October 1982), 33–37, 39.
Gadpaille, W. J. "Graffiti: Its Psychodynamic Significance." *Sexual Behavior* (November 1971), 45–51.
Gans, Herbert J. *Popular Culture and High Culture*. New York: Basic Books, 1975.
Goldstein, Richard. "The Fire Down Below." *Village Voice* 25 (December 24, 1980), 55.
———. "This Thing Has Gotten Completely Out of Hand." *New York Magazine* (March 26, 1973), 33–39.
Gonos, George, Virginia Mulkern, and Nicohlas Poushinski. "Anonymous Expression: A Structural View of Graffiti." *Journal of American Folklore* 89 (January–March 1976), 40–48.
"Graffiti on the Canvas." *Newsweek* (April 18, 1983), 94.
Greenstein, M. A. "A Conversation with Timothy Treacy." *Artweek* 23 (April 9, 1992), 22–23.
Hager, Steven. *Hip Hop: The Illustrated History of Break Dancing, Rap Music, and Graffiti*. New York: St. Martin's Press, 1984.
Hammerstein, Richard, and Maria N. Haan. *Graffiti in the Big Ten*. New York: Warner Books, 1981.
———. *Graffiti in the Ivy League, Seven Sisters, and Thereabouts*. New York: Warner Books, 1981.
———. *Graffiti in the PAC Conference*. New York: Warner Books, 1981.
———. *Graffiti in the Southwest Conference*. New York: Warner Books, 1981.
Haring, Keith. *Art in Transit: Subway Drawings by Keith Haring*. New York: Harmony Books, 1984.
Horowitz, Carl F. "Portrait of the Artist as a Young Vandal: The Aesthetics of Paint Graffiti." *Journal of American Culture* 2 (Fall 1979), 376–91.
Huber, Jocrg. *Paris Graffiti*. London: Thames and Hudson, 1986.
Ingham, Curtis. "Graffiti: The Soapbox of the Seventies." *Ms.* 4 (September 1975), 65–67.
Jameson, Fredric. "Postmodernism and Consumer Society." In *The Anti-Aesthetic*, ed. Hal Foster. Port Townsend, Wash.: Bay Press, 1983, 111–25.
Jundis, Orvy. "Graffiti Cartoons and Comics: Is There a Connection?" *Witty World* 3 (Spring 1988), 18–19.
Leary, Bill. *Graffiti*. Greenwich, Conn.: Fawcett, 1969.
Ley, David, and Roman Cybriwsky. "Urban Graffiti as Territorial Markers." *Annals of the Association of American Geographers* 64 (December 1974), 491–505.
Lomas, Harvey D. "Graffiti: Some Observations and Speculations." *Psychoanalytical Review* 60 (Spring 1973), 71–89.

Lucie-Smith, Edward. *American Art Now*. New York: William Morrow, 1985.
Mailer, Norman. *The Faith of Graffiti*. New York: Praeger, 1974. Also published in *Esquire* 81 (May 1974), 77–88, 154, 157–58.
MLA International Bibliography of Books and Articles on the Modern Languages and Literatures. New York: Modern Language Association of America, 1921– .
Mockridge, Norton. *The Scrawl of the Wild: What People Write on Walls—and Why*. New York: Paperback Library, 1969.
Moufarrege, Nicholas A. "Lightning Strikes (Not Once but Twice): An Interview with Graffiti Artists." *The Arts* (November 1982), 87–93.
Nadelman, Cynthia. "Graffiti Is a Thing That's Kind of Hard to Explain." *ARTnews*, 81 (October 1982), 76–78.
Nye, Russel B. *The Unembarrassed Muse: The Popular Arts in America*. New York: Dial Press, 1970.
Ong, Walter J. "Subway Graffiti and the Design of the Self." In *The State of Language*, ed. Christopher Ricks and Leonard Micheals. Berkeley: UC Berkeley Press, 1990, 400–407.
Posener, Jill. *Spray It Loud*. London: Routledge and Kegan Paul, 1982.
Psychological Abstracts. Arlington, Va.: American Psychological Association, 1927– .
Read, Allen Walker. *Lexical Evidence from Folk Epigraphy in Western North America: A Glossarial Study of the Low Element in the English Vocabulary*. Paris: Privately printed, 1935.
Readers' Guide to Periodical Literature. Bronx, N.Y.: H. W. Wilson, 1890– .
Reisner, Robert. *Graffiti: Two Thousand Years of Wall Writing*. Chicago: Cowles Book, 1971.
Reisner, Robert, and Lorraine Wechsler. *Encyclopedia of Graffiti*. New York: Macmillan, 1974.
Ricard, René. "The Radiant Child." *Artforum* 20 (December 1981), 35–43.
RILA: Repertoire international de la litterature de l'art. Williamstown, Mass.: J. Paul Getty Trust, 1975– .
Rosenberg, Harold. *Art on the Edge*. Chicago: University of Chicago Press, 1971.
Serra, Richard. "Tilted Arc Destroyed." *Art in America* (May 1989), 34–45.
Sheff, David. "Just Say Know. 'You Use Whatever Comes along,' Says Artist Keith Haring about the Path His Career Has Taken. Now, Living with AIDS, He Sums up His Life and Times." *Rolling Stone* (August 10, 1989), 59–66, 102.
Siegal, Nina. "Extending the Life and Lore of Graffiti." *New York Times*, January 25, 2001: D1.
Small, Michael. "Drawing on Walls, Clothes and Subways, Keith Haring Earns Favor with Art Lovers High and Low." *People Weekly* (December 5, 1983), 147.
Stella, Frank. *Working Space*. Cambridge: Harvard University Press, 1986.
Stocker, Terrance L., Linda W. Dutcher, Stephen M. Hargrove, and Edwin A. Cook. "Social Analysis of Graffiti." *Journal of American Folklore* 85 (October/December 1972), 356–66.
"Taki 183 Spawns Pen Pals." *New York Times*, July 21, 1971: 37.

"The Talk of the Town: Taking Action." *The New Yorker* (August 15, 1983), 25–26.

Thrumbo, Hurlo. *The Merry-Thought, or The Glass-Window Bog House Miscellany*. London: 1731. Reprint. Los Angeles: Augustan Reprint Society, 1982.

Tomkins, Calvin. "The Art World: Up from the I.R.T." *The New Yorker* (March 26, 1984), 98–102.

Uehling, Mark D., and Maggie Malone. "Making War on Graffiti." *Newsweek* (August 11, 1986).

Periodicals

Art and Design. London, 1985– .

Art Direction. New York, 1949– .

Artforum. New York, 1962– .

Art in America. Marion, Ohio, 1913– .

ARTnews. Farmingdale, N.Y., 1902– .

Arts. New York, 1983– .

Artweek. Oakland, Calif., 1970– .

Bolletino d'Arte. Rome, 1907– .

Domus. Milan, 1950– .

Flash Art. Milan, 1977– .

Journal of American Culture. Bowling Green, Ohio, 1978– .

Journal of American Folklore. Washington, D.C., 1888– .

Journal of Popular Culture. Bowling Green, Ohio, 1967– .

Los Angeles: The Magazine of Southern California. Los Angeles, 1960– .

Los Angeles Times. 1881– .

Maledicta. Waukesha, Wis., 1977– .

New York Magazine. New York, 1968– .

New York Times. New York, 1851– .

Print. Bethesda, Md., 1940– .

Studio International. New York, 1893– .

Village Voice. New York, 1955– .

HOUSING

Benyamin Schwarz and Ruth Brent

> A good house is a created thing made of many parts economically and meaningfully assembled. It speaks not just of the materials from which it is made, but of the intangible rhythms, spirits, and dreams of people's lives. Its site is only a piece of the real world, yet this place is made to seem like an entire world. In its parts it accommodates important human activities, yet in sum it expresses an attitude toward life.
>
> Charles Moore, Gerald Allen, and Donlyn Lyndon

As a field of research, housing draws on many disciplines: anthropology, political science, sociology, architecture, urban planning, economics, geography, law, social work, public administration, psychology, and public administration, among many others. This chapter attempts to capture the multidisciplinary essence of housing as a complex system that seeks to meet the objectives of a variety of users. While this chapter strives to be a comprehensive guide to the field of housing studies, it is by no means exhaustive. Limitation of scope necessitates selection of topics within the broad, interdisciplinary research and practice of the field of housing in order to create this short reference guide.

The chapter starts with a short history of housing in the United States and moves on to issues of race and class as they are reflected in housing. The third section reviews design and construction, and the fourth discusses policy and economics of housing. The two following sections are dedicated to psychological aspects of housing; the first one in this sequence discusses the cognitive evaluation of housing, and the second reviews the concept of home. Neighborhoods and communities are reviewed in the next section, and the last part of this chapter discusses housing for special populations such as elderly and children.

HISTORICAL OUTLINE

The historical evolution of the American house, from early settlements to our time, is richly discussed in the literature. Fish's (1979) *The Story of Housing* and Foley's (1980) *The American House* are recommended for the novices in the field. In the span of 200 years, society in the United States transformed from a rural, agricultural, individualistic group of colonists into an urban, highly industrialized, independent nation. This evolution can be demonstrated by the fact that while in 1790 only 5 percent of the population lived in urban settings, in 1990 less than 5 percent were still farming. This complete reversal of occupation, lifestyle and location as well as the growth of the population from 4 million in 1790 to more than 270 million in 1998 has shaped the story of housing. Waves of immigrants, internal migration, wars, changing economic situations, and political turbulence all influenced the way that Americans were housed.

Resources about the history of housing in the United States may be found, among others, in Ford and Ford (1984) *Classic Modern Homes of the 30's*; Jones (1987) *Authentic Small Houses of the Twenties*; Radford (1983) *Old House Measured and Scaled*; Scully (1988) *American Architecture and Urbanism*; Walker (1981) *American Shelter*; Handlin (1979) *American Home: Architecture and Society, 1815–1915*; and Rowe (1993) *Modernity and Housing*.

Sources emphasizing the evolution of historic housing styles include McAlester and McAlester's *A Field Guide to American Houses* (1984), Rifkind's *Field Guide to American Architecture* (1998), and Whiffen's *American Architecture since 1780* (1968, rev. ed. 1992). In addition to the historic style of exterior housing, resources on historic interiors are William Seale's *Recreating the Historic House Interior* (1979) and Calloway and Cromley's *Elements of Style* (1991). The prolific writer Edith Wharton, who published, as her first book with Ogden Codman, *The Decoration of Houses* (1897, reprinted in 1997), produced a canon of interior decoration for affluent homes. This book was influential reading for Elsie de Wolfe and her cohort of decorators in the early 1900s. See Banham (1997) *Encyclopedia of Interior Design* and Brown (1982) *Sixty Years of Interior Design*. Taking the modernist perspective, Rogers (1962) examines the family and the house in the twentieth century, the house plan, and its furnishings in *The Modern House, U.S.A.*

ISSUES OF RACE AND CLASS

A different perspective of the history of housing can be found in studies about the adequacy and affordability of housing in the United States. The inability of parts of the U.S. population to obtain adequate housing because of their class, race, or ethnicity is central to this line of inquiry. Books that discuss these issues include Doucet and Weaver (1991) *Housing the North American City*; Friedman (1968) *Government and Slum Housing: A Century of Frustration*; Hirsch (1983) *Making the Second Ghetto: Race and Housing in Chicago, 1940–1960*; Jackson (1976) *A Place Called Home: A History of Low Cost Housing in Manhattan*; Jackson (1985) *Crabgrass Frontier: The Suburbanization of the United States*; Lubove (1962) *The Progressives and the Slums: Tenement House Reform in New York City, 1890–1917*; Mitchell (1985) *Federal Housing Policy and Programs: Past and Present*; Radford (1997) *Modern Housing for America: Policy Struggles in the New*

Deal Era; and Wright (1981) *Building the Dream: A Social History of Housing in America*.

According to these authors, housing is shaped by social, political, and economic forces that embody the values and relations of race, class, gender, occupation, age, and disability in the society. Creating housing involves moral choices that reflect and reinforce the nature of human inequality in the social context of the built environment (Weisman, 1992). The goal of decent, safe, and sanitary housing for all Americans has not been achieved after decades of federal legislation, presidential mandates, and government initiatives. Clearly, many of the nation's racial and ethnic minorities have not benefited from the changing housing opportunity structure to the same extent as their white counterparts. By all standards of measurement, a significant disparity in housing conditions by race, ethnicity, and income persists in the United States. "Too many people in our country are badly housed," stated Davis in 1967. The U.S. census for 1990 showed that the housing needs of America's poor and moderate-income families were still immense and growing. While the nation spends nearly $100 billion on housing, too little of it is used to meet the needs of people who are homeless or those who live in dilapidated homes or housing that they cannot afford. Stegman (1991), in his background paper on the limits of privatization, considers the national commitment to provide more housing and to provide it more fairly.

Housing has always been considered in connection with its location. The quality of residential environment declines with increasing size of settlements and with increasing centrality within settlements (Dahmann, 1985). Berry and Kasarda (1977) pointed out that older sites often bear the stamps of "obsolescence, high density, high industrialization, and aging inhabitants" (221). Several architects and urban designers share their ecological approach to cities, with the addition of skepticism about big initiatives and sweeping programs. In an article in *Progressive Architecture*, Fisher (1994) reports on a symposium at Yale in which the questions of violence and depopulation of America's inner cities were raised. Design professionals in this symposium tended to portray cities as physical artifacts used to create and sustain culture. In contrast, most economists and policy analysts perceived cities as places of economic exchange or social conflict. While designers believe that cities demand a high concentration of diverse people in close proximity, economists argue that if the global economy no longer needs dense cities, then they can be changed, and if keeping the peace means separating or dispersing people, then it should be done.

Several studies addressed issues of minority housing. The sociological concept of minority relates to power differentials and the difference in power rather than in numbers. The treatment of minorities results in their physical separation and segregation in the society. Minorities have been held back in terms of their education and employment opportunities, as well as countless other ways, by inadequate and segregated housing. Books and articles about minorities and public housing include Bingham's *Public Housing and Urban Renewal: An Analysis of Federal-Local Relations*; Bratt's "Controversies and Contributions: A Public Housing Critique"; Kamin's "Public Housing in 1999: A Hard Assessment"; Klutznick's "Poverty and Politics: The Challenge of Public Housing"; Meehan's "Is There a Future for Public Housing?"; Struyk's "Public Housing Modernization: An Analysis of Problems and Prospects"; and Weidemann et al.'s "Residents' Perceptions of Satisfaction and Safety: A Basis for Change in Multifamily Housing."

Women tend to be confined to the traditional division of labor within the family and to limited labor force participation, in part as a result of housing design and location (Hayden, 1981; Weisman, 1992). Housing patterns tend to keep classes, races, and subcultures separate and often antagonistic. In this way, the housing crisis today expresses and perpetuates the economic and social divisions that exist within the society as a whole (Achtenberg and Marcuse, 1981).

Residential segregation has been studied intensely by social science scholars over the past fifty years. Housing segregation is defined as "the spatial separation of different population groups with a given geographical area" (Saltman, 1991: 1). Spatial segregation of living quarters occurs in all human societies. What differs from one society to another are the extent of segregation, the patterns of segregation, and the specific basis for it. That basis is rooted in the history of each society. In the United States, ethnic and racial minorities are clustered in different parts of the country. However, most of the problems associated with segregation occur in areas within cities and metropolitan regions where minorities are concentrated. Sociopsychological explanations of residential segregation focus on human preferences and choices of locations. One explanation of segregation in the United States refers to the preference of whites for all-white neighborhoods and their exclusion of blacks from their neighborhoods. A study by Schuman, Steeh, and Babo (1985) proved that whites perceive blacks as holding different and undesirable values. Studies show that whites associate racial integration with neighborhood decline and rising crime.

Issues of housing segregation of minorities are discussed in the following books and articles: Huttman's edited book *Urban Housing Segregation of Minorities in Western Europe and the United States*; Blalock's "Segregation and Intergroup Interactions" in his book *Race and Ethnic Relations*; Darden in his numerous articles on segregation of blacks, Hispanics, American Indians, and Asians; Hirsch's book *Making the Second Ghetto: Race and Housing in Chicago, 1940–1960*; Massey's several publications such as "A Research Note on Residential Succession: The Hispanic Case"; Spriggs' "Measuring Residential Segregation: An Application of Trend Surface Analysis"; and Taeuber's "Racial Segregation: The Persisting Dilemma."

Several studies attempted to answer the analytic question of whether and to what extent the legislative and political history of federal public housing influenced the segregated character of public housing. Books and articles concerning minorities, housing policy, and housing politics include the following: Darden's "Demographic Changes 1970–1980: Implications for Federal Fair Housing"; Glaszer's "Dilemmas of Housing Policy"; Goering's "Race, Housing, and Public Policies: A Strategy for Social Science Research"; Hartman's *Housing and Social Policy*; Kivisto's "An Historical Review of Changes in Public Housing Policies and Their Impacts on Minorities"; and Marcuse's chapter "United States of America" in van Vliet's *International Handbook of Housing Policies and Practices*.

Homelessness is an extreme instance of poverty. Although not a recent phenomenon, homelessness today involves a full range of household types, ages, and races. According to Hopper and Hamberg (1986), the homelessness phenomenon stems from changes in the housing market, in the labor market, in the structure of American urban areas, and in public policies designed for "dependent" popu-

Neighborhood in Levittown, Pennsylvania, 1959. Courtesy of the Temple University Press Library, Urban Archives

lations. The problem of homelessness is not confined to one area in the nation. "The driving dynamic behind it is a widening gap for many households between the cost of their subsistence needs and the resources available to meet them. The growing scarcity of affordable housing operates in reciprocal fashion with the progressively deteriorating situation of individual households. The upshot is the dearth of housing as a procurable good" (14). Books and articles regarding homelessness include Bassuk's "The Homelessness Problem"; Baxter and Hopper's "The New Mendicancy: Homeless in New York City"; Crystal's "Homeless Men and Homeless Women: The Gender Gap"; Goldman and Morrissey's "The Alchemy of Mental Health Policy: Homelessness and the Fourth Cycle of Reform"; and Hombs and Snyder's *Homelessness in America: A Forced March to Nowhere.*

Demographic trends, economic changes, and public policies determine housing in the United States. Clearly, the housing experience of any given individual is shaped by systems that generate diversity, inequalities, and contradictions. Some Americans live in the most luxurious housing in the world, while others can hardly find minimal shelter. The future of housing in the United States holds the promises for the balance between healthy diversity and social downfall.

DESIGN AND CONSTRUCTION

"Long before governments and housing agencies took to supplying housing, people were constructing houses for themselves. Such housing of, by, and for the people, designed and constructed without the help of specialized professionals, such as formally trained designers, architects, planners, and engineers, is called *traditional*, or more broadly, *vernacular housing*" (Mazumdar, 1998: 623). Vernacular housing is defined by cultural values and beliefs and based on structural techniques and design solutions. This housing is often built in forms and materials, using the patterns and aesthetic ideals that are carried in memories. Vernacular houses continue to be constructed without government agencies or trained designers, reflecting traditions, customs, local climate and lifestyles that influence the choice of architectural solutions. As a result, the self-expression of vernacular housing is innovative, diverse, and often unregulated. Readings about vernacular housing may be found in Rapoport's *House Form and Culture* (1969); Rudofsky's *Architecture without Architects* (1964); Marshall's chapter in *Popular American Housing* (1995); McAlester and McAlester's *A Field Guide to American Houses* (1984); Clark's *The American Family Home 1800–1960* (1986); Jakle, Bastian, and Meyer's *Common Houses in America's Small Towns* (1989); and Gottfried and Jennings' *American Vernacular Design 1870–1940* (1985).

While architects and interior designers plan a small fraction of the housing built in the United States, their influence is significant on types and forms of housing built by builders, contractors, and tradespeople. A comprehensive monograph about the participation of professional architects in the housing industry is Gutman's *Design of American Housing* (1985). Dictionary and encyclopedia sources provide an overview of the field and details related to aspects of building, technology, and construction. These include *A Dictionary of Architecture and Building* (1902) by Sturgis; *Encyclopedia of Architecture* (1988) by Wilkes; *Construction Materials* (1978) by Hornbostel; *Housing: A Multidisciplinary Dictionary* (1987) by Sayegh; and *The Construction Glossary* (1993) by Stein.

While several books on housing design focus on the practical design essentials, others center on more poetic aspirations, attempting to teach how to design dwellings that resonate with the life of the people within them. One highly acclaimed book of the latter kind is *The Place of Houses* by the three architects Moore, Allen, and Lyndon. Other books that address design elements and processes through the eyes of designers include *The Essential House Book* and *New House Book* by Conran; *House Design: Art and Practice* by De Vido; *Small Houses for the Next Century* by Dickinson; *The Not So Big House* by Susanka; *The Complete Home Style Book* by Grey and her colleagues; and *A Natural System of House Design* by Woods. Readers who are interested in houses designed by contemporary architects will be fascinated by two series: *One House*, published by Monacelli Press, and *Ten Houses*, published by Rockport. Other sources in the same vein are *American House Now* by Doubilet and Boles and *The New American House*, *The New American House 2*, and *The New American Apartment*, all edited by Ojeda.

Minimum space requirements and standards for activities are found in graphic standards books for architects, interior designers, and landscape architects. These books offer detailed space planning standards for a variety of settings, including residential housing. Examples of the most widely used standards books for architecture, landscape architecture, and interior design, respectively, are *Architectural Graphic Standards* by Ramsey; *Graphic Standards for Landscape Architecture* by Austin et al.; *Interior Graphic and Design Standards* by Reznikoff; and *Time-Saver Standards for Housing and Residential Development* by De Chiara, Panero, and Zelnik. *Time-*

Saver Standards for Architectural Design Data by Callender includes basic data on such topics as industrialized building systems and solar angles, structural design, building materials, components and techniques such as flashing and roofing, and environmental controls such as acoustics, heating, air conditioning, and ventilation systems.

The definition of building materials for construction is another approach for framing the issue of construction. One general reference for building materials that is thorough in its discussion and is set up like an expanded dictionary is *Construction Materials: Types, Uses and Applications* by Hornbostel. The format and detail in definitions make the source appropriate as a starting point for a search of various topics. A second excellent dictionary is *Housing: A Multidimensional Dictionary* by Sayegh. Designed for both housing professionals and students, the dictionary includes over 28,000 key terms entered alphabetically. It lists many interdisciplinary perspectives on housing such as legal, social, economic, and philosophical aspects. It is also most useful for construction and building terminology. *Construction Glossary: An Encyclopedic Reference and Manual* by Stein is a detailed source, perhaps best suited for experienced builders and readers with a significant interest in the building trades.

The following books address construction of residential as well as commercial buildings: Allen's *Exercises in Building Construction, Fundamentals of Building Construction*, and *The Professional Handbook of Building Construction*; Ambrose's *Building Construction and Design*; Anderson's *Wood-Frame House Construction*; Benson's *The Timber-Frame Home*; Berglund's *Stone, Log and Earth Houses: Building with Elemental Materials*; Breyer's *Design of Wood Structures*; Ching's *Building Construction Illustrated*; Dietz's *Dwelling House Construction*; Feirer's *Carpentry and Building Construction*; Parker's *Simplified Design of Structural Wood*; Mann's *Illustrated Residential and Commercial Construction*; Russell's *Building Systems, Industrialization, and Architecture*; Iselin and Lemer's *The Fourth Dimension in Building: Strategies for Minimizing Obsolescence*; Hounshell's *From the American System to Mass Production (1800–1932)*; Fitch's *American Building*; Elliott's *Techniques and Architecture*; Newman's two books *Standard Handbook of Structural Details for Building Construction* and *Design and Construction of Wood-Framed Buildings*; Parker and Ambrose's *Simplified Engineering for Architects and Builders*; Sherwood's *Wood Frame House Construction*; and Thallon's *Graphic Guide to Frame Construction*.

Interior construction and finishes are included in *Building Construction: Interior Systems* by Ambrose; *Architectural Interior Systems* by Flynn, Segil, Kremers, and Steffy; *Construction Materials for Interior Design* by Rupp and Friedmann; *A Manual of Construction Documentation* by Wiggins; *Interior Construction and Detailing for Designers and Architects* by Ballast; *Materials and Components of Interior Design* by Riggs; and *Graphic Guide to Interior Details* by Thallon. Other books about residential design from an interior design perspective include *Inside Today's Home* (1954; now in its sixth edition of 1994) by Nissen, Faulkner, and Faulkner; *Time Saver Standards for Interior Design and Space Planning* (1991) by DeChiara, Panero, and Zelnik; *The Good House* (1990) by Jacobson; *Kitchens and Baths* (1993) by Jankowski; *Household Equipment in Residential Design* (1986) by Pickett, Arnold, and Ketterer; and *Interior Design* (1995) by Pile.

Guide to Popular U.S. Government Publications by Bailey includes a section on housing with subsections on construction and building techniques, home improvement, maintenance and repair, home heating, cooling, and energy conservation. Each subsection lists many references designed for general consumers and homeowners. Other sections cover construction reports on housing starts, new residential construction in selected geographic areas, housing completions, price indexes of new homes sold, and expenditures for housing upkeep and improvement. This source also provides statistical information to the building industry.

The specification of materials and products is often dictated by building and housing codes. Various national codes published by the Building Officials and Code Administrators International (BOCA) are regularly updated to reflect changes. Examples of national codes include the *BOCA National Building Code*, *BOCA Basic/National Plumbing Code*, *BOCA Basic/National Energy Conservation Code*, *BOCA National Fire Prevention Code*, *BOCA National Mechanical Code*, *BOCA National Plumbing Code*, and *BOCA Basic/National Code Interpretations*.

Construction cost estimators such as the *Means* cost data series are widely used in the building industry. Annual editions available in this series include *Means Interior Cost Data*, *Means Site Work Cost Data*, *Means Mechanical Cost Data*, *Means Landscape Cost Data*, *Means Square Foot Cost Data*, and *Means Building Construction Cost Data*. Each *Means* cost data book includes sections on how to use the book, unit prices of components, assemblies (i.e., the costs of construction systems made up by combining unit prices), references that explain the unit price data, and alternative pricing systems.

The Sweet's Group of the McGraw-Hill publishing house is an industry source of construction and interior data. The books may be helpful in both understanding the complexity of building systems and specifying products. *Sweet's Group Industrial Construction and Renovation* is an annual, several-volume product selection guide. *Sweet's Contract Interiors* is an annual, two-volume set that includes finishes, equipment, furnishings, mechanical systems, and electrical systems, among other topics.

Since the Industrial Revolution of the late eighteenth century, industrialization in housing construction reduced costs, increased speed, and improved quantity and quality. Industrialized housing is the production of large, expensive, and complex building elements that are prefabricated in factories. While many U.S. consumers are unwilling to accept factory-built housing, mobile homes and modular construction homes have a place in the housing industry. See, for example, Bruce and Sandbank, *A History of Prefabrication* (1972); Russell, *Building Systems, Industrialization, and Architecture* (1981); and Habraken, *Transformations of the Site* (1988).

Levels of industrialization in housing, from custom-built to precut, panelized and modular, represent a major market in housing production. While industrialized housing dates back to the 1920s and even earlier, more recent industrialized techniques can be explored by looking at the 1960s federal program Operation Breakthrough. Operation Breakthrough was a $60 million project under the auspices of the then recently formed cabinet-level Department of Housing and Urban Development (HUD). It was designed to explore the possibilities of systems building to create new and better forms of housing production at less cost and to alleviate consumer fears and misconceptions about "prefab" housing. *Housing Perspectives: Individuals and Families* (1st ed.), edited by Wedin and Nygren, provides historical reference on a variety of housing topics, including Operation Breakthrough. A good source for current industrialized housing resources is *Affordable Housing: A Resource Guide to Alternative and Factory-Built Houses, New Technologies, and the Owner-Builder Option* by Burns.

In exploring construction process periodicals, the titles may be indicative of the intended audience. For example, *Custom Builder* is intended for builders, but its features include case studies of homes; descriptions of new products; heating, ventilation, and air conditioning (HVAC); technology; and design, among other topics of interest to a more general audience. *Builder*, *Building Design*, and *Qualified Remodeller* are also useful periodicals for construction processes. *The Directory of International Periodicals and Newsletters on the Built Environment*, by Gretes, lists 1,199 titles with regard to the topics of construction. The reference includes a user's guide and sections on building types, building and construction, building services and systems, housing, and engineering. Many construction process, technology, and environmental design periodicals are cited in the Vance Bibliography series. The series includes 2,386 architecture subject bibliographies published between 1978 and 1990.

In recent history, interest in historic preservation, renovation, and restoration of older housing has increased. The main purpose of those who attempt to preserve and restore old buildings has always been to ensure that older structures will be saved for present and future use and studies. It has also been a strategy in revitalizing neighborhoods, particularly with the U.S. Internal Revenue Service historic preservation tax credit program first enacted by Congress in 1976. See Advisory Council on Historic Preservation's *The Contribution of Historic Preservation to Urban Revitalization* (1979), Andrews' *Tax Incentives for Historic Preservation* (1981), Escherich's *Affordable Housing through Historic Preservation* (1996), and Maddex's *All about Old Buildings: The Whole Preservation Catalog* (1985). The U.S. Department of the Interior publishes *The Secretary of the Interior's Standards for the Treatment of Historic Properties: With Guidelines of Preserving, Rehabilitating, Restoring and Reconstructing Historic Buildings*, codified in the Federal Register as 36 CFR 68, and the slightly different standards for rehabilitation, which apply to the tax-credit program, codified as 36 CFR 67. See Web site for the *Heritage Preservation* section of the *National Park Service*: www.cr.nps.gov. Technical information on historic preservation has also proliferated throughout American popular culture. Offering technical advice about historic structures are the periodicals *The Old House Journal* and *Association for Preservation Technology (APT) Bulletin* and Bob Vila's popular television series *This Old House*.

General technical books that include discussions of energy topics related to housing include Brawne's *From Idea to Building: Issues in Architecture*, Guise's *Design and Technology in Architecture*, and Reid's *Understanding Buildings*. A sample of books from the solar heyday of the mid-1980s includes Hunt's *Handbook of Conservation and Solar Energy: Trends and Perspectives; The Complete Passive Solar Home Book* by Schepp and Hastie; and *The Passive Solar Construction Handbook* by Levy. *Passive and Low Energy Architecture* by Suzuki reflects a 1990s evolution in thinking in energy saving and is a good example of case studies of energy-saving architecture. Other books that cover interior and environment control include Anderson's *Solar Building Architecture*; Balcomb's edited book *Passive Solar Buildings*; Bobenhausen's *Simplified Design for HVAC Systems*; and Olgyag's *Design with Climate*.

Numerous books have been published on energy-saving strategies for homeowners. *Energy-Saving Home Improvements: A Dollars and Sense Guide*, published by the U.S. Department of Housing and Urban Development, is one of many publications available from the federal government. *The Energy Resources Center Illustrated Guide to Home Retrofitting for Energy Savings* by Knight is another useful government publication. *Movable Insulation: A Guide to Reducing Heating and Cooling Losses through the Windows in Your Home* by Langdon is published by Rodale Press, a publishing house with many energy and housing titles. Other good sources for insulation are *Superinsulated Design and Construction: A Guide for Building Energy-Efficient Homes* by Lenchek, Mattock, and Raabe and Brand's *Architectural Details for Insulated Buildings*. Time-Life Books has a series on home improvement and repair, which includes many construction titles, including a general energy efficiency book entitled *Weatherproofing*. Although beyond the scope of this chapter, local energy and housing organizations are also a good source for reference materials. These sources often reflect the specific geographic, climatic, and housing stock issues of a particular area.

Managing residential heating and cooling is a broad topic in building literature. *Environmental Control Systems: Heating, Cooling, Lighting* by Moore is one of the best reference books on this topic. Other sources on heating and cooling include Flynn et al.'s *Architectural Interior Systems: Lighting, Acoustics, Air Conditioning*; Lechner's *Heating, Cooling, Lighting: A Guide of Qualitative Design Methods for Architects*; and Stein and McGuiness' *Mechanical and Electrical Equipment for Buildings*.

Resources on residential lighting range from picture books of lighted interior and exterior spaces to technical data sourcebooks for lighting calculations and engineering. The Illuminating Engineering Society of North America, with its national office located in New York City, has a publications list that includes many sources, both for a general audience and for those who are technically proficient in lighting. General Electric and other major manufacturers of lamps also offer publications on their products and on lighting applications. Useful books on lighting include the general sources *Designing with Light: Residential Interiors* by Jankowski. *Interior Lighting for Environmental Designers* by Nuckolls is one of the best sources for technical lamp, luminaire, and calculation information. Also see *Bringing Interiors to Light: The Principles and Practices of Lighting Design for Interior Designers* by Smith and Bertolone; Gardner and Hannaford's *Lighting Design: An Introductory Guide for Professionals*; Lam's *Perception and Lighting as Formgivers for Architecture*; Schiler's *Simplified Design of Building Lighting*; and Steffy's *Architectural Lighting Design*.

POLICY AND ECONOMICS

Homeownership—particularly of a single-family dwelling—is an American Dream. With the National Housing Act establishing the Federal Housing Administration (FHA) in the 1930s, mortgage insurance and the long-term amortized mortgagee were realized. The tax system allowed homeowners to deduct interest payments on mortgage debt and mortgage credit and thereby stimulated the increase of homeownership. Recent homeownership trends indicate that more people own their own home and own it for longer periods of time during their lifetime. Owner occupancy makes families more active in neighborhood associations, decreases residential mobility, and sustains consumer demand and economic growth in a community. See Clark's *The American Family Home, 1800–1960*, Hayden's *Redesigning the American Dream: The Future of Housing, Work, and Family Life*, and Saunders' *A Nation of Home Owners*.

Periodicals covering the economics and demographics of homeownership include: *Journal of Urban History*; *Journal of Urban Affairs*; *Annals, Association of American Geographers*; *Housing and Society*; *Housing Policy Debate*; and *Urban Studies*. (See also Gretes [1986], *The Directory of International Periodicals and Newsletters on the Built Environment*).

Rental housing is usually the poor alternative to homeownership in the United States. More poverty-stricken individuals rent than own a home. Publications in this area include Appelbaum and Gilderbloom's *Rethinking Rental Housing*; Dolbeare's *The Widening Gap*; Downs' *Residential Rent Controls*; Joint Center for Housing Studies' annual *The State of the Nation's Housing*; Kemeny's *From Public Housing to Social Housing: Rental Policy Strategies in Comparative Perspective*; and Stone's *Shelter Poverty*.

Because housing costs rose faster than incomes in recent years, housing affordability became a chief housing problem in the United States within the last decades of the twentieth century. A consumer's housing costs in relation to his or her income and resources derive housing affordability. For those with lower incomes, one coping strategy is to pay a larger expenditure-to-income ratio on housing than the generally recommended 30 percent. Nevertheless, the American Housing Survey data for 1993, for example, indicated that 6.9 million renter households were paying 50 percent or more of their income for housing. Background regarding these topics can be found in the Joint Center for Housing Studies of Harvard University's *The State of the Nation's Housing*; Stone's *Shelter Poverty: New Ideas on Housing Affordability*; Van Vliet's *Affordable Housing and Urban Redevelopment in the United States*; and the U.S. Department of HUD's *Worst Case Needs for Housing Assistance in the United States*.

Additional means of coping among low-income families include living in substandard housing, sharing housing with others, or combining both of these strategies. The literature on substandard housing suggests that it is a result of poor workmanship, compromises in the interest of profit, obsolescence, disinvestment, changing standards, and changing values. See Deforest and Veiller's *The Tenement House Problem*, Riis' *How the Other Half Lives*, and Rosenberry's *Housing Issues of the 1990s*. Information specifically on shared housing alternatives include Franck and Ahrentzen's *New Households, New Housing*; Hemmens, Hoch, and Carp's *Under One Roof: Issues and Innovations in Shared Housing*; Horne and Baldwin's *Home-Sharing and Other Lifestyle Options*; Jaffe's *Shared Housing for the Elderly*; and Streib, Folts, and Hilker's *Old Homes—New Families: Shared Living for the Elderly*. The problem of poor quality of housing in urban areas has marred the history of U.S. housing. Substandard housing has at times been the result of absentee, greedy landlords squeezing what is possible from the low-income rental market. In the aftermath, housing is abandoned in the last stage of ownership as rental housing. Housing abandonment is discussed in Bratt's *Rebuilding a Low-Income Housing Strategy*; Salins' *The Ecology of Housing Destruction*; Smith's *Uneven Development*; Stegman's *Housing Finance and Public Policy*; and Sternlieb's *The Tenement Landlord* and *The Urban Housing Dilemma*.

Because housing abandonment can be contagious within a neighborhood, leading to thinned-out sections of crumbling buildings and vacant parking lots, urban redevelopment legislation for slum clearance was enacted as early as 1949. During the 1960s however, urban renewal schemes to displace neighborhood residents were reexamined, and subsequent legislation focused on community preservation, rehabilitation rather than demolition, and resident participation. In the 1970s Community Development Block Grant funds were introduced for redevelopment activities such as housing rehabilitation. Neighborhood organizations began their own revitalization efforts as community development corporations (CDCs). Background work can be reviewed in Fainstein and Fainstein's *Restructuring the City*; Frieden and Sagalyn's *Downtown, Inc.*; Gelfand's *A Nation of Cities*; Judd and Parkinson's *Leadership and Urban Regeneration*; Mollenkopf's *The Contested City*; Squires' *Unequal Partnerships*; Stone and Sanders' *The Politics of Urban Development*; and Wilson's *Urban Renewal: The Record and the Controversy*.

Mortgage finance tightly binds "housing as shelter" with "housing as big business." The United States has a highly regulated system of mortgage instruments and financial intermediaries supported by a secondary market of Wall Street investors. Mortgage debt stimulates consumers and developers to finance the purchase, construction, or rehabilitation of a home over several years with little cash. The current mortgage finance system is greatly influenced by the stock market crash of 1929, the high demand for housing after World War II, the savings and loan industry problems in the 1970s and early 1980s, and the continuing problem of racial discrimination. Clearly, mortgage lending is inextricably linked to the U.S. capitalist economy. Resources for further study include Brueggeman and Fisher's *Real Estate Finance and Investments*; Dennis and Robertson's *Residential Mortgage Lending*; Florida's *Housing and the New Financial Markets*; and Squires' *From Redlining to Reinvestment*.

COGNITIVE EVALUATION

Since housing constitutes a major unresolved societal problem, it attracted considerable investigation from psychological perspectives. Cooper noted in her *Easter Hill Village: Some Social Implications of Design* that housing represents one of the most sociobehavioral, salient, and complex classes of built environments. Weideman and her colleagues (1982) expressed similar ideas. The following section deals with housing perception, preference, satisfaction, meaning, and symbolism.

Housing perception research represents one of the aspects of cognitive evaluation that describe parameters of dwelling. Marans reviewed this issue in "Perceived Quality of Residential Environments: Some Methodological Issues." Other researchers who have discussed some of the parameters of perception include Garling, who has studied the variation, shadows, and openness in "Studies in Visual Perception of Architectural Spaces and Rooms: Aesthetic Preference"; Nasar, who researched diversity, clarity, and decreasing building prominence in his dissertation, titled "The Impact of Visual Aspects of Residential Environments on Hedonic Responses, Interests, and Fear of Crime"; Tobey, who investigated housing as symbol, art, and social status in "Connotative Messages of Single Family Homes: A Multidimensional Scaling Analysis"; Gobster, who reported on complexity, contrast, naturalness, and visible development as predictors of suitability of residential structures; Canter, Gilchrist, Miller, and Roberts, who discussed in

Habitat for Humanity. © AFP/CORBIS

"An Empirical Study of the Focal Point in the Living Room" the influence of attention and activity on defining the focal point of a room; and Volkman, who in "User Perceptions of Underground Houses and Implications for Site Planning" referred to issues of cleanliness, silence, privacy, energy efficiency, concerns with window views, and possible lowered socioeconomic class associations among residents of underground housing. Another book that can be added to this list is Wood and Beck's *Home Rules*, which describes and analyzes every room in one house as the manifestation of meanings and values of its inhabitants.

Many studies in England, Australia, and the United States indicate that the freestanding single-family house with a yard represents the ideal housing form that most people seek. Authors who have written about this preference include Michelson in his *Environmental Choice, Human Behavior and Residential Satisfaction*; Ward in *The Home of Man*; Kaplan in *The Dream Deferred: People, Politics and Planning in Suburbia*; and Cooper Marcus and Sarkissian in "The House as Symbol of the Self." Irregular forms of housing and those with lowest levels of massing are also preferred, as Faletti argued in "An Experimental Investigation of Cognitive Processing Underlying Judgments of Residential Environments by Different Observer Groups." In some cases, studies refer to the nonpreference for multifamily housing, because such dwellings reduce residents' control and lack properties of self-expression (Robinson 1980). People prefer styles of houses that bolster their image of themselves, as noted by Cherlnik and Wilderman in "Symbols of Status in Urban Neighborhoods: Contemporary Perceptions of Nineteenth-Century Boston" and Nasar in "Symbolic Meanings of House Style."

A variety of studies on housing prove the anecdotal evidence that home buyers select the house that they want on the basis of its aesthetic appeal. Nasar's chapter "Connotative Meanings of House Styles" addressed this issue by looking at similarities and differences in preference and meaning across sociocultural groups and regions. In the same book, *The Meaning and Use of Housing*, Arias explored the role of housing preference in design. In his chapter he discusses how consumer preference is altered by the outcomes of a design process. Sanoff examined significant factors that influence housing preferences among teenagers in conjunction with the types of houses reported in "Youth's Perception and Categorization of Residential Cues." Issues such as modernism, humanism, stimulus-seeking/exploratory behavior, and territoriality were central preference factors.

Housing satisfaction is another area of concentration related to cognitive evaluation. Reference to satisfactory management–tenant concerns appeared in Cooper's "Resident Dissatisfaction in Multi-Family Housing"; Newman's *Defensible Space*; and Anderson and Weidemann's "Development of an Instrument to Measure Residents' Perceptions of Residential Quality." Comparison with other alternatives of residence seems to be another factor in housing satisfaction. If, for instance, the dwelling compared is perceived to be equal to, or better than, the current dwelling, residents probably report satisfaction. However, if the dwelling compared is inferior, then it is likely that residents experience dissatisfaction. Writers who focused on these aspects include Campbell, Converse, and Rogers in *The Quality of American Life: Perceptions, Evaluations, and Satisfactions*; Michelson in *Environmental Choice, Human Behavior, and Residential Satisfaction*; and Saegert in "Masculine Cities and Feminine Suburbs: Polarized Ideas, Contradictory Realities." Several researchers dealt with housing satisfaction based on the characteristics of the physical setting. They refer to the availability of storage places, types of furniture, and room arrangement as indicators for satisfaction. Authors who approached satisfaction from this perspective include Lansing, Marans, and Zehner in *Planned Residential Environments*; Hanna and Lindamood in "Components of Housing Satisfaction"; Mackintosh in "High in the City"; and Morrissy and Handal in "Characteristics of the Residential Environment Scale: Reliability and Differential Relationship to Neighborhood Satisfaction in Divergent Neighborhoods."

Most writers reviewed here tended to characterize settings in terms of stimulus dimensions and how these dimensions affect individuals who are exposed to them. Their approach emphasizes, most often, housing as systems that individuals adapt to by conforming to demands from environmental stimuli or by changing the environment, causing it to conform to their needs by adjustment. A good collection is *Housing, Culture, and Design*, edited by Low and Chambers. Each chapter in this book highlights a different dimension of cultural analysis of housing, such as sociopolitical, cognitive, symbolic, and interpretive. Another point of view within the field of environment and behavior is the one taken by physical designers. Designers are responsible for the success or the failure of housing environments to meet the needs, goals, and day-to-day behaviors of their inhabitants. Written from this perspective is Raymond Studer's chapter "Design of the Built Environment: The Search for Usable Knowledge" in the *Handbook of Housing and the Built Environment in the United States*. Studer's chapter focuses on the issues and processes involved in the design of housing with emphasis on the sociophysical knowledge and its utilization in the design process of housing environments. John Zeisel is a researcher who tried to provide directions to overcome the impasse that seems to exist between theoretical knowledge-generation and its utilization in the design field. Zeisel's *Inquiry by Design* and Zeisel and Griffin's *Charlesview Housing: A Diagnostic Evaluation* are good examples that demonstrate the effort to close the gap between theory and practice. Brill in his *Do Buildings Really Matter? Economic and Other Effects of Designing Behaviorally Supportive Buildings* and Cooper Marcus and Sarkissian in their *Housing As If People Mattered* made similar attempts.

Meaning is a concept that is used in association with cognitive evaluation research of housing as well. The use of housing gives it its meaning, and at the same time meaning influences the way that housing is used. In *The Meaning and Use of Housing*, edited by Arias, one can find a collection of chapters by various contributors who focused their discussions on the interplay between cognitive and emotional reaction to housing as well as the actions that are supported by the sociophysical settings. In the same book, Francescato argued in his chapter "Meaning and Use: A Conceptual Basis" that the term "meaning" signals the intention to approach housing from the communication point of view. According to Sadalla, Vershure, and Burroughs in "Identity Symbolism in Housing," houses and their contents are part of the language of signs and gestures that individuals use to communicate with each other. Rubinstein and Parmelee argued in "Attachment to Place and the Representation of the Life Course by the Elderly" that the orientation toward environmental meaning versus environmental function is a relatively new line of inquiry in the field of environment and behavior. Studies have indicated that environmental meaning results from individual experiences and factors such as personal and cultural filters or social constructs. This theme is central in Rapoport's classic *The Meaning of the Built Environment: A Nonverbal Communication Approach*. The book describes how the environment takes on special human meanings in different social and physical settings. The approach to housing through its meaning raises questions such as meaning for whom (residents, architects, policymakers, housing managers, or other customers of the housing system); scale of reference (home, building, complex, neighborhood, community, city); use; and time.

CONCEPT OF HOME

A considerable amount of literature investigating person–environment relationships has attempted to answer questions regarding the meaning of "home." Several studies such as Sebba and Churchman in "The Uniqueness of the Home," Sixsmith in "The Meaning of Home: An Exploratory Study of Environmental Experience," Csikszentmihalyi and Rochberg-Halton's *The Meaning of Things: Domestic Symbols and the Self*, and Benjamin in his edited book *The Home: Words, Interpretations, Meanings, and Environments* have identified general categories of behavioral interpretations of home and its meaning to its occupants.

Després has listed certain categories in the article "The Meaning of Home: Literature Review and Directions for Future Research and Theoretical Development." The categories include home as a center of control and security for the individual; home as a symbol and reflection of one's ideas and values; home as a basis for physical, financial, and emotional involvement; home as a familiar place that provides its occupants with sense of belonging, rootedness, and place attachment; home as a place to secure and develop relationships with people for whom one cares; home as a setting for work, hobby, and leisure activities; home as a haven or a place where one can control levels of social interaction, privacy, and independence; home as a place to symbolize social status; home as a material structure; and home as a place to own.

A variety of writers have discussed the centrality of home in the human existence. Norberg-Schultz's book *Existence, Space and Architecture*; Dovey's article "Home: An Ordering Principle in Space"; and Seamon's article "The Phenomenological Contribution to Environmental Psychology" discuss the centering qualities of home. Tuan's book *Space and Place: The Perspective of Experience* as well as Dovey's chapter "Home and Homelessness" in Altman and Werner's book *Home Environments* refer to the concept of rootedness and the implications of home as a place from which to reach out and to which to return. The central nature of home is addressed in Jung's autobiography *Memories, Dreams and Reflections*, which influenced Bachelard's book *The Poetics of Space*. Bachelard also recognized the significance of experiences in people's childhood home on their other life experiences.

Security and control are defined in the literature as outcomes of needs to satisfy human territorial needs. Taylor and Brower (1985) discussed the perceived and actual control of dwellers as a result of the definition of territory. People's desire to modify their home environment, to place items with special attributes or meaning within the house or around it, and to rearrange their furniture has been interpreted as territorial behavior referred to as personalization. The definition of territory by markers in the neighborhood and the house boundaries, as well as in the interior of the house, was also discussed by Brown and Altman (1981, 1983) and Brown and Werner (1985) and in Brown's chapter "Territoriality" in Stokols and Altman's *Handbook of Environmental Psychology*. In 1966, anthropologist Hall published *The Hidden Dimension* and introduced the concept of proxemics. Hall explored the meanings that people from many different cultures attach to the use of space. Closely related to Hall's studies of the spatial norms of people is the concept of personal space. In *Personal Space: The Behavioral Basis of Design*, written in 1969, Sommer defined it as the area around a person's body into which others may not intrude without provoking discomfort. These two now-classic books spurred considerable interest in the area of human spatial behavior and have led to the accumulation of a large number of studies during the past decades.

It was proposed that a home fulfills a hierarchy of human needs. On the very elementary basis it provides a shelter. On an additional level it provides psychological comfort by satisfying the human needs of light, comfortable temperatures, cleanliness, and eased movement (Appleyard 1979). Rybczynski in his *Home: A Short History of an Idea* attempted to discover the meaning of comfort as a central concept in the home environment. The home also provides a center for the family and friends and a focal point for maintaining social interaction (Werner 1987). As much as the home serves the human needs for social intercourse, it also provides the psychological needs for privacy and retreat. It is assumed that the home is where privacy is most needed. Privacy is an interpersonal boundary control process designed to pace and regulate interactions with others. Desired levels of privacy and achieved levels of privacy are conceived of as an interplay of dialectic forces involving different balances of opening and closing the self to others. Home is a place where persons can control and achieve their privacy goals through personal space, or the area immediately surrounding persons and groups. An uncontrollable feeling of privacy may be a result of isolation or too many interactions, as Westin described in *Privacy and Freedom*. Westin provided systematic analysis of the concept of privacy as well as four functions of privacy that he defined as personal autonomy, emotional release, self-evaluation, and limited and protected communication. Anthony suggested in her article "The Role of the Home Environment in Family Conflict: Therapists' Viewpoints" that home environment may have a role in regulating family conflicts over issues of privacy.

Homeownership is associated with privacy in that ownership is perceived as a higher level of boundary regulation process than renting. Writers concerned with the issues of ownership include Pynoos, Schafer, and Hartman, editors of *Housing Urban America*; Altman and Gauvain in their chapter "A Cross-Cultural and Dialectic Analysis of Homes"; Korosec-Serfaty and Bolitt in "Dwelling and the Experience of Burglary"; and Lawrence in "What Makes a House a Home?" In some cases, people prefer to own a house just for the sake of investment. Agnew's chapter "Home Ownership and Identity in Capitalist Societies" suggested that owners' motivations of that sort predispose them toward a reduced sense of attachment to place.

Attachment to place has been defined as a positive affective association between persons and a geographic location. Shumaker and Taylor in their article "Toward a Classification of People–Place Relationships: A Model of Attachment to Place" discussed the aspects of attachment to place in residential environments and the evolutionary advantages inherent in these strong bonds between people and places. In "The Home Environments of Older People: A Description of the Psychological Process Linking Person to Place," Rubinstein described the characteristics of four different levels of attachment to place: knowing the place with no feelings or memories associated with it; having personalized attachment where an individual has memories of place that are inseparable from personal experiences; experiencing highly emotional memories with place referred to as extension; and embodying the boundaries between the person and the environment that become blurred (the most intense level). Similar experiences of individuals who have spent a lifetime in a house and elicited feelings of attachment, where their personal identity became interwoven with the place identity, were described also by Howell in her chapter "The Meaning of Place in Old Age." The passage of time appears to be central in the process of developing attachment to place. Consequently, elderly people are often the most strongly attached to their homes. Rowles' study "Growing Old 'Inside': Aging and Attachment to Place in an Appalachian Community"; Taylor's book *Human Territorial Functioning*; and Rubinstein's chapter coauthored with Parmelee "Attachment to Place and the Representation of the Life Course by the Elderly" are three examples out of many in this field. Last in this section is Altman and Low's edited book *Place Attachment* in the series "Human Behavior and Environment: Advances in Theory and Research."

Home is also important in maintaining the bonds among people in their social circles. Most of the family life, family and marital relations, and relationships between people and their children occur within the home context. Saile's chapter

"The Ritual Establishment of Home" reflects a person's place in the family and role of the home in preserving the family's social fabric. Extensive research literature exists on these topics. Writers concerned with the concept of home as a set of social interactions include Cooper Marcus and Sarkissian, "The House as Symbol of the Self"; Horwitz and Tognoli's "Role of Home in Adult Development: Women and Men Living Alone Describe Their Residential Histories"; Csikszentmihalyi and Rochberg-Halton's book *The Meaning of Things: Domestic Symbols and the Self*; Tognoli and Horwitz's chapter "From Childhood Home to Adult Home: Environmental Transformations"; and Staines and Pleck's publication *The Impact of Work Schedules on the Family*.

Home in sociocultural context attracted many anthropologists, who often refer to the terms "house" or "dwelling" rather than "home." Rapoport wrote extensively on the connections among *House Form and Culture*. He claimed that physical features such as climate, construction methods, and availability of materials might have a secondary role in the construction of houses. According to Rapoport, sociocultural factors such as way of life, societal ordering, attendance to basic needs, family structure, position of women and men, privacy, territoriality, and social organization and social relations are the primary factors in the interplay of environmental and cultural interaction. In a later chapter written for Duncan's *Housing and Identity*, Rapoport argued that the dwelling is an inseparable part of the culture in which it is located. He noted that sociocultural identity of the dwelling was partly expressed according to ordering systems such as front–back, male–female, sacred–profane, and good–bad. A pivotal concept in Rapoport's chapter "Thinking about Home Environments" is his conceptual framework that stressed the fact that "in reality the main effect of environment on people is through choice or habitat selection," where choice applies to issues such as design, habitat selection at various scales, modification, furnishing, and other existing components of home environments.

The terms "home" and "house" seem to be used too often in the literature interchangeably. Altman and Chemers, for instance, in *Culture and Environment* treated house and home as synonymous terms when they proposed several categories for classifying homes according to their permanence, portability, homogeneity, and communality. They suggested that North American homes tend to be permanent, specialized/differentiated, and noncommunal. Likewise, Rapoport treated the concept of the home environment as "part of a larger, culturally variable system of settings within which a particular set of activities takes place." Other writers, however, preferred different definitions. Dovey (1985) asserted that "the phenomenon of home is an intangible relationship between people and places in which they dwell; it is not visible nor accurately measurable." A good collection of essays that reflect the tensions, arguments and enthusiasms about the topic of "home" in recent decades is *The Home: Words, Interpretations, Meanings, and Environments*, edited by Benjamin.

While "home" is both a physical place and a cognitive concept, "housing" is a term that can be many different things to different people. The very multiplicity of meanings and uses of housing can be seen as a defining characteristic of the field. It may be defined as a form of built environment. But housing is not just hardware. It is also more than just the "dwelling." Housing in this context is a term that defines the public, rather than the private, realm. The following section reviews articles and books that emphasize the psychosocial aspects of housing as a set of physical and spatial parameters of human habitats.

NEIGHBORHOODS AND COMMUNITIES

In examining residential environments, one has to address the impact of the location and the impact of neighborhood as a central factor in housing quality. For city planners, the neighborhood "has been conceived as a building block in creating larger communities and has been defined by particular physical boundaries and specific number of people" (Marans, in "Perceived Quality of Residential Environments" 132). Other researchers such as Gans in *Urban Villagers* or Lee in "A Theory of Socio-Spatial Schemata" suggest that this conception may be less meaningful to residents than a group of houses or one or two blocks. Connerly and Marans described in "Neighborhood Quality: A Description and Analysis of Indicators" neighborhood quality in four primary dimensions: (1) the quality of the physical environment; (2) proximity and convenience to shopping or work; (3) the quality of local services and facilities; and (4) the quality of the neighborhood's social and cultural environment. Other studies that attempted to develop systematic methods for observing neighborhoods include Clay's *Close-Up: How to Read the American City* and Jacobs' *Looking at Cities*. Several researchers argued that using data to describe quality of neighborhoods has to be indicative of the quality of neighborhood life as experienced and perceived by the residents living there. The works of Marans and Rodgers in "Toward an Understanding of Community Satisfaction" and Brudney and England's "Urban Policy Making and Subjective Service Evaluations: Are They Compatible?" are samples of this theme.

Goffman distinguished as early as 1959 in *The Presentation of Self in Everyday Life* between the "front regions" of the house, which are constantly exposed to the public, and the "back regions," which usually are off-limits to visitors and where residents feel higher levels of privacy. It seems obvious that through physical proximity, residents of one house are forced to interact with those living in nearby houses. Festinger, Schacter, and Back found in their classic study, *Social Pressures in Informal Groups*, that friendships are influenced by nearness of distance and shared paths. Neighborhood can be described in terms of physical characteristics such as size and area, type and condition of housing, and location, as Taylor mentioned in "Neighborhood Physical Environment and Stress." Researchers such as Greenberg, Rohe, and Wilson have related neighborhood to crime in their report *Informal Citizen Action and Crime Prevention at the Neighborhood Level*. Other researchers described neighborhoods in terms of their social organization. Warren, in *Helping Networks*, developed a typology of neighborhoods based on interaction, identification, and connections. He found that the social organization of a neighborhood was related both to the reciprocity among the neighbors and to general well-being.

Neighbors often serve as support systems for individuals, providing emotional and material aid. Therefore, many researchers studied the concept of neighboring. The list includes Gans in *The Urban Villagers: Group and Class in the Life of Italian Americans*; Jacobs in *The Death and Life of Great American Cities*; Suttles in *The Social Order of the Slum*; Michelson in *Man and His Urban Environment: A Sociological Analysis*; Heuman in "Racial Integration in Residential Neighborhoods: Towards More Precise Measures and Analysis"; and Argyle and Henderson in "The Rules of Friendship." Altman and Gauvain studied the time and the expense that homeowners in middle-class suburban areas devote to the upkeep of the front of their houses. They argue in Liben, Patterson, and Newcombe's edited book *Spatial Representation across the Life Span* that by maintaining the yard and displaying appropriate amounts of holiday decorations, people show what "good neighbors" they are. All these writers emphasize social interaction that derives from community.

Neighborhoods provide shelter and essential commodities for residents. The dual phenomena of neighborhood and neighbors reflect on a social foundation and interchange across individuals and groups that constitute the commerce of neighborhood life. Rivlin suggested in "The Neighborhood, Personal Identity, and Group Affiliations" that it is possible to consider neighbors as more than residents of a defined locale. The people who provide services or those who "hang out" in an area help to define the social neighborhood's borders by their interaction with the local residents.

For some cultural groups, the area of residence incorporates all aspects of life. Their neighborhood is where they shop, nurture children, acquire social services, celebrate holidays and events, recuperate from illness and tragedy, and enjoy recreation. However, this is not the typical experience of neighborhoods today. Out-migration and turnover have become more familiar patterns of neighborhoods. Changes in family structure and residential patterns have changed the function of local areas, as Horwitz and Tognoli noted in "The Role of Home in Adult Development: Women and Men Living Alone Describe Their Residential Histories." Members of families are dispersed, and older adults stay in "naturally occurring retirement communities." Articles regarding these topics include Riche's "Retirement's Lifestyle Pioneers" and Hunt and Ross' "Naturally Occurring Retirement Communities: A Multiattribute Examination of Desirability Factors." Other neighborhood changes have come from the use of the automobile, which has extended people's horizons beyond their immediate areas. It has altered not only families' recreation patterns but also people's shopping habits. The introduction of the mall and the recreational shopping contrasted sharply with the neighborhood-based stores and the open markets of the past, as Sommer argued in "The Behavioral Ecology of Supermarkets and Farmer's Markets."

In his book *The Fall of Public Man*, Sennett analyzed the "end of public culture" and the increasing privatization of life. Whether using computers for virtual reality shopping and spending more hours in front of television sets will affect community life is a matter for speculation and further research. However, with the invasion of electronics and sophisticated technology into shopping, entertainment, and communication, there is little doubt about the major alterations in people's relationships to their homes and neighborhoods. In spite of the changes in human life and the fact that the local area is no longer the focus, as most people move across the environment to work, seek entertainment, visit families, and find other services, the neighborhood remains the model for urban planning. Neighborhoods still form the basis for new towns in the United States and abroad, as noted by Banerjee and Baer in *Beyond the Neighborhood Unit: Residential Environments and Public Policy* and Keller in *The Urban Neighborhood: A Sociological Perspective*.

The role that community and neighborhood play in people's lives has attracted several studies. Proshansky, Fabian, and Kaminoff described the contribution of the physical setting in forming persons' place identity in "Place-Identity: Physical World Socialization of the Self." The neighborhood is a part of the social, emotional, and cognitive experience of children as they grow up, as Unger and Wandersman noted in "The Importance of Neighbors: The Social, Cognitive and Affective Components of Neighboring" and by Seamon in his phenomenological study *A Geography of the Lifeworld*. The immediate area of neighborhoods affects not only children. Levinson has pointed out in "A Conception of Adult Development" the relationships of people living in a community with others across the life cycle. Carp and Carp examined in "Perceived Environmental Quality of Neighborhoods" the specific role of the neighborhood in the housing experience of older people. Rowles has identified in his article "Toward a Geography of Growing Old" qualities of residents' geographic experiences that "expressed a subtle meshing of place and time, embracing not only physical and cognitive involvement within their contemporary neighborhood, but also vicarious participation in an array of displaced environments" (57).

It is difficult to find consensus for the term "community." Hillery in his classic "Definitions of Community: Areas of Agreement" reviewed ninety-four definitions of community found in the literature. He noted that the three most commonly mentioned elements that define community are (1) social interaction; (2) common ties in the sense of a shared value system; and (3) geographical area. Warren, in *The Community in America*, mentioned additional community function such as community in the sense of production, distribution, and consumption of goods and services, socialization, social control, and mutual support. Research on community sentiment was divided by Shumaker and Taylor in "Toward a Classification of People–Place Relationships: A Model of Attachment to Place" into three broad approaches: those focusing on community satisfaction, community attachment, and identity and community life. Researchers of community satisfaction include Campbell, Converse, and Rodgers in their book *The Quality of American Life*; and Herting and Guest in "Components of Satisfaction with Local Areas in the Metropolis." Researchers of community attachment include Gerson, Steuve, and Fischer in their chapter "Attachment to Place"; and Sampson in "Local Friendship Ties and Community Attachment in Mass Society: A Multilevel Systematic Model."

Authors who discussed identity, place, and community sentiment include Lavin and Agatstein in "Personal Identity and the Imagery of Place: Psychological Issues and Literary Themes"; Rapoport in "Identity and Environment" in Duncan's edited book *Housing and Identity*; Cochrane's "Place, People, and Folklore: An Isle Royale Case Study"; Goldfield's chapter "Neighborhood Preservation and Community Values in Historical Perspective"; and Rivlin's chapter "The Neighborhood, Personal Identity, and Group Affiliations" in Altman and Wandersman's edited book *Neighborhood and Community Environments*; Landman in her ethnographic study *Creating Community in the City: Cooperatives and Community Gardens in Washington D.C.*; and Hummon in his book *Commonplaces: Community Ideology and Identity in American Culture*.

Van Vliet and Burgers argued in "Communities in Transition: From the Industrial to the Postindustrial Era" that a combination of political lobbying, economic pressures, and the cultural climate in North America has driven the extensive residential development. However, single-family dwellings, built in low densities, have characterized this development. The authors claim that these patterns of population densities do not provide sufficient critical mass of people to support services and jobs in concentrated areas because of the segregated land use. Authors who have studied the community concept at the neighborhood level share similar ideas. Works of this category include Banerjee and Baer's *Beyond the Neighborhood Unit: Residential Environments and Public Policy*; Hallman's *Neighborhoods: Their Place in Urban Life*; and Wireman's *Urban Neighborhoods, Networks, and Families: New Forms for Old Values*. Social scientists have found the concept of neighborhood useful to describe the intermediate level of social organization between home and city. Neighborhoods allow people to achieve a sense of community, as McAndrew noted in his book *Environmental Psychology*. The concept "sense of community" appeared in Holahan and Wandersman's "The Community Psychology Perspective in Environmental Psychology" and Nisbet's *Community and Power: A Study in the Ethics of Order and Freedom*. Chavis, Hogge, McMillan, and Wandersman defined the term in "Sense of Community through Brunswik's Lens: A First Look" as "a feeling that members have of belonging and being important to each other, and a shared faith that members' needs will be met by their commitment to be together" (25).

Taylor in *Human Territorial Functioning* argued that street blocks are the focus of neighborhood ties and that street blocks are physically bounded behavior settings that encourage territorial control by inhabitants. Neighborhood norms develop on what constitutes acceptable behavior. Neighborhood turnover, instability, and lower-quality housing decrease territorial marking, resident satisfaction, and the appearance of control, as Taylor argued in "Toward an Environmental Psychology of Disorder: Delinquency, Crime and Fear of Crime." Research confirms the notion that neighborhoods consisting of multistory apartments are less cohesive and have less of a sense of community than neighborhoods with single-family dwellings. See, for instance, Weenig, Schmidt, and Midden in "Social Dimensions of Neighborhoods and the Effectiveness of Information Programs."

Neighborhood design is associated with the mistakes made in the design of public housing projects in many American cities. Errors in the design of public housing projects are magnified by the unfortunate circumstances faced by the residents of these types of housing. Sadly, the demographic profile of people who most often need public housing consists of low-income and unemployed residents, elderly, females, and members of minority groups. The location of many of the public housing projects near areas with a high crime rate combined with the lack of social networks in these neighborhoods breeds feelings of fear and danger. Analysis of residents' experiences in neighborhoods of public housing may be found in the work of Greenberg and Rohe, "Informal Social Control and Crime Prevention in Modern Neighborhoods." Social scientists have tied the illnesses of life in public housing projects to the physical environment of their settings. The best-known account of life in public housing and its linkage to the architecture occurred in the Pruitt-Igoe housing project in St. Louis, Missouri. Yancey described in "Architecture, Interaction, and Social Control: The Case of a Large-Scale Public Housing Project" the fearful life of assault, rape, and drugs of Pruitt-Igoe residents. Rainwater in *Behind Ghetto Walls: Black Family Life in a*

Federal Slum provided a full description of the institutions and processes that determined the content and style of minority lower-class life in 1970s America. Many environmental and behavioral researchers jumped onto the theme that the design of Pruitt-Igoe did not consider the social and cultural needs of the prospective tenants and was not "defensible space," as Newman defined it in his *Defensible Space: Crime Prevention through Urban Design*. The "failure" of much of public housing has been attributed to the failure of policymakers and architects to understand the activity systems and aesthetic values of people in whose culture they themselves were not saturated. The breakdown of life in public housing projects was linked with economically built, badly maintained, dangerous-to-live-in, high-rise vertical structures. While the criticisms have some validity, they overlook a more fundamental issue. In contrast to many forms of housing in the United States, these large-scale, high-rise projects are publicly owned. Public ownership, usually in the form of municipal authorities, creates dependency upon public appropriation to fund regular maintenance and all degrees of rehabilitation and improvement. There is little doubt about the need of environmental designers to nurture a sensitivity to places in terms of their own experiences and to realize the experiences of the recipients of their design. One possible direction for housing design that enables people to make their own choices regarding their housing may be found in Turner's *Housing by the People*; Turner and Fichter's *Freedom to Build*; and Habraken's *Supports: An Alternative to Mass Housing*. According to Habraken, for example, architects should be responsible only for the overall framework of housing, and the inhabitants should be responsible for the infill. This approach to housing design limits the role of environmental designers to exterior structures and leaves the interiors for people's desires and needs. Nevertheless, the physical design of public housing is only one factor in its success or failure, but the discussion of this important issue is beyond the scope of this chapter.

The New Towns of the 1970s combined construction processes with community and regional issues. This housing program included thirteen new community projects funded by HUD. New Towns were planned to have combinations of dwellings with workplaces for both social and resource benefits. Another social goal was to create communities that would integrate people from various racial, ethnic, and income backgrounds. A third goal was the provision of better land use planning. Although idealistic in principles and planning, most of the New Towns failed due to problems with bureaucratic delays and inflation, difficulties with coordination of federal agencies, and corruption in the administrative and building agencies. A look at the New Towns program is provided in three articles in Wedin and Nygren's *Housing Perspectives: Individuals and Families* (1st ed.). The articles, written several years apart, range from an idealistic discussion of the potential of the New Towns program, to a "how did it happen?" account of the failure of the program. The history of the New Towns program is examined also in *New Towns: Journal Articles, 1980–1988* by Vance and in Huttman's chapter "New Communities in the United States."

Two trends toward the restoration of community and concern for a more sustainable environment appear to address in their own ways crucial issues of our time. One is the New Urbanism movement, which tries to suggest alternatives to the present decline of America's cities and its poorly planned suburban growth.

Peter Katz's book *The New Urbanism: Toward an Architecture of Community* provides a guide to this emerging movement through documented case studies of new designs that integrate housing, shops, workplaces, parks, and civic facilities into new communities. A closely related concept is hybrid housing, which is "a residential structure which contains both residential and business spaces and activities; residents of that structure occupy and manage both spaces; and such housing is intentionally designed to incorporate both spaces" (Ahrentzen, 1991: 1).

The second trend is manifested in the collaborative communities, which attempt to take a holistic approach to housing by combining housing with gardening, shopping, and workplaces. The essence of collaborative housing is that meeting everyday needs in a communal way creates community. In her book *Collaborative Communities: Cohousing, Central Living and Other New Forms of Housing with Shared Facilities*, Fromm describes communities where residents enjoy the advantages of private homes and the convenience of shared services and amenities. In spite of their vast differences, these trends exemplify the search for alternatives to the present sprawl and isolation of existing American suburbs.

HOUSING FOR SPECIAL POPULATIONS

A number of architects and social scientists have contended that by incorporating social-behavioral sciences into the architectural design process, the resulting buildings would function better for users and occupants. An examination of the literature in environment-behavior studies reveals that some housing types were researched more than others and that still other areas were left almost untouched. It appears that the requirement for matching the needs of human beings with the environment is more urgent in the cases of housing for special populations.

In the past thirty years several groups have protested the ways in which American society has attempted to exclude people with disabilities. They have pointed to the architectural environment as the most obvious symbol of how the able-bodied population handicaps the disabled. For a brief history of the various social movements of the 1960s and 1970s as they relate to physically disabled people's activism, see DeJong's *Environmental Accessibility and Independent Living Outcomes: Directions for Disability Policy and Research*. Nevertheless, the recent passage of civil laws—the Americans with Disabilities Act and the Fair Housing Amendments Act—has extended accessibility into every realm of the built environment, both public and private.

The concept of designing for people of all ages and abilities, known as universal design, is a meaningful response to the law as well as to the changing demographics of the American aging society. Universal design is a holistic approach to creating environments and products that are usable by all people regardless of their abilities or age. *Rethinking Architecture* by Lifchez discusses the issues in his book about an innovative experiment in architectural education that took place at the University of California, Berkeley.

Another enlightened approach to housing accessibility is what is called adaptive housing. Mace (1990) contended that "this approach specifies that some common access features will be fixed and installed at construction time and that others be made adjustable, and a few other specific features could be added or removed when needed by particular occupants" (50). Three books that stress the approach

Boarding school for Native Americans with teepees in front, Pine Ridge, South Dakota, 1891. Courtesy of the Denver Public Library

that barrier-free design can improve accessibility without compromising aesthetics are *Beautiful Barrier-Free* by Leibrock, *Beautiful Universal Design* by Leibrock and Terry, and *High-Access Home* by Riley.

The Elderly

The subfield of environment and aging developed from the same awareness of the two-way character of the transaction between the person and the environment. Still, from its early stages it dealt with the reality that elderly are, statistically speaking, more vulnerable to environmental pressures than the young. Therefore, the impact of deficits in the environment on their behavior is greater. Implicit in the provision of housing for the elderly and the research on their impact was the assumption that physical as well as interpersonal aspects of the environment affect outcomes, as Carp observed in "Environment and Aging." Pastalan in "Architectural Research and Life-Span Changes" argued that the research paradigm, or model that links life-span changes to design, must match "the demands of the physical environment with the competence level of the individual over the life span" (200).

Several investigators developed theoretical models that directly address the definitions of personal and environmental competence. These studies include Lawton and Nahemow's ecological model described first in "Ecology and the Aging Process"; Kahana and Kahana's "Environmental Continuity, Futurity and Adaptation of the Aged"; Carp and Carp's "A Complementary/Congruence Model of Well-Being or Mental Health for the Community Elderly"; Schooler's "Response of the Elderly to Environment: A Stress-Theoretical Perspective"; Scheidt and Windley's "The Ecology of Aging"; and Moos and Lemke's "The Multiphasic Environmental Assessment Procedure" and also their "Supportive Residential Settings for Older People." The essence of most of these models suggests that the ability of individuals to function within any environmental setting depends on their capabilities and the characteristics of the setting. Gelwicks and Newcomer in their work *Planning Housing Environments for the Elderly* have drawn on the work of Lawton and Nahemow and suggested a model that takes into account an individual's competence to cope with environments and views the problem of functioning as one of matching individuals to the most appropriate setting. The model suggests that the ability to function is the result of interaction between individual capabilities, such as physical health and environmental support, and resources and incentives in the environment for use of services. Describing the model, Faletti noted in his chapter "Human Factors Research and Functional Environments for the Aged" that matches of individual capabilities with an environment of a particular structure happen within a zone or range of adaptability. Mismatches that create oversupport lead to dependency, whereas those that create undersupport can result in diminished levels of functioning and increased levels of stress.

In *Environment and Aging Theory: A Focus on Housing*, Scheidt and Windley have compiled a collection of seven essays highlighting the seminal theory-driven research that has underwritten the field of environment and aging. Since its beginning more than three decades ago, this multidisciplinary field has focused on theoretical and practical strategies for matching the needs of older persons with their residential environments.

As people age, they must make a fundamental decision whether to stay in their existing dwelling and to age in place or to move to a new location that may offer a completely different type of living accommodation. In his book *Housing America's Elderly: Many Possibilities/Few Choices*, Golant reviewed the options that confront older people seeking to bring their housing situation to fit their changing lifestyles. Golant listed under the housing options that encourage residential relocation by older persons: age-segregated conventional shelter strategies, such as planned retirement communities; financial strategies, like low-rent, government-subsidized rental accommodations; household strategies, such as relocation to a child's residence; and group shelter strategies which include congregate housing, board and care, assisted-living facilities, continuing care retirement communities, and nursing homes. Under the housing options allowing older people to stay put in their current dwelling Golant listed five categories of aging in place: (1) financial strategies; (2) household strategies, such as family caregiving assistance; (3) home-based service strategies, like home nursing care or case management; (4) community-based service strategies, such as respite care or adult day care; and (5) group shelter strategies, such as assisted-living facilities in congregate housing facilities.

In spite of the numerous options, the available housing alternatives for the elderly are far from being perfect. Older people discover that their lifestyles, values, attitudes, personalities, and mental and physical disabilities clash with the features of most available options. As Golant noted, "They find that most options require them to sacrifice something: their control, autonomy, or privacy; the rhythms of their everyday life; their ability to be alone; their capacity to act spontaneously; their familiar surroundings; their sense of being conventional; and their attachment to people and objects of their past" (11). Many researchers explored this fundamental issue in housing for the elderly.

There is little doubt that the focus on the functional aspects of person–environment relations in late life has generated important insights. Nevertheless, the functional orientation ignored meaningful facets of elderly people's lives. As Lawton noted in "Environment and the Need Satisfaction of the Aging":

> The docility and proactivity conceptions underline what I see as a basic dialectic in conceptualizing services for the elderly: support versus autonomy. Decline and deprivation demand support, but the human spirit demands autonomy. The view that either aspect of this duality tells the whole story is sheer fantasy. Proactive environments, such as institutions, were not constructed to crush human spirit but to attempt to adjust the average press level of vulnerable people to one consistent with their competence. Our errors have come in assuming that all forms of press are negative and that autonomy ends once competence is low enough to require a specialized environment. (37–38)

Older people tend to understate their housing problems, as several studies observed. These include Golant's article "Subjective Housing Assessments by the Elderly: A Critical Information Source for Planning and Program Evaluation"; Lawton's chapter "Housing and Living Environments of Older People"; and Rabushka and Jacobs' book *Old Folks at Home*. The reasons and factors that appear to be responsible for it may be found in Golant's chapter "The Effects of Residential and Activity Behaviors on Old People's Environmental Experiences" in Altman, Lawton, and Wohlwill's *Elderly People and the Environment*; and Lawton's classic *Environment and Aging*. Several studies identified an array of physical conditions that create difficulties or uncomfortable occupancy and use of housing. Of these works Hiatt's "Understanding the Physical Environment" and Regnier and Pynoos' book *Housing the Aged: Design Directives and Policy Considerations* are good examples. Several books and articles concerning psychological aspects may be found in the field of psychology of aging. In fact, one may find chapters related to housing issues in each one of the editions of the *Handbook of the Psychology of Aging*, edited by Birren and Schaie. Because of the nature of the field of aging and the environment, some of the books and articles mentioned may be more theoretical in their content. One example of this sort is the edited book titled *Aging and the Environment* by Lawton, Windley, and Byerts, which through theoretical models, deals with environments inhabited by older persons. "For both the researcher and the designer, the instance of environmental match and mismatch, if examined within a more general theoretical framework, are highly instructive and pave the way toward improving the environment for people of all ages" (vii).

The need to be in control of one's life is particularly important in old age, as Langer noted in *The Psychology of Control*. Other books and articles that explored aspects of control and dependency in aging include Baltes and Werner-Wahl's "Dependence in Aging"; Seligman's *Helplessness: On Depression, Development, and Death*; Perlmuter, Monty and Chan's "Choice, Control, and Cognitive Functioning"; Rodin's "Health, Control, and Aging"; White and Janson's "Helplessness in Institutional Settings: Adaptation or Iatrogenic Disease?"; and Fry's edited book *Psychological Perspectives of Helplessness and Control in the Elderly*. Closely related to the issue of control is the issue of autonomy, which attracted several studies. Articles and books about autonomy include Hofland's introduction to the *Generation* supplement about "Autonomy and Long-term Care Practice"; Collopy's "Autonomy in Long-Term Care: Some Crucial Distinctions"; Agich's book *Autonomy and Long-Term Care*; and *Aging, Autonomy and Architecture*, edited by Schwarz and Brent.

Older people list six factors to the mismatch between their neighborhoods and their competence level: (1) poor location; (2) alternative transportation options; (3) limited choice of nearby alternative housing accommodations; (4) dislike of the people in the neighborhood; (5) high crime level; and (6) inadequately maintained houses and apartments. Authors who wrote about these issues include Carp in her chapter "Neighborhood Quality Perception and Measurement" in the book *Housing an Aging Society: Issues, Alternatives, and Policy*, edited by Newcomer, Lawton, and Byerts; Golant in *Housing America's Elderly*; Struyk and Soldo in their book *Improving the Elderly's Housing*; and Ward, LaGory, and Sherman in the book *The Environment for Aging: Interpersonal, Social, and Spatial Contexts*. When their physical or mental impairments become unmanageable, older people may have to relocate to more appropriate settings. This may be a cause for stress and anxiety, as observed in Pastalan's "Environmental Displacement" and Tobin and Liberman's *Last Home for the Aged*. The alternative for moving to an undesired setting may be found in several options of aging in place.

Aging in place is a strongly held preference of older persons. The concept represents a transaction between an aging individual and his or her residential environment. Most simply, the term "aging in place" "means not having to move from one's present residence in order to secure necessary support services in response to changing needs," as Pastalan defined it in *Aging in Place: The Role of Housing and Social Supports*. According to Pynoos' "Public Policy and Aging in Place: Identifying the Problems and Potential Solutions," aging in place has emerged as a social problem due to three factors: (1) existing housing units are not designed to meet physical, social, and service needs of their aging occupants; (2) many frail elderly in nursing homes could be cared for in noninstitutional settings; and (3) forces in the housing market such as rising rents and increased property taxes affect the ability of older persons to remain in their homes. Additional chapters in the book *Aging in Place: Supporting the Frail Elderly in Residential Environments*, edited by Tilson, explore the issue from different perspectives. Other works that dealt with the concept of aging in place and its implications include Miller's *Community-Based Long-Term Care: Innovative Models*; Holshouser in *Aging in Place: The Demographics and Service Needs of the Elderly in Urban Public Housing*; and Cohen and Weisman in *Holding on to Home: Designing Environments for People with Dementia*.

Two other topics are characterized by Cohen and Weisman's book: design guidelines for housing for the elderly and special care units for people with dementia. Design guidelines that address physical, psychological, and social needs of older persons were written by researchers, consultants, and organizations and associations focused on the market of elderly housing. In many of these publications one can find the essence of environment and behavior design. Books of this sort include Zeisel, Epp, and Demos' *Low-Rise Housing for Elderly People: Behavioral Criteria for Design*; Zeisel, Welch, Epp, and Demos' *Mid-Rise Elevator Housing for Older People*; Valins' *Housing for the Elderly People: A Guide for Architects and Clients*; Weal and Weal's *Housing for the Elderly: Options and Design*; Howell's *Designing for Aging: Patterns for Use*; and Carstens' *Site Planning and Design for the Elderly: Issues, Guidelines, and Alternatives*.

Special care units for people with dementia have been built in recent years all around the United States and in other parts of the world. Consequently, the topic attracted research that may be found in the literature, as the trend to develop facilities is growing. Thoughtfully designed architectural environments represent potentially valuable, albeit typically underutilized, therapeutic resources in the care of people with dementia. It has been argued that many of the behaviors attributed to Alzheimer's disease are, in part, a consequence of countertherapeutic settings. This notion and the hope that the physical environment combined with policies, programming, and management of facilities may assist in the therapy of dementia are in many publications, for example, Coons' *Specialized Dementia Care Units*; Lawton, Fulcomer, and Kleban's "Architecture for the Mentally Impaired Elderly"; Sloane and Mathew's *Dementia Units in Long-Term Care*; Calkins' *Design for Dementia: Planning Environments for the Elderly and the Confused*; Hiatt's "Environmental Design and Mentally Impaired Older People"; and Cohen and Day's *Contemporary Environments for People with Dementia*.

Other books that are directed toward the audiences of environment-behavior researchers, designers, and care providers include Koncelik's *Designing the Open Nursing Home*; Pastalan and Carson's *Spatial Behavior of Older People*; Hoglund's *Housing for the Elderly: Privacy and Independence in the Environments for the Aging*; Raschko's *Housing Interiors for the Disabled and Elderly*; Spivac and Tamer's *Institutional Setting: An Environmental Design Approach*; Golant's *Place to Grow Old: The Meaning of Environment in Old Age*; Rowles and Ohta's *Aging and Milieu*; Willcocks, Peace, and Kellaher's *Private Lives in Public Places*; Regnier, Hamilton, and Yatabe's *Best Practice in Assisted Living: Innovations in Design, Management and Financing*; and Regnier's *Assisted Living Housing for the Elderly: Design Innovations from the United States and Europe*. Regnier's book is written from an architectural and interior design standpoint about an emerging model of residential care for frail elderly, which is defined as "any residential group program that is not licensed as a nursing home, that provides personal care to persons with need for assistance in daily living, and that can respond to unscheduled needs for assistance that might arise" (Kane and Wilson, 1993: xi). More information about the topic may be found in Mollica and Snow's *State Assisted Living Policy*; Wilson's "Developing a Viable Model of Assisted Living"; Newcomer's "Best Practices in Residential Care for the Elderly: Draft Notes"; and Schwarz and Brent's *Aging, Autonomy and Architecture*.

Children

Children are a significant user group of housing. Still, descriptions of life among children in residential environments are uncommon. Children spend most of their days in institutional environments such as school, and when they lead a "normal" life in their homes, they have relatively few degrees of freedom, as Michelson observed in *From Sun to Sun: Daily Obligations and Community Structure in the Lives of Employed Women and Their Families*. Ahrentzen offered one of the most comprehensive collections about this topic in her *Children and the Built Environment: An Annotated Bibliography of Representative Research of Children and Housing, School Design and Environmental Stress*. Research about children and the environment has focused on schools and, to a lesser extent, playgrounds. However, schools represent only a fraction of the environments to which children are exposed, as Zimring, Carpman, and Michelson noted in "Design for Special Populations: Mentally Retarded Persons, Children, Hospital Visitors." Several researchers discussed children within their family's context. Barker and Wright, for example, studied the behaviors and activities of children using a process of simple observations of all the activities of a single child during a whole day in *One Boy's Day*.

Children often use neighborhood spaces for recreational and social activities. Lynch has described in *Growing Up in Cities: Studies of the Spatial Environment of Adolescents in Cracow, Melbourne, Mexico City, Salta, Toluca, and Warszawa* how children in different cities around the world, including in the United States, engage with the built environment. Michelson, Levine, and Michelson's *The Child in the City: Changes and Challenges* approached the issue from a somewhat different perspective. Children can turn any part of the built environment into a setting for play. However, research has shown that children in low-rise apartment complexes have much easier access to play areas. Cooper Marcus and Sarkissian in "Children's Play Behavior in Low-Rise Inner-City Housing Development" concluded that this is also one of the reasons that parents prefer to live in these settings over high-rise apartments, where access to the outdoors as well the control of children are more limited.

Explaining the rationale and the purpose of their book *Housing As If People Mattered: Site Design Guidelines for Medium-Density Family Housing*, Cooper Marcus and Sarkissian wrote: "The book is primarily about housing for families with children. This group forms the majority of households needing public and private housing" (12). The book emphasizes children's needs "not because they are the chief users of outdoor common space, and most influenced by their design, but because designers frequently ignore their needs" (13).

A significant amount of research exists in the field of environmental cognition in childhood, which incorporates in it aspects of housing environments. Examples of research of this kind include Beil's study of judgments of relative distance from one point in a child's neighborhood to two others reported in "Children's Spatial Representation of Their Neighborhood: A Step towards a General Spatial Competence"; Cousins, Siegel, and Maxwell's study of assessment of landmark, route, and configurational knowledge, based on walks over terrain near school, reported in "Way Finding and Cognitive Mapping in Large Scale Environments: A Test of a Developmental Model"; and other studies presented in Heft and Wohlwill's chapter "Environmental Cognition in Children." These studies add the empirical dimension to the notion that many individuals' most powerful memories revolve around environments associated with their childhood. People remember the houses where they grew up, the neighborhoods where they played, the secret places of childhood and adolescence, as Cooper Marcus and Sarkissian described in "Environmental Memories" in Altman and Low's *Place Attachment*. The meaning of childhood home and children's special affinity or bond for certain places was explored by Sebba in "The Landscapes of Childhood: The Reflection of Childhood's Environment in Adult Memories and in Children's Attitudes" and by Chawla in a chapter titled "Childhood Place Attachment." In "Home Is Where You Start From: Childhood Memories in Adult Interpretations of Home," Chawla examined some major cultural interpretations of the significance of remembered childhood homes through four case studies.

Boschetti in "Memories of Childhood Homes: Some Contributions of Environmental Autobiography to Interior Design Education and Research" proposed that an environmental autobiography can generate useful concepts for interior designers. Environmental autobiography is one method of research used for the studies of children and the environment. Other methods and studies may be found in Altman and Wohlwill's *Children and the Environment* and in the chapter "Children and Built Environments: A Review of Methods for Environmental Research and Design" by Ziegler and Andrews in Bechtel, Marans, and Michelson's book *Methods in Environmental and Behavioral Research*.

BIBLIOGRAPHY

Books and Articles

Achtenberg, Emily P., and Peter Marcuse. "Toward the Decommodification of Housing: A Political Analysis and a Progressive Program." In *America's Housing Crisis: What Is to Be Done?*, ed. Chester Hartman. Boston: Routledge and Kegan Paul, 1981.

Advisory Council on Historic Preservation. *The Contribution of Historic Preservation to Urban Revitalization*. Washington, D.C.: Government Printing Office, 1979.

Agich, George J. *Autonomy and Long-Term Care*. New York: Oxford University Press, 1993.

Agnew, James. "Home Ownership and Identity in Capitalist Societies." In *Housing and Identity: Cross-Cultural Perspectives*, ed. James S. Duncan. New York: Holmes and Meier, 1982, 60–97.

Ahrentzen, Sherry. *Children and the Built Environment: An Annotated Bibliography of Representative Research of Children and Housing, School Design and Environmental Stress*. Architecture Series, NO A-764. Monticello, Ill.: Vance Bibliographies, 1982.

———. *Hybrid Housing: A Contemporary Building Type for Multiple Residential and Business Use*. Milwaukee: Center for Architectural and Planning Research, University of Wisconsin-Milwaukee, 1991.

Allen, Edward. *Exercises in Building Construction*. New York: Wiley, 1990.

———. *Fundamentals of Building Construction: Materials and Methods*. New York: John Wiley and Sons, 1999.

———. *The Professional Handbook of Building Construction*. New York: Wiley, 1985.

Altman, Irwin. *Environment and Social Behavior: Privacy, Personal Space, Territory, and Crowding*. Pacific Grove, Calif.: Brooks/Cole, 1975.

Altman, Irwin, and Martin Chemers. *Culture and Environment*. Monterey, Calif.: Brooks/Cole, 1980.

Altman, Irwin, and Mary Gauvain. "A Cross-Cultural and Dialectic Analysis of Homes." In *Spatial Representation and Behavior across the Life Span: Theory and Application*, ed. Lynn Liben, Arthur Patterson, and Nora Newcombe. New York: Academic Press, 1981, 283–320.

Altman, Irwin, M. Powell Lawton, and Joachim F. Wohlwill. *Elderly People and the Environment*. New York: Plenum Press, 1984.

Altman, Irwin, and Setha M. Low, eds. *Place Attachment*. New York: Plenum Press, 1992.

Altman, Irwin, and Abraham Wandersman, eds. *Neighborhood and Community Environments*. New York: Plenum Press, 1987.

Altman, Irwin, and Carol M. Werner. *Home Environments*. New York: Plenum Press, 1985.

Altman, Irwin, and Joachim F. Wohlwill. *Children and the Environment*. New York: Plenum Press, 1978.

Ambrose, J. *Building Construction: Interior Systems*. New York: Van Nostrand Reinhold, 1991.

———. *Building Construction and Design*. New York: Van Nostrand Reinhold, 1992.

Anderson, B. *Solar Building Architecture*. Ed. C. A. Bankston. Cambridge, Mass.: MIT Press, 1990.

Anderson, E. N. "Some Chinese Methods of Dealing with Crowding." *Urban Anthropology* 1 (1972), 143–150.

Anderson, James, and Sue Weidemann. "Development of an Instrument to Measure Residents' Perceptions of Residential Quality." Paper presented at the International Conference on Housing. Miami, Fla., 1979.

Anderson, L. O. *Wood-Frame House Construction*. Carlsbad, Calif.: Craftsman, 1990.

Andrews, Gregory, ed. *Tax Incentives for Historic Preservation*. Washington, D.C.: Preservation Press, 1981.

Anthony, Kathryn H. "The Role of the Home Environment in Family Conflict: Therapists' Viewpoints." In *EDRA 15—1984 Proceedings: The Challenge of Diversity*, ed. Donna Duerk and David Campbell. Washington, D.C.: Environmental Design Research Association, 1984, 219–26.

Appelbaum, Richard P., and John I. Gilderbloom. *Rethinking Rental Housing*. Philadelphia: Temple University Press, 1988.

Appleyard, D. "Home." *Architectural Association Quarterly* 11 (1979), 4–20.

Argyle, Michael, and M. Henderson. "The Rules of Friendship." *Journal of Social and Personal Relationships* 1 (1984), 211–37.

Arias, Ernesto G. "User Group Preferences and Their Intensity: The Impacts of Residential Design." In *The Meaning and Use of Housing*, ed. Ernesto Arias. Brookfield, Vt.: Ashgate, 1993, 169–199.

———, ed. *The Meaning and Use of Housing*. Brookfield, Vt.: Ashgate, 1993.

Austin, Richard L., et al. *Graphic Standards for Landscape Architecture*. New York: Van Nostrand Reinhold, 1986.

Bachelard, Gaston. *The Poetics of Space*. Boston: Beacon, 1969.

Bailey, W. G. *Guide to Popular U.S. Government Publications*. Englewood, Colo.: Libraries Unlimited, 1990.

Balcomb, D., ed. *Passive Solar Buildings*. Cambridge, Mass.: MIT Press, 1992.

Baldassare, Mark. "Residential Crowding in the United States: A Review of Research." In *Handbook of Housing and the Built Environment in the United States*, ed. Elizabeth Huttman and Willem van Vliet. Westport, Conn.: Greenwood Press, 1988.

Ballast, D.K. *Interior Construction and Detailing for Designers and Architects*. Belmont, Calif.: Professional, 1994.

Baltes Margret M., and H. Werner-Wahl. "Dependence in Aging." In *Handbook of Clinical Gerontology*, ed. Laura L. Carstensen and Barry A. Edelstein. New York: Pergamon Press, 1987, 204–221.

Balton, Richard E. *Houses and Households: A Comparative Study*. New York: Plenum, 1994.

Banerjee, Tridib, and William C. Baer. *Beyond the Neighborhood Unit: Residential Environments and Public Policy*. New York: Plenum Press, 1984.

Banham, Joanna, ed. *Encyclopedia of Interior Design*. London: Fitzroy Dearborn, 1997.

Benjamin, David N., ed. *The Home: Words, Interpretations, Meanings, and Environments*. Brookfield, Vt.: Avebury, 1995.

Barker, Roger G., and Herbert F. Wright. *One Boy's Day*. New York: Harper and Row, 1951.

Bassuk, Ellen L. "The Homelessness Problem." *Scientific American* 25 (1984), 40–46.

Baum, Andrew, and Glenn E. Davis. "Spatial and Social Aspects of Crowding Perception." *Environment and Behavior* 8 (1976), 527–44.

Baum, Andrew, and Paul B. Paulus. "Crowding." In *Handbook of Environmental Psychology*, ed. Daniel Stokols and Irwin Altman. New York: John Wiley and Sons, 1987.

Baxter, Ellen, and Kim Hopper. "The New Mendicancy: Homeless in New York City." *American Journal of Orthopsychiatry* 52 (1982), 393–408.

Bechtel, Robert, Robert Marans, and William Michelson, eds. *Methods in Environmental and Behavioral Research*. New York: Van Nostrand Reinhold, 1987.

Beil, Anders. "Children's Spatial Representation of Their Neighborhood: A Step towards a General Spatial Competence." *Journal of Environmental Psychology* 2 (1982), 193–200.

Benjamin, David N., ed. *The Home: Words, Interpretations, Meanings, and Environments*. Brookfield, Vt.: Avebury, 1995.

Benson, T. *The Timber-Frame Home: Design, Construction, Finishing*. Newtown, Conn.: Taunton, 1990.

Berglund, M. *Stone, Log and Earth Houses: Building with Elemental Materials*. Newtown, Conn.: Taunton, 1986.

Berry, Brian Joe Lobley, and John D. Kasarda. *Contemporary Urban Ecology*. New York: Macmillan, 1977.

Bingham, Richard D. *Public Housing and Urban Renewal: An Analysis of Federal-Local Relations*. New York: Praeger, 1975.

Birren, James E., and K. Warner Schaie, eds. *Handbook of the Psychology of Aging*. New York: Van Nostrand Reinhold, 1990.

Blalock, Hubert M., Jr. *Race and Ethnic Relations*. Englewood Cliffs, N.J.: Prentice-Hall, 1982.

Bobenhausen, W. *Simplified Design for HVAC Systems*. New York: Wiley, 1992.

Booth, Alan. *Urban Crowding and Its Consequences*. New York: Praeger, 1976.

Boschetti, Margaret. A. "Memories of Childhood Homes: Some Contributions of Environmental Autobiography to Interior Design Education and Research." *Journal of Interior Design Education and Research* 13 (1987), 27–36.

Brand, R. *Architectural Details for Insulated Buildings*. New York: Van Nostrand Reinhold, 1989.

Bratt, Rachel G. "Controversies and Contributions: A Public Housing Critique." *Journal of Housing* 42 (1985), 165–73.

———. *Rebuilding a Low-Income Housing Strategy*. Philadelphia: Temple University Press, 1989.

Brawne, M. *From Idea to Building: Issues in Architecture*. Stoneham, Mass.: Butterworth-Heinemann, 1992.

Brent, Ruth, and Benyamin Schwarz, eds. *Popular American Housing: A Reference Guide*. Westport, Conn.: Greenwood Press, 1995.

Breyer, D.E. *Design of Wood Structures*. New York: McGraw-Hill, 1993.

Brill, Michael. *Do Buildings Really Matter? Economic and Other Effects of Designing Behaviorally Supportive Buildings*. New York: Educational Facilities Laboratories, Academy for Educational Development, 1982.

Brower, Sidney. *Design in Familiar Places: What Makes Home Environments Look Good*. New York: Praeger, 1988.

Brown, Barbara B. "Territoriality." In *Handbook of Environmental Psychology*, ed. Daniel Stokols and Irwin Altman. New York: John Wiley and Sons, 1987.

Brown, Barbara B., and Irwin Altman. "Territoriality and Residential Crime: A Conceptual Framework." In *Environmental Criminology*, ed. Paul J. Brantingham and Patricia Brantigham. Beverly Hills, Calif.: Sage, 1981, 55–76.

———. "Territoriality, Street Form, and Residential Burglary: An Environmental Analysis." *Journal of Environmental Psychology* 3 (1983), 203–20.

Brown, Barbara B., and Carol M. Werner. "Social Cohesiveness, Territoriality, and Holiday Decorations: The Influence of Cul-de-Sacs." *Environment and Behavior* 17 (1985), 539–65.

Brown, Erica. *Sixty Years of Interior Design*. New York: Viking Press, 1982.

Bruce, Alfred, and Harold Sandbank. *A History of Prefabrication*. New York: Arno (originally published in 1944), 1972.

Brudney, Jeffrey L., and Robert E. England. "Urban Policy Making and Subjective Service Evaluations: Are They Compatible?" *Public Administration Review* 42 (March/April 1982), 127–35.

Brueggeman, William B., and Jeffrey D. Fisher. *Real Estate Finance and Investments*. New York: McGraw-Hill, 2001.

Building Officials and Code Administrators International. *The BOCA Basic/National Plumbing Code*. Country Club Hills, Ill.: BOCA, 1983– .

———. *The BOCA Basic/National Energy Conservation Code*. Country Club Hills, Ill.: BOCA, 1984– .

———. *The BOCA Basic/National Code Interpretations*. Country Club Hills, Ill.: BOCA, 1985– .

———. *The BOCA National Building Code*. Country Club Hills, Ill.: BOCA, 1986– .

———. *The BOCA National Fire Prevention Code*. Country Club Hills, Ill.: BOCA, 1986– .

———. *The BOCA National Mechanical Code*. Country Club Hills, Ill.: BOCA, 1986– .

———. *The BOCA National Plumbing Code*. Country Club Hills, Ill.: BOCA, 1986– .

Burns, B. *Affordable Housing: A Resource Guide to Alternative and Factory-Built Houses, New Technologies, and the Owner-Builder Option*. Jefferson, N.C.: McFarland, 1989.

Calkins, Margaret. *Design for Dementia: Planning Environments for the Elderly and the Confused*. Owing Mills, Md.: National Health, 1988.

Callender, J.H., ed. *Time-Saver Standards for Architectural Design Data*. 6th ed. New York: McGraw-Hill, 1982.

Calloway, Stephen, and Elizabeth Cromley. *Elements of Style*. New York: Simon and Schuster, 1991.

Campbell, Angus, Philip E. Converse, and Willard L. Rodgers. *The Quality of American Life: Perceptions, Evaluations, and Satisfactions*. New York: Russel Sage Foundation, 1976.

Canter, David., J. Gilchrist, J. Miller, and N. Roberts. "An Empirical Study of the Focal Point in the Living Room." In *Psychology and the Built Environment*, ed. David Canter and Terence Lee. New York: Halsted, 1974, 29–37.

Canter, David, and David Stea, eds. *Housing: Design, Research, Education*. London: Avebury, 1993.

———. *The Meaning and Use of Housing: International Perspectives, Approaches and Their Applications*. London: Avebury, 1993.

———. *Placemaking: Production of Built Environment in Two Cultures*. London: Avebury, 1993.

———. *Vernacular Architecture*. London: Avebury, 1990.

Carp, Frances Merchant. "Environment and Aging." In *Handbook of Environmental Psychology*, ed. Daniel Stokols and Irwin Altman. New York: John Wiley and Sons, 1987, 329–360.

———. "Neighborhood Quality Perception and Measurement." In *Housing an Aging Society: Issues, Alternatives, and Policy*, ed. Robert J. Newcomer, M. Powell Lawton, and Thomas O. Byerts. New York: Van Nostrand Reinhold, 1986.

Carp, Frances Merchant, and Abraham Carp. "A Complementary/Congruence Model of Well-Being or Mental Health for the Community Elderly." In *Elderly People and the Environment*, ed. Irwin Altman, Joachim Wohlwill, and M. Powell Lawton. New York: Plenum, 1984.

———. "Perceived Environmental Quality of Neighborhoods: Development of Assessment Scales and Their Relations to Age and Gender." *Journal of Environmental Psychology* 2 (1982), 295–312.

Carpelan, Bo. *Vuodet Kuin Lehdet*. Trans. Michael Wynne-Ellis. Helsinki: Otava, 1989.

Carstens, Diane. *Site Planning and Design for the Elderly: Issues, Guidelines, and Alternatives*. New York: Van Nostrand Reinhold, 1985.

Chavis, David M., James H. Hogge, David W. McMillan, and Abraham Wandersman. "Sense of Community through Brunswik's Lens: A First Look." *Journal of Community Psychology* 14 (1986), 24–40.

Chawla, Louise. "Childhood Place Attachment." In *Place Attachment*, ed. Irwin Altman and Setha M. Low. New York: Plenum Press, 1992.

———. "Home Is Where You Start From: Childhood Memories in Adult Interpretations of Home." In *The Meaning and Use of Housing: International Perspectives, Approaches and Their Applications*, ed. Ernesto G. Arias. Brookfield, Vt.: Ashgate, 1993.

Cherlnik, Paul D., and Scott K. Wilderman. "Symbols of Status in Urban Neighborhoods: Contemporary Perceptions of Nineteenth-Century Boston." *Environment and Behavior* 18 (1986), 604–22.

Ching, F. *Building Construction Illustrated*. New York: Van Nostrand Reinhold, 1991.

Clark, Clifford E. *The American Family Home 1800–1960*. Chapel Hill: University of North Carolina Press, 1986.

Clay, Grady. *Close-Up: How to Read the American City*. Chicago: University of Chicago Press, 1980.

Cochrane, T. "Place, People, and Folklore: An Isle Royale Case Study." *Western Folklore* 46 (1987), 1–20.

Cohen, Uriel, and Kristen Day. *Contemporary Environments for People with Dementia*. Baltimore: Johns Hopkins University Press, 1993.

Cohen, Uriel, and Gerald D. Weisman. *Holding on to Home: Designing Environments for People with Dementia*. Baltimore: Johns Hopkins University Press, 1991.

Collopy, Bart J. "Autonomy in Long-Term Care: Some Crucial Distinctions." *Gerontologist* 28, suppl. (June 1988), 10–17.

Connerly, Charles E., and Robert W. Marans. "Neighborhood Quality: A Description and Analysis of Indicators." In *Handbook of Housing and the Built Environment in the United States*, ed. Elizabeth Huttman and Willem van Vliet. Westport, Conn.: Greenwood Press, 1988.

Conrads, Ulrich. *Programs and Manifestoes on 20th-Century Architecture*. Cambridge: MIT Press, 1970.

Conran, Terence. *The Essential House Book: Getting Back to Basics*. New York: Crown Trade, 1994.

———. *New House Book*. New York: Crown Trade, 1999.

Coons, Dorothy H., ed. *Specialized Dementia Care Units*. Baltimore: Johns Hopkins University Press, 1991.

Cooper, C. "Resident Dissatisfaction in Multi-Family Housing." In *Behavior, Design and Policy Aspects of Human Habitats*, ed. W. M. Smith. Green Bay: University of Wisconsin–Green Bay Press, 1972, 119–45.

———. *Easter Hill Village: Some Social Implications of Design*. New York: Free Press, 1975.

Cooper Marcus, Clare, and Wendy Sarkissian. "Children's Play Behavior in Low-Rise Inner-City Housing Development." In *Man-Environment Interactions: Evaluations and Applications*, ed. Daniel Carson. Washington, D.C.: Environmental Design Research Association, 1974.

———. "Environmental Memories." In *Place Attachment*, ed. Irwin Altman and Setha M. Low. New York: Plenum Press, 1992.

———. "The House as Symbol of the Self." *Design and Environment* 3 (1974), 30–37.

———. "The House as Symbol of the Self." In *Designing for Human Behavior*, ed. Jon T. Lang, Charles Burnette, Walter Moleski, and David Vachon. Stroudsburg, Pa.: Dowden, Hutchinson, and Ross, 1974, 130–46.

———. *Housing As If People Mattered: Site Design Guidelines for Medium-Density Family Housing*. Berkeley: University of California Press, 1986.

Cousins, Jennifer H., Alexander W. Siegel, and Scott E. Maxwell. "Way Finding and Cognitive Mapping in Large Scale Environments: A Test of a Developmental Model." *Journal of Experimental Child Psychology* 35 (1983), 1–20.

Crystal, Stephen "Homeless Men and Homeless Women: The Gender Gap." *Urban and Social Change Review* 17 (1984), 2–6.

Csikszentmihalyi, Mihaly, and Eugene Rochberg-Halton. *The Meaning of Things: Domestic Symbols and the Self.* New York: Cambridge University Press, 1981.

Dahmann, Donald C. "Assessments of Neighborhood Quality in Metropolitan America." *Urban Affairs Quarterly* 20 (1985), 511–535.

Darden, Joe T. "Accessibility to Housing Differential Residential Segregation for Blacks, Hispanics, American Indians, and Asians." In *Race, Ethnicity, and Minority Housing in the United States*, ed. Jamshid A. Momeni. Westport, Conn.: Greenwood Press, 1986.

———. "Blacks in the Suburbs: Their Number Is Rising, but Patterns of Segregation Persist. What Are the Causes?" *Vital Issues* 27 (1977), 1–4.

———. "Demographic Changes 1970–1980: Implications for Federal Fair Housing." In *Shelter Crisis: The State of Fair Housing*, ed. U.S. Commission on Civil Rights. Washington, D.C., 1983.

———. "The Residential Segregation of Blacks in Detroit, 1960–1970." *International Journal of Comparative Sociology* 17 (1976), 84–91.

———. "The Residential Segregation of Hispanics in Cities and Suburbs of Michigan." *The East Lake Geographer* 18 (1983), 25–37.

Davis, T. L. "Cooperative Self-help Housing." *Law and Contemporary Problems* 32 (1967), 409–415.

De Chiara, Joseph, Julius Panero, and Martin Zelnik. *Time-Saver Standards for Housing and Residential Development*. New York: McGraw-Hill, 1991.

———. *Time Saver Standards for Interior Design and Space Planning*. New York: McGraw-Hill, 1991.

DeForest, Robert W., and Lawrence Veiller. *The Tenement House Problem*. 1900. Manchester, N.H.: Ayer, 1974.

DeJong, Gerben. *Environmental Accessibility and Independent Living Outcomes: Directions for Disability Policy and Research*. East Lansing: University Center for International Rehabilitation, Michigan State University, 1981.

Dennis, Marshall W., and Michael J. Robertson. *Residential Mortgage Lending*. Mason, Ohio: South-Western Thomson, 1994.

Després, Carol. "The Meaning of Home: Literature Review and Directions for Future Research and Theoretical Development." *The Journal of Architectural and Planning Research* 8:2 (Summer 1991), 96–115.

De Vido, Alfredo. *House Design: Art and Practice*. New York: John Wiley, 1996.

Dickinson, Duo. *Small Houses for the Next Century*. New York: McGraw-Hill, 1995.

Dietz, A. *Dwelling House Construction*. Cambridge, Mass.: MIT Press, 1991.

Dolbeare, Cushing. *The Widening Gap: Housing Needs of Low Income Families*. Washington, D.C.: Low Income Housing Information Service, 1992.

Doubilet, Susan, and Daralice Boles. *American House Now: Contemporary Architectural Directions*. New York: Universe, 1997.

Doucet, Michael J., and John C. Weaver. *Housing the North American City*. Montreal: McGill-Queen's University Press, 1991.

Dovey, Kim. "Home: An Ordering Principle in Space." *Landscape* 22 (1978), 27–30.

———. "Home and Homelessness." In *Home Environments*, ed. Irwin Altman and Carol M. Werner. New York: Plenum, 1985.

Downs, Anthony. *Residential Rent Controls: An Evaluation*. Washington, D.C.: Urban Land Institute, 1988.

Duncan, James S., ed. *Housing and Identity: Cross-Cultural Perspectives*. New York: Holmes and Meier, 1982.

Elliott, Cecil D. *Techniques and Architecture*. Cambridge: MIT Press, 1992.

Escherich, Susan M. *Affordable Housing through Historic Preservation*. Upland, Pa.: Diane, 1996.

Fainstein, Norman I., and Susan S. Fainstein. *Restructuring the City*. Rev. ed. New York: Longman, 1986.

Faletti, M. V. "An Experimental Investigation of Cognitive Processing Underlying Judgments of Residential Environments by Different Observer Groups." Doctoral diss., University of Miami. *Dissertation Abstracts International* 40 (1979), 1924B–25B.

———. "Human Factors Research and Functional Environments for the Aged." In *Elderly People and the Environment*, ed. Irwin Altman, M. Powell Lawton, and Joachim F. Wohlwill. New York: Plenum, 1984.

Feirer, John L. *Carpentry and Building Construction*. New York: McGraw-Hill, 1993.

Festinger, Leon, S. Schacter, and K. Back. *Social Pressures in Informal Groups: A Study of Human Factors in Housing*. Stanford, Calif.: Stanford University Press, 1950.

Fish, Gertrude S., ed. *The Story of Housing*. New York: Macmillan, 1979.

Fisher, Thomas. "Bosnia in America?" *Progressive Architecture* (May 1994), 25, 32.

Fitch, James Marsten. *American Building: The Environmental Forces That Shape It*. New York: Schocken, 1947.

Fleming, India, Andrew Baum, and Linda Weiss. "Social Density and Perceived Control as Mediators of Crowding Stress in High-Density Residential Neighborhoods." *Journal of Personality and Social Psychology* 52 (1987), 899–906.

Florida, R.L., ed. *Housing and the New Financial Markets*. New Brunswick, NJ: Center for Urban Policy Research, 1986.

Flynn, J., A. Segill, J. Kremers, and G. Steffy. *Architectural Interior Systems: Lighting, Acoustics, Air Conditioning*. 3rd ed. New York: Van Nostrand Reinhold, 1992.

Foley, Mary Mix. *The American House*. New York: Harper and Row, 1980.

Ford, James, and Katherine Ford. *Classic Modern Homes of the 30's*. New York: Dover, 1984.

Francescato, Guido. "Meaning and Use: A Conceptual Basis." In *The Meaning and Use of Housing*, ed. Ernesto G. Arias. Aldershot, England: Avebury, 1993.

Franck, Karen A. "Women's Housing and Neighborhood Needs." In *Handbook of Housing and the Built Environment in the U.S.*, ed. Elizabeth Huttman and Willem Van Vliet. Westport, Conn.: Greenwood Press, 1988.

Franck, Karen, and Sharon Ahrentzen. *New Households, New Housing*. New York: Van Nostrand Reinhold, 1991.

Fried, M. "Residential Attachment: Sources of Residential and Community Satisfaction." *Journal of Social Issues* 38 (1982), 107–200.

Frieden, Bernard J., and Lynne B. Sagalyn. *Downtown, Inc.* Cambridge: MIT Press, 1990.

Friedman, Lawrence Meir. *Government and Slum Housing: A Century of Frustration*. New York: Arno, 1968.

Fromm, Dorit. *Collaborative Communities: Cohousing, Central Living and Other New Forms of Housing with Shared Facilities*. New York: Van Nostrand Reinhold, 1991.

Fry, Prem S., ed. *Psychological Perspectives of Helplessness and Control in the Elderly*. North Holland: Elsevier Science Publishers B. V., 1989.

Gans, Herbert J. *The Levittowners*. New York: Pantheon, 1967.

———. *The Urban Villagers: Group and Class in the Life of Italian Americans*. New York: Free Press, 1962.

Garber, Marjorie. *Sex and Real Estate: Why We Love Houses*. New York: Pantheon Books, 2000.

Gardner, C., and B. Hannaford. *Lighting Design: An Introductory Guide for Professionals*. New York: Halsted, 1993.

Garling, Tommy. "Studies in Visual Perception of Architectural Spaces and Rooms: Aesthetic Preference." *Scandinavian Journal of Psychology* 13 (1972), 222–27.

Gelfand, Mark. *A Nation of Cities: The Federal Government and Urban America, 1933–1965*. New York: Oxford University Press, 1975.

Gelwicks, Louis E., and Robert J. Newcomer. *Planning Housing Environments for the Elderly*. Washington, D.C.: National Council on the Aging, 1974.

Gerson, Kathleen, Ann C. Steuve, and Claude S. Fischer. "Attachment to Place." In *Networks and Places: Social Relations in the Urban Setting*, ed. Claude S. Fischer, R. M. Jackson, Ann C. Steuve, Kathleen Gerson, Lynne M. Jones, and Mark Baldassare. New York: Free Press, 1977.

Glaszer, Nathan. "Dilemmas of Housing Policy." In *Toward a National Urban Policy*, ed. Daniel P. Moynihan. New York: Basic Books, 1970.

Gobster, Paul H. "Judged Appropriateness of Residential Structures in Natural and Developed Shoreland Settings." In *EDRA 1983: Proceedings of the 14th International Conference of the Environmental Design Research Association*, ed. Doug Amedeo, James B. Griffin, and James J. Potter. Washington, D.C.: Environmental Design Research Association, 1983, 105–12.

Goering, John M. "Race, Housing, and Public Policies: A Strategy for Social Science Research." *Urban Affairs Quarterly* 17 (1982), 463–89.

Goffman, Erving. *The Presentation of Self in Everyday Life*. New York: Doubleday, 1959.

Golant, Stephan M. "The Effects of Residential and Activity Behaviors on Old

People's Environmental Experiences." In *Elderly People and the Environment*, ed. Irwin Altman, M. Powell Lawton, and Joachim Wohlwill. New York: Plenum, 1984.

———. *Housing America's Elderly: Many Possibilities/Few Choices*. Newbury Park, Calif.: Sage, 1992.

———. *Place to Grow Old: The Meaning of Environment in Old Age*. New York: Columbia University Press, 1984.

———. "Subjective Housing Assessments by the Elderly: A Critical Information Source for Planning and Program Evaluation." *Gerontologist* 26 (1986), 122–27.

Goldfield, David R. "Neighborhood Preservation and Community Values in Historical Perspective." In *Neighborhood and Community Environments*, ed. Irwin Altman and Abraham Wandersman. New York: Plenum Press, 1987.

Goldman, Howard H., and J. P. Morrissey. "The Alchemy of Mental Health Policy: Homelessness and the Fourth Cycle of Reform." *American Journal of Public Health* 75 (1985), 727–31.

Gordon, Paul. *Developing Retirement Facilities*. New York: Wiley, 1988.

Gottfried, Herbert, and Jan Jennings. *American Vernacular Design 1870–1940: An Illustrated Glossary*. New York: Van Nostrand Reinhold, 1985.

Greenberg, Stephanie W., and William M. Rohe. "Informal Social Control and Crime Prevention in Modern Neighborhoods." In *Urban Neighborhoods: Research and Policy*, ed. Ralph Taylor. New York: Praeger, 1986.

Greenberg, Stephanie W., William M. Rohe, and Jay R. Wilson. *Informal Citizen Action and Crime Prevention at the Neighborhood Level*. Research Triangle Park, N.C.: Research Triangle Institute, 1984.

Gretes, Frances C. *The Directory of International Periodicals and Newsletters on the Built Environment*. New York: Van Nostrand Reinhold, 1986.

Grey, Johny, Susanne Ardley, Dinah Hall, Sylvia Katz, Sarah Gaventa, and Barbara Weiss. *The Complete Home Style Book*. New York: DK, 1998.

Guise, D. *Design and Technology in Architecture*. New York: Van Nostrand Reinhold, 1991.

Gutman, Robert. *The Design of American Housing: A Reappraisal of the Architect's Role*. New York: Design Arts Program of the National Endowment for the Arts, Publishing Center for Cultural Resources, 1985.

Habraken, John. *Supports: An Alternative to Mass Housing*. New York: Praeger, 1972.

———. *Transformations of the Site*. Cambridge: Awater Press and MIT Department of Architecture, 1988.

Hall, Edward Twitchell. *The Hidden Dimension*. New York: Doubleday, 1966.

Hallman, Howard W. *Neighborhoods: Their Place in Urban Life*. Beverly Hills, Calif.: Sage, 1984.

Handlin, David P. *American Home: Architecture and Society, 1815–1915*. Boston: Little, Brown, 1979.

Hanna, Susan, and Suzanne Lindamood. "Components of Housing Satisfaction." Paper presented at the 12th Environmental Design Research Association Conference, Iowa State University, Ames, 1981.

Hartman, Chester. *Housing and Social Policy*. Englewood Cliffs, N.J.: Prentice-Hall, 1975.

Hayden, Dolores. *The Grand Domestic Revolution: A History of Feminist Designs for American Homes, Neighborhoods, and Cities*. Cambridge: MIT Press, 1981.

———. *Redesigning the American Dream: The Future of Housing, Work, and Family Life*. New York: Norton, 1984.

Heft, Hassy, and Joachim F. Wohlwill. "Environmental Cognition in Children." In *Handbook of Environmental Psychology*, ed. Daniel Stokols and Irwin Altman. New York: John Wiley and Sons, 1987.

Hemmens, George C., Charles J. Hoch, and Jana Carp, eds. *Under One Roof: Issues and Innovations in Shared Housing*. New York: State University of New York Press, 1996.

Herting, Jerald R., and Avery M. Guest. "Components of Satisfaction with Local Areas in the Metropolis." *The Sociological Quarterly* 26 (1985), 99–115.

Heuman, Leonard F. "Racial Integration in Residential Neighborhoods: Towards More Precise Measures and Analysis." *Evaluation Quarterly* 3:1 (1979), 59–79.

Hiatt, Lorraine G. "Environmental Design and Mentally Impaired Older People." In *Alzheimer's Disease: Problems, Prospects and Perspectives*, ed. Harvey J. Altman. New York: Plenum, 1987, 309–20.

———. "Understanding the Physical Environment." *Pride Institute Journal of Long Term Home Health Care* 4 (1985), 12–22.

Hillery, George A. "Definitions of Community: Areas of Agreement." *Rural Sociology* 20 (1955), 111–23.

Hirsch, Arnold R. *Making the Second Ghetto: Race and Housing in Chicago, 1940–1960*. New York: Cambridge University Press, 1983.

Hiss, Tony. *The Experience of Place*. New York: Knopf, 1990.

Hofland, Brian, ed. "Autonomy and Long-term Care Practice." *Generations* 14 (1990), 91–94.

Hoglund, David. *Housing for the Elderly: Privacy and Independence in the Environments for the Aging*. New York: Van Nostrand Reinhold, 1985.

Holahan, Charles J., and Abraham Wandersman. "The Community Psychology Perspective in Environmental Psychology." In *Handbook of Environmental Psychology*, ed. Daniel Stokols and Irwin Altman. New York: John Wiley and Sons, 1987, 827–61.

Holshouser, William L., Jr. *Aging in Place: The Demographics and Service Needs of the Elderly in Urban Public Housing*. Boston: Citizens Housing and Planning Association, 1988.

Hombs, Mary Ellen, and Mitch Snyder. *Homelessness in America: A Forced March to Nowhere*. Washington, D.C.: Community for Creative Non-Violence, 1983.

Hopper, Kim, and Jill Hamberg. "The Making of America's Homeless: From Skid Row to New Poor, 1945–1984." In *Critical Perspectives on Housing*, ed. Rachel Bratt, Chester Hartman, and Ann Meyerson. Philadelphia: Temple University Press, 1986.

Hornbostel, Caleb. *Construction Materials: Types, Uses and Applications*. New York: John Wiley and Sons, 1978.

Horne, Jo, and Leo Baldwin. *Home-Sharing and Other Lifestyle Options*. Washington, D.C.: Scott, Foresman, 1988.

Horwitz, Jaime, and Jerome Tognoli. "Role of Home in Adult Development:

Women and Men Living Alone Describe Their Residential Histories." *Family Relations* 31 (1982), 335–41.

Hounshell, David A. *From the American System to Mass Production (1800–1932).* Baltimore: Johns Hopkins University Press, 1984.

Howell, Sandra. *Designing for Aging: Patterns for Use*. Cambridge: MIT Press, 1980.

———. "The Meaning of Place in Old Age." In *Aging and Milieu: Environmental Perspectives on Growing Old*, ed. Graham Rowles and Russell J. Ohta. New York: Academic Press, 1983.

Hummon, D. M. *Commonplaces: Community Ideology and Identity in American Culture*. Albany: State University of New York Press, 1990.

Hunt, Michael E., et al. *Retirement Communities an American Original*. New York: Haworth Press, 1984.

Hunt, Michael E., and L. E. Ross. "Naturally Occurring Retirement Communities: A Multiattribute Examination of Desirability Factors." *Gerontologist* 30 (1990), 667–74.

Hunt, V.D. *Handbook of Conservation and Solar Energy: Trends and Perspectives*. New York: Van Nostrand Reinhold, 1982.

Huttman, Elizabeth. "New Communities in the United States." In *Handbook of Housing and the Built Environment in the United States*, ed. Elizabeth Huttman and Willem van Vliet. Westport, Conn.: Greenwood Press, 1988.

———, ed. *Urban Housing Segregation of Minorities in Western Europe and the United States*. Durham, N.C.: Duke University Press, 1991.

Huttman, Elizabeth, and Willem Van Vliet, eds. *Handbook of Housing and the Built Environment in the United States*. Westport, Conn.: Greenwood Press, 1988.

Institute of Medicine Staff. *The Social and Built Environment for an Aging Society*. Washington, D.C.: National Academy Press, 1987.

Iselin, Donald, and Andrew Lemer, eds. *The Fourth Dimension in Building: Strategies for Minimizing Obsolescence*. Washington, D.C.: National Academy Press, 1993.

Jackson, Anthony. *A Place Called Home: A History of Low Cost Housing in Manhattan*. Cambridge: MIT Press, 1976.

Jackson, Kenneth T. *Crabgrass Frontier: The Suburbanization of the United States*. New York: Oxford University Press, 1985.

Jacobs, Alan B. *Looking at Cities*. Cambridge: Harvard University Press, 1985.

Jacobs, Jane. *The Death and Life of Great American Cities*. New York: Random House, 1961.

Jacobson, Max. *The Good House: Contrast as a Design Tool*. Newtown, Conn.: Taunton, 1990.

Jaffe, Dale J. *Shared Housing for the Elderly*. New York: Greenwood, 1989.

Jakle, John A., Robert W. Bastian, and Douglas K. Meyer. *Common Houses in America's Small Towns: The Atlantic Seaboard to the Mississippi Valley*. Athens: University of Georgia Press, 1989.

Jankowski, Wanda. *Designing with Light: Residential Interiors*. New York: PBC, 1991.

———. *Kitchens and Baths*. New York: PBC, 1993.

Joint Center for Housing Studies of Harvard University. *The State of the Nation's Housing*. Cambridge: Author, 1994.

Jones, Robert, ed. *Authentic Small Houses of the Twenties*. New York: Dover, 1987.

Judd, Dennis, and Michael Parkinson, eds. *Leadership and Urban Regeneration*. Newbury Park, Calif.: Sage, 1990.

Jung, Carl Gustav. *Memories, Dreams and Reflections*. New York: Vintage, 1963.

Kahana, Eva, and Boaz Kahana. "Environmental Continuity, Futurity and Adaptation of the Aged." In *Aging and Milieu*, ed. Graham D. Rowles and Russell J. Ohta. New York: Academic Press, 1983, 205–28.

Kamin, Blair. "Public Housing in 1999: A Hard Assessment." *Architectural Record* 11 (1999), 77–83, 200–202.

Kane, Rosalie A., and Keren Brown Wilson. *Assisted Living in the United States: A New Paradigm for Residential Care for Frail Older Persons?* Washington, D.C.: American Association of Retired Persons, 1993.

Kaplan, Samuel. *The Dream Deferred: People, Politics and Planning in Suburbia*. New York: Random House, 1977.

Katz, Peter. *The New Urbanism: Toward an Architecture of Community*. New York: McGraw-Hill, 1994.

Keller, Susan. *The Urban Neighborhood: A Sociological Perspective*. New York: Random House, 1968.

Kemeny, Jim. *From Public Housing to Social Housing: Rental Policy Strategies in Comparative Perspective*. New York: Routledge, 1994.

Kent, Susan, ed. *Domestic Architecture and the Use of Space*. Cambridge: Cambridge University Press, 1990.

Kivisto, Peter. "An Historical Review of Changes in Public Housing Policies and Their Impacts on Minorities." In *Race, Ethnicity, and Minority Housing in the United States*, ed. Jamshid A. Momeni. Westport, Conn.: Greenwood Press, 1986.

Klutznick, Philip M. "Poverty and Politics: The Challenge of Public Housing." *Journal of Housing* 42: 1 (1985), 9–12.

Knight, P.A. *The Energy Resources Center Illustrated Guide to Home Retrofitting for Energy Savings*. Washington, D.C.: Hemisphere, 1981.

Koncelik, Joseph. *Designing the Open Nursing Home*. Stroudsburg, Pa.: Dowden, Hutchinson, and Ross, 1976.

Korosec-Serfaty, Perla, and Dominique Bolitt. "Dwelling and the Experience of Burglary." *Journal of Environmental Psychology* 6 (1986), 329–44.

Lam, W.M. *Perception and Lighting as Formgivers for Architecture*. New York: Van Nostrand Reinhold, 1992.

Landman, Ruth H. *Creating Community in the City: Cooperatives and Community Gardens in Washington D.C.* Westport, Conn.: Bergin and Garvey, 1993.

Langdon, W.K. *Movable Insulation: A Guide to Reducing Heating and Cooling Losses through the Windows in Your Home*. Emmaus, Pa.: Rodale, 1980.

Langer, Ellen J. *The Psychology of Control*. Beverly Hills, Calif.: Sage, 1983.

Lansing, John B., Robert W. Marans, and Robert B. Zehner. *Planned Residential Environments*. Ann Arbor: Institute for Social Research, University of Michigan, 1970.

Lavin, Marjorie W., and Frederic Agatstein. "Personal Identity and the Imagery of Place: Psychological Issues and Literary Themes." *Journal of Mental Imagery* 8 (1984), 51–66.

Lawrence, Roderick J. "What Makes a House a Home?" *Environment and Behavior* 19 (1987), 154–68.

Lawton, M. Powell. *Environment and Aging*. Monterey: Brooks Cole, 1980.

———. "Environment and the Need Satisfaction of the Aging." In *Handbook of Clinical Gerontology*, ed. Laura L. Carstensen and Barry A. Edelstein. New York: Pergamon Press, 1987, 33–40.

———. "Housing and Living Environments of Older People." In *Handbook of Aging and the Social Sciences*, 2nd ed., ed. Robert H. Binstock and Ethel Shanas. New York: Van Nostrand Reinhold, 1985, 450–78.

———. *Planning and Managing Housing for the Elderly*. New York: Wiley and Sons, 1980.

Lawton, M. Powell, Mark Fulcomer, and Morton Kleban. "Architecture for the Mentally Impaired Elderly." *Environment and Behavior* 16 (1984), 730–57.

Lawton, M. Powell, and Lucille Nahemow. "Ecology and the Aging Process." In *Psychology of Adult Development and Aging*, ed. Carl Eisdorfer and M. Powell Lawton. Washington, D.C.: American Psychology Association, 1973.

Lawton, M. Powell, Paul G. Windley, and Thomas O. Byerts, eds. *Aging and the Environment*. New York: Springer, 1982.

Lechner, H. *Heating, Cooling, Lighting: A Guide of Qualitative Design Methods for Architects*. New York: Wiley, 1991.

Lee, Terence R. "A Theory of Socio-Spatial Schemata." In *Humanscape: Environments for People*, ed. Stephen Kaplan and Rachael Kaplan. North Scituate, Mass.: Duxbury Press, 1978.

Leibrock, Cynthia. *Beautiful Barrier-Free: A Visual Guide to Accessibility*. New York: Van Nostrand Reinhold, 1993.

Leibrock, Cynthia, and James Evan Terry. *Beautiful Universal Design*. New York: John Wiley, 1999.

Lenchek, T., C. Mattock, and J. Raabe. *Superinsulated Design and Construction: A Guide for Building Energy-Efficient Homes*. New York: Van Nostrand Reinhold, 1987.

Levinson, Daniel J. "A Conception of Adult Development." *American Psychologist* 41 (1986), 3–13.

Levy, M.E. *The Passive Solar Construction Handbook*. Emmus, Pa.: Rodale, 1983.

Liben, Lynn, Arthur H. Patterson, and Nora Newcombe, eds. *Spatial Representation across the Life Span: Theory and Application*. New York: Academic, 1981.

Lifchez, Raymond. *Rethinking Architecture. Design Students and Physically Disabled People*. Berkeley: University of California Press, 1987.

Low, M. Setha, and Erve Chambers, eds. *Housing, Culture and Design*. Philadelphia: University of Pennsylvania Press, 1989.

Lubove, Roy. *The Progressives and the Slums: Tenement House Reform in New York City, 1890–1917*. Pittsburgh: University of Pittsburgh Press, 1962.

Lynch, Kevin, ed. *Growing Up in Cities: Studies of the Spatial Environment of Adolescents in Cracow, Melbourne, Mexico City, Salta, Toluca, and Warszawa*. Cambridge: MIT Press, 1977.

Mace, Ronald L. "Design for Special Needs." In *Housing: Symbol, Structure, Site*, ed. Lisa Taylor. New York: Rizzoli, 1990.

Mackintosh, Elizabeth. "High in the City." In *Knowledge for Design: Proceedings of the 13th Environmental Design Research Association Conference*, ed. Polly Bart, Alexander Chen, and Guido Francescato. Washington, D.C.: Environmental Design Research Association, 1982, 424–34.

Maddex, Diane, ed. *All about Old Buildings: The Whole Preservation Catalog*. Washington, D.C.: Preservation Press, 1985.

Mann, P. *Illustrated Residential and Commercial Construction*. Englewood Cliffs, N.J.: Prentice-Hall, 1989.

Marans, Robert W. "Perceived Quality of Residential Environments: Some Methodological Issues." In *Perceiving Environmental Quality: Research and Applications*, ed. Ervin Craik and Kenneth Zube. New York: Plenum, 1976, 123–47.

Marans, Robert W., and W. Rodgers. "Toward an Understanding of Community Satisfaction." In *Metropolitan America in Contemporary Perspective*, ed. Amos Hawley and Vincent Rock. New York: John Wiley and Sons, 1975, 299–352.

Marcuse, Peter. "United States of America." In *International Handbook of Housing Policies and Practices*, ed. Willem van Vliet. Westport, Conn.: Greenwood Press, 1990.

Marshall, Howard. "Vernacular Housing and American Culture." In *Popular American Housing*, ed. Ruth Brent and Benyamin Schwarz. Westport, Conn.: Greenwood Press, 1995.

Massey, Douglas S. "A Research Note on Residential Succession: The Hispanic Case." *Social Forces* 61:3 (1983), 825–33.

Mazumdar, Sanjuy "Vernacular Housing." In *The Encyclopedia of Housing*, ed. Willem van Vliet. Thousand Oaks, Calif.: Sage, 1998.

McAlester, Virginia, and Lee McAlester. *A Field Guide to American Houses*. New York: Alfred A. Knopf, 1984.

McAndrew, Francis T. *Environmental Psychology*. Pacific Grove, Calif.: Brooks/Cole, 1993.

Meehan, Eugene J. "Is There a Future for Public Housing?" *Journal of Housing* 40:3 (1983), 73–76.

Michelson, William. *Environmental Choice, Human Behavior, and Residential Satisfaction*. New York: Oxford University Press, 1977.

———. *From Sun to Sun: Daily Obligations and Community Structure in the Lives of Employed Women and Their Families*. Totowa, N.J.: Rowman and Allenheld, 1985.

———. *Man and His Urban Environment: A Sociological Analysis*. Reading, Mass.: Addison-Wesley, 1976.

Michelson, William, Saul V. Levine, and Ellen Michelson. *The Child in the City: Changes and Challenges*. Toronto, Canada: University of Toronto Press, 1979.

Miller, Judith Ann. *Community-Based Long-Term Care: Innovative Models*. Newbury Park, Calif.: Sage, 1991.

Mitchell, J. Paul, ed. *Federal Housing Policy and Programs: Past and Present*. New Brunswick: Rutgers, State University of New Jersey, Center for Urban Policy Research, 1985.

Mollenkopf, John. *The Contested City*. Princeton, N.J.: Princeton University Press, 1983.

Mollica, Robert, and Kimberly Irvin Snow. *State Assisted Living Policy*. Portland, Maine: Center for Vulnerable Populations: National Academy for State Health Policy, 1996.

Momeni, Jamshid A. *Housing and Racial/Ethnic Minority Status in the United States. An Annotated Bibliography with a Review Essay*. New York: Greenwood Press, 1987.

Moore, Charles, Gerald Allen, and Donlyn Lyndon. *The Place of Houses*. New York: Henry Holt, 1974.

Moore, F. *Environmental Control Systems: Heating, Cooling, Lighting*. New York: McGraw-Hill, 1993.

Moos, Rudolf H., and Sonne Lemke. "The Multiphasic Environmental Assessment Procedure." In *Community Mental Health*, ed. Abraham Jeger and Robert Slotnick. New York: Plenum, 1980.

———. "Supportive Residential Settings for Older People." In *Elderly People and the Environment*, ed. Irwin Altman, Joachim Wohwill, and M. Powell Lawton. New York: Plenum, 1984.

Morrissy, Eugene, and Paul Handal. "Characteristics of the Residential Environment Scale: Reliability and Differential Relationship to Neighborhood Satisfaction in Divergent Neighborhoods." *Journal of Community Psychology* 9: 2 (1981), 125–32.

Myers, Dowell, ed. *Housing Demography: Linking Demographic Structure and Housing Markets*. Madison: University of Wisconsin Press, 1990.

Nasar, Jack L. "Connotative Meanings of House Styles." In *The Meaning and Use of Housing*, ed. Ernesto G. Arias. Brookfield, Vt.: Ashgate, 1993, 143–67.

———. "The Impact of Visual Aspects of Residential Environments on Hedonic Responses, Interests, and Fear of Crime." Doctoral diss., Pennsylvania State University. *Dissertation Abstracts International* 40: 4 (1979), 1963B.

———. "Symbolic Meanings of House Style." *Environment and Behavior* 21 (1989), 235–57.

National Association of Homebuilders. *Seniors Housing: A Development and Management Handbook*. Washington, D.C.: NAHB, 1987.

Newcomer, Robert. "Best Practices in Residential Care for the Elderly: Draft Notes." Mimeo. University of California at San Francisco, Institute for Health and Aging, 1992.

Newcomer, Robert J., M. Powell Lawton, and Thomas O. Byerts, eds. *Housing an Aging Society*. New York: Van Nostrand Reinhold, 1986.

Newman, M. *Design and Construction of Wood-Framed Buildings*. New York: McGraw-Hill, 1994.

———. *Standard Handbook of Structural Details for Building Construction*. New York: McGraw-Hill, 1993.

Newman, Oscar. *Defensible Space: Crime Prevention through Urban Design*. New York: Macmillan, 1972.

Nisbet, Robert A. *Community and Power: A Study in the Ethics of Order and Freedom*. New York: Oxford University Press, 1962.

Nissen, Luann, Ray Faulkner, and Sarah Faulkner. *Inside Today's Home*. 6th ed. Fort Worth, Tex.: Harcourt, Brace College, 1994.

Norberg-Schultz, Christian. *Existence, Space and Architecture*. New York: Praeger, 1971.

Nuckolls, J.L. *Interior Lighting for Environmental Designers*. New York: Wiley, 1976.

Ojeda, O. Riera, ed. *The New American Apartment: Innovations in Residential Design and Construction*. New York: Watson-Guptill, 1997.

———. *The New American House: Innovations in Residential Design and Construction*. New York: Watson-Guptill, 1995.

———. *The New American House 2: Innovations in Residential Design and Construction*. New York: Watson-Guptill, 1997.

Olgyag, V. *Design with Climate: A Bioclimatic Approach to Architectural Regionalism*. New York: Van Nostrand Reinhold, 1992.

Parker, Harry. *Simplified Design of Structural Wood*. New York: John Wiley, 1988.

Parker, Harry, and J. Ambrose. *Simplified Engineering for Architects and Builders*. New York: Wiley, 1994.

Parmelee, Patricia A., and M. Powell Lawton. "The Design of Special Environments for the Aged." In *Handbook of the Psychology of Aging*, 3rd ed., ed. James Birren and K. Warner Schaie. San Diego: Academic Press, 1990, 464–88.

Pastalan, Leon A. *Aging in Place: The Role of Housing and Social Supports*. New York: Haworth Press, 1983.

———. "Architectural Research and Life-Span Changes." In *Architectural Research*, ed. James C. Snyder. New York: Van Nostrand Reinhold, 1984.

———. "Environmental Displacement." In *Aging and Milieu*, ed. Graham D. Rowles and Russell J. Ohta. New York: Academic Press, 1983, 189–203.

Pastalan, Leon A., and Daniel H. Carson, eds. *Spatial Behavior of Older People*. Ann Arbor: University of Michigan Press, 1970.

Peloquin, Albert A. *Barrier-Free Residential Design*. New York: McGraw-Hill, 1994.

Perlmuter, Lawrence C., Richard A. Monty, and Florentius Chan. "Choice, Control, and Cognitive Functioning." In *Aging and the Psychology of Control*, ed. Margeret M. Baltes and Paul B. Baltes. New York: Lawrence Erlbaum Associates, 1986.

Pickett, Mary S., Mildred G. Arnold, and Linda E. Ketterer. *Household Equipment in Residential Design*. New York: John Wiley and Sons, 1986.

Pile, John. *Interior Design*. Englewood Cliffs, N.J.: Prentice-Hall, 1995.

Professional Builder. "What 1986 Buyers Want in Housing." *Professional Builder* (1985), 50, 68–85.

Proshansky, Harold M., Abbe K. Fabian, and Robert Kaminoff. "Place-Identity: Physical World Socialization of the Self." *Journal of Environmental Psychology* 3 (1983), 57–83.

Pynoos, John. "Public Policy and Aging in Place: Identifying the Problems and Potential Solutions." In *Aging in Place: Supporting the Frail Elderly in Residential Environments*, ed. David Tilson. Glenview, Ill.: Scott, Foresman, 1990.

Pynoos, John, Robert Schafer, and Chester W. Hartman, eds. *Housing Urban America*. Chicago: Aldine, 1973.

R. S. Means Company. *Means Building Construction Cost Data*. Kingston, Mass.: Author, annual.

———. *Means Interior Cost Data*. Kingston, Mass.: Author, annual.

———. *Means Landscape Cost Data*. Kingston, Mass.: Author, annual.

———. *Means Mechanical Cost Data*. Kingston, Mass.: Author, annual.

———. *Means Site Work Cost Data*. Kingston, Mass.: Author, annual.

———. *Means Square Foot Cost Data*. Kingston, Mass.: Author, annual.

Rabushka, Alvin, and B. Jacobs. *Old Folks at Home*. New York: Free Press, 1980.

Radford, Gail. *Modern Housing for America: Policy Struggles in the New Deal Era*. Chicago: University of Chicago Press, 1997.

Radford, William A. *Old House Measured and Scaled*. New York: Dover, 1983.

Rainwater, Lee. *Behind Ghetto Walls: Black Family Life in a Federal Slum*. Chicago: Aldine, 1970.

Ramsey, Charles George. *Architectural Graphic Standards*. New York: John Wiley, 2000.

Rapoport, Amos. *History and Precedent in Environmental Design*. New York: Plenum, 1990.

———. *House Form and Culture*. Englewood Cliffs, N.J.: Prentice-Hall, 1969.

———. *The Meaning of the Built Environment: A Nonverbal Communication Approach*. Beverly Hills, Calif.: Sage, 1982.

Raschko, Bettyann Boettic. *Housing Interiors for the Disabled and Elderly*. New York: Van Nostrand Reinhold, 1982.

Regnier, Victor. *Assisted Living Housing for the Elderly: Design Innovations from the United States and Europe*. New York: Van Nostrand Reinhold, 1994.

———. *Behavioral and Environmental Aspects of Outdoor Space Use in Housing for the Elderly*. Los Angeles: School of Architecture, Andrus Gerontology Center, University of Southern California, 1985.

Regnier, Victor, Jennifer Hamilton, and Suzie Yatabe. *Best Practice in Assisted Living: Innovations in Design, Management and Financing*. Los Angeles: National Eldercare Institute on Housing and Supportive Services, 1991.

Regnier, Victor, and John Pynoos, eds. *Housing the Aged: Design Directives and Policy Considerations*. New York: Elsevier, 1987.

Reid, E. *Understanding Buildings*. Cambridge, Mass.: MIT Press, 1989.

Reznikoff, S.C. *Interior Graphic and Design Standards*. New York: Whitney Library of Design, 1986.

Riche, Martha Farnsworth. "Retirement's Lifestyle Pioneers." *American Demographics* 8:1 (1986), 42–44, 50, 52–54, 56.

Rifkind, Carole. *Field Guide to American Architecture*. New York: Dutton, 1998.

Riggs, J.R. *Materials and Components of Interior Design*. Englewood Cliffs, N.J.: Prentice-Hall, 1989.

Riis, Jacob A. *How the Other Half Lives*. 1849. New York: Viking Penguin, 1997.

Riley, Charles A. *High-Access Home: Design and Decoration for Barrier-Free Living*. New York: Rizzoli, 1999.

Rivlin, Leanne G. "The Neighborhood, Personal Identity, and Group Affiliations." In *Neighborhood and Community Environments*, ed. Irwin Altman and Abraham Wandersman. New York: Plenum Press, 1987.

Robinson, Julia. "Images of Housing, Minneapolis: A Limited Study of Urban Residents' Attitudes and Values." Master's thesis, University of Minnesota, Minneapolis, 1980.

Rodin, Judith. "Health, Control, and Aging." In *Handbook of Clinical Gerontology*, ed. Laura L. Carstensen and Barry Edelstein. New York: Pergamon Press, 1986.

Rogers, Kate Ellen. *The Modern House, U.S.A.: Its Design and Decoration*. New York: Harper and Brothers, 1962.

Rosenberry, Sara, ed. *Housing Issues of the 1990s*. Westport, Conn.: Greenwood Press, 1989.

Rotton, James. "Hemmed in and Hating It: Effects of Shape of Room on Tolerance for Crowding." *Perceptual and Motor Skills* 64 (1987), 285–86.

Rowe, Peter G. *Modernity and Housing*. Cambridge: MIT Press, 1993.

Rowles, Graham D. "Growing Old 'Inside': Aging and Attachment to Place in an Appalachian Community." In *Transition of Aging*, ed. Nancy Datan and Nancy Lohmann. New York: Academic Press, 1980.

———. "Toward a Geography of Growing Old." In *The Human Experiences of Space and Place*, ed. Anne Buttimer and David Seamon. New York: St. Martin's Press, 1980, 55–72.

Rowles, Graham D., and Russell J. Ohta, eds. *Aging and Milieu*. New York: Academic Press, 1983.

Ruback, R. Barry, and Christopher A. Innes. "The Relevance and Irrelevance of Psychological Research: The Example of Prison Crowding." *American Psychologist* 43 (1988), 683–93.

Ruback, R. Barry, and Janak Pandey. "Crowding, Perceived Control, and Relative Power: An Analysis of Households in India." *Journal of Applied Social Psychology* 21 (1991), 315–44.

Rubinstein, Robert L. "The Home Environments of Older People: A Description of the Psychological Process Linking Person to Place." *Journal of Gerontology* 34 (1989), 545–53.

Rubinstein, Robert L., and Patricia A. Parmelee. "Attachment to Place and the Representation of the Life Course by the Elderly." In *Place Attachment*, ed. Irwin Altman and Setha M. Low. New York: Plenum Press, 1992.

Rudofsky, Paul. *Architecture without Architects*. New York: Doubleday, 1964.

Rupp, W., and A. Friedman. *Construction Materials for Interior Design*. New York: Whitney Library of Design, 1989.

Russell, Barry. *Building Systems, Industrialization, and Architecture*. New York: John Wiley, 1981.

Rybczynski, Witold. *Home: A Short History of an Idea*. New York: Penguin Books, 1986.

Sadalla, Edward K., Beth Vershure, and Jeffrey Burroughs. "Identity Symbolism in Housing." *Environment and Behavior* 19 (1987), 569–87.

Saegert, Susan. "Masculine Cities and Feminine Suburbs: Polarized Ideas, Contradictory Realities." *Signs: Journal of Women in Culture and Society* 5 (1980), 96–111.

Saile, David G. "The Ritual Establishment of Home." In *Home Environments*, ed. Irwin Altman and Carol M. Werner. New York: Plenum, 1985.

Salins, Peter. *The Ecology of Housing Destruction*. New York: New York University Press, 1980.

Saltman, Juliet. *A Fragile Movement: The Struggle for Neighborhood Stabilization*. New York: Greenwood Press, 1990.

———. "Theoretical Orientation: Residential Segregation." In *Urban Housing Segregation of Minorities in Western Europe and the United States*, ed. Elizabeth D. Huttman. Durham, N.C.: Duke University Press, 1991.

Sampson, Robert J. "Local Friendship Ties and Community Attachment in Mass Society: A Multilevel Systematic Model." *American Sociological Review* 53 (1988), 766–79.

Sanoff, Henry. "Youth's Perception and Categorization of Residential Cues." In *Environmental Design Research*, vol. 1: *Proceedings of the 4th Environmental Design Research Association Conference*, ed. W.E.F. Preiser. Stroudsburg, Pa.: Dowden, Hutchison, and Ross, 1973.

Saunders, Peter. *A Nation of Home Owners*. London: Unwin Hyman, 1990.

Sayegh, Kamel S. *Housing: A Multidisciplinary Dictionary*. Ottawa, Ontario: ABCD-Academy, 1987.

Scheidt, Rick J., and Paul G. Windley. "The Ecology of Aging." In *Handbook of the Psychology of Aging*, 2nd ed., ed. James Birren and Warner Schaie. New York: Van Nostrand Reinhold, 1985.

———. *Environment and Aging Theory: A Focus on Housing*. Westport, Conn.: Greenwood Press, 1998.

Schepp, B., and S.M. Hastie. *The Complete Passive Solar Home Book*. Blue Ridge Summit, Pa.: Tab, 1985.

Schiler, M. *Simplified Design of Building Lighting*. New York: Wiley, 1992.

Schooler, Kermit K. "Response of the Elderly to Environment: A Stress-Theoretical Perspective." In *Aging and the Environment: Theoretical Approaches*, ed. M. Powell Lawton, Paul G. Windley, and Thomas O. Byerts. New York: Springer, 1982.

Schuman, Howard, Charlotte Steeh, and Lawrence Babo. *Racial Attitudes in America*. Cambridge: Harvard University Press, 1985.

Schwarz, Benyamin, and Ruth Brent, eds. *Aging, Autonomy and Architecture: Advances in Assisted Living*. Baltimore: Johns Hopkins University Press, 1999.

Scully, Vincent. *American Architecture and Urbanism*. New York: H. Holt, 1988.

Seale, William. *Recreating the Historic House Interior*. Nashville, Tenn.: American Association for State and Local History, 1979.

Seamon, David. *A Geography of the Lifeworld*. New York: St. Martin's Press, 1979.

———. "The Phenomenological Contribution to Environmental Psychology." *Journal of Environmental Psychology* 2 (1982), 119–40.

Sebba, Rachel. "The Landscapes of Childhood: The Reflection of Childhood's Environment in Adult Memories and in Children's Attitudes." *Environment and Behavior* 23 (1991), 395–442.

Sebba, Rachel, and Arza Churchman. "The Uniqueness of the Home." *Architecture and Behavior* 3 (1986), 7–24.

Seligman, Martin E. P. *Helplessness: On Depression, Development, and Death*. San Francisco: Freeman.

Sennett, Richard. *The Fall of Public Man*. New York: Vintage, 1978.

Sherwood, R., ed. *Wood Frame House Construction*. National Association of Home Builders Staff. New York: Delmar, 1991.

Shumaker, Sally A., and Ralph B. Taylor. "Toward a Classification of People–Place Relationships: A Model of Attachment to Place." In *Environmental Psychology*, ed. Nickolaus R. Feimer and E. Scott Geller. New York: Praeger, 1983.

Sixsmith, Judith. "The Meaning of Home: An Exploratory Study of Environmental Experience." *Journal of Environmental Psychology* 6 (1986), 281–98.

Sloane, Philip D., and Laura J. Mathew, eds. *Dementia Units in Long-Term Care*. Baltimore: Johns Hopkins University Press, 1991.

Smith, F.K. and F.J. Bertolone. *Bringing Interiors to Light: The Principles and Practices of Lighting Design for Interior Desginers*. New York: Whitney Library of Design, 1986.

Smith, Neil. *Uneven Development*. New York: Basil Blackwell, 1984.

Sommer, Robert. "The Behavioral Ecology of Supermarkets and Farmer's Markets." *Journal of Environmental Psychology* 1 (1981), 13–19.

———. *Design Awareness*. San Francisco: Reinhart, 1972.

———. *Personal Space: The Behavioral Basis of Design*. Englewood Cliffs, N.J.: Prentice-Hall, 1969.

Spivac, Mayer, and Joanna Tamer. *Institutional Setting: An Environmental Design Approach*. New York: Human Sciences Press, 1984.

Spriggs, William. "Measuring Residential Segregation: An Application of Trend Surface Analysis." *Phylon* 45 (1984), 249–63.

Squires, Gregory D. *From Redlining to Reinvestment*. Philadelphia: Temple University Press, 1992.

———, ed. *Unequal Partnerships*. New Brunswick, N.J.: Rutgers University Press, 1989.

Staines, Graham L., and J. H. Pleck. *The Impact of Work Schedules on the Family*. Ann Arbor: University of Michigan, Institute for Social Research, Survey Research Center, 1983.

Steffy, Gary R. *Architectural Lighting Design*. New York: Van Nostrand Reinhold, 1990.

Stegman, Michael. *Housing Finance and Public Policy: Cases and Supplemental Readings*. New York: Van Nostrand Reinhold, 1986.

———. *More Housing, More Fairly: Report of the Twentieth Century Fund Task Force on Affordable Housing*. New York: Twentieth Century Fund Press, 1991.

Stein, B., and W. McGuiness. *Mechanical and Electrical Equipment for Buildings*. New York: Wiley, 1992.

Stein, J. Stewart. *The Construction Glossary: An Encyclopedic Reference and Manual*. New York: John Wiley and Sons, 1993.

Sternlieb, George. *The Tenement Landlord*. New Brunswick: Rutgers, State University of New Jersey, Center for Urban Policy Research, 1965.

———. *The Urban Housing Dilemma*. New Brunswick: Rutgers, State University of New Jersey, Center for Urban Policy Research, 1969.

Stokols, Daniel. "On the Distinction between Density and Crowding: Some Implications for Future Research." *Psychological Review* 79 (1972), 275–77.

Stokols, Daniel, and Irwin Altman, ed. *Handbook of Environmental Psychology*. New York: John Wiley and Sons, 1987.

Stone, Clarence, and Heywood Sanders, eds. *The Politics of Urban Development*. Lawrence: University Press of Kansas, 1987.

Stone, Michael. *Shelter Poverty: New Ideas on Housing Affordability*. Philadelphia: Temple University Press, 1993.

Streib, Gordon Franklin, Edward Folts, and Mary Anne Hilker. *Old Homes—New Families: Shared Living for the Elderly*. New York: Columbia University Press, 1984.

Struyk, Raymond J. "Public Housing Modernization: An Analysis of Problems and Prospects." *Journal of Housing* 37 (1980), 492–96.

Struyk, Raymond J., and Beth Soldo. *Improving the Elderly's Housing*. Cambridge, Mass.: Ballinger, 1980.

Studer, Raymond G. "Design of the Built Environment: The Search for Usable Knowledge." In *Handbook of Housing and the Built Environment in the United States*, ed. Elizabeth Huttman and Willem Van Vliet. Westport, Conn.: Greenwood Press, 1988.

Sturgis, Russell. *A Dictionary of Architecture and Building: Biographical, Historical and Descriptive*. 3 vols. London: Macmillan, 1902.

Susanka, Sarah. *The Not So Big House*. Newtown, Conn.: Taunton, 1998.

Suttles, Gerald. *The Social Order of the Slum*. Chicago: University of Chicago Press, 1968.

Suzuki, S. *Passive and Low Energy Architecture*. Tokyo: Process Architecture, 1991.

Sweet's Group. *Contract Interiors*. 2 vols. New York: McGraw-Hill, annual.

———. *Industrial Construction and Renovation*. 3 vols. New York: McGraw-Hill, annual.

Taeuber, K.E. "Racial Segregation: The Persisting Dilemma." *Annals of the American Academy of Political and Social Science* 422 (November 1975), 87–96.

Taylor, Ralph B. *Human Territorial Functioning*. Cambridge: Cambridge University Press, 1988.

———. "Neighborhood Physical Environment and Stress." In *Environmental Stress*, ed. Gary W. Evans. New York: Cambridge University Press, 1982.

———. "Toward an Environmental Psychology of Disorder: Delinquency, Crime and Fear of Crime." In *Handbook of Environmental Psychology*, vol. 2, ed. Daniel Stokols and Irwin Altman. New York: John Wiley and Sons, 1987.

Taylor, Ralph B., and S. Brower. "Home and Near-Home Territories." In *Home Environments*, ed. Irwin Altman and Carol M. Werner. New York: Plenum, 1985.

Thallon, Rob. *Graphic Guide to Frame Construction*. Newtown, Conn.: Taunton Press, 2000.

———. *Graphic Guide to Interior Details*. Newtown, Conn.: Taunton Press, 1996.

Tilson, David. *Aging in Place: Supporting the Frail Elderly in Residential Environments*. Glenview, Ill.: Scott, Foresman, 1990.

Time-Life Books: Home Repair and Improvement Service. *Weatherproofing*. Alexandria, Va.: Time-Life, 1977.

Tobey, Henry N. "Connotative Messages of Single Family Homes: A Multidimensional Scaling Analysis." In *Knowledge for Design: Proceedings of the 13th Environmental Design Research Association*, ed. Polly Bart, Alexander Chen, and Guido Francescato. Washington, D.C.: Environmental Design Research Association, 1982.

Tobin, Sheldon S., and Morton A. Liberman. *Last Home for the Aged*. San Francisco: Jossey-Bass, 1976.

Tognoli, Jerome, and Jaimie Horwitz. "From Childhood Home to Adult Home: Environmental Transformations." In *Knowledge for Design: Proceedings of the 13th Environmental Design Research Association Conference*, ed. Polly Bart, Alexander Chen, and Guido Francescato. Washington, D.C.: Environmental Design Research Association, 1982.

Tuan, Yi-Fu. *Space and Place: The Perspective of Experience*. Minneapolis: University of Minnesota Press, 1977.

Turner, John F. C. *Housing by the People*. New York: Pantheon Books, Mansell Publishing, 1976.

Turner, John F. C., and Robert Fichter, eds. *Freedom to Build*. New York: Macmilllan, 1972.

Unger, Donald G., and Abraham Wandersman. "The Importance of Neighbors: The Social, Cognitive and Affective Components of Neighboring." *American Journal of Community Psychology* 13 (1985), 139–60.

Urban Land Institute. *Housing for Maturing Population*. Washington, D.C.: Urban Land Institute, 1983.

U.S. Department of Housing and Urban Development. *Energy-Saving Home Improvements: A Dollars and Sense Guide*. New York: Drake, 1977.

———. *Worst Case Needs for Housing Assistance in the United States*. Office of Policy Development and Research. Report to Congress, 1994.

U.S. Department of the Interior. *The Secretary of the Interior's Standards for the Treatment of Historic Properties: With Guidelines of Preserving, Rehabilitating, Restoring and Reconstructing Historic Buildings. Federal Register* 36 CFR 68; 36 CFR 67.

Valins, Martin. *Housing for the Elderly People: A Guide for Architects and Clients*. New York: Van Nostrand Reinhold, 1988.

Van Vliet, Willem. *Affordable Housing and Urban Redevelopment in the United States*. Thousand Oaks, Calif.: Sage, 1997.

———. *The Encyclopedia of Housing*. Thousand Oaks, Calif.: Sage, 1988.

Van Vliet, Willem, and Jack Burgers. "Communities in Transition: From the Industrial to the Postindustrial Era." In *Neighborhood and Community Environments*, ed. Irwin Altman and Abraham Wandersman. New York: Plenum Press, 1987.

Vance, Mary. *New Towns: Journal Articles, 1980–1988*. Monticello, Ill.: Vance Bibliographies, 1988.

Volkman, Nancy. "User Perceptions of Underground Houses and Implications for Site Planning." In *Design Research Interactions: Proceedings of the 12th Environmental Design Research Association Conference*, ed. Arvid E. Osterberg, Carole P. Tiernan, and Robert A. Findlay. Washington, D.C.: Environmental Design Research Association, 1981.

Walker, Lester. *American Shelter*. New York: Overlook, 1981.

Ward, Barbara. *The Home of Man*. New York: Norton, 1976.

Ward, Russell A., Mark LaGory, and Susan Sherman. *The Environment for Aging: Interpersonal, Social, and Spatial Contexts*. Tuscaloosa: University of Alabama Press, 1988.

Warren, Donald I. *Helping Networks*. Notre Dame, Ind.: University of Notre Dame Press, 1981.

Warren, Roland L. *The Community in America*. 3rd ed. Chicago: Rand McNally, 1978.

Weal, Francis, and Francesca Weal. *Housing for the Elderly: Options and Design*. New York: Nichols, 1988.

Wedin, Carol S., and L. Gertrude Nygren. *Housing Perspectives: Individuals and Families*. 1st ed. New York: Burgess, 1976.

———. *Housing Perspectives: Individuals and Families*. 2nd ed. New York: Burgess, 1978.

Weenig, Mieneke W. H., Taco Schmidt, and Cees J. H. Midden. "Social Dimensions of Neighborhoods and the Effectiveness of Information Programs." *Environment and Behavior* 22 (1990), 27–54.

Weidemann, Sue, James R. Anderson, Dorothy I. Butterfield, and Patricia M. O'Donnell. "Residents' Perceptions of Satisfaction and Safety: A Basis for Change in Multifamily Housing." *Environment and Behavior* 14 (1982), 695–724.

Weisman, Leslie Kanes. *Discrimination by Design. A Feminist Critique of the Man-Made Environment*. Urbana: University of Illinois Press, 1992.

Welch, Polly, V. Parker, and John Zeisel. *Independence through Interdependence*. Boston: Department of Elder Affairs, Commonwealth of Massachusetts, 1984.

Wener, Robert, and Franciesca Szigeti, eds. *Cumulative Index to the Proceedings of Environmental Design Research Association: Volumes 1–18, 1969–1987*. Washington, D.C.: EDRA, 1988.

Werner, Carol M. "Home Interiors: A Time and Place for Interpersonal Relationships." *Environment and Behavior* 9 (1987), 169–79.

Westin, Alan F. *Privacy and Freedom*. New York: Atheneum, 1967.

Wharton, Edith, and Odgen Codman Jr. *The Decoration of Houses*. New York: Charles Scribner's Sons, 1897.

———. *The Decoration of Houses*. Rev. and expanded Classical America Edition. New York: W. W. Norton, 1997.

Whiffen, Marcus. *American Architecture Since 1780: A Guide to the Styles*. 1968. Rev. ed. Cambridge: MIT Press, 1992.

White, Charles B., and Philip Janson. "Helplessness in Institutional Settings: Adaptation or Iatrogenic Disease?" In *Aging and the Psychology of Control*, ed. Margaret M. Baltes and Paul B. Baltes. New York: Lawrence Erlbaum Associates, 1986.

Wiggins, G.E. *A Manual of Construction Documentation*. New York: Whitney Library of Design, 1989.

Wilkes, Joseph A. *Encyclopedia of Architecture: Design, Engineering and Construction*. 5 vols. New York: John Wiley and Sons, 1988.

Willcocks, Dianne M., Sheila Peace, and Leonie Kellaher. *Private Lives in Public Places*. New York: Tavistock, 1987.

Wilson, James Q., ed. *Urban Renewal: The Record and the Controversy*. Cambridge: MIT Press, 1966.

Wilson, Keren B. "Developing a Viable Model of Assisted Living." In *Advances in Long-Term Care*, ed. Paul Katz, Robert L. Kane, and Mathy Mezey. New York: Springer, 1993.

Wireman, Peggy. *Urban Neighborhoods, Networks, and Families: New Forms for Old Values*. Lexington, Mass.: D. C. Heath, 1984.

Wood, Denis, and Robert Beck. *Home Rules*. Baltimore: Johns Hopkins University Press, 1994.

Woods, C. G. *A Natural System of House Design: An Architect's Way*. New York: McGraw-Hill, 1997.

Wright, Gwendolyn. *Building the Dream: A Social History of Housing in America*. Cambridge: MIT Press, 1981.

Yancey, William L. "Architecture, Interaction, and Social Control: The Case of a Large-Scale Public Housing Project." *Environment and Behavior* 3 (1971), 3–21.

Zeisel, John. *Inquiry by Design: Tools for Environment-Behavior Research*. Monterey, Calif.: Brooks/Cole, 1981.

Zeisel, John, Gayle Epp, and Stephen Demos. *Low-Rise Housing for Elderly People: Behavioral Criteria for Design*. Washington, D.C.: Government Printing Office, #HUD-483, September 1977.

Zeisel, John, and Mary Griffin. *Charlesview Housing: A Diagnostic Evaluation*. Cambridge: Harvard University, Architecture Research Office, 1975.

Zeisel, John, Polly Welch, Gayle Epp, and Stephen Demos. *Mid-Rise Elevator Housing for Older People*. Boston: Building Diagnostics, 1983.

Ziegler, Suzanne, and Howard F. Andrews. "Children and Built Environments: A Review of Methods for Environmental Research and Design." In *Methods in Environmental and Behavioral Research*, ed. Robert B. Bechtel, Robert W. Marans, and William Michelson. New York: Van Nostrand Reinhold, 1987.

Zimring, Craig, Janet R. Carpman, and William Michelson. "Design for Special Populations: Mentally Retarded Persons, Children, Hospital Visitors." In *Handbook of Environmental Psychology*, ed. Daniel Stokols and Irwin Altman. New York: John Wiley and Sons, 1987.

Zube, Ervin, and Gary T. Moore, eds. *Advances in Environment, Behavior, and Design*. New York: Plenum Press, 1989.

Zuravin, Susan J. "Residential Density and Urban Child Maltreatment: An Aggregate Analysis." *Journal of Family Violence* 1 (1986), 307–22.

Periodicals

Activities Adaptation and Aging
Adult Residential Care Journal
AIA Journal
American Anthropologist
American Behavioral Scientist
American Journal of Orthopsychiatry
American Journal of Psychiatry
American Journal of Psychotherapy
American Journal of Sociology
American Psychologist
American Sociological Review
Annals, Association of American Geographers
Annual Review of Psychology
Applied Ergonomics
Architectural Forum
Architectural Psychology
Architectural Record
The Architectural Review
Architecture and Comportment
Archives of Environmental Health

Association for Preservation Technology (APT) Bulletin
Behavior Analyst
Behavioral Analysis and Social Action
Behavioral Science
Builder
Building Design
Built Environment
Children's Environments Quarterly
Clinical Social Work Journal
Criminal Behavior and Mental Health
Custom Builder
Design Research News
Ekistics: The Problems and Science of Human Settlements
Environment and Behavior
Environmental Design Research Association (EDRA) (Proceedings)
Environmental Psychology
Ergonomics
Generations
Geographical Review
The Gerontologist
Good Housekeeping
Hastings Center Studies
House and Garden
House Beautiful
Housing and Society
Housing Policy Debate
Housing Studies
Human Behavior and Environment Advances in Theory and Research
Human Relations
International Journal of Aging and Human Development
International Journal of Comparative Sociology
International Journal of Technology and Aging
International Social Science Journal
Journal of Abnormal Psychology
Journal of Aging and Health
Journal of Applied Behavioral Science
Journal of Applied Gerontology
Journal of Applied Social Psychology
Journal of Architectural and Planning Research
Journal of Architectural Education
Journal of Community Psychology
Journal of Consulting and Clinical Psychology
Journal of Contemporary Ethnography
Journal of Educational Research
Journal of Environmental Education
Journal of Environmental Psychology
Journal of Experimental Research in Personality
Journal of Gerontological Social Work

Journal of Health and Social Behavior
Journal of Housing
Journal of Housing for the Elderly
Journal of Human Ecology
Journal of Interior Design Education and Research
Journal of Leisure Research
Journal of Psychology
Journal of Psychomatic Research
Journal of Social Issues
Journal of Sociology and Social Welfare
Journal of the American Institute of Planners
Journal of the American Medical Association
Journal of the American Planning Association
Journal of the Society of Architectural Historians
Journal of Urban Affairs
Journal of Urban Economics
Journal of Urban History
Journal of Vocational Behavior
Journals of Gerontology
Lifestyles
Man Environment Systems
Old House Journal
Perceptual and Motor Skills
Physiology and Behavior
Progressive Architecture
Psychology Today
Psychosocial Rehabilitation Journal
Qualified Remodeller
Social Forces
Social Indicators Research
Social Problems
Social Science International
Social Work
Sociological Focus
Sociological Forum
Urban Affairs Quarterly
Urban and Social Change Review
Urban Anthropology
Urban Studies
Woman's Home Companion (Ladies' Home Companion)
Women and Environments

Birthplace of John Adams, Quincy, Massachusetts. Courtesy of the Library of Congress

An Italian ragpicker's home, ca. 1907. Courtesy of the Library of Congress

The Chinese colony in New York, Mott Street, 1896. Courtesy of the Library of Congress

Modern Chinatown, in New York, Mott Street, 1996. Courtesy of the Library of Congress

Victorian-style mansion in Los Angeles. © Painet

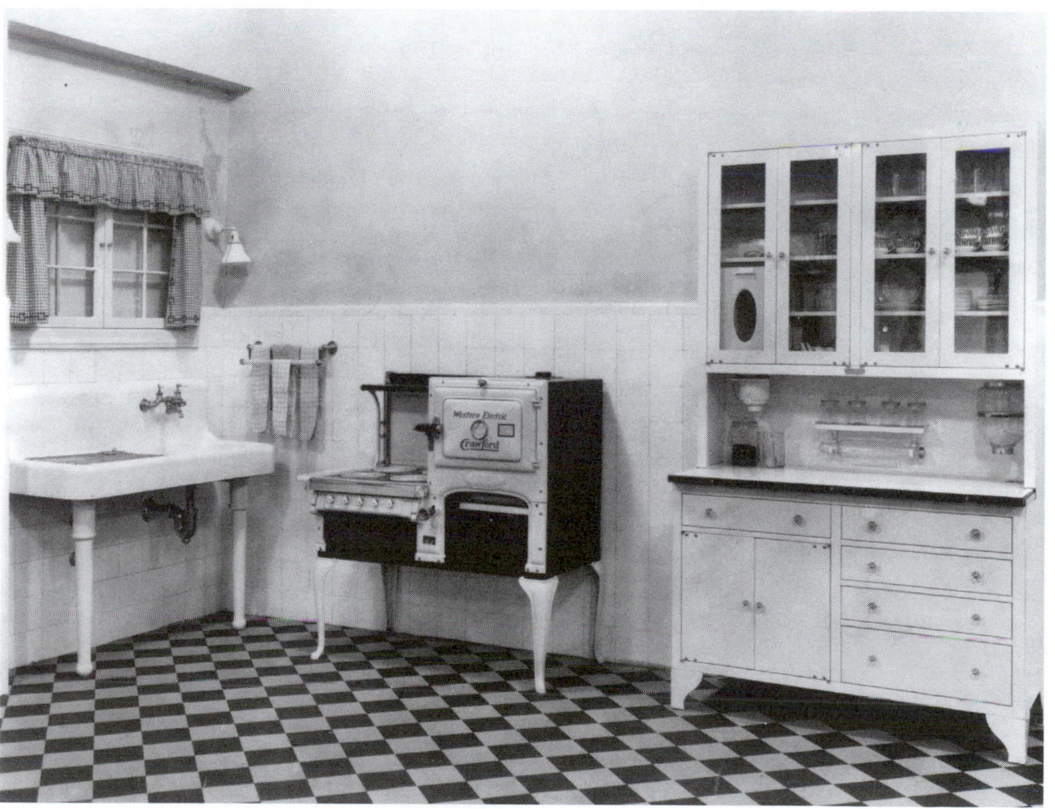

1950s kitchen, Philadelphia. Courtesy of the Library of Congress

Low income housing in Seattle. © Painet

Crowded neighborhood in West Virginia. © Painet

Trailer park. © Painet

Pueblo house in New Mexico. © Painet

Poster from the Work Projects Administration. Courtesy of the Library of Congress

ILLUSTRATION

James J. Best

Popular illustration refers to artwork intentionally designed for mass market consumption by means of reproduction on paper, that is, magazine and book illustrations and posters. The illustrations may be created using a wide variety of media, but the reproduction is done on paper. The job of the illustrator is to create images that can be used in whole or in part to tell stories and re-create events in ways that are intelligible to a mass audience. Unlike the easel artist, who has few constraints on how, what, when, why, or for whom he or she paints, the illustrator is constrained by his or her subject matter, the way that the illustration will be reproduced, where it will be reproduced, the audience for the illustration, the art editor overseeing the creative process, publication deadlines, and illustration pay rates.

To the extent that illustrators are successful in their task, the vehicles for their illustrations—illustrated books, magazines, and posters—become art galleries for the mass public. In the days before television, before radio, even before photography, illustrations had an enormous impact on American society and culture. During the golden age of American illustration (1890–1920) U.S. illustrators were far better known to the American public than their contemporaries in the fine arts; more people saw Howard Pyle's illustrations on the pages of *Harper's Monthly* than saw the 1913 Armory Show in New York City. Charles Dana Gibson's "Gibson Girls" set the standard for beauty and hairstyling at the turn of the century.

Popular illustration requires a literate public, the technology for the inexpensive reproduction of artwork, and the means for inexpensive distribution to the public. Because of these constraints, the content, techniques, and vehicles for popular illustration have varied through time; as popular tastes have changed, so have the popularity of various illustrators and sources of illustration. The historical outline that follows charts many of these changes.

Unfortunately, popular illustration has not been the subject of extensive or intensive scholarly research. The recent resurgence of interest in illustration—signaled by an increasing number of museum exhibits, new books dealing with an increasingly wider array of illustrators, and the republication of a number of illustrated "classics"—may give legitimacy and interest to the study of popular illustration, past and present. To the extent that popular illustration is artwork for a mass public, it is important that we understand its content and style as well as its most successful practitioners. The sections that follow contain discussions of the major written works, scholarly research reports, and various research sites for the study of popular illustration.

Several topics are not covered in this review. There is little or no discussion of etchings from the last century, of movie and other genre posters, or of computer graphics from this century.

HISTORICAL OUTLINE

The history of popular illustration in the United States dates from the eighteenth century (one of the first was an etching by Paul Revere), but illustrations were not widely used until the Civil War, when technological developments, growing print and picture literacy, and popular demand resulted in an enormous growth in their use. As with many American cultural phenomena, the roots of American popular illustration can be traced to England, where illustrations by leading English illustrators of the mid-1800s were "copied" (frequently without attribution) by American engravers. Alexander Anderson was the first American to achieve stature as a "native" American illustrator, but F.O.C. Darley was the first illustrator of importance whose work was widely recognized and rewarded—to the extent that he received credit for his artwork on the title pages and covers of the books that he illustrated. During the period 1840–1860 Darley dominated the field of American illustration, illustrating works by Washington Irving, Francis Parkman, and James Fenimore Cooper, as well as a number of volumes of *The Library of Humorous American Works* (1846–1869). His illustrations were distinctly "American" in style, unpretentious, frontier-oriented, and humorous in an earthy way; they appealed to readers who recognized themselves in the pictures that Darley created, pictures that were both familiar and "real."

The Civil War and an increasingly literate public created a demand for comprehensive coverage of Civil War battle action, in both words and pictures. *Harper's Weekly* and *Leslie's Illustrated Weekly* dispatched reporters and artists to cover major battles, and readers saw pictures of battles within weeks of their occurrence. Battlefield illustrators did rough sketches that were dispatched to New York, where engravers, frequently using their imagination to fill in voids in the artwork, translated the rough sketches into front-page visual images of recently completed battles. So successful was *Harper's Weekly* that its press run at the peak of the Civil War reached 250,000 copies, and its Civil War issues represent a vivid pictorial history of the period. The best of the war illustrations can be found in commemorative volumes published by the two weeklies *Harper's Illustrated History of the Civil War* (1895) and *Frank Leslie's Illustrated History of the Civil War* (1895), which feature illustrations by the best battlefront illustrators of the period.

The artistic and financial success of *Harper's Weekly* during the Civil War led the House of Harper to expand its use of illustrations in its monthly magazine, *Harper's Monthly*, its children's magazine, *Harper's Young People*, and its books.

Sketch made during the Civil War, Battle of Cedar Creek. Courtesy of the Library of Congress

Under the direction of art editor Charles Parsons, Harper's recruited a staff of full-time professional illustrators—most notably, Edwin Abbey, A. B. Frost, Alfred Kimble, and Howard Pyle—who became leading figures in the golden age of American illustration. As Harper's magazine circulation increased, two other monthlies, *Century* and *Scribner's*, entered the field of high-quality illustrated magazines. These three magazines represented the "elite" of American magazine illustration during the golden age, and an illustrator whose work was published in any of these three was a "recognized" illustrator.

Although magazine illustration provided the most fruitful field for illustrators, demanding and consuming thousand of illustrations every year, book illustration was more prestigious. Book illustration paid more, meant more work on a particular topic, and allowed greater artistic freedom as to which scenes to illustrate. Not all of the leading magazine illustrators were also successful book illustrators; only a handful achieved recognition in both fields. Most notable among this select group were Howard Pyle, N. C. Wyeth, Howard Chandler Christy, Harrison Fisher, Charles Dana Gibson, Jessie Wilcox Smith, and Maxfield Parrish.

Preeminent among this group of illustrators was Howard Pyle. Pyle received recognition for his early book illustrations for *Robin Hood* (1883), *Pepper and Salt* (1886), *The Wonder Clock* (1888), and *Otto of the Silver Hand* (1888), as well as his many black-and-white illustrations for *Harper's Monthly*. More important, Pyle established the first school devoted to the training of professional illustrators, and his success as a teacher was reflected in the work of his students. N. C. Wyeth, Frank Schoonover, Elizabeth Shippen Green, Jessie Wilcox Smith, and Thornton Oakley were among his students at Chadds Ford, Pennsylvania, and in his Wilmington, Delaware, studio, and their artwork appeared in all the major illustrated magazines and books of the day. Pyle's emphasis on capturing the essence of the action in a story, on involving the reader in the illustration, and on historical accuracy resulted in illustrations that were stylistically different from those of their contemporaries. One has only to contrast the women portrayed by Elizabeth Shippen Green and Jessie Wilcox Smith with the Gibson and Christy "American Beauty" girls to see the differences.

While Pyle was preaching romantic realism to his students, a tradition of western or "cowboy" illustration was developing, led by Frederic Remington and

Charles Russell and continued by Will James and Harold Von Schmidt. For many of these "cowboy" illustrators, a trip to the West was a necessary part of their training—Remington took two trips prior to 1900, N. C. Wyeth spent time in the still-Wild West of 1904, and Frank Schoonover spent almost two years in the back country of Canada. Of the initial "cowboy" illustrators, only Russell was truly a cowboy. For the rest, the trips that they made West provided them with enough material for a continuing series of western illustrations.

The golden age of American illustration was far more reflective of American society than it was of European illustration. Pyle and his students, with their emphasis on romantic realism, and Howard Chandler Christy, Charles Dana Gibson, Harrison Fisher, and James Montgomery Flagg, with their idealization of the American woman, were quite different in content and style from the leading English and continental illustrators of the period, who were illustrating fantasy worlds of fairies and elves (Arthur Rackham, Edmund Dulac, and W. Heath Robinson) or introducing art nouveau to the world (Aubrey Beardsley, Alphonse Mucha, and Kay Nielsen). Rackham's illustrations for *Alice's Adventures in Wonderland* (1909) and *Peter Pan in Kensington Garden* (1906); Dulac's illustrations for *Tanglewood Tales* (1918) and *Stories from the Arabian Nights* (1907); W. Heath Robinson's pen-and-ink illustrations of *Shakespeare's Comedy of a Midsummer Night's Dream* (1914); Beardsley's drawings in line for *The Rape of the Lock* (1896); and Kay Nielsen's color work for *East of the Sun and West of the Moon* (1922) are decidedly different from those of their American contemporaries in both content and style. The most popular American illustrators at the turn of the century were the romantic realists, led by Pyle and his students, primarily concerned with accurately depicting the historical past, which their readers had never seen, or idealizing the present, to which their readers could aspire. Even the fantasy illustrations of W. W. Denslow in the most popular children's book of the period, *The Wonderful Wizard of Oz* (1900), placed a very real girl from Kansas (and her dog) in the company of a scarecrow, a lion, and a tin woodsman. Dorothy is certainly different from the girls found in Kate Greenaway's *Under the Willows* (1879) and *The Pied Piper of Hamlin* (1888), the most popular English children's books of the time.

In one area of popular illustration—poster art—American illustrators were influenced by the styles and techniques of their European counterparts. The modern poster dates from France in the 1870s and 1880s, when Cheret and Toulouse-Lautrec created a new form of popular illustration. British poster art developed differently from the French. French posters were gay and colorful, full of life and color and activity, while British poster artists, more heavily influenced by Japanese block prints, made extensive use of large masses of solid color. As a result, the posters of Cheret are quite different from those of his British contemporaries John Hassall, Dudley Hardey, and the Beggarstaffs. The most prominent American poster artists of the period were Will Bradley, Edward Penfield, and Maxfield Parrish. In the posters of Will Bradley for the *Inland Printer* and Penfield's for *Harper's Magazine* one can see the impact of European poster art.

World War I had a major impact on American illustration. While a number of illustrators reached their nadir doing war posters, World War I marked the end of the golden age of American illustration, signaling a change in the demand for, and use of, illustrations. Never again were posters as popular as an advertising medium. The nature of magazine illustration changed as well. Whereas the first decade of the twentieth century saw *Century*, *Harper's*, and *Scribner's* as the leading illustrated magazines, by the 1930s these three had been replaced by the *Saturday Evening Post, Collier's, Cosmopolitan, Woman's Home Companion, Redbook, Ladies' Home Journal*, and *American* magazines, general mass market or women's magazines that published the greatest number of illustrations. Equally important, the number of illustrated magazines and the demand for illustration artwork, always costly to reproduce well, declined during the depression. Color artwork appeared only as covers, so doing covers for the remaining magazines was a mark of distinction and success for an illustrator. Norman Rockwell's success as an illustrator can be measured by the number of covers that he did for the *Saturday Evening Post* during the 1930s. Surprisingly few illustrators whose magazine artwork was popular before World War I continued that success into the 1930s; two exceptions were Norman Rockwell, whose artwork displayed an amazing ability to change content and style to keep pace with a changing society, and J. C. Leyendecker, who was to men's fashions in the 1930s what Charles Dana Gibson was to women's fashions decades earlier. Between them Leyendecker and Rockwell each completed more than 300 *Saturday Evening Post* covers.

With the decline in the number and quality of illustrated magazines, many illustrators shifted their energies to new markets. In the twenty years following World War I specialized magazines printed on cheap paper—the "pulps"—proliferated, creating an increasing demand for illustrators who could work quickly and cheaply and whose covers would attract newsstand readers. Although this market was not as prestigious as doing covers for the *Post*, covers for pulp magazines provided a livelihood for many illustrators. But most of these illustrators labored in anonymity. For an excellent review of these artists, see Steven Heller and Seymour Chwast's *Jackets Required: An Illustrated History of American Book Jacket Design, 1920–1960* and Wendell Minor's *Art for the Written Word: Twenty-Five Years of Book Cover Art*.

The nature of book illustration changed as well. The economies of publishing during the depression dictated that book illustration be done in black and white rather than in the more expensive color processes and on the same paper stock as the text. As a result, line drawings and black-and-white illustrations returned, and full-page color plates printed on slick paper virtually disappeared. The *Oz* books, published almost yearly from 1900 into the 1940s, clearly show this transformation. Some illustrators handled the demands of this genre well, notably Rockwell Kent and Lynd Ward. Kent's *Salamina* (1934) and *N by E* (1930) as well as Ward's *Mad Man's Drum* (1930) and *Song without Words* (1936) are striking for their effective use of black-and-white figures against stark, contrasting backgrounds.

With the changing market for illustrations, many illustrators moved into other areas of illustration, namely, advertising art and children's book illustration, particularly "picture" books for younger readers. A number of illustrators who had achieved success prior to World War I found themselves doing at least some advertising art after the war. Frank Schoonover adapted some of his western illustrations for Colt Firearms, Maxfield Parrish did advertisements for Jello, N. C. Wyeth did calendar art for Mazda-Edison light bulbs, Coles Phillips used his "fadeaway" illustrations to sell silverware and lingerie, and J. C. Leyendecker did Arrow shirt advertisements.

Children's books became an even larger market for illustration than ever before,

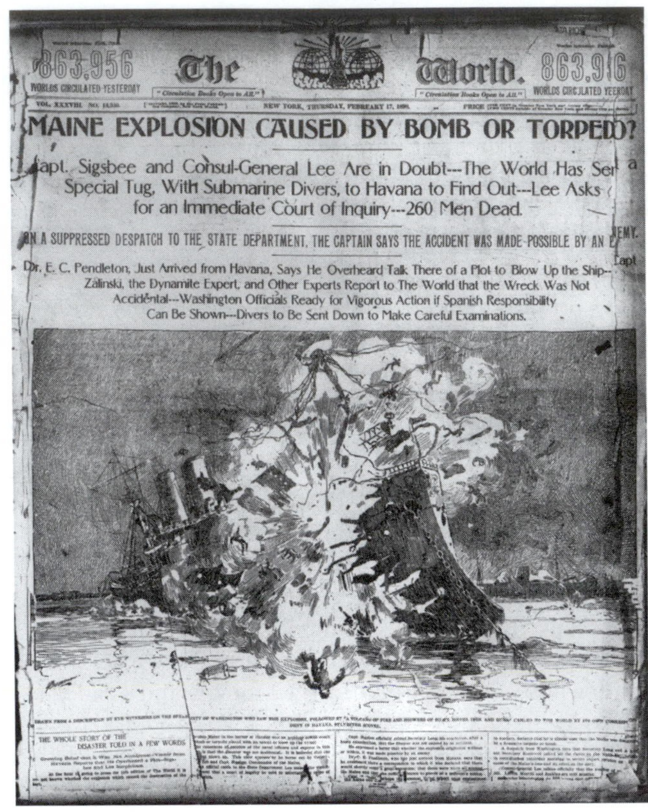

863,956 The World. 863,9[illegible]6
WORLDS CIRCULATED YESTERDAY
"Circulation Books Open to All."
NEW YORK, THURSDAY, FEBRUARY 17, 189[illegible]

MAINE EXPLOSION CAUSED BY BOMB OR TORPEDO?

Capt. Sigsbee and Consul-General Lee Are in Doubt---The World Has Sent a Special Tug, With Submarine Divers, to Havana to Find Out---Lee Asks for an Immediate Court of Inquiry---260 Men Dead.

IN A SUPPRESSED DESPATCH TO THE STATE DEPARTMENT, THE CAPTAIN SAYS THE ACCIDENT WAS MADE POSSIBLE BY AN ENEMY.

Dr. E. C. Pendleton, Just Arrived from Havana, Says He Overheard Talk There of a Plot to Blow Up the Ship--Zalinski, the Dynamite Expert, and Other Experts Report to The World that the Wreck Was Not Accidental---Washington Officials Ready for Vigorous Action if Spanish Responsibility Can Be Shown---Divers to Be Sent Down to Make Careful Examinations.

THE WHOLE STORY OF THE DISASTER TOLD IN A FEW WORDS

Newspaper illustration of the explosion of the *Maine*. Courtesy of the Library of Congress

and a new generation of illustrators emerged as a pack, with no one figure or "school" dominating as Howard Pyle and his students had a generation earlier. The older illustrators were replaced in the 1920s and 1930s by Johnny Gruelle and his Raggedy Ann and Andy books, Jean de Brunhoff's Babar the Elephant series, Ernest Sheppard and his illustrations for the Winnie-the-Pooh series, and books illustrated by the Disney studio based on Disney cartoon characters and movies, as well as books illustrated by Ludwig Bemelmans, Wanda Gag, Willy Pogany, Helen Sewell, and Morris Artzybasheff.

During World War II, poster art briefly reemerged as a major form of popular illustration, although it never achieved the importance and status—or the artistic impact—of World War I poster art. During World War II, the U.S. government had other, more efficient media for communicating with, and mobilizing, the citizenry, namely, movies and radio. As a consequence, the war posters that were produced were comparatively few in number, and the quality of poster art was not particularly high.

The last half century has seen fundamental changes in the content and form of popular illustration. Children's illustrated books have retained their importance as sources of illustration art, and many of the most creative illustrations are to be found there, illustrations of increasing beauty, sophistication, and subtlety. Certainly, the fantasy illustrations of James Christenson and Chris Van Allsburg are superb examples of the genre. While book illustration has not experienced a renaissance (somewhat surprising considering the popularity of "art" and "coffee-table" books), the market for magazine illustrations has remained strong, but the nature of that demand has changed. Long gone are the national mass market magazines; *TV Guide* is one of the few national magazines that occasionally use artwork for their covers. The demand for magazine illustrations comes from the quality "specialty" magazines—*Sports Illustrated*, for example, uses artwork on a weekly basis. Poster art is still a popular medium, but, like that for magazine artwork, the demand is to fill certain niches: rock music, science fiction, and political protest. New markets for illustration artwork have also developed; the demand for paperback book covers, record album (vinyl, cassette, and CD) covers, and advertising art has developed or expanded to create demand for more illustration. The development and application of new illustration techniques—computer graphics, claymation, animation, airbrush, and computer-enhanced photographic illustration—have served to blur the distinction between what is illustration and what is not. Can the cartoon sitcoms on television and the movie *Toy Story* be classified as illustrations?

With the increased diversification of outlets for popular illustration and illustration techniques, it is no longer possible for one illustrator (Howard Pyle or Norman Rockwell) or a school of illustrators to dominate the field of illustration, as was true before World War I, or even to be recognized outside their field. It would take a true *cognoscente* of American illustration to recognize all of the Society of Illustrators' major award winners. Contemporary illustrators now use a variety of styles, techniques, and publication outlets to convey their messages. As our society has become more artistically and technologically sophisticated and more visually oriented, the nature of American popular illustration has evolved.

REFERENCE WORKS

To date, there is no single comprehensive bibliographical source that lists the major illustrators and all their published works. Compiling such a list would be a valuable, but monumental, task; my research on magazine illustrators in *Century*, *Harper's*, and *Scribner's* found that 252 illustrators contributed almost 5,000 illustrations to those three periodicals alone during the five-year period 1906–1910. The increase in outlets for illustrations would make the task even more daunting. Nonetheless, two basic types of bibliographies do exist: reasonably complete bibliographies of books illustrated by a selected set of illustrators (children's book illustrators, etc.) and complete bibliographies of illustrations for a single illustrator.

In the first group are the major bibliographies of selected illustrators. Theodore Bolton's *American Book Illustration* is a bibliographical checklist of 123 American illustrators and the books that they illustrated; it lists each illustrator alphabetically along with the major illustrated books, including the number and type of illustrations as well as where the illustrations had been previously published. The work is time-bound, however, with its coverage ending in the mid-1930s, and even its coverage of this period is incomplete. Bertha E. Mahoney, Louise Latimer, and Beulah Folmsbee's *Illustrators of Children's Books, 1744–1945* and the 1958 and

1968 supplements constitute one of the best bibliographic sources on children's illustrated books. These works contain brief bibliographies of more than 500 illustrators as well as bibliographies organized by author and illustrator. In addition, several excellent bibliographic essays analyze trends in children's book illustration. As with the Bolton book, however, there is no coverage of magazine illustrations, particularly important since a number of illustrators at the turn of the century published much of their artwork in children's magazines. This defect is remedied, in part, by John M. Shaw's *The Poems, Poets and Illustrators of St. Nicholas Magazine, 1873–1943*, which lists the illustrators and their contributions to this important children's magazine. Some books have taken a less illustrator-specific approach to children's book illustration, focusing instead on analyzing the styles and content rather than the illustrators per se. Two of the best of these books are Barbara Bader's *American Picture Books from Noah's Ark to the Beast Within* and Trinkett Clark and H. Nichols Clark's *Myth, Magic, and Mystery: 100 Years of American Children's Book Illustration*. Both authors analyze how different types of children's books have been illustrated by different illustrators, with the purpose of making generalizations about various aspects of the genre of children's book illustration. Bader's book is somewhat more scholarly, but the Clarks' book contains more current illustrators. Jeff Dykes' *Fifty Great Western Illustrators* is a welcome bibliography of yet another illustration genre, covering the major western illustrators of the past 100 years. There are some interesting inclusions. N. C. Wyeth, whose western illustrations encompass a comparatively small proportion of his total artistic output, is included. Dykes' bibliography is unusually comprehensive for these fifty illustrators; it lists not only books illustrated but also exhibits in which the artwork appeared and articles written by and about the illustrator, but, like most other bibliographies, there is very little attention given to magazine illustrations. Harold McCracken's *Frederic Remington: Artist of the Old West* remedies this defect by listing Remington's many magazine illustrations, as does Yost's excellent bibliography of Charles M. Russell.

There are a number of more or less complete bibliographies for selected individual illustrators. One of the most useful (because of Darley's influential role in the early development of American illustration) is Theodore Bolton's *The Book Illustrations of Felix Octavius Carr Darley*, which lists all his major illustrated books and includes an excellent bibliographic essay detailing his development as an illustrator as well as tracing his role in American illustration. An excellent addition to Bolton's work is Christine Anne Hahler's exhibition catalog . . . *Illustrated by Darley*, which provides a more extended bibliographic essay and 152 examples of his illustrations. A third work on Darley, by Ethel King, *Darley, the Most Popular Illustrator of His Time*, is poorly written, rambling, frequently incorrect, and often irrelevant.

The work of Howard Pyle and some of his students is well documented. The basic bibliographic reference work for Pyle's published material is Willard S. Morse and Gertrude Brinckle's *Howard Pyle: A Record of His Illustrations and Writings*, one of the most comprehensive bibliographies on any one illustrator ever compiled. It lists almost all magazines and books that published Pyle's written and illustration art, describing them in terms of the title of the illustrations, size, and color. Together with Henry C. Pitz's *Howard Pyle*, Charles D. Abbot's *Howard Pyle: A Chronicle*, and the Delaware Art Museum catalog *Howard Pyle: Diversity in*

Depth, edited by Rowland Elzea, there is now an impressive listing analysis of his life and works. The Pitz volume is probably the best general-purpose reference book on Pyle, including an incomplete list of his students and an incomplete bibliography of his book and magazine illustrations.

A number of excellent books have dealt individually with Pyle's students. John P. Apgar's *Frank Schoonover, Painter-Illustrator: A Bibliography* lists the number and type of illustrations for each book illustrated by Schoonover but does not include his many magazine illustrations, while Cortland Schoonover's *Frank Schoonover, Illustrator of the North American Frontier* provides an excellent cross-section display of his artwork, as well as a biography and numerous statements of his illustration philosophy.

The Allens' book *N. C. Wyeth* contains the best-organized bibliography of an American illustrator and is a model of what can be done. In addition to listing the books that he illustrated by title and type of illustration—with cross-references when illustrations were later published as part of another publication—the book lists magazine illustrations, advertising art, murals, calendar art, and even the one plate for which Wyeth did the illustration artwork. Betsy James Wyeth's sensitive editing of her father-in-law's letters in *The Wyeths* gives a uniquely personal perspective on Wyeth's forty-year career as an illustrator, particularly his relationship with his mentor, Howard Pyle, and the continual struggle between Wyeth's desire to do "fine art" and the continued demand for his illustration artwork. Wyeth's relationship with Pyle and members of his own family, his parents and his children, is explored by David Michaelis in *N. C. Wyeth: A Biography*. Based on thousands of letters written between Wyeth and family members, the Michaelis biography is a major attempt to understand what factors influenced Wyeth's personal and artistic development and the role that he played in the development of his children. The picture that emerges from this biography is like pictures that N. C. Wyeth painted—the hero is larger than life, capable of herculean effort. That was Wyeth and the N. C. Wyeth most frequently written about. Michaelis' book shows a more complex, brooding, darker picture—of the hero as human being. This is not a book about Wyeth the artist (although there is a list of his books) so much as it is about N. C. Wyeth the person, the family that he came from, and the family that he produced. For another perspective on Wyeth, see Betsy James Wyeth's essay on N. C. Wyeth in *Wondrous Strange: The Wyeth Tradition*, an essay that she titles "In a Dream I Met N. C. Wyeth."

Coy Ludwig's *Maxfield Parrish* contains a brief biography and a comprehensive bibliography of Parrish's published artwork, including his very substantial calendar and advertising output, while Paul Skeeters' *Maxfield Parrish: The Early Years* reproduces in folio size many of Parrish's book illustrations as they appeared in many of his early books.

Pyle's women students have received comparatively little attention from writers, with most of the writing dealing with the most successful of his students, Elizabeth Shippen Green and Jessie Wilcox Smith. Three of Pyle's women students formed their own studio, Cogslea, on the Philadelphia Main Line, and Catherine Connell Stryker's exhibition catalog, *The Studios at Cogslea*, contains a reasonably complete bibliography of the book illustrations of Jessie Wilcox Smith, Elizabeth Shippen Green, and Violet Oakley. S. Michael Schnessel's *Jessie Wilcox Smith* contains the most comprehensive bibliography of her work and describes in passing the work of many of Pyle's other students.

A number of other illustrators, particularly the "American Beauty" illustrators, have had books devoted to their lives and work. Among the best are Fairfax Downey's *Portrait of an Era as Drawn by C. D. Gibson*; Michael Schau's two books *All American Girl: The Art of Coles Phillips* and *J. C. Leyendecker*; Susan Meyer's *James Montgomery Flagg*; Henry Reed's *The A. B. Frost Book*; Carl J. Weinhardt's *The Most of John Held, Jr.*; Walt Reed's *Harold Von Schmidt*; and the two books devoted to Frederic Remington and Charles M. Russell, mentioned earlier. Norman Rockwell's prolific career has produced a spate of books dealing with one or more aspects of his career. Three of the best are Christopher Finch's *Norman Rockwell's America* and Thomas Buechner's two books *Norman Rockwell: Artist and Illustrator* and *Norman Rockwell: A Sixty Year Perspective*. Each of these works gives the reader a reasonably good picture of the scope of the illustrator's life and work, often with pictorial examples.

There are comparatively few published works dealing in depth with various poster artists. Probably the best is Clarence Hornung's *Will Bradley: His Graphic Art*, which deals with Bradley's posters, magazine covers, and book illustrations but does not provide a detailed bibliography of his work. Dover Publications has published a series of poster books that provide examples of the major categories of poster art, as has Avon Books.

Even less has been published on advertising art. The seminal theoretical work is still Marshall McLuhan's *The Mechanical Bride*. Perhaps the most useful single volume on advertising art and popular culture is Robert Atwan, Donald McQuade, and John W. Wright's *Edsels, Luckies and Frigidaires*, which reviews 100 years of advertising art through the medium of 250 commercial ads. Given the enormous changes that have taken place in advertising art over the past several decades, the need for a definitive work in this field is becoming ever more apparent.

RESEARCH COLLECTIONS

It is difficult to do research on American illustration artwork because much of it no longer exists. Until the early 1900s, illustrations were the property of the publisher rather than the artist, and many publishing houses had vast and fast-growing collections that were periodically weeded out, art editors and publishers keeping choice pieces and disposing of the remainder to friends or the trash heap. When color illustrations became more prevalent, publishers frequently sold an artist's artwork to help defray the cost of commissioning it; by 1920 N. C. Wyeth's paintings for *Scribner's* were being sold by the publisher for $200 apiece. As a result, comparatively few illustrations exist, even in museums, and in many instances, particularly for lesser-known illustrators, no one knows if the original artwork still exists and, if so, where. Even when the original artwork was returned to the illustrator, the illustrator frequently did not keep it; Cortland Schoonover found that his father, Frank Schoonover, kept only 800 of the approximately 6,000 illustrations that he had published during his lifetime.

Researchers who wish to study the original illustration artwork of specific illustrators must focus on those large-scale collections that are accessible to the public. Very few collections are either complete or comprehensive, however. The Delaware Art Museum, which holds over 700 sketches and almost 500 pieces of

Howard Pyle illustration, "A Famous Chapbook Villain" (*Harper's New Monthly Magazine*, vol. 81, no. 482, July 1890). Courtesy of the Library of Congress

illustration artwork by Howard Pyle, does not have several of the most important Pyle illustrations, which reside in the Brandywine River Museum, the Philadelphia Free Library, or private collections. The Brandywine River Museum, frequently thought of by the public as the "Wyeth" museum (the Wyeths still live nearby in Chadds Ford, Pennsylvania), contains over 300 paintings, of which fewer than 20 are by N. C. Wyeth. Other important Wyeth artwork is housed in the Delaware Art Museum, the Children's Room of the Philadelphia Free Museum, the Center for the Wyeth Family at the Farnsworth Art Museum in Rockland, Maine, and private collections. The Center for the Wyeth Family, opened in 1998, contains a gallery and study center devoted to the Maine artwork of Andrew Wyeth as well as N. C. and Jamie. The Norman Rockwell Museum in Stockbridge, Massachusetts, contains some of Rockwell's most famous paintings and an excellent permanent exhibit devoted to Rockwell's artwork from the 1960s and 1970s that had more political and social issues content. In addition, the Rockwell Museum has relocated Rockwell's studio onto its grounds and has an excellent display of historic artifacts devoted to offering a look at the artistic, business, and social aspects of his life. The ability of these illustrator-focused museums to create specialty exhibits with donations from a number of sources makes them and their exhibition catalogs an important source of information about illustrators and their artwork. The Norman Rockwell Museum, for example, has been able to gather together for special exhibits all 322 covers that Rockwell did for *The Saturday Evening Post*.

The problems associated with studying other, less visible illustrators are enormous. In one exhibition mounted by the Delaware Art Museum, fifty-four of fifty-five pieces of artwork came from private collections, and thirty-nine of forty pieces of artwork by W.H.D. Koerner were loaned by private collectors, and in a major exhibition of one of Pyle's leading students, Stanley Arthurs, only nine of the seventy-two paintings came from the museum's holdings.

A number of sources contain a few pieces of artwork each for a large number of illustrators. The Print Division of the Library of Congress contains 60,000 American and foreign posters dating from 1850 to the present, one of the largest and most comprehensive collections in the nation, if not the world. The Brooklyn Museum, the Thornton Oakley Collection of the Philadelphia Free Library, the Philadelphia Art Museum, the New York Public Library, the Grunwald Center for Graphic Arts at UCLA, the F. R. Gruger Collection at the University of Oregon, and the Museum of American Art in New Britain, Connecticut, contain major and important collections of illustration artwork. The Amon Carter Museum of Art in Fort Worth, Texas, and the Buffalo Bill Cody Museum in Cody, Wyoming, are two important research centers for western illustration artwork. Lastly, the Society of Illustrators Museum in New York City contains a large collection of paintings, drawings, and sketches by twentieth-century illustrators, including a wide cross-section of editorial, advertising, and book illustration artwork. The society's yearly traveling exhibition of the year's best illustration artwork is an excellent vehicle for keeping up with who are the best illustrators in the field.

Fortunately, technology has made viewing available artwork somewhat easier. Many of the major repositories of illustrator artwork have Web sites on the World Wide Web, providing differential access to viewing pictures of the artwork. Some Web sites merely provide information on holdings and exhibitions, while others provide a great deal of useful information for the researcher. The Delaware Art Museum (www.delart.mus.de.us), for example, provides access to pictures of some of its artwork, while the Brandywine River Museum (www.brandywinemuseum.org) has a very extensive and useful listing of its exhibition catalogs on the Wyeths as well as other American artists, dating back to the 1970s.

The best source for studying illustrations is the books and magazines in which they originally appeared, and the best single collection of such material is the Library of Congress, which contains copies of all U.S. copyrighted materials. In addition there are several specialized collections in the Library of Congress that are of limited interest. The Lessing J. Rosenwald Collection may be the best collection of illustrated books, ranging from the fifteenth through the twentieth centuries. Unfortunately, its strengths are outside the field of American illustration—fifteenth-century woodcut books, early sixteenth-century illustrated books, and twentieth-century *livres des peintres*—with the major emphasis on books produced by the earliest printers and outstanding presses of later periods. Also of marginal interest is the Caroline and Erwin Swann Collection of Caricature and Cartoon in the Prints and Photographs Division, with over 2,000 drawings, prints, and paintings related to the arts of caricature, cartoon, and illustration, spanning the years 1780 to 1977. Most of the images are cartoons, comic strips, and periodical illustrations drawn by American artists between 1890 and 1970, with the major emphasis on cartoons and comic strips.

Most other libraries lack the breadth or depth of the Library of Congress collection, but some of the best holdings of published illustrated materials are in the

Spenser Collections of the New York Public Library, the Philadelphia Free Library, the Newberry Library in Chicago, the Cleveland Public Library, the Detroit Public Library, the Minneapolis Public Library, and the Metropolitan Museum of Art in New York City. There are also substantial holdings at the university libraries at UCLA, Princeton, Johns Hopkins, the Children's Collection at the University of Toronto, and the Anne B. Moore Collection at Columbia Teachers College.

One frequently overlooked source is the specialized holdings in the possession of individual book collectors or dealers in illustrated books. Many book collectors have better collections of illustrated materials than nearby public or university libraries and frequently allow researchers limited access to their holdings. Book dealers who specialize in illustrated books are knowledgeable and usually possess bibliographies and other materials of interest to researchers. Equally important, their catalogs are invariably excellent sources of information about the most collectible illustrators and their books. Joanne Reisler of Vienna, Virginia, and Helen Younger of Aleph-Bet Books in Valley Cottage, New York, publish periodic catalogs worth subscribing to. Booksellers who list their wares on the Internet, on Bibliofind, ABEbooks, and Alibris can prove to be excellent sources of information, depending on how detailed their catalog descriptions are, but a search for "illustrated books" on these three databases provides hundreds of listings.

The researcher who seeks to go beyond the artwork and published materials will find the task very difficult indeed. Records, correspondence, diaries, and daybooks of individual illustrators and publishers have been fragmented or destroyed. Howard Pyle's wife destroyed much of his correspondence after his death. Some of Frank Schoonover's papers are at the Delaware Art Museum, some at the Philadelphia Free Library, and some in the possession of his son, Cortland Schoonover. F. R. Gruger's materials are currently housed at the University of Oregon, and much of Norman Rockwell's correspondence is at the Norman Rockwell Museum in Stockbridge, Massachusetts. The Society of Illustrators has an archive of materials from Arthur William Brown, Wallace Morgan, Rene Clarke, William Meade Prince, Charles Dana Gibson, and James Montgomery Flagg, who were founders, members, or benefactors of the society. The materials on Gibson and Flagg are particularly important since they were founders and early presidents of the society as well as major illustrators. The Archives of American Art, with depositories in a number of American cities, has significant collections of manuscript material available on microfilm for research. There may be hitherto unknown or untapped sources of materials. N. C. Wyeth's biographer, David Michaelis, discovered the Wyeth Family Archive, with more than 10,000 items, containing the written records of five generations. Finding that the Family Archive existed was one feat, but gaining access to it was another; his description of this process in the Acknowledgments of his biography is a must-read for any cultural or art historian wanting to research original source materials.

Another source of information, the records of publishing companies, particularly those that were major printers of illustrated work, are frequently missing or incomplete. Scribner's Publishing Company donated its early company records, including correspondence with authors and illustrators, to Firestone Library at Princeton University, but that holding is incomplete; a file cabinet listing thousands of illustrations published by the firm, who did them, in what medium, and for what price on filing cards found its way to the Brandywine River Museum in Chadds Ford, Pennsylvania. But what has happened to the records of the *Saturday Evening Post*, *Life*, *McClure's*, and *Century*—magazines no longer in publication? It was only through the tireless efforts of an Akron, Ohio, book dealer and the head of special collections at nearby Kent State University that the Saalfield Publishing Company records were purchased and moved to Kent State. These company records are crucial for researchers who want to understand the role of illustration in American popular culture and the publishers who published those illustrations.

HISTORY AND CRITICISM

Because of the large numbers of illustrations and the lack of comprehensive bibliographies, even for the most prolific of illustrators, there have been few attempts to write the definitive history of American popular illustration. The several attempts merit discussion, however.

Walter Reed edited one of the more ambitious attempts, *The Illustrator in America: 1900–1960*, which provides a decade-by-decade capsule description of the major illustrators and their work. At the beginning of each decade chapter, an illustrator provides a historical and artistic overview of the decade. This is followed by very brief biographies of major illustrators of the decade, which tell where their artwork was published and detail changes in illustration; the decade-by-decade presentation of illustration artwork does more to demonstrate the continuities and changes in illustration over the sixty-year period than do the historical overviews written by practitioners. There are a number of problems with Reed's book. It is now dated, a particular problem given the changes in illustration that have occurred since 1960. The book also focuses on magazine illustrators (in contrast to many bibliographies that ignore this artwork), thereby overlooking illustrators who worked primarily in books or poster art. Finally, for illustrators like Norman Rockwell, whose careers spanned more than one decade, it is difficult to surmise in which decade chapter they are to be found.

Another mode of analysis is to focus on the "great" illustrators in American history. Susan Meyers' *America's Great Illustrators* is the leading example of this genre. She analyzes in some depth ten "great" American illustrators—Howard Pyle, N. C. Wyeth, Frederic Remington, Maxfield Parrish, J. C. Leyendecker, Norman Rockwell, Charles Dana Gibson, Howard Chandler Christy, James Montgomery Flagg, and John Held Jr.—and provides examples of their work and a comparative chronology. Perhaps the most useful aspect of this book, since much of the information and artwork is available elsewhere, is the Introduction, where Meyers compares and contrasts the artwork and approaches to illustration of the ten men. Obviously, one can always argue with her choice of "great" illustrators. Why did she choose three American Beauty illustrators (Gibson, Christy, and Flagg)? Why didn't she choose any women? Why John Held, Jr.? Nonetheless, Meyers' book provides an insightful and well-written overview of American illustration during the first forty years of the twentieth century.

Henry C. Pitz's *200 Years of American Illustration*, a celebration of the seventy-fifth anniversary of the Society of Illustrators that contains 850 reproductions by 530 American illustrators, is a stunning visual treat. The 325 pages of illustrations—line drawings, halftones, and color—represent the most comprehensive display of the breadth and depth of American illustration artwork yet published. Arranged by decades, the book attempts to show the best illustration artwork by the leading illustrators. In addition, he has written a series of essays providing brief historical descriptions of major developments in the field, analyzing major illustrators, and looking at alternative uses of illustrations as magazine covers, posters, advertisements, and humor. Aside from the necessary brevity of the essays and Pitz's emphasis on Howard Pyle, the book also suffers from some factual errors and the mislabeling of some of the illustrations. Nonetheless, this increasingly scarce work is a sheer visual treat.

A Century of American Illustration, a catalog of an exhibition at the Brooklyn Museum of Arts and Sciences in 1972, contains 119 illustrations that show the scope of American illustration between 1850 and 1972. The period is divided into two eras—1850–1920 and 1920–1972—with each period receiving a brief analysis. Although the analysis is cursory, the illustrations show much of the diversity in illustration artwork during the period. A more limited time period is covered by Rowland Elzea's catalog for a 1972 exhibition at the Delaware Art Museum, *The Golden Age of American Illustration, 1880–1914*, a good survey of the leading illustrators of the period as well as an informed analysis of the development of illustration during its golden age, particularly the important role played by magazines in that development. As with most exhibition catalogs, there is a multitude of illustrations, by illustrators whose works hang in the Delaware Art Museum or who studied with Howard Pyle.

The role of magazines is examined in still another Delaware Art Museum exhibition catalog, edited by Dorey Schmidt in 1979, *The American Magazine, 1890–1940.* This catalog uses the slick-paper magazine format to introduce readers to the exhibit and a very solid collection of articles on magazines and their role in American popular culture. There are several articles relating to magazine illustration; Margaret Cohen discusses the importance of cover art for magazine sales, Rowland Elzea analyzes the contributors to the early *Life* magazine, and Elizabeth Hawkes writes an analysis of magazines and their illustrations, raising a number of interesting questions.

The Brandywine River Museum has published an interesting series of illustrator-specific exhibit catalogs. Among the male illustrators with catalogs are Clifford Ashley (1973), Charles Livingston Bull (1981), W. W. Denslow (1996), Harvey Dunn (1974), A. B. Frost (1985), Peter Hurd (1977), Arthur I. Keller (1988), John McCoy (1982), Thornton Oakley (1983), Maxfield Parrish (1974), Joseph Pennell (1986), Henry C. Pitz (1988), Howard Pyle (1980 and 1987), Frank Schoonover (1979), and William T. Smedley (1981). More important are the exhibition catalogs devoted to women's illustrations, beginning with *Women Artists in the Pyle Tradition* (1975) and *America's Great Women Illustrators* (1985), and those examining Charlotte Harding (1982), Rose O'Neill (1989), and Alice Barber Stevens (1984).

There has been little systematic empirical research on American illustration. One of the few is James J. Best's "The Brandywine School and Magazine Illustration: *Harper's*, *Scribner's*, and *Century*, 1906–1910," which counts the number, type, and source of 5,000 illustrations that appeared in the three major monthly illustrated magazines of a five-year period. The research shows that the illustration

Vaudeville poster, 1899. Courtesy of the Library of Congress

content for each magazine was decidedly different, with *Harper's* publishing a substantially greater proportion of illustrations by Howard Pyle and his students than the other two magazines. Rowland Elzea's piece in Dorey Schmidt's *The American Magazine, 1890–1940* notes a similar specialization in *Life* magazine, with one-third of the illustrators doing two-thirds of the illustrations. Both of these students raise interesting questions about the relationship between magazine art editors and professional illustrators, the two people who determined what appeared in illustrated magazines at the turn of the century.

Most of the biographies mentioned earlier are uncritical in their evaluation of their subjects and their artwork. Henry C. Pitz's two books on Howard Pyle and his students, *Howard Pyle* and *The Brandywine Tradition*, do a good job of analyzing the relationship between Pyle and his students, particularly Pyle's unique teaching style and philosophy of illustration. N. C. Wyeth's edited letters in *The Wyeths* discuss Wyeth's ambivalence toward Pyle and illustration, among other topics. Michaelis' biography, *N. C. Wyeth*, is a first-rate biography, critically examining Wyeth's personal and professional life. Much of the analysis of Wyeth's artwork and his relations with Pyle is not new, but placing them in the context of his relationships with his family gives them new and fresh significance. The two books dealing with Pyle's women students, *Jessie Wilcox Smith* by S. Michael Schnessel and *The Studios at Cogslea*, an exhibition catalog by Catherine Connell Stryker, deal sensitively and critically with the relationships between Pyle and his women students and also analyze illustration as a professional career field for women at the turn of the century. Christopher Finch's *Norman Rockwell's America* discusses how and why Rockwell's illustrations changed through time in terms of style, and he makes well-considered judgments on which of Rockwell's many illustrations are his best.

Historically, various magazines have published articles dealing with American illustration and illustrators. The *Quarterly Illustrator* and *Monthly Illustrator* were short-lived efforts to provide information about, and analysis of, contemporary illustrators during the 1890s. The *Studio* and *International Studio* periodically published critiques of American illustration during the early part of the twentieth century. Since the 1930s the *American Artist* has periodically reviewed the illustrations of various illustrators, with many of these reviews written by Henry C. Pitz. The February 1975 issue, for example, is devoted to tracing the familial ties and artistic heritage of the Wyeth family. Contemporary illustration is reviewed and displayed in *Illustrators*, an annual of American illustration.

The history of poster art is examined in detail in a number of books. Bevis Hillier's *Posters* examines the development of poster art in France and England from before World War I into the post–World War II era. Victor Margolin's book *American Poster Renaissance* focuses more narrowly on the development of poster art in America in the 1890s. Margolin identifies three different styles of poster art—decorative, descriptive, and illustrative—and shows examples of each style by their leading exponents, Will Bradley, Edward Penfield, and Maxfield Parrish, respectively. In addition to delineating the major styles of the period, Margolin analyzes the roles that poster art played in American life at the turn of the century. Ervine Metzl's *The Poster: Its History and Art* goes one step further to develop an aesthetic for judging poster art; the poster should not be overburdened with detail, should not be too literal, must enlist the viewer as participant, must imply a world of continuing action, and must sell a product. This last criterion is crucial, for it is possible to have posters that are good art but bad advertising, just as it is possible to have bad art that nonetheless sells a product. The ideal poster is both good art and good advertising. From this aesthetic perspective Metzl can evaluate the leading poster artists of the turn of the century, and he concludes that some, notably the Beggarstaffs (John Pryde and William Nicholson) in Britain, did posters that were good art but bad advertising. Gary Yanker's *Prop Art* seeks to develop a similar analysis of the role and function of contemporary propaganda posters, examining what propaganda posters are designed to do, how they seek to achieve their effects, and how well they do.

Unfortunately, no one has developed a similar framework for analyzing and evaluating the quality of magazine and book illustrations. For many years illustrators debated whether they were "artists," whose illustrations were not limited by the text, or "illustrators," whose artwork was tied to, and reflective of, the printed word. This question, whether illustration could be or was "high" rather than "popular" art, was bothersome for many illustrators, most notably, Charles Dana Gibson, James Montgomery Flagg, N. C. Wyeth, and F. R. Gruger, who each took leave of his illustrations work to do "fine art," traveling to Paris to paint or to study with leading easel artists of the day. The comparatively high salaries of illustrators and the disdain with which they were frequently held by poorer, but high-status, "fine" artists compounded their discomfort. Some artists—William Glackens, Winslow Homer, and John Sloan, to name the most prominent—began their careers as illustrators and then made the transition to "fine" art. Very few "fine" artists were interested in long-term careers as illustrators, however, although

Edward Hopper began his career as a "fine" artist, was unsuccessful, and turned to illustration before returning to "fine" art.

Because illustrations serve to visualize a print medium, Rowland Elzea, in *The Golden Age of American Illustration*, suggests that illustrators, as opposed to easel painters, must satisfy themselves, the text, and the public in order to be successful. Doing so requires a knowledge of the dramatic points in the text and the artistic ability to convey that drama pictorially to the reader and to involve the reader in a visual image of the story in a way that the reader understands and enjoys. At the same time illustrators must have the artistic freedom to illustrate what they want in their own style—to remain true to themselves. According to Charles D. Abbot in *Howard Pyle: A Chronicle*, Pyle sensed what is central to both the artist and the illustrator: "For after all, a man is not an artist by virtue of clever technique or brilliant methods; he is fundamentally an artist in the degree that he is able to sense and appreciate the significance of life that surrounds himself, and to express that significance to the minds of others" (226). The major difference between the artist and the illustrator in their fulfillment of this central task is that the illustrator is constrained by the text to be illustrated, whereas the artist is constrained only by his or her imagination.

The idea that the illustrator must deal with a text and can be judged on the basis of how well his or her work conveys the author's intent has not been used very often as the basis for evaluating the artwork of various illustrators. This is surprising since many illustrators have worked on more than one topic, and many of the literary classics have been illustrated by more than one illustrator. Little comparative analysis has been done, however. Frederick Joseph Harvey Darton, in *Modern Book Illustration in Great Britain and America*, has a critical review of four illustrated versions of Chaucer, and John Lewis, in *The Twentieth Century Book*, compares ten different illustrated editions of *Treasure Island*, showing how illustrative styles changed between 1884 and 1963.

Perhaps the best test of the success of an illustrator (but not an artist) is whether the illustrations were popular with the public and whether they remain popular today. If we use the test of longevity as the measure of illustration success, the honor roll of American illustrators would be comparatively short. But perhaps the best measure of success is how popular the illustrator was in his or her own time. We run the risk of arguing that the most popular and successful illustrators were those whose work was published and that only those whose works were published were popular and successful—a tautology. Nonetheless, whose work appeared most frequently in their time must be accounted as successes in their day, if not ours.

BIBLIOGRAPHY

Books and Articles

Abbott, Charles D. *Howard Pyle: A Chronicle*. New York: Harper and Brothers, 1925.

Allen, Douglas, and Douglas Allen Jr. *N. C. Wyeth*. New York: Bonanza Books, 1972.

Apgar, John P. *Frank Schoonover, Painter-Illustrator: A Bibliography*. Morristown, N.J.: Author, 1969.

Atwar, Robert, Donald McQuade, and John W. Wright. *Edsels, Luckies and Frigidaires*. New York: Delacourt Press, 1979.

Bader, Barbara. *American Picture Books from Noah's Ark to the Beast Within*. New York: Macmillan, 1976.

Best, James J. *American Popular Illustration: A Reference Guide*. Westport, Conn.: Greenwood Press, 1984.

———. "The Brandywine School and Magazine Illustration: *Harper's*, *Scribner's* and *Century*, 1906–1910." *Journal of American Culture* 3 (Spring 1980), 124–44.

Blackbeard, Bill. "The Pulps." In *The Handbook of Popular Culture*, vol. 1, ed. M. Thomas Inge. Westport, Conn.: Greenwood Press, 1978, 195–223.

Blanck, Jacob. *Peter Parley to Penrod*. New York: Bowker, 1939.

Bland, David. *The Illustration of Books*. London: Faber and Faber, n.d.

Blewett, David. *The Illustration of Robinson Crusoe, 1719–1920*. Gerrards Cross, England: Colin Smythe, 1995.

Bolton, Theodore. *American Book Illustration: Bibliographical Checklist of 123 Artists*. New York: Bowker, 1938.

———. *The Book Illustrations of Felix Octavius Carr Darley*. Worcester, Mass.: American Antiquarian Society, 1952.

Broder, Patricia James. *Dean Cornwell, Dean of Illustrators*. New York: Watson-Guptill, 1978.

Brokaw, Howard Pyle. *Howard Pyle and the Golden Age of Illustration*. Billings, Mont.: Yellowstone Art Center, 1984.

———. *The Howard Pyle Studio: A History*. Wilmington, Del.: Studio Group, 1983.

Brown, Arthur W. "Howard Chandler Christy." *American Artist* 16 (January 1952), 50–51, 68.

Buechner, Thomas. *Norman Rockwell: Artist and Illustrator*. New York: Henry Abrams, 1970.

———. *Norman Rockwell: A Sixty Year Perspective*. New York: Henry Abrams, 1972.

Cirker, Haywood, and Blanche Cirker. *The Golden Age of the Poster*. New York: Dover, 1971.

Clark, Trinkett, and H. Nichols Clark. *Myth, Magic, and Mystery: 100 Years of American Children's Book Illustration*. New York: Rinehart, 1996.

Darracott, Joseph, ed. *The First World War in Poster*. New York: Dover, 1974.

Darton, Frederick Joseph Harvey. *Modern Book Illustration in Great Britain and America*. London: The Studio, 1931.

Downey, Fairfax. *Portrait of an Era as Drawn by C. D. Gibson*. New York: Scribner's, 1936.

Dykes, Jeff. *Fifty Great Western Illustrators: A Bibliographical Checklist*. Flagstaff, Ariz.: Northland Press, 1975.

Ellis, Richard W. *Book Illustrations*. Kingsport, Tenn.: Kingsport Press, 1952.

Finch, Christopher. *Norman Rockwell's America*. New York: Henry Abrams, 1975.

Frank Leslie's Illustrated History of the Civil War. New York: Mrs. F. Leslie, 1895.

Gallo, Max. *The Poster in History*. New York: American Heritage, 1972.

Gowan, Alan. *The Unchanging Arts*. New York: J. B. Lippincott, 1971.

Guptill, Arthur. *Norman Rockwell: Illustrator*. New York: Watson-Guptill, 1946.
Halsey, Ashley, Jr. *Illustrating for the Saturday Evening Post*. Boston: Arlington House, 1951.
Harper's Illustrated History of the Civil War. New York: Harper and Bros., 1895.
Hassrick, Peter H. *The Way West: Art of Frontier America*. New York: Harry Abrams, 1977.
Heller, Steven, and Seymour Chwast. *Jackets Required: An Illustratred History of American Book Jacket Design, 1920–1960*. San Francisco: Chronicle Books, 1996.
Hillier, Bevis. *Posters*. New York: Stein and Day, 1969.
Hornung, Clarence. *Will Bradley: His Graphic Art*. New York: Dover, 1974.
Hurd, Peter. *Peter Hurd: Sketchbook*. Chicago: Swallow Press, 1971.
King, Ethel. *Darley, the Most Popular Illustrator of His Time*. Brooklyn, N.Y.: T. Gaus' Sons, 1964.
Kingman, Lee. "The High Art of Illustration." *Horn Book Magazine* 50 (October 1974), 94–103.
Kingman, Lee, Joanna Foster, and Ruth Giles Lontoft. *Illustration of Children's Books, 1956–66*. Boston: Horn Book, 1968.
Klemin, Diana. *The Illustrated Book*. New York: Charles Potter, 1970.
Lewis, John. *The Twentieth Century Book*. London: Studio Vista, 1967.
Loughery, John. *John Sloan: Painter and Rebel*. New York: Henry Holt, 1995.
Ludwig, Coy. *Maxfield Parrish*. New York: Watson-Guptill, 1973.
Mahoney, Bertha E., Louise P. Latimer, and Beulah Folmsbee. *Illustrators of Children's Books, 1774–1945*. Boston: Horn Books, 1947.
Margolin, Victor. *American Poster Renaissance*. New York: Watson-Guptill, 1975.
McCracken, Harold. *Frederic Remington: Artist of the Old West*. New York: Lippincott, 1947.
McLuhan, Herbert Marshall. *The Mechanical Bride*. New York: Vanguard Press, 1951.
Metzl, Ervine. *The Poster: Its History and Art*. New York: Watson-Guptill, 1963.
Meyer, Susan. *America's Great Illustrators*. New York: Henry Abrams, 1978.
———. "Howard Chandler Christy." *American Artist* 42 (May 1978), 42–47, 98–101.
———. *James Montgomery Flagg*. New York: Watson-Guptill, 1974.
———. "Three Generations of the Wyeth Family." *American Artist* 39 (February 1975).
Michaelis, David. *N. C. Wyeth: A Biography*. New York: Alfred A. Knopf, 1998.
Minor, Wendell. *Art for the Written Word: Twenty-Five Years of Book Cover Art*. New York: Harcourt, Brace, 1995.
Morse, Willard S., and Gertrude Brinckle. *Howard Pyle: A Record of His Illustrations and Writings*. Wilmington, Del.: Private printed, 1921. Reprint. Detroit: Singing Treee Press, 1969.
Mott, Frank Luther. *A History of American Magazines: Vol. V, 1905–1930*. Cambridge: Harvard University Press, 1968.
Peppin, Brigid. *Fantasy: The Golden Age of Fantastic Illustration*. New York: New American Library, 1976.
Perlman, Bernard. *The Golden Age of American Illustration: F. R. Gruger and His Circle*. Westport, Conn.: Northern Lights, 1978.

Pitz, Henry C. "Book Illustration since 1937." *American Artist* 31 (April 1967), 64–71, 101.
———. *The Brandywine Tradition*. New York: Weathervane Books, 1968.
———. "George Harding." *American Artist* 21 (December 1957), 29–35.
———. *Howard Pyle*. New York: Clarkson and Potter, 1975.
———. "Millions of Pictures, Part I." *American Artist* 15 (November 1961), 35–39, 76–77.
———. "Millions of Pictures, Part II." *American Artist* 15 (December 1961), 52–57, 85–88.
———. "N. C. Wyeth." *American Heritage* 17 (October 1965), 36–55, 82–84.
———. *The Practice of Illustration*. New York: Watson-Guptill, 1947.
———. *200 Years of American Illustration*. New York: Random House, 1977.
Reed, Henry. *The A. B. Frost Book*. Rutland, Vt.: Charles E. Tuttle, 1972.
Reed, Walt. *Harold Von Schmidt*. Flagstaff, Ariz.: Northland Press, 1972.
———. ed. *The Illustrator in America: 1900–1960*. New York: Reinhold, 1966.
Schau, Michael. *All American Girl: The Art of Coles Phillips*. New York: Watson-Guptill, 1975.
———. *J. C. Leyendecker*. New York: Watson-Guptill, 1976.
Schnessel, S. Michael. *Jessie Wilcox Smith*. New York: Crowell, 1977.
Schoonover, Cortland. *Frank Schoonover, Illustrator of the North American Frontier*. New York: Watson-Guptill, 1976.
Shaw, John M. *The Poems, Poets, and Illustrators of St. Nicholas Magazine, 1873–1943*. Tallahassee: Florida State University Press, n.d.
Shinn, Everett. "William Glackens as an Illustrator." *American Artist* 9 (November 1945), 22–27, 37.
Skeeters, Paul. *Maxfield Parrish: The Early Years*. Secaucus, N.J.: Chartwell Books, 1973.
Smith, F. Hopkinson. *American Illustrators*. New York: Scribner's, 1893.
Viguers, Ruth Hill, Marcia Dalphin, and Mertha Mahoney Miller. *Illustrators of Children's Books, 1946–56*. Boston: Horn Books, 1958.
Watson, Ernest W. "Harvey Dunn: Milestone in the Tradition of American Illustration." *American Artist* 6 (June 1942), 16–20, 31.
Weinhardt, Carl J. *The Most of John Held, Jr.* Brattleboro, Vt.: Stephen Greene Press, 1972.
Weitenkampf, Frank. *American Graphic Art*. New York: Scribner's, 1912.
———. *The Illustrated Book*. Cambridge: Harvard University Press, 1938.
Wyeth, Betsy James. "In a Dream I Met N. C. Wyeth." In *Wondrous Strange: The Wyeth Tradition*. Boston: Little, Brown, 1998, 56–58.
———, ed. *The Wyeths*. Boston: Gambit Press, 1971.
Yanker, Gary. *Prop Art*. New York: Darien House, 1972.

Museum Catalogs

Alice Barber Stephens, a Pioneer Woman Illustrator. Essay by Ann Barton Brown. Chadds Ford, Pa.: Brandywine River Museum, 1984.
The American Personality: The Artist-Illustrator of Life in the United States: 1860–1930. Los Angeles: Grunwald Center for the Graphic Arts, 1976.

America's Great Women Illustrators. Chadds Ford, Pa.: Brandywine River Museum, 1985.

The Art of American Illustration. Essay by Joan H. Gorman. Chadds Ford, Pa.: Brandywine River Museum, 1976.

The Art of Rose O'Neill. Essay by Helen Goodman. Chadds Ford, Pa.: Brandywine River Museum, 1989.

Arthur Burdett Frost. Essay by Gene E. Harris. Chadds Ford, Pa.: Brandywine River Museum, 1985.

Arthur I. Keller. Essay by Gene E. Harris. Chadds Ford, Pa.: Brandywine River Museum, 1988.

The Artist and the Book: 1860–1960. Boston: Museum of Fine Arts and Harvard University Library, 1961.

A Century of American Illustration. Brooklyn, N.Y.: Brooklyn Museum of Arts and Sciences, 1972.

Charles Livingston Bull, Illustrator. Essay by Peter White. Chadds Ford, Pa.: Brandywine River Museum, 1981.

Charlotte Harding. Essay by Ann Barton Brown. Chadds Ford, Pa.: Brandywine River Museum, 1982.

Clifford Ashley. Essay by Wilton W. Hall. Chadds Ford, Pa.: Brandywine River Museum, 1973.

Elzea, Rowland, ed. *Howard Pyle: Diversity in Depth*. Wilmington: Delaware Art Museum, 1973.

———. *The Golden Age of American Illustration, 1880–1914*. Wilmington: Delaware Art Museum, 1972.

Frank Schoonover, Illustrator. Essay by Ann Barton Brown. Chadds Ford, Pa.: Brandywine River Museum, 1979.

Gorman, Joan H. *The Art of American Illustration*. Chadds Ford, Pa.: Brandywine River Museum, 1976.

Hahler, Christine Anne, ed. . . . *Illustrated by Darley*. Wilmington: Delaware Art Museum, 1979.

Harvey Dunn. Essay by Robert Karolevitz. Chadds Ford, Pa.: Brandywine River Museum, 1974.

Henry C. Pitz. Essay by Patricia Likos, Chadds Ford, Pa.: Brandywine River Museum, 1988.

Howard Pyle: A Teacher. Chadds Ford, Pa., and Wilmington: Brandywine River Museum and Delaware Art Museum, 1987.

Maxfield Parrish: Master of Make-Believe. Essay by Maxfield Parrish Jr. Chadds Ford, Pa.: Brandywine River Museum, 1974.

Peter Hurd. Essay by Paul Horgan. Chadds Ford, Pa.: Brandywine River Museum, 1977.

Schmidt, Dorey, ed. *The American Magazine, 1890–1940*. Wilmington: Delaware Art Museum, 1979.

Stryker, Catherine Connell, ed. *The Studios at Cogslea*. Wilmington: Delaware Art Museum, 1976.

Thornton Oakley. Essay by Gene E. Harris. Chadds Ford, Pa.: Brandywine River Museum, 1983.

William Thomas Smedley, Illustrator. Essay by Alan M. Pensler. Chadds Ford, Pa.: Brandywine River Museum, 1981.
Women Artists in the Pyle Tradition. Chadds Ford, Pa.: Brandywine River Museum, 1975.